Business Intelligence
Guidebook

Business Intelligence Guidebook
From Data Integration to Analytics

Rick Sherman

AMSTERDAM • BOSTON • HEIDELBERG • LONDON
NEW YORK • OXFORD • PARIS • SAN DIEGO
SAN FRANCISCO • SINGAPORE • SYDNEY • TOKYO

Morgan Kaufmann is an imprint of Elsevier

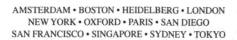

Acquiring Editor: Steve Elliot
Editorial Project Manager: Lindsay Lawrence
Project Manager: Punithavathy Govindaradjane
Designer: Matthew Limbert

Morgan Kaufmann is an imprint of Elsevier
225 Wyman Street, Waltham, MA, 02451, USA

Library of Congress Cataloging-in-Publication Data
Sherman, Rick.
   Business intelligence guidebook : from data integration to analytics/Rick Sherman.
      pages cm
   ISBN 978-0-12-411461-6
   1. Business intelligence. I. Title.
      HD38.7.S52 2014
      658.4'72–dc23

                                              2014031205

British Library Cataloguing-in-Publication Data
A catalogue record for this book is available from the British Library.

ISBN: 978-0-12-411461-6

For information on all MK publications
visit our website at www.mkp.com

Contents

PART III   ARCHITECTURAL FRAMEWORK

PART IV   DATA DESIGN

PART V   DATA INTEGRATION DESIGN

Foreword

There are many books explaining the need for BI, its methodology, and the myriad designs and implementation pathways that can be taken. The missing book is one that covers all of these from start to finish in a complete, detailed, and comprehensive fashion. From justifying the project, gathering requirements, developing the architectural framework, designing the proper approach for BI data models, integrating the data, generating advanced analytics, dealing with "shadow systems," understanding and dealing with organizational relationships, managing the full project life cycle, and finally creating centers of excellence—this book covers the entire gambit of creating a sustainable BI environment.

It is the one book you will need to create and maintain a world-class data warehouse environment. Rick's deep understanding of technical implementations is only matched by his understanding of the history behind many of the decision points in the development of the BI components. This history will help you determine the best deployment options for your specific situation—so invaluable in today's confusing and mixed messages BI world!

I highly recommend this book to anyone just starting out in BI, who has a legacy environment that needs renovating or just wants to understand the entire implementation picture from start to finish. Rick's mastery of all the critical implementation activities means you are receiving the best advice for creating a world-class BI environment that will last for long haul. Nicely done, Rick.

Claudia Imhoff
President of Intelligent Solutions, Inc. and
Founder of The Boulder Business Intelligence Brain Trust.

How to Use This Book

I wrote this book to fill in the gap between books that focus on the concepts of business intelligence (BI) and the nitty gritty of vendor tool training. It does not just provide a foundation, it shows you how to apply that foundation in order to actually get your work done. After this book, you should be ready to learn specific tools. As you do that, you'll see how the concepts and the step-by-step instructions mesh together.

See www.BIguidebook.com for companion material such as templates, examples, vendor links, and updated research. There, you will be able to subscribe to an email list and receive notices of updates, additions, and other occasional news that relates to the book. I will also use my blog at www.datadoghouse.com to post updates.

If you are a professor choosing this book as a text book, contact us at BIguidebook@athena-solutions.com for a syllabus.

Note: You may notice that this book does not use the word "user" any more than absolutely necessary. I explain my reasons in Chapter 17: People, Process and Politics, but, briefly, it is because we are building BI solutions for *people*. This is an important mind-set, seeing as BI projects are about people as much as they are about technology.

For this book and other related titles, see the publisher's website: http://booksite.elsevier.com/9780124114616.

CHAPTER SUMMARIES

BI projects require the participation of both business and IT groups. The simplistic view is that business people are the customers and IT people deliver the solution. The reality is that business people need to participate in the entire process. Below you will find summaries and guidance on how business and IT people can use this book.

Chapter 1: The Business Demand for Data, Information, and Analytics sets the stage, and is important background for all audiences. It explains how the deluge of data and its accompanying need for analysis makes BI critical for the success of today's enterprise. There is a big difference between raw data and actionable information. While there are attempts to circumvent BI with operational systems, there really is no good substitute for true BI.

Chapter 2: Justifying BI helps the BI team make both the business and technical case to determine the need, identify the benefits, and, most importantly, set expectations. Identifying risks and an organization's readiness is critical to determining realistic expectations. This chapter covers determining the scope, plan, budget, and return on investment.

Chapter 3: Defining Requirements—Business, Data, and Quality discusses the process of creating the foundation of a successful BI solution by documenting what you are planning to build. The development team then uses these requirements to design, develop, and deploy BI systems. This is one of the most people-oriented processes in a project, making it especially tricky. Use this chapter to understand the roles and workflow, and how to conduct the interviews that are the basis for the requirements you will be documenting.

Chapter 4: Architecture Introduction helps everyone understand the importance of a well-architected foundation. The architecture sets your directions and goals. It is a set of guiding principles, but is flexible enough to allow for incremental growth. One of the key concepts discussed in this chapter is that of the accidental architecture, which is what happens when there is no plan.

Chapter 5: Information Architecture introduces the framework that defines the business context—"what, who, where, and why"—necessary for building successful BI solutions. An information architecture helps tame the deluge of data with a combination of processes, standards, people, and tools that establish information as a corporate asset. Using a data integration framework as a blueprint, you can transform data into consistent, quality, timely information for your business people to use in measuring, monitoring, and managing the enterprise. This gives your enterprise a better overall view of its customers and helps consolidate critical data.

Chapter 6: Data Architecture explains that data architecture is a blueprint that helps align your company's data with its business strategies. This is where the book gets more technical, as it delves into the history of data architecture, the different choices available, and details on the analytical data architecture. It covers types of workflows, then explains operational data stores. It introduces the hybrid dimensional-normalized model.

Chapter 7: Technology and Product Architecture gets into the nitty gritty of the technology and product architectures and what you should know when you are evaluating them. It does not name products and vendors, as these can change frequently as companies merge and are acquired. If you want names, see the book Web site www.BIguidebook.com.

Chapter 8: Foundational Data Modeling, **Chapter 9: Dimensional Modeling,** and **Chapter 10: Advanced Dimensional Modeling** are aimed at technical members of the BI team who will be involved with creating data models, which are the cornerstone to building BI applications.

Chapter 8: Foundational Data Modeling describes the different levels of models: conceptual, logical and physical; the workflow, and where they are used. It explains entity relational (ER) modeling in depth,and covers normalization, the formal data modeling approach for validating a model.

Chapter 9: Dimensional Modeling compares ER versus dimensional modeling and provides details on the latter that is better suited to BI. Dimensional modeling uses facts, dimensions, and attributes, which can be organized in different ways, called schemas. The chapter covers dimensional modeling concepts such as date, time, role-playing, and degenerative dimensions, as well as event and consolidated fact tables.

Chapter 10: BI Dimensional Modeling gives you a strong understanding of how to develop a dimensional model and how dimensional modeling fits in your enterprise. It covers hierarchies, slowly changing dimensions, rapidly changing dimensions, causal dimensions, multivalue dimensions, and junk dimensions. The chapter also takes a closer look at snowflakes, as well as concepts such as value-band reporting, heterogeneous products, hot swappable dimensions.

Chapter 11: Data Integration Design and Development introduces data integration (DI), where the bulk of the work in a BI project lies. The best approaches are holistic, incremental, and iterative. The DI architecture represents the workflow of source data as it is transformed to become actionable information. The chapter covers the DI design steps for creating each stage's process model and determining the design specifications. Standards are important for successful DI and it covers how to develop and apply them. Because historical data is often needed, it explains what to watch out for when loading it. It wraps up with discussions on prototyping and testing.

Chapter 12: Data Integration Processes takes the DI discussion to the next level, covering why it is best to use a DI tool (as opposed to hand-coding) and how to choose the best fit. These tools cover many services, including access and delivery, data profiling, data transformation, data quality, process management, operations management, and data transport; the data ingestion services change data capture, slowly changing dimensions, and reference look-ups.

Chapter 13: BI Applications talks about specifying the content of the BI application you are building, and the idea of using personas to make sure it resonates with your intended audience. It guides you on designing the layout as well as the function and form of the data. Matching the type of visualizations you create to the analysis that will be done makes the application much more effective.

Chapter 14: BI Design and Development covers the next step, which is to design the BI application's visual layout and how it interacts with its users. This includes creating and adhering to standards for the user interface and standards for how information is accessed from the perspectives of privacy and security. You will learn the different methods for working on the design of the components, prototyping, developing the application, and then testing.

Chapter 15: Advanced Analytics shows how you can use analytics not just to learn about what has happened, but also to gauge the future and act on predictions. Predictive analytics includes the processes by which you use analytics for forecasting and modeling. Analytical sandboxes and hubs are two self-service data environments that help business people manage their own analytical needs, although IT is needed to create the data backbone. The chapter addresses the challenges of Big Data analytics, including scoping, architecting, and staffing a program.

Chapter 16: Data Shadow Systems sheds light on these frequently-seen departmental systems (usually spreadsheets) that business groups create and use to gather and analyze data on their own when they do not want to work with IT or cannot wait for them. Data shadow systems create silos, resulting in inconsistent data across the enterprise. The BI team needs to identify them and either replace them or incorporate them into the overall BI program.

Chapter 17: People, Process, and Politics delves into the stickiest of BI project issues. Technology is easy; it is people that are hard. This chapter lays out the relationship between the business and IT groups, discussing who does what, how they interact, and how to build the project management and development teams. It covers training for both business and IT people and provides a firm foundation in data governance—a people-centric program that is critical for transforming data into actionable information.

Chapter 18: Project Management stresses the need for an enterprise-wide BI program, which helps the BI project manager better plan and manage. The assessment is another arrow in the project manager's quiver, helping to create a project plan that meets its requirements. The chapter gets into details on the work breakdown structure and project methodology choices. It guides you through all phases of the project and its schedule.

Chapter 19: Centers of Excellence discusses these organizational teams that address the problem of disconnected application and data silos across an enterprise. The business intelligence center of excellence (BI COE) coordinates and oversees BI activities including resources and expertise. The data integration COE (DI COE) team focuses specifically on data integration, establishing its scope, defining its architecture and vision, and helping to implement that vision.

Acknowledgments

Although this book is about learning, I am the one who has learned so much, starting with the folks at Project Software & Development, Inc., who took a chance on an industrial engineer whose only work experience was with companies that made grinding wheels and bubble gum. My then manager said he could train an engineer to program but he could not train a programmer to be an engineer.

Digital Equipment Corporation got me into data warehousing, with a 150-Gb warehouse, one of the largest nongovernment data warehouses in the world at the time—now it would fit on my smartphone. The consulting I have done since then, including with CONNECT: The Knowledge Network (Maureen Clarry), PriceWaterhouseCoopers Consulting and through Athena IT Solutions has given me the privilege of working with customers and fellow consultants who have taught me so much. I have been fortunate to work with people who would later become thought leaders in industry research firms.

The people who have published my articles, podcasts, webinars, and videos over the years have been a great source of encouragement. Mary Jo Nott was the first, way back when *DM Review* was a thick, printed monthly magazine. Eric Kavanaugh, Hannah Smalltree, and Craig Stedman have been and continue to be strong supporters and I appreciate their enthusiasm.

The team at Morgan Kaufmann had great patience with my loose interpretation of deadlines. Steve Elliot and Lindsay Lawrence, particularly, somehow managed to keep the book on track despite me.

A special thanks to my editor and marketing communications expert, Andrea Harris, who has transformed this book, and all my other writing, from the prose of an engineering term paper to a more readable form for people who are not nerds (like me!). Andrea also deserves far more thanks from me, as she has been married to me for quite some time.

And thanks to my sons, Jake and Josh, for humoring me and pretending that they are interested in what I do.

CONCEPTS AND CONTEXT

THE BUSINESS DEMAND FOR DATA, INFORMATION, AND ANALYTICS

INFORMATION IN THIS CHAPTER:

- The data and information deluge
- The analytics deluge
- Data versus actionable information
- Data capture versus information analysis
- The five Cs of data
- Common terminology

JUST ONE WORD: DATA

> "I just want to say one word to you. Just one word… Are you listening? … Plastics. There's a great future in plastics."
>
> ***Mr. McGuire in the 1967 movie The Graduate.***

The Mr. McGuires of the world are no longer advising newly-minted graduates to get into plastics. But perhaps they should be recommending data. In today's digital world data is the key, the ticket, and the Holy Grail all rolled into one.

I do not just mean it's growing in importance as a profession, although it is a great field to get into, and I'm thrilled that my sons Jake and Josh are pursuing careers in data and technology. Data is where the dollars are when it comes to company budgets. Every few years there is another report showing that business intelligence (BI) is at or near the top of the chief information officer's (CIO) list of priorities.

Enterprises today are driven by data, or, to be more precise, information that is gleaned from data. It sheds light on what is unknown, it reduces uncertainty, and it turns decision-making from an art to a science.

But whether it's Big Data or just plain old data, it requires a lot of work before it is actually something useful. You would not want to eat a cup of flour, but baked into a cake with butter, eggs, and sugar for the right amount of time at the right temperature it is transformed into something delicious. Likewise, raw data is unpalatable to the business person who needs it to make decisions. It is inconsistent, incomplete, outdated, unformatted, and riddled with errors. Raw data needs integration, design, modeling, architecting, and other work before it can be transformed into consumable information.

This is where you need data integration to unify and massage the data, data warehousing to store and stage it, and BI to present it to decision-makers in an understandable way. It can be a long and complicated process, but there is a path; there are guidelines and best practices. As with many things that are hard to do, there are promised shortcuts and "silver bullets" that you need to learn to recognize before they trip you up.

It will take a lot more than just reading this book to make your project a success, but my hope is that it will help set you on the right path.

WELCOME TO THE DATA DELUGE

In the business world, knowledge is not just power. It is the lifeblood of a thriving enterprise. Knowledge comes from information, and that, in turn, comes from data. It is up to a BI team to gather and manage the data to empower the company's business groups with the information they need to gain knowledge—knowledge that helps them make informed decisions about every step the company takes.

Enterprises need this information to understand their operations, customers, competitors, suppliers, partners, employees, and stockholders. They need to learn about what is happening in the business, analyze their operations, react to internal and external pressures, and make decisions that will help them manage costs, grow revenues, and increase sales and profits. Forrester Research sums it up perfectly: "Data is the raw material of everything firms do, but too many have been treating it like waste material—something to deal with, something to report on, something that grows like bacteria in a petri dish. No more! Some say that data is the new oil—but we think that comparing data to oil is too limiting. Data is the new sun: it's limitless and touches everything firms do. Data must flow fast and rich for your organization to serve customers better than your competitors can. Firms must invest heavily in building a next-generation customer data management capability to grow revenue and profits in the age of the customer. Data is an asset that even CFOs will realize should have a line on the balance sheet right alongside property, plant, and equipment" [1].

It can be a problem, however, when there is more data than an enterprise can handle. They collect massive amounts of data every day internally and externally as they interact with customers, partners, and suppliers. They research and track information on their competitors and the marketplace. They put tracking codes on their websites so they can learn exactly how many visitors they get and where they came from. They store and track information required by government regulations and industry initiatives. Now there is the Internet of Things (IoT), with sensors embedded in physical objects such as pacemakers, thermostats, and dog collars where they collect data. It is a deluge of data (Figure 1.1).

DATA VOLUME, VARIETY, AND VELOCITY

It is not only that enterprises accumulate data in ever-increasing volumes, the variety and velocity of data is also increasing. Although the emerging "Big Data" databases can cause an enterprise's ability to gather data to explode, the volume, velocity, and variety are all expanding no matter how "big" or "small" the data is.

Volume—According to many experts, 90% of the data in the world today was created in the last two years alone. When you hear that statistic you might think that it is coming from all the chatter on social media, but data is being generated by all manner of activities. For just one example, think about the emergence of radio frequency identification (RFID) to track products from manufacturing to purchase. It is a huge category of data that simply did not exist before. Although not all of the data gathered is significant for an enterprise, it still leaves a massive amount of data with which to deal.

Velocity—Much of the data now is time sensitive, and there is greater pressure to decrease the time between when it is captured and when it is used for reporting. We now depend on the speed of some of this data. It is extremely helpful to receive an immediate notification from your bank, for example, when a fraudulent transaction is detected, enabling you to cancel your credit card immediately. Businesses across industry sectors are using current data when interacting with their customers, prospects, suppliers, partners, employees, and other stakeholders.

Variety—The sources of data continue to expand. Receiving data from disparate sources further complicates things. Unstructured data, such as audio, video, and social media, and semistructured data

FIGURE 1.1

Too much information.

like XML and RSS feeds must be handled differently from traditional structured data. The CIO of the past thought phones were just for talking, not something that collected data. He also thought Twitter was something that birds did. Now that an enterprise can collect data from tweets about its products, how does it handle that data and then what does it do with it? Also, what does it do with the invaluable data that business people create in spreadsheets and Microsoft Word documents and use in decision-making? Formerly, CIOs just had to worry about collecting and analyzing data from back office applications, but now their data can come from people, machines, processes, and applications spread across the world.

Unfortunately, enterprises have not been as good at organizing and understanding the data as they have been at gathering it. Data has no value unless you can understand what you have, analyze it, and then act on the insights from the analysis.

See the book's companion Website www.BIguidebook.com for links to industry research, templates, and other materials to help you learn more about business intelligence and make your next project a success.

To receive updates on newly posted material, subscribe to the email list on the Website or follow the RSS feed of my blog at www.datadoghouse.com.

TAMING THE ANALYTICS DELUGE

With this flood of data comes a flood of analytics. Sure, enterprises are adept at gathering all sorts of data about their customers, prospects, internal business processes, suppliers, partners, and competitors. Capturing data, however, is just the beginning. Many enterprises have become overwhelmed by the information deluge, and either cannot effectively analyze it or cannot get information that is current enough to act on.

This is a massive, potential headache for CIOs. According to the *2014 State of the CIO Survey* [2], leveraging data and analytics is the most important technology initiative for 2014, with 72% of CIOs surveyed stating that it is a critical or high priority. Gartner concurs, with the prediction that BI and analytics will remain a top focus for CIOs through 2017, and that the benefits of fact-based decision-making are clear to business managers in a broad range of disciplines, including marketing, sales, supply chain management (SCM), manufacturing, engineering, risk management, finance, and HR [3].

Adding to the complexity, now many more people in an organization need the information that comes from all this data. Where in the past only a few managers received information to analyze, now business people at all levels are using analytics in their jobs. For example:

- Shipping data extends far beyond the shipping department to include outside shipping carriers and customers.
- Website analytics are no longer just the domain of webmasters looking at "hits"—marketing managers use them to measure the success of sales and social media campaigns.
- Medical information is shared not just with doctors, but also with hospital networks, patients, and insurance companies.
- TV streaming services compile data on everything we watch and use that to recommend other movies and shows it thinks we would like.

All of this information has had a tremendous impact on businesses' ability to make informed decisions. According to a study conducted by *The Economist* [4], the flood of information and analytics has had these effects:

- The majority of companies (58%) claim they will make a bigger investment in Big Data over the next 3 years.
- Two-thirds of executives consider that their organizations are "data driven."
- Over half (54%) say that management decisions based purely on intuition or experience are increasingly regarded as suspect.
- The majority of executives (58%) rely on unstructured data analysis including text, voice messages, images, and video content.
- Although 42% of executives say that data analysis has slowed down decision-making, the vast majority (85%) believe that the growing volume of data is not the main challenge, but rather being able to analyze and act on it in real time.
- As organizations increasingly look to the output from analytics to automate decision making, data quality is seen as a major hurdle.

THE IMPORTANCE OF ANALYTICS

Businesses cannot underestimate the importance of their analytics initiatives. While enterprises still need leaders and decision-makers with intuition, they depend on data to validate their intuitions. In this sense, data becomes a strategic guide that helps executives see patterns they might not otherwise notice. A study from Bain found that enterprises with the most advanced analytics capabilities outperformed competitors by wide margins, with the leaders showing these results [5]:

- Twice as likely to be in the top quartile of financial performance within their industries
- Five times as likely to make decisions much faster than market peers
- Three times as likely to execute decisions as intended
- Twice as likely to use data very frequently when making decisions.

ANALYTICS CHALLENGES

The use of analytics is not just growing in volume; it is also growing more complex. Advanced analytics is expanding to include predictive analytics, data visualization, and data discovery.

Analytics is not just about numbers; it is about brainpower. More companies are realizing they need to hire a new class of data-savvy people to develop complicated analytics models; these people are often referred to as data scientists. A McKinsey report stated that "By 2018, the United States alone could face a shortage of 140,000 to 190,000 people with deep analytical skills as well as 1.5 million managers and analysts with the know-how to use the analysis of Big Data to make effective decisions"[6]. Are companies worried about this? You bet! According to the 2014 Gartner CIO Agenda Report, "Fifty-one percent of CIOs are concerned that the digital torrent is coming faster than they can cope, and 42% don't feel they have the right skills and capabilities in place to face this future"[7].

Our industry has faced a shortage of skilled people in business intelligence, analytics, and data integration that has kept business from effectively using the data they already have. With the onslaught of Big Data and the advanced skills it requires, it is important that more people learn how to work with these advanced analytics solutions.

ANALYTICS STRATEGY

Business analytics is indispensable for analyzing this data and using it to make informed business decisions. A Forrester report [8] highlights some of the reasons why BI analytics is so critical:

- Many business decisions remain based on intuitive hunches, not facts
- Analytics lessens the discontinuity between intuition and factual decision-making
- Competitive differentiation can be achieved by more sophisticated data usage
- Big Data enables new use cases but will require analytics to take full advantage of its potential.

To make the most of the power of analytics, an enterprise needs a strategy based on how its business people interact with and use data. Chapter 15 will cover this topic in detail, but to sum up, an analytics strategy may include:

- Designing a data architecture that enables reporting, analytics, predictive modeling, and self-service BI
- Architecting a BI portfolio
- Architecting solutions with data discovery, data visualization, and in-memory BI
- Enabling operational and analytical BI
- Designing and implementing analytical sandboxes and hubs
- Creating data and analytical governance programs
- Creating shared BI metadata environments.

TOO MUCH DATA, TOO LITTLE INFORMATION

As the sailor in The Rime of the Ancient Mariner said, "Water, water, everywhere, nor any drop to drink." How about "Data, data everywhere, but not any of the right information I need to do my job?" Businesses may be awash with data, but that does not necessarily mean they have useful *information* (Figure 1.2).

My son Jake's first job out of college was at a firm that analyzed large volumes of data for resume parsing and job matching. His boss voiced a similar lament when he said "What's the use of Big Data if it's just a lot of data? We need information we can analyze, not just a big pile of data."

THE DIFFERENCE BETWEEN DATA AND INFORMATION

There is a big difference between data and information, although the terms are often used interchangeably. Data is raw, random, and unorganized. Information is data that has been organized, structured, and processed. Information is what you use to gain knowledge. We all eat, so let us look at how a foodie would approach these concepts:

- **Data:** a collection of ingredients sitting on the counter. They include carrots, onions, leeks, garlic, and potatoes from the farmer's market, and a package of chicken, a box of rice, and some cans of broth from the grocery store. *In the data warehousing (DW)/BI world, this is like source data from different operational systems.*

FIGURE 1.2

No water to drink; no information to consume.

- **Information:** then you get everything ready by washing, peeling, and cutting up the vegetables, cutting up the chicken, and opening the cans of broth. You put it all in the pot and turn on the heat where it cooks and becomes soup. *In the DW/BI world, the data has been moved into the ETL (extract, transform, and load) system and is transformed into information.*
- **Knowledge:** Now the soup is ready to be put into bowls and eaten. *In the DW/BI world business people consume the information in reports to gain knowledge that helps them make informed business decisions.*

THE ROLE OF BI IN CREATING ACTIONABLE INFORMATION

BI turns data into "actionable" information—information that is useful to the business and helps it gain knowledge. Business demand for actionable information is ever expanding. With business managers and workers seemingly connected 24/7 via their smartphones, tablets, and other devices, expectations are being raised even further for BI systems that can go beyond basic reporting and provide analytics capabilities at the speed of thought.

It is good that enterprises have recognized the significant business value of analyzing the surging amount of information and then acting on that analysis. It is a bad thing, however, when enterprises become so overwhelmed by the information deluge that they cannot effectively analyze it or receive current enough information on which to act.

Enterprises are in this position because many are still using the standard techniques and technologies that became mainstream in BI and DW before the current information deluge. Enterprises have been encountering significant increases in volume, variety, and velocity over the last several years as they have expanded from integrating data from internal operational systems to data interchange with customers, prospects, partners, suppliers, and other stakeholders.

Once the necessary data is located and evaluated, work often needs to be done to turn it into a clean, consistent, and comprehensive set of information that is ready to be analyzed.

THE INFORMATION BACKBONE

No matter what the BI request, the right business information must be available. That does not mean that all you need to do is to grant a business person access to a database. Comprehensive, consistent, conformed, clean, and current data does not happen without a strategy to manage the information.

Once the information is in order, then business people can plug into the information backbone through many BI tools such as data discovery, data visualization, ad hoc query, dashboards, scorecards, OLAP analysis, predictive analytics, reports, and spreadsheets. An enterprise's data demands are ever expanding and evolving—meaning that the information backbone is likewise expanding. This often requires data integration, data cleansing, data profiling, and, most importantly, data governance.

DATA CAPTURE VERSUS INFORMATION ANALYSIS

You know you need BI to arm your enterprise's business people with knowledge, but there are some gray areas where BI might not seem like the optimal method. This is where many people become confused. Before explaining this, we will introduce the differences between BI and transaction processing systems, and data capture versus information analysis.

THE ROLES OF BI AND OPERATIONAL SYSTEMS

To understand the role of a BI system versus a transaction processing system, start with data—there is a big difference between just capturing data and using it for analysis. Capturing data means converting or translating it to a digital form. For example, when you scan a printed bar code at the grocery store checkout, it captures data on the item's price. When you use your smartphone to scan the QR code on a movie poster, it captures that data and sends you to a web video with a preview of the movie. When you use your phone to scan a check for online deposit, and then you key in the deposit amount, that information is captured and sent to the bank.

Captured data is input into operational systems. These are the systems that perform the day-to-day transactions of a business, such as deposits in a bank, sales in a store, and course registrations in a university. These are also called transaction processing systems, because it is where the enterprise processes its transactions.

Contrast this with business intelligence, which is the applications used for reporting, querying, and analytics. This category also includes data warehousing, which is the database backbone to support BI applications. A data warehouse is not the only data source used by BI, but it remains a key ingredient to an enterprise-wide solution providing clean, consistent, conformed, comprehensive, and current information, rather than yet another data silo.

Traditionally, operational systems had only limited reporting capabilities. This is understandable; they are built for transactional processing, after all. An enterprise's data can be scattered across many different operational systems, making it very hard to gather and consolidate. In a big medical center, for instance, one system could process data related to patient accounts, another could be delegated to medical research data, and another used for human resources. The systems are built to process large amounts of data, and do it quickly.

The answer to the need for better reporting was BI—and it is still the answer. But there is also a middle ground, called operational BI, which causes a lot of confusion.

OPERATIONAL BI BLURS THE LINES

Operational BI (also sometimes called real-time BI) shifts queries and reporting to the operational systems themselves. On the positive side, this allows queries on real-time data and immediate results. On the negative side, it causes confusion. I've worked with clients where people did not understand the boundaries between data capture and analysis; they thought the same data could be used for both transaction processing and analysis. The reality is that data still must be structured for analysis—hence the conundrum of data capture versus information analysis.

It is dangerous when an enterprise considers operational BI as a panacea for its business information needs. Too often, the latest technology is seen as a solution that avoids all that tough, time-consuming, data integration stuff we have been doing for years. It is not a shortcut. IT and business still need to communicate and agree on the data definitions and data transformations for business information.

WHERE DATA WAREHOUSING FITS IN

It is easy to see why the idea of simply accessing enterprise data where it is stored in the operational systems sounds so appealing. Operational BI does have many benefits, such as the simplicity of a single suite of BI tools for accessing, reporting, and analyzing data. But it is a big mistake to think it makes data warehousing obsolete. Not even close. Data warehousing is a necessary part of an enterprise's information management strategy for many reasons.

- Operational data is different from analytical data in several ways:
  - Operational data is structured for efficiently processing and managing business transactions and interactions, whereas data in data warehouses is structured for business people to understand and analyze.
  - Operational systems live in the here and now, whereas data warehousing must support the past, present, and future. Operational systems record the business event as is, whereas data warehousing tracks changes in dimensions—products, customers, businesses, geopolitical, account structures, and organizational hierarchies—so that information can be examined as is, as was, and as will be.
  - Operational data typically contains a relatively short time span, whereas analytical data is historical. A business needs to perform period-over-period analysis or examine trending using historical data.
  - The data for many of the attributes that the business wants to analyze is neither needed nor available in an operational system.
- Operational data is spread out over many source systems, making it hard to bring together and analyze. The more sources you have, the more data integration you will need.
- Every enterprise, no matter how large or small, must perform data integration to ensure that its data is consistent, clean, and correct.
- There are many business algorithms used to transform data to information outside of operations systems. Finance, sales, marketing, and other business groups each must transform the data into the business context they need to perform their work.
- There are both enterprise-wide and business group-specific performance measures of key performance indicators (KPIs) that need to be derived outside of operational systems.

There have been numerous times when vendors proclaim that data warehousing is no longer needed. Over the years, we have heard them talking about middleware, virtual data warehouses, conformed data marts, enterprise information integration (EII), enterprise application integration (EAI), service oriented architectures (SOA), data virtualization, and real-time access from every generation of BI tools. In fact, it is a recurring theme. There is no "silver bullet" that helps an enterprise avoid the hard work of data integration. Information that is clean, comprehensive, consistent, conformed, and current is not a happenstance; it requires thought and work.

Whatever silver-bullet promises you may hear, the answer has nothing to do with connectivity, bandwidth, memory, or slick interfaces. The reality is that a lot of analysis is needed in order to make sense of the data scattered across silos both in and outside of enterprises. Operational systems lack many key attributes and do not support all the necessary business transformations to handle this analysis.

Enterprises need both operational and analytical BI. Chapter 5 will cover operational BI in more detail, and will include its benefits, risks, and guidelines for doing it right.

THE FIVE Cs OF DATA

Before a BI/DW program can deliver actionable information to business people, it must whip the enterprise's data into shape. Data that has been whipped into shape will be clean, consistent, conformed, current, and comprehensive—the five Cs of data.

- **Clean**—dirty data can really muddy up a company's attempt at real-time disclosure and puts the CFO at high risk when signing off on financial reports and even press releases based on incorrect information. Dirty data has missing items, invalid entries, and other problems that wreak havoc with automated data integration and data analysis. Customer and prospect data, for example, is notorious for being dirty. Most source data is dirty to some degree, which is why data profiling and cleansing are critical steps in data warehousing.
- **Consistent**—there should be no arguments about whose version of the data is the correct one. Management meetings should never have to break down into arguments about whose number is correct when they really need to focus on how to improve customer satisfaction, increase sales, or improve profits. Business people using different hierarchies or calculations for metrics will argue regardless of how clean the transactional data is.
- **Conformed**—the business needs to analyze the data across common, shareable dimensions if business people across the enterprise are to use the same information for their decision-making.
- **Current**—the business needs to base decisions on whatever currency is necessary for that type of decision. In some cases, such as detecting credit card fraud, the data needs to be up to the minute.
- **Comprehensive**—business people should have all the data they need to do their jobs—regardless of where the data came from and its level of granularity.

So much is riding on your data. No one can afford to be sloppy or wasteful in their BI and data integration strategies. Mistakes are expensive and it is highly embarrassing when a customer finds errors before you do. Businesses, now more than ever, need to understand who their current and potential customers are as well as how much revenue and profit each product or service line generates. This demands clean, consistent, conformed, current, and comprehensive data.

Do not be swayed by vendor sales pitches for quick-hit solutions that promise short cuts. Prepackaged analytics and corporate dashboards offer the allure of off-the-shelf solutions that appear to take almost no work and instantly provide the business with the answers to all their questions. If the solution looks too good to be true, step back and ask some questions. Read the fine print, such as the qualifiers that everything works fine only if all your data is clean, all the data is included in the supported sources, and your business analytics match the prebuilt models. In short, the prebuilt solution works if you already have all your data in place. These quick and dirty solutions often have the unintended consequence of creating more data silos.

It would be great if all it took was buying the right tool to provide your business with comprehensive, cleansed, consistent, conformed, and current business information from source data. You do need to buy tools, but it does not happen in minutes, hours, or days. It takes time and hard work.

The best situation for an enterprise is when, in addition to using clean, consistent, conformed, current, and comprehensive data, they are routinely using analytic-driven processes to manage and grow the business. Advanced analytics tools such as data visualization, predictive analytics, and data discovery often play a large role in this. The reality is that most enterprises are not in this state of "analytical nirvana," but it should always be their goal.

Their path should include:

- **Getting serious about data governance.** Data governance, both for data definitions and for business agreed-on metrics, is foundational because if data is not consistent, then slick visualizations do not matter. The old school term was GIGO (garbage in, garbage out). You do not have to make everything perfect for BI to be useful, but if business people spend their time debating the numbers or reconciling data (because they do not trust it), then foundational work must be done. It is not glamorous, but it is essential.

- **Getting serious about data integration.** Most enterprises have a data integration backlog, but keep getting distracted by industry pundits and vendors that claim that this time, with the latest and greatest analytic tools, they do not need to integrate (gather, cleanse, standardize, conform, and transform from multiple business processes) data but can simply "point and click" to get their answers. It is not that easy.
- **Getting serious about spreadsheets.** Spreadsheets are often used for reporting, but it is a problem when they are used as the data integration and transformation tool without any governance or architecture. If a spreadsheet is used to analyze the same consistent, comprehensive, clean, and current data as the dashboard, data discovery, and data visualization applications then it is a viable tool. Many business people gravitate to it since it is truly pervasive.

COMMON TERMINOLOGY FROM OUR PERSPECTIVE

The three core building blocks of a DW/BI program are data integration, DW, and BI. Data integration is the foundation of DW, which, in turn, is the foundation of BI. (See Chapter 18 to learn why an enterprise should set up a BI program, as opposed to tackling projects individually and tactically.)

See Figure 1.3 for a visual representation of how they interrelate.

Data integration—combining data from different sources and bringing it together to ultimately provide a unified view. Data integration and data shadow systems are often at opposite ends of the DW/BI spectrum. If an enterprise has inconsistent data, it is highly likely that it has a data integration problem. The components of data integration include the data sources; the processes to gather, consolidate, transform, cleanse, and aggregate data and metadata; standards; tools; and resources and skills.

Data warehousing—the process of storing and staging information, separate from an enterprise's day-to-day transaction processing operations, and optimizing it for access and analysis in an enterprise. In this process, data flows from data producers to the data warehouse, where it is transformed into information for business consumers. It encompasses all the data transformations, cleansing, filtering, and aggregations necessary to provide an enterprise-wide view of the data.

As for reporting and decision-support systems, historically it was a centralized database. In the classic definition from Bill Inmon's book *Building the Data Warehouse* it is:

- Integrated—data gathered and made consistent from one or more source systems
- Subject oriented—organized by data subject rather than by application
- Time variant—historical data is stored (Note: in the beginning, enterprise applications often only stored a limited amount of current and historical data online.)
- Nonvolatile—data did not get modified in the DW, it was read-only.

BI—to present data to business people so they can use it to gain knowledge. BI enables access and delivery of information to business users. It is the visible portion of the corporate data systems, as opposed to data warehousing, which is in the "back room." BI is what business people see via tools and dashboards. The data comes from relational data sources or enterprise applications such as enterprise resource planning (ERP), customer resource management (CRM), and SCM. The source of the data can be a "black box" from the business person's perspective; they mainly care about what it is, not where it came from.

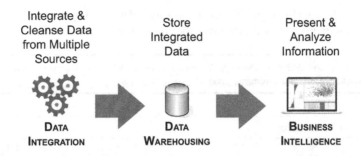

FIGURE 1.3

How BI, DW and DI fit together.

A few of the key terms are depicted in Figure 1.4. Some enterprises will use data warehousing as the umbrella term for everything depicted in that diagram while others will use BI instead. As long as it is designed, developed, tested, and deployed either term is fine. Table 1.1 presents some of the key

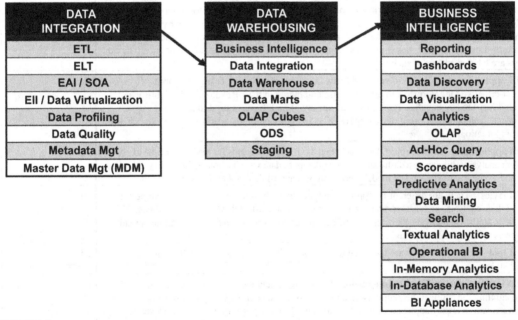

FIGURE 1.4

Categorizing BI, DW, and DI terminology.

terms and the discipline to which they apply.

Each building block includes a host of different technologies, many listed in Table 1.1. Although there is overlap, we have tried to group them by BI, DW, and data integration. This is not meant to be an all-inclusive list or definitions, but rather our perspective on some of the bigger terms. The rest of this book shows how these technologies are put into action and where they fit with one another. Becoming familiar with these terms now will help make the concepts easier to understand.

> Note that much of what is covered here is technology. As you'll read in Part VII, technology is the easy part of a DW/BI program. It is the people, process, and governance issues that are the hard part.

Table 1.1 Common Terminology

Term	Applies to BI, DW, and/or DI
Ad hoc query—People use SQL to make ad hoc queries to a database when the need arises. This is the opposite of predefined queries, which are performed routinely and known ahead of time. Tools for ad hoc querying can help you manipulate data for analysis and report creation. Most business people, however, do not really need ad hoc querying; they do fine with interactive reporting and data discovery.	BI
Analytics—The examination of information to uncover insights that give a business person the knowledge to make informed decisions. Analytics tools enable people to query and analyze information using data visualization to communicate findings in an easy-to-understand way. There are different analytical types: descriptive (what happened), diagnostic (why it happened), predictive (what is likely to happen) and prescriptive (what actions should be taken). Descriptive analytics is the most common and considered foundational or core. The others are labeled advanced analytics.	BI
BI appliance—Bundled hardware and software aimed at making it easier and more cost-effective for enterprises to purchase, use and maintain their BI solution. Scalability and flexibility are key benefits. There is a wide variety of architectures used in appliances, so a formal evaluation and proof of concept (POC) are highly recommended to ensure a match with your situation.	BI
BI application—Any BI project deliverable that the BI team develops for business people to use in their analysis. This can be a dashboard, scorecard, report, data visualization, ad hoc query, OLAP cube, predictive model, or data model. There can be many BI deliverables in an application.	BI
BI styles—There are different BI application types that a business person may use in performing their analysis, such as: reporting, dashboards or scorecards, OLAP or pivot analysis, ad-hoc query, statistical analysis, alerting or notifications, data discovery, data visualization, spreadsheets and advanced analysis.	BI
BI tool—A vendor's software tool used to develop the BI application and deliver one or more BI styles.	BI
EAI (enterprise application integration)/SOA—Tools and methods for consolidating and integrating the applications that exist in an enterprise. The goal is usually to protect the investment in legacy applications and databases while adding or migrating to a new set of applications that exploit the Internet, e-commerce, extranet, and other new technologies.	DI
Dashboards—This BI tool displays numeric and graphical informations on a single display, making it easy for a business person to get information from different sources and customize the appearance. This is often a mashup of other BI styles.	BI
Data cleansing—The process of finding and fixing errors, inconsistencies and inaccuracies in data. The level of cleanliness required depends on each industry's best practices. Data quality tools are used for the more complex processing while data integration tools performs basic processing.	DI

Table 1.1 Industry Terms—cont'd	
Term	**Applies to BI, DW, and/or DI**
Data franchising—Packages data into a BI data store so business people can understand and use it. Although this creates data that is redundant with what's in the data warehouse, it is a controlled redundancy. The data stores may be dependent data marts or cubes. Data franchising takes place after data preparation.	DW
Data mart—A subset of a data warehouse that's usually oriented to a business group or process rather than enterprise-wide views. They have value as part of the overall enterprise data architecture, but can cause problems when they sprout uncontrolled as data silos with their own data definitions, creating data shadow systems.	DW
Data mining—This process analyzes large quantities of data to find patterns such as groups of records, unusual records, and dependencies. Data mining helps businesses sift through data to find patterns and relationships they do not yet know, such as "what is the likelihood that a customer who buys our hammer will also buy our nails?"	BI
Data quality—Achieved when data embodies the "five Cs": clean, consistent, conformed, current, and comprehensive.	DW
Data preparation—The core set of processes for data integration. These processes gather data from diverse source systems, transform it according to business and technical rules, and stage it for later steps in its life cycle when it becomes information used by information consumers.	DW
Data profiling—An essential part of the data quality process; this involves examining source system data for anomalies in values, ranges, frequency, relationships, and other characteristics that could hobble future efforts to analyze it. It enables early detection of problems.	BI
Data governance—A process that enforces consistent definitions, rules, business metrics, policies, and procedures for how an enterprise treats its data. It can encompass many areas including data creation, movement, transformation, integration, definitions, all the way to consumption. A data governance program helps the organization treat its data as a corporate asset and maximize its value, but the process of governance is challenged by data that is unstructured and from the cloud, as well as by Big Data.	DI
Data visualization—Presenting data in a visual way, such as with graphs and charts, helps business people glean insights they might not otherwise discern from tabular data. Dashboards and self-service BI use data visualization, but it is only as effective as the quality of the data it draws upon.	BI
Data virtualization—Retrieving and manipulating data without requiring details of how it is formatted or where it is located. It enables enterprises to expand the data used in their analysis without requiring that it be physically integrated. They do not have to get IT involved (via business requirements, data modeling, and ETL and BI design) every time data needs to be added, allowing them to focus more on data discovery. Also called data federation and formerly called enterprise information integration (EII).	BI
Dimensional modeling—A generally accepted practice in the data warehouse industry to structure data intended for user access, analysis, and reporting in dimensional data models.	DI
ETL (extract, transform, and load)—The process in which data is taken from the source system, configured, and stored in a data warehouse or database. ETL tools automated data integration tasks.	DW

Continued

Table 1.1 Industry Terms—cont'd

Term	Applies to BI, DW, and/or DI
In-memory analytics—Leveraging advances in memory to provide faster and deeper analytics by querying a system's random-access memory (RAM) instead of on disks. In-memory analytics architectural options include in-memory analytics in the BI tools, as part of the database or on the BI appliance platform.	BI
MDM (master data management)—The set of processes used to create and maintain a consistent view, also referred to as a master list, of key enterprise reference data. This data includes such entities as customers, prospects, suppliers, employees, products, services, assets, and accounts. It also includes the groupings and hierarchies associated with these entities.	DI
Metadata management—The classic definition of metadata as "data about the data." metadata, is a means to an end—an enabler to the desired goal of making decision-support data accessible to the business community throughout an enterprise. In managing metadata, an enterprise needs to understand what the data means, how it was transformed from creation to consumption, and its associated data quality.	DI
ODS (operational data store)—A type of database sometimes used in a BI data architecture. Unlike a data warehouse, an ODS may serve both analytical and operational functions.	DW
OLAP (online analytical processing)—This technique for analyzing business data uses dimensional models often deployed as cubes, which are like multidimensional pivot tables in spreadsheets. It often answers the question "Tell me what happened and why." OLAP tools can perform trend analysis and enable drilling down into data. They enable multidimensional analysis such as analyzing by time, product, and geography. The two OLAP camps are MOLAP (multidimensional) and ROLAP (relational). HOLAP (hybrid) combines them.	BI
Operational BI—Queries and reporting are performed on operational systems themselves, as opposed to the data warehouse. Most enterprises need a mix of operational BI and analytical BI from the DW.	BI
Predictive analytics—An advanced form of analytics that uses business information to find patterns and predict future outcomes and trends. Determining credit scores by looking at a customer's credit history and other data is a typical use for predictive analytics.	BI
Report (or analytical) governance—BI deliverables need solid report governance in order to provide consistent information with which the business can make decisions. Report governance includes managing not only reports but also dashboards, scorecards, self-service BI, ad hoc query, OLAP analysis, predictive analytics, data visualization, data mining, and spreadsheets along with the data used. It is more accurate to refer to this as "analytical governance" rather than just report governance.	DI
Reporting—Collecting data from various sources and presenting it to business people in an understandable way so they can analyze it. This is the core BI style. Reports were initially static with predefined formats but have become interactive and customizable.	BI
Scorecards—Performance management tools that help managers track performance against strategic goals. These may be considered a type of dashboard.	BI
Self-service BI—Intuitive tools that allow BI consumers to obtain the information they need without the help of the IT group. People still need the IT group for the hard work of making the data clean, correct, consistent, current, and comprehensive.	BI

Continued

Table 1.1 Industry Terms—cont'd

Term	Applies to BI, DW, and/or DI
Structured data—Data that can be organized in a pre-defined record or file and may be stored in a database or spreadsheet. Some examples of structured data are an enterprise's sales, employee and financial data.	DI
Text or textual analytics—The use of data mining for analysis of unstructured textual data such as emails. Text mining tools help find, for example, instances of fraud in thousands of emails or mentions of a company's name in social media.	BI
Unstructured data—Data that is free form or unorganized. Email messages, tweets, PowerPoint, Word documents, or video images are examples of unstructured data.	DI

REFERENCES

[1] Gualtieri M, Yuhanna N, Kisker PhD H, Curran R, Murphy D. Customer data should be the lifeblood of your enterprise. Forrester Research, Inc.; June 11, 2014. Web.
[2] 2014 state of the CIO survey. CIO magazine; January 2014. PDF.
[3] Gartner predicts business intelligence and analytics will remain top focus for CIOs through 2017. Press release; December 16, 2013. Web.
[4] The deciding factor: big data & decision making. Capgemini and the Ecomomist; June 26, 2012. Web.
[5] Pearson T, Wegener R. Big data: the organizational challenge. Bain & Company; 2013. PDF.
[6] Manyika J, Chui M. Big data: the next frontier for innovation, competition, and productivity. McKinsey Global Institute; May 13, 2011. Web.
[7] Taming the digital dragon: the 2014 CIO agenda. Gartner; 2014. Web.
[8] Kisker PhD H, Green C. TechRadar™: BI analytics, Q3 2013. Forrester Research, Inc.; July 11, 2013. PDF.

BUSINESS AND TECHNICAL NEEDS

JUSTIFYING BI: BUILDING THE BUSINESS AND TECHNICAL CASE

INFORMATION IN THIS CHAPTER:

- Building the business case
- Building the technical case
- Assessing readiness
- Creating a high-level BI road map
- Developing scope, preliminary plan, and budget
- Obtaining program and project approval
- Justification pitfalls

WHY JUSTIFICATION IS NEEDED

You have read all the press proclaiming the importance of business intelligence (BI) and analytics for enterprises of all sizes and across all industries. You have done your homework on how it will benefit your company, and the rest of the IT group agrees. Your business executives have also joined the bandwagon because they understand that BI will provide the edge that they need to be competitive or to grow their business. Everyone agrees that BI has been consistently listed among the top technology projects for organizations over the last decade.

So it seems like a no-brainer to skip the justification process and proceed directly into the project, right? Not so fast.

Although enthusiastic business executives or chief information officers (CIOs) can make it possible to get BI projects approved without much formal justification effort, it is not a good idea. Project approval is not the only reason to go through this process. A careful, well-documented justification can help prevent your project from being labeled a failure.

According to studies, the majority of BI projects fail. These projects fail not because of technology shortcomings but from an expectations shortfall. In addition, BI projects have a tendency to be late and over budget. Many of these problems stem from failing to establish what needs to be built from a business perspective, and then managing the project's scope and change management based on these flawed expectations.

The BI team needs to make both the business and technical case to determine the need, identify the benefits, and, most importantly, set expectations. With the case established, the BI team needs to estimate scope, costs, schedule, and a return on investment (ROI). Identifying risks and an organization's readiness is critical to determining how realistic expectations are.

This chapter will review the common pitfalls that BI teams encounter when they shortchange the project justification process. Although a BI justification is generally regarded only as a selling device, its importance as a vehicle to set expectations and guide the BI project cannot be overlooked.

BUILDING THE BUSINESS CASE

Although most organizations need to justify and get approval for investments in IT projects, such as BI, it is surprising how many are able to do so without building a business case, or by presenting only high-level, intangible benefits. BI projects can get approved without a business case when the business sponsors or CIOs think it is obvious that a BI investment will pay off. They have read numerous BI articles in the press, their peers are doing it, or they were involved in BI projects in previous jobs. But even if a BI effort can get approval and funding without justification, it is crucial to build a business case and get stakeholders to agree on it.

There are many hidden dangers for an organization that kicks off a BI project without developing a business case. During the first generation of data warehousing, many BI groups made this mistake when they fell into the trap of assuming it was obvious that a data warehouse (DW) was needed. Typically, the "if we build it they will come" approach resulted in projects that were too big and long, missed expectations as businesses were sold an information nirvana where everyone gets all the information they need, and spawned alternate reporting solutions such as spreadmarts or data shadow systems (those pesky one-off spreadsheets that business groups created in frustration when the DW project took too long).

The business case needs to answer the following in respect to the BI solution:

- What business problems or opportunities are being addressed?
- Who will use it?
- What are the anticipated business benefits?
- Were there any prior BI initiatives that failed, and if so, why?

After answering these questions, the BI team needs to get business sponsorship, involvement, and commitment to the BI effort. It is a common mistake to think that getting the budget approved is the sponsor's only deliverable. Although business sponsors do need to come up with the money, they also have to commit business resources to work with the BI team throughout the project, engage in politics to ensure money and resources are maintained for the long haul, and provide support when there are inevitable hiccups.

To answer these questions and define the business case, you will need to:

- Review the organization's business initiatives
- Enlist a BI sponsor
- Connect with BI stakeholders
- Identify business processes affected by BI
- Document business benefits

The BI effort needs to be based on supporting the needs of business initiatives, business drivers, and business processes. The focus is on solving business problems, not IT issues such as what BI tool should be used. By putting the business first, you encourage the business to value and use the resulting BI solution.

REVIEW ORGANIZATION'S BUSINESS INITIATIVES AND PROCESSES

The success of BI lies in addressing the organization's key business needs and priorities. The best way to understand these needs is to learn what your organization faces in terms of:

- Strategic business initiatives and their underlying data needs
- Current business processes being hindered by analytical bottlenecks

Business Initiatives

Most organizations perform business planning for strategic initiatives with a minimum time horizon of the next couple of fiscal years. These business initiatives have been prioritized, approved, funded, and scheduled. In today's data-driven climate, it is almost a certainty that these initiatives need data and analytics. If BI is not pervasive in an organization, however, these needs are probably not being adequately planned for. The BI team needs to do their due diligence and determine how BI would support these business initiatives. They can then use this information to help build a business case.

Business Processes

Chances are, the organization has business processes that are constrained by limitations in the data and its analysis. For example, an inability to analyze a customer's sales across all of your organization's channels with the profit margins of the products purchased keeps the business from determining the lifetime value of that customer. Again, if BI is not pervasive, then it may not be readily apparent to the business that analytics has become a gating factor in these business processes. Adding the current analytical bottlenecks along with the business initiatives needing analytics can help strengthen the business case.

Be aware, however, that listing the business initiatives and bottlenecked processes may generate an overwhelming business demand for BI that an organization will not be able to deliver all at once. This list should be the foundation for a long-term BI program (discussed in Chapter 18) with priorities matched to business demand.

In the short term, prioritize the list and reduce it to a set of business requirements that this BI justification will address. Bear in mind that, for the long term, there may be other opportunities for BI that you need to plan for. There may be emerging initiatives and processes that cannot be addressed now, but will need BI down the road.

SOLICIT BI SPONSORSHIP

The next step is to solicit and engage business sponsors. Use your list of business needs (above) to identify the business people you will approach as potential business sponsors. The sponsor needs to either have the budgetary authority to fund the BI project or be an influential leader who can get funding approved. Beyond the initial funding, a business sponsor needs to secure the commitment of resources from the business stakeholders and users (below) to ensure BI success.

Key characteristics of a business sponsor are being politically astute, enthusiastic, and realistic. The first two characteristics are obvious, but it is important that neither the sponsor nor the BI team gets carried away with being overly optimistic. Although having a gung ho sponsor may seem appealing, setting realistic expectations is necessary for BI success. In addition, a realistic sponsor will understand that there may be problems or setbacks during the BI project that will need to be handled. Getting support for the typical issues that one always encounters during a BI project will be extremely helpful.

Ideally, a BI project has the support of the CIO, but that person should not be the sole sponsor of the project. The risks of a CIO-only sponsored BI project can include that it:

- Is perceived as technology driven
- Does not get business commitment and involvement
- Has an unlimited scope and is difficult to manage

The BI project needs at least one committed business sponsor and, if possible, multiple business sponsors representing a cross-section of the organization. This is a balancing act, where one sponsor may create the impression that the BI effort is geared exclusively to that sponsor's business group, or too many sponsors create friction with conflicting priorities. The best case is one primary sponsor with a couple of secondary sponsors.

The BI team needs to interview business sponsors (see Chapter 3) to determine the business initiative and current analytical pain points that they would like to address, set priorities, and help establish the scope of the BI project. This is where you start to build a solid working relationship with your sponsors. The conversations will be more productive if you have done your due diligence and explored what business initiatives and analytical pain points your sponsor(s) will likely discuss.

ENLIST BI STAKEHOLDERS

With the business sponsors engaged and their priorities established, the next step is to enlist the business stakeholders who will be affected by the BI project. They include the business people who will be either direct users of the BI solution or whose work will be affected by the BI solution, as well as those working on data governance.

Getting the business stakeholders involved while building the business case enables more detailed business input and may help identify gaps and risks. In addition, the stakeholders will likely be the primary input for detailed business requirements later in the project (see Chapter 3).

One of the most frequent mistakes made when engaging business stakeholders is relying exclusively on a business group's "power users," i.e., the go-to people in the organization who get the data needed for others' analysis. The power users typically use spreadsheets or build spreadmarts to provide reporting to their organization. You should engage these folks, but if you limit yourself to them then you may encounter several problems:

- You never know what other stakeholders really need to do their jobs since you just may be hearing filtered requirements from the power users.
- Business power users, being data and tool savvy, are not necessarily representative of the other stakeholders' abilities and needs.
- Power users built the spreadmarts, and, sometimes very subtlety, they become obstacles to replacing those spreadmarts with the BI solution.

IDENTIFY BUSINESS PROCESSES AFFECTED BY BI

When creating the BI business case, it is important to identify the key business processes that are affected and organize your project to support them. Business processes are the collection of tasks that an organization performs for operations and management, including order processing, customer acquisition, budgeting, expense management, customer support, and marketing campaigns. Business processes create data that needs to be captured, monitored, and measured. Business processes generate the business measures and key performance indicators (KPIs) that are so common in BI deliverables.

Organizing your business case, and later your project deliverables, around business processes offers many advantages because that is how the organization works. Using business processes as the BI building blocks enables you to better identify the business people who will use your BI solution and how it will be used in their jobs. Too often, business cases and BI projects are oriented around BI's technical deliverables, such as reports and dashboards, rather than a business deliverable. Business focus creates a more compelling business case and often gets business stakeholders more involved in getting BI integrated into their jobs.

Focusing on business processes also makes it easier to identify business benefits resulting from the use of BI in the organization.

DOCUMENT BUSINESS BENEFITS

You need to formalize the business case for BI projects, otherwise, several problems can arise:

- Overblown expectations, which cannot be met
- Underfunding for BI initiative and the ongoing BI team
- Continued use or expansion of data shadow systems
- Inability to garner business support for data governance initiatives
- BI is seen as expensive overhead and not an enabler supporting business
- BI is viewed as a mere report generator

DETERMINE BUSINESS VALUE (TANGIBLE BENEFITS)

An organization should not proceed with a business case based solely on intangible benefits such as providing "a single version of the truth" or "better decision making." Although the BI solution likely will deliver these benefits, they are highly subjective and difficult to substantiate. This makes them more than likely a recipe to disappoint business stakeholders who expected something else or something more. Instead, base the business case on tangible or quantifiable business benefits. See Figure 2.1.

Tangible benefits for BI typically fall into several broad categories:

- Revenue optimization
- Cost reductions
- Risk reduction
- Regulatory compliance
- Ability to enter new markets and develop new products

One of the benefits of aligning the BI business case with business initiatives is that the initiatives have likely already been justified and have tangible benefits assigned to them. If BI becomes an essential component of those initiatives, then the work of assigning tangible benefits has already been done for you.

There will also be tangible benefits associated with the business processes that the BI solution is going to affect—you've already identified these processes in the business case. Have a discussion with the business stakeholders to determine exactly what tangible benefits are associated with those processes.

CATEGORIES OF BUSINESS BENEFITS	EXAMPLES
Revenue optimization	• Increase sales revenue amount per $ spent on sales campaign • Increase up-sell & cross-sell revenue per account manager visits
Cost reductions	• Reduce time and people involved in expense reporting • Reduce inventory costs by using predictive analytics to reorder
Risk reduction	• Automate fraud detection with the use of predictive analytics • Reduce loan defaults using customer analytics
Regulatory compliance	• Determine contractual metrics to get best payment terms enhancing revenue • Comply with governmental regulatory reporting requirements avoiding penalties
Ability to enter new markets and develop new products	• Determine new territories or industries to target with specific products • Design new products based on customer, product and competitive analytics

FIGURE 2.1

Business benefits matrix.

Analytics and data-driven decision making has become invaluable to organizations of all sizes and across all industry categories. There are countless articles and case studies proclaiming the business value resulting from BI projects. You should have no problem gathering a list of business benefits that your BI project can deliver.

BUILDING THE TECHNICAL CASE

A BI project will introduce new technologies and products into an enterprise across a variety of BI, data integration, database, and infrastructure categories. Even if your organization has been providing BI solutions for years, new technologies and products will likely need to be added to your BI tool portfolio to increase business value, use, and productivity.

TECHNOLOGY AND PRODUCT SHORT LISTS

With each new technology and product, the best practice is to conduct an evaluation and, if possible, a proof of concept. The evaluation should have stakeholders, both technologists and business people, involved throughout the process. It is important to involve the people who are going to use these technologies in their day-to-day jobs, whether it is the business person who will perform analysis or the developer who will use the tools to create the BI environment. Involve the management personnel, business power users, and architects (if you have them). Be very cautious, however, if they are the only people involved, because their ability to learn new tools may be far better than that of the people who will really use the tools. BI projects can flounder because business people cannot get used to the interface and capabilities of a new tool.

As shown in Figure 2.2, the product evaluation process will involve these steps:

- Gather and prioritize requirements
- Establish success and value criteria
- Select short list of product candidates
- Conduct product reviews with hands-on proofs of concept, if possible
- Score and rank products
- Review results and select product(s)
- Haggle with product vendors over pricing

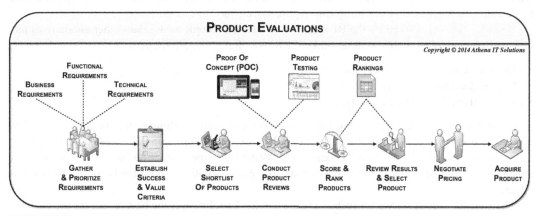

FIGURE 2.2

Selecting product short list(s) workflow.

The costs for these technologies ranges from free (at least in respect to licensing costs) to very expensive. Prior to creating your product short list, you need to get a ballpark estimate on what your organization would likely spend and what the products will cost. You probably will not tell the vendor what your budget is, but you need to filter products based on what you can afford or are willing to spend. It does not make sense to evaluate products that you will not realistically purchase unless it is part of your bargaining strategy with the vendor. The book discusses product evaluations in Chapter 7.

Most evaluations have a long list of functional and usability criteria from both technology and business perspectives. After the product reviews, score each product according to this criterion and then rank them, creating a final score that identifies the winner. An objective evaluation will help lead to the best solution for the organization.

There are two mind-sets regarding when product evaluations will occur. (See Chapter 18.) Some organizations will conduct the evaluations during the BI justification phase in order to determine the specific products and their costs. In this scenario, the organization knows it needs a BI project, but more details are necessary for specific projects to be approved. The other approach, which is more common, is to perform an abbreviated evaluation that would document:

- List of technologies needed
- Short list of products that will evaluated with winner(s) used in BI project
- Range of high-level cost estimates for above

The first step toward building your technical case is selecting the products and technologies, or at least narrowing down a short list, but as we will discuss in the next two subsections, you still need to convince business people and technologists that they ought to *use* these tools.

CONVINCING BUSINESS PEOPLE

Business management is likely very excited about the BI hype that they have read or heard. Business power users who love new toys are also very interested. But that interest is before people start adding up the time, costs, and resources for the BI project. More importantly, it is before people start considering the changes that will be needed and the associated business opportunity loss that will happen during that change. Saying "yes" to one thing can require saying "no" to others.

What is often overlooked by the BI team is that business people may select other alternatives that they consider "good enough" because unlike the BI solution, those alternatives:

- Do not require a significant investment
- Can be done more quickly
- Do not require retraining and change

An alternative to using new technology can even mean doing nothing (continue to use what you have) or use substitutes. These substitutes can include expanding operational reporting or using more data shadow systems. These "good enough" alternatives may mean that the business does not fully engage during the BI project or that they use the alternative solution more than BI solution once it is operational.

The BI team needs to make the technical case that the BI solution is the best choice for the business user. This is where the business case needs to be tightly coupled with the technical case. The BI team has to justify or explain why the BI solution will be more effective at meeting the goals of the business case from functional, productivity, and long-term cost perspectives. This is not a feature comparison like the tool evaluation but rather a comparison of alternatives. Often, the technologists and business power users are so enamored with the new tool that they have no idea that the business community would consider "inferior" alternatives.

Operational systems are typically bundled with reporting capabilities. (Operational BI is discussed further in Chapter 5.) Business people may complain about these systems, but the short-term benefit is that they are inexpensive and may be producing some value. If the business choses the alternative of expanding these reporting capabilities, it will likely be cheaper and faster than a BI solution, at least initially. Likewise, it is almost guaranteed that business people have been using spreadsheets to do reporting and, if the reporting complexity warranted it, they also built data shadows systems. However, cheaper and faster stops looking so attractive when you look at the medium term, which is more expensive for IT support, and the long term, which is far more expensive and less agile as you attempt to expand with all those data shadow systems.

The technical case, therefore, does not end with comparing different BI tools and selecting the "best," but rather needs to compare BI tools with alternatives that business people are inclined to use. This comparison is not a feature checklist bake-off; it is a reality check of what would convince business people to actually use the BI tool. The BI evaluation can give a false impression that just because a tool has many features it will be preferable to what the business users have available now. It is not the best tool if the business people will not use it.

The business community has to invest time in learning the new BI tools and changing existing business processes to take advantage of them. They also have to spend time waiting for the new BI solution to be built while the business climate—sales, operations, competitors, the economy, and government regulations—keeps changing. That time is an opportunity loss that must be factored into the cost–benefit calculations. In fact, the first generation of DWs often failed for the very reason that they took too long to build and the businesses could not wait.

CONVINCING THE TECHNOLOGISTS

All the technology stakeholders in your organization are saying that they are excited about the BI project, especially about learning and using the new technology and products. You are thinking that there may be business people resistant to change, but the technologists are on board and looking forward to change.

But below the surface, you might be surprised that there is resistance to change, possibly even some passive aggressive behavior. The people who say that they are excited may not even realize that when it comes down to it, they do not really want to change. You have to be thinking, "Why would technologists not want new toys?" The answer: basic human behavior. This is a phenomenon that surprises and thwarts many a BI effort. You can avoid this by making the technical case for the technologists.

First, you need to get the technologists involved in the technology and product selection process. In this phase, you will need to:

- Determine the technologies required
- Create a short list of product candidates

BI projects, especially the first one for the organization, often need to introduce many new technologies such as various categories of business intelligence, data integration, database, and infrastructure tools. List the technologies that will be needed to fulfill business requirements and classify them as must-haves versus nice-to-haves. Your business requirements are very high level at this point, but should be enough to develop these lists.

Once you have determined the technology categories for the BI project, you need to create a short list of products from those categories.

Second, despite the current state of reporting, the technologists are probably "king of the hill" with their business users and their management. They are the firefighters who people depend on because they are the only ones who understand how to create reports with the current technology. There may be long queues for getting reports from them, and the resulting data may be limited, but nobody blames them for that. Instead, they get rewarded for whatever they can do. But when new products are introduced, they will be novices again. Even if there is no intention of replacing them, that has to be in the back of their minds.

Finally, it takes time to become proficient at a new product. During that time, they will likely keep thinking that they could do things faster the old way. Developers can crank out code pretty quickly. In addition, although there may be product training, there usually is no training for designers and developers on BI concepts, processes, and architectures. This lack of fundamental and architectural training usually results in solutions built the old way—without leveraging the new products. This further reinforces the reluctance to embrace the new tool.

You have to sell the technologists that these new products will not only help the business, but also themselves. I am not trying to be cynical, but it does come down to "what's in it for me" with the technologists. This is not to say they are thinking this outwardly, but deep down they are experts in the current environment, and no matter how bad that is, they are still the gurus. You can pitch all the business benefits and productivity gain, but if that means they are novices again or worse, they will be reluctant. As discussed earlier, it is most helpful to have a powerful sponsor who can guarantee that people will commit their time and will have enough of their other tasks freed up for them to work on this project.

You need to use care in selecting and using these new tools, and try to help the technologists become even more valuable in their current organization and in their industry. Learning new skills and then becoming an expert in that tool does make them more marketable. You need them to not only help in the selection but advocate their use.

ASSESSING READINESS

Even if you have built a terrific business case and have strong business enthusiasm, you still need to critically examine your organization's readiness for BI. Realistically assess its readiness for the following areas:

- Data
- Expertise and experience
- Analytical commitment
- Organizational and cultural change
- Financial commitment

Many people refer to the above as a risk assessment, and would potentially list risk mitigation strategies. If you look at the above areas optimistically, then you are determining:

- Your organization's current state
- What you need to be to be successful in BI
- The gap
- How you bridge that gap

Your BI justification and project plan must include what your organization needs to do in order to be ready to design, build, and implement BI successfully.

DATA AND DATA QUALITY

Many a BI project has been blindsided by data and data-quality issues. Often these issues are not apparent until business people start testing the BI solution just before going "live." These unfortunate surprises happen when people fail to assess the current state of their organization's data and instead get enamored with the flash of BI products such as dashboards and data visualizations. Product demos should always contain a disclaimer that business people can only use them if the underlying data accurately reflects the business processes relevant to decision making.

The key data attributes that need to be assessed are the 5C's (covered in detail in Chapter 1):

- Clean—is the data error free?
- Consistent—are there many overlapping sources for data with inconsistent data?

- Conformed—can the business analyze it across common, sharable dimensions?
- Current—is the data updated and available in the frequency needed?
- Comprehensive—is the data needed for analytics even available or collected at this time?

You need to review the current state of the data by talking to subject matter experts on source systems and potentially performing a high-level data profiling exercise. A critical assessment of the 5 C's will provide a data-quality baseline. From this, you can determine the scope of the data integration and cleansing efforts that the BI project will need to provide the analytics that the business is requesting.

Determining the scope will typically involve many back-and-forth discussions with the business. The initial request will likely ask for a level of the 5 C's that is too time consuming and costly. Unrealistic data-quality requirements can be the downfall of a BI project. After discussing the trade-offs, you should be able to achieve a mutual agreement on data-quality requirements with associated costs.

EXPERTISE AND EXPERIENCE

If an organization is just starting its BI initiative, there are not only new technologies to learn but also a significant amount of new architectural, design, and development concepts and techniques that are associated with successful implementations. These include:

- Data architecture and data modeling to support new processing such as data integration, data warehousing, master data management (MDM), and analytics
- Data integration
- BI

In addition, business people also will be introduced to new BI technologies and analytical techniques such as data visualization and predictive analytics.

Be aware of these risks:

- Organizations will not have the expertise to use the tools
- Organizations will not have the expertise in the new concepts and techniques to effectively use the new tools
- Business people will not understand how to leverage the new BI technologies and analytics to obtain business value

Most organizations recognize the first risk and take steps to mitigate it. Organizations get training for their staff, supplement their staff with consultants, or have consultants perform all the work with the new technologies. Getting the staff trained is a terrific long-term solution to obtaining the needed expertise, but in the short term, people who have only just been trained will not be as productive and will likely make rookie mistakes, putting the BI project at risk. Augmenting staff or having only experienced consultants work with the new technologies helps mitigate those risks.

One of the risks organizations often do not recognize is not having the expertise in the new architectural design and development concepts and processes needed to effectively use these new technologies and implement BI. First-generation DWs and BI solutions are typically built the way developers had always been building systems, resulting in systems that take longer to build than they should, perform poorly, or do not work at all. In addition, without BI expertise, the new BI team may not know that it should be performing better. "You don't know what you don't know" is the phrase that rings true.

Finally, business people are the ultimate BI consumers. As with technologists, it is recognized that business people using the BI tools need product training, but conceptual training on the use of analytics in one's job is not typically addressed. There are many analytical techniques offered through BI tools today such as data visualization and statistical analysis. If your business case relies on these techniques being used but your business people do not currently have the expertise, you need to address this in the BI justification and planning.

ORGANIZATIONAL AND CULTURAL CHANGE

In order for BI to succeed, your organization needs to be committed to or strive to become a data-driven and analytical culture. This may be quite different from the current state if the organization has been operating by making decisions with incomplete data. If decision making has been based on "gut feelings," then the organization may need to make a tectonic cultural change. Most organizations need to make this change in today's business climate but will only do so if it is recognized and planned for.

The BI center of excellence (described in Chapter 19) is one example of an organizational change that can help increase the success of BI in the enterprise while also allowing different groups to share the success and risks.

You have identified the business processes that will be affected by BI. The people working on these business processes need to understand and be committed to the changes that will occur. These changes will often involve much more time and resources than simply using a new BI tool. You need to factor these costs and additional work resulting from the impact of these changes into the BI justification.

FINANCIAL AND RESOURCE COMMITMENT

Obviously, you are getting financial and resource commitments, but these efforts can fall short for two reasons:

- A total cost of ownership (TCO) is not completed
- A budget is approved, but resources are not committed and people do not free up their time

You need to develop cost estimates for the full life cycle of a BI solution from design through implementation and ongoing support. Almost everyone will include software, infrastructure, and external labor costs, but you need to include internal costs for both IT and business people. You need to do this even if your financial justification does not need to include the internal costs so that your organization's management understands the full cost. Often there is sticker shock; that is fine, as it generates conversations on what the business is really willing to spend. You will need to adjust scope appropriately if your financial commitment is smaller than you had planned for.

The other problem that BI projects run into is that although business people and other technologists outside the BI team are assigned to work on the project, these stakeholders are already fully committed to other work. You need their management to free up their time so they can work on the BI project—otherwise it will never succeed.

CREATING A BI ROAD MAP

According to a Chinese proverb, a journey of a thousand miles begins with a single step. BI is a journey that is not going to be completed with a single BI project; if you are successful, BI will continually expand with new data, technologies, analytics, and business uses. With this in mind, a mistake organizations often make when starting their BI journey is to trying to "boil the ocean" with their first BI project.

The journey requires you to create an overall BI program. This should include a road map for your BI program over the next couple of years, or whatever time frame is typically used for your IT-related programs. The underlying reason for this is that BI should be built incrementally and iteratively. The overall BI program becomes the framework of the journey, with individual BI projects building out specific portions of that road map, relying on tactical decisions that are appropriate for that particular project at that particular time. The road map is similar to software firms gradually building their product capabilities out one release (project) at a time.

The BI road map lists projects with the following attributes:

- Key business initiatives supported and business processes involved
- High-level business deliverables
- Data source feeds (at the application level, not tables or files)
- Technology introduced
- Business groups involved

See the book Web site www.BIguidebook.com for a sample BI road map template.

The BI road map is a living vision that will evolve, reacting to changes in business, organization, economy, and technology. In addition, as an organization sees the business value from BI, new and expanded business uses for BI will become apparent. With each new BI project and justification, the BI road map should be revised to reflect the current BI vision and analytical demand.

DEVELOPING SCOPE, PRELIMINARY PLAN, AND BUDGET

Developing the preliminary scope, plan, and budget (see Chapter 18) is a mix of art and science. You need to develop these with high-level and incomplete information, but then you will be held accountable for both the timeline and budget of the BI project. Many BI projects are over budget and late not because the BI project team "messed up," but because preliminary plans were too optimistic, overly aggressive, or just plain naïve.

It may sound like "Mission Impossible," but with some guidelines you should be able to set proper expectations.

A BI assessment helps answer questions about the project, such as what is the scope? How should we proceed? What will it cost? See Chapter 18 for a section on BI assessments.

Keep it simple. Do not get bogged down in trying to formulate detailed plans and costs when you simply are not going to have the information to do so at this point. You only have to develop high-level plans and a ballpark estimate with upper and lower bounds for costs. You should be able to explain the scope, plan, and budget each on one presentation slide.

Be conservative. No matter how many superstars you have working on the BI project, there are so many new technologies, products, and process changes affecting business people and technologists that you have to plan on activities taking longer than normal because most people will be novices.

Expect the unexpected. Every project has some combination of data, source system, database and data integration, and business processes surprises. BI teams are always complaining that the business is adding or changing its requirements well after development has started. You need to include time in the plan for contingencies, because the inevitable is going to happen. You need to just say no to the business sponsor or CIO when they say you do not need to add this time, because you absolutely do.

PROJECT SCOPE

The project scope lays out the subset of the BI road map that you are planning on delivering in the next project, using the same context in which it was discussed:

- Key business initiatives supported and business processes involved
- High-level business deliverables
- Data source feeds
- Technology introduced
- Business groups involved

  In addition to the above, document the following in order to establish scope:

- Business objectives
- Targeted business users
- Stakeholders
- Assumptions
- Risks
- Success criteria
- What is out of scope

PROJECT PLAN

You need to create a project milestone plan indicating the completion of project phases. If your organization has a project methodology that has successfully dealt with uncertainty, you should use it, otherwise use the BI project methodology described in Chapter 18. We advocate an incremental and iterative project methodology that leverages a waterfall framework for the overall project (especially when data integration tasks are involved) and an agile-style approach for individual BI applications. Key milestones in the overall project will include, at a minimum: when you define requirements, design the system, develop the code, conduct business user acceptance testing, perform systems testing, and deploy the BI solution to its users. Of course, the only date most business people will hear is when they will have the BI solution.

It is also worth noting that including a defined change management process will help with resetting expectations along the way. The scope always creeps, so plan for it.

> See the book Web site at www.BIguidebook.com for a sample BI project milestone plan that you can use to get your own plan started.

There are two opposing approaches to developing a milestone plan: delivery-based versus time-based. Many technologists feel a delivery-based approach is very logical and therefore the most sensible to use. The reality is that you do not really know the detailed requirements at this time, and they are likely to change and expand during the course of the project. Using an iterative and incremental project methodology mixed with agile enables the time-boxed approach to incrementally build the individual BI applications while managing within an overall milestone project schedule.

A very successful approach is to create the initial project milestone plan based on the high-level deliverables known at that time, but manage the project as a time-based (and budget-limited) approach. The reasons are: (1) business users' expectations are fixated on the project completion date and the business sponsors are focused on the budget, and (2) BI is never done, so if you keep pushing back the schedule to accommodate changes, you may never be done. In addition, if you push back the completion date, the business will more likely remember you are late rather than that you added more functionality for them. One of the key purposes of the BI road map is to enable additional functionality to move into subsequent releases, and not to have to have everything get done at one time. This allows you to manage scope changes successfully.

PROJECT BUDGET

The typical costs components for your budget include:

- Labor
  - Internal resources—IT and business
  - External resources—typically technologists
  - Training—IT and business
- Software
  - Licensing or subscription costs
  - Maintenance or upgrade costs
- Infrastructure
  - Capital purchases, expenses or subscriptions
  - Maintenance or upgrade costs
- Software
  - Capital or expenses, on premise versus cloud
  - Maintenance or upgrade costs
- Additional expenses
  - Examples: travel and communication
- Ongoing support
  - Labor, software, and infrastructure costs to sustain BI after deployment

You might think it would be a straightforward exercise to determine the cost of your BI project, but at this point there are many unknowns and alternatives, such as:

- Software (Chapter 7 will explain these in detail.)
  - What technologies and product categories do you need?
  - Do you buy software suites or bundles versus individual products?
  - How many licenses for business users and developers?
  - Should you deploy in cloud versus on premise?
  - Should you use BI appliances versus the traditional BI approach where software and hardware are not prepackaged?
- Infrastructure
  - What do you need in regard to processing, memory, storage, and network bandwidth?
  - Should you deploy in cloud versus on premise?
  - How and when do you plan to increase infrastructure?
- Labor
  - What will be the size of your internal development team?
  - How many business people will be involved and in what roles?
  - How many IT people outside of the BI team will be involved and in what roles?
  - Will you use external consulting resources and, if so, how?
  - What training will be needed for technologists and business people?
- Product costs
  - Vendor pricing schemas are often complex and confusing
  - Estimating pricing may be difficult because discounting, if applicable, may not occur until you are closer to purchasing
  - You have a wide range of cost of products from open source to very expensive proprietary products, although there is typically a wide range of prices in proprietary products too
- Do you capitalize (CAPEX) or expense (OPEX) items? This is a decision that the finance group will make. They need to be engaged in the financial justification.

After thinking about these unknowns and alternatives, you might consider it a daunting task to estimate your BI project's costs and create a budget. Do not worry, it is really not as hard as it seems. First, you need a ballpark estimate rather than an exact cost. It is best to provide a range of costs with upper and lower bounds to reflect different options that are available.

Second, and most important, this task is especially difficult (and maybe impossible at this point in the process) if you try to calculate the costs bottom-up, i.e., determining the individual component costs and then summing them for a total. Instead, you should develop a project budget by using a top-down approach of estimating cost *categories* rather than individual components. This is similar to how you would work with an architect in developing a budget for building a house. You would discuss with the architect the type and size of the house, the number and types of rooms, and overall quality of the house, but you would not start pricing out shingles, electrical wiring, and plumbing fixtures. You would get to those details later, just as you will with the BI project; the initial planning is to develop a ballpark budget within a cost range. Once you agree on that budget and blueprints are created, you can start to price out the details.

Remember to work with your organization's finance group. It is likely that there are standards that you need to follow for estimating budgets and costs.

CALCULATING BENEFITS AND ROI

Estimating benefits and calculating a ROI is often a very difficult task because business people, although very helpful in identifying requirements when formulating the business case, struggle with quantifying the financial return. For example, if the BI solution will improve up-selling and cross-selling to customers, can they tell you by how much and over what period of time? Those numbers might be difficult to determine, especially if your organization does not have a way to compare the results with and without using the BI solution. Another interesting twist: if the business people being asked to estimate the financial return are compensated based on these estimates, they may be reluctant to perform them, or they may want to keep the estimates low to guarantee that there is a measurable ROI. Nothing changes behavior in business more than something that is tied to compensation.

The reality is that BI is an enabler for business people making decisions and taking the actions that will create business value. This means that the BI solution is valuable for its users to do their jobs and, ideally, improve their performance. Just as we approach the cost side of the equation by ball parking the estimates, you should do the same when working on the business value. Ask the business people what the BI solution is worth to them. Consider this discussion a negotiation. If they cannot articulate how the BI solution will provide value, you may need to shift your focus to other business people who can. There is no question that the BI project offers value, you just need to quantify the value for your organization. Do not beg for business people to fund and use your BI solutions; rather, work with those who do see the value.

How do you calculate the ROI of a successful project? It is going to be different for every situation. Here are some potential business benefits (you will need to quantify them for your own organization):

- How many days have you reduced from the budget, planning, and forecasting cycle? How much time have you reduced from the monthly budget-to-actual review cycle? What is the value of shifting your financial group from gathering data to analyzing it? What is the value to the business groups scattered across your enterprise of being able to manage their business rather than playing with spreadsheets?
- How much do you save by meeting financial reporting and regulatory compliance with consistent information and automated analysis, validation, and distribution of your reports without any scrambling or tense, late nights?
- How much impact can marketing have on profitability now that you've reduced report time from weeks to minutes, giving them real-time visibility into the impact of the new pricing and promotional strategies they are experimenting with?
- What is the top-line impact knowing that a certain product is now selling like hotcakes in a previously untapped geography, and being able to shift stock, reprice the product to remain competitive and profitable, and provide manufacturing with the data it needs to plan for ramping up inventory?
- How many data shadow system spreadsheets did you eliminate, thereby ensuring that everyone is using the same data? How many arguments over who has the right data has this eliminated? How much did those conflicting decisions cost the enterprise before?

OBTAINING APPROVAL

No matter how formal a process your enterprise requires for your budget requests, it is important to document the BI justification for project management, scope management, and communication. The BI justification needs to include:

- Overview
- Business problem or opportunities
- Situational analysis
- Solution alternatives
- Project description—plan and budget
- Cost–benefit analysis
  - Initial investments
  - TCO
- Risks and issues
- Business sponsors and stakeholders

> See the book Web site www.biguidebook.com for a BI justification template that will help you get started.

The purpose of the BI justification is to get funding approval, but resource commitments are also critical. Of course, you need to get your internal staffing and external resources approved for BI development, but you also need time commitment for the business people and other technologists who will be involved. Frequently, stakeholders are already fully committed to their own jobs and do not have time for the BI project. You need to ensure realistic commitments.

In addition to budget and resource approvals, you also need to get agreement on who is responsible for sign-off on the following:

- Follow-on detailed project requirements and priorities
- Scope change
- User acceptance testing
- System testing
- Deployment

COMMON JUSTIFICATION PITFALLS

You will find failed BI projects in all sizes of companies, in all industries. There are dozens of reasons why BI projects fail, and a flawed justification process is just one of them. Justification problems are usually related to issues with people, not technology. You can blame many of these problems on the following justification pitfalls:

- Overzealous business sponsors
- The CIO is the sole sponsor
- Intangible benefits
- Confusion between BI technology and business value

Why else do BI projects fail to meet expectations? The list could go on forever, but here are a just a few, in no particular order:
- Scope creep is not managed and controlled
- Organizational issues and politics
- Assuming technology alone can solve anything
- Lack of awareness, education, and internal marketing of the project
- Lack of communication
- Training focuses on the tool, skipping concepts and fundamentals
- Focusing on power users instead of everyone else in the business group
- Data quality is not addressed properly
- Business group does not commit resources
- Lack of oversight from a steering committee
- Too big, too fast—rather than taking an incremental approach
- Ignoring data shadow systems

I often write about these issues and many, many more on my blog, www.datadoghouse.com.

OVERZEALOUS BUSINESS SPONSOR

It is great to have an enthusiastic business sponsor, but it is a mixed blessing if enthusiasm overrides realism. Successful projects are grounded with realistic expectations—and with business sponsors who realize that things do not always go according to plan, especially when they ask to change the scope.

CIO IS SOLE SPONSOR

As I discussed earlier in this chapter under *Solicit BI sponsorship*, there are risks to having the CIO be the only sponsor. This is a red flag not matter how terrific the CIO is, as it harkens back to the early days of data warehousing when people believed "if we build it they will come." If your enterprise truly needs BI, then its BI efforts should be business driven rather than technology driven. Successful projects are sponsored by the business groups that will benefit the most from them.

INTANGIBLE OR TOO HIGH-LEVEL BENEFITS

It is not very realistic to state that the BI project will deliver "one version of the truth," faster time to market and better decision making, although these are worthy goals. Ultimately, you are going to be asked about tangible benefits like increased sales, greater profits, and reduced costs.

BI projects may get approved with these intangible benefits, but if an organization does not know what the tangible benefits are, then how will they know how much to invest, how to measure success, and whether more investments are wise? Successful projects have tangible benefits that you can measure.

CONFUSION BETWEEN BI TECHNOLOGY AND BUSINESS VALUE

Do not fall into the trap of assuming that implementing BI tools creates business value by itself. Business value results when the analytics enabled by BI tools are used in business processes or in decision making. It is those business decisions that create the business value. The BI project simply supports those business processes. Successful projects are those that improve processes no matter what technology they use—arming business people with better data to make more informed decisions.

DEFINING REQUIREMENTS— BUSINESS, DATA AND QUALITY

THE PURPOSE OF DEFINING REQUIREMENTS

While groups might feel that they can take shortcuts and skip the justification process, almost no one is going to suggest skipping the process of defining requirements. They might, however, try to cut corners, which will hobble the project with murky requirements that put it on the path to failure.

It sounds pretty simple—defining requirements creates the foundation of a successful business intelligence (BI) solution by documenting what you are planning to build. The development team then uses these requirements to design, develop, and deploy BI systems. Traditionally, a business analyst (or someone in that role) handles this phase, which takes place early in the project and includes a lot of document writing.

Here is where it can get complicated, however. This is the most people-oriented process in BI development. It is where IT works most closely with business people and puts technology on the back burner. It can be a little tricky because politics between groups may influence behavior, attitudes, and discussions in subtle ways. Issues with people and politics may be out of the comfort zone of many in IT, resulting in land mines that can sink a BI project.

> Ideally, if you are in a larger company, there is a BI program that has laid out the strategic vision and guidelines for enterprise-wide BI. See Chapter 18 to learn about the role of the BI program and why it is preferable to the alternative of tackling projects tactically without this oversight.

Most BI failures are not related to technology shortcomings but rather to a failure of meeting expectations or of requirement surprises toward the end of the BI project. (Oh, you wanted the dashboard to include customer lifetime value? Sorry, no one told us that.) The result is projects that fall short of business needs, are late, and are over budget. You can justly blame poorly defined requirements for all these problems.

It is also important that the business people know enough to know what to ask for with the new project. They cannot ask for something if they have not had any training or orientation that would show them that it is possible.

The most common mistakes in defining requirements are that they:

- Are not detailed enough to clarify what is needed and set expectations
- Restrict their focus to just business requirements
- Are not refined and changed as the project changes
- Do not involve business power users or BI designers and developers
- Re-create the existing system with its warts and inefficiencies

Making these mistakes can prevent you from delivering what the business needs within the agreed-upon time frame and cost. You would not think of building a house without a blueprint, so you should not proceed without a signed set of documented requirements. The documented requirements are used to guide the project, manage scope, and provide the input to the BI development team just as blueprints are used for building your house.

This chapter presents an approach and the best practices to define requirements and avoid these all-too-common mistakes.

GOALS

The primary goal is to define the set of requirements that will be used to design, build, and implement BI solutions within an agreed-upon project timeline and budget. From a business perspective, it gets agreement on the business needs and their priorities, while from a technology perspective, it establishes what needs to be built in the three pillars of BI: data model, data integration, and analytical processes.

A BI assessment provides a road map to achieve your business and technical objectives in as cost- and resource-effective manner as possible. The subject areas it covers are:
- Business and IT requirements
- Architectures (data, information, technology, and products)
- Organization and skills
- Program, project, processes, and policies
See Chapter 18 for a section on BI assessments.

The secondary goal is for the BI team to establish the working relationships with its sponsors, stakeholders, and others that support the BI project. This phase is often the first opportunity for everyone in the project to work together:

- Business people who will ultimately be the information consumers
- Business and technology people who are subject matter experts (SMEs) in the analytical requirements, data source systems and data shadow systems
- IT staff members who support the applications and infrastructure for the BI solution

Initially, it is usually easy to identify the people involved, especially if the BI team has already been working in the organization. When more project details are uncovered, however, it can be necessary to engage additional people in the project.

This phase is the bridge between defining the project scope and designing the data model, data integration, and BI processes. Defining requirements often encounters the "Goldilocks syndrome" of being too hot or too cold, but never "just right."

When too hot, the requirements process suffers from analysis paralysis, takes too long, and appears too bureaucratic. Although a waterfall-style software development life cycle (explained in Chapter 18) has many benefits, this project approach can be accompanied by an inordinate amount of documents that need to be filled out completely as to whether they are applicable to the BI project and its scope. This approach puts the emphasis on completing a checklist of documents rather than getting the right content to build a BI solution on time and within budget.

When too cold, the requirements are too high level, creating ambiguity both with the business and the people building the BI solution. The primary danger is that the business expectations do not match what gets built. In addition, BI developers will need to interpret high-level requirements, which takes additional time and can introduce errors. Most BI project failures are not caused by technology but rather a failure to meet business expectations. This is often caused by high-level requirements that lack the necessary detail to reduce ambiguity.

DELIVERABLES

The primary deliverable is a set of requirements that business sponsors, stakeholders, and IT management have agreed upon. A supporting deliverable will be a revised project plan including budget and resource commitments based on these requirements.

The BI requirements documentation should include the following:

- Project description: Brief explanation of the project goals and objectives.
- Project functionality: Overview of key deliverables.
- Project assumptions: Outline of dependencies or prerequisites.
- Authors and contributors: List of people working on or assisting in documentation.
- List of inputs for requirements, such as:
  - Interviewee lists
  - List of databases and files examined
  - Data source systems documentation
  - List of reporting systems, reports, and data shadow systems examined
- Requirements: (see below)
- Requirement priorities: Subjective priority of requirements based on sponsor and users' preferences.
- Issues and concerns: Resources, budget, schedule, scope, etc.
- Change management: Need to track changes (additions, modifications, and deletions) from requirements and when they occurred.
- Sign-offs: List of who and when requirements and changes approved.

The requirements need to be in sufficient detail to move on to following steps of designing the data model, data integration processes, and BI applications. A complete set of requirements would include the following subjects:

- Business requirements
  - High-level business requirements
  - Business processes supported
  - Business rules and metrics
- BI functional requirements
  - Use cases
  - Process workflow and user interaction
  - Analytical styles and functionality
- Data requirements
  - Data sources
  - Data conformance, consistency, and currency
  - Data integration
  - Data quality
- Regulatory and compliance requirements
  - Country
  - Industry
  - Privacy and security
- Technical requirements
  - Infrastructure standards
  - Technology directions

The scope of the BI project will dictate which of the above subjects need to be included. The most extensive scope, requiring all of the above, would be for a first-time BI, data warehouse (DW), or master data management (MDM) initiative. A BI project that is expanding existing analytics on data already in the DW would be able to simply expand existing requirements documentation. The BI, DW, or MDM program should establish a library of documentation available for review, feedback, and leveraging follow-up projects.

The BI team will initially gather business requirements and then delve deeper into the details to define the associated data and functional requirements. This approach is referred to as stepwise refinement or functional decomposition, as shown in Figure 3.1.

Traditionally, the BI team follows a top-down process, gathering high-level requirements and then refining or decomposing them into more levels of detail. Sometimes, however, there is a need to work bottom-up by reverse engineering existing reporting systems or data shadow systems and then aggregating these details into higher-level requirements. Choose this approach when existing reporting systems are not documented but need to be replaced.

The best practice for defining requirements is a combination of bottom-up and top-down:

- Gather *new* requirements bottom-up to ensure that needed features in the existing systems become part of the new solution and are not lost.
- Determine *existing* requirements top-down to ensure that all business stakeholders have their say and you get to validate and fine tune the requirements through feedback loops.

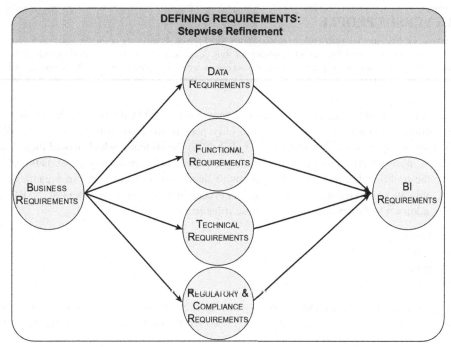

FIGURE 3.1

Requirements—stepwise refinement.

ROLES

It is important to spell out who does what, so no one is surprised. This project phase requires a lot of interaction between the BI team and people from other business and IT groups. This may be a time when the BI team feels out of their comfort zone because many of the activities involve people and politics rather than technology. Chapter 17 provides more details about the various roles on the project team.

BI TEAM PARTICIPANTS

A business analyst (or business systems analyst) takes the lead on defining requirements for the BI team. Depending on the scope and the business management level involved, the lead business analyst may need to be a very seasoned professional.

The key skills of the business analyst include:

- Ability to communicate with both business and IT people, including senior level management if necessary
- Knowledge of the overall business model and specific business processes in order to understand where the use of BI fits
- Being data savvy in order to explore data sources and metrics in detail

ROLES VERSUS PEOPLE

Note that there is a difference between a role or responsibility and a person. Particularly in smaller companies or teams, one person may fill two or more roles. The responsibility for something can be spread across multiple people. This is not just the case while you are defining requirements—it is quite common during implementation of the project as well.

Traditionally, the business analyst role was the primary role filled by the BI team in defining requirements. Sometimes the business analyst was the only person involved from the BI team. With this approach, a set of business requirements was handed off to the BI team, which would then design the BI solution. A more effective approach for defining requirements significantly expands those requirements over the traditional approach both in terms of depth (more details) and in breadth (business, functional, and data requirements). With this new approach in mind, more members of the BI team get involved. In addition to the business analyst, these roles include:

- Data architect
- Data modeler
- ETL designer
- BI designer

These additional BI roles are not likely to participate in the initial interviews to gather business requirements but get involved as more detailed data and BI functional requirements are defined.

BUSINESS PARTICIPANTS

Although it seems obvious to say this, you have to talk to business people to get their requirements. It may be tempting to rely on BI developers or business analysts as proxies for business people, but this is a dangerous shortcut.

The business participants should be sponsors, stakeholders, or users of the proposed BI solution. These are the people who have a vested interest in getting their requirements fulfilled. The initial discussions may generate a huge wish list of everything the business ever wanted in a BI solution. In that case, figure out the priorities along with project planning that balances functionality, time, and cost before signing off on the BI project's requirements. Even in the initial wish list, it is a good practice to have the business classify requests as must-haves and nice-to-haves to get them used to the idea of trade-offs in this process. (You will ask them to prioritize requirements in the final requirements document, as explained in Prioritizing Requirements, later in this chapter.)

The order of interviews will likely follow the stepwise refinement approach, where business management provides their business requirements and then you get more details from their staff and other business people who are directly involved in business analysis. The business roles often included are business analysis, financial analysis, and business management. Although not an official title, business "power users" are key participants.

When interviewing an executive, invite the person on her staff who she relies on for analysis. Although you will likely be meeting with that "go-to" person in follow-up meetings anyway as more detailed are defined, it is good to have him in the initial meeting so he can step in as needed to clarify the executive's business requirements.

OTHER IT PARTICIPANTS

Besides business people, there are other stakeholders from the IT group who should be interviewed to assist in gathering more detailed data and functional requirements. The IT roles that may be included are subject matter experts (SMEs) for the following areas:

- Data source systems
- Applications used in applicable business processes
- Existing reporting systems
- Infrastructure and services

DEFINING REQUIREMENTS WORKFLOW

To build the BI solution, the BI team needs to gather the business, functional and data requirements from business and IT in sufficient detail. The process is depicted in Figure 3.2.

The process starts with defining business requirements, followed by defining data, functional, regulatory/compliance, and technical requirements. If there are existing undocumented reporting applications or data shadow systems, you need to reverse engineer them. You can do these three tasks in parallel if you have enough resources, but be sure to coordinate and share findings.

See the book Web site www.BIguidebook.com for the BI requirements template that helps you document the various categories of requirements during this process.

BUSINESS REQUIREMENTS

The initial task in this process is to obtain business requirements from the business sponsors, stakeholders, and BI users. Gathering requirements is done primarily though interviewing, which is discussed in the following section.

Business requirements typically are associated with particular business processes and business groups. This association identifies who and what will be affected by the BI solution. This potentially expands the stakeholders who need to be included in discussions and the interconnections other systems may have with the BI solution. Ensure that requirements address the change-management issues affecting these business processes and groups.

Business requirements may depend on new or revised business processes, along with new transactional systems or modifications to them. If these changes are occurring, then the BI project scope is more than just the BI solution; it may be highly dependent on the success of the new business processes or enterprise applications implementation.

While defining business requirements, it is crucial to define the business metrics—also referred to as performance metrics, measure or key performance indicators (KPI)—that will be required in the BI solution. Business is driven by these metrics, and they are the cornerstone of analytics. Too often, the details of these business metrics, particularly what data is needed and how it needs to be transformed, is either discovered very late in the BI development process or not at all. This is a very real risk. If it is missed entirely, then business people will be very frustrated that they cannot perform the analysis they need with the new BI solution.

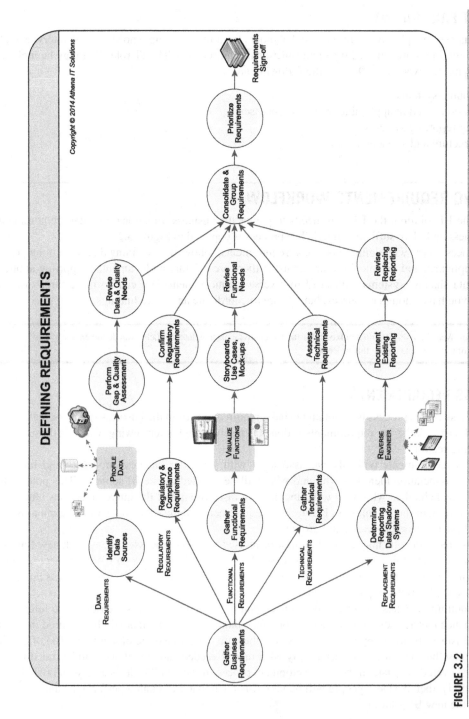

DEFINING REQUIREMENTS

Copyright © 2014 Athena IT Solutions

FIGURE 3.2

Defining requirements workflow.

Defining metrics often gets into details that the initial business interviewees do not know. You will need to get the details from the business power users who have been calculating the metrics manually or by reverse engineering existing reporting or data shadow systems.

DATA (AND DATA QUALITY) REQUIREMENTS

Business requirements need to be detailed enough to identify the data sources or systems of record (SOR), such as applications, databases, or files needed to build the BI solution. (The SOR is, by definition, the authoritative data source.) Defining data requirements means drilling into the data sources to identify detailed data content, such as columns within tables or fields within files, and the transformations that are needed for consistency, conformance, or to calculate the business metrics.

In the early days of data warehousing, IT generally extracted all the data that was available in SORs in case it would be needed in the future. Nowadays, most enterprises have too much data in their SORs to just dump it in the DW, so the BI team needs to be more judicious in selecting what is really needed for analytics. There has been a trend to focus too narrowly when extracting data from SORs, resulting in BI projects continually revising their extracts as each new data requirement arises. The best practice is to extract the data needed by current requirements but also to include related data.

The other area too often overlooked is examining the source systems' data quality in relation to what is being requested for analytics. If there are gaps caused by data quality issues or the data content does not even exist, then the impact on requirements needs to be addressed. These gaps may require:

- Identifying new sources
- Defining data cleansing processes
- Defining MDM processes
- Creating new data capture applications (outside the scope of the BI project)
- Dropping the data requirement until it can be fulfilled

The reason why this analysis is skipped is because people feel that the source systems own their data quality issues and the BI team is just bringing in the data as is. Although the BI team cannot be blamed for the data quality issues, it can be blamed for not identifying and addressing the problems while defining data requirements. Quite a few BI projects have been waylaid by source–system data quality issues identified very late in the project, and there is no excuse for this.

DATA QUALITY CONFUSION

People tend to have several misconceptions about data quality. These are covered in Chapter 12 and summarized briefly below:
- Data quality problems originate in the data warehouse. (Try blaming the conflicting data silos instead.)
- Data quality problems are the result of data entry or acquisition errors. (Rarely, but usually it is because data is inconsistent, incomplete, irrelevant, and outdated.)
- Source system data is always excellent. (But it can still be inconsistent or old.)
- You cannot blame the data warehouse because it does not alter data. (Yes, but it is the BI program's problem to fix.)
- Data cleansing tools will fix any data quality problems. (If only this were true!)

Do not assume anything about the state of the data. The areas where data quality and inconsistency problems lurk include:

- Data quality within SOR may be "masked" by corrections made within existing reports or spreadsheets created from this data. The people using these reports or spreadsheets might not even be aware of these "adjustments."
- Data does not age well. Although data quality may be fine now, there is always the chance that you will have problems or inconsistencies with the historical data. Over time, fields are sometimes used for different content or have different business rules applied to them.
- Data quality may be fine within each SOR application, but may be very inconsistent across applications. Many companies have problems with inconsistent master data in product, customer, and other dimensions that will not be apparent until the data is loaded into the enterprise DW. Data inconsistency needs to be identified as part of the data requirements process.

The BI team needs to perform data profiling or source systems analysis to determine the current state of data quality and its consistency within and across source systems. Traditionally, this type of analysis, if it was done at all, involved manually querying databases and examining files to determine their structure and content. This process was labor intensive and only sampled a portion of the data due to the time it took. Currently, there are various categories of tools that automate data profiling and are quite exhaustive in examining content both within and across source systems. We will discuss this in more detail in Chapter 12.

Based on the data profiling results, perform a gap analysis to determine the current state of data quality within and across source systems regarding the data requirements. With the gap analysis, determine what corrective action, if any, can be done to plug the gaps.

Review the gap analysis and potential corrective actions with the business, asking them to determine if and how the gaps affect their requirements. The business options are to continue with the data quality as is, change their data requirements, or take some corrective action. If they are interested in taking corrective action, then they need to assign a value to that action to determine if it is a must-have. When the BI team revises the project plan and budget after defining the requirements, you want to identify the cost of these corrective actions and get final business sign-off.

FUNCTIONAL REQUIREMENTS

There is a tendency for functional requirements to be very generic, such as providing the ability to "drill down into data details," "access multiple sources," and "perform role-based security." These types of generic functions should be evaluation criteria for BI products rather than BI functional requirements. Without more details, how does the BI development know what to build?

This is a symptom of oversimplifying BI as if it is nothing more than accessing data. BI is a lot more complicated than that—it supports business processes and decision making by giving a business person the ability to analyze data. Functional requirements are a description of that analytical process.

BI functional requirements need to include the following:

- BI use cases
- Analytical process workflow and user interaction
- Analytical styles needed

BI use cases document the why, where, and how of business people using the BI applications while performing their jobs. High-level examples of this include sales pipelines, supply chain management, emergency room wait time, and product profitability analysis. Of course, use cases should get more detailed than these examples and provide information such as who the users are, what data is needed, and what metrics need to be examined.

See the book Web site www.BIguidebook.com for examples of BI use cases.

The next portion of the functional requirements is describing the analytical process workflow and user interactions. Once you identify the business processes involved, it becomes clear that analyzing data and metrics is rarely a one-time occurrence. Rather, it is a succession of analyses that are often interconnected. Documenting the workflow and dependencies enables you to design a more productive BI environment for the people using it. Two common techniques, described in more detail in Chapter 14 are:

* Business process modeling
* Storyboarding

Although process modeling has been the traditional approach, storyboarding is becoming the best practice; it is easier for nontechnical folks to understand, enabling better interaction and feedback. Storyboarding is a very effective tool at documenting the process the business person goes through when planning to use BI.

REGULATORY/COMPLIANCE REQUIREMENTS

An enterprise's adherence to laws, regulations, guidelines, and specifications is going to vary depending on a range of variables including the countries that are involved, the industry, the individual business, and the type of data. The complete checklist for all compliance and regulatory requirements is beyond the scope of this book, but some common examples include:

* Sarbanes-Oxley Act of 2002—retention of financial data for seven years.
* USA Patriot Act—access to data by U.S. law enforcement and national security agencies.
* Health Insurance Portability and Accountability Act (HIPAA)—rules such as encryption for the security and privacy of health data.
* Markets in Financial Instruments Directive (MiFID)—a European law dictating transparency requirements for investment firms.
* Basel Committee on Banking Supervision—international standards for handling risk in the banking industry.
* Payment Card Industry (PCI)—data protection and security standards for credit, debit, and other payment cards.

When you are gathering requirements, be aware that people you are working with either may not know all the relevant and required compliance and regulatory rules or may assume that you already know them.

Make note of security and privacy requirements when working within a supply chain or when the enterprise shares data with suppliers and partners. There can be issues with compliance, information exchange, and country boundaries. For example, a call center in one country may need to comply with different rules as to what employee data can be shown in a dashboard.

TECHNICAL REQUIREMENTS

You may need to follow technical requirements, standards, or guidelines that you are not even aware of. These requirements could be issued by the CIO, an IT group with responsibility for infrastructure or architecture, or the business group you are working with. There may be no discretionary leeway for these, so be sure to ask about them up front.

Technical requirements can include:

- New technology directions, such as whether work is done in the cloud or on the premises
- Policies on where the data centers are located
- What vendor hardware and software can be used
- If BI appliances are required
- If Web services are required
- Rules on who can access the databases (some enterprises only allow one group to access the database, so you will have to work with them)

REVERSE ENGINEERING (WHEN NECESSARY)

It is rare to create a BI solution with no existing reporting capability in place. The existing reporting system may be part of the operational application, it might have been a previous attempt at BI, or it might be a data shadow system (also called a spreadmart) created by business users. In most cases, if the analytical need is important enough, then the business has been doing something, no matter how imperfect, to get data and analyze it.

Almost no data shadow system is documented, and many older reporting systems might likewise have little or out-of-date documentation. With this in mind, there are two reasons why the BI team will need to reverse engineer some or all of the existing reporting or data shadow systems:

- First, for comparison—although business users may complain about their existing reports or data shadow system, they have been using them for analysis for some period of time, so these systems are now the benchmark for comparison. This comparison happens even when the BI team believes and has documented that the new BI solution is better in terms of data quality, consistency, currency, and completeness than the old. The only effective way to compare and contrast systems will require the older system be reverse engineered.
- Second, for better understanding—even when the old systems are being discarded and the business is providing "new" requirements, it is fairly common for many of the business rules and data used by the business in the old systems to be relevant. The problem is that often the business person providing the new requirements either forgot about those business rules and data or just assumed that the BI team would understand what those rules and data were. Reverse engineering fills in the inevitable gaps in detailed requirements, keeping the new BI solution from being derailed when business users start using it.

The bad news is that reverse engineering takes time and is not something IT folks are especially excited about doing. The good news is that the bulk of the work should be able to be done by the business power user who created or is maintaining the data shadow system. In addition, enlisting the power user brings that person into the BI virtual team, creating an advocate for the new BI solution and presenting the business with their "trusted advisor" in relation to this analysis. If the power user blesses the new solution, then business adoption is almost guaranteed.

PUTTING IT ALL TOGETHER

You will need to collect business, data, functional, regulatory, technical, and, if applicable, existing reporting requirements from different business groups and people who may have different needs or at least different viewpoints regarding those needs. As the scope of the BI solution expands, so too does the diversity of business groups and requirements you gather.

> See the book Web site www.BIguidebook.com for the BI requirements template that helps you document the various categories of requirements during this process.

It is crucial to consolidate and coordinate the varied requirements into a cohesive BI project requirements document. This is the only way to "see the forest from the trees" and determine which requirements truly drive value. The consolidation process identifies overlapping, redundant, outdated, and conflicting requirements. It also identifies gaps and missing elements based on dependencies that might not have been apparent before the consolidation.

Consolidate and cross-reference (or tag) the requirements along the following dimensions:

- Business value
- Business processes
- Business group
- Data sources
- Analytical functionality

Is the business driving projects within strategic business plans? If so, you will need to categorize requirements by this information in addition to the above criteria. This will be discussed in Chapter 18.

PRIORITIZING REQUIREMENTS

Although business and technology participants should validate business, functional, and data requirements as soon as they are gathered and documented, make sure the consolidated requirements documentation is made available for final review and feedback. This process enables the team to validate consolidated requirements, clarify misunderstandings, correct mistakes, make revisions, and, if appropriate, add requirements. The method for collecting the feedback will depend on what the BI team established in their initial project plan.

With the consolidated requirements documentation validated, the next step is to meet to review and prioritize those requirements. The discussions should include the following:

- Who was interviewed
- List of business requirements by business process
  - Brief description
  - Commonality of requirement across business groups
  - Feasibility

- List of data sources
  - Commonality of requirement across business groups
  - Brief description of data gaps and data quality issues
  - Dependent corrective actions, if applicable
- Brief description of functional requirements
  - Commonality of requirement across business groups

As we discuss in Chapter 18, the best practice is to develop BI within the context of a BI program with iterative and incremental BI projects gradually building out the long-term BI vision. Within this context, the business will understand that rather than trying to do everything at once, they need to set priorities.

Never accept that every requirement is a top priority. At a minimum, the business needs to classify the requirements in its initial reviews as:

- Must-have
- Should-have
- Nice-to-have
- Forget about it

This classification is solely from the business perspective. You also need to assess business and technical dependencies that may impact prioritization.

You should have developed an initial project plan and budget when the BI project was scoped and justified. The BI team will need to review the consolidated requirements prioritization to determine what can be done within the existing project plan and budget. If all the must-haves can be developed, then it is likely that the BI team will have the approval to proceed. If, however, not all of the must-haves can be developed within existing project constraints, then business sponsors' choices are:

- Proceed with a set of must-haves that can be accomplished within the existing plan and budget. If there are alternative selections, then the business and BI team need to agree on the list of requirements that will be delivered.
- Reduce the scope of some of the must-have requirements so that they can be accomplished within the existing plan and budget. This might be possible, for example, by implementing with a reduced number of data sources for the initial project iteration.
- Increase the budget and lengthen the schedule based on a revised list of requirements for the BI project.

Regardless of what choices are made in the prioritization process, it is crucial to get a business sign-off on the requirements for the BI project. The BI team and it sponsors should consider this a contract between them.

INTERVIEWING

The primary technique for gathering business and functional requirements is interviewing. This section will discuss how to:

- Prepare for the interviews
- Conduct the interviews
- Follow up after the interviews

PREPARATION FOR INTERVIEWS

The BI team members conducting the interviews need to prepare to make them productive and engaging. There are three preparation areas:

1. Background information on the enterprise and interviewees
2. Creating a list of subject areas and, ideally, specific questions to be covered in the interview
3. Inviting participants and providing the information from above

First, the background information check for requirement interviews is similar to what one would do for a job interview. The BI team needs to be somewhat knowledgeable about the following subjects as they apply to the proposed BI solution heading into the interviews:

- Enterprise's business and customers
- Business and technology initiatives
- Business terminology and acronyms
- Business processes that proposed BI solution will be used to support
- Interviewees' title, organization, and background

Performing due diligence on these areas is important. If the BI team is familiar with these subjects and interviewees, then this part of the preparation will be brief. Background information on the organization, its business, financial performance, its industry, its competitors, and its customers is available on its Web site and outside financial sites. Other information may be on its intranet: business and technology initiatives, business terminology and acronyms, business processes, and organizational information. In addition, do not overlook business-oriented social media sites as a great source of background on your interviewees.

Second, the BI team needs to determine what subject areas they will focus on during the interviews. If possible, it is useful to know what business processes and existing reporting or data shadow systems the interviewees use in order to better focus the discussion and make it more productive.

Some sample questions for business interviewees can include:

- What are your roles and responsibilities?
- In each area:
  - What information do you need?
  - How is that information gathered and analyzed?
  - What reports or data shadow systems do you use?
  - What information do you lack and how valuable is it to you?
  - What new types of business analysis would be useful to you and how?
  - Do you rely on others to perform this analysis? If so, who does it?
  - If a specific report or information is no longer available, what is your backup plan?

When interviewing technology people, it is extremely important to have an understanding of a person's background and what systems or processes they are involved in that relate to the BI project. BI people find these interviews easier than interviewing business people because they "speak the same language," i.e., technical jargon, and they often know more about the systems in which these people are involved. The line of inquiry will be to examine the applications and databases that they work with that are relevant to the BI project.

Finally, even if interviewees have already been asked to attend requirements-gathering discussions, send a formal invitation to all potential attendees. This invitation should include:

- Meeting time, location, and list of potential attendees
- Brief overview of BI project
- Goals and expectations of meeting and participants
- List of subject areas to be discussed (if known)
- Sample of list of questions (if available)
- A list of decisions that need to be made

The interviewees' time is valuable; allowing them to prepare for the meeting is well advised. Often the attendees do not really prepare for the interview sessions but, at a minimum, the invitation gives them a chance to at least glance at what the interview sessions are about. In addition, the invitation content is an excellent framework for the meeting agenda regardless of the attendees' preparation.

CONDUCTING THE INTERVIEWS

Whether the interview is a one-on-one discussion or a group meeting, the agenda published in the meeting invitation should guide the meeting. It is important to take notes and, if possible, record the meeting (with permission). There are many conference, tablet, and smartphone applications for recording, but for greater productivity, I prefer a smartpen application that synchronizes the recording with bookmarks in my notes.

When interviewing business people, a common mistake is to ask an open-ended question such as, "What do you want in regard to reporting and analytics?" This inquiry generally results in a business person either being focused on current limitations in their existing reports or asking for every piece of data their enterprise has and maybe more. In either case, the BI team often feels like the business person does not know what they want or does not understand what BI can do for them. The problem is not with the interviewee, but rather with the interviewer who abdicated responsibility to direct the discussion. A better question would be something specific like, "What is the most valuable report that you currently run from your data shadow system or on your own spreadsheets?"

Ideally, the interviewers are prepared with subject areas to discuss and a list of questions. But the questions are just a starting point; the interviewee needs to delve into the areas that will yield the most information regarding the interviewee's requirements. Interviewing is an invaluable skill and includes an element of detective work. The interviewer needs to be flexible and follow the line of inquiry to where it leads.

REVIEWING INTERVIEW CONTENT

Try to review your notes (and recording, if you have it) as soon as possible after the interview. Although it is tempting to schedule interview sessions back-to-back, there are several good reasons to leave yourself time in between them to review what was discussed. First, you need to be very attentive during each interview; a day-long series of meetings will tire even the most dedicated person. Second, there may be overlap between what interviewees discuss—this will all blur together if you have meetings back-to-back. Finally, the interview may raise questions or ideas that you are going to want to write down and digest before you lose those trains of thought.

If there was more than one interviewer or BI team member in the interviews, then you should hold debriefing meetings where all present review their interview notes. It is best to conduct the interview and then hold a debriefing meeting immediately afterward (before the next interview session).

When reviewing your notes, either individually or in a debriefing meeting, you need to perform the following:

- Complete partial notations. Often you will be scribbling something when one of the interviewees says something else that you need to capture. Try to complete these partial thoughts while you remember them.
- Identify areas where there is confusion or potential misunderstanding (if team members have different interpretations).
- Identify data sources, business processes, and business initiatives involved in BI.
- Identify stakeholders and business people who will be using the BI solution.
- Identify common, repetitive themes among interviewees.
- List business issues, concerns, or risks discussed.
- Determine (or agree upon) key findings or issues from the interview.
- Identify conflicting information or requirements among interviewees.

After the interviews, you should send a thank-you note and, if at all possible, attach a quick summary of the interview, listing topics discussed, agreed-upon action items, and outstanding issues. If you cannot do both at the same time, please do them as soon as possible. This is not meant to be the interview write-ups that you will review with the interviewees (below), but rather a quick acknowledgment of the interview. This is a similar practice that a job candidate would do after a job interview.

INTERVIEW FOLLOW-UPS

You will need to have follow-up discussions with interviewees to clarify items, resolve disparities, and to expand upon the topics discussed. These discussions need not be formal meetings, but may be handled more effectively with one-on-one or informal group conversations. The reason for this approach is that often the questions are very specific to particular people or topics.

In addition, schedule follow-up meetings with subject matter experts (SMEs) to discuss data sources, functionality, or existing reporting in more detail. This is the stepwise refinement process where you start with business requirements, and then develop more detailed requirements on data, functionality, and current reporting systems applicable to the BI project. These follow-up meetings help you define requirements in sufficient detail to guide the project.

It is a best practice to document the interview and include the following:

- Interviewees, titles, responsibilities
- Business objectives
- Business initiatives
- Business processes
- Data subjects and sources such as application and databases, if possible
- Stakeholders and business groups that will use BI

- Issues, concerns, or risks
- Success factors

After documenting the interview, send a copy to the interviewees and conduct a follow-up meeting with them to validate the content. Revise the document as necessary, and then, most importantly, get the interviewees to sign off on the document. This serves two purposes: first, it ensures that the interviewees do indeed agree on the content, and second, it serves as explicit permission to publish the document for other stakeholders to review. If there are materials that are not meant to be shared, be sure to clear them up prior to publishing.

It is tempting to be less formal and skip the interview documentation step—resist those urges! BI projects too often fail to meet expectations and deliver what the business is asking for precisely because this step was not taken seriously, allowing misunderstandings to arise and kill the project.

DOCUMENTING REQUIREMENTS

The process of collecting requirements involves a stepwise refinement, starting with business requirements and then delving into more details on data and functional requirements, followed by a review of the current state of reporting. You should document each of these processes during the requirements workflow, gathering feedback from applicable stakeholders and refining the document throughout the process. It is much easier and productive to create the documentation while you go rather than waiting until you have completed all the tasks. If you wait, it is guaranteed that you will forget things and risk shortchanging the process by getting behind schedule.

The key topics in the requirements documentation include:

- Business requirements
- Data requirements
- Current state reporting assessment
- Feasibility analysis
- Critical success criteria

In the "dark ages," documentation meant an excessively long Microsoft Word document that few people read, and that was likely very verbose or poorly written. People spent way too much time on writing prose, editing it, and then finally giving up on it altogether. Once reviewed, the document went into a folder never to be seen again. This is bad practice!

The best practices today are to use collaborative tools to manage the content and as many visual tools or techniques as possible. Although visual techniques reduce writing, the primary benefits are improved communication and increased productivity.

There are many collaborative tools that can be used in documenting requirements. The simplest technique is to have a documentation tool with revision capabilities to track changes and enable the document owner to accept or reject changes from each reviewer. There are many sophisticated collaborative tools from general purpose to those geared to project management and requirements documentation; price tags range from free to expensive. You can also find collaborative tools that work in the cloud and on mobile devices; these may improve access and participation. If your firm has adopted a collaborative tool, then use it.

Using a collaborative tool is recommended for documentation, but do not rely on it for gathering requirements, especially business requirements, since nothing replaces interactive discussions between the stakeholders and you.

There are specific techniques or tools that you can use when gathering various requirements:

- Business requirements
  - Storyboards
  - BI mock-ups
  - Prototyping BI objects
- Data requirements
  - Data profiling
  - Output from data modeling, ETL, and BI tools
- Functional requirements
  - Storyboards
  - BI mock-ups
  - Prototyping
- Current state of reporting
  - Sample reports or spreadsheets
  - Sample data

If you choose the type of project methodology we discuss in Chapter 18, using storyboarding, mock-ups, or prototyping is an extremely effective method to gather, validate, and document functional requirements. These visual techniques are a much better way to communicate and establish joint expectations than writing dozens of pages of prose. Similarly, data profiling and output from BI tools is a great communication tool when working with the BI developers throughout the BI project.

After all the collaboration in defining and documenting the requirements, this phase should be completed with the business sponsor(s) and key stakeholders signing off on the requirements documentation. This sets expectations and establishes a baseline to manage the project as it progresses.

ARCHITECTURAL FRAMEWORK III

III

ARCHITECTURAL
FRAMEWORK

ARCHITECTURE FRAMEWORK

THE NEED FOR ARCHITECTURAL BLUEPRINTS

BI environments and houses have something in common. When you plan to build a house, you start with its purpose: a place to live, a place to live and work, a place to raise kids, a place to grow old, etc. Knowing that, you put together a wish list on the architectural style, size, and types of rooms. Then you hire an architect to design the house and create a detailed blueprint. The architect gives you feedback on how the various rooms can fit together, what the building codes are, and how to fit in the infrastructure such as wiring and plumbing. Most importantly, the architect advises you on what is really possible or practical given your location, house size, wishes, budget, and timetable. In addition, she offers ideas for things you had not thought of.

What happens if you skip the architect and go straight to a builder? The house may not meet building codes, the flow of the rooms will be awkward, and the style will not be as attractive. The process will take longer as the builder tries to figure out what you want. Meanwhile, you do not really know what you want until you see it, and then you probably do not like what you see. And, you certainly do not like paying for all this extra time.

Like the unfortunate house without blueprints, many enterprises today have a BI environment that did not have the benefit of an architecture. It is a hodgepodge of the following pieces:

* Many application-specific reporting environments in addition to an enterprise BI environment. Business people are forced to switch between these environments based on what they are trying to analyze.
* Various databases created for BI outside the application environments (above) that were created at different times, by different teams for different purposes. These databases might be referred to as data warehouses (DW), data marts, operational data stores (ODS), repositories, online analytical processing (OLAP) cubes, or by some internal acronym.

65

- Several different BI tools, either associated with the application-specific reporting environments or the enterprise BI solution. It is not unusual to see the enterprise BI environment supporting several BI tools because different BI tools were designated as the enterprise standard at different times. And once a BI tool becomes a standard, it is likely to become entrenched in an enterprise for a long time, even if a new BI tool has been selected as the new or latest standard.
- A data-integration tool selected as the enterprise standard for loading the DW, yet people use a lot of manually created custom SQL code or other extract transform and load (ETL) tools to load the databases used by the BI tools.

Business people are grouped by business function and processes, so enterprises tend to build (or purchase) business applications in discrete silos. The initial wave of reporting that business people use is from these application silos. Enterprises then try to expand this reporting, but they typically focus the BI projects on the same applications that the business groups have been using without examining how these projects should fit into an overall architecture. As a result, many BI environments have become a collection of technology, product, and data silos that are loosely connected and require an intensive commitment of resources to operate, upgrade, maintain, and enhance.

Business people are frustrated with the state of their BI environments, which take longer and longer to enhance over time, and are always a release away from becoming pervasive throughout the enterprise. They remember the significant investments of time, resources, and budget for BI projects, and they ask why they still have to use spreadsheets (i.e., data shadow systems or spreadmarts) as the superglue for reporting and analysis.

IT people are also frustrated as more and more of their time is spent on reconciling data between these silos and maintaining these systems rather than expanding the breadth and value of BI for the business. The temptation, too often reinforced by industry hype, is that an enterprise can get out of this mess by simply using the latest technology marvel; but it always ends up as the next silo.

ARCHITECTURAL FRAMEWORK

Successful enterprise BI solutions with enduring business value are not completed in a "one and done" project, but rather evolve over time. BI will, if done right, expand in terms of the number of business people using it, business processes affected, data consumed, and analytics performed. An architectural framework, i.e., a set of architectural blueprints, is needed as each new BI project is undertaken to enable these projects to complement each other and create a cohesive, cost-effective BI solution. The framework needs to be designed to accommodate expansion and renovation based on evolving requirements, capabilities, and skills. Although the framework designer will not know the future, she can design the framework to meet those challenges. Besides adding BI capabilities for the enterprise, the designer needs to include support for development, testing, ongoing operations, performance monitoring, and documentation. Many of these areas get shortchanged or overlooked if the focus is merely on blueprints for implementing only the current project.

As shown in Figure 4.1, BI framework is composed of four architectural layers:

1. Information architecture
2. Data architecture
3. Technical architecture
4. Product architecture

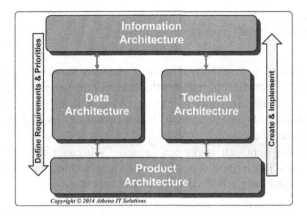

FIGURE 4.1

The four architecture categories.

These four architecture categories are discussed below and covered in detail in Chapters 5, 6, and 7.

INFORMATION ARCHITECTURE

The information architecture defines the "what, who, where, and why" for BI or analytical applications:

- **What** business processes or functions are going to be supported, **what** types of analytics will be needed, and **what** types of decisions are affected
- **Who** (employees, customers, prospects, suppliers, or other stakeholders) will have access
- **Where** the data is now, **where** it will be integrated, and **where** it will be consumed in analytical applications
- **Why** the BI solution(s) will be built—what the business and technical requirements are

The information architecture defines the business context necessary for successful BI solutions to be built on a sustaining basis. Too often, IT skips the information architecture and goes directly to designing the technology and product architectures. The rush to technology is because it is IT's comfort zone and a way to avoid engaging in business process discussions to design the information architecture. But it is also easier for business people, especially BI power users, to focus on products because they typically only see the BI tools and not the underlying architectures. Product evaluations and selection then become the focus of the initial BI planning and design effort, with information architectural design getting shortchanged.

If you listen to industry hype, you might think that simply picking the best products will solve your problems. Beware of this trap. When BI solutions fall short of expectations, are late, or go over budget, it is easy to blame the products. I call this the "Twilight Zone" never-ending trap:

1. Evaluate and select "best" products
2. Implement BI solution without an information architecture
3. BI project is late and costs more than planned
4. BI solution fails to meet expectations and active adoption

5. Blame current products used

6. Evaluate and select a new "best" product

7. Go back to step 2

Enterprises have business applications that perform the many business processes needed for their operations. The information architecture enables the business to perform analytics on these diverse processes whether they are selling a product, monitoring a patient's vital stats, posting students' grades, or tracking the performance of financial accounts. It is tempting to look at each of these processes as unique and implement each BI application independently. If there is an overarching information architecture, the project-oriented approach works well, especially because it concentrates on supporting specific business processes. But if there is no information architecture, the result will be silos, which thwart effective analytics and carry a high cost in time and opportunity lost.

DATA ARCHITECTURE

The data architecture defines the data along with the schemas, integration, transformations, storage, and workflow required to enable the analytical requirements of the information architecture. The scope of the data architecture starts where data is created in the source systems by information providers and ends where the business person (or information consumer) performs data analysis. The source system data definitions are obtained from information providers, while business metrics, dimensions, transformations, and measures are obtained from information consumers based on information architecture requirements.

THE RISE OF THE ENTERPRISE DATA WAREHOUSE

Years ago it became apparent that there needed to be a database, called an enterprise data warehouse (EDW) (see Figure 4.2), for reporting purposes separate from the data source systems (also known as systems of record (SOR)). There are several compelling reasons for separating reporting data from SORs and creating an EDW.

First, source systems, such as enterprise resource planning (ERP), customer relationship management (CRM), and supply chain management (SCM), are built for data capture and processing transactions rather than for reporting and analytics. Although they may both be on relational databases, they are structured, logically and physically, quite differently based on their respective objectives: data creation versus information analysis. The differences between data capture and analytical data structures became even greater as the variety of data sources expanded to include unstructured data and then Big Data including Web, social media, and machine data.

Second, data across SORs is often inconsistent. These inconsistencies may be the result of differences in form, structure, data relationships, business definitions, or transformations. Data inconsistency is not the same as data quality (next issue), with the former being the result of differences that may indeed be quite valid from a business perspective and the latter being the result of errors or gaps in data. Getting data consistent is a significant focus of data warehousing because it is a critical requirement for business analytics. Master data management (MDM) has emerged as a specialization within data warehousing to address significant inconsistencies in data.

Third, data quality within and across SORs is a challenge that data warehousing addresses. The mantra in the early days of data warehousing was that data in the EDW was read-only and any data-quality issues

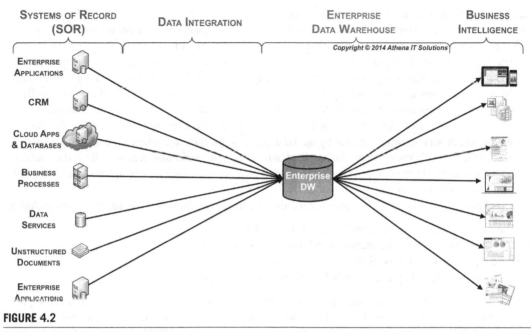

FIGURE 4.2

Enterprise data warehouse.

needed to be pushed back to the SORs to be fixed. Although SORs have improved significantly in eliminating data entry errors, data quality and completeness is still a problem. From a pragmatic perspective, it turned out that the EDW became the preferred location to perform data quality processing. An EDW is the "canary in the coal mine" regarding data quality because many of these issues do not become visible or affect others until the data is extracted from its source and integrated with data from other SORs. Data-quality problems are often the result of changes occurring in the data structures and usage over time, which is why it is stated that data does not age well. When the data was current it would have processed fine with the SORs' business processes; it is only after it has aged, i.e., become historical data, that it negatively affects reporting such as trending performance over time or performing a predictive analysis. Since it is only the reporting processes that are affected, in many cases data quality processes have shifted to data warehousing rather than SORs.

Finally, it is more difficult and sometime impossible, to access all the SORs directly in real time rather than having a separate EDW to access for reporting. Some of the inhibitors to direct access are:

- Too many SORs to access from the BI tool at once
- Specific data varieties that are not accessible
- One or more of the SORs will be adversely impacted
- Privacy or security policies

DATA WAREHOUSING REPLACES THE DATA WAREHOUSE

Over the years, many technologies and approaches to providing analytics have prompted people to proclaim the death of the data warehouse. Although these DW killers have been able to provide analytics, they have not been able to support enterprise-wide analytics with its accompanying need for consistent, comprehensive, clean, conformed, and current data. Their best results might have provided terrific analytics, but they did it in yet another silo (that then needed to be integrated with the other silos!).

The key fallacy of the push to replace the concept of separating reporting data from transactional data was that it was only being done for technological reasons. If that were true then data warehouses would have died long ago. The underlying reason for the separation is business and data needs. Business processes and applications have different business rules, data definitions, and transformations that create inconsistency. Data ages poorly and its completeness varies based on business need. Many of these differences need to be discovered by the BI team to be used in data integration and business intelligence applications. If only it was so easy that business people could just access all their data sources in a BI tool that would magically know what needed to be transformed and how, then that tool would replace a DW. But, of course, it is not that easy.

The classic EDW as depicted in Figure 4.2 is a single, centralized database. The data workflow includes:

- Data being created, updated, and modified in the SORs
- Data from SORs being integrated, transformed, and cleansed
- Data being loaded into the EDW
- Data being accessed by the BI tools for reporting and analysis

Advances in technology have prompted the evolution from the classic EDW model to more sophisticated data architecture. Figure 4.3 illustrates some of the other data stores that are being used today to replace an EDW-only structure. These data stores may include: ODS, MDM, data marts, OLAP cubes, staging data stores in addition to the EDW. The data stores' characteristics vary: they may be persistent or transient; may be stored in a database, file structure, or memory; may be distributed or centralized;

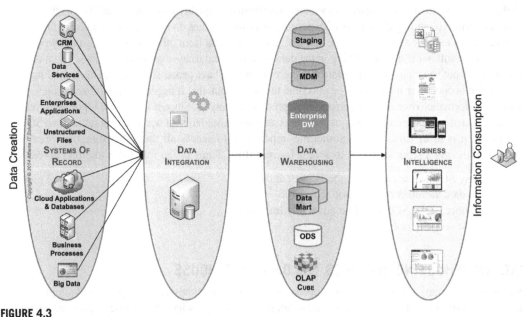

FIGURE 4.3

Data architecture workflow.

etc. Each of these data stores has specific use cases that an enterprise will leverage based on its needs. We will discuss these in more detail in the follow-on chapters in the architecture section.

This evolution from a single centralized EDW to a set of architectural options is what I call the shift to data warehousing, i.e., many data stores, from a data warehouse. One of the best practices for a BI data architecture is to have the EDW serve two different data roles: systems of integration (SOI) and systems of analytics (SOA). Figure 4.4 depicts the three roles that occur in the BI data architecture. The purpose of each role is as follows:

- **Systems of Record (SOR)**—data is captured and updated in operational and transactional applications. These applications are designated as the SOR so that people and processes know what the authorized sources are for any particular data subject. This implies an expectation level in regards to the integrity and legitimacy of the data. For example, an application would be designated as the SOR for accounting data.
- **System of Integration (SOI)**—gathers, integrates, and transforms data from SORs into consistent, conformed, comprehensive, clean, and current information. Similar to the SOR, this designation implies a particular level of integrity and legitimacy of the integrated data. It also implies that if a person or process needs integrated data, then the SOI should be the source used.
- **System of Analytics (SOA)**—provides business information that has been integrated and transformed to BI applications for business analysis. Similar to the SOR, this designation implies a particular level of integrity and legitimacy of the information being used in BI. Although BI applications will directly access SORs for operation reporting, if integrated and transformed data is needed, the SOA needs to be the source.

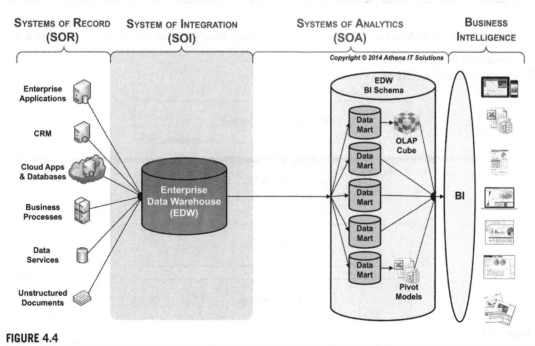

FIGURE 4.4

BI data architecture—roles of data systems.

Note: The hub and spoke (or EDW to data marts) depicted in Figure 4.4 is a logical depiction of the BI architecture. This is done to simplify the diagram and focus on the data-related functions rather than display physical databases.

Just as the data sources depicted in Figure 4.4 are the SOR for operational processes, the BI architecture needs to establish the EDW as the SOI—where data gets integrated—and the SOA—where BI and analytical application go for integrated data.

TECHNICAL ARCHITECTURE

The technical architecture defines the technologies that are used to implement and support a BI solution that fulfills the information and data architecture requirements. These technologies cover the entire BI life cycle of design, development, testing, deployment, maintenance, performance tuning, and user support.

Note: The following section introduces the technologies used in BI, data integration and data warehousing. The figures presented in this section are high-level or simplified versions of what will be examined in more detail in the follow-on architecture chapters or sections on data, data integration, and BI design.

PRODUCTS VERSUS TECHNOLOGIES

Note that it is a common mistake to confuse the technical architecture with the products themselves. This typically happens because people associate products with specific technologies. It is important to remember that products may incorporate many technologies, especially with vendors extending their product lines and supporting a wide range of technologies. Resist the urge to evaluate products immediately. Determine your information and data needs, and then select the technologies that will support them.

The BI technical architecture is composed of four major functional layers, as shown in Figure 4.5:

1. Business intelligence (and analytical applications)
2. Data warehouse and BI data stores

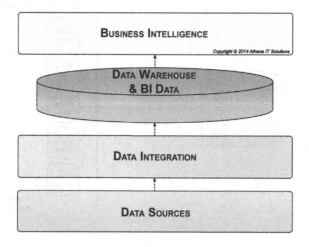

FIGURE 4.5

BI technical architecture.

3. Data integration
4. Data sources

For many years, or in the "old days" as industry veterans like to describe it, the answer to what was in each of these layers was straightforward, as shown in Table 4.1.

Table 4.1 Classic BI Technology Choices	
Functional Layer	**Classic (Old School) Technological Choices**
BI	BI reporting tool and later a BI OLAP tool
DW & BI data store	Enterprise DW on a relational database
Data integration	ETL tool running in batch updating the DW overnight
Data sources	ERP system(s) running in that enterprise's data center

It is no longer quite so simple. The demands on information and data architectures have significantly expanded, as you can see in Figure 4.6. Not only have data variety, volume, and velocity grown

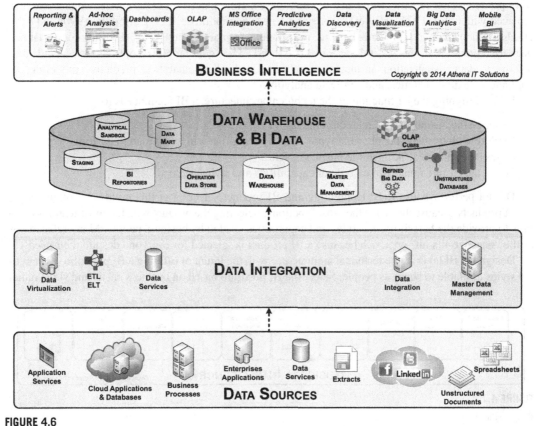

FIGURE 4.6

BI technical architecture categories.

substantially, but there has been substantial growth in the need to include data from outside an enterprise and interact with customers, prospects, suppliers, and many other stakeholders.

There are two opposing viewpoints that often sabotage BI initiatives. First, many describe the BI industry as mature and past its prime. This viewpoint overlooks the significant advances in each of the functional layers. BI teams with this viewpoint rely on the same old technologies in the same old ways, which significantly constrains business value and hinders return on investment (ROI).

The other viewpoint assumes that the latest products eliminate the need to do the fundamentals, so a team can skip tasks such as designing the information and data architectures. The product sales pitch is that "this time it is different" and business and IT no longer need to interact. This approach also fails to achieve business value and ROI because products, in the long run, cannot make up for wrong data, or data that is inconsistent, incomplete, or poor quality.

BUSINESS INTELLIGENCE

Although BI tools have been around for a couple of decades, the depth, breadth, and variety of BI capabilities and styles continues to expand and change. This is illustrated in Figure 4.7.

For much of their history, BI applications were built by the IT group, which then published reports for business people using detailed report requirements for content and layout. In the beginning, these were printed (often called "green bar") reports; these were replaced by PDF reports, which were then replaced with online (Web browser) reports and now even mobile devices. During the 1990s and early 2000s, dashboards and scorecards became very popular, replacing the typical reporting tools that had been used previously. This was followed by OLAP and ad hoc query tools. BI options now include data discovery, data visualization, in-memory analytics, in-database analytics, predictive modeling, BI appliances, textual analytics, and Big Data analytics.

When designing the BI function of the technical architecture, a BI team needs to:

- Examine the business and data requirements
- Explore with business people what types of analytical processing they plan to perform
- Assess the analytical skills of the business users
- Select the BI functionality, i.e., type of capabilities and styles, needed

Do not perform both the BI technology and BI product selection at this point. Too often people select products because they have the most functions. Selecting the product with the most features often fails to provide the best fit for the styles and capabilities needed by business people. Many refer to this as the "one-size-fits-all" approach because a BI product is selected for everyone despite their needs.

Design the BI layer of the technical architecture with the intent of offering a BI portfolio of analytical styles available to business people. Select the BI portfolio based on business needs and skills rather

FIGURE 4.7

BI analytical styles.

than on the latest product hype or marketing pitch. It is a good idea to build the BI portfolio iteratively with additions or modifications based on value and changes in needs.

DATA WAREHOUSE AND BI DATA STORES

The relational database has been the primary database technology used since the beginning of data warehousing. As depicted in Figure 4.8, most of the potential data stores used in this architectural layer are housed in relational databases.

When enterprises first started using relational databases for their DW, relational technology was primarily used for transactional processing, so its functionality was geared for that purpose. Since then, however, relational databases have become very common for BI, data integration, and DW. It now has many features and enhancements oriented to those needs, including sophisticated indexing, partitioning, compression, materialized views, in-memory processing, in-database analytics, and relational online analytical processing (ROLAP). Advances in hardware, memory, storage, networks, and many other infrastructural components have greatly expanded relational technologies' capability and performance.

Its extensive use in BI has allowed for the growth of a skilled workforce and many best practices that enterprises can leverage to increase business value and lower costs. In addition, the relational database market is competitive with several large vendors along with open source and niche products.

Despite the dominance of relational databases in BI, there has been a growing number of alternative technologies. These technologies are often targeted to particular BI uses and thereby do not eliminate the use of relational; rather, they replace it in portions of the technical architecture.

Some of the alternative technologies, which will be discussed in Chapter 7, include:

- OLAP databases
- Massively parallel processing (MPP) databases
- Data virtualization
- In-database analytics
- In-memory analytics
- Cloud-based BI, DW, or data integration
- NoSQL databases

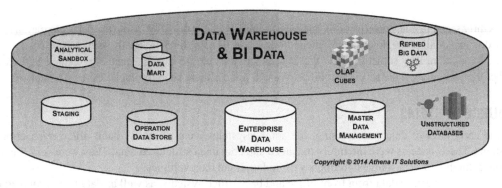

FIGURE 4.8

Data warehouse & BI data store layer.

A BI or DW appliance is another growing technology category. These products are combinations of hardware, software, and systems integration designed to improve the business value and lower the total cost of ownership (TCO) of BI implementations. BI appliances typically bundle one or more of the emerging technologies that we have discussed. They also may include combinations of commodity hardware, open source software, and proprietary components that might be hardware or software. We will discuss these further in Chapter 7.

DATA INTEGRATION

Data integration suffers from an image problem. It has become synonymous with ETL. Likewise, ETL has been regarded as a data warehousing technology. Both of these viewpoints fail to reflect current capabilities, and they greatly inhibit enterprises in their attempt to integrate data to provide the information their business needs.

A further stereotype is the classic ETL use of loading the EDW on a daily basis in batch mode. Many enterprises have increased the update frequency to near real time, but are still operating with the same type of ETL processing. Just as relational database technology has adapted and expanded to support the increasing demands of BI, data integration and ETL has likewise expanded to meet the ever-increasing data volumes, variety, and velocity facing enterprises.

Data integration has grown to encompass many different technologies and capabilities beyond ETL. In fact, you can consider classic ETL as just one use case of data integration. Today the high-end tools are considered data-integration suites encompassing many integration technologies such as the ones depicted in Figure 4.9. The high-end data-integration suites historically started as ETL tools, so many in IT still have a limited view of what the suites can accomplish. We will discuss these further in Chapter 7.

FIGURE 4.9

Data integration layer.

A dirty secret in many enterprises is that even though they load the EDW using the data-integration tool, they do most or all of the downstream integration to load BI data stores manually using custom code with SQL. In addition, they sometimes use the data-integration suite to execute manually created SQL code rather than actually use the suite capabilities. We will discuss these shortcomings further in Chapter 6.

SOURCE SYSTEMS

In the early days of data warehousing, the source systems were primarily back office transactional systems. These systems were internally managed and contained structured data. They were very limited in their number of data sources, frequency of updates, and data volumes.

Nowadays we have data from front office and back office systems, as well as data that is sourced or exchanged externally with customers, prospects, suppliers, partners, and other stakeholders. We also have structured, unstructured, and semistructured data that may need to be integrated on a real-time basis. Data is now created in all types of business and people activities, thus greatly expanding the data volumes that need to be integrated. Figure 4.10 depicts just a small sample of these new data sources.

We will discuss the impact of these data sources on the other three architectural layers in Chapter 6.

FIGURE 4.10

Data sources layer.

BI TECHNOLOGY KEEPS EVOLVING

Figure 4.11 shows a brief and high-level historical view of the evolution of data-related technology. The diagram provides a sampling of some of the technology milestones that occurred in data management, data

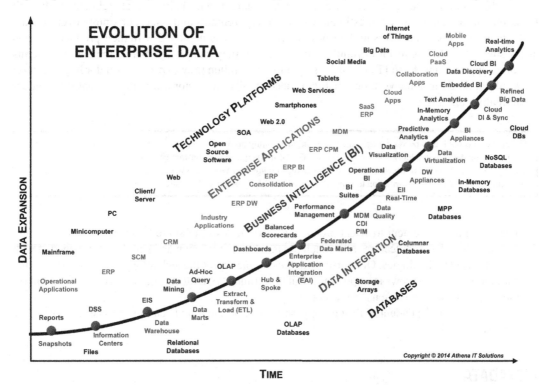

FIGURE 4.11

Evolution of data technology over time.

integration, business intelligence, and enterprise applications as the volume, variety, and velocity of data have also expanded over the years. It shows the progression of the sustained innovation that the industry has produced and, from a relative time perspective, the technology starting to make an impact on BI. The figure is not meant to imply that each new technology innovation is better than or replaces the previous innovation. Often the latest innovation becomes another option for an enterprise to use in its technology architecture. We will discuss the data technologies further in Chapter 7.

PRODUCT ARCHITECTURE

The product architecture defines the products, their configurations, and how they are interconnected to implement the technology requirements of the BI framework.

In Figure 4.1, the line on the left indicates that an enterprise defines its requirements and priorities from the top down, moving from the information, data, technology, and finally product architecture. On the right side of the diagram, we implement bottom-up and follow the architectures in reverse order.

Unfortunately, enterprises often rush to select products before defining the other components of this architecture. They issue product RFPs before examining their information, data, and technology needs and then end up with an architecture determined by the vendor. They then conform or contort their architecture, project, resources, time frame, and budget to fit their product architecture. It is all too common for vendors to underestimate your data requirements and issues, or simply overestimate what their products can do. It is in their best interest to get you deployed with their products as soon as possible. If problems result or numbers do not align, they can always blame the source systems and other applications. Both IT and business groups have fallen prey to product vendor hype because they did not do their homework on what their needs really were, nor did they vet what the vendors could realistically do.

> The goal of this book is to be vendor agnostic and avoid mentioning products and associated vendors so the content does not become outdated as products and vendors evolve. The BI marketplace is a constant churn of mergers and acquisitions, making it very difficult not to become outdated. This book's companion Web site www.BIguidebook.com will contain product and vendor-related information to support discussion of the product architecture.

The premature movement to select products is also the result of some biases against architecture. There is a feeling that architectures take much too much time to design and simply are not needed with today's advanced technologies. Of course, with the complexity of the technology, data, and people, the need for an architecture grows in importance. But the attitude "Architecture...we don't need no stinkin' architecture!" occurs more often than it should.

As a final note, independent analyst groups that review products and vendors are an excellent source of information in this area.

METADATA

Metadata management is not at the top of most BI teams or business people's priority lists. However, like flossing, it is one of those things you just have to do—and for good reason. The architectural framework needs to incorporate a strategy for handling metadata because it is essential to implementing and managing the underpinnings of technology and products.

The classic definition of metadata is "data about data." Metadata is the description of the data as it created, transformed, stored, accessed, and consumed in the enterprise. Business people need to know what the data represents—where it came from, how it was transformed, and what it means—if they hope to perform meaningful business analytics. IT people need to know what happened to the data from the point of capture through its consumption by the business in their reports and analysis if they are to provide consistent, comprehensive, conformed, clean, and current data for business analytics.

In essence, metadata is one of the key ingredients to enabling a data-driven enterprise. That is the carrot, while the stick is the many governmental and industry regulations that require an enterprise to manage and audit its data. How does that happen without metadata?

WHAT IS IT?

There are two types of metadata: technical and business. This distinction has been poorly understood and has caused much confusion, especially with IT and software vendors.

- **Technical metadata** is the description of data as it is processed by software tools. Databases, for example, need to define columns (format, size, etc.), tables, and indexes; ETL tools need to define fields, mappings between source and targets, transformations, and workflows; and BI tools need to describe fields and reports. All of this metadata is used to enable the software tools (not people) to understand and process data.
- **Business metadata**, in contrast, is the description of information from the business perspective (e.g., the business context of the inventory turns, weekly sales, or budget variance reports). Some of the metadata that describes a report is technical, such as field size and type. However, most of the data the business person cares about is not used by the software tools. BI tools have implemented "semantic layers," where text can be associated with fields to allow the input of business descriptions. While helpful, this is not nearly extensive enough to encapsulate the full business metadata needed.

WHAT TO DO ABOUT IT

Managing metadata can be a dirty job, but a few guidelines can smooth out the process.

First, manage the scope. If you try to "boil the ocean," you will get burned. Unless budget is not an issue, constrain your goals in the beginning. This will keep you from spending too much time and money, wasting resources, and delaying the project. You will probably only get one chance, so start small with a project guaranteed to succeed in a short period of time.

Second, address the cultural and political issues. Know who owns the data, who has time to define it, and if management really is committed to the project. It is nice to get everyone excited about metadata management, but is it on someone's priority list? Is it considered someone's real job?

Establish standards and processes that ingrain metadata management into business and IT people's jobs. Standards and processes need to be part of what we do, no excuses. The incentive of Sarbanes-Oxley and other regulations should spur management to back a reasonable metadata initiative.

 Finally, do not count on technology to be a silver bullet for metadata management. It is dirty, it is ugly, and you typically need to piece together a solution. In addition, a lot of the work involves talking with business people about what the data means and finding where the metadata is. Do not be scared away. Keep the scope small enough that your technology can handle it without significant custom software development.

 Metadata management is covered in Chapter 5.

SECURITY AND PRIVACY

With massive amounts of data flowing around the world and being consumed by governments, businesses, and people for legitimate and not-so-legitimate reasons, enterprises need to have security and privacy foremost in their architectural framework. It is essential given the adverse impact on your enterprise if security or privacy is compromised, with stark examples in the media of millions of people's data breached from enterprises in the retail, health care, insurance, and finance industries. Besides these adverse events, there are governmental and industry-specific regulations that need to be complied with.

 Security and privacy used to be simple in BI because there were only a few trusted people accessing a limited account of data that typically was not sensitive. In addition, those people were inside the enterprise firewall and they were generally using prebuilt reports or dashboards that did not allow any data discovery, meaning their data access was controlled.

 But since those early days, BI has become more pervasive, with many people within an enterprise taking on the role of BI consumer. Furthermore, many enterprises are also offering BI capabilities to their stakeholders, such as customers, prospects, partners, suppliers, and investors. Not only are there many more people, but there is much more data available and much more analytical capability. Without security and privacy constraints, this provides more opportunities for people to discover data that they are not supposed to see.

 Security and privacy are not just a BI concern; this obviously needs to be elevated to an enterprise-wide policy and program. Typically, it is in the CIO's domain, but regardless of who manages it, the BI initiative needs its security and privacy policies to follow enterprise standards and become active participants to get BI data and applications included into this domain.

GETTING STARTED

It can be complicated to design and implement BI and DI to conform to existing enterprise security and privacy policies, and it is also complicated if there are no policies and you need to create new ones. Many technologies have security access mechanisms associated with them, including networks, servers, notebooks, mobile devices, business applications, portable storage, BI tools, spreadsheets, data integration tools, and any other tool that can access data such as data profiling and data modeling. Cloud applications, databases, and analytic applications add complexity.

 An enterprise needs to determine where in the technology stack to implement security, how many layers of security are needed, and what types of security should be implemented in those layers. BI requires multiple layers of security implemented to access data and applications.

To design for and implement security and privacy, a BI team needs to determine the what, who, why, and how:

- **What** data is being used in building the BI applications—not just the data the BI consumers use directly but all the data gathered from the SORs, transformed, and then accessed in BI application
- **Who** is going to get access to the data
- **Why** are these people getting access to the data and what can they do to it
- **How** can the data be secured, and of the security options available, what should they use

IMPLEMENTING THE PLAN

Figuring out the what, who, and why is the easiest part of the equation; the difficult part is determining how security will be applied in relation to people and data.

First, the BI team needs to determine what data needs to be secured and what does not. Imposing the highest level of security for all data is not only impractical, it would constrain analytics and be much too costly to implement. There is always a trade-off between implementing tight security and providing high-performance access. The data inventory needs to classify data into security levels based on regulations, reputation, and negative impact if exposed. Specific employee and financial data will certainly be in the most sensitive category, but marketing data may be secured from external access and internal access may not be as much a concern.

Second, the BI team needs to examine what type and level of security could be implemented at each BI layer, such as in the database, analytics application, and network access.

Third, they need to examine the cost/benefit trade-off of what could be done and determine what makes the most sense from a business value perspective. For example, a BI team could use database security to limit user access by table and column, but that might be too time-consuming to implement and slow analytical analysis to a crawl.

Next, implement the security and privacy in the BI architecture.

Finally, communicate those policies to all BI stakeholders and enlist their vigilance in enforcing those policies in what they do.

AVOIDING ACCIDENTS WITH ARCHITECTURAL PLANNING

Unfortunately, many enterprises evolve their DW and BI projects without a planned architecture. This evolution is the result of developing tactical projects while chasing the latest technology proclaimed by analysts, columnists, and the vendors offering these solutions.

The random walk that creates this accidental architecture may have solved some immediate, tactical needs, but the expenditure of time, resources, and budget does not deliver ROI. Even worse, each new project results in a new stovepipe of data and technology that requires increasing resources to integrate. It also makes business users more likely to develop data shadow systems to perform their own integration.

How do you break the cycle of dependency on hype and the allure of silver bullet technologies? In order to correct a problem, you first have to recognize you have a problem. Both business and IT need to confront the accidental architecture addiction and resolve to work a better way—without finger-pointing.

THE SIGNS OF ACCIDENTAL ARCHITECTURE ADDICTION

How do you know you are facing an accidental architecture? Ask these questions:

- Do you have multiple BI and performance management (PM) tools or applications scattered throughout your enterprise?
- Do your business groups continually engage vendors to bring in new BI solutions to make up for the current environment's shortcomings?
- Have your business groups built many data shadow systems—and continue to build more—to do their reporting and analysis?
- Are people assuming that technologies such as Big Data, service-oriented architecture, software as a service or on-demand software, enterprise service bus (ESB), master data management, customer data integration, or open source software will deliver information nirvana, solving all your information needs?

If any of these are true, your company has probably developed an accidental architecture for your DW/BI environment. Even if each DW/BI project was well thought out and designed, you still have multiple DW/BI silos. You use different technologies, products, and data architectures for each one. Each project was going to solve the shortcomings of past initiatives. The sum of the parts, i.e., projects, does not add up to what the business was expecting.

If you are still in denial, let us probe a little deeper. From an IT perspective, ask yourself:

- Can IT provide the data models for your DW, data marts, cubes, and all the other data structures used for reporting and analysis, including Microsoft Access, SAS, and Microsoft Excel files?
- Can IT provide the extract, transform, and load (ETL) workflows documenting the data integration, starting from your data sources all the way to where the business consumes the information, including your DW, data marts, cubes, and any other data structures used for reporting and analysis?
- Does IT use an ETL product to load your DW, data marts, cubes, and other data structures? Or, is the ETL tool only used for loading the DW? If hand coding is involved, is it documented and managed?
- Can IT document all the processes and data used to build reports or perform analysis?
- Can IT identify and document your data shadow systems?

Answering these questions can make the IT group very nervous. They may be able to generate the ETL workflow from data sources to the DW (they can have their ETL tool generate that) and they sometimes have a DW data model (but it is usually not current). But the travels and transformation of the data from the DW to business reports and analysis, especially in spreadsheets, are generally a mystery.

If the IT group built the DW/BI environment according to an architecture, you would have all this information at your fingertips. But if your enterprise is like most, you probably do not.

The enterprise has evolved an accidental architecture, and it is time to break the cycle of dependency. There are no silver bullets that will solve these problems, but there is a road to recovery. It takes hard work, resources, and commitment, but it is worth it.

RECOVERING FROM AN ACCIDENTAL ARCHITECTURE

Do not make the mistake of thinking you can use a "green field" solution to fix an accidental architecture. Be realistic. You do not have a green field, and it is not practical to start from scratch. You have various silos of data and technologies, including data shadow systems. Whatever your solution architecture, you need to plan on building it iteratively and replacing or integrating your silos incrementally. Your solution architecture needs to be built using a program approach; it will evolve as your business and technology evolve.

Take these steps toward developing the architecture:

- Review your documentation of existing systems.
- Reverse engineer any systems without updated documentation or where there are gaps in the documentation.
- Gather and prioritize business requirements.
- Gather and prioritize technology considerations.
- Design your architecture.
- Determine the gaps between your current systems and your solution architecture.
- Develop a program plan, including budget, resources, and timetable to get you toward that architecture.
- Start your first project.

It is important to remember that the architecture has four components: information, data, technology, and products. Resist the urge to evaluate and select products. You need to first understand and agree on the information architecture that your business needs. Then determine the data you need, the condition of that data, and what you need to do to cleanse, conform, and transform that data into business information.

Next, determine what technologies (not products) are required by the information and data architectures. Finally, almost as an afterthought, evaluate and select products that match your architectural needs. Consider the products you already have in your silos as incumbent candidates, and determine if they will do the job. Do not chase the latest and greatest if your incumbent products can get the job done.

Designing an architecture to support your enterprise reporting and analytical needs is a significant project that will result in correspondingly significant business ROI, if you do it right. Do not be intimidated or overwhelmed. Too many people will decide that they do not have the time or money for this and will go back to the tactical project approach. That is shortsighted and will result in greater time and money spent on results that are far short of what you should be achieving.

DO NOT OBSESS OVER THE ARCHITECTURE

Whatever you do, do not get too wrapped up in the architecture. Some companies will get so fixated on the final architecture that they take months or years trying to develop it. Imagine what that does to a budget and project schedule!

The architecture is not the result of your BI/DW project, but rather a means to an end. Do not spend time on a monstrous, complicated architecture that solves world hunger; design something that you can start developing toward and that you can evolve over time. The architecture sets your direction and goals. It is a set of guiding principles, but should be flexible enough to allow for incremental growth. The world is not set in stone. You will be faced with changing business conditions and new technology. A rigid architecture will not be able to accommodate the changes.

Table 4.2 sums up all the various steps of creating your architecture, but it leaves room for flexibility.

Table 4.2 Summary of Architecture Action Plan	
Architecture	**Deliverables**
Data	• Define what data is needed to meet business user needs. • Examine the completeness and correctness of source systems that are needed to obtain data. • Identify the data facts and dimensions. • Define the logical data models. • Establish preliminary aggregation plan.
Information	• Define the framework for the transformation of data into information from the source systems to information used by the business users. • Recommend the data stages necessary for data transform and information access. • Develop source-to-target data mapping for each data stage. • Review data quality procedures and reconciliation techniques. • Define the physical data models.
Technology	• Define technical functionality used to build a data warehousing and business intelligence environment. • Identify available technologies available and review trade-offs associated between any overlapping or competing technologies. • Review the current technical environment and company's strategic technical directions. • Recommend technologies to be used to meet your business requirements and implementation plan.
Product	• List product categories needed to implement the technology architecture. • Review trade-offs between overlapping or competing product categories. • Outline implementation of product architecture in stages. • Identify a short list of products in each of these categories. • Recommend products and implementation schedule.

INFORMATION ARCHITECTURE

5

INFORMATION IN THIS CHAPTER:

- Information architecture purpose
- Data integration framework (DIF)
- Data preparation
- Data franchising
- BI and analytics
- Data management
- Metadata management
- Operational BI versus analytical BI
- Master data management (MDM)

THE PURPOSE OF AN INFORMATION ARCHITECTURE

Despite the data deluge (discussed in Chapter 1) and the investment to analyze this data, typical business analysts and managers spend a quarter of their time hunting, gathering, importing, integrating, and transforming data in spreadsheets just to keep their enterprise running. Note that these managers and analysts, the people reporting to vice presidents or chief financial officers, are the backbone of the knowledge workers in most corporations today, so if *they* are bogged down hunting and gathering data, then *corporations* are bogged down.

> Remember that *data* is not what business people can use to perform analysis, gain insight, and then act on that insight. Data becomes valuable to an enterprise when it is transformed into *information* and put into context with other information. This information then helps create *knowledge*.

Enterprises have business applications that perform the many business processes needed for their operations. The information architecture enables the business to perform analytics on these diverse processes, whether they are selling a product, monitoring a patient's vital stats, posting a student's grades, or tracking the performance of financial accounts. It is tempting to look at each of these processes as unique and implement each business intelligence (BI) application independently. If there is an underlying information architecture, the project-oriented approach works well, especially because it concentrates on supporting specific business processes. But if there is no information architecture, the result will be silos, which thwart effective analytics and carry a high cost in time and opportunity lost.

The information architecture defines the business context—"what, who, where and why"—necessary for building successful BI solutions. Table 5.1 lists the key questions that need to be addressed when designing the information architecture.

Table 5.1 The Information Architecture Questions

Question	Description
WHAT	• What business processes or functions are going to be supported • What types of analytics will be needed • What types of decisions are affected
WHO	• Who will have access—employees, customers, prospects, suppliers, or other stakeholders
WHERE	• Where is the data now • Where will it be integrated • Where will it be consumed in analytical application
WHY	• Why will the BI solution(s) be built, i.e. what are the business and technical requirements

This chapter introduces the key areas you need to examine when designing the information architecture:

- Data integration framework (DIF), which includes data preparation, data franchising, BI and analytics, data management, and metadata management
- Operational BI and its role versus analytical BI
- Master data management (MDM)

DATA INTEGRATION FRAMEWORK

The DIF is a combination of architecture, processes, standards, people, and tools used to transform enterprise data into information for tactical operations reporting and strategic analysis. People tend to equate data integration with an extract, transform, and load (ETL) tool. Although ETL tools can automate specific functions and improve BI development productivity, they are only one element within a DIF. Oversimplifying data integration creates the impression that it is quick and easy if you buy the right tool. This leads to false business hopes and makes it more difficult to explain why you have multiple information silos.

The DIF is a blueprint and set of guidelines to transform data into consistent, conformed, comprehensive, clean, and current information for your business people to use in measuring, monitoring, and managing your enterprise. The components of DIF are outlined in Table 5.2.

The discussion on information architecture follows; the other DIF components are covered in more detail further in this book:

- Processes and Standards—Part IV, Part V, Part VI
- Resources and Skills—Chapter 17
- Tools—Chapter 7

Table 5.2 DIF Building Blocks

Building Blocks	Purpose
Information architecture	Staging data from data sources to "information consumers"
Processes	Gathering, consolidating, transforming, cleansing, and aggregating data and metadata
Standards	Ensuring data consistency, accuracy, integrity, and validity
Tools	Assisting in the creation, deployment, management, and expansion of this framework
Resources and skills	Correct use of the tools and successful implementation of the architecture, processes, and standards

DIF INFORMATION ARCHITECTURE

The DIF information architecture's objective is to gather data that is scattered inside and outside an enterprise and transform it into information that the business uses to operate and plan for the future. Data is gathered, transformed using business rules and technical conversions, staged in databases, and made available to business users to report and analyze. Data flows from creation through transformation to information, just as materials flow from the supplier (enterprise resource planning systems, transaction systems), to factory (data integration), to warehouses (data warehouses (DWs)), and finally to retail stores (data marts and business analytic applications).

The DIF information architecture depicted in Figure 5.1 illustrates the processes that transform data into useful information as it progresses from source systems to the BI tools where business people

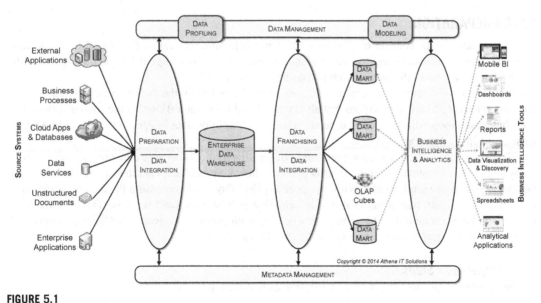

FIGURE 5.1

DIF information architecture.

analyze that information. The diagram shows a simplified version of a conventional hub-and-spoke architecture with an enterprise data warehouse (EDW) feeding multiple data marts. These concepts will be covered in more detail in Chapter 6. You will learn about the data integration workflow and all the potential data stores that may be included in an enterprise's data architecture such as sub-marts, federated DWs, operational data stores (ODSs), closed-loop systems, and analytic applications.

The DIF information architecture is composed of:

1. **Data preparation**: the first data integration stage includes gathering, reformatting, consolidating, transforming, cleansing, and storing data – both in staging areas and in the DW.
2. **Data franchising**: the second data integration stage reconstructs data into information for reporting and analysis with BI tools. Often, data is franchised from a DW into data marts or cubes. The data is filtered, reorganized, transformed, summarized/aggregated, and stored.
3. **Business intelligence and analytics**: these processes retrieve the data stored in the information architecture and delivers it to business users using BI applications. These applications can take the form of reports, spreadsheets, alerts, graphics, analytic applications, and slice-and-dice cubes. BI tools, spreadsheets, and analytic applications enable these processes, sometimes doing so through portals.
4. **Data management**: the processes and standards used to define, govern, and manage an enterprise's information assets (within the BI domain.) This establishes the specifications for what data will be selected and how it will be transformed for analysis in BI applications.
5. **Metadata management**: similar to software development management, is the behind-the-scenes processes, procedures, and policies that define and manage the metadata used and exchanged within the DIF. Metadata defines the data flowing from source systems, transformed in DIF components, and finally consumed by business people in their analysis with BI tools.

DATA PREPARATION

Data preparation is the core set of processes for data integration that gather data from diverse source systems, transform it according to business and technical rules, and stage it for later steps in its life cycle when it becomes information used by business consumers.

There are no shortcuts with data preparation. Don't be lulled by the "silver bullet" a vendor or a consultant may try to sell you, saying that all you need to do is point a BI tool at the source system and your business group will have what it needs. That oversimplifies data integration into a connectivity issue alone. It's a lot more than that.

The reason the solution is not just point-and-click with a BI tool is because data preparation involves many steps. The complexity of these steps depends on how your business operates, as well as how your business systems are implemented within your enterprise. Physically accessing the data in source systems is the easy part; transforming it into information is where the hard work is. This is something people don't appreciate if they have only been dealing with proofs of concept (POCs) or departmental business solutions rather than enterprise-wide, real data solutions.

Data Preparation Steps

The processing steps involved in data preparation as depicted in Figure 5.2 are:

• **Gather and extract data from source systems.** An enterprise's source systems may have a mix of custom-built, on-premise, and cloud-based applications along with many external

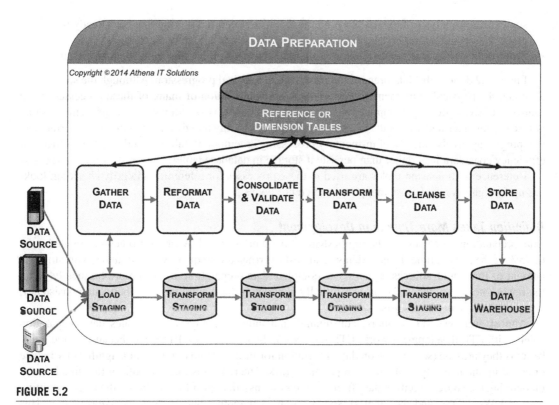

FIGURE 5.2

Data preparation processes.

sources. Although it is generally easy to get data out of any of these sources, it is still time-consuming to understand and obtain definition of its content. The best practice is to designate a subject matter expert to get that information and, if it is an internal system, to make the group maintaining that source system responsible for its extraction processes. They might not code it, but they own it.

- **Reformat data.** The source systems' data needs to be converted into a common format and schema to be fed into a DW. This is essential but straightforward provided there are schema and column definitions.
- **Consolidate and validate data**—Multiple data sources may need to be consolidated and standardized to provide a single, consistent definition for business consumers to use in their analysis. The data is validated by querying dimensions or reference files to determine if it conforms to specific business rules. The validation process ensures referential integrity in database terms.
- **Transform data**—Business transformations turn data into business information. These transformations include business rules, algorithms, and filters that convert data into a business context. Transformation may also associate a business transaction in a dimensional context such as the region, business division, or product hierarchy it is associated with.
- **Data cleansing**—Much of the simpler data quality checking, such as reformatting, consolidation, validation, and transformation, has already taken place. Data cleansing involves a more

sophisticated analysis of the data beyond the record-by-record checking that has already taken place. Name-and-address cleansing and customer householding are two examples.

- **Store data**—Data is stored to make it available for further processing in the data architecture.

Figure 5.2 depicts the data preparation processes in a logical progression. Although the sequence is accurate, the physical implementation may involve a combination of many of these processes into a sequence of source-to-target mapping operations or workflows. Also, although the diagram implies that you're storing intermediate results in a staging database, it's only a logical representation. Intermediate mappings may involve the use of in-memory processing or temporary tables based on performance and efficiency considerations rather than persistent storage in database tables.

Reference or dimension tables are used in these processes for referential integrity checking, looking-up foreign keys, and cross-mapping to reference codes.

Definition Takes More Time than Development

Data preparation processes are the lion's share of the work of any DW or BI project—estimated at 60 to 75% of the project time. Project delays and cost overruns are frequently tied to underestimating the amount of time and resources necessary to complete data preparation or, even more frequently, to do the rework necessary when the project initially skimps on these activities and then data consistency, accuracy, and quality issues arise.

Almost everyone—IT, vendors, consultants, and industry analysts—associates data preparation solely with ETL development work. ETL tools are indispensable in a BI project because of the many benefits they provide (see section on data integration for further details), but do not significantly reduce or speed up the majority of the data preparation work. The reason is that the bulk of the time is spent on defining the sources (getting data from source systems), data profiling, defining the targets (putting data in DWs, ODSs, and data marts), source-to-target mapping, and business transformations. This definitional work is time-consuming because it involves meeting, discussing, and obtaining consensus on the definitions and transformations with source systems' subject matter experts and business people. As the number of systems and people expands, these activities expand disproportionally.

Consolidating and Cleansing Data

Although the data gathering, reformatting, transforming, and storing data processes are straightforward, the consolidation and data cleansing processes are typically much more complex. Many BI projects oversimplify these processes and fail to design the data preparation processes that will result in consistent, conformed, and clean data.

Ensuring data quality is a part of the data preparation process that is required for the business to effectively use the data. Most people consider data quality to be checking for error conditions, data format conversions and mappings, and conditional processing of business rules based on a combination of dimension values or ranges. These types of data quality processes can be adequately performed with an ETL tool if planned for and designed into the overall data preparation architecture. A more important aspect of data quality, however, is data consistency rather than simply error detection or data conversion. Data may be valid in its transactional form when brought into a DW, but become inconsistent (and incorrect) when transformed into business information. Data preparation needs to take into account these transformations and ensure data quality and consistency. Tools alone will not enforce this consistency unless it is defined and then designed into the processes.

There are certain types of data quality that are better handled by special-purpose data cleansing tools rather than ETL. Data cleansing tools manage a wide variety of complex data quality issues that companies encounter, particularly those related to customer data such as cleansing customer names and addresses. A customer name and address may be input in different variations across source systems. Examples: a company may be stored as IBM, IBM Corp., or International Business Machines Corporation, while an address might be input as "12 Main Street," "12 Main St," or "12 Main Street, Suite 135." Although we can visually match these variations, it is not as straightforward a task with ETL tools or SQL. Because of this, companies facing problems like large lists of customer names and addresses can purchase specialized data cleansing software to perform this matching and standardization into one representation in the BI environment.

Another example of specialized data cleansing is the householding that financial service firms and retailers perform. The household process links family members' personal and business accounts or purchases together both for their customers' convenience and for their own convenience in promoting a full range of their products or services to their customers. Householding offers business value because it improves the ability of an enterprise to cross-sell and up-sell, and reduces redundancy. You know a company is not doing householding right when it mails both you and your spouse the same promotional brochure.

Data cleansing tools are important additions to enterprises' arsenals for ensuring data quality and consistency. Be careful, however, not to equate data cleansing tools with data quality. While the data cleansing tools provide data preparation processes for data quality, they are not the only processes that are needed in that area. Many see the data cleansing tool as a silver bullet. Others feel that if they cannot afford those tools (or they are not applicable to their situation), then they can forget about data quality. You can never forget about data quality, and you have to build data quality processes throughout data preparation.

DATA FRANCHISING

Data franchising takes place after data preparation has gathered and transformed data from source systems into a DW. Data franchising takes the data from the DW and transforms it into the information consumed in business analysis by using BI tools. Granted, this creates data that is redundant with what is in the DW, but it is a controlled redundancy with the first stage being data preparation and data franchising the second stage. The downstream target may be either a dependent data mart or a on-line analytical processing (OLAP) cube.

The Need for Data Franchising

A DW stores enterprise-wide data, both current and historical, gathered from many source systems in a manner that is efficient for IT to define, manage, and control. Data franchising packages data from the DW for several reasons:

- **Business people can understand the data.** The DW-tier in the BI data architecture (see Chapter 6) needs to be subject-oriented or both application- and business-process-neutral. If the DW does not provide neutrality, then it does not serve an enterprise role. Problems arise when a BI team concentrates on designing a DW to solely meet the needs of a specific business function, such as finance, or business process, such as supply chain management. The BI team's intent is to include others later, but the DW becomes so specific to the business group or process that it is not really usable by others. Instead, the business transformations, business rules, filters, hierarchies, and aggregations that are specific to a business group or process should be implemented in the data franchising processes to create data marts or cubes that are oriented toward them. The resulting data stores are in the business context of their consumers—people from business groups or involved in business processes—making it more easily understood and analyzed by them.

- **BI tools can more effectively present the data.** Of all the DIF components, data franchising is the most likely to be influenced by tools – in this case, the BI tools that you deploy in your DIF architecture. You need to design the data stores used by BI tools in a manner that most effectively exploits their capabilities. You can split BI tools into two categories based on what schemas they will work best with:

1   Dimensional models deployed in data marts
2. OLAP cubes or other proprietary schemas

When the BI tools work well with dimensional models, there are performance and usability considerations regarding the physical schema loaded through data franchising. Although your BI tool may be able to point at almost any data source and query it, the reality is that the data needs to be packaged appropriately. Design considerations in dimensional schema may include the following (see the data modeling chapters for detailed description of these concepts):

- Star versus snowflake
- Pre-built aggregated tables
- Handling hierarchies
- Shrunken dimensions
- Slowly changing dimensions
- Rapidly changing dimensions
- Multi-valued dimensions

When tools, such as OLAP, require proprietary schemas, you will need to use data franchising processes to load the data into the proprietary schema (tool-specific) in addition to performing the business-specific processes. Typically, the proprietary schemas will have their own design, tuning, and operational environment similar to relational databases. There may be advantages to using cubes rather than data marts, but that decision needs to be made based on business and technical considerations (see Chapter 7).

- **Improves business and IT productivity.** Having data franchising perform business-specific filtering, transformations, metrics calculations, and aggregation improves business and IT productivity. To understand this, it is best to examine what happens in its absence:
  - IT builds BI applications with embedded filtering, business transformations, metrics calculations, and aggregations.
  - Business people repeatedly filter, perform transformations, create metrics, and aggregate data to tailor data specific to their business group or process.

Embedding the processing logic in the BI applications that would have been implemented in data franchising has three drawbacks:

  - First, the logic is often repetitive and redundant across multiple reports, particularly when used by business groups or processes. To avoid repetitive logic built into each BI report or executed with each query generated from BI analysis, it often makes sense to stage data for further analysis. When data is *not* staged, you have to repeat the same steps for every report or analysis. Generally, business groups need the same data analysis over and over again, so it's a lot more efficient to just stage it once.

    To illustrate, look at a simplified example that includes only one of the many dimensions that business users need. Consider a company with global sales data that wants to franchise a

U.S. sales-by-product-line data mart. The data franchising process would begin by filtering only U.S. sales records and associating them with product information. This would reorganize the data so that sales transactions (facts) would be coupled (denormalized) with product-related information (dimensions). There may be certain business rules or transformations that would associate sales transactions with specific business units, product categories, or some other grouping. Data may be stored in an aggregated or summarized state to improve performance, or that might be done later when a report or analysis is generated. Without data franchising, each BI application would need to embed this logic.

- The second drawback is that when the logic is embedded in BI applications, it is executed at analysis instead of being pre-built once in the data mart or cube prior to the business person using the BI application. Business people are quite sensitive to BI dashboards taking too long to start up or to query data after they have made their selections. Adverse BI application performance has driven many business people to abandon BI applications and retreat back to their spreadsheets.
- The third drawback is that the logic needed in a BI application may be too complex to widely deploy or maintain. There are three problems with doing complex transformations in a BI report. First, it becomes expensive to maintain. Second, and more important, the reports get out of sync with one another and have conflicting numbers. As soon as the business users see inconsistent numbers in their reports, they'll question their integrity. Then, someone has to do a costly reconciliation to determine which numbers are right. Third, the logic is seldom documented in business terms, creating business risks.

- **Enables pervasive self-service BI.** BI tools continue to become easier for business people to use, but BI self-service remains an elusive goal in many enterprises. BI teams are often quite encouraged with the reception received with initial BI self-service attempts using pilot or POC projects to evaluate these tools. However, the BI team becomes frustrated when the enterprise-wide deployment is unsuccessful. A key reason for this is not because of the tool, but rather the business context of the data. In the pilot, the business people saw the data relevant to them, while during the enterprise-wide deployment they were accessing the DW. Using data franchising to deploy business-specific data marts enables BI self-service to be successful on an enterprise level.

There is an unfortunate tendency for people to overlook data franchising. They focus on the huge data volumes in their DW and assume that data integration is complete. However, *data* is not transformed into *information* until the business person obtains it, examines it, and acts upon it. Too often, business people do much of this data franchising by pulling data into a spreadsheet and transforming, aggregating, and summarizing it manually or by creating macro filters. Currently, it is possible to automate, document, and manage most of the data franchising used in a corporation. The more data is automated and managed, the more information quality and consistency are improved. Business-user productivity improves dramatically when work is shifted from data gathering and messaging to information analysis and action.

Data Franchise Steps

As shown in Figure 5.3, data franchising involves data filtering, reorganizing, transforming, summarizing, aggregating, and storing data generally extracted from a DW or ODS. Sometimes, external data sources are introduced either to increase dimensionality or to add attributes for analysis that may not have been in the original source systems. For example, a company might purchase or use external data for customer demographics or credit scoring.

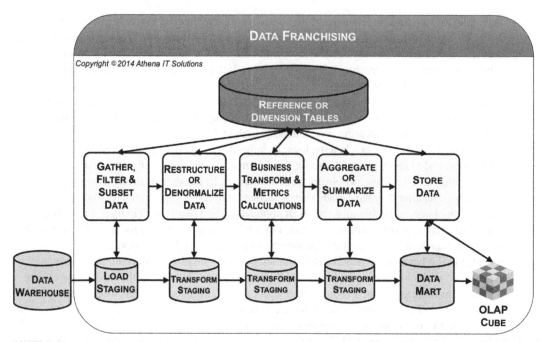

FIGURE 5.3

Data franchising processes.

The data franchising processes are:

- **Gather, filter, and subset data.** With the presumption that the data gathered has already undergone data preparation so it is consistent, conformed, clean, and current, then the focus shifts to rather straightforward processing. You are typically getting the data from one source and then filtering it by rows and columns to gather just what is needed by the target data store.
- **Restructure or denormalize data.** The target schemas will be different from the source in terms of content (subset) and possibility structure if non-relational databases are used. This process performs the source and target mappings.
- **Perform business transformations and metrics calculations.** Data marts and cubes typically support specific business processes. This process will perform the business transformations and metrics calculations that are used by these specific business processes.
- **Aggregate or summarize data.** Depending on the BI tool you're using, you may need to create aggregations or summarizations to improve query response time, especially when dashboards or scorecards display aggregated data into which the business person can drill down.
- **Store data.** The primary target data stores are data marts and OLAP cubes.

Dimension or reference tables are used in the data franchising processes for:

- Referential integrity
- Lookups and cross-maps
- Business transformation

- Business metric calculation
- Query selection criteria
- Aggregations
- Report value bands

The steps for staging data stores for loading and transforming are depicted in Figure 5.3. They are typically transient rather than persistent—the opposite of data preparation—because data volumes and data integration processing are not sufficient to warrant persistent storage.

Differences between Data Franchising and Data Preparation

Data franchising is the aggregation, summarization, and formularization of data for use with BI tools. This process overlaps with data preparation with regard to extracting the data from a data source and reformulating it into a data mart. The data franchising component, however, does not need to perform many of the more sophisticated data integration functions of data preparation processes. There are four main differences:

- First, the data sources used by data franchising are often the DW or ODS rather than the many, and sometimes conflicting, data sources used to initially build the DW or ODS.
- Second, the data preparation stage performs the data cleansing processing necessary to accumulate data from its sources. This means that the data franchising component is dealing with clean data (or at least does not need to perform those functions).
- Third, data preparation has already performed such processes as conforming dimensions, managing slowly changing dimensions, updating dimensional hierarchies, and handling all the intricacies of historical data. Again, data franchising starts processing when these more difficult issues have been addressed.
- Fourth, the DW or ODS is stored in a relational database with a documented data model and its associated data definitions. The best practice, as explained in the section on data design, is for the DW to be designed with a hybrid (or advanced) dimensional model and any data mart to use a standard dimensional model. The processing of this data is more straightforward than in the data preparation stage, so you have a wider range of tools from which to choose. Although you may be more productive if you use a single ETL tool for both data preparation and data franchising, it may be more economical and faster to use a less robust ETL tool or do custom coding.

You may find yourself with a target database requiring special processing that a general-purpose ETL tool cannot provide. Examples are multidimensional online analytical (MOLAP) BI tools that store their data in cubes and relational online analytical (ROLAP) BI tools that store their data in a relational database but need it set up a specific way in order to work. Often, an OLAP BI tool includes ETL tools or utilities that move data into its databases so that BI tools can access them. In other cases, you may need to create custom code.

BI AND ANALYTICS

Two roles of BI in the information architecture are to provide:

- Back-end processes that select, retrieve, and transform the data stored in the information architecture.

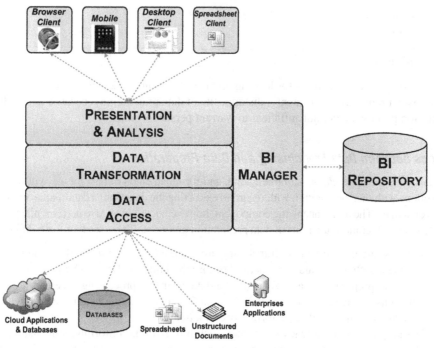

FIGURE 5.4

BI tool components.

- Front-end processes visible to BI application users to interact with, analyze, and present results in graphic or tabular form.

BI applications are the only portion of the information architecture that the business person interacts with. It is common to hear the business refer to the overall environment by the name of the BI product being used.

Although many refer to the BI and analysis as the presentation layer of the information architecture, that is too simplistic and ignores the information processing that occurs in this layer. Figure 5.4 depicts the various components that process the information that the business person selects, transforms, presents, and analyzes:

- **BI manager:** The application controller that orchestrates the BI processes and interfaces with the BI repository and its supporting metadata.
- **BI repository:** Stores the metadata used by the application. This may include screen layouts, data definitions, filters, measures, annotations, scheduling, workflow, version control, access control lists, and data access specifications. The repository uses a database or files for storing its metadata.
- **Data access:** Retrieves data from the various data sources specified in the application. BI tools will bring the data into memory, a database, or file structure for transformations, presentation, and analysis. The data brought in for these purposes may be either transient or persistent based on the specific BI tool used.

FIGURE 5.5

BI interface analytical styles.

- **Data transformation:** Enables the application to transform data based on the analytical needs of the business. There will typically be many pre-built capabilities offered by the BI tool, but most tools enable manually coded transforms. The coding may use a tool's proprietary language or an industry standard such as SQL or multidimensional expressions (MDX).
- **Presentation and analysis:** The component the business person interacts with to select, view, and analyze data. One or more of the BI styles depicted in Figure 5.5 will be available for those interactions.

The powerful transformation capabilities are both a blessing and a curse in the information architecture. From a positive perspective, it provides more processing options in the architecture to transform data tailored to the needs of business processes, groups, or people. The dangers are how that is accomplished or to what extent it is relied upon.

When transforming data, the objectives should be that it is shared, reusable, and documented. It is very important that metadata about the transformation is available to enable tracing the flow of data from source to its analysis. To ensure the information 5 C's, it is ideal to perform the transformation once and use it many times. This "do once and use many times" approach is what the various data stores in the BI data architecture accomplish and what we strive to extend throughout the entire information architecture. A guiding principle is to shift data transformation as far upstream—from BI to data franchising to data preparation—as it makes sense. Moving this processing upstream increases the extent of reusability, improves the probability of consistency and likely will be more efficient in terms of resources – both people and infrastructure.

The most significant risks when transforming data in BI processes occur when it is done with manual coding: it may not be reusable, it won't be visible to anyone other than the developer, and it might not be documented. This creates a black hole where we do not know what happens to this data; it's a similar situation to when data is manipulated in a spreadsheet with macros without anyone other than the spreadsheet owner knowing what happened. Using extensive manual coding increases the overall costs of developing and maintaining the BI application, eliminates the ability to perform impact or where-used analysis on the data, and can adversely affect upgrades, migration, and enhancements to the BI application.

DATA MANAGEMENT

Data management encompasses the policies, procedures, and standards used to design and manage the other information architecture processes: data franchising, data preparation, BI, and metadata management. This is a very broad category that can sometimes make you feel like you are trying to boil the ocean. To try and make the task more manageable, you can select what you will do by prioritizing these activities based on their long-term business impact and return on investment. Too often we fall into the trap of choosing one extreme or the other. We either try to do too much and end up accomplishing nothing, or we ignore data management altogether and face significant business risks and costs.

The key joint business and IT initiative to implement data management is data governance. This process drives the prioritization of the data management policies, procedures, and standards. Chapter 17 describes data governance in more detail.

Two data management processes that are too often ignored or shortchanged are data modeling and data profiling. As depicted in Figure 5.6, they are used to understand existing data and then define the data in the BI environment. Data profiling and data modeling are two processes that go hand-in-hand with data preparation. Data profiling is a precursor to data preparation because it helps you understand the data in the source system in order to prepare it for BI. Data modeling complements data integration by defining the target data structures it will load.

> ### AVOID REWORK WITH DATA PROFILING AND DATA MODELING
>
> When I was a neophyte software engineer, my first manager told me that there are two approaches to developing software: design and code or code and rework. The latter appears to be initially faster, but the former gets you there sooner with quality, consistent code. In addition, constant rework raises the overall cost and reduces the trust people have in your code.

METADATA MANAGEMENT

As discussed in Chapter 4, metadata is the description of the data and information processes that affect it as it moves from data sources to information consumption. Metadata is generated by many of the tools used in the BI environment, and also created by design, development and deployment activities such as gathering business requirements.

Metadata Categories

You should capture and manage the following categories of metadata within the information architecture:

Data definitions—Documenting data element descriptions should be part of the requirements gathering of any BI project. As such, you have already done the heavy lifting for this type of metadata. This is where most metadata initiatives start, and typically you create a data dictionary. Although the data elements are initially documented in the project's business requirements document, they are usually stored and queried from a data modeling tool or BI tool accessing a customized data dictionary stored in a relational database. More sophisticated projects may have purchased and deployed a metadata repository.

ETL source-to-target mapping—If you have used an ETL tool rather than custom code, this should be an easy step. Your ETL tool should have a catalog that you can use for documentation and examining the ETL workflow. You can examine and query data lineage, at least within the context of your ETL code, to determine how a data element was transformed, as well as the impact of a change on

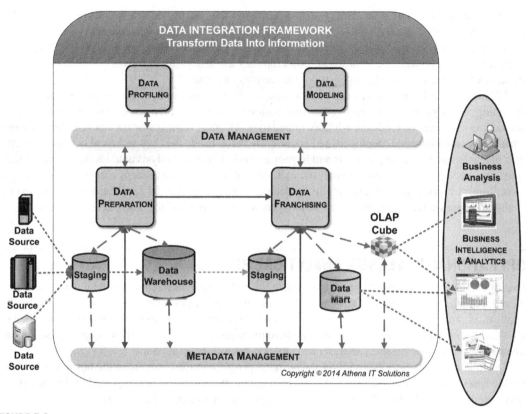

FIGURE 5.6

Data management processes.

that data element or workflow. This metadata, although of interest to business, is generally an IT tool and improves their productivity.

BI applications—This metadata includes cataloging the data accessed by BI applications, filters, and queries used; workflow of data processes; and data transformations. Most of today's top-tier BI products come with BI repositories that store the metadata. In addition, portals are also available within these BI product suites that allow grouping of reports, queries, and data elements that business people can access.

These metadata categories are typically straightforward to gather and maintain as separate entities by using the appropriate BI, ETL, and database tool features. These tools typically manage metadata only in their domain, so without a metadata repository product the BI team will need to manage this metadata in silos.

Metadata Value

Metadata management provides value to both the business and IT:

Business value—For the business people using the BI environment, metadata should serve as their documentation and reference materials. We may complain about the quality of the documentation we receive from vendors, but what about the documentation that we provide to the business people? No matter how powerful or easy a BI tool is, business people need to know what data they are using with it. We need to provide the business metadata, i.e., the BI's documentation, along with the BI applications for them to understand what the information they are analyzing represents. Where did it come from, how was it transformed, and what does it mean as they use it?

IT value—For IT, metadata management coupled with source code management is essential for designing, developing, and managing the information management processes. Business requirements and coding specifications indicate what we intend to build, but it is the metadata that actually describes what has been built, tested, deployed, and is currently being used. Two key technical benefits of metadata management are lineage analysis and impact analysis. Lineage analysis enables the tracing of data from its source to eventual use in analysis, including all the processing steps that were taken to get there. Impact analysis provides the ability to determine how ETL and BI applications are affected by changes in data sources along with how an analysis will be affected if the data selected is altered.

OPERATIONAL BI VERSUS ANALYTICAL BI

One of the ongoing struggles enterprises wrestle with is the clash between operational versus management reporting. Operational reporting is tied to specific applications and is typically provided by the application vendor as a pre-built offering. Management reporting spans applications, is typically tied to a DW, and is custom-built using BI tools. The term management refers not only to an enterprise's management staff, but also business analysts and any non-operational personnel.

Operational reporting is essential for the business people involved in running the business on a day-to-day basis. Business transactions and events are captured, monitored, and reported on by the operational applications. The benefits of relying on the application's operational reports are:

- Pre-built reporting that does not require an IT project to custom-build the reports or load the data into a DW
- Real-time data access, enabling the business to get the most up-to-date data.
- Integration and cooperation with operational processes, to streamline and expedite these processes.
- Data that is presented in the terminology of the underlying application that is well understood by its business users.

Because enterprises have multiple source systems, management reporting used DWs that were devised to integrate the source systems and provide the business with the five C's of data: consistent, conformed, comprehensive, clean, and current.

For quite a while these two worlds—DW versus applications—were clearly separate domains with their own business consumers, IT staffs, budgets, and expertise. There was no overlap between the people using it, the tools, the data, or the expertise needed. The closest these groups came to working together was the scheduled feeds from the application to the DW, but even these were generally hand-offs to the BI team, which then went about doing its own thing.

The BI landscape has changed over time in several ways:

- Business people need both operational and management reporting
- Application vendors adopted BI tools in their operational reporting offerings (or the largest application vendors acquired the BI tool vendors themselves)

- Some application vendors even built their own DW product offering
- The data currency gap—the frequency of updating the data has narrowed or has been eliminated in some instances.

The application vendor landscape has changed with a split between mega-vendors offering applications with a significant enterprise footprint across many business processes and specialty application vendors targeting specific business processes or industries. Enterprises encounter a proliferation of applications, often a mix of on-premise and cloud-based, each with their own operational reporting environment.

The result of these changes has been the rise of many reporting silos providing overlapping and inconsistent data when compared to the enterprise BI environment using a DW. With the 5 C's of data broken in this landscape of data silos, what is IT to do? Assuming that it is not acceptable to continue to maintain the status quo of reporting silos, these are the alternatives:

- Shift business users to a specific application reporting silo and supplement the operational reporting with data from other applications
- Shift all reporting to the DW-based BI environment
- Blend application-specific and DW BI environments

SHIFT ALL REPORTING TO THE APPLICATION-SPECIFIC ENVIRONMENT

There are two types of application vendors where this scenario get serious consideration:

1. **Mega-application vendor.** This type of application vendor has a significantly robust application that spans many business processes, offers its own DW environment, and may even sell one of the major BI tools in the marketplace (a tool that it acquired when it purchased the original BI vendor).
2. **Application vendor supporting cross-function business process.** This type of application vendor has a significant business footprint in an enterprise, offers capability to import other application data, has an application development platform, and likely has cloud-based support.

A key—and erroneous—assumption in this scenario is that the application-specific reporting platform can be a substitute for the DW or even make it obsolete. Although it's possible to bring data into the application environment, you've got to ask if it can do an adequate job or even try to. Nearly every enterprise, no matter how large or small, needs a significant data integration effort to create data consistency, data integrity, and data quality. It doesn't happen overnight and it takes substantial resources with 60–75% of a DW effort spent on data integration, not creating reports. Even if the application's data integration capabilities were up to the task, why would an enterprise shift its focus from supporting business processes to being a DW? Why would an enterprise migrate its DW environment to the application when there would be such a large cost, loss in time, and drain on resources? And if the DW was not replaced, then the enterprise is, in effect, expanding its multiple reporting silos to multiple DW silos. This makes no sense.

A second erroneous assumption is that all business people need real-time data from an application. Certainly many applications, such as call centers and inventory management operations, truly benefited from the real-time information. But then everyone wanted real-time data. Operational BI was seen as the way to get it.

The reality is that most business analysis does not need real-time data. In fact, real-time data would cause problems or create noise, e.g., inconsistent data results, that would have to be filtered out. Much of what business people do is examine performance metrics, trend reports, and exception reporting. Most are looking at daily, weekly, monthly, and year-to-date analysis, not hourly analysis or trends. There are some industries where that would be useful, but with most it doesn't matter what was sold between 9:05 a.m. and 9:30 a.m. today.

Remember, you build performance management and BI solutions to satisfy a business need. Real-time BI often is suggested because it can be done technically, not because of a business need. Do you really want to spend the resources, time, and budget for something the business doesn't need?

SHIFT ALL REPORTING TO THE DW-BASED BI ENVIRONMENT

Although there are many DW zealots that state that all reporting should come from the DW, there are many practical reasons why this, like the shift to exclusively using applications-based reporting previously discussed, should not be pursued.

With advances in data integration capabilities and productivity, enterprise BI environments can capture data near-time or even real-time if there is a business need. This removes one of the technical constraints on the DW's ability to provide operational reporting, but there are other considerations.

The primary reason to not have a DW assume all operational reporting is simply, "If it ain't broke, don't fix it." If the application's pre-built reporting is being used and relied on, particularly if it has been embedded in an enterprise's business processes, you should not pursue a replacement project with the associated expense, time, and resources to duplicate something that is working. This would result in a lost opportunity to invest those resources into expanding an enterprise's overall BI capability and usage.

In addition, the application vendor will likely be expanding, updating, and maintaining its operational reporting offering, which means that shifting this reporting to the DW would be a continuing drain to duplicate what the vendor is providing.

BLEND APPLICATION-SPECIFIC AND DW BI ENVIRONMENTS

With the understanding that neither the DW nor the application-based operational reporting will be sufficient unto themselves, the solution is to blend these together. Although an enterprise could just keep each environment in its own silo, it is very likely that business people will not see consistent information in each silo. In addition, with totally separate silos, the business consumers need to know which one to use under what conditions and their experience within each silo will be different. Leaving the silos as is will be a drain on both IT and business productivity.

The recommendations for creating a blended environment, as depicted in Figure 5.7, are to:

- **Create a data architecture** for your business users that includes the enterprise applications, DWs, data marts, cubes, and even spreadsheets that are needed to enable both operation and management reporting (see Chapter 6).
- **Create a technical architecture** that enables data to be transformed and moved in whatever manner is appropriate for the business purpose (see Chapter 7). There are many times that data should be queried from the enterprise application directly rather than insisting that the data be moved to a DW before the business people can access it. Data virtualization, for example, enables querying across disparate data sources, i.e., enterprise applications, where in the past the data had to be physically moved into a common database using an ETL tool.

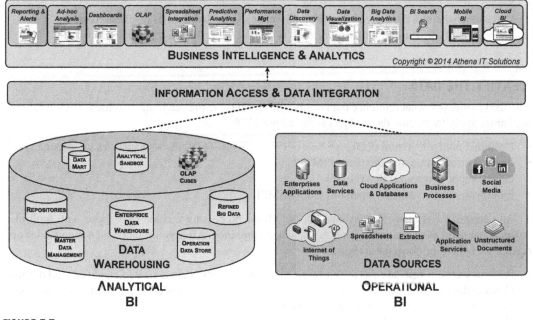

FIGURE 5.7

Blended BI environment.

- **Create an information architecture** that enables a BI portfolio for your business people that spans operational and management reporting. Business people do not need to understand the differences. They simply need to perform their analysis regardless of where the data is located in your data architecture.
- **Leverage common BI tools** across your BI portfolio. Business people should be able to use the same BI tools for their reporting and analysis, regardless of where the data comes from. They should not need to change their behavior based on where in the data portfolio their analysis needs are met. Simplify their lives by letting them go to one place and use one set of tools.

There should not be a business distinction between operational and analytical BI when it's properly designed into your information, data and technology architectures.

MASTER DATA MANAGEMENT

MDM is the set of processes used to create and maintain a consistent view, also referred to as a master list, of key enterprise reference data. This data includes such entities as customers, prospects, suppliers, employees, products, services, assets, and accounts. It also includes the groupings and hierarchies associated with these entities. The need for MDM arises when there are multiple, independent sources for an entity.

Many enterprises need MDM as part of their information architecture to create consistent and conformed reference data. When designing an information architecture, follow these steps with respect to MDM:

- Identify what reference data needs MDM.
- Determine where in the information lifecycle inconsistent data creates business risks.
- Assess what type of information processing is needed to create consistent reference data.

IDENTIFY THE DATA

You need to identify what reference data needs MDM. MDM is the catch-all term used, but the following names apply to specific data subject areas within MDM:

- Customer data integration (CDI)
- Product information management (PIM)
- Global supplier management (GSM)
- Enterprise master patient (or person) index (EMPI)

An enterprise has many dimensions, but for MDM processing include only those with multiple, independent sources that create inconsistency when combined. After you select which dimensions are needed for MDM, perform these tasks:

- Perform source system analysis to determine where and how this data is created, modified, and deleted.
- Conduct data profiling to examine what has already been stored, its current state, and its data structures.
- Get business people to sign-up for data ownership responsibilities
- Document definitions and business processing rules
- Establish data governance processes for MDM

Never assume that technology will solve your MDM problems without significantly including people, processes, and politics in the equation. Data governance, with the business taking ownership of the data and IT becoming the custodian, is needed to successfully design, deploy, and sustain an MDM solution.

Business people need to help IT identify master data, define it, and assist in determining what the resultant master list should be. Managing master data needs business commitment if it is to be treated as the corporate asset that it is. It is important to note that this is no different from anything else in the DW/BI world – information is an important business asset, but if the IT and business groups don't work together this asset will be wasted.

MDM requires that the data governance processes are part of an enterprise information management initiative to actively update and maintain the data definitions that the business creates. Data governance is an enabling process, but too often falls short because its deliverables are not incorporated into information management.

FIND THE PROBLEM AREAS

You need to determine where inconsistent data creates business risks in the information lifecycle. Although MDM is typically thought of as separate from BI, the reality is that for many years, whether people realized it or not, EDW has served as the default MDM application. With its role of integrating data from many source systems, the EDW serves as the "canary in the coal mine" by being the first place, sometimes only place, where the disparate data is brought together and the inconsistencies become visible. Typically, a particular source system's reference data is correct in its own silo, but creates inconsistency problems for the enterprise when other data sources' reference data is commingled with it. Because there is no incentive for a source system to undertake MDM with other source systems if it is performing its business functions with its own reference data, the EDW is forced to take on this responsibility.

Just because the EDW has become the default MDM does not mean that it should remain so. But you can't fix the problem until you figure out where it is, which is going to be where the business pain is most evident. There are three potential areas to address: operational, analytical, or enterprise (both). You should focus on managing reference data in your operational systems, such as your ERP application, if data synchronization across systems is inhibiting the business from running the business. Many companies spend a lot of time integrating product lists, for example, between various enterprise applications to keep them consistent. This is a flag that you should look at a solution that concentrates on systematically improving application integration of reference data.

If your operational systems are working fine but your business is struggling with inconsistent reference data in BI applications because of conflicting data sources, then you should concentrate your efforts to manage reference data in the EDW. This activity is referred to as conforming dimensions in dimensional modeling terminology.

If your company is having issues in managing reference data in both your operational and analytic systems, then you need a stand-alone MDM application. A word of caution: in this situation, you need to limit your scope if you want to have a fighting chance of success, so start with the area causing the most significant business pain.

ASSESS A SOLUTION

You'll need to assess what type of information processing is needed to create consistent reference data. There are two levels of information processing that may be needed to manage master data.

First Level

The first level is the integration processes that conform dimensions and standardize facts when an EDW is being loaded from multiple data sources and the enabling dimensional schema. For these processes you need to:

- Profile each data source
- Define data and business rules with the business
- Create a conformed dimension
- Create a cross-reference that maps the data source to the target conformed dimension
- Develop an integration processes to load the data using the cross-map

In addition, as we discuss in the data modeling section, you'll implement both slowly changing dimensions and hierarchy management processes to manage the conformed dimensions. This level of processing will likely address most, if not all, of your MDM requirements.

Second Level

The second level of integration processes includes data cleansing and data enrichment processes. These processes demand more extensive tools than just ETL tools that load a DW. If you already have extensive data integration processes and expertise, then you should add data cleansing and data enrichment tools to your environment. The data integration suite you use may have these tools as options to add, which would be the direction you will likely pursue. If, however, you do not have a robust data integration environment, your existing data integration suite does not have these options or your organization's skills are not extensive in this area, then you are a candidate to purchase and implement a full-fledged MDM application. See Chapter 7 for further discussion.

The second level of processing may be necessary for specific data domains. CDI is by far the most likely data domain that would require integration processing beyond the first level.

Customer data has many characteristics that differ from other reference data:

- First, many key attributes, such as name and address, are textual in nature and may vary between sources. A name could be Richard, Rick, Rich, Dick, or R. An address might be listed as a 12 Main Street, 12 Main St, or 12 Main. Although we can visually identify similar names or addresses, ETL programs and SQL statements do not deal with this ambiguity as well. Also, it is common for these attributes to be filled in by people at different points in times on different input devices, increasing the opportunity for variations. Name and address matching is the process that deals with this problem.
- The second characteristic of customer data is that customers are typically associated with locations such as their home, place of work, or where they purchase a product or service. They may also input incorrect or incomplete data if accuracy is not needed to complete the action for which they are inputting the data. This may result in ambiguity, especially if customers or salespeople input the data.
- The third customer data characteristic is that customers are related to other customers. A business making a transaction may be part of a larger business entity that is not evident by its business name. A person may have a spouse, former spouse, or children that your business would like to know about to determine what to sell to them. This process is called householding, where a family is connected together in customer data even if they do not all have the same last name.

DATA ARCHITECTURE

6

INFORMATION IN THIS CHAPTER:

- Data architecture purpose
- History of data architecture
- Various architectural choices
- Analytical data architecture (ADA)
- Data integration (DI) workflows
- Operational data store (ODS)

THE PURPOSE OF A DATA ARCHITECTURE

Data is everywhere in the enterprise, from large legacy systems to departmental databases and spreadsheets. No one controls all of it, it's often duplicated erratically across systems, and the quality spans a wide range. Despite the tendency for chaos, the bulk of data is the lifeblood of an enterprise. If it is not clean, current, comprehensive, and consistent, the enterprise is in trouble. This makes data architecture all the more important.

The data architecture defines the data along with the schemas, integration, transformations, storage, and workflow required to enable the analytical requirements of the information architecture. A solid data architecture is a blueprint that helps align your company's data with its business strategies. The data architecture guides how the data is collected, integrated, enhanced, stored, and delivered to business people who use it to do their jobs. It helps make data available, accurate, and complete so it can be used for business decision-making.

DATA ARCHITECTURE VERSUS DATA MODELING

Don't confuse data architecture with data modeling. *Data architecture* applies to the higher-level view of how the enterprise handles its data, such as how it is categorized, integrated, and stored. *Data modeling* applies to very specific and detailed rules about how pieces of data are arranged in the database. Where data architecture is the blueprint for your house, data modeling is the instructions for installing a faucet.

Data architecture is important for many reasons, including that it:

- Helps you gain a better understanding of the data
- Provides guidelines for managing data from initial capture in source systems to information consumption by business people
- Provides a structure upon which to develop and implement data governance

- Helps with enforcement of security and privacy
- Supports your business intelligence (BI) and data warehousing (DW)activities, particularly Big Data

HISTORY

> "Those who cannot remember the past are condemned to repeat it."
>
> **George Santayana, "The Life of Reason", 1905.**

There are many myths and misconceptions in BI today that were formed during the evolution of DW. Although most of the people in BI today were not involved in its formative stages, folklore from DW evolution still haunts and ultimately hinders BI architecture, reducing its business value, lowering productivity, and increasing costs.

This section's goal is to provide commentary on the what, why, and how of DW evolution. Follow-on sections will describe the best practices that have resulted from these lessons. The first lesson to learn is that the initial use of the terms does not necessarily represent the way they relate to current best practices. To paraphrase a movie disclaimer: any resemblance to current terminology is purely coincidental.

PREHISTORY

HOW LARGE WERE GREEN-BAR REPORTS?

My first software development job was in a funky modern building in Harvard Square, Cambridge, Massachusetts. We couldn't adjust the overly cold air conditioning, and several people on my floor started blocking the floor vents in their offices with thick stacks of green-bar reports. So, all the cold air was redirected into the office of the one freezing-cold programmer who didn't know how useful green-bar reports could be!

In the early days, IT groups built reports for specific business applications. Large and cumbersome, these "green bar" reports were a voluminous dump of data printed on wide, continuous sheets of green-striped paper using dot-matrix printers. Business people had to thumb through thick stacks to get the information they were looking for. As IT generated more reports, it put a huge strain on the CPUs that the business applications ran on. This then prompted IT groups to create nightly snapshots of business applications on a separate CPU, and then run the reports the next day using the snapshot. The snapshot offloaded the reporting and improved the business application performance, but it did not change the way reports were created or used.

IN THE BEGINNING

In the 1980s, a group of companies—Digital Equipment Corporation (DEC), Apple, and Motorola— decided that reporting had to fundamentally change. The common characteristics of these technology companies were that they were engineering-oriented and sold hardware and software. They had vibrant IT staffs that thrived in a corporate culture that embraced innovation. Their quest for innovation was fueled by nearly unlimited access to all the hardware and software they wanted. Budgets are far tighter nowadays, but you might see this freedom and embrace of innovation in an open source environment.

These companies collaborated on a technical architecture that separated transactional processing of the business applications and the reporting environments. This architecture involved extracting data from the transactional systems to a DW (and they did indeed call it a data warehouse). The architecture further evolved to the two data tiers in DW with a wholesale DW feeding downstream retail DWs. This was before the term data mart was coined, and likely was the first hub-and-spoke architecture.

There were no data integration (DI) and business integration tools then, so everything was done by building custom code. The IT environment was fragmented in many ways:

- Relational databases had not yet become mainstream, and many nonrelational databases were being used for transactional systems
- Structured query language (SQL) was not yet pervasive in relational databases, so proprietary interfaces needed to be used for each database
- No pervasive database connectivity application programming interfaces (APIs) existed so, just as with database access, proprietary APIs were used

Developing a DW was laborious, requiring a very tech-savvy IT staff with access to a lot of resources, including highly skilled people, time and significant investments in infrastructure such as hardware, storage, databases, extract, transform, and load (ETL) tools, and BI tools. The technology companies just mentioned continued evolving their reporting architectures, but it was invisible to the overall marketplace and mainstream IT.

DATA WAREHOUSING GOES PUBLIC

The early 1990s were dawn of DW for the masses. This occurred when IBM endorsed the concept and Bill Inmon started evangelizing it. IBM saw DW (it used the term "information warehouse") as a great approach for its customers to address their expanding reporting needs and, of course, a terrific opportunity to sell their mainframe as the host platform for a central (or corporate) DW (CDW). Centralizing data, in what would years later be referred to as the "single version of the truth," would enable business people to gain an enterprise view of the business.

Bill Inmon promoted DW by speaking at technical conferences, talking with large companies about its values, and writing books explaining what it was. Inmon is often referred to as the "Father of Data Warehousing" not because he invented it, but because he was its evangelist. Inmon's devotion to the cause was critical for the emergence and widespread popularity of DW.

The classic definition from Inmon's 1991 book *Building the Data Warehouse* [1] was that the DW data has the following attributes:

- Integrated—data gathered and made consistent from one or more source systems
- Subject-oriented—organized by data subject rather than by application
- Time-variant—historical data is stored (Note: in the beginning, enterprise applications often only stored a limited amount of current and historical data online.)
- Non-volatile—data did not get modified in the DW, they were read-only

Companies beyond the technology sector started implementing DWs. These DWs were centralized databases, often referred to as CDWs. Figure 6.1 shows a typical CDW. (With Big Data, people now call them enterprise data warehouses (EDWs).) These DWs extracted data from many transactional systems to enable cross-functional reporting. At the time, many transactional systems did not retain history on-line, so a key feature of CDWs was that they kept historical data available.

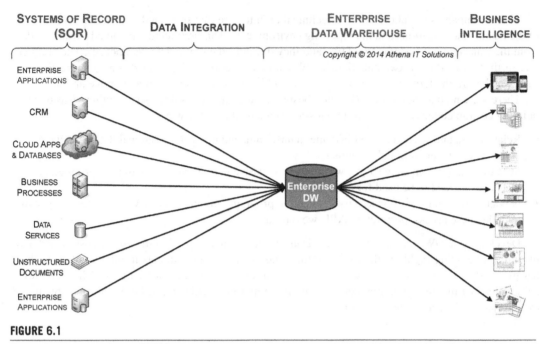

FIGURE 6.1

Enterprise data warehouse (EDW).

Designing, building, and implementing CDWs took a long time—months and maybe years. Some of the reasons for the lengthy time to deliver a CDW were:

- IT's use of the waterfall project methodology
- Everything had to be manually coded
- Much of the database, access, and networking standards that we take for granted today had not yet evolved, requiring the use of specific propriety APIs

The biggest reason why CDW projects took so long was IT's misguided attempt to gather all the requirements and implement an entire CDW in one "big bang" project. With an enterprise-wide scope, the project was destined to consume many resources, be late, and exceed the budget. An even worse outcome was that while the lengthy project was under way and after business requirements were documented, the business changed—invalidating many of the requirements.

Being an early adopter always carries some risk, and this was no exception. In addition to missing deadlines and running over budgets, CDW projects tended to under-deliver on expectations. And that was for the projects that actually were completed; many simply fizzled out. It is worth noting that many other big corporate projects in the 1990s encountered similar fates. There were scattered success stories, but, in general, the underwhelming results gave CDWs a bad reputation. It was inevitable, therefore, that there would be a backlash.

THE DATA MART

The next era was the rise of data marts. Data marts promised to be quicker and cheaper to build, and provided many more benefits—including the benefit of actually being able to finish building them! The data mart was primarily a backlash to the big, cumbersome CDW projects, with the key difference being that its scope was limited to a single business group rather than the entire enterprise. Of course, that shortcut did speed things up, but at the expense of obtaining agreement on consistent data definitions, thereby guaranteeing data silos.

Although the early-adopter technology companies and Bill Inmon both advocated that data marts should be fed from the EDW, the rest of the industry was pushing data marts based on a different architecture where they were fed directly from source systems. Instead, data mart vendors and pundits stated there was no real architectural difference between a DW and data mart. As Figure 6.2 shows, the data mart, just like the DW, sourced data from SORs, used a waterfall project methodology and had to use quite a bit of manually-created custom code. The pundits' sales pitches said that the data mart was just like a DW – using the same tools, data models and design principles – but simpler and faster to build.

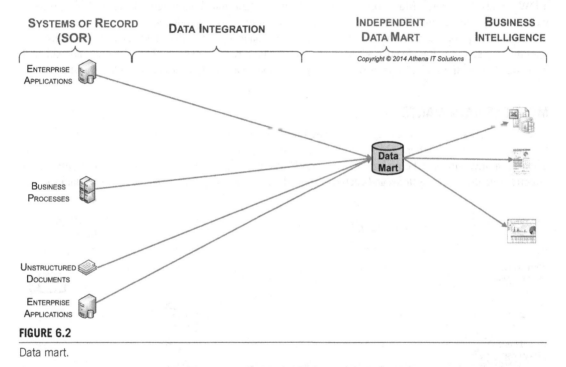

FIGURE 6.2

Data mart.

By the time data mart projects were starting to be widely built, two trends were also occurring: the emergence of BI tools and the use of relational databases to build new source systems. These trends resulted in a much shorter time to build a data mart than a CDW, aided, of course, by the fact that data marts have a more limited scope than CDWs.

Rather than being part of an overall enterprise data architecture, data marts were the architecture. You could build them faster and cheaper because you did not take the whole rest of the enterprise into account. This meant you could take shortcuts and avoid the most difficult part of DW: DI and reaching agreement on data definitions and metrics across business groups. As a result, data marts were built for the parochial interests of their sponsors rather than for the enterprise.

Companies sprouted multiple data marts, each built to accommodate only their sponsor with their own data definitions, data transformation, reporting, and technical platform. We moved from trying to achieve one version of the truth to building multiple single versions of the truth—an oxymoron. To top it off, many of these projects overpromised and under-delivered, just like the CDW projects.

Data mart projects exacted another toll. The tradeoff for being able to deliver cheaper and faster was to severely limit scope of the breadth and depth of data, their integration, their quality, and the analytical capability offered to business users. Initially, data marts were perceived as a great success—until business groups realized they were debating in meetings which one of their reports (and associated data marts) had the "right" numbers. Each group had its own data silo.

In the end, data marts left their business users wanting more, which often meant building another round of data silos with more disjointed data marts or data shadow systems and more versions of the truth. At this point there started to be a debate within the industry on whether enterprises should build a DW versus data marts. Many vendors jumped on the data mart bandwagon because those projects were initially successful and they could therefore sell more of their products.

Later, this type of data mart would be become known as an independent data mart versus a dependent data mart that is part of a hub-and-spoke architecture. This meant it was independent from the DW and extracted data directly from the source systems rather than pulling the data from (and being dependent on) the DW.

MULTIPLE DATA MARTS

After the initial success of creating a data mart for a specific business group within an enterprise, more business groups wanted them and IT obliged. Each subsequent data mart was a success in its own right, at least initially, with each being built independently. As depicted in Figure 6.3 each data mart pulled data directly from the source systems and each report used one of the independent data marts as its data source.

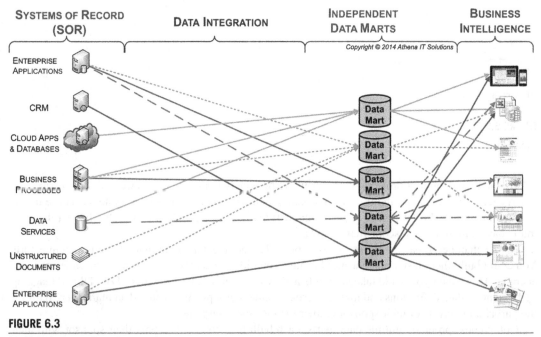

FIGURE 6.3

Multiple independent data marts.

After the independent data marts started proliferating in an enterprise, business people quickly started seeing differences in the reported business metrics they obtained from different data marts. The independent data marts became the new data silos for an enterprise. Each business group defined different business rules to filter, select, and transform the data in their data mart, causing greater disparity. Business people started debating the numbers in meetings and spent increasing amounts of time reconciling the data between reports that were generated from different independent data marts.

Although it was good that independent data marts could be built rather quickly and create business-group-specific reporting, it was at the expense of data consistency. It created new data silos with inconsistent reporting metrics across the enterprise. There is a phrase now about BYOD (bring your own device), but at that time the independent data marts (data silos) resulted in business groups debating BYOR (bring your own results).

In addition to the data silos created, there was a tendency for each data mart project to select its own tools (database, ETL, and BI) based on the myopic scope of a single business group. The result was an "accidental data architecture" for the enterprise. (The accidental architecture is discussed further in this chapter and in detail in Chapter 4.)

OPERATIONAL DATA STORE (ODS)

A new data architecture component called an ODS (see Figure 6.4) emerged in the early days of DW. The primary ODS objective was to bring data together from multiple source systems on as close to a

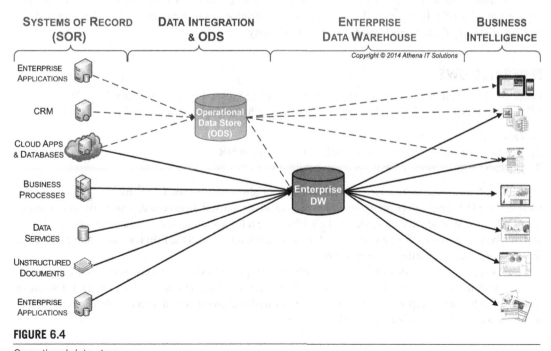

FIGURE 6.4

Operational data store.

real-time basis as possible to enable specific business processing or operational reporting. The typical ODS business requirements differed from a DW in these ways:

- Loading the data into one location, the ODS, for ease of access without any extensive DI or transformation. It was generally desirable for the data to remain as is rather than the usual cleansing, conforming, and transforming needed for a DW.
- Loading current data but generally not maintaining historical data.
- Loading application-specific data that supported business processes rather than a DW's business subject orientation.

The industry best practice was to use the ODS as the SOR to the EDW for the data it extracted from the source systems. The EDW would extract data from the source systems that the ODS did not use and would also extract data from the same source systems as the ODS if there was data needed by EDW that was not loaded into the ODS.

Enterprises with both an EDW and ODS could get their reports from:

- ODS only
- EDW only
- ODS and EDW

Although it was possible to manage reporting applications to avoid overlap and maintain integrity, just like ETL processing, it was all too common for the overlapping data sourcing options to create inconsistency.

An ODS may be a viable data architectural component; however, the architecture using an ODS and EDW without data marts suffered the same BI limitations as an EDW-only architecture such as not supporting robust BI; being inflexible with the inevitable changes in data and analytical requirements; and not adversely impacting IT and business productivity.

FEDERATED DWS

Federated DW is another architecture option that emerged. (See Figure 6.5) Federated DWs split the EDW into multiple physical DWs, using some of the following options to make the divisions:

1. Geographical regions or countries
2. Business functions such as finance, sales, marketing, or HR
3. Business entities such as divisions or subsidiaries

Although this data architecture was considered an alternative to the CDW by most people in the industry, the DW early adopters in the 1980s did not make a distinction between an EDW and a federated DW. The early adopters considered the EDW to be a logical entity that could be physically federated if it better supported that enterprise's BI requirements, and indeed the firm I worked in implemented that data architecture during that timeframe.

The best practice is to design EDW logically as a single data store, but physically implement it as either one data store or federated based on performance and business needs. Further, as I discuss in Chapter 7, when an enterprise is sourcing both structured and unstructured data into its BI architecture, it should use federated DWs based on the structures.

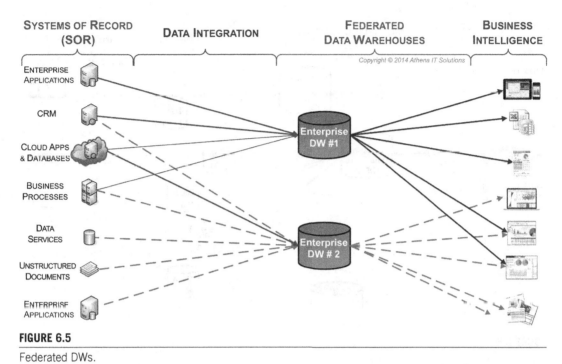

FIGURE 6.5

Federated DWs.

The federated DW suffers the same limitations as any of the other data architectures that do not use data marts to enable BI. These include performance issues, lack of DI, and no reliable source of historical data.

BI ACCIDENTAL ARCHITECTURE

The reaction to the independent data marts was to create DWs or operational data stores and drop them into an architectural smorgasbord, typically without redesigning the data marts. As depicted in Figure 6.6, it was common for an enterprise to have a patchwork of DWs, ODSs, and data marts along with multiple databases, ETL tools, and BI products. The idea of the accidental architecture is explained in detail in Chapter 5.

The current reality of many enterprise data landscapes is data silos that include overlapping and redundant DWs, ODSs, independent and dependent data marts, OLAP cubes, other reporting databases, and data shadow systems. A typical scenario could include the following:

- Sales and Finance have each built their own DWs independently without synchronizing data or transformations.
- The enterprise builds one or more ODS to handle near real-time updates.
- Other departments build multiple data marts, cubes, and spreadsheets for their specific business needs, and these systems have overlapping and sometimes conflicting data.

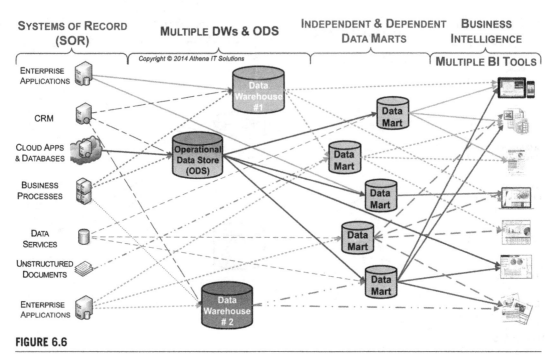

FIGURE 6.6

Multiple built BI silos & multiple BI tools.

Each of these BI data silos addressed a specific need, but looked at holistically they created their own silo problems. Despite the best intentions of each of the project-based BI applications, they were centered on the parochial interests of a specific business group and there was no overarching data architecture. It is inevitable that the solutions end up producing more harm than good when examined from an enterprise perspective.

HUB-AND-SPOKE

An answer to the data mart problem was needed. Two competing architectural approaches emerged: a data bus with conformed data marts versus a hub-and-spoke with a data warehouse feeding data marts, as shown in Figure 6.7. This set up the classic Kimball vs. Inmon (CIF) debate.

The conformed dimensions approach tied disparate data marts into a logical "single version of the truth" without the need for a DW, which appealed to those who still had a bias against DWs. The ETL layer staged all the data from the source systems and then directly parsed the data to the data marts. It was intellectually very appealing, but there were crucial stumbling blocks to implementing this approach:

- Only a small percentage of companies had the discipline to design and implement the required data integration processes.
- Inconsistency and data quality needed overly complex real-time DI that was beyond the ETL tools' capabilities at that time.

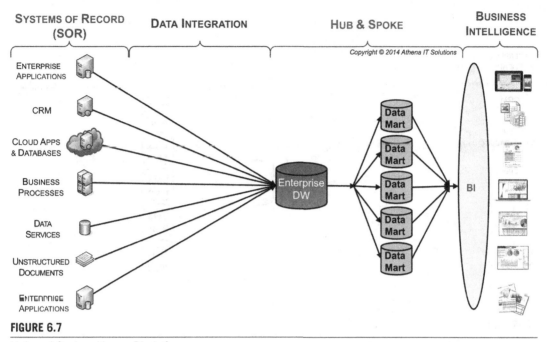

FIGURE 6.7

Hub-and-Spoke with one BI platform.

- In the real world, the timing of transactional data and the updates of its associated reference data were often out of sync, preventing the on-the-fly validation and integration of data from multiple source system to multiple data marts.

The hub-and-spoke approach became more popular, judging by the number of companies that adopted it; it ultimately became part of the architectural best practices. Successful hub-and-spoke implementations borrowed heavily from the conformed dimension approach by using its data modeling and integration techniques. The key difference was that the hub-and-spoke built a physical DW (data hub) rather than trying to achieve a virtual hub. That virtual hub was simple to draw but difficult to achieve in real-world situations.

Despite the adoption of the hub-and-spoke approach to unify data, however, the data silo genie was already out of the bottle. By the time companies adopted hub-and-spoke, they had already built countless ODS systems, DWs, data marts, online analytical processing (OLAP) cubes and data shadow systems. They didn't have the time or resources to bring these databases into the hub-and-spoke fold.

Although the hub-and-spoke enables the 5C's of information (consistent, clean, comprehensive, conformed, and current), some enterprises delegate BI application development and tool selection to departmental groups. This typically results in the scenario shown in Figure 6.8, multiple BI silos not only of different BI tools, but more damaging redundant and inconsistent reporting. Although the cause is organizational, it is important to consider this possibility even when an enterprise has achieved the 5C's. Refer to Chapter 19 on organizational best practice to avoid this scenario.

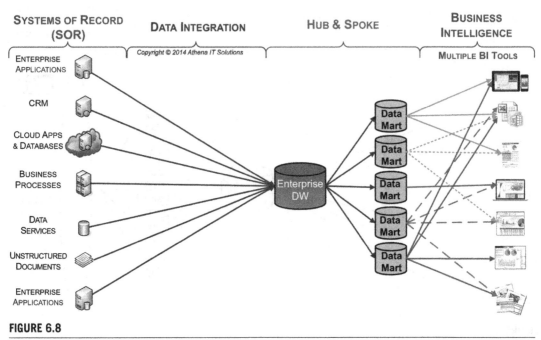

FIGURE 6.8

Hub and spoke with multiple BI tools.

DATA ARCHITECTURAL CHOICES

Various different data architectures have been used to implement enterprise BI solutions throughout the years. These architectures have evolved and often blended together, reducing many of the differences between them. Best practices have emerged, and, from a high-level perspective, include the recommended DI workflow and supporting data stores. From a lower level of detail, the best practices include the recommended DI processes, analytical processes, and the data schemas needed to support them.

Even with a long list of best practices, there still is much confusion and misleading concepts in the industry. The primary reasons for this confusion include the following:

- **Too much emphasis on technology**—there is still too much of an orientation toward technical architectures and products rather than information and data architectures. The reliance on technical wizardry may appear to work in the short run; sometimes "horsepower" can temporarily overcome poor design. But in the long run, without a fundamental data information architecture, the solutions tends to create costly application and data silos that are then replaced by the next round of overhyped technology.
- **Misunderstanding**—Without understanding the underlying data architecture best practices, such as data models and process workflows, designers who think they're building a particular architecture may actually build a system that is drastically different than what they thought they were building. This misapplication of best practices results in inferior solutions and gives them an undeserved bad reputation.

- **Old biases die hard**—initial reputations can be difficult to overcome, even for people who weren't directly affected. The underlying infrastructure (hardware, storage, networks, databases, interoperability, etc.), when much of the BI, DW, and DI concepts were initially introduced, was vastly inferior in comparison with today's standards. My iPhone has more memory, storage, processing power, and interoperability than the first DW environment I helped implement in the 1980s.

DATA CATEGORIES

There are three categories of data management processing based on business objectives and use cases:

- Data capture
- Data integration
- Information analysis (BI and analytics)

Regardless of advances in technology and products, these fundamental data management categories form the basis of an enterprise's data architecture and its information management. In the BI domain, the data architecture needs to address DI and information analysis, while the data capture category is managed by operational systems.

Since the beginning of DW, there have been significant technological advances as people expanded interoperability capabilities and learned from their mistakes and successes. But through all those changes and advances, the following fundamental concepts still need to be incorporated into designing data architectures:

- **There's a significant difference between data capture and information consumption in regard to their business uses and functional requirements**. Data capture is about creating, updating, or deleting data about a business event, transaction, or description of attributes relating to entities involved in those events or transactions. Information consumption is about analyzing those events, transactions, or descriptions in a context that is not material to it or may not even apply at the time. In addition, information consumption looks at data that is related to the business relationships and transformations that is not applicable at the point of capture.
- **Data captured at a point in time is a historical record that does not change**. (Although it may be altered because of error, other changes that are the result of subsequent events or transactions do not change the underlying historical event.) But with information consumption, data does change—it evolves as the context of business data relationships changes. These changes can include product hierarchies, sales territories, contractual relationships, organizational structures, and customer attributes.
- **DI keeps getting more complex** not because of volume or velocity, as that can generally be handled by technology advances, but rather because of the variety and diversity of sources and business interpretation. Data silos keep propagating because of politics and parochial interests, requiring ever-increasing DI.

SELECTING A DATA ARCHITECTURE

The major competing data architectures are:

- EDW
- Independent data marts

- Enterprise data bus architecture—Ralph Kimball [1]
- Hub-and-spoke, corporate information factory (CIF)—Bill Inmon [2]
- Analytical data architecture (ADA)

The history lesson earlier in this chapter covered the EDW and independent data marts. Although they provide reporting, they are not likely to provide the five information C's (consistent, clean, comprehensive, conformed, and current). Each of these architectures is too focused on only one of the two data management categories:

- **EDW-only architecture addresses DI**, but makes it extremely difficult for business people to use it for information analysis. Historically, when IT was responsible for creating all reports, this was acceptable because they could navigate the labyrinth of a DW schema. But now that we have self-service BI, it's no longer viable to have data discovery and data visualization tools accessing the EDW.
- **Independent data marts address information analysis** but at the expense of not integrating data and creating silos. In the short term, this approach may create reporting applications, but it lessens business productivity with the time lost on reconciliation and debating the numbers; costs more because of overlapping and redundant activities; and poses too much business risk due to inconsistent, inaccurate and incomplete data. The resulting data silos create more problems than they solve and increase the need for further DI.

The two divergent BI camps emerged in the 1990s to address the limitations of the EDW-only and independent data mart architectures:

- Bill Inmon's CIF, as shown in Figure 6.9.
- Ralph Kimball's enterprise data bus architecture, as shown in Figure 6.10.

See the book website www.biguidebook.com for more on the Bill Inmon's CIF and Ralph Kimball's enterprise data bus architectures. Figures 6.9 and 6.10 are my simplification of these architectures and represent the "evolved," rather than the initial, versions.

Table 6.1 lists the key differences between Inmon's CIF architecture and Kimball's enterprise data bus architecture.

The fundamental differences of their approaches are:

- CIF started out with the EDW as the core of the architecture, while Kimball's architecture focused on the BI (and business-oriented) data marts.
- CIF is a top-down design creating an enterprise-wide data model from the source systems to design the EDW, while Kimball uses a bottom-up business requirements-driven approach to design schemas for the data marts. The key assumptions when the respective architectures were introduced were:
  - Inmon's architecture created an EDW organized by subject areas containing detailed data and departmental databases. These were organized by their parochial interests, typically with summarized or aggregated data.
  - Kimball's architecture assumed the ETL system could perform the 5C's (consistent, clean, comprehensive, conformed, and current) either on-the-fly or using a staging area and thus making the need for an EDW superfluous.

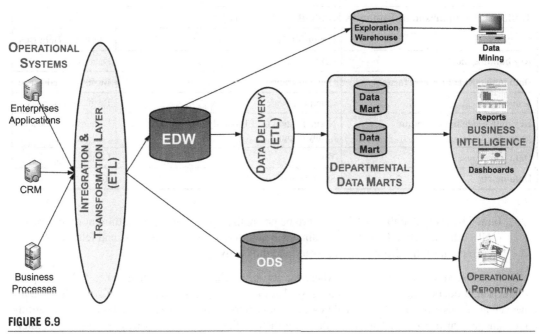

FIGURE 6.9

Inmon's CIF architecture.

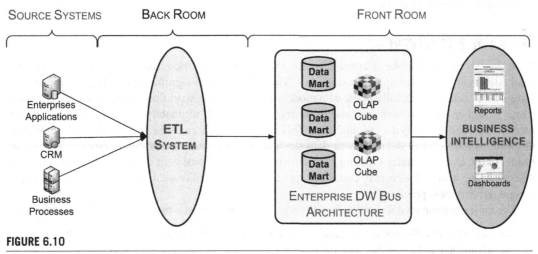

FIGURE 6.10

Kimball's enterprise data bus architecture.

Table 6.1 Comparison of Inmon vs Kimball Architecture

Concepts	Inmon's CIF	Kimball's Data Bus
Key building block	EDW	Data marts
Data management process focus	Data integration	Business intelligence
Scope	Enterprise-wide	Business processes
Key data modeling technique	Normalization for EDW only; marts can be any design	Dimensional models
Data warehouse	Yes	Unnecessary
Data marts	Summarized from DW	Yes

- Inmon believed that the EDW needed to be normalized, i.e., implement a third normal form (3NF) schema, while Kimball used dimensional models for the data marts and felt the 3NF requirement of the CIF was unnecessary and too costly to create.

Both architectures have evolved to where the use of an EDW and data marts, i.e., hub-and-spoke architecture, is not only acceptable but recognized as the most pragmatic approach. There is still debate, however, about 3NF versus dimensional models. Both camps have taken a more holistic view regarding data management processes, but they still retain their initial biases to a particular data management category.

Despite the history, the hub-and-spoke architecture with an EDW feeding data marts was created in the mid- to late 1980s. Industry best practices have finally evolved to embrace the hub-and-spoke architecture of the earliest adopters.

THE SAME BUT DIFFERENT

Even though hub-and-spoke is considered the industry best practice, the results and costs can be vastly different even in comparable situations. This is because of significant variations in the underlying design details, especially in the data models and processing workflow. Many of these variations result in higher costs, slower response to business needs, and, ultimately, the BI system not being used or regarded as the system of analytics. This encourages the creation of more data silos either in the form of independent data marts or data shadow systems, resulting in higher costs and a loss in productivity, and potentially creating business risks due to inconsistent or incomplete information. These varying design details may cause enterprises to have an unfavorable view of what is otherwise a good industry best practice.

The most common mistakes made by enterprises implementing the hub-and-spoke architecture are:

- Designing the EDW using a "standard" 3NF schema (Chapter 8 explains 3NF) rather than a hybrid dimensional-normalized model
- Allowing the business BI consumers to perform self-service BI from EDW
- Designing a separate data mart or BI data structure for each dashboard or report
- Designing data marts to support many business processes or entire business groups
- Thinking that a BI product eliminates the need to design a logical dimensional data model

The most common mistakes made by enterprises implementing Kimball's architecture are:

- Designing each data mart to be so parochial to a department's terminology and business definitions that conformed dimensions and facts across data marts are impossible
- Designing a separate data mart for each dashboard or report
- Abandoning dimensional models by denormalizing data to ease report development or improve query performance
- Failing to implement slowly changing dimensions (SCD) to track historical changes in data (this often happens because departments did not initially think they needed it for their reporting)
- Thinking that a BI product eliminates the need to design a logical dimensional data model

In the beginning of DW, many enterprises built or bought transactional systems that used a variety of database and file structures that did not use a 3NF schema. With the source systems having a variety of schemas, it was a best practice to build the EDW using a 3NF schema, as that was the only location in the enterprise that the data was normalized. (The benefits of normalization are presented in Chapter 10.) Bill Inmon's CIF architecture was conceived in this era and thus its normalization requirement for the EDW was an industry best practice.

As the 1990s progressed, the following major trends in the scope and structure of operational systems affected the design of DWs:

- Enterprises replaced legacy operational systems that were often custom-built with enterprise resource and planning (ERP) systems that they bought from IT vendors.
- IT vendors built their ERP systems using relational databases with 3NF schemas.
- The ERP systems consolidated many previously silo'd operational systems into an application that had a more enterprise-wide scope.

These trends eventually shifted the responsibility of designing a 3NF data model from the EDW to source systems, such as ERP applications. During this transition, best practices emerged for data integration, BI and advanced dimensional modeling that enabled the standard 3NF being used in EDW to evolve to a hybrid dimensional-normalized data model (explained later in this chapter.)

During the early phases of the rise of ERP systems, IT vendors sold the idea of one-stop shopping for operational systems with their own dedicated reporting. This resulted in warring IT camps between the ERP and BI implementations, with each side feeling they were developing the "single version of the truth" and competing data silos. Eventually, IT vendors came to the realization that the ERP systems did not, and likely would never, contain all the data than an enterprise needed for reporting. With this realization, the IT vendors that sold ERP systems embraced DW and sold their own BI solutions. Unfortunately, IT groups designing DWs have often continued to use 3NF schemas even though it is no longer necessary or the best practice because 3NF is what they are familiar with.

ANALYTICAL DATA ARCHITECTURE (ADA)

I recommend the implementation of the ADA depicted in Figure 6.11. This architecture represents the evolution of best practices for BI, DI, and DW with a framework that can leverage current and future technologies in its implementation. Keep in mind that with a high-level diagram like this many of the underlying design best practices and exceptions are not visible.

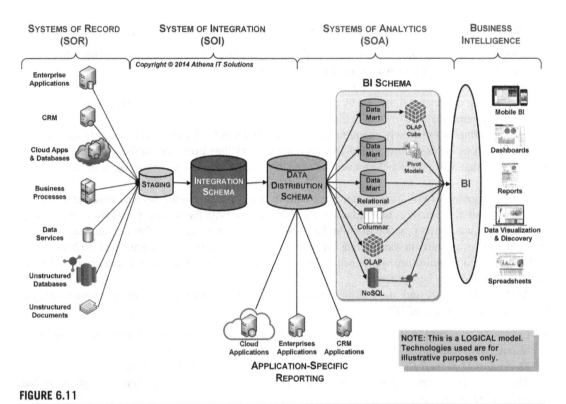

FIGURE 6.11

Analytical data architecture (ADA).

There are three layers of data that enable BI:

1. **Systems of record (SOR)**—source systems where data is created, updated and deleted. This layer is the source of data for systems of integration (SOI) layer but is managed outside the ADA.
2. **Systems of integration (SOI)**—data structures used to integrate data to enable the 5C's of information: consistent, clean, comprehensive, conformed and current.
3. **Systems of analytics (SOA)**—data structures used by BI application to enable analytics

Several aspects of the underlying design details are explained in other portions of this book:

- Data integration workflow—the next section.
- Data schemas—Chapter 10.
- Technologies—Chapter 7.

Enhanced Hub-and-Spoke Model

The SOI replaces a lone physical EDW with SOI feeding the SOA. The goal of the SOI is to integrate data to create comprehensive, current, clean, and consistent information for the enterprise. The goal of the SOA is to enable BI by providing business-oriented information for analysis.

The SOI logically contains an integration schema and staging area. The integration schema will be a physical data store, while the staging area may be persistent or transient based on use cases. The latter is the case when the DI processes do not need persistent data stores for acquiring or integrating data.

The SOA contains the logical data distribution schema that potentially feeds data marts that, in turn, may feed sub-marts such as OLAP cubes or pivot tables. The SOA is a source of BI data either by BI tools accessing the data or by operational applications receiving distributed data from the data distribution schema. The latter would prevent operational applications from redundantly sourcing data from other applications when the EDW has already done so.

Enterprise Data Warehose (EDW)

The EDW is split into two schemas with different data objectives. The two schemas are:

- EDW integration schema—its purpose is to enable the enterprise DI processes.
- EDW data distribution schema—its purpose is to distribute the data downstream to the data marts so BI consumers can analyze the data or do application-specific reporting and advanced analytics that support the business.

Although the EDW is the source of the enterprise's integrated 5 C's data, it is pragmatic to recognize that not all data needed for analytics will be available in the EDW. The intent of this chapter is to discuss how the integrated data that does flow though the EDW will be designed and processed. Using data both from the EDW environment and directly from data sources is discussed in Chapter 15. The Information (Chapter 5) and Technology (Chapter 7) Architectures discussed in this book also incorporate analytics accessing data from the EDW and other data sources.

Data Marts

The EDW data distribution model represents the enterprise dimensional model that feeds both data marts and application-specific reporting. Data marts are designed to support business processes or business groups. Sub-data marts are created to support different types of analysis performed within a business process or a business group. These sub-data marts are fed from data marts and derived by applying additional filters, business rules, and transformations that are specific to a particular business line of analysis.

The dimensional model and data workflow depicted in the ADA are logical rather than physical. The logical dimensional model may be implemented in a variety of database technologies and the data workflow may be built in one or more databases (and database technologies). Both are discussed further in this chapter.

Data Schemas

The EDW staging area, if it is a persistent data store, may use a variety of schemas such as relational, flat file, or XML, depending on its use case. There may be a variety of EDW staging area data stores to support acquiring data from a similar variety of different source systems.

The EDW integration schema uses a hybrid dimensional-normalized data model. This schema needs to be built from a 3NF or normalized data model representing the entities, attributes, and relationships from the source systems that are relevant to BI with model extensions (see below). If the underlying source systems do not have supporting 3NF data models, then create those models from the extracted data. There are several key purposes for using a hybrid model:

- Leverage 3NF design principles to promote normalization.
- Leverage advanced dimensional modeling constructs to enable tracking dimensional model changes and eliminating hierarchical structure changes.
- Implement data lineage, auditing, cleansing, and tracking in data integration and BI workflow.

Although not depicted in the diagram, if an ODS is used in the ADA, its schema will be based on its intended use and the database technology it is implemented with. The ODS schema could range from a 3NF in a relational database to a schema-less NoSQL database.

The EDW data distribution schema, data marts, OLAP cubes, and any other SOA data store use a logical dimensional model. This becomes a physical dimensional model if a relational database is used, however, different technologies may physically deploy other schemas such as multidimensional OLAP cubes, columnar databases, in-memory databases, and semi-structured or unstructured databases. See Table 6.2.

Table 6.2 BI Data Stores and Data Model	
Data Store	**Data Model**
Staging	Same as source system
ODS	3NF or alternate schema based on its use
EDW: Integration schema	3NF or hybrid dimensional-normalized
EDW: Distribution schema	Hybrid dimensional-normalized
Data mart (relational)	Dimensional
OLAP cube, columnar, in-memory and other non-relational BI data stores	Logically dimensional
MDM (for source system applications)	3NF
MDM (for BI only)	Hybrid dimensional-normalized

Understanding the Hybrid Dimensional-Normalized Model

I have been able to persuade both normalization and dimensional zealots to design, develop, and deploy EDWs with this hybrid dimensional-normalized model. Rather than compromising their respective viewpoints, this hybrid model leverages the best of both to integrate data in an EDW.

From a 3NF modeler's viewpoint, this model leverages a 3NF data model while also:

- Grafting on several advanced dimensional modeling constructs (below).
- Extending the data model to track data integration and analytical processes.
- Consolidating 3NF entities when specific entity relationships and other entities are not relevant to BI.

From a dimensional modeler's viewpoint, this hybrid model leverages a standard dimensional data model while also:

- Using advanced dimensional modeling constructs (below).
- Extending the data model to track data integration and analytical processes.

- Normalizing dimensions using outriggers when dimension tables have groups of attributes at different grains or are updated at much different frequencies (referred to as rapidly changing dimensions).
- Avoiding the use of summarizations or aggregations unless required by a business transformation.

The advanced dimensional constructs include:

- Implementing a date dimension and add date dimension foreign keys for each of the date attributes in fact tables while retaining the original data attributes.
- Creating slowly changing dimension (SCD) data models to track historical changes to dimensional values. This leverages documented processes that are built into data integration processes.
- Using bridge tables to model hierarchies rather than using separate tables for each hierarchy level. This avoids changing the physical number of entities in the model, as the number of hierarchy levels inevitably changes.
- Using bridge tables to many-to-many valued relationships.
- Creating surrogate keys, independent of source systems' natural keys, for all tables, not just tables that are considered dimensions, to facilitate independence from source systems.
- Logically classifying entities as dimensions, facts, bridges, or other types of tables. This assists in following the best practices for data integration and conversion to dimensional models for BI.

The extensions to the data model, as discussed in Chapters 10–12, include such attributes as data integration process identifiers, time stamps for when data was created or modified, source system identifiers, error handling, data cleansing, security and privacy roles, and other BI/DW life cycle-specific attributes.

Source systems, especially ERP, SCM, and CRM applications, may have 3NF data models that contain thousands or tens of thousands of entities and relationships. A significant portion of those entities and relationships are needed by application-, transaction- or business-event-processing, but are not relevant to BI. This creates a subset of entities, attributes, and relationships relevant for BI that can be consolidated. Although this consolidation might be considered denormalizing the 3NF since entities, attributes, and relationships have been eliminated, the integrity of the 3NF model is maintained.

BI Sources

In the early days of DW there was a presumed edict that all reporting and analysis, i.e., BI, would be sourced solely from the DW environment. There are two primary reasons why this is not practical:

1. Is highly unlikely that the BI environment will source all the data that any business person would need to analyze at any time.
2. Much of an enterprise's operational reporting and analysis can be accomplished by directly accessing the operational systems, provided that these systems have all the data needed for analysis.

When either of these two conditions occurs, the BI tools will need to directly access the operational source systems. As discussed in Chapter 7, tools such as data virtualization make that access easier and more transparent to the business person. The enterprise IT group must handle both types of analysis in the data management framework.

Physical Data Store Combinations

EDW data distribution schema, data marts, OLAP cubes, and any other SOA data stores are logical, not physical, and based on the data use case, one or more of these data stores may not need to be made a persistent physical data store.

Each of the data stores may actually be split into federated entities. For example, the EDW may be split into federated DWs based on such criteria as geographic regions, business functions, and business organizational entities or to support structured versus non-structured data.

On the other end of the spectrum, the entire set of data stores may be implemented on a single database platform, with each data store being represented as a schema within that database.

DATA INTEGRATION WORKFLOW

The data architecture enables the transformation of data into consistent, conformed, comprehensive, clean, and current information for business analysis and decision-making. The diagram in Figure 6.12 illustrates the flow from data creation in the SOR through information consumption by business people

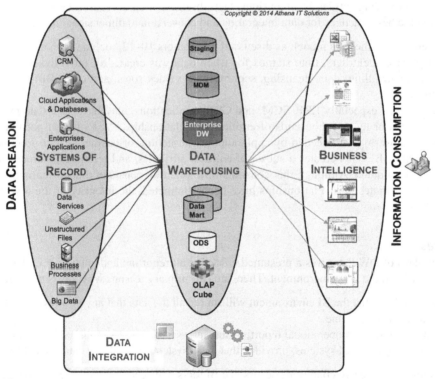

FIGURE 6.12

Data integration workflow.

using BI. Data is transformed into information by DI processes (depicted in the example's data warehousing section) that:

- Gather data
- Integrate and transform data using business rules and technical conversions
- Store it in various data stores
- Make it available to business users with BI tools

An analogy to this process is the material flow of a consumer product from the supplier (SOR), to factory (DI), to warehouses (DW), and finally to retail stores (BI applications), where consumers buy it (business analysis).

The following sections progressively explain in more detail the various data stores that may be deployed within the ADA.

DATA INTEGRATION WORKFLOW—HUB-AND-SPOKE

The initial starting point for discussion of the DI workflow is a classic hub-and-spoke architecture, with an EDW gathering data from SORs and then feeding data marts that are accessed by business people using BI, as shown in Figure 6.13. The central premise of this architecture is that the heavy-duty DI activities, i.e., data preparation, are completed as the data moves from source systems into the DW where it becomes the SOI. Once done, the data is propagated, i.e., data franchised, from the DW into the data marts. Data franchising packages the data via filtering, aggregation and transformations into SOA to be consumed by BI.

This diagram begins the discussion on the functionality and supporting data stores for the DI workflow, while the following sections will decompose the SOI and SOA into more detail.

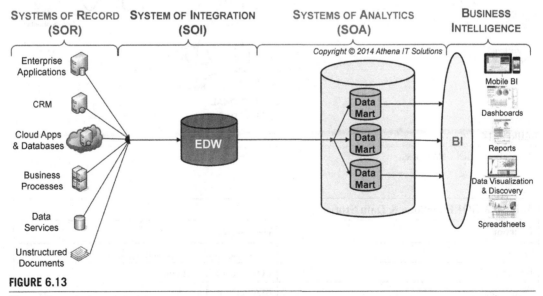

FIGURE 6.13

DI workflow—hub-and-spoke.

DATA WORKFLOW OF THE SYSTEM OF INTEGRATION (SOI)

The SOI has three primary functions:

1. Gather data from the SORs—stage
2. Perform data preparation—integrate
3. Serve as a data hub for the SOA—distribute

Figure 6.14 depicts the breakdown of the SOI from the EDW by itself into three data stores that support its primary functions. Table 6.3 pairs function and data store in tabular form. These data stores are logical entities that may become either a physical, persistent or a virtual, transient entity. At a minimum, the EDW will be a physical entity, whereas the staging area may be transient.

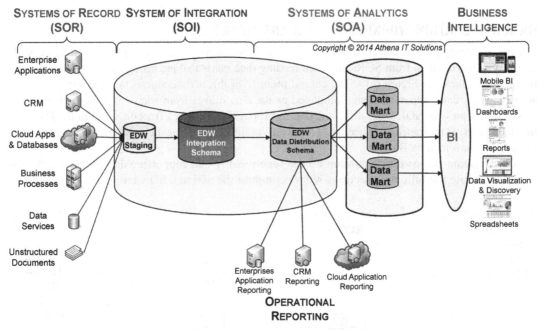

FIGURE 6.14

DI workflow—SOI data stores.

Table 6.3 SOI Functions & Data Stores	
Function	**Data Store**
Stage	Staging area (also called landing area)
Integrate	EDW integration schema
Distribute	EDW distribution schema

Staging (or Landing) Area

With today's database connectivity and API access to most of the widely-used ERP applications, it is relatively easy to directly connect, query, and extract data. In addition, many DI tools enable the use of memory and parallel processing when gathering and integrating data from multiple sources. It would seem, therefore, that physically staging data would no longer be necessary, but for a variety of reasons it is often a best practice to maintain a staging area feeding the EDW.

There might be a requirement to stage data during other DI or access processes throughout the DI workflow; however, those are typically handled by transient data stores or processed in memory.

There are several reasons to implement a physical staging area: audits; recover and restart; referential integrity; data quality; recycling rows and error handling; and enterprise standard or source system requirement.

- **Audit**—Auditing enables you to provide detailed documentation of the workflow of data from source systems through information consumption. This provides several benefits such as:
  - Impact analysis to determine the effect of changes in source system data on the BI solution
  - "Where used" search capability so that IT and business people can examine where the data they are using originated
  - System documentation for maintenance and enhancement.
  - Regulatory and legal requirements to provide auditing

A DATA AUDITABILITY STORY

A former colleague of mine experienced first-hand one of the pitfalls of not knowing the lineage of a client's data. The project was to replace a spreadsheet-based budgeting, planning, and forecasting system (data shadow system) with a performance management solution at a multi-billion dollar company. He spent 10 hours in a client meeting—one of those painful marathon meetings—where they were discussing the design of the new system and poring over the data in the client's spreadsheets to understand how the data was transformed and manipulated.

The meeting dragged on through lunch, and then dinner. Finally, a senior manager from the client said "Hey, wait a minute. This isn't even the right set of spreadsheets!" Everything that the dozen people at the meeting—half from the client's finance staff and the other half highly paid consultants—had just done over the past 10 hours was a total waste of time.

The sad truth is that my colleagues and I see many clients who honestly have no idea how their data got into their reports or Microsoft PowerPoint slides. They may know what enterprise application the data originated in and can get their IT staff to document how the data was loaded in their DW, but then the trail goes cold.

Under the circumstances, the staging area will follow enterprise standards relating to backups and archiving. This further ensures you can audit historical extracts or perform disaster recovery processing.

- **Recovery and restart**—Although it is generally possible to re-query the source systems if there is a failure when loading the EDW, sometimes it is preferable to maintain a copy of the data extracted from the source systems in the staging area to be used when recovery and restart is necessary. The criteria to select this approach are:
  - When loading a periodic snapshot, i.e., a data snapshot, at a point in time
  - When a stage copy would avoid having to redo lengthy extraction times
  - When there are limited times when the source systems are available for extraction
  - To enable debugging loading failures

- **Referential integrity**—It is a BI best practice to enforce referential integrity during DI processing rather than using database constraints. Enforcing referential integrity requires that the attribute that the foreign key is related to, typically a dimensional attribute, is available for validation at the point in time that the foreign key needs to be checked. Dimensional reference data used in this validation is often managed by separate business processes other than transactional or operational systems. Under those conditions it is common to have early-arriving facts or late-arriving dimensions, necessitating the need to stage data to make it possible to validate referential integrity in real time.
- **Data quality**—The bulk of the data quality and cleansing processes occur in data preparation (see Chapter 12). There are conditions, however, when it is better to perform this during the initial loading process into the staging area. The general rule of thumb in quality processing is to correct errors as soon as possible, as they get more expensive and difficult to correct the longer it takes. It is best to use the staging area for data quality processes in those cases when waiting until later would make it much more complex or potentially even impossible to correct.
- **Recycling rows and error handling**—As mentioned in the referential integrity bullet, there may be circumstances where DI workflow encounters early-arriving facts or late-arriving dimensions. When these conditions occur, the referential integrity checks would flag an error in processing and prevent it from moving the data forward in the workflow. At this point, DI processes need to know how to proceed. The most extreme option would be to stop processing all the data in the load at the time of a referential integrity error. Although this is a viable option in certain circumstances, in general the offending rows are rejected and processing continues. The next decision is what to do with the rejected rows. The options are to just ignore them as if nothing happened (the least likely alternative), load the offending data with an indicator to flag the error condition, or suspend the data and attempt to reprocess it on subsequent data loads. This last condition is a typical practice that requires the suspended data to be stored in the staging area.

The process used to handle referential integrity errors should be defined in the business requirements that the BI team obtains while working with the business. Typically this level of detail is not obtained when requirements are initially documented, so the BI team will need to revisit this with the business to make sure these processing requirements follow business rules.

- **Enterprise standard or source system requirement**—Often a staging area is required due to an enterprise IT standard or source system requirement. The SOR, for example, may not be available for direct access, or for performance reasons, no direct access is allowed by the BI team's DI processes. Under these conditions the SOR application team will provide required extracts, typically in files that are placed in the staging or landing area.

Splitting the EDW

The EDW has two distinct functions: integrating the data and then distributing it. Although one schema could support both of these functions, is much better to divide the EDW into two schemas, each supporting one function.

The purpose of the EDW integration schema is to enable the data preparation integration processes and to manage historical data. The hybrid dimensional-normalized model is the most effective at performing these processes:

- Tracking the inevitable changes in business and data relationships
- Minimizing or possibly eliminating the need for data structures with routine business changes.

The EDW integration schema's hybrid dimensional-normalized model is not as complex in terms of tables and data relationships as a normalized model, but it is much more complex than the data models that are required in the SOA data stores. The data franchising process takes data from the EDW and propagates it into each of the data marts in the SOA. Besides the business transformations that the data franchising processes perform specific to each data mart, every data franchising process needs to perform data restructuring between the EDW and the data mart schemas. The restructuring converts the hybrid dimensional-normalized model into a standard dimensional model by denormalizing or flattening the structures. In addition, most of the data marts will not require the structures used to track changes in hierarchies or other historical attributes. The data restructuring process is redundant across each of the data franchising processes and needs to be re-created every time a new data mart is created.

It is best practice to perform the data restructuring once and reposition the data franchising processes to concentrate on the business-specific transformations from the EDW to individual data marts. Creating an EDW data distribution schema with the type of dimensional model that is used in data marts enables the data restructuring to execute once when it gets loaded from the EDW integration schema and then be used many times as the data franchising processes load data marts.

In addition to being the source of data for the SOA, the EDW data distribution schema also serves as a data hub to operational reporting.

DATA WORKFLOW OF THE SYSTEM OF ANALYTICS (SOA)

The primary goal of the SOA is to enable business people using BI to analyze information, make more informed decisions, and potentially improve the operations or profitability of the enterprise. This is accomplished by taking the data from the SOI and performing data franchising processes to package data to support analysis for specific business processes or business functions.

The classic diagram illustrated in Figure 6.13 depicts an EDW feeding a single tier of data marts that are then accessed by BI. This is a good starting point to explain the need for data marts in the purpose of data franchising, but it is a too simplistic approach for most enterprises, whether they are Fortune 500 or small to medium business (SMB) enterprises.

As depicted in Figure 6.15, the SOA has multiple tiers of data marts. The diagram provides a logical depiction of many data stores, but there are several implementation choices available:

- One physical data store, such as a database housing all the logical data stores represented by separate schemas. This physical data store could also include the SOI data stores.
- Multiple physical data stores all using the same technology, such as a database.
- Multiple physical data stores using different combinations of technologies, such as relational database, columnar database, OLAP cube or an in-memory database managed by a BI tool, spreadsheet, or BI appliance.

Different physical schemas may be required by these technologies. But, regardless of the physical implementation, each of the SOA data stores should have a logical dimensional model that defines the schema in the context of business rules and relationships.

The first tier of the SOA is the EDW data distribution schema (enterprise data mart). (Note: when discussing why we split the EDW in Figure 6.14 we placed the EDW data distribution schema in the SOI, but its proper positioning in the analytics data architecture is the SOA.) As previously discussed, this is primarily used to improve the efficiency of schema transformations that are required when moving from an EDW integration schema to the data mart's dimensional models.

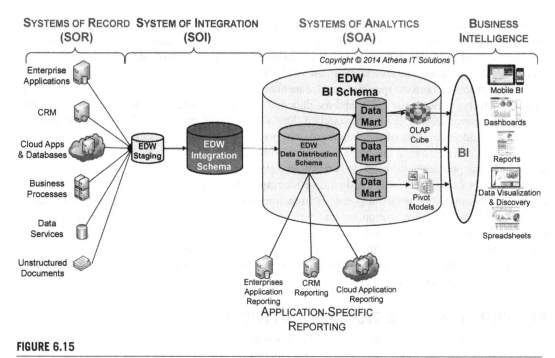

FIGURE 6.15

DI workflow—SOI & SOA.

In the second tier of the SOA are the classic data marts that are built by franchising data from the EDW data distribution schema (enterprise data mart) to support analysis for specific business processes or business functions. Subsequent tiers, i.e., sub-data marts, are created by applying additional data franchising processing that further refines the data for a particular analysis that a subset of business people using the original data mart need. This is a stepwise refinement process that continues to find new analytical uses for the data in the SOA.

The Need for the SOA

The stepwise refinement process of creating multiple tiers of data marts takes more time in the short run than constructing the classic single tier of data marts. This approach, however, is a very efficient method to prepare the data for reporting and analysis that business people perform in their jobs. Without these multiple tiers, every report and business analysis would need to repeatedly perform the same filters, aggregations, and transformations of data—work that could have been done once in a sub-data mart.

If you do not design and deploy multiple tiers in the SOA, then each BI application (e.g., reports, dashboards, data discovery tools, and data visualizations) will need to embed the data franchising process logic that would have been used to build the sub-data marts. This means that the BI applications are more complex to design, build, and maintain; queries are slower; and analysis is more difficult because business people need to understand much more complex data structures. The multi-tier data stores, on the other hand, are prebuilt for better understanding and easier access, and they are customized for their customers. They boost productivity for both IT and business because the logic to build the sub-data marts needs to be done only once.

By adopting a single tier of data marts, enterprises shift the burden of data franchising onto their BI tools and, ultimately, their business users. This has the following two significant adverse effects:

- **BI applications take more time to build, operate, and maintain.** You shift the cost of building a data mart once to building the same logic many times into a BI report or business user's analysis. From a total cost of ownership (TCO) perspective, this shift increases an enterprise's cost of providing the data for analysis and reduces the productivity of the business as it tries to analyze the data.
- **Creation of data shadow systems.** The second and more costly result of a single tier of data marts is shifting the data franchising processes from IT creating the multi-tier data stores to the business creating multiple data shadow systems. Chapter 16 describes these systems and their adverse impact on the enterprise. In particular, data shadow systems create data silos of inconsistent information, reversing the benefit of having a BI solution.

Benefits of the SOA

Although the classic single tier of data marts is simpler to implement in the short-term, the BI team should strive to explain and justify the more sophisticated and robust SOA architecture.

The benefits of SOA's multi-tier data stores are:

- **Enables self-service BI**—BI tools are continuously evolving to improve their ease of use and increase their business analytical capabilities with the goal of providing self-service BI. Regardless of BI tool capabilities, in order for self-service BI to occur, the data architecture needs to provide the 5C's of information (consistent, comprehensive, conformed, clean, and current). But an additional C is needed: context. Each data franchising process and SOA data store provides greater business context that improves understandability and business productivity, increasing the likelihood that self-service BI succeeds.
- **Increases business productivity**—If the enterprise does not create the tiered data stores with the data franchising processes, the burden of re-creating those processes will be on the shoulders of the business person who is performing analysis using BI tools. It means that every time that person goes into a data discovery, data visualization, or dashboard tool, she needs to re-create the filters, groupings, business transformations, and aggregations that could have been prebuilt in a data store.
- **Enables more efficient data processing**—By shifting the data franchise processing from the IT developer creating a BI application or the business person using a self-service BI tool to the SOA, overlapping or redundant data franchising processing is eliminated. This improves overall processing efficiency. Similar to an EDW that sources integrated data once for the enterprise so it can be used many times, the SOA formulates preconfigured data stores once so multiple business people can use them repeatedly, using many BI applications.
- **Lowers TCO and increases business return on investment (ROI)**—On the cost side of the equation, improved processing efficiency reduces the cost and support of additional infrastructure that will be needed without the SOA. In addition, improved business productivity should also reduce overall costs or at least shift activities back to business people's "real" jobs because they're no longer spending time processing data.

Self-service BI and more understandable business information will prove the business value of BI and, in turn, increase its ROI.

DATA WORKFLOW—RISE OF EDW AGAIN

The industry has adopted the hub-and-spoke architecture as a best practice, and the ADA is a more detailed refinement of that approach. Although Chapter 7 will review technologies in more detail, there is one trend that needs to be addressed in designing the SOA: the rise of the EDW.

The industry has shifted back and forth between a centralized and distributed deployment of a BI architecture. The first wave of BI was a distributed architecture, primarily because the technology firms that were the earliest adopters were using servers, at that time called minicomputers, for implementation. The second wave in the 1990s was spearheaded by using mainframes to implement a centralized DW. The third wave in the timeline reverted to the distributed architecture model with, initially, the use of client/server, and then evolving to use many distributed devices and services.

The industry is currently undergoing a fourth wave where, due to advances in databases, storage, network, and server capabilities, it is often more effective to deploy the hub-and-spoke all on the same database, BI appliance, or cloud platform (as depicted in Figure 6.16) rather than store the EDW (hub) and data marts (spokes) on separate servers and databases. Although this is often a very cost-effective approach from an operational deployment perspective, it appears that once the BI architecture is deployed on a single platform the BI team forgets the fundamental aspects of that architecture.

Physically storing all the data on a single platform appliance can be done, but often when companies deploy this architecture, they forget why they split the data into a hub-and-spoke. What often happens is the EDW and data mart-oriented data get mixed together or, worse, the data mart tables or

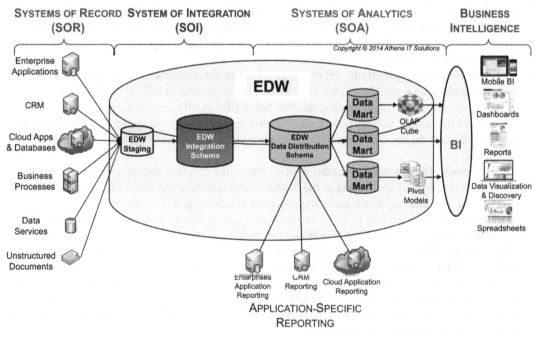

FIGURE 6.16

DI workflow—it's different this time.

cubes do not get built at all. Instead, people start trying to use the EDW schema for all reporting and analysis needs, eliminating distinction and functionality of the SOI and SOA. This shifts the architecture back to the old-school idea of a centralized DW, as depicted in Figure 6.17, trying to be all things for all purposes and generally getting none of it right.

Although the single platforms that enterprise are using are very powerful, that still does not negate the functional needs and benefits of separating the SOI and SOA data architectural components. I do not advocate physically separating them on different platforms, but to maintain their logical separation, and segment them on that platform by their schema and functionality. Although there are advantages to using a single platform, the risks are greater: the danger of misusing this technology and sending an enterprise BI effort back to the days of the EDW-only architecture, when it was harder for the business to leverage it for BI.

OPERATIONAL DATA STORE

No BI term has been muddied and misused more than ODS. There are consensus definitions for DW and data mart; however, an ODS seems to mean anything that isn't a DW or data mart. Whereas people understand how to architect, design, and build a DW and data mart, they are stumped when it comes to an ODS. IT departments, enterprise application vendors, and BI vendors have been very busy building ODS in the absence of a clear definition or agree-upon architecture.

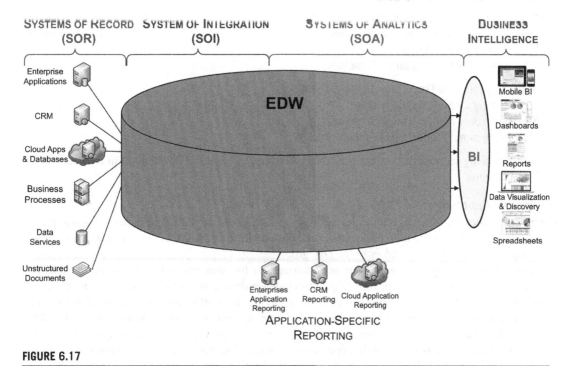

FIGURE 6.17

DI workflow—back to the future.

Although ODS designs vary widely, an ODS typically has these characteristics:

- Integrates data from multiple source systems
- Enables consolidated reporting
- Offers pre-built reporting or integration solution for enterprise applications
- Uses a data schema similar to source systems

ODS systems are usually distinct and separate from an enterprise's BI architecture. Because an ODS is created either by the IT group managing operation applications or the vendors that sell these same applications, they are usually extensions of operational applications that are not designed along BI architectural principles. Historically, the tools used for development were those used with the ERP systems, and the data schema was similar to the operational application. With different tools, database design principles, and groups developing the ODS and BI, it is no wonder they were not engineered to work in the same architecture and became data silos.

The methods used for building the ODS have changed dramatically over the years due to advances in technologies and industry knowledge in BI and data management. Many of the conditions that applied years ago when many ODSs were built don't apply anymore. The following sections will review the reasons for building ODS, examine whether those reasons are still applicable, and, if so, how these requirements should be addressed.

THE RATIONALE FOR AN ODS

ODS definitions have fallen short because they mainly explain what has been built rather than why it was built. As a result, people tend to define an ODS by its characteristics rather than the business or technical reasons for building it.

The reasons for building an ODS include:

- Providing integrated reporting across application.
- Establishing an SOR for dimensions.
- Creating a data hub for a business process.
- Achieving more frequent updates than an EDW.

The following sections discuss the reasons for building an ODS and how they fit in an enterprise's data architecture.

Integrated Reporting

ODS systems got their start by supporting reporting requirements across multiple transactional applications. They helped fill a gap in fulfilling DI across these multiple applications because it was not within the scope of the application vendors or the DW groups.

The vendors were too busy expanding or acquiring new functionality and modules, not focusing on integration and reporting across them. DW groups tended to draw a line between management reporting (what they did) and operational reporting (what they did not do). DW teams were occupied by building and maintaining their existing projects without taking on the burden of operational reporting. In addition, updating the data more often than once a day, or in real time, was more than many of them could handle. Thus, the group maintaining the applications managed integrated reporting activities. As a result, the worlds of ODS and DW diverged into different, overlapping, and counterproductive approaches.

Today, enterprise application and BI vendors use ODSs to develop integrated reporting solutions:

Enterprise application vendors have built ODSs into their products to meet their customers' ever-growing demands for reporting. A pre-built ODS is a way for these vendors to integrate across their own modules and their competitors' products. With so many of these applications created through mergers and acquisitions, an ODS is a very expeditious systems-integration approach for the vendor. These ODS systems are architected as the applications reporting solution and are typically designed with a schema similar to the operational applications. The solutions work well for application users and can be very cost-effective, helping avoid the need to build custom operational reporting systems.

BI vendors have developed corporate performance management (CPM) solutions that support both operational and management processes. The underlying ODS integrates data and enables real-time updates. These CPM solutions provide an alternative to custom-built solutions on top of enterprise applications.

SOR for Dimensions

When used as an SOR for categories of data, an ODS collects, integrates, and distributes current information and provides an enterprise view of it. Common examples are customer and product data. Business groups, such as divisions or subsidiaries, may be responsible for managing a subset of this data, but no single group is responsible for managing the overall customer or product lists.

Data categories such as customers or products are often referred to by different names (dimensions, reference data, or master data) based on your application background, as shown in Table 6.4.

Table 6.4 Data Category Descriptions

Role	Description
BI team & data modelers	Dimensions
Business people & application developers	Reference data (also cross-reference or look-up data)
ERP vendors	Master data

Regardless of what it is called, this data is typically scattered across multiple applications or source systems. For accurate reporting and analysis, an enterprise needs to make sure this data is consistent. For those in the BI, making this data consistent is referred to as conforming dimensions.

Historically, the BI group received de facto responsibility for making this data consistent. This is a great use of an ODS—where the ODS becomes the SOR for this consistent data or conformed dimensions. ERP vendors have recognized this need and offer master data management (MDM) solutions across their application modules through their own pre-built ODS solutions. When an enterprise's needs are greater than one ERP vendor's applications, a custom ODS may be required.

Establish a Data Hub for Updates

One of the most prominent purposes for an ODS is to provide DI, data distribution, and reporting to support specific business processes and associated data. The two most common examples are customer relationship management and budgeting/forecasting. Both of these involve integrating front-office applications rather than the back-office applications that are the mainstay of DW. With the front-office applications, many people need up-to-the-minute updates on information that is relevant to their business function. With customer-facing applications, such as a call center, the business people need data on all aspects of their customers, but that data is spread across many applications.

The ODS provides the ability to act as a data hub to collect, update, and redistribute the data to people and the applications that they use. As a data hub, the ODS may be connected to various enterprise applications, DWs, and data marts, using them as both sources and targets (for data updates) in various business processes. This is similar to how budgeting and forecasting can be serviced by an ODS. The budgeting applications will use the ODS as the initial source of information, update the data through these applications, and then use the ODS to distribute these updates to the DW. In all cases, the ODS is used for the immediate reporting needs of its constituents.

Update Data More Frequently than a DW

A very common rationale used for creating an ODS is that the DW cannot handle either the data volumes or update frequencies required to support the operational reporting demands. This can be the case when a DW was originally designed to update data daily, but doesn't have the hardware capacity to expand, or if it does, the performance would degrade. On the other hand, even if the capacity exists, handling operational data may be outside the charter of the DW group, and should be assigned to the application group.

ODS REEXAMINED

Several advances in technologies and BI knowledge have significantly affected the "why" and "how" of building an ODS. The following sections will look at the previous reasons for using an ODS to determine if they are still applicable.

Integrated Reporting

Although there are still many ODS-based integrated reporting solutions offered by enterprise application and BI vendors, many of the early adopters have replaced their operational data stores with BI architectures such as DWs, data marts, and cubes using the same technologies recommended in Chapter 7. They have done this for several reasons:

- The evolution of BI best practices and the technologies to support them
- Industry pushback against the technology and data silos that the ODS-based solutions created
- A cross pollination of BI knowledge and a desire to offer an integrated BI architecture as mergers and acquisitions have blended ERP, BI, and DI vendors together.

There is still a tendency for IT vendors or IT groups who work exclusively with operational systems to initially design ODS-based solutions for integrated reporting, but those typically become stop-gap approaches until they can shift to a BI architecture.

SOR for Dimensions

There are two approaches available based on the business and technical requirements:

First, if the data volumes, frequency of updates, and type of data cleansing needed justify it, then an enterprise should invest in an MDM solution that manages data on their customers, prospects, products, or employees. These types of solutions and their architectures are discussed in Chapter 5.

Second, if a full-fledged MDM is not needed, the enterprise should build a solution based on the principles of conforming dimensions using a hybrid dimensional-normalized schema. This solution can be built in either the overall BI architecture within the EDW integration schema or in a schema within an enterprise application. The recommended approach is within the EDW, but there may be conditions, such as the hosting environment, that push an enterprise to host that solution in an enterprise application.

Establish a Data Hub for Updates

DI used to be limited to batch-driven ETL processes. Because of this, people used ODS data hubs to enable near real-time data updates. Today, however, significant advances in integration technologies have replaced this approach:

- DI has expanded to include many real-time processes such as data services that can query and update data.
- Data virtualization has become much more robust: it handles larger volumes, a variety of data sources both structured and unstructured, and it can be incorporated into a BI architecture.

Update Data More Frequently than a DW

In the past, creating an ODS to handle real-time or near real-time updates was a pragmatic approach because ETL and database technologies were not robust enough to update a DW with that frequency. However, these technology reasons for creating an ODS do not apply because advances in infrastructure, DI, and databases can support real-time DW updates if the enterprise has the business requirements and is willing to make the required investments.

There are conditions when real-time or near real-time updates need to be segmented from the core EDW integration schema. One of these conditions occurs when the dimensional and transactional data has inconsistent times, causing referential integrity issues. These inconsistencies are addressed when the underlying applications are synchronized, but until that happens they can remain inconsistent throughout the day. Based on business needs, the BI environment supporting the more traditional periodic updates should continue to provide analytics to the business while the business processes that need to use the real-time updates should be aware of and handle the inconsistencies.

Segmenting real-time data from the EDW integration schema is a prime scenario where an ODS-like application is justified. The ODS should adopt a hybrid dimensional-normalized model and be adopted into the BI architecture.

A caveat is that before building this solution, an enterprise should consider if data virtualization would be a better alternative.

Sourcing Unstructured or Semi-structured Data for Analytics

An ODS has often been used as a way to perform a non-traditional EDW function or capability. Supporting Big Data analysis of semi-structured or unstructured data is the latest capability that does not lend itself to traditional EDW schemas today. For example:
- A NoSQL database may be used to capture semi-structured or unstructured data
- Textual analysis is performed on the captured data
- Results of textual analysis are stored in an ODS that might use any of a variety of database technologies based on its intended usage

ODS IS DEAD, LONG LIVE ODS

Much of the technological rationale for building ODSs has dissolved, and advances in BI best practices provide a blueprint on how to address the business requirements that an ODS met.

That is, of course, for the ODSs that were built in the past. An ODS was always a pragmatic approach to addressing the shortcomings in the technology and state of BI expertise at that moment in time. There will continue to be new data analysis requirements that cannot be addressed at the moment, and it is likely that an ODS will arise to meet that need. Already, ODS-like structures are filling some of the gaps in Big Data and cloud-based data solutions.

When asked what an ODS is the answer will likely be "We will know it when we see it." And just as likely, the industry will respond to fill the gaps that the ODS pragmatically plugs.

REFERENCES

[1] Kimball R, Ross M. The data warehouse toolkit: the definitive guide to dimensional modeling. Wiley; 2013.
[2] Inmon WH. Building the data warehouse. Wiley; 1991.

TECHNOLOGY & PRODUCT ARCHITECTURES

INFORMATION IN THIS CHAPTER:

- Evolution of technology and products
- BI and analytics
- Information access and data integration
- Relational databases and alternatives
- Big Data
- BI appliances
- Product and technology evaluations

WHERE ARE THE PRODUCT AND VENDOR NAMES?

The quick answer is, you won't find them here. A key objective of this book is to be product and vendor agnostic. In fact, I have strived to not mention any business intelligence (BI), data integration, or database product or vendor in this book. It was not easy! It would have been so much easier to use their names.

But the BI world moves fast. There are mergers and acquisitions every month, therefore any discussion that mentions product and company names can be quickly rendered out of date. The concepts of BI, however, have a much longer shelf life. So, this book discusses concepts and how to apply them regardless of the specific product you choose. There are plenty of books, online tutorials, and web videos to help you learn about a product and, quite frankly, this book could not be long enough to teach you how to do all things BI in all products.

Most of my previous articles and blogs have been vendor neutral. Generally, to be fair, one should either mention no vendors or mention all of them. This is where the book's companion website, www.biguidebook.com and my blog www.datadoghouse.com become useful.

The companion Website www.biguidebook.com will provide:

- Positioning of products and vendors in the BI architecture
- Links to independent research reviews and articles
- Technology-related updates
- Descriptions of most effective technology use cases
- Discussions of best practices

The blog www.datadoghouse.com will continue to offer a mix of posts that are neutral and those that name products and vendors. I will also continue to write about mergers and acquisitions in the industry.

You can keep track of updates by following the blog's RSS feed or subscribing to the e-mail list on www.biguidebook.com.

EVOLUTION NOT REVOLUTION

BI's history spans several decades. Enterprises developed data warehouses using relational databases to support management reporting in the late 1980s, long before anyone called them data warehouses (DWs). As the years progressed, the industry created terminology to describe the existing technologies: business intelligence, data marts, and dimensional models. Over the last decade, BI has been one of the top, if not the top information technology (IT) initiative, according to various industry analyst surveys of chief information officers (CIOs). Regardless of economic conditions, BI has continued to grow faster than the overall IT spending, as enterprises across industries view BI as a strategic requirement to operate and grow.

BI is mature in many respects, but it is a significant mistake to equate this maturity with being stodgy or stagnant. BI is a market that has experienced sustaining innovation throughout its history, as depicted in Figure 7.1. Each wave of innovation has unleashed the power of increased analytical capabilities, and is then soon followed by even greater demands for more data and greater insights.

The diagram illustrates the innovation of several technology categories. The technology categories that have supported BI and data integration are:

- Technology platforms
- Enterprise applications
- Databases

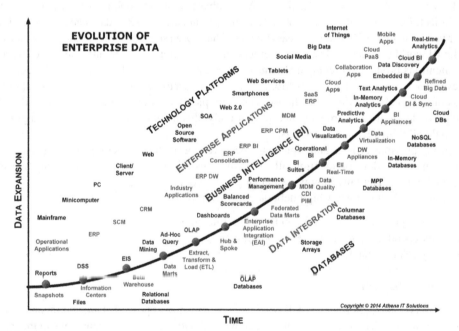

FIGURE 7.1

Evolution of enterprise data.

Enterprises' data and analytical needs have driven the advances in these technology areas; in turn, the advances in these technology areas has affected the evolution of BI and data integration. To understand BI and its future, one needs to briefly examine the evolution of these related technology areas.

TECHNOLOGY PLATFORMS

The evolution of the technology platforms depicted in Figure 7.1 has given rise to the data deluge that enterprises are dealing with. As Chapter 1 explained, the ever-increasing data volumes, variety, and velocity are the result of this evolution.

In the early days of data warehousing, the mainframe was the primary computing platform with mini-computers, PCs, and client/server computing emerging to expand the implementation options available to IT. Enterprise networking expanded, supporting client/server computing and a proliferation of servers and PCs.

It is hard to imagine that data warehousing preceded the dot-com bubble and the now ubiquitous Web by more than a decade. As the Web expanded into commerce, technology trends such as service-oriented architecture (SOA) and Web services expanded the capabilities of both BI and data integration. With exposure to the Web industry, open source software (OSS) became a viable option for IT with OSS databases, extract, transform and load (ETL) and BI emerging.

With over one billion smartphones and tablets sold in 2013, it is easy to overlook the fact that the first iPhone was introduced in 2007. Since that time, smartphones, tablets, and a wide variety of mobile devices have become a new source of data for enterprises to analyze.

With the Web and mobile devices, social media exploded onto the scene, creating new data exceeding the amount of data that enterprises had previously been capturing and analyzing. And the challenge isn't just the amount of data; it's the type. This data is unstructured, very different from the structured data that everyone was accustomed to working with. This then led to the creation of Big Data platforms and tools.

With the expansion of these technology platforms, businesses and consumers are expanding the use of networked devices that monitor, measure, and transmit data related to all types of human and machine activities. This has been labeled the *Internet of Things* (IoT) and is the latest technology platform evolution that will significantly impact data.

Although BI's original technology platforms are drastically different today, people still need to monitor, measure, analyze, and act on that data. There are people who would label some of the changes in technology platforms as revolutionary, but the reality is that, at least from the BI context, each new extension fed the sustaining innovation in that field.

BI's demand and supply have been significantly impacted by the technology platform changes. This does not discount that the changes to our lives and businesses may have been disruptive innovation (or revolution), but that is different from what BI experienced.

On the demand side, we face a data deluge that does not seem to be abating any time soon. Fortunately, the supply side has experienced a significant expansion in technology capabilities in CPUs, networking, memory, storage, and other infrastructure components.

ENTERPRISE APPLICATIONS

When data warehousing began, enterprises were using applications (often custom built) that were narrowly focused on supporting specific business functions. At that time, DWs were typically updated monthly to align with the accounting cycle. The data came exclusively from internal sources.

Beginning in the 1990s and accelerated by the Y2K scare, the enterprise resource planning (ERP) market significantly altered enterprises' internal systems, as they replaced almost all of the legacy function-oriented applications. Vendors promised that ERP systems would be one-stop shops for all the applications managing enterprise systems, hence all the data as well.

After the initial migration wave, ERP vendors introduced additional applications such as customer relationship management (CRM), supply chain management (SCM), corporate performance management (CPM) and master data management (MDM) over the next decade or so. This significantly increased the amount of data that enterprises generated and needed to report on.

The hype proclaiming the ERP application to be a one-stop shop for an enterprise proved illusionary. First, with significant merger and acquisition activity, many of the ERP applications were collections of acquired modules that were not tightly integrated. Second, ERP applications were implemented as modules serving specific functions, much like their predecessors, thereby fragmenting data and workflows. Finally, much of the innovation and new functionality came from startup or smaller enterprise application firms, meaning the large ERP vendors were not the one-stop shop.

ERP vendors offer reporting capabilities bundled with their applications for operational purposes. It is fairly typical for the ERP-bundled operational reporting to be less robust than what standalone BI tools provide. After more than a decade of this situation, the largest ERP vendors acquired the largest independent BI vendors and bundled their tools with the ERP applications. The ERP vendors continue to sell these BI products as standalone products. Many of the smaller ERP vendors have shifted from building homegrown reporting capabilities and partnered with standalone BI vendors to provide operational BI.

Another significant trend that permeated the ERP application market occurred when the vendors started offering prebuilt data warehouses, operational data stores (ODS), or data marts to the customers. Prior to that trend, ERP vendors had fought the need for data warehousing but came to recognize that their ERP data was not structured for analytics, and the customers had many sources of data beyond their ERP applications. The ERP vendors' prebuilt DWs have proved to be fairly effective at supporting operational BI for the application-centric data, but most enterprises have built DWs that are customized to their enterprise's data, metrics, and analytical needs.

DATA MANAGEMENT

From a technology perspective, the ERP applications built with relational databases swept away the legacy systems, which had used network databases, hierarchical databases, and file-based systems. This was the beginning of the relational era, which, after two decades, continues to thrive, expand, and adapt.

During the initial ERP migration wave, the knock on relational databases (from the competing database technologies) was that they could not handle the transaction activity that many enterprises experienced. Relational vendors responded with innovations that cemented their databases as the bedrock for transactional processing across enterprises of all sizes. There have been many database challengers to relational databases in the analytics space over the years, including online analytical processing (OLAP) cubes, columnar databases, massively parallel processing (MPP) databases, in-memory databases, and BI appliances (covered further in this chapter). Relational database vendors have responded with sustained innovations built to enhance their products' BI and analytics capabilities. Indexing, partitioning, optimization, in-database analytics, and in-memory databases are just some of the enhancements that have been made into relational technology. The top relational vendors are high-tech titans who respond to innovative competitors by either copying the technologies—I am not implying intellectual property (IP) infringement—or acquiring the products with their vendors. The relational databases of today are significantly different from what I first started using decades ago; they will likely change as the future unfolds.

A cornerstone of using relational databases for BI has been the adoption of dimensional modeling. This, as we discuss in Chapter 10, enables business relationships and rules to be represented in the database schemas that BI and analytical tools query. Many of the data integration design principles that are covered in Chapter 13 also rely on dimensional schemas. With BI and data integration tools leveraging dimensional modeling and relational databases in a symbiotic relationship, there have been continual improvements in the effectiveness and ROI of BI applications.

During BI's history, there has been a steady improvement in infrastructure, networks, and CPU power, but the two most significant breakthroughs in this area for BI have been (1) the arrival of storage arrays and (2) significant expansion of available memory for computing with the adoption of 64-bit operating systems. These innovations, and many that followed, address the two key historical constraints on BI implementations: disk I/O and memory limitations. These capabilities have become so pervasive that enterprises of all sizes can leverage faster I/O and memory in querying or loading data.

One area where relational database technology has not been able to adapt, nor will it, is to capture and manage unstructured data, i.e., *Big Data* (covered further in this chapter). Although some relational database vendors have expanded their offerings by including NoSQL technology, this is a coexistence strategy recognizing that relational databases will not adequately handle unstructured data.

Also, although this book discusses how relational database technology has innovated to keep up with OLAP cubes, columnar databases, MPP databases, in-memory databases, and BI appliances, it does not mean that relational databases are the only alternative to use in BI; quite the contrary, we discuss some of these alternatives to relational technology later in this chapter.

TECHNOLOGY ARCHITECTURE

There are four technology layers, as depicted in Figure 7.2 that form the BI technology architecture:

- **Business intelligence and analytics**: the tools that a person or process uses to analyze information.
- **Information access and data integration:** the tools used to gather, integrate and transform data into information, and then make it accessible.
- **Data warehousing:** any database or file that is used to store integrated data that would then be consumed by BI and analytics.
- **Data sources:** any data source that captures data that will be used by an enterprise.

There are several key differences between the conventional view of BI technologies and what is shown in Figure 7.2. The conventional wisdom regarding BI is much too narrow, and has led not only to data silos but also to analytic, integration, and application silos resulting in higher costs, low productivity, inconsistent information, and smaller returns on investment (ROI). The key differences from conventional wisdom are:

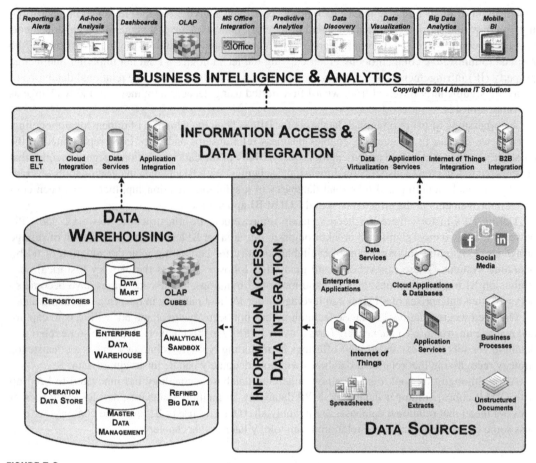

FIGURE 7.2

Technology architecture.

- **Information access and data integration:** Rather than the conventional view that narrowly defines data integration to be batch-driven ETL processes, the recommended technology architecture in the figure includes all tools used to query, gather, integrate, cleanse, and transform data into information that is delivered to a person, a process, or database.
- **Data warehousing:** The conventional view portrays the enterprise data warehouse (EDW) at the center of BI efforts along with data marts and OLAP cubes being loaded from the EDW. The recommended expanded technology architecture encompasses all databases where data has been transformed for analytics from other sources or integrated from multiple data sources. Collectively, this data represents an enterprise's logical data warehouse (LDW), creating the data foundation for its analytics platform. Based on its requirements and capabilities, the enterprise would decide to implement its LDW as a tightly integrated or a loosely federated platform.

In addition to the EDW, data marts and OLAP cubes, the LDW may include:

- **Analytical sandboxes**
- **Refined Big Data** (unstructured data that has been reduced or refined)
- **MDM**
- **ODS**
- **Repositories**, which include those used to store metadata for BI, analytics, data integration, and data virtualization
- **Data sources**: Conventional wisdom has always been that data should be stored only once to support both data capture and information consumption, whether it is a relational database, NoSQL database, or something else. The recommended technology architecture, however, recognizes that there are times when information consumption is limited to querying directly from the data capture database, but for those other times, integrating and transforming data into information is required. When integration occurs, the recommended technology architecture assumes the data is moved into a data warehousing environment. This does not mean that data capture and information consumption cannot use the same database technologies, but that they need to be structured and stored differently.

BUSINESS INTELLIGENCE AND ANALYTICS

An enterprise's business community will have a very diverse set of analytical needs and work styles. The type of analysis they perform will vary based on the depth, subject, volume, and structure of the data used, as well as the business processes: examining salespeople's performance, providing customer support, predicting customer behavior, etc. Business people will also approach analysis differently based on their background and experience. In Chapter 13, we describe those different approaches to analysis as the following BI personas: *casual consumers*, *analysts*, *power users*, and *data scientists*. The BI personas are helpful when designing BI applications and selecting BI tools.

Although BI tools have been around for a couple of decades, the depth, breadth, and variety of BI capabilities and styles continue to expand and change. The BI marketplace has responded to the diverse set of BI personas, application needs, and type of analysis that a business person will perform by creating a variety of BI analytical styles, as depicted in Figure 7.3.

FIGURE 7.3

BI analytical styles.

Previously, dashboards and scorecards were the rage versus the typical reporting tools at that time; these tools were followed by OLAP and ad-hoc query tools. BI options now include data discovery, data visualization, in-memory analytics, predictive modeling, BI appliances, and Big Data analytics. Below, we describe the most common BI styles.

Reporting and alerts: This is the traditional and most pervasive BI style in an enterprise. Reports have a preset format, sometimes requiring pixel-perfect design if delivered to customers, and are used by a variety of enterprise stakeholders. There are several delivery options:

- Static reports pushed to users via e-mail: These reports may be "burst" with each user's report only containing the data pertinent to them.
- Parameter-driven reports run on-demand by user to filter and sort data.
- Drill-down capabilities, although not historically a reporting capability, are often available when users are interactively using the report.
- Alerts, sent via email or other messaging, signaling specific events or data values.

Ad hoc analysis: Rather than presenting data in a prebuilt report, ad hoc analysis presents the data to the users, who then create their own custom reports with queries and data they select. This is a report builder geared to the business person, and was the precursor to OLAP analysis and data discovery. Typically, the business person using this BI style is a power user.

Dashboards and scorecards: These styles are a mashup of other BI styles presented on a single page or screen. Originally used to provide executives with an at-a-glance view of corporate performance metrics or balanced scorecards, dashboards have expanded to display other BI styles in their panels and to support people at all levels of the enterprise. Typical characteristics include:

- Two to six panels on the page with combinations of data charts, tabular grids, or other data visualizations
- The first dashboard a user sees displays summarized information and exceptions, and then the user drills down into details in other dashboards that are linked through a drill path.
- May be updated periodically using a time-based schedule, triggered by an event, or run on-demand by a user.

OLAP analysis: This is a more structured approach providing a form of ad hoc reporting, in which users can select various combinations of dimensions and measures for their analysis. The following terms are often used to describe the query capabilities:

- Drill-down: drilling down a dimensional hierarchy to get more details
- Drill-across: querying across multiple dimensions
- Slice and dice: use drill-down and drill-across capability

This style was named after the type of data it queried from, which historically was a multidimensional (or OLAP) cube. An OLAP cube is no longer a requirement, because relational, columnar, and in-memory structures are now used to support this type of analysis. A pivot table in a spreadsheet is an example of this BI style, and it is why many business users are very comfortable using it.

Spreadsheet integration: This BI style enables spreadsheets to use the data derived from BI queries, so that the spreadsheet becomes the user interface (UI). In the early days of BI, many BI vendors considered spreadsheets competition, there was no integration, and business people simply cut and pasted data from their BI application display into a spreadsheet. Since that time, based on business demand, most BI tools offer integration with spreadsheets.

Predictive analytics: This is more of a BI analytical process. It is a distinct BI style that combines statistical analysis, data visualizations, and either ad hoc query or data discovery. This is discussed in Chapter 15. Data scientists use predictive analytics to create predictive models or forecasts. These models are then used by other business people in their business analysis and may be built into processes such as credit scoring and fraud detection. This falls in the category of advanced analytics.

Data discovery: Although some may view this BI style as a disruptive innovation (compared to conventional BI), this style is really an evolution from using OLAP analysis (without the cube) to select data and a mashup of data visualizations and dashboards to present the data. This BI style follows the tradition of the latest BI generation being easier than the last from a business user perspective. The key difference from other BI styles is the visual self-service UI to select data; however, the analytical presentation itself does not deviate from the BI styles it mashes up.

Big Data analytics: This is narrowly focused to the exclusive BI analytical style offered, which is textual analytics. This type of analytics searches for patterns in unstructured data that meet query criteria by the business person. This item is not about an all-inclusive Big Data analytics platform, nor is it about a variety of BI analytical styles which that platform may support.

BI search: This BI style has been the Holy Grail of many business users. They wonder why they cannot simply type a few words in a Web browser and the search engine returns a list of useful results. Searches of unstructured data use Big Data or text analysis as the BI capability. Structured data, however, becomes a problem in this situation. Whereas the textual search compares what you typed with lots of text out on the Web, it is indeed looking for matches based on keywords and linguistic knowledge. Structured data, however, is different. First, structured data is stored as columns of numbers and text; all you see are column names, not a human language. Second, and more important, how does the BI search engine know what one business person means by the word "profit" versus another business person? One of the key reasons BI takes so much hard work is precisely because the business terms that a person would use are imprecise or inconsistent.

Mobile BI: This is more about where business people perform their analysis—a smartphone or a tablet—than it is about a particular type of analytics. A smartphone, even the largest one sold, has too small a UI to provide rich graphics or detailed tabular data, but instead is perfect for receiving alerts about exceptions and events. A tablet, on the other hand, provides a rich graphical platform capable of displaying data visualizations and tabular data. Consider that the business person may not always be connected to a network to access or update the data.

Cloud BI: This is more about the back end of how the BI tool operates than it is what analytics it delivers on the front end. The only caveat is that the first generation of a product vendor's cloud application typically offers the business person less functionality than a comparable on-premise tool. Based on experience with other application categories, however, cloud BI will likely become on par with on-premise offerings as the product vendors upgrade it.

INFORMATION ACCESS AND DATA INTEGRATION

The conventional view of a BI environment is that an ETL tool loads a DW by integrating data from many source systems, and then a business person uses a BI tool to query the DW to perform analysis. That view is correct, but it does not tell the full story of what should or could be happening in the BI architecture. This oversimplified view creates misperceptions that constrain how enterprises approach

BI and integration projects. It causes them to create integration and data silos due to overlapping integration projects. It raises the enterprise's overall costs and reduces the effectiveness of both BI and integration. The misperceptions caused by this oversimplified view are:

- A business person is always the BI consumer
- BI and analytics applications merely query data
- BI tool is always the destination of data in the BI architecture
- Data integration is always an ETL batch process
- BI is the only enterprise project that needs data integration

A more comprehensive view of a BI technology architecture is depicted in Figure 7.4. This architecture breaks from the conventional view in many ways.

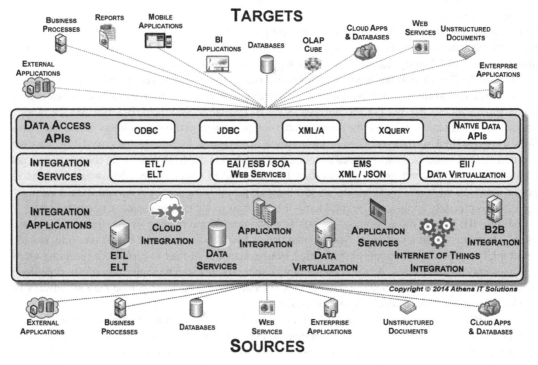

FIGURE 7.4

BI's information access & data integration layer.

BI Targets

A business person using a BI tool is a typical BI consumer or delivery target just as the conventional wisdom portrays. However, business processes and applications are increasingly important BI targets, particularly as BI expands into internal operations and interacts with external enterprise stakeholders. BI may be embedded into business processes or used to communicate with business applications, both of which potentially trigger actions based on its data. In Figure 7.4, nonpeople BI targets include external applications, business processes, cloud applications and databases, Web services, unstructured documents, enterprise applications, OLAP cubes, and databases.

Data Access APIs

Many data access Application Programming Interfaces (APIs) are used in information access and data integration. The most common protocols include:

- **Open Database Connectivity (ODBC):** standard middleware API used to access databases. ODBC was developed to be database and operating system independent, replacing database-specific APIs.
- **Java Database Connectivity (JDBC):** data access API used by Java programming languages.
- **XML for Analysis (XML/A):** industry standards for accessing analytical data sources such as OLAP and data mining. It is based on industry-standard Extensible Markup Language (XML), SOAP, and HTTP. It can execute several query languages such as Multidimensional eXpressions (MDX), SQL, Data Analysis eXpressions (DAX), and Data Mining eXtensions (DMX).
- **XQuery:** query language used to extract and transform data from XML data sources and Simple Object Access Protocol (SOAP) and Representational State Transfer (REST) web services. There is a variety of structured and unstructured data sources that can be viewed as XML.
- **Native database or data APIs:** these APIs access specific data or database sources whose providers may feel these APIs provide better functionality than industry standard APIs, or that they cannot conform to those standards.

Integration Services

There are two reasons that there should be a variety of integration services much more expansive than the conventional view. First, although BI and analytics applications always query data, they may also need to integrate and transform data to complete a business analysis. The integration may take place at the beginning of, or during the business analysis process. Under these circumstances, data access APIs will not be sufficient to complete the analysis. Second, when BI was limited to accessing integrated data from internal enterprise applications, batch-driven ETL was typically sufficient. However, with data sources spanning a wide variety of locations, protocols, data types, security, and currency, there is a need for a variety of integration services.

The types of integration services in a BI architecture include:

- **Enterprise application integration (EAI)** including enterprise service bus (ESB), service oriented architecture (SOA), and Web (or data) services. EAI is a group of integration approaches to provide interoperability between the multiple disparate systems. One of the key characteristics of the EAI approach is a loose coupling of integration tasks rather than using point-to-point integration tasks; this results in more flexibility and reliability. The earliest versions of EAI used a broker-based architecture, but that approach was very costly and complex, and there was a high project failure rate. EAI applications have evolved to the bus-based architecture or ESB, which is the most common approach used in application integration. ESBs are scalable, distributable, expandable, and support SOA. For BI, this provides an application-centric integration capability rather than the database-centric approach used with ETL. There are many use cases, often real-time, where sources such as business processes, B2B integration, cloud applications, and IoT should be integrated using data services. In addition, if an enterprise is using an ESB application, then leveraging the technology and skills will accelerate integration efforts.

- **Enterprise message services (EMS)** including XML and JavaScript Object Notation (JSON). Although similar to an ESB, the EMS focuses solely on providing messaging between disparate applications using structured formats such as XML and JSON. EMS is a very quick and scalable approach to interapplication communication. The message queue sometimes becomes a bottleneck, with the result that EMS is often used in conjunction with an ESB implementation. For BI, EMS offers a lightweight integration service that can very effectively provide real-time data updates from disparate data sources.
- **Enterprise information integration (EII)** including data virtualization and data federation. The earliest generations of EII applications enabled access to an enterprise's disparate data sources and presented a unified view of that data to its users, but only provided limited integration. This flavor of EII was called *data federation*, as it loosely coupled the sources together. Supported by advances in access (data and network) standards and memory capabilities, EII has significantly evolved its access and integration capabilities. EII, or *data virtualization* as it is now called, provides both data abstraction and data services layers to a wide variety of data sources: structured, semistructured, and unstructured. The BI use cases include:
  - Create a logical data warehouse, virtually integrating EDW and other data stores used for BI and analytics.
  - Virtually integrate Big Data, cloud application or MDM application with EDW.
  - Create virtual BI data stores to supplement DW.
  - Create or supplement virtual data marts or operational data stores.
  - Enable self-service BI by providing business people with a virtual data catalog that can access and integrate BI data stores and operational data sources.
- **ETL and extract, load & transform (ELT):** This is the primary data integration tool used in BI and data warehousing. As the name implies, the data from source systems is extracted, transformed from raw data into the information 5Cs (although typically the data undergo multiple transformation processes), and loaded into the target database. Historically, ETL was run in batch on a periodic basis, often nightly, with all the data integration processes taking place at that time. The nightly load would source all data and then iteratively load the staging area, DW, data marts, and OLAP cubes. Nowadays, much of the ETL processing is still run in batch, but the periods have gotten more frequent with many enterprises running ETL process every few minutes to provide near real-time data updates. The book discusses data integration processes and their workflow in Chapter 11.

Data Integration Suites

Many ETL products have evolved into data integration suites with a portfolio of integration services: ETL, ELT, EAI, ESB, EMS, EII and other data integration services. In addition, many of these suites include other services such as data cleansing, data profiling, and MDM. Unfortunately, many people still think of these data integration suites as just ETL tools, and use them only as batch-driven ETL tools. Underutilizing (or worse, misusing) the data integration suites lowers developer productivity, increases data integration costs, lengthens project time, and lessens the amount of information with the 5Cs available to business people.

This raises the issue of whether an enterprise should use one data integration suite to perform all of the integration services discussed above, or use separate products for each integration service. This is the classic software suite versus best-of-breed scenario; however, some of the data integration suites offer one integration service that is best-of-breed. Typically, buying a suite lowers the total cost of ownership (TCO), leverages skill sets across services, and avoids the creation of integration and data silos. An enterprise's decision, however, needs to be based on its business and technical needs, and generalities may not apply to its situation. Undertake a product evaluation (as discussed later in this chapter) if new types of integration services need to be used in the enterprise.

Many enterprises have already invested in different products to implement each of the integration services discussed. Enterprises that implement a significant number of integration services with different products and have expertise in those products will most likely continue using them. In this scenario, the recommendation is to perform an integration assessment to position each integration service within an overall architecture and determine, based on use cases, when a particular integration service should be used. This will result in a more cost- and resource-effective architecture that better addresses the information integration needs of the enterprise. The integration services assessment tasks are:

- Examine and prioritize the enterprise's integration needs.
- Create a vendor-neutral integration architecture based on needs.
- Take an inventory of the products and integration services currently being used in the enterprise.
- Position existing products and integration services within the integration architecture.
- Identify any overlaps or misuse of products and make appropriate adjustments in their use.
- Identify any gaps.
- Conduct a product evaluation to select what will be used to fill those gaps.

An enterprise that needs multiple integration services and is using different integration products should implement a data integration center of excellence (DI COE). We discuss this topic in Chapter 19.

Integration Applications

We have looked at things from the viewpoint of a technology architect. Now we switch to that of an application developer. An enterprise may need to deploy one or more of the following integration applications in its BI architecture:

- ETL or ELT
- Cloud integration
- Data services
- Application integration
- Data virtualization
- Application services
- IoT integration
- B2B integration

ETL versus ELT

The same data integration processes are performed using either ETL or ELT products, but the differences are in the where, when, and how they are performed. The classic ETL architecture is depicted in Figure 7.5, while the ELT architecture is depicted in Figure 7.6.

The initial generation of ETL products comprised code generators that created COBOL or C code with a graphical interface, and then deployed it on source and target servers. These tools helped improve developer productivity and code reusability, but did not offer any specialized data integration functionality.

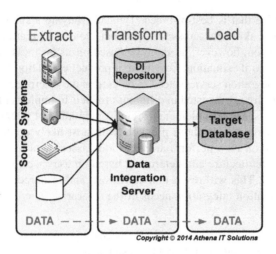

FIGURE 7.5

ETL architecture.

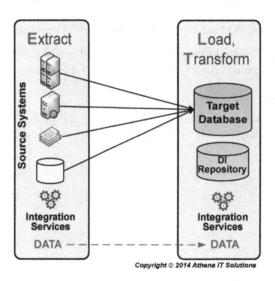

FIGURE 7.6

ELT architecture.

The next generation of ETL products, as depicted in Figure 7.5, introduced the data integration server dedicated to performing the transform or integration services. Vendors improved this generation of ETL products with innovations such as increased integration capabilities built into the data integration server. Many of the innovations in processing data, such as parallel processing, originated in these products and were later implemented in database management systems (DBMSs). ETL products using this architecture were chosen as a best practice for data integration. The data integration products at the top of the industry analyst charts for more than a decade have used this architecture as they have evolved into the data integration suites (discussed above).

As the advanced integration capabilities were adopted by DBMSs, an opportunity arose that spawned the ELT architecture. ELT, as depicted in Figure 7.6, does not have a dedicated data integration server, but instead runs integration services on either the source or target database servers, leveraging their integration capabilities. ELT is a more lightweight architecture than ETL because it does not require a dedicated data integration server. It also has a lower TCO because it does not require the specialized database and data integration server expertise that is required of an ETL product.

Although ELT products have a cost advantage, ETL products typically have the advantage of greater integration capabilities and better performance. The key criteria for product selection should be established according to which data integration product and architecture are the best fit for an enterprise, rather than which product has the most features or the best performance. The trade-off is between capabilities and performance versus cost and complexity. The enterprise should perform a product selection to make that determination.

Data Integration Expanding from BI

With the emergence of the more powerful suites, data integration has moved beyond BI to include other integration initiatives in an enterprise, such as:

- Data migration
- Application consolidation
- Operational and real-time BI
- MDM, customer data integration (CDI), and product information management (PIM)

Enterprises often undertake data migration or application consolidation projects because of mergers and acquisitions, or because they need to streamline applications. In the past, these projects were seen as one-offs and typically hand coded. As systems integrators (SIs) became proficient in ETL tools from BI projects, they realized that they would be much more productive in data migrations and application consolidation projects if they used these same data integration tools. Even though the projects were one-offs, data integration tools enabled the SIs to reuse code, leverage prebuilt transformations, better manage processes, and produce documentation without laborious manual effort. In addition, they did not have to deploy a cadre of coding gurus, but could leverage the data integration developers they already employed.

Several market forces have converged to produce the perfect storm, enabling operational or real-time BI with the same data integration and BI tools as used in DW projects. These forces include enterprise applications built on relational databases and data integration tools no longer bound to batch ETL constraints. In addition, with the major enterprise application vendors also bundling data integration and BI tools, this convergence is leading to more consistent, comprehensive, and current information (business benefit) with the same data integration and BI infrastructure (IT benefit).

MDM, CDI, and PIM all deal with conforming and maintaining master data or reference data for data subjects, such as customers and products. The initial wave of technology solutions bundled a set of tools and applications that were business process-specific or industry-specific. What got lost in many of the initial implementations was that these applications relied heavily on data integration, and that it made sense to leverage a company's existing data integration platform to create MDM, CDI, and PIM solutions.

DATABASES

For decades, enterprises have been storing increasing amounts of data captured in their ERP, CRM, SCM, and other applications used to manage operations and interface with stakeholders such as customers, suppliers, partners, and investors. This data predominantly represents the transactions and events that occur within an enterprise and among its stakeholders. External data, such as customer demographic and economic data, captured by other entities is used to supplement the data captured by an enterprise. A key characteristic of most of this data is that it is structured and its integrity needs to be guaranteed.

In today's environment, much of the data being gathered by enterprises is unstructured, and that can be a game changer. Yesterday's enterprise, with its transactional systems and relational databases, was well poised to collect and store structured data such as sales figures, prices, and addresses. But today's enterprise is gathering more unstructured data from sources such as e-mails, social media, patient records, and legal documents. Also, the IoT with networked devices monitoring, measuring, and transmitting data about all sorts of things may exponentially expand the pool of data being generated yet again. Figure 7.7 depicts a sample of some of the data that an enterprise may use for data capture and analytics.

With the data spanning structured, unstructured, and semistructured formats, enterprises need to examine what technologies and products they will use to capture and analyze that data. Today there is a wide variety of database and file system technologies available for these purposes. It is a lot more complicated now; it is no longer strictly selecting the right database or file system and operating it on a general-purpose server and storage devices. Now, there are many more choices with a variety of combinations of hardware and software configured to handle data capture or analytics.

When examining database choices to be used in the BI technology architecture, base the selection on analytical rather than data capture capabilities. Even when the same database technology is used for both data capture and analytics, analytical data (depicted as data warehousing in Figure 7.2) is stored separately from the data capture (depicted as data sources). Real-time queries and operational BI will take place on the data capture database while analytical BI accesses the analytical data that has been integrated and transformed from the data capture databases. (Refer to Chapter 6 for more details on the concept of using the same database for data capture and analytics, and the sections on data modeling explaining the different schemas that data capture and analytics use.)

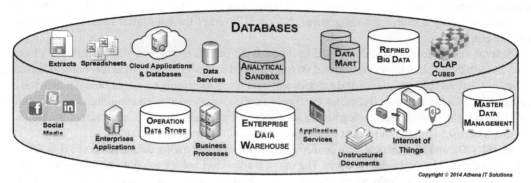

Copyright © 2014 Athena IT Solutions

FIGURE 7.7

Technology architecture - databases.

Relational

We are in the relational database era, with IT using it as the database engine for the majority of data capture and analytical operations. With a significant installed base that works well, and an extensive body of skilled resources and BI tools built with relational in mind, these databases continue to dominate with structured and potentially semistructured data.

There were many relational database vendors in the 1990s, but since the dot-com bubble, the top three relational vendors, who are high-tech titans, broke out of the pack and have dominated market share. Open-source databases are being used in many Web-related applications, but are not significant players in the BI market even though they have sufficient capabilities to handle many BI workloads. Open source may be constrained because IT staffs favor a particular relational database vendor, and they do not see the business value in migrating to another product.

Since the top-tier relational vendors are high-tech titans, they have the resources to continually invest in sustaining innovation and acquiring other vendors with technology to enhance their product. The relational vendors continue to improve workload management, query and load processing, parallelization, and systems administration. In addition, they have been able to leverage advances in infrastructure such as CPUs, memory, network bandwidth, and storage.

As part of their sustaining innovation efforts, relational vendors also use other technologies such as BI appliances, in-memory analytics, in-memory databases, and MPP in various combinations with their relational databases to better support their customers.

Relational Alternatives for BI

There are various technologies that are used as an alternative to relational databases. These can also be combined with relational databases or each other to better support enterprise BI.

Online Analytical Processing

This technology was developed to provide query and analysis of data in a multidimensional schema. Initially, OLAP applications were nonrelational, and created physical multidimensional databases called *cubes*. Later on, some OLAP applications allowed the data to be stored in a relational database and created a logical multidimensional schema using a metadata layer. The person creating the schema would assign which tables were facts and dimensions, define hierarchies and drill-paths, create calculated measures, and specify aggregations. Eventually there would be three types of OLAP:

- Multidimensional OLAP (MOLAP): creates physical cubes.
- Relational OLAP (ROLAP): data stored in relational with logical schema.
- Hybrid OLAP (HOLAP): mixture of ROLAP for detailed data and MOLAP for aggregations.

OLAP applications are widely used, in BI especially, by business power users. Since a spreadsheet pivot table visually represents a multidimensional schema, it is easily understood by business people who are quite comfortable using it. Besides OLAP UIs and spreadsheets, many other styles of BI, such as data discovery, have adopted the multidimensional or pivot table UI when providing self-service BI capabilities. Table 7.1 compares and contrasts each type of OLAP with each of the other types and with relational database systems. All three types have proven to be popular with business people, and various vendors have chosen to offer a particular type.

The MDX language is a specialized language to query and manipulate multidimensional data. Although it was not introduced as an open standard, it has been widely adopted in the industry. Later,

Table 7.1 OLAP Comparisons

Characteristics	MOLAP	ROLAP	HOLAP
Query performance	Fastest	Fast	Faster
Well-defined model, definitions and rules	Yes	Yes	Yes
Data volumes	Limited by physical cube	Limited by relational database	Limited by relational database
Needs to be rebuilt when data change	Yes	No	Only aggregations
Primary disadvantages vs relational	Cube "explosion," i.e., must build many cubes because of size limitations	Need to manage both relational DBMS and metadata layer	Need to manage both relational DBMS and metadata layer

XMLA, based on industry standards such as XML, SOAP, and HTTP, was created as an industry standard for accessing analytical applications, such as OLAP and data mining. With XMLA referencing the MDX query language, MDX became a standard and widely used. MDX is the multidimensional equivalent of SQL.

Columnar Databases

Columnar databases turn the row-based orientation of relational databases on its side, instead storing data vertically by columns. An example of customer data stored on a relational table is depicted in

Customer ID	First Name	Last Name	Marital Status	Gender	Education	City	State
11019	Luke	Lal	S	M	High School	Langley	British Columbia
11027	Jessie	Zhao	M	M	Partial College	Warrnambool	Victoria
11057	Carl	Andersen	M	M	Graduate Degree	Lane Cove	New South Wales
11167	Jasmine	Barnes	S	F	Bachelors	Issaquah	Washington
11175	Luis	Wang	S	M	Partial College	Beverly Hills	California

FIGURE 7.8

Customer data on a relational table.

Figure 7.8, whereas the same data stored in columnar format is depicted in Figure 7.9.
Query processing is sped up in a columnar database because:

- All columns are indexed automatically.
- With all the data in a columnar table having the same data type, there can be significant data compression reducing the amount of data that is processed by a query.
- Most queries only use a subset of the columns in a table, so by having the columns already separated, the queries only need to retrieve exactly the data they need, whereas a relational database reads the entire row and then reduces the results.

Customer ID	First Name	Last Name	Marital Status	Gender	Education	City	State
11019	Luke	Lal	S	M	High School	Langley	British Columbia
11027	Jessie	Zhao	M	M	Partial College	Warrnambool	Victoria
11057	Carl	Andersen	M	M	Graduate Degree	Lane Cove	New South Wales
11167	Jasmine	Barnes	S	F	Bachelors	Issaquah	Washington
11175	Luis	Wang	S	M	Partial College	Beverly Hills	California

FIGURE 7.9

Customer data stored in columnar tables.

The columnar approach is based on analytical usage patterns and essentially indexes all of the data automatically. This reduces the laborious effort needed to tune relational databases to run specific queries in data marts, and can also lower the number of skilled database administrators needed to do the tuning work. In fact, many enterprises have found that they can combine their various relational data marts into just one columnar database.

It is important to note that column-oriented databases can be accessed by BI and advanced analytics tools in the same manner that they access relational databases. This means that a shift to columnar database technology, or indeed to other types of analytical database platforms, typically does not require an organization to change the reporting, query, and analytics software it uses.

Columnar databases actually predate relational databases, but for decades they languished in relative obscurity. The reason was that businesses primarily needed databases to handle the steadily rising demands of transaction processing from enterprise applications, which was the strength of the relational database, not the columnar database. Today, most enterprises have robust transaction processing operations and are instead focused on trying to meet the analytical demands of the exploding volumes of data.

As with much of this technology, there is a good deal of mixing and matching when vendors are building their products. In-memory, MPP, and BI appliances have all been coupled with columnar databases in different products and in different combinations. There's a full range of capabilities, from spreadsheets with in-memory columnar databases to large-scale BI appliances with MPP columnar databases. In a BI architecture, columnar databases are well suited to providing data mart and OLAP cube functionality. Depending on which columnar product is used, a columnar database could function as an enterprise-wide data mart, eliminating the need for multiple data marts or cubes.

In-database Analytics

Just as database vendors have implemented integration services in their DBMS, they have also been implementing BI and analytical services into their DBMS. With in-database analytics, compute-intensive analytical processing is moved directly into a data warehouse built on top of an analytical database. This shift eliminates having to transform and move data between a database and a separate analytical application.

The in-database approach can reduce both setup and data retrieval times, ultimately resulting in much faster analytics performance. It also simplifies the BI data architecture by:

- Eliminating the need to preaggregate data.
- Reducing the need for multiple data marts, since the analytical processing is shifted from the ETL process to the in-database analytical process.

The most significant advantages are achieved when in-database analytics are combined with BI appliances that leverage MPP and other advanced technologies that expand scalability and performance of databases.

In-memory Databases

Traditionally, databases stored their content on disk because it was the most cost-effective and reliable option. Storing data on nonvolatile disks ensured that it was persistent (excluding disk failure), whereas data would be lost if power was cut off to volatile memory. Also, there are capacity issues with how much data can reside in memory. But the key constraint on database performance has always been I/O to disk, and despite advances in storage technology, the goal continues to be storing the data in memory.

With the advent of 64-bit architectures, multicore processing, and advances that enable data to persist in memory indefinitely, the technological barriers have been broken. The amount of data from a database that can be put into main memory continues to increase, although it will continue to be more expensive than storing data on disk.

Database vendors have been enabling their DBMSs to store some or all of the system's data in memory. The hybrid approach is storing the most frequently used data in memory while the rest uses disk. Enterprises that experience trouble achieving the database performance that the business needs should consider in-memory databases. Those enterprises will need to examine the performance versus price curve of the in-memory databases compared to what they currently use to determine if it is a cost-effective solution. If an enterprise is considering moving to an in-memory database, then they need to calculate database migration costs in their database evaluations. If the enterprise's current database vendor is offering in-memory capabilities with their DBMSs, the cost of upgrading to a version of the database software may be less than the cost of migrating to another DBMS.

Massively Parallel Processing

There are two hardware-related architectural approaches to DBMSs:

- Symmetric multiprocessing (SMP)
- Massively parallel processing (MPP)

An SMP databases operates on one or more identical CPUs sharing a common operating system, memory, I/O resources, and disks. When SMP databases are running on more than one server, it is called a clustered configuration. SMP databases always assign tasks to a single CPU. The SMP architecture is called a "shared everything" system. By contrast, MPP databases use multiple CPUs, each having their own operating system, memory, disks, and I/O resources. This architecture is called a "shared nothing" system. The data in an MPP database is spread across processes. The MPP system has software that splits processing and coordinates communication between CPUs. The primary constraint on SMP databases is memory, whereas MPP scales linearly as CPUs are added. SMP databases typically cost less than MPP databases and require less expertise to operate.

SMP databases are typically used for transaction processing systems and are very common in BI implementations, since the top relational vendors by market share offer this architecture. MPP systems have been around a while, but because of their cost, their use had been limited to the most demanding database applications. With the cost of processors, memory and disks declining and with data volumes soaring, MPP databases are being more widely used. The BI market has responded by building many of the BI appliances, columnar databases, and NoSQL databases using an MPP database architecture.

Big Data

Enterprises have been experiencing an ever-increasing rise in data volumes, data variety (source and formats), and data velocity (the need for real-time updates.) This phenomena has been labeled *Big Data*. This trend started when enterprises created more data from their operations, exploded with Web and social media data and is expanding with the IoT, creating more and more networked devices feeding even more data.

There are three categories of data based on its form in the primary source:

- Structured: transactional data from enterprise applications
- Semistructured: machine data from the IoT
- Unstructured: text, audio and video from social media and Web application

Relational database technology is terrific at handling structured data and has the following attributes:

- Large installed base of applications, often running key business processes within an enterprise.
- Large pool of experienced people with skills such as DBA, application developer, architect, and business analyst.
- Increasing scalability and capability due to advances in relational technology and underlying infrastructure that it uses.
- Large pool of BI, data integration, and related tools that leverage the technology.
- Requires a schema with tables, columns, and other entities to load and query database.
- For transactional data, it provides ACID (atomicity, consistency, isolation, and durability) support to guarantee transactional integrity and reliability. The terms making up the acronym "ACID" stand for:
  - Atomic: Entire transaction succeeds or it is rolled back.
  - Consistent: A transaction needs to be in a consistent state to be completed.
  - Isolated: Transactions are independent of each other.
  - Durable: Transactions persist after they are completed.

For all its strengths with structured data, relational technology cannot handle unstructured data effectively. NoSQL databases, rather than relational databases, are being used to handle unstructured data such as Web and social media. NoSQL databases are referred to as "Not Only" SQL databases, because SQL is not required but may be used for some of these databases. NoSQL databases have the following attributes:

- Significant installed base of systems, particular websites, using a NoSQL database.
- Supports distributed, scalable, and real-time data updates.
- Schema-free design that provides flexibility to start loading data and then changing it later.
- Provides BASE (basically available, soft state, eventual consistency) rather than ACID support (yes, someone appears to be a high school chemistry nerd!). This eventually consistent model informally guarantees that if no changes occur in the intervening time span, then eventually all access queries will return the latest data values. The terms in the acronym "BASE" stand for:
  - Basically available: high availability of 24/7, for example, demanded for most transactional systems, is relaxed.
  - Soft state: database may be inconsistent at any point in time.
  - Eventually consistent: at some point in time the data will be consistent.

There are product market differences between relational and NoSQL:

- Relational has a few dominant products and vendors, as the vendor market has thinned considerably since its early days, while there are over 150 NoSQL products in the market.

- Although there are several OSS relational products, the market is dominated by proprietary software. On the other hand, many of the top NoSQL products are either OSS or have their origins in OSS.

NoSQL databases fall into several technology architectures categories:

1. Key-Value
2. Column-Family
3. Document
4. Graph

Key-Value: This database works by matching keys with values. The key, typically unique, serves as the index to search for a value. Key-value databases use an associative array, also called a map or dictionary, to represent a collection of key-value pairs. Some implementations have extended the key-value model to include ordering the keys to allow for range searches. This is considered the most basic implementation of NoSQL.

Column-Family: This database extends the simple key-value model by creating a collection of one or more key-value pairs that match a record. Each column of each record can be different. Column-family databases contain two-dimensional arrays with each key (row) having one or more key-value pairs. These databases are extremely powerful and are used to keep very large amounts of important data.

Document: This database works in a similar manner to column-family databases, but enables much deeper nesting and complex structures. The nesting allows for the value associated with a key to contain structured or semistructured data. Unlike a key-value database, a document database allows queries on both the structure of a document and the elements within it. A liability of this database is that queries and updates need to access most or all of the complex structure, regardless of what portion is really needed. The advantage of these databases is that they are quite effective at separating a large amount of unrelated, complex information that has highly variable structures.

Graph: This database does not involve key-value pairs like the others, but instead uses treelike structures or graphs with nodes (also referred to as *edges*) that are linked to other nodes through relationships. This model, more so than key-value pairs, enables the ability to more easily link and group related data.

If an enterprise needs to capture and analyze unstructured data, then it need a NoSQL database. Use a product evaluation to determine which type of NoSQL database should be used and the specific product to implement.

BI Appliances

BI appliances are a combination of products designed to improve performance and increase scalability for BI and analytical applications. There are also comparable appliances built to do the same for data warehousing, Big Data, and transaction processing.

There are significant differences between BI appliances. To start with, an appliance typically includes hardware and software components, but there are some that are software only. All will have specialized components to improve something by making it better, faster, or less expensive, but each BI appliance takes a different approach to achieving those benefits. Increasingly, BI appliances are taking advantage of the declining costs of hardware—processors, memory and disks—by using commodity products in their configurations. In addition, some BI appliances leverage OSS for its operating system or its database.

Some BI appliances have redesigned hardware, such as specially designed chips that handle analytical I/O and compression techniques, to increase capacity and throughput. Incorporating this capability into hardware speeds up business analytical processing even before it hits a database or disk. This means that a business person's dashboard or other analytical application is quicker "out of the box" with BI appliances designed with these components.

Other BI appliances have gone further than these hardware advances and have reduced the reliance on relational databases to enable business analytics. Columnar databases, MPP, and in-memory analytics are all designed to speed up processing and reduce (or eliminate) the time necessary to build specially designed and tuned relational databases or OLAP cubes to support BI behind the scenes. These technologies enable business analytics by supporting the onslaught of variety, volume, and velocity of data. Business people always wish to examine data in new ways to meet changing market conditions and customer needs. These technologies enable self-service business analytics by eliminating reliance on newly designed and tuned BI data structures every time a business person wants to examine data in a different way.

A WORD OF CAUTION:

When you are examining and evaluating the use of BI appliances to implement an enterprise's business analytical needs, be sure to look under the covers to determine what the true innovation is, both in terms of hardware and software, in the BI appliance's architecture. There are a few BI appliance pretenders whose vendors have merely bundled existing hardware and software into a product offering, using the BI appliance label.

Make sure you understand what is being offered in the BI appliance architecture, how it addresses your business analytical needs, the impact on speed to implementation, and how/if it lowers the TCO compared to the traditional "roll your own" BI systems, for which you pick each component separately.

PRODUCT AND TECHNOLOGY EVALUATIONS

BI has had a long history of sustained and disruptive innovations that continue to improve an enterprise's ability to meet the challenge of increasing data volumes, velocity, and varieties, while at the same time returning more value to its stakeholders. The BI industry also has a long and sustained history of technology and product hype resulting in too many inflated expectations and project failures— not because of technology, but rather from missed expectations.

BI PRODUCT VENDORS

Interestingly, each BI style was introduced by a new generation of BI vendor responding to the perceived limitations of the existing popular BI styles. There have been hundreds of BI vendors over the last couple of decades with one of the following outcomes:

- The most successful or innovative of the vendors are acquired by larger BI vendors who then incorporate their product into their BI product suite. Usually, there is a product roadmap that shows the product becoming part of the BI suite over the span of several product releases. Often, the level of integration is far from seamless, and customers end up implementing the product in the BI suite separately.
- Some BI vendors and products fade away.
- Surprisingly, many BI vendors and their products linger on for years with sales in the tens or hundreds of millions of dollars and a very loyal customer base. These vendors do not "break out" to dominate the BI industry, but remain niche players. Often, the vendors specialize in an industry and offer terrific customer service to retain their customers and their loyalty.

After determining your BI requirements (data to be accessed, type of analysis to be performed, number and diversity from a skills perspective of your BI business consumers and the BI styles they need), you need to look at which products and vendors in the marketplace can meet your needs. We will discuss product evaluations later in this chapter. The vendors in the BI marketplace—BI, data integration and databases—can be split into the following categories:

High-tech titans: These are the largest technology firms that offer the full range of BI technologies plus other software categories, services, and potentially hardware. Some of these titans also sell ERP systems that use their BI tools, but those tools can be purchased independently. These vendors may also offer BI appliances.

Enterprise application stack vendors: These companies will offer applications for ERP, CRM, SCM, specific industries or other business processes along with BI applications. Their tools may be homegrown or they may partner with an independent BI vendor to use their tools. Sometimes a DW, data mart, or ODS is prebuilt to support standardized BI applications that can be customized later.

Independent BI vendors: These companies may offer the complete spectrum of BI technologies, or they may specialize in specific technologies such as data integration, data discovery, or predictive analytics. These vendors' offerings will fall into one or more of the following categories:

- Full BI stack
- BI and analytic specialists
- Data integration specialists
- OSS
- Cloud or SaaS (software as a service)
- Big Data specialists

Enterprises have a wide variety of BI products and vendors that will meet their business and technical requirements. When conducting a technology or product evaluation, examining the product vendor is a critical to positioning their product(s) in your architecture, assessing their ability to execute now and in the future—and, determining if the level of support you will likely get matches your needs. It is generally safe to pick the largest vendor, although that vendor might not necessarily be the best for your enterprise.

DAZED AND CONFUSED

Each new generation of BI vendors, consultants, and pundits boldly proclaim that they have discovered BI's Holy Grail and can implement BI in minutes or hours with their latest BI tool, technique, or service. Their sales people have slick demos that show BI applications being built instantly without the need for those stodgy IT folks who are clinging to the last generation's tools, techniques, or services. These generations occur every 3 to 5 years, because that is typically how long it takes for the last wave's BI Holy Grail to become part of the mainstream. Each generation has indeed expanded and improved BI's capability, its use and its value, but none have eliminated the BI backlog in enterprises or the hard work involved with integrating data.

There are foundational concepts that keep eluding each new generation of BI pundits:

- **It's the data.** Each new generation keeps approaching the development of a BI application as if the fundamental issue is the business user accessing data. Accessing data is easy; accessing the correct information and understanding what it means is the tough part. The reason that data management and data integration work requires lengthy discussions with business people to define data is that the business needs some or all of the 5C's—clean, comprehensive, consistent, conformed, and current—when it comes to information to be used for analysis, not just data access.

- **Data capture is different from information consumption.** Data is captured in the context of a business transaction, an event, or an act by someone or something. The information consumed in business analysis is in the context of the person performing the analysis. That analysis involves data relationships, business rules, and business measures that typically are of no relevance or may not have even existed at the time of data capture. The same information may be analyzed many different ways by different people for different purposes.

- **The tail does not wag the dog.** Each new generation blames the previous generations of tools for the reasons various BI techniques and approaches were followed, claiming that now it eliminates the need for them. Relational databases, ETL tools, and existing BI tools are blamed for the need for dimensional models, data integration, data warehouses, and many other things. But with BI's rich history of evolution to meet increasing business demands, it is more accurate to assume that these techniques are based on business needs, not the demands of the technologies. It is not the tail wagging the dog—i.e., technologies dictating BI best practices—but rather these practices that are driving the direction of the technologies.

Without these foundational concepts, much of what occurs in data management, data integration, and BI seems superfluous. The newest generation of BI tools has great demos and they work well in their initial projects because they primarily deal with one group of business people that performs analysis on a data silo. But once the BI tool starts being used beyond the data silos, the same data issues appear as with the previous tools, and then we wait for the next newest generation to appear.

Beware the hype.

TECHNOLOGY AND PRODUCT EVALUATIONS

With each new technology and product, the best practice is to conduct an evaluation and, if possible, a proof of concept (POC). The evaluation should have stakeholders, both technologists and business people, involved throughout the process. The people who are going to use these technologies in their day-to-day jobs need to be engaged in the evaluation, whether it's the business person who will perform analysis or the developer who will use the tools to create the BI environment. Management personnel, business power users, and architects (if you have them) should be involved, but if they are the only people involved, then the results may not be the best fit for purpose and might be rejected by the people who will really use the tools.

Product evaluation tasks include:

Gather and prioritize requirements: This includes business, data quality, and analytical needs along with volumetric estimates such as data volume, frequency of updates, number of data sources, and number of business users (total, active, average and maximum at any time).

Establish success and value criteria: Although numeric scores look quantitative and scientific, they are often subjective, and many times attributes that are not needed or will never be used end up influencing the selection decision. To avoid these shortcomings, it is best to establish, at a minimum, the following classifications: (1) must have, (2) nice to have, and (3) will not use. Numeric scores can still be used, but they can be judged within these classifications instead of just by themselves.

Select shortlist of product candidates. It is a good practice to conduct a quick survey of the many products available with their vendors placed in the categories we previously discussed (high-tech titan or independent BI vendor). This list should be reduced to, at most, three to five candidates before any detailed due diligence begins. If there is a legacy BI product being used, include it, if only for a baseline (unless it is hated). Also, include only products and vendors that have a chance of being selected, For example, if your enterprise will not use OSS products or buy from a vendor whose sales do not meet a specific threshold, then do not waste your time or theirs in the evaluation.

Conduct product reviews. The first step is to examine online demos or have the vendor perform them for you, followed by a question and answer session. The next step is to have hands-on experience with the product. Some vendors may offer a very robust demo environment where business people can interact with the product using various BI styles, performing different types of analysis, and with different types of data. Of course, that type of demo is for using the product, not building the BI or data integration applications, so in those cases you may be able to use a trial version of the product and any available tutorials to become familiar with it. The final step, if time and resources allow, is to conduct a POC or pilot using your enterprise's data, and creating sample BI or data integration applications that demonstrate your specific needs. The scope can vary greatly, but if there are more than two vendors involved, you should keep the scope limited. After all, the goal is to eventually develop BI applications for your enterprise, not to spend all your time conducting product evaluations.

Score and rank products. All stakeholders should have some someone representing them in this process. Classify as (1) must have, (2) nice to have, or (3) will not use. Assign numeric scores or grades to each attribute that is being examined based on guidelines created before the scoring begins. Most evaluations have a long list of functional and usability criteria from both technology and business perspectives. After product reviews, each product is scored according to this criterion and then ranked, creating a final score that identifies the winner. The evaluation team should feel that it has been very objective and has arrived at the best solution for the organization.

Review results and select product(s). Although the evaluation process tries to be as objective and democratic as it can, the reality is that there is subjectivity, as we are humans. As long as there is no appearance that the process was "rigged," then a little bias is fine and unavoidable.

Hassle with product vendors over pricing. Although this is not generally discussed, it is what happens. Sorry, product vendors! That is why the task above was to select the top two products. The goal will be to come to terms with the top product from an evaluation perspective, but purchasing departments like this scenario.

There is a wide range of costs for almost all these technologies. They range from free (at least in respect to licensing costs) to very expensive. Prior to selecting your product shortlist, you need to get a ballpark estimate on what your organization would likely spend and what the products will cost. You probably will not tell the vendor what your budget is (I would not), but you need to filter products based on what you can afford or are willing to spend. Do not evaluate products that are not realistically within your budget. As an aside, if you are engaging an outside consultancy or independent consultant in the product evaluation, tell them what your product budget is, otherwise they may waste everyone's time, including that of the vendors selling the products that you cannot afford.

PRODUCT MIGRATION

Many times, an enterprise is new to a particular technology, so there are no legacy products in their enterprise. But when there is, take special considerations.

Many large enterprises, for instance, already have more than six BI tools in use by various business people. If your existing BI, ETL, or database product is indeed not able meet your enterprise business needs or is too costly, then it is time to replace it. However, many times when new products are evaluated and selected, it is based on unrealistic expectations or product hype.

Although I would never discourage a product evaluation to determine if there is a better tool to meet business requirements or to lower costs, it is a best practice to include the costs of product migration if you do chose to replace your existing product. Some of the considerations and costs include:

- New product licensing (or subscription) and support costs.
- Cost of expertise. New skills or expertise will be needed and previous skills no longer needed. Existing staff are not likely to be experts in the new technology or product. Options:
  - Bring in new people and let go of the existing staff. Add in hiring and firing costs.
  - Keep the existing staff but retrain them. The costs are:
    - Training: Include both formal and on-the-job training for IT and business people.
    - Lost productivity: It takes time to become an expert and it takes longer to get things done.
    - Quality issues: Deliverables are not likely to be done well at first and lots of foundational work will be shabby and difficult, or costly to replace or improve later on.
- Consulting costs, if you choose to have outside resources with expertise augment your staff.
- Cost of lost opportunity. Rather than working on business needs during the migration, the focus is on technology, not business. What could have been built or improved for the business has to be part of the cost of migration. If you migrate what you have and the result is the same business functionality on a new platform, then there is no gain to the business. "If it ain't broke, don't fix it." Why migrate to another technology or product if the existing one works well and there is no significant gain to migrating to the new platform?

DATA DESIGN

IV

FOUNDATIONAL DATA MODELING

THE PURPOSE OF DATA MODELING

A well-designed data model is the cornerstone to building business intelligence (BI) and data warehousing (DW) applications that provide significant business value. Effective data modeling results in transforming data into an enterprise information asset that is consistent, comprehensive, and current. Data is transformed from operational or source systems into a data warehouse, data marts, or online analytical processing (OLAP) cubes for analysis.

This chapter discusses the first of two logical data modeling approaches: entity-relationship (ER) modeling, also referred to in the industry as relational modeling. (The next chapter will cover the other approach, dimensional modeling.) ER modeling is used to establish the baseline, operational data model, while dimensional modeling is the cornerstone to BI and DW applications. These modeling techniques have expanded and matured as best practices have emerged from years of experience in data modeling in enterprises of all sizes and industries. These techniques improve the business value of the data, enhance project productivity, and reduce the time to develop applications.

DEFINITIONS—THE DIFFERENCE BETWEEN A DATA MODEL AND DATA MODELING

Before reading any further, it is a good idea to learn how we define a data model and data modeling.

A *data model* is a specification of the data structures and business rules representing business requirements. One of the first things you do when developing an application is talk to the business group about their requirements, then document them. In addition to those requirements, there will be a set of data that is required to run that application, whether it is a reporting, analysis, or transaction processing system. In addition to this necessary data, there will be business rules that define the relationship between the various data entities or objects that are required. The data model represents the data portion of those rules and the relationships between those structures.

The data model's primary job is to be the data design specification for an IT application. The team meets and develops the reporting or application specifications for the code. But that code needs to operate on data. And the data model is the data design specification for that portion of the application.

Data modeling is a structured approach to identify and analyze those data components of the information system specifications. This approach involves close work between the business and IT groups and adherence to a best practices approach to ensure that the data model is most appropriate for building the application.

The data model provides a method to visually communicate the data that is needed, collected, and used by an organization. Data modeling tools present visual representations of data models. As your data model gets used in dozens or even thousands of tables, the visual representation is very important as it shows the relationships between the tables—relationships that would not show up if it was just text.

As a communication tool, the data model is best used for discussions between developers, database analysts, and business analysts during design and application development. Although there are some business people with whom the models can be shared, it can be too complex for most and should be limited to the technical members of the team. The conceptual data model, described below, is an exception to this.

THREE LEVELS OF DATA MODELS

There are three levels of data models, which grow increasingly complex: conceptual, logical. and physical. Figure 8.1 shows how they relate to one another.

The **conceptual data model** represents the high-level business view. This is very effective for communicating with the business to understand and define the business processes within the enterprise.

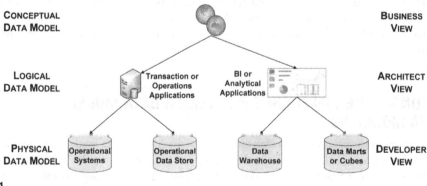

FIGURE 8.1

Three levels of data models.

The **logical data model** is the next layer down, and is the one we are most involved in when designing the BI application. It helps us understand the details of the data, but not how it is implemented. The logical data model is the architect or designer view of the data. This chapter covers two use cases:

1. Transactional or operation applications such as enterprise resource planning (ERP) systems.
2. BI or analytical applications such as DW, data marts, and OLAP cubes.

The **physical data model** makes up the third tier. The logical data model is used as the blueprint of what data is involved while the physical data models detail how that data will be implemented. Then database administrators and application developers will convert the logical data model into the tables, columns, keys, and other physical entities of a database. The database design for operational and transactional systems is derived from ER logical data models while BI-related databases use logical dimensional models. Application developers use the physical data model to design, build, and test application systems.

CONCEPTUAL DATA MODEL

The conceptual data model is a structured business view of the data required to support business processes, record business events, and track related performance measures. This model focuses on identifying the data used in the business but not its processing flow or physical characteristics. This model's perspective is independent of any underlying business applications. For example, it allows business people to view sales data, expense data, customers, and products—business subjects that are in the integrated model and outside of the applications themselves.

The conceptual data model represents the overall structure of data required to support the business requirements independent of any software or data storage structure. The characteristics of the conceptual data model include:

- An overall view of the structure of the data in a business context.
- Features that are independent of any database or physical storage structure.
- Objects that may not ever be implemented in physical databases. There are some concepts and processes that will not find their way into models, but they are needed for the business to understand and explain what is needed in the enterprise.
- Data needed to perform business processes or enterprise operations.

The conceptual data model is a tool for business and IT to define:

- Data requirements scope.
- Business terms and measures across different business units and those that are agreed upon for enterprise-wide usage.
- Names, data types, and characteristics of entities and their attributes.

LOGICAL DATA MODEL

The logical data model is the one used most in designing BI applications. It builds upon the requirements provided by the business group. It includes a further level of detail, supporting both the business system-related and data requirements.

The business rules are appropriated into the logical data model, where they form relationships between the various data objects and entities. As opposed to a conceptual data model, which may have very general terms, the logical data model is the first step in designing and building out the architecture of the applications.

Like the conceptual data model, the logical data model is independent of specific database and data storage structures. It uses indexes and foreign keys to represent data relationships, but these are defined in a generic database context independent of any specific DBMS product.

The characteristics of the logical data model include:

- Features independent of specific database and data storage structures.
- Specific entities and attributes to be implemented.
- Identification of the business rules and relationships between those entities and attributes.
- Definitions of the primary keys, foreign keys, alternate keys, and inversion entities.

The logical model is used as a bridge from the application designer's view to the database design and the developer's specifications. This model should be used to validate whether the resulting applications that are built fulfill business and data requirements.

PHYSICAL DATA MODEL

Implementing the physical data model requires understanding the characteristics and performance constraints of the database system being used. Quite often, it is a relational database, and you will have to understand how the tables, columns, data types, and the relationships between tables and columns are implemented in the specific relational database product. Even if it is another type of database (multidimensional, columnar, or some other proprietary database), you need to understand the specifics of that DBMS in order to implement the model.

Designing the physical data model requires in-depth knowledge of the specific DBMS being used in order to:

- Represent the logical data model in a database schema.
- Add the entities and attribute definitions needed to meet operating requirements.
- Configure and tune the database for performance requirements.

The characteristics of the physical data model include:

- DBMS-specific definitions.
- Table, column, and other physical object definitions in the DBMS that represent the entities and attributes in the logical data model. Column attributes such as data types are defined and implemented differently across specific DBMSs.
- Referential integrity rules establishing the relationships between the tables and columns. Referential integrity will include foreign keys, constraints, and triggers that vary across specific databases.
- Performance and optimization entities based on specific DBMS functionality, such as indexes, triggers, procedures, table spaces, partitions, and materialized views. The initial design is based on estimates of data volumes and update frequency; these physical entities are likely to be modified based on changes encountered in deployment and operation.

DATA MODELING WORKFLOW

The data modeling workflow progresses from business requirements to physical implementation of the database. From a high level, data modeling is a process that you use to:

- Gather business requirements.
  - Analyze the data needed by the business requirements.
  - Identify data relationships.
- Create the various data models needed.
  - Conceptual
  - Logical
  - Physical
- Support the application development.
  - Create application specifications
  - Develop applications
  - Deploy applications

As Figure 8.2 shows, the workflow starts with gathering the business requirements. This is where you talk to the business group and ask what they need for the application.

After gathering requirements, you develop the conceptual data model. For this stage, you need to know what business subjects are being captured in the data requirements, what they mean, where the data is, and what some of the relationships are in that data.

Then you create the logical data model, which is the bulk of the data modeling work. It includes taking what you learned in the business requirements gathering and conceptual data model stages and discerning the detail of the entities and relationships present in the conceptual model. From this you create the application specifications. The whole point of creating a logical model is to make a blueprint that guides the development of your application code and ensures it works correctly.

After creating the logical data model and application specs, the next step is actually designing the physical data model. This includes adding the partitioning, indexing, table spaces, and whatever else is necessary in order to generate optimal performance. This is followed by physically developing the applications.

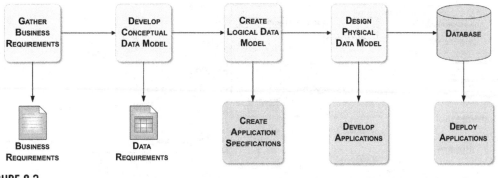

FIGURE 8.2

Data modeling workflow.

Developing the logical data model is an iterative process. Once you have started application development, you may uncover new relationships, algorithms, or dependencies that were not apparent during the first discussions of logical data modeling. This is very common and is not a major problem. In fact, this iterative process is a powerful stepwise refinement of both the logical and physical model that occurs during application development and testing. The end result is a validated physical data model used to implement the business and data requirements in the application.

THE DATA MODEL IS CRITICAL

When consulting, I see cases where the IT group completed all the work to create specifications for their code and reviewed it, but when I ask them for a data model there is a sheepish laugh; they admit that they do not really have one or that they do not have a current one. That is not a good sign. It is important to manage and spec the code within your data model—logically or physically. The code has to operate that data, and you need to save that data model just as you save the specs. The data model is part of the spec; it is a key part of your communication vehicle and your maintenance package.

WHERE DATA MODELS ARE USED

Data models are a key component of relational databases, which are the workhorses of enterprise applications today. There are two primary areas in which relational databases are used—transactional processing (also called operational systems) and BI:

- **Transactional processing and operational systems**—the class of applications built to support these transactions is ERP systems. These systems process the business transactions and business events that occur throughout an enterprise. When a customer places an order, when an employee is paid, and when a mortgage is processed, all those types of transactions are handled by the operational systems.
- **BI applications**—these applications are used for reporting, querying, and analytics. This category also includes data warehousing, which is the database backbone to support BI applications.

These two uses for relational databases correspond to the two primary modeling approaches used for data: entity-relationship (ER) models and dimensional models. The point of Figure 8.3 is to show them at a high level; the dimensional model on the right is much simpler.

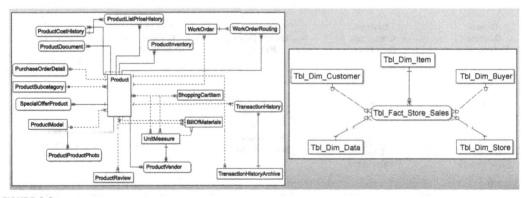

FIGURE 8.3

Entity vs dimensional at a glance.

Entity-relationship models are used primarily for transactional processing systems. As the figure shows, the ER model gets very complex with many entities, even for the simple example provided, which is related to a product. In most enterprises, these models get quite complex and contain hundreds, if not thousands, of entities.

Dimensional modeling is used primarily for BI applications. It was designed to represent data more simply in a business context than an ER model. Dimensional models have far fewer entities and are visually easier to understand than ER models. Dimensional models were designed for better BI performance and BI tools; likewise, they were designed to leverage these models for better performance. Although many enterprises have used ER models, we recommend the hybrid dimensional-normalized model discussed in Chapter 6.

There are several reasons why it is important to understand both ER modeling and dimensional modeling to design, develop, and deploy BI applications:

- First, most source systems feeding into a BI environment use ER models. Knowing how these source systems are structured will help in understanding business requirements and performing source systems analysis for data integration.
- Second, ER modeling provides the foundation for many dimensional modeling concepts.
- Finally, hybrid dimensional modeling, the recommended approach to DW design, blends both ER and dimensional modeling.

ENTITY-RELATIONSHIP (ER) MODELING OVERVIEW

ER modeling is a logical design modeling technique. After the business requirements and data requirements are gathered and you understand the business rules, you will start developing your logical data model.

> An ER model is often referred to as a 3NF, or third normal form, or sometimes just a normalized model for short. It is also sometimes referred to as a relational model, which is incorrect. Although it is implemented in a relational database, it is not the sole data modeling technique that could be used in a relational database.

ERP systems nearly always uses ER models. These systems often have thousands of tables, and some even have tens of thousands. Certainly, with that complexity, using a structured approach and technique is critical. Because of the size of these applications, it is important to eliminate data redundancy. The enterprise also likely needs to have its transactions input immediately. With so many tables to deal with, ER models need to enable fast loading and updates.

ER BUILDING BLOCKS

The three building blocks of an ER model are entities, relationships, and attributes (see Figure 8.4).

An entity is a person, place, thing, event, or concept about which the business keeps data. For example, an enterprise keeps track of its products, customers, employees, suppliers, sales, expenses, and interactions with partners, the government, and other people or business entities. The enterprise needs all these things, or entities, to operate and manage its business.

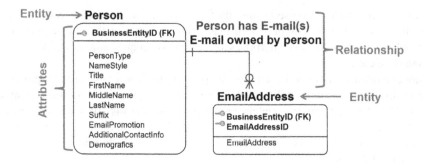

FIGURE 8.4

ER modeling building blocks.

Relationships show how the entities are related to one another. Relationships are the logical links between the entities that represent the business rules or constraints. For example, a customer's relationship to a product is that she buys it; an enterprise's relationship to an employee is that it pays her. These links have business rules, which are captured in the data model.

An attribute is a distinct characteristic of an entity for which data is maintained. For example, if the entity is a person, the attributes may be birthday, marital status, and address. If the entity is a product, the attributes may be price, color, and size. These attributes are characteristics the enterprise needs to capture in order to understand the business.

The example in Figure 8.4 shows a simple example of two entities, a person and an email address:

- The person has various attributes, starting with type (*PersonType*), which could categorize a role within the enterprise, such as a salesperson or a manager. Then it shows the person's title, name, and additional contact information and demographics. All are attributes related to a person. The person entity's primary key is *BusinessEntityID*.
- The email address entity simply has the attributes of *EmailAddressID* and the email address itself. The email address entity's primary key is a combination of *BusinessEntityID* and *EmailAddressID*.

In between these two entities is the relationship. One example of a relationship is that a person can have one or multiple email accounts, but an email account is owned by one person. Similarly, a product has relationships with other entities such as other products, customers, and salespeople. All relationships are defined by particular business rules.

TYPES OF ENTITIES AND ATTRIBUTES

There are two types of entities, independent and dependent:

- Independent entities can survive on their own and do not need any children.
- Dependent entities are child records that need a parent record to exist.

Figure 8.5 shows the *SalesOrderHeader* entity. It may have one or more *SalesOrderDetail* entities; each of those line items in the order detail needs to have the *SalesOrderHeader* entity to exist. This makes them dependent entities. The *SalesOrderHeader* entity itself is an independent entity.

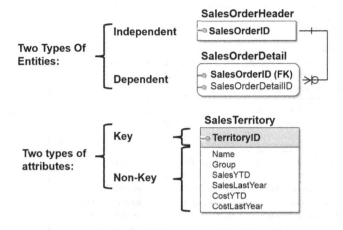

FIGURE 8.5

Entity and attribute types.

There are also two types of attributes in an entity: key or non-key. The figure shows the *SalesTerritory* entity with a key attribute of *TerritoryID* and the non-key attributes of *Name*, *Group*, *SalesYTD*, etc. Unlike key attributes, non-key attributes do not uniquely identify an attribute. Similarly, we can have a product with a product ID and the product attributes, or a person with person attributes as shown in Figure 8.4. Keys are important, and will be covered in more detail later in this chapter.

RELATIONSHIP CARDINALITY

Cardinality is defined as the number of instances of an entity in a relationship with another entity. There can be one or many instances. For example, with a parent-child relationship, cardinality defines, on both the parent and child sides, how many occurrences can take place between these entities. There are four options, described in Table 8.1: one-to-one, one-to-many, many-to-one, and many-to-many.

In addition to these four types of cardinality, note that relationships can also be recursive. With self-referencing, or recursive, relationships, the same entity can be in both ends of the relationship. In other words, there may be more than one relationship between entities. A parent-child relationship could also have a child-parent relationship, and they do not have to be the same. The classic example of this is an employee who reports to another employee (a manager). So you have an entity with an employee ID, then you would have a second employee ID for the manager, and then that manager has a manager that he reports to, etc. So you could have a relationship that just points to itself.

TYPES OF RELATIONSHIP MODELS

An entity-relationship model has four basic types of relationships: identifying, nonidentifying (either optional or mandatory), and many-to-many relationships. Cardinality imposes itself on these various relationships.

Table 8.1 Cardinality

Type	Crow's Foot Notation
One-to-one—One instance of the first entity, the parent, corresponds to only one instance of the child or the second entity. If you have one, you have to have the other. For example, one employee has one employee ID number.	
One-to-many—The example in Figure 8.5 shows the relationship between an order header item and an order detail item. The parent is *SalesOrderHeader*: there is only one of them. The children are *SalesOrderDetail*: there can be many of them.	
Many-to-one—There is more than one instance of the first entity, the parent, but it corresponds to only one instance of the second entity. For example, there can be many survey responses to one question. Or there are multiple reasons why a person buys one product. The difference between one-to-many and many-to-one depends on what side of the relationship you are looking at. For example, one department has many employees (one-to-many), but many employees work in one department (many-to-one).	
Many-to-many—The most complex is the many-to-many relationship. There is more than one instance of the first entity corresponding to more than one instance of the second entity. The classic example of this is a sick patient visiting the doctor. The patient can have many symptoms and diagnoses. There can be many procedures that apply to each of those diagnosis. These are the most complex relationships to implement in a relational database. But there are techniques, covered later under dimensional modeling, that show how to handle them.	

A data modeling tool helps to specify the type of these relationships in a data model; it then builds the SQL data definition code corresponding to the relationships' constraints.

Identifying Relationship

As the name implies, the identifying relationship establishes the parent as a way to identify and classify the child. In this type of relationship, the primary key from the parent migrates through the relationship to become part of the primary key, or identity, of the child. Therefore, the child entity is dependent upon the parent for its identification or classification, and it cannot exist without the parent.

Figure 8.6 shows the highest level entity, *BusinessEntity*. This entity can define multiple types of entities, such as an organization, asset, or person. *BusinessEntity* is the top-level parent and identifies the child entity *Person*, which uses the *BusinessEntityID* as one of its primary keys. Next, the *Employee* entity is the child of the *Person* entity that then defines the *Employee* entity. Each of these entities has different attributes that are inherited by the children under them, as well as their identity. It is a classic object-oriented development approach called inheritance, and it is a way to reuse attributes and entity characteristics.

Nonidentifying Mandatory Relationship

To understand the nonidentifying mandatory relationship, you need to understand its two aspects, nonidentifying and mandatory:

- It is nonidentifying because the parent entity's primary key migrates as a non-key attribute to the child but does not identify the child. The non-key attribute means it is a foreign key pointing back to the parent entity. But it is not used as part of the primary key.

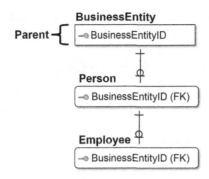

FIGURE 8.6

Identifying relationship.

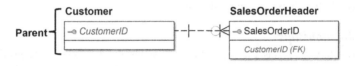

FIGURE 8.7

Non-identifying mandatory relationships.

- The relationship is mandatory because the child is independent of the parent for its identification, but it cannot exist without a parent.

The example in Figure 8.7 shows that *Customer* is the parent; customers can exist whether they buy a product or not. *SalesOrderHeader*, which is the child record, migrates from the *CustomerID*, a non-key attribute, as a foreign key to then point back at *Customer*. *Customer* can exist without *SalesOrderHeader*. However, it is mandatory that *SalesOrderHeader* has a *CustomerID*.

The nomenclature on the sales order side shows crow's feet, which means many orders can be placed by one customer. The circle over the crow's feet means it is not mandatory. On the other side of the equation, one customer must exist. This is a one-to-many relationship.

Nonidentifying Optional Relationship

In a nonidentifying optional relationship, the parent entity has a primary key that migrates, as a non-key attribute, to the child but does not identify the child. In other words, the child is independent of its parents for its identification. Also, the child may exist without parent information.

Figure 8.8 shows the parent entity *ProductModel*, which can exist on its own. *ProductModel* has *ProductModelID* as its primary key and some attributes (*Name*, *CatalogDescription*, and *Instruction*).

The child record is the entity *Product*. The *ProductID* is its primary key identifying the product entity. It has various attributes, including the *ProductModelID*, which is the foreign key and migrated from the parent entity. But that *ProductModelID* is not necessary to identify the product. It may indeed be null, and it does not even need to exist.

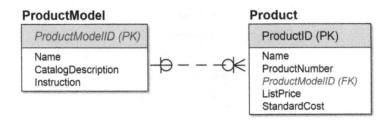

FIGURE 8.8

Non-identifying optional relationship.

On the child side are the crow's feet, which means "many," so one *ProductModel* can have many *Products*. There is a circle over the crow's feet, meaning it is optional.

On the parent side, a single line indicates a "one" relationship, so it is one-to-many (one from the parent, many for the children). The circle indicates that it is optional. There are optional relationships on both sides. Each entity can exist without the other one.

Many-to-Many Relationships

The many-to-many relationship has a nonspecific relationship in which primary keys do not migrate as foreign keys. There must be two verb phrases to explain the relationship because it is many-to-many, representing a relationship for both the parent and child sides. Each phrase must state the rule from the perspective of first the parent to the child and then the child to the parent.

Figure 8.9 is for a company that sells multiple products listed on entity *Tbl_Dim_Product* with *SK_Product_ID* as the primary key. It also has an entity of vendor, which produces various product IDs, with other attributes relating to the vendor.

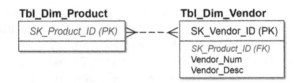

FIGURE 8.9

Many-to-many relationship.

The two verb phrases identifying the relationships for this example are:

- A product may be purchased from one or more vendors.
- A vendor may produce one or more products.

This is a classic retailer model. The vendor or supplier produces multiple products, which the company (in this example a retailer) acquires and then resells. The product may be produced by multiple vendors. This makes it a many-to-many relationship, and the nomenclature in the figure shows crow's feet on either side with no mandatory or optional symbols (circles). The many-to-many relationship is the most difficult to implement in a relational database. The next chapter, on dimensional modeling, will discuss how to simplify that relationship and how to implement it in a dimensional model.

Recursive Relationships

After a many-to-many relationship, one of the more difficult relationships to express in SQL is a recursive relationship. This is a nonidentifying, nonmandatory relationship in which the same entity is both the parent and the child.

Figure 8.10 shows the entity *DimEmployee*, with *EmployeeKey* being the primary key. It has various attributes, including *ManagerKey*, which is actually another *EmployeeKey*. So you are an employee, and your manager is also an employee, and that is in the same dimension. That manager is an employee who most likely will have a manager and so on up the organizational structure. The parent entity instance primary key has migrated to the non-key area of the child entity instance.

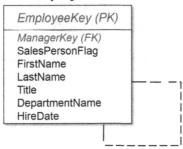

DimEmployee

FIGURE 8.10

Recursive relationship.

Each migrating primary key attribute must be given a role name to clarify the attribute's foreign key role. So we did not simply have *EmployeeKey*; we could not have the same attribute again called *EmployeeKey*. In essence, we created and renamed it *ManagerKey*, which is a foreign key.

This is also referred to as a self-referencing relationship. It is used frequently in ER and dimensional modeling in enterprises because many business relationships are represented by recursive hierarchies. However, it is one of the areas that is difficult to handle in standard SQL code as you are moving up and down a tree, without either custom coding or using a DBMS with added SQL extensions to support this recursive processing.

ER Model Example

The previous sections have covered the different types of relationships. So how do they all fit together? Figure 8.11 provides a view of how the various relationships and cardinality fit in. Pieces of this example have already appeared in previous figures.

The example shows a business event, in this case a sale being made to a customer who buys various products. *SalesOrderHeader* defines what the sales transaction is. There is a one-to-many relationship between *SalesOrderHeader* and *SalesOrderDetail*. So, a customer can buy one or more products in that order. The crow's feet signify the "many," the single line underneath *SalesOrderHeader* shows "one," and the circle over the crow's feet indicates an optional relationship between *SalesOrderHeader* and the *SalesOrderDetail*.

Similarly, we have the one-to-many optional relationship between the customer who buys the products and the sales order (*Customer* to *SalesOrderHeader*). We have a customer who can exist

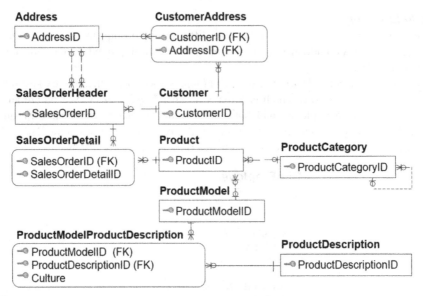

FIGURE 8.11

ER model example.

independent of the sales order, but the sales order must have a customer associated with it. Similarly, *SalesOrderDetail* is where the products are listed as foreign keys, and we have the one-to-many relationship between *Product* and *SalesOrderDetail*. Just like the customer, products can exist outside of the orders, but an order detail line item must have a product.

The figure also shows the example of a product model (*ProductModel*); *Product* may have *ProductModelID* and even multiple *ProductModelIDs* related to it. *ProductModel* will then potentially have one-to-many product descriptions (*ProductModelProductDescription*). In this example, people took out the commonality of product descriptions, which might be used across products, and separated that as a separate entity itself, another one-to-many relationship.

Going back up to *Product*, the example shows that many products may be related to one category (*ProductCategory*). "May" is an important distinction, indicated by the circles showing both relationships are optional.

But, *ProductCategoryID* shows multiple levels of product categories that a product can be grouped in. This means that a product can be grouped in one set, a number of products grouped into a product category, and the product category itself could have a hierarchy. In the lower right-hand corner of that product category entity is a recursive, or self-referencing, relationship, which indicates it could move up the hierarchy.

Finally, above *SalesOrderHeader*, the example shows that there could be multiple addresses associated with the sales order. There could be ship-to addresses, bill-to addresses, and other related addresses. There is also a specific customer address related to a customer ID, and there might be multiple addresses related to it. That customer address is then related to the business entity address that is set up in the upper left-hand corner.

The example shows that a simple sales order has a number of relationships; this is how an entity relationship model is built with the various relationships discussed in this chapter.

KEYS

Learning about keys gets you closer to learning how to build a physical data model. This section describes the process of using a logical model to decide which attributes are used for keys. There are four types of keys: candidate, primary, alternate, and foreign.

Candidate Key

The candidate key is the attribute or group of attributes that can uniquely identify each instance of an entity.

There may be more than one key that can accomplish this. This is often the case where there is a transaction-related key. In Figure 8.12 *SalesOrderHeader* has the candidate key of *SalesOrderNumber*, which may be generated by the transaction, assumed to be unique. You would also potentially have *SalesOrderID*, which may be an identity key or a surrogate key that is generated to uniquely identify the transaction later on.

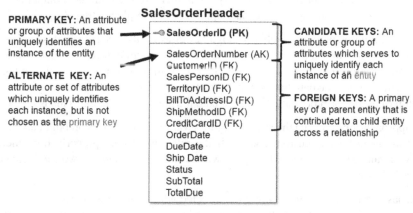

FIGURE 8.12

Key types.

Primary and Alternate

The primary key (PK) is the attribute or group of attributes that is chosen to uniquely identify each instance of an entity. If there is a list of candidate keys, then one needs to be designated as the PK.

The alternate key (AK) is the attribute or group of attributes that is not chosen as a primary key to uniquely identify each instance of an entity. There are alternate keys when there are more than one candidate key that may be chosen to be the primary key.

It is important to pick a primary key that is the most efficient for the application. The decision between which key will be primary and which will be alternate in a BI application is usually based on which one is best for querying, especially when many joins are used. The best key in this scenario has a numeric or integer data type, because it is much more efficient for indexing, sorting, and joining.

Foreign Key

The foreign key (FK) is a primary key of a parent entity that is contributed to a child entity across a relationship. That means there are attributes, such as customer ID, salesperson ID, territory ID, and bill-to address ID, that are primary keys in various other entities. There is a customer entity and a salesperson entity that have those keys as primary keys. They are placed in the sales order header, so they identify who bought it, who sold it, and what territory it was bought in. This is the quick way to be able to join those entities and collect the attributes that are related to the foreign key, which could be customer, salesperson, territory, or something else.

REFERENTIAL INTEGRITY

Referential integrity (RI) is a term used with relational databases to describe the integrity of the business relationships represented in the schema. It ensures that relationships between tables remain consistent. As it applies to a logical data model, RI encompasses the rules that determine the actions that are taken when parent or child rows are inserted, updated, or deleted in a database. None of these actions—inserting, updating or deleting—can violate the relationships that have been defined.

RI includes enforcing relationship cardinality rules (e.g., one-to-many, many-to-one, etc.) and the various types of relationship models (e.g., identifying, nonidentifying optional, nonidentifying mandatory, and many-to-many). There are two primary approaches to implementing RI:

1. Leverage database functionality, such as foreign key constraints and triggers. Using this approach, when data is inserted, updated, or deleted in the database, it will enforce referential integrity.
2. Develop data integration processes such as ETL code. With this approach, the data integration processes will examine the data that is being inserted, updated, or deleted; determine what the relationship rules are for processing; and then take the appropriate action. This is the best practice.

The first approach appears to be the most straightforward because it uses prebuilt database functionality without the need for any custom coding. If the relationships are properly implemented in the database, it is guaranteed that referential integrity will be enforced. There are two significant drawbacks to this approach, however:

- First, database performance can be adversely affected when using this approach.
- Second, and most importantly, database inserts, updates, and deletions can only occur if all the data related to the relationships is available at the same time. Although this condition is met in transaction processing, it is often not the case in BI applications where data is being gathered from many different source systems that have different update frequencies and operate under different business rules. This means that if you use the first method, many BI-related database updates might not be completed, which then results in significant amounts of data never being updated or made available for analysis. Under these conditions, it is best to choose the second approach of developing code.

For these reasons, transactional applications commonly enforce referential integrity by using the first method of relying on the database. In BI implementations, the best practice has been the second method of developing data integration code that can systematically process data under agreed-upon rules to enforce referential integrity. An emerging best practice has been to define database referential integrity and then to turn it off during loads if ETL-enforced RI is needed to load data.

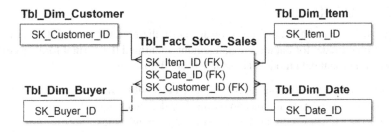

FIGURE 8.13

Referential integrity.

Figure 8.13 shows a fact table for store sales—*Tbl_Fact_Store_Sales*. Four entities surround *Tbl_Fact_Store_Sales* with the following relationships:

- One-to-many relationship between the entity table item *Tbl_Dim_Item*, which is the product being sold at the store.
- One-to-many relationship between the entity of date *Tbl_Dim_Date*, which is when the product was sold at the store.
- One-to-many relationship between the entity of customer *Tbl_Dim_Customer*, which is the customer who bought the product.

Within *Tbl_Fact_Store_Sales* are three foreign keys that are used to define the primary key of that particular entity. Any of those three entities (*SK_Item_ID*, *SK_Date_ID*, or *SK_Customer_ID*) can exist on their own. But you cannot have a store sale without selling a product to a customer at a particular point in time. That is how referential integrity is defined. The store sale cannot occur unless those three foreign keys are brought into the entity.

Additionally, the example shows the buyer (*Tbl_Dim_Buyer*), which is a one-to-many relationship, but is optional in this case. There could be a buyer who actually bought the product from another company, or the purchase could have been in another business transaction. So, this is an optional relationship that is not enforced through referential integrity.

NORMALIZATION

The ER model is used for transactional systems primarily because it minimizes data redundancy and ensures data integrity. The approach to reduce redundancy is called normalization, which is a formal data modeling approach to examining and validating a model and putting it into a particular normalized form. The ER model is often called a third normal form (3NF) or a normalized model. The advantage of this process is that each attribute that belongs to an entity is going to be assigned a unique position within the data model. The goal is to have minimal or no redundancy throughout the data model, and normalization helps achieve this goal.

The downside of normalization is that it can adversely affect performance and deadlines if strictly enforced. ERP systems can have tens of thousands of tables. This, of course, has an impact on performance anyway based on the number of joins and tables that have to be updated. Adding the effort of normalizing a large model can take an inordinate amount of time to design and to code.

NORMALIZATION LEVELS

There are precise definitions and approaches toward normalizing a database. Edgar Frank Codd, who invented the relational model for database management, identified the normal forms as different states of the normalized relational data model. Those levels are defined as:

- First normal form (1NF), which has no repeating groups within it.
- Second normal form (2NF), which has no partial-key dependencies.
- Third normal form (3NF), which has no non-key interdependencies.
- Fourth normal form (4NF), which has no independent multiple relationships.
- Fifth normal form (5NF), which has no semantically-related multiple relationships.

Like cardinality, normalization is an obscure concept that requires close examination to really understand the differences. Fortunately, this classic, yet challenging modeling technique leads to whatever level of normalization is required. The application of the normalization rules are cumulative from 1NF to 5NF.

Most operational systems or transactional systems are implemented in the third normal form. 3NF is considered the best practice in that it enables transactional integrity while balancing complexity and performance. Although there are higher levels of normalization, they are rarely used in transactional systems and never used in BI applications.

NORMALIZING AN ENTITY

There are three steps to develop a third normal form database. They are shown at a high level below, and then in further detail in the subsequent sections.

1. 1NF—Eliminate repeating groups. Make a separate table for each set of attributes (in essence, this is creating an entity). Identify a primary key for each table. If you cannot define a primary key, then you have not split up the tables into the sets of related attributes creating an entity, and you need to repeat this step.
2. 2NF—Eliminate redundant data stored in different entities. If an attribute depends on anything other than the primary key (could be a compound key), then remove it as a separate table.
3. 3NF—Eliminate non-key interdependencies. If you have defined the primary key and the keys within that, then all the attributes in that entity need to be related to that key. For example, if you have customer or product, you can only have attributes that are related to the customer or the product within the entity. Otherwise, remove them and put them into a separate table, as they are most likely separate entities. With these steps completed, you have defined a 3NF schema.

FIRST NORMAL FORM—1NF

The first step to ultimately normalize a database to third normal form is to eliminate repeating groups, creating a first normal form.

Refer to Figure 8.14 and ask the following question for each attribute: does this attribute occur more than once for any instance?

- If it does not, then you have no repeating groups, and you can move on.

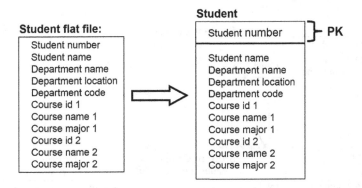

FIGURE 8.14

1NF example.

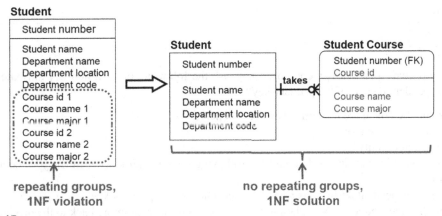

FIGURE 8.15

1NF example continued.

- If it does, you need to:
  - Build a new entity.
  - Move all the repeating attributes to the new entity.
  - Set the attributes for the new entity's primary key.
  - Build an identifying relationship from the original entity (the one that had the repeating groups to begin with) to the new entity, where you moved those repeating attributes.

As shown in Figure 8.15, you slowly decompose the entities until you have no repeating attributes, so each entity stands alone by itself.

SECOND NORMAL FORM—2NF

The second step is to eliminate redundant data and get into second normal form (see Figure 8.16). If attributes are not dependent on the primary key, place them into a separate entity. For only those entities

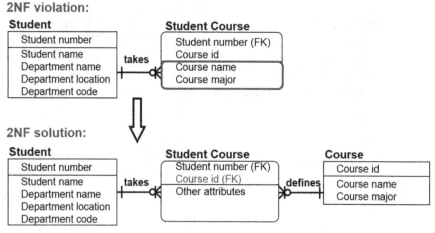

FIGURE 8.16

2NF example.

that have a primary key that is a composite key, ask the following of each non-key attribute: is this attribute dependent on part of the primary key?

- If it is not, then there are no partial-key dependencies.
- If it is, then you need to:
  - Build a new entity.
  - Move out all the attributes that have the following same partial-key dependency to the new entity.
  - Use the dependent attribute as a key or determine a better primary key.
  - Build, name, and identify a relationship from the new entity pointing back to the original entity that had the partial-key dependencies.

As Figure 8.16 shows, a stepwise refinement further decomposes the entities, so they can stand on their own.

THIRD NORMAL FORM—3NF

The final step is to eliminate the columns not dependent on the key, which creates the third normal form as shown in Figure 8.17. For each non-key attribute, ask the following: does this attribute depend on some other non-key attribute?

- If it does not, then there are no non-key interdependencies.
- But if it does, once again, you need to:
  - Build a new entity to contain all attributes with this same non-key dependency.
  - Use the dependent attribute as the primary key.
  - Build and name a nonidentifying, nonmandatory (meaning optional) relationship from the new entity back to the original entity.

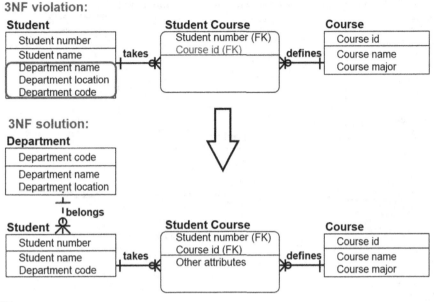

FIGURE 8.17

3NF example.

So the third step, to recap, is to decompose an attribute and spin it off when there are attributes that depend on the non-key attributes. Attributes that are related to one another get split out into their own entity.

After the three normalization steps, you reach the third normal form data model, which is generally the area of normalization that is needed to support enterprise applications.

ER MODEL RECAP

The examples up to this point have shown the various building blocks of the ER model. See Figure 8.18 to see how it all comes together with the attributes, not just the entity and the primary keys, defined.

The example shows a sales order with various products purchased by a customer. It shows *SalesOrderHeader*, which has the ID (the primary key) and various attributes related to the order ship date, due date, status of the order, purchase order number, the account number, the customer ID, etc. It has a one-to-many relationship with *SalesOrderDetail*, which has the product ID, order quantity, unit price, and other items related to line item details of the sale.

Putting it into real-world terms helps put the elements of the example into perspective, so you can see how it all comes together:

- The customer order, which is *SalesOrderHeader*, has a one-to-many relationship to *SalesOrderDetail*, because a customer makes the purchase, creating the sale.
- There are attributes related to the *Customer* entity, because customers are people with attributes such as first name, last name, and email address.
- The sales order, *SalesOrderDetail*, has attributes, such as quantity ordered and unit price.

Sales Order bought by a Customer with various Products in it:

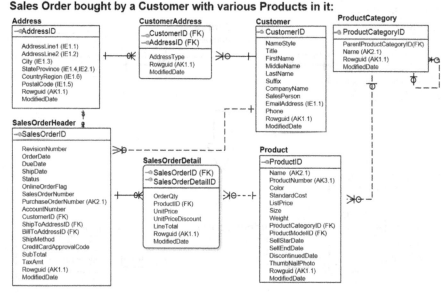

FIGURE 8.18

ER model recap.

- The *Product* entity shows the details of a typical product, such as color, standard cost, list price, size, and weight.

Taking the entity model and expanding it to include the attributes shows how much sense the model makes:

- There is *Product*, which becomes part of the product category that was a self-referencing (or recursive) relationship, where multiple products are grouped in product categories that are then grouped in product categories themselves.
- There is *Customer*, which has a customer address, and some attributes related to it.
- There is the generic *Address*, which is referenced by the *CustomerAddress* and also referenced by *SalesOrderHeader*, because the order header has multiple related addresses (ship-to address, bill-to address, etc.)

Although data modeling often seems esoteric, it is an effective data design technique to represent data in its business context. Reviewing the above example illustrates how the company sales can be represented with entities such as *Customer*, *Product*, *Address*, *SalesOrderHeader*, and *SalesOrderDetail*.

LIMITS AND PURPOSE OF NORMALIZATION

There are issues with normalization. The structures can get very complex when ERP applications have thousands of tables. It can be difficult to understand a model that large. Of course, performance can be an issue: querying is especially difficult when you have so many tables to join.

Fortunately, for those of us working in BI, most ER modeling is done for transactional systems, so we do not have to create models for thousands of tables. But it is good to understand the model, because we need to access, reference, and use those enterprise applications, and we should know how they are constructed.

Understanding ER modeling also helps you learn dimensional modeling, because the entity, relationship, and attributes are all building blocks for the dimensional model. This will be covered in the next chapter.

The obvious question is why you should go through the process of normalization, especially to third normal form. The reason is that normalization creates the cleanest entity relationship model available. The entities only have attributes related to the entities themselves, and you can establish relationships between the entities that make sense. This makes it easier to define the data, and the relationships and interdependencies are more clearly identified. Because only the attributes within the entities exist, the ambiguities are resolved. The data model can be more flexible, and it is easier to maintain, not only because of the lack of redundancy, but also because the entities, the attributes, and the relationships are clearly defined.

DIMENSIONAL MODELING

INFORMATION IN THIS CHAPTER:

* Dimensional modeling
* Facts
* Dimensions hierarchies and keys
* Schemas
* ER vs. dimensional modeling
* Purpose of dimensional
* Fact tables
* Consistency and conforming
* Advanced dimensions and facts

INTRODUCTION TO DIMENSIONAL MODELING

Like enterprise relationship (ER) modeling, dimensional modeling is a logical design technique. Dimensional modeling is much better suited for business intelligence (BI) applications and data warehousing (DW). It depicts business processes throughout an enterprise and organizes that data and its structure in a logical way. The purpose of dimensional modeling is to enable BI reporting, query, and analysis. The hybrid dimensional-normalized model is best for supporting DW integration demands.

The key concepts in dimensional modeling are facts, dimensions, and attributes. There are different types of facts, depending on whether they can be added together. Dimensions can have different hierarchies, and have attributes that define the who, what, where, and why of the dimensional model. The grain, or level of granularity, is another key concept with dimensional modeling, as it determines the level of detail.

Facts, dimensions, and attributes can be organized in several ways, called schemas. The choice of schema depends on variables such as the type of reporting that the model needs to facilitate and the type of BI tool being used. Building a dimensional model includes additional puzzle pieces such as calendar and time dimensions, and more complicated pieces such as degenerative dimensions and consolidated fact tables.

In addition to explaining these concepts, this chapter will compare the approach between an ER model and a dimensional model.

See the book's Website www.BIguidebook.com for data modeling templates.

HIGH-LEVEL VIEW OF A DIMENSIONAL MODEL

As shown in Figure 9.1, there are two key entities in a dimensional model: facts (measures) and dimensions (context). The example shows these elements:

- The fact *Tbl_Fact_Store_Sales* is at the core of the dimensional model.
- Four surrounding dimensions that define and put into context the store sales:
  - On the upper right corner is the item *Tbl_Dim_Item*, which is what products were sold.
  - Below that is the date, *Tbl_Dim_Date*, which is when those products were sold.
  - On the lower left corner is the customer, *Tbl_Dim_Customer*, who bought the products.
  - On the upper left corner is the buyer, *Tbl_Dim_Buyer*, who bought the product for the store.

In context, the example shows that when someone buys a product we can use this model to capture information about that business process. The details will be covered in much greater detail in the following sections.

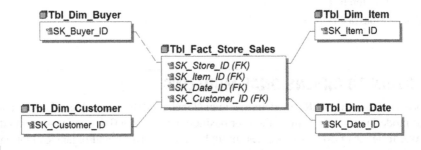

FIGURE 9.1

Dimensional modeling overview.

FACTS

A fact is a measurement of a business activity, such as a business event or transaction, and is generally numeric. Examples of facts are sales, expenses, and inventory levels. Numeric measurements may include counts, dollar amounts, percentages, or ratios.

Facts can be aggregated or derived. For example, you can sum up the total revenue or calculate the profitability of a set of sales transactions. Facts provide the measurements of how well or how poorly the business is performing. A fact is also referred to as organizational performance measure.

Fact tables are normalized and contain little redundancy. Fact table record counts can become very large. Ninety-percent of the data in a dimensional model is typically located in the fact tables. The key dimensional modeling design concerns when working with the data in fact tables are how to minimize and standardize it and make it consistent.

FACT TABLE KEYS

Fact tables are composed of two types of columns: keys and measures. The first, the key column, consists of a group of foreign keys (FK) that point to the primary keys of dimensional tables that are associated with this fact table to enable business analysis. The relationships between fact tables and the dimensions are one-to-many, as explained in the ER modeling section of Chapter 8.

Figure 9.2 shows the key columns in a fact table of sales (*Fact_OnlineSales*):

- *DateKey*—Date and time purchase was made
- *StoreKey*—Online store in which purchase was made
- *ProductKey*—Product that was bought
- *CustomerKey*—Customer who made purchase
- *PromotionKey*—Sales promotion
- *CurrencyKey*—Currency used to make purchase

The primary key of a fact table is typically a multipart key consisting of the combination of foreign keys that can uniquely identify the fact table row. This key may also be referred to as a compound or concatenated key. The multipart key may be a subset of the foreign keys such as in our example: *DateKey*, *StoreKey*, *ProductKey*, and *CustomerKey* may uniquely identify each row in the sales fact table.

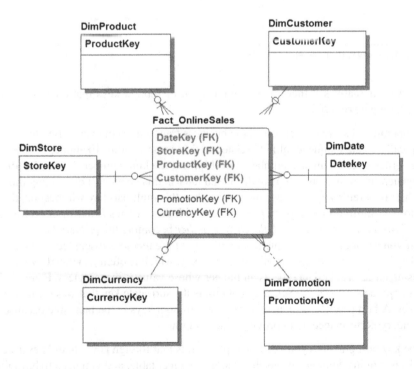

FIGURE 9.2

Fact table—keys.

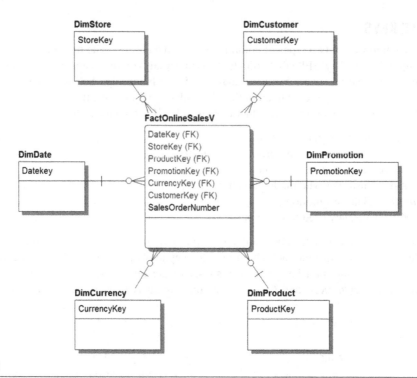

FIGURE 9.3

Fact tables—primary key with degenerative dimensions.

You have two alternatives if there is no combination of foreign keys that creates the uniqueness required for creating a primary key:

- First, the operational systems that record the business transactions or events used to populate fact tables typically create unique identifiers related to those transactions. Examples of these identifiers are a sales order number, invoice number, and shipment tracking number. These identifiers are called degenerative dimensions and are discussed later in this chapter. If combining this identifier with a subset of foreign keys creates uniqueness, then this multipart key will become the primary key. Figure 9.3 illustrates this type of primary key with the columns *DateKey*, *StoreKey*, *Product-Key*, and *CustomerKey* paired with *SalesOrderNumber* becoming the primary key.
- Second, if you cannot identify unique rows with any of the methods discussed so far, create a primary key based on a surrogate key. A surrogate key, which is often generated by the database system using an IDENTITY data type, is an integer whose value is meaningless. Figure 9.4 illustrates this approach. The *OnlineSalesKey* column is the surrogate key that was created as the primary key. A best practice is to index each of the foreign keys in the fact table because this will speed up query performance by improving joins and filters.

One of the key best practices you need to implement is that foreign keys should never be null. Performing analysis requires joining various dimensions to a fact table, and you need to have the value of the foreign key in order to guarantee valid business results. Each of the foreign keys points back to a

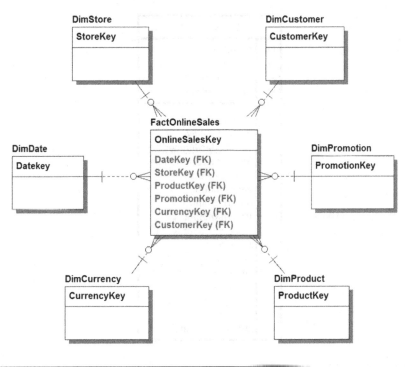

FIGURE 9.4

Fact table—primary key is a surrogate key.

corresponding dimension, which provides attributes relevant to the internet sales event such as who the customer is, where he or she lives, his or her age, and other demographic attributes.

FACT TABLE MEASURES

The second type of column in a fact table is the actual measures of the business activity such as the sales revenue and order quantity. Every measurement has a grain, which is the level of detail in the measurement of an event such as a unit of measure, currency used, or ending daily balance of an account. For example, the grain of currency could be to the dollar amount, or be more granular and include cents. Granularity is determined by its data source.

The circled portion in Figure 9.5 shows several measures of an internet sale: *SalesQuantity*, *SalesAmount*, *ReturnAmount*, *ReturnQuantity*, *DiscountAmount*, *DiscountQuantity*, and *TotalCost* that apply to a customer for a product purchased at a specific time. All of these measures are related to the business event (the sale) that the fact represents and they have a level of granularity related to that event.

When creating and defining columns and measures, ensure that all rows have a single, uniform grain. In other words, they must be relevant. If the example is buying a product, you must have measures that are relevant to that particular purchase in order for the query and the report to make any sense to a business person. In this example, the fact table should have total cost rather than unit cost when

	Fact_OnlineSales
PK	DateKey
PK	StoreKey
PK	ProductKey
PK	CustomerKey
	CurrencyKey
	PromotionKey
	SalesOrderNumber
	SalesOrderLineNumber
	SalesQuantity
	SalesAmount
	ReturnQuantity
	ReturnAmount
	DiscountQuantity
	DiscountAmount
	TotalCost
	UnitCost
	UnitPrice
	DW_ETLLoadID
	DW_LoadDate
	DW_UpdateDate

FIGURE 9.5

Fact table—granularity.

comparing it with sales quantity and sales amount; otherwise, business ratios and aggregating orders will result erroneous measures.

It's an accepted best practice to store the lowest, or the most detailed grain captured in the business process. In Figure 9.5, this would be storing order line level detail rather than summarized order header details. Historically, data warehousing and business intelligence used summarized data, so queries and reports were less detailed. That practice was based on infrastructure and processing limitations that no longer are applicable. Now, it's an established practice to store at the lowest transactional level of detail that's available from a transactional or operational systems. This enables the most flexibility, because as soon as you summarize something, you lose the detail, making the data less useful. Granularity allows extensibility; having the lowest level of detail allows you to aggregate and manipulate facts or measures.

TYPES OF FACTS

After you've defined the measures and their level of grain in the facts, you need to determine the numeric attributes of the types of measures that are being stored in the fact. There are three types of measures: additive, semiadditive, and nonadditive.

Additive Facts

An additive fact is the easiest to define and manage. It's simply a measure of the fact table that can be added across all dimensions. The simplest example of an additive fact is the quantity of items you bought in an online store—such as the number of books. Additive measures enable the fact to be aggregated by all applicable dimensions, which in our example is customer, store, product, and date.

Semiadditive Facts
Semiadditive facts are measurements in the fact table that can be added across some dimensions but not others. Examples of these measures are bank account balances, the number of students attending a class, or inventory levels. You can't simply add 12 months of account balances and get how much money somebody has in a bank account. In this case, you would average those balances over 12 months. However, at the point in time that they were measured (at the end of the month), you could add the account balances of all your customers and get the total account balances at that point in time.

Nonadditive Facts
Nonadditive facts are measures in fact tables that can't be added across any dimensions. Examples of these include unit prices, ratios, and temperatures; even though they are numbers they aren't supposed to be added. In a real-life example, a client of mine was taking samples of water levels in a particular state, and those ratios and water levels couldn't just be added together. They had to look at them from a scientific perspective. Nonadditive facts can't be added like a typical SQL query that is simply summed across a column.

It's important to understand the concepts of additive, semiadditive, and nonadditive facts because aggregating or summarizing data is a big part of reporting and analysis. It's one of the key benefits of using dimensional models, and one of the things for which it is most often used. After you define measures and determine whether they are additive, nonadditive, or semiadditive facts, you need to establish how they can be analyzed in BI. It is the BI team's responsibility to ensure that the business people performing the analysis know what type of measure they are accessing to prevent the risk of using data inappropriately.

DIMENSIONS
A dimension is an entity that establishes the business context for the measures (facts) used by an enterprise. Dimensions define the who, what, where, and why of the dimensional model, and group similar attributes into a category or subject area. Examples of dimensions are product, geography, customers, employees, and time. Whereas facts are numeric, dimensions are descriptive in nature (although some of those descriptions, such as a product list price, may be numeric). Creating a dimension enables facts to store attributes in a single place, rather than multiplying them redundantly across the rows of the fact tables. The way they are connected is through the foreign key in the fact tables, which links back to the dimension table. This is a level of normalization—it eliminates redundancy.

Another benefit of dimensions is that in addition to saving storage space and reducing bandwidth for repeatedly moving those attributes across the network, it enables dimensional attributes to change without having to alter the underlying facts—avoiding potentially complex and time-consuming processing.

Dimensions keep the database from being overrun with redundant data. With all the attributes in a dimension table, they don't have to be repeated in the fact tables. Take Amazon, for example. The data for an individual sale will contain the product identification number, but will not repeat all the attributes of the product (color, description, reviews, etc.). Those attributes are in a dimension, and each individual sale of that product just points to them.

From a business perspective, the key purpose of dimensions it to use their attributes to filter and analyze data based on performance measures. In Figure 9.6, the dimension is a product, *DimProduct*, with its attributes including name, weight, size, color, and list price. When the product dimension is joined with a sales fact table, a business person could examine sales based on one or more of these specific product attributes, such as analyzing sales by color or size.

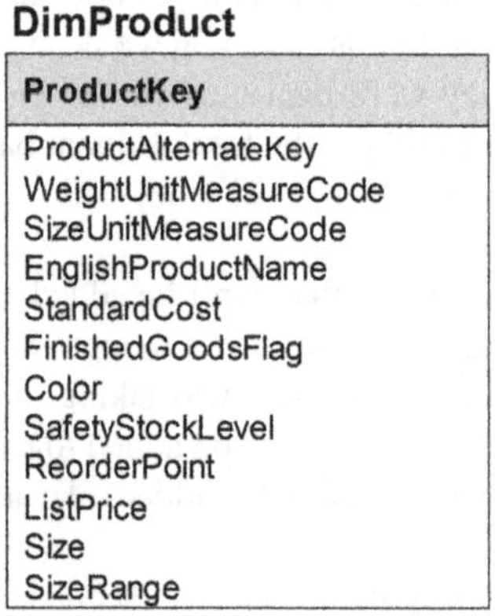

DimProduct

ProductKey
ProductAltemateKey
WeightUnitMeasureCode
SizeUnitMeasureCode
EnglishProductName
StandardCost
FinishedGoodsFlag
Color
SafetyStockLevel
ReorderPoint
ListPrice
Size
SizeRange

FIGURE 9.6

Dimension—basic example.

To be useful in analysis a dimensional attribute needs these key characteristics:

- Descriptive, so business people and those designing the BI applications can understand it.
- Complete, with no missing values.
- Unique, because it's critical that values are uniquely identifiable.
- Valid, so the data is useful to the business.

DIMENSION HIERARCHY

Another aspect of the business context created by dimensions is that they are often hierarchical; they group things together in ways that an enterprise would measure itself. These hierarchies represent many-to-one relationships. Examples of hierarchies include:

- Organizational structures, such as a marketing or sales organization.
- Product or service categories.
- Geographic groupings such as sales territories.
- Time. Years breaks down to quarters, months, weeks, hours, days, minutes, on down to seconds. This is the classic hierarchy.

Figure 9.7 shows the geography dimension *DimGeography* with attributes that define a hierarchy. The highest level of the hierarchy is a country or region (*CountryRegionCode*) that then breaks down to a state or province (*StateProvinceCode*), then breaks down to a city, and finally into a postal code.

DimGeography

GeographyKey
PostalCode
City
StateProvinceCode
StateProvinceName
CountryRegionCode

FIGURE 9.7

Dimensional hierarchy.

This example works for the United States and Canada, but may need to be modified for other countries.

The geography example shows the hierarchy and how, using BI terminology, you can drill up and down and across. For example, you can view sales at the country level or drill down to the detailed state level, city level, and finally down to postal code. This allows you to aggregate the data. You would use a SQL "Group By" for example, if the data was organized correctly to group the data by a particular column or attribute within that hierarchy and to sum the data appropriately. That summing would use additive facts or measures.

DIMENSION KEYS AND SURROGATE KEYS

A key concept in constructing dimensions is that each row of a dimension table is unique. In a dimension table, the primary keys are a single field compared to facts, which use a grouping of foreign keys as their primary key.

Figure 9.8 shows two dimensions, *DimProduct* and *DimGeography*. Each has single fields, *ProductKey* for *DimProduct* and *GeographyKey* for *DimGeography* that are used as the primary key for those respective tables.

DimProduct

ProductKey
ProductAlternateKey
WeightUnitMeasureCode
SizeUnitMeasureCode
EnglishProductName
StandardCost
FinishedGoodsFlag
Color
SafetyStockLevel
ReorderPoint
ListPrice
Size
SizeRange

DimGeography

GeographyKey
PostalCode
City
StateProvinceCode
StateProvinceName
CountryRegionCode

FIGURE 9.8

Dimension keys.

Surrogate Keys

One of the best practices to emerge for dimensions is using a surrogate key as the primary key as depicted in Figure 9.8. A surrogate key, which is often generated by the database system, is an integer whose value is meaningless (see the following section on smart keys for an explanation). Date and time dimensions are accepted exceptions to the meaningless value criteria, and are covered later in this chapter.

Note: if the maximum number of rows in a table is greater than 2.1 billion, you need to use a bigint or equivalent data type rather than int.

In Chapter 8, we discussed how the processes for designating a primary key for ER modeling involves selecting a key that uniquely identifies the entity. If there is more than one possibility they are called candidate keys, and the keys not selected are alternate keys. Even though transactional systems will have already created primary keys that can be used in a dimensional model, it has become best practice to designate that key as an alternate key and create a surrogate key as the primary key instead.

The reasons to create a surrogate key are:

- When gathering dimensional data from multiple source systems, there are often inconsistent or incompatible primary keys used across these systems.
- Primary keys from source systems often change over time with different naming or numbering conventions being used at different times. Additionally, over time, source applications may be replaced by newer systems, or mergers may create the need to replace systems.
- Primary key consistency may be maintained by source systems for shorter periods than the enterprise analytical needs dictate.
- Source systems may be using smart keys.

An additional best practice is to maintain the source system's primary key as an alternate key in the dimension. This is also called the source system's natural key. If there are multiple source systems with natural keys you should add an attribute that identifies the source system. This results in a multipart alternate key to identify the natural keys. In Figure 9.9, *CustomerSK* is the primary key in the customer dimension, *CustomerNK* is the natural key in the dimension and primary key in the source system, *SOR_NK* is the SOR (systems of record) indicator and the multipart alternate key is the *SOR_NK* and *CustomerNK* columns.

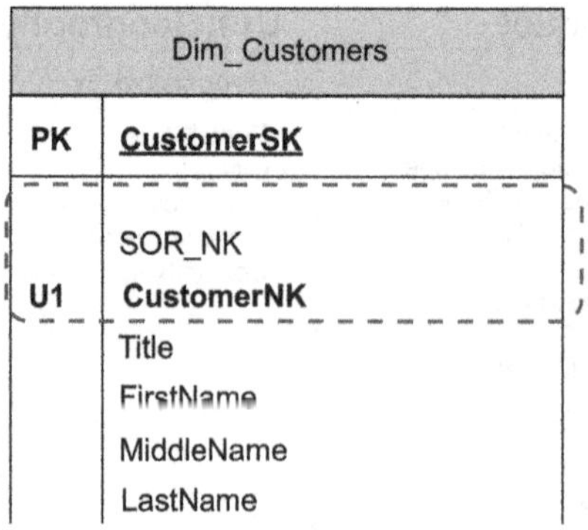

FIGURE 9.9

Surrogate and natural keys.

Smart Keys

Operational and transactional systems sometimes define or identify items such as products with smart keys. These are alphanumeric strings, maybe 24 or 40 characters in length. The character string is typically divided into substrings. The substrings have meaning, hence the word smart key. For example, the first three characters might designate what manufacturing plant the product was built in. The next five characters might designate the materials that were used to construct the product. The next 10 might designate the size or some other characteristics of the construction of the product, and so on.

In the 1990s and 2000s, when some operational systems were developed, smart keys were a way to put a lot of intelligence in the key, especially because of limited memory and storage. But today that intelligence has worked against most of the operational systems. There are two main reasons for this:

- First, in most operational systems, the smart keys change over time. The substrings and their meanings and definitions change. So when you're trying to get historical view of that smart key, you'll have considerable inconsistencies.
- Second, because each operational system has its own arbitrary definition of what those smart keys mean, when you had an enterprise that had multiple operational systems (and many enterprises do), there were inconsistencies in the keys that made it difficult to uniquely identify a product across an enterprise.

The solution to the smart key problem was to create the surrogate key—a meaningless key that would be the consistent and unique identifier in a dimension.

Not NULL Values

The foreign keys used as the primary key in fact tables should never contain null values. For an example of how a null value gets assigned, suppose a row in a sales fact table has a null value in the customer identifier column that is the foreign key linked to the customer dimension. The null value was input into that column when, loading the data from the source systems, the ETL process could not find a customer associated with that sale because the value was unknown, missing or invalid.

Null values are confusing to both people and BI tools. If you understand SQL, you know there's a difference between querying results when joining on keys with null or nonnull values. Using our example again, a join between a sales fact and a customer dimension would only include the sales rows that had a value (nonnull) in the customer key. This means that if a business person was trying to analyze total sales she would be missing those sales with null customer keys. This condition clearly results in misleading analysis that potentially creates business risk. And this condition can be exacerbated if other foreign keys also have nulls.

The best practices that address this potential business risk include:

- Create row(s) in each dimension that are used when dimensional values are unknown, missing, invalid, or other conditions in which referential integrity is not met.
- Because the numbering convention for surrogate keys is a positive integer, use negative integers such as −999 for "missing" row keys.
- Dimensional rows have surrogate keys along with attributes used for naming and describing them. Create a standard name and description for these rows used across all dimensions, e.g., "Missing," "Unknown," or "Invalid."

- At a minimum, designate one row per dimension table for missing values, but if it is important to be able to identify different conditions then use multiple rows. If there are multiple conditions handled then use standard numbering and naming for each of these conditions across all dimensions.

This may seem trivial, but BI tools, just like SQL queries with joins, will result in misleading or inaccurate results if nulls exist in the fact table foreign keys. This exposes the business to needless risks.

Benefits

The primary benefit of using a surrogate key as a dimension's primary key is to provide an identifier that is consistent and unique across source systems and time, and that is independent of business systems. An additional benefit of the surrogate key is that, being integer-based, it is a great data type to index and join in a relational model.

To summarize, dimensions should have the following characteristics:

- Unique rows
- Surrogate keys used as primary keys
- Non-NULL primary keys

SCHEMAS

You've now learned about dimensions, facts and attributes. It's time to put those pieces together and fill out the dimensional data model jigsaw puzzle. There are three types of schemas for building a dimensional model: star schema, a snowflake schema, and multidimensional schema.

You choose which schema to use when building the dimensional model by considering these questions:

- What kind of analysis are you trying to perform on that data and how complex is it?
- What are the analytical requirements and restrictions?
- How consistent is the data you want to query and analyze?
- What BI tool do you plan to use? Although different tools may appear to show the same type of data, results, and graphs, they can be very different under the covers, and rely on a specific schema for the best results.

STAR SCHEMA

The star schema is the most common schema for dimensional models. It is a fact table surrounded by multiple dimension tables, as shown in Figure 9.10.

The example shows a fact, *FactInternetSales*; this example is about selling products online. The multiple dimension tables for this fact are:

- *DimSalesTerritory*—where the sales territory is located
- *DimPromotions*—what promotions are selling products
- *DimCurrency*—what currency is being used, such as dollars or pounds
- *DimCustomer*—who's buying it
- *DimDate*—when it's being sold
- *DimProduct*—what products they are selling

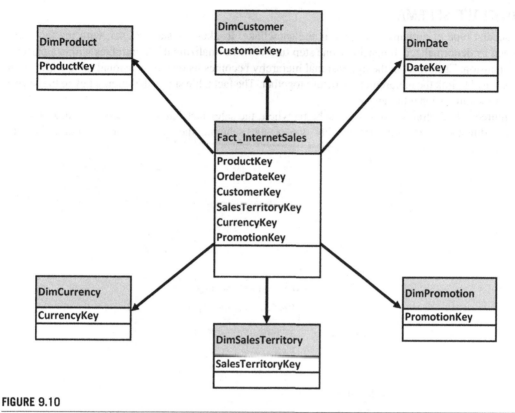

FIGURE 9.10

Star schema.

And, of course, filtering or grouping by attributes in different dimension tables enables a business person to analyze who is buying what, where are they located, when they are buying, and if they are buying using promotions.

The star schema is a compromise between a fully normalized and a denormalized model. Fact tables are where the majority of the data stored in the dimensional model is located, so it's important that facts are stored in normalized tables. This normalization is essential for minimal redundancy, ease of maintenance, and improved query performance.

Dimensions, on the other hand, are denormalized tables containing attributes that are often spread out across multiple tables if a 3NF data model is used. In Figure 9.10, each of the dimensions listed has descriptive attributes in a denormalized or "flattened" table. Even hierarchies that have each of their levels represented by a separate entity in an ER model are flattened into one dimensional table in a star schema.

The advantages of the star schema are that it's great for query, performance, and analytics. It supports tasks that business people normally perform when they are using pivot tables in spreadsheets, so it is very intuitive to them. It's easy for business people to use and has fast query performance because BI tools are built to take advantage of the star schema construct.

SNOWFLAKE SCHEMA

The second type of dimension schema is the snowflake. It takes the star schema, with the facts surrounded by denormalized dimensions, one step further by normalizing the hierarchies within a particular dimension. Each level in the dimensional hierarchy becomes its own dimensional table with parent keys created to link the hierarchical structure together. The fact table stores the foreign key to the lowest level of the dimensional hierarchy.

Figure 9.11 illustrates a snowflake schema where the sales fact *FactInternetSales*, is linked to the product dimension, *DimProduct*. If this was a star schema, the fact would just point back to

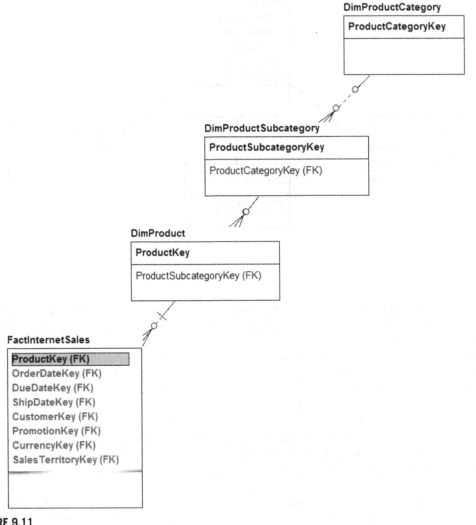

FIGURE 9.11

Snowflake schema.

DimProduct, just as the first table above it does in Figure 9.10. But in a snowflake schema, the dimensional product table is split into subsequent levels of a product hierarchy. Its parts include:

- *DimProduct*, which is the core or bottom level of the hierarchy. If this was a bike store this might be the specific bike, biking shorts, or water bottle sold.
- *DimProductSubcategory*, the next level, which rolls out of various products into subcategories. For the bike store, the bike-related subcategories might be road, mountain, and hybrid.
- *DimProductCategory*, the highest level of the hierarchy. For the bike store, the top-level categories might be bikes, clothing, and accessories.

In this example, the product dimension in a star schema is split into three tables representing the three levels of the hierarchy—product, product subcategory, and product category in a snowflake schema. Summarizing by product data for internet sales would require joining the sales fact table to each level of the product hierarchy until the highest level required for the summarization is reached.

This approach is most often used with dimensions that have a very large number of rows with deep hierarchies that are relatively static. If the number of levels in the hierarchy is relatively constant, developers prefer this type of model, because it's closer to the ER model used in the source systems.

Some BI tools are built specifically to leverage snowflake schemas. The tools use metadata—definitions about the dimensional snowflake model—in order to generate reports and queries. Most BI tools, however, will require the BI developer to "flatten" the hierarchy (see Chapter 14).

Although developers prefer snowflake schemas because they're easier to design, business people find them more difficult to use in analysis. For this reason, the practice is generally discouraged in the dimensional modeling domain. But it still gets used because of the advantages and speed it offers with a particular BI product. Chapter 10 will cover the reasons why it is used.

MULTIDIMENSIONAL SCHEMA

The third dimensional model is the multidimensional schema. It is a hierarchical database that consists of one structure, a multidimensional array. To help understand a multidimensional schema, conceptualize it as a spreadsheet pivot table, which is an approximation of a multidimensional cube. It contains all the detailed and summarized data at the various levels in an array. It's like a big Rubik's Cube,® as shown in Figure 9.12.

The example shows sales facts with dimensions for product, date, and geography; there can be many additional dimensions on the other "sides" of the cube. Each cell of the cube is an actual measure. Depending on what data someone needs to get in that cube, the combination of the different dimensions would get them to the cell with the data they need in that multidimensional array. Dimensional attributes and hierarchies are defined in the multidimensional product's metadata.

Star and snowflake schemas are traditionally stored in relational databases (see Chapter 7 for discussions of other options), whereas multidimensional schemas are stored in multidimensional databases, also called online analytical processing (OLAP) cubes. Whereas relational databases use SQL and specific structural standards—tables, columns, foreign keys—multidimensional database structures vary widely and are proprietary. Multidimensional databases store and aggregate data at the various levels in the hierarchy. They enable drill up and drill down, meaning you can go from the lowest level or the most detail, all the way to summarize data, then back down again through the hierarchy. These databases are specifically designed to understand the multidimensional arrays, the

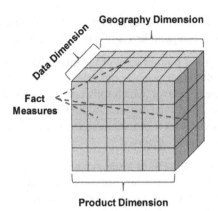

FIGURE 9.12

Multidimensional schema.

hierarchies, what can be added, what's semiadditive, and what's not additive in the cube. Just as tables, columns, constraints, and so on need to be defined for a relational database, the facts, dimensions, hierarchies, and so on need to be defined in the multidimensional database's metadata repository.

MULTIFACT STAR MODELS

Examples of dimensional models, whether star, snowflake, or multidimensional, usually depict them with a single fact table surrounded by dimensions. Although this is a popular illustration and a terrific approach that simplifies explanations, the reality is that data in an enterprise requires multiple facts. Examples of facts are sales, expenses, inventory, and the many other business events associated with running an enterprise.

Figure 9.13 shows two facts: store sales and store inventory (*Tbl_Fact_Store_Sales* and *Tbl_Fact_Store_Inventory*). On the right side are three dimensions that both facts share: the item dimension, the

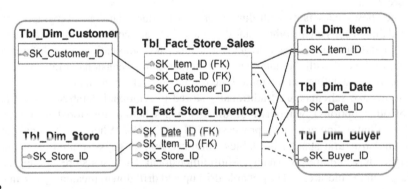

FIGURE 9.13

Multifact star models.

date dimension, and the buyer dimension. The shared dimensions are referred to as conformed dimensions, a concept covered later in this chapter.

On the left side of the example are the customer and store dimensions that are not shared across the two facts. The *Tbl_Dim_Customer* is related to *Tbl_Fact_Store_Sales*, whereas the *Tbl_Dim_Store* is related to *Tbl_Fact_Store_Inventory*.

In a real-world example there might be hundreds or thousands of tables with many different combinations of dimensions sharing various combinations of facts. Although the models get complex, it helps to visualize subsets of the data models as a stars to better understand and validate the models.

ENTITY RELATIONSHIP VERSUS DIMENSIONAL MODELING

ER and dimensional models both depict the same business processes, but as Figure 9.14 shows, the ER model has significantly more entities and relationships than the dimensional model. (You're not expected be able to see the details in the example, this is just to show, at a high level, the difference in complexity.) You saw a similar comparison of ER and dimensional modeling in the previous chapter: Figure 8.3.

In the dimensional model, the dimensions are denormalized and the facts are normalized. Further, in the dimensional model only a subset of facts is selected from the operational system based on analytical need and to reduce complexity. The dimensional model is clearly simpler, easier to navigate, and more understandable than the ER model.

It's important to note that most operational systems today are purchased, whereas most analytical systems are custom-built by the information technology group. So, most information technology groups will be familiar with, or will be using the dimensional modeling approach as opposed to the ER model approach.

COMPARING APPROACHES

ER modeling, sometimes referred to as normalized modeling, is the standard for transactional systems (also called operational or online transactional processing (OLTP) systems). Dimensional modeling is the best practice for BI and OLAP systems. The reason for this stems from how the two systems process and manipulate data.

The data in operational systems is being constantly updated. The main job of these workhorses is transaction throughput. They have to maintain and update a large number of records, so they have to be able to handle high amounts of consistent throughput with large volumes.

Compare that with the BI and reporting systems, which are generally not updating data. Rather, they are copying, extracting, transforming, and loading from operational systems. They are not doing real-time updates like operational systems. The focus is not on transactional throughput once the data is loaded. The focus is on query performance, and gathering and aggregating large sets of data. That's a critical operation. Transactional systems update a small number of data records quite often, whereas BI systems gather and aggregate large sets of data records, but not so often—sometimes over large spans of time. The data from the BI system then get used for reports. See Table 9.1 for a summary of the differences.

The operational system and its accompanying normalized models have minimal redundancy to support the high transaction throughput. Its limited indexes and efficient use of storage space eliminate the

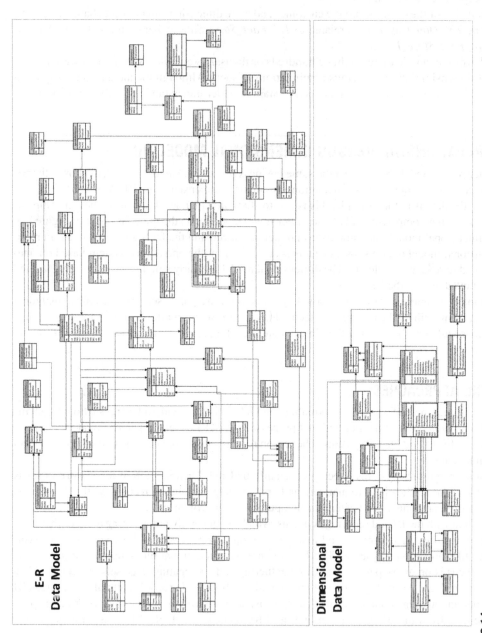

**E-R
Data Model**

**Dimensional
Data Model**

FIGURE 9.14

ER and dimensional models.

Table 9.1 Comparing Operational and BI	
Operational Systems	**BI and Analytics**
Normalized models are standard for OLTP	Dimensional models are standard for BI and OLAP
Highly volatile	Generally not updated
Transaction throughput (updating and maintaining numerous records) is critical	Query performance (gathering and aggregating large sets of records) is critical
Characteristics supporting use of normalized models:	**Characteristics supporting use of dimensional models:**
Minimal redundancy (normalization)	Increased redundancy (denormalization)
Limited index use	Increased index use
Efficient use of storage space	Increased storage space
Eliminate inconsistent data	Consolidate inconsistent data
Few maintenance concerns	Increased maintenance issues

need for consistent data, also contributing to the fast transaction throughput. The system is able to update and maintain records instantaneously.

On the other hand, in BI reporting, there is a lot of redundancy. After all, the warehouse and data marts and whatever else you store on the reporting side are all copies of data that originally was in the operational systems. The BI system depends heavily on indexes and partitioning because it needs much more storage space for reporting, whereas the operational system only needs internal consistency—it doesn't have to be consistent with other systems' data. BI needs to have consistent data consolidated from multiple operating systems, so the inconsistency might not be just in the individual system, but across the various systems. Many of the dimensional constructs are set up to support consistent information.

Because the operational system has no redundancy and limited index usage, there are fewer maintenance concerns. A BI system, however, has more maintenance issues than an operational system because it's storing data over a long period of history, and data does not age well.

WHY THE STRUCTURES MATTER

An important questions is: why do these structures matter for data modeling? Each structure has its purpose, and you need the right structure for the job at hand. The choice is highly dependent on the way the data is used and the type of data warehousing or business intelligence tool. The best practice is to use a normalized ER model for OLTP systems. An operational data store often mirrors the OLTP structure and is geared for operational reporting of OLTP systems.

BI applications and BI-related data stores, on the other hand, are better served with dimensional data models. BI tools will give the best performance with star or snowflakes in querying the relational database. Or, if the BI application is a multidimensional model, then you need to select the proper BI tool that uses that particular multidimensional model.

Figure 9.15 shows, on the ER side, a smaller subset of data with a store's database implemented in an ER model. This example shows a business process. At the top of the example, the customer makes a call; this call has a type. That customer call is related to the customer, which then relates to a customer

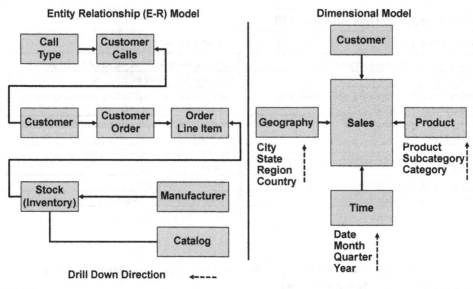

FIGURE 9.15

ER versus dimensional example.

order entity, which then relates to order line item entity, which then relates to where that line item was chosen, which is out of stock. Then, the example relates that to the manufacturer of the catalog that the item was in. It's very process-oriented, and the entities are updated as the business activities progress through a particular business process.

On the dimensional side of the example, the subset of the store's database looks very different from the ER side. At the center of it, the fact is a sales cell. The sales fact table and has four keys to the customer, the geography, the time, and the product. So whereas on the left side in the ER model there is a process- and application-specific design, the right side with the dimensional model has a data- and subject area–driven design. The dimensional model has fewer tables, is more understandable, and is less process-focused.

PURPOSE OF DIMENSIONAL MODELING

Now that you understand why dimensional modeling is the best choice for BI, it's important to understand its purpose and how it fits in with business reporting. The business people in an enterprise will probably never see the actual data models, but they certainly will use the reports or dashboards that are built. So it's important that the models can help generate clear, effective reporting and analysis that will ultimately help business people view the data and make informed decisions for the enterprise. Dimensional modeling is well-suited to the generation of exactly the kind of information business people need to see. Common business uses for these models are displaying the facts (measures) and dimensions in BI reports, OLAP analyses, or spreadsheets. This visualization of the data is very common to the millions of spreadsheet jocks who are analyzing data every day.

MAPPING TO A BUSINESS REPORT

Figure 9.16 shows a business report displaying top employees and top stores ranked by sales revenue. The sales revenue of the top employees is displayed both in tabular form and by a bar chart. The top store sales revenue is displayed in a tabular form and in a pie chart. Facts (measures) are displayed as numbers in the table and graphically as the size of the bars or pie slices. The list of employee and store names are attributes from the *Employee* and *Store* dimensions, respectively. Although not displayed in this example, it would be common for the report to provide filters allowing the business person to select specific attributes of either employees or stores for more detailed analysis. Chapter 14 discusses BI interface design options.

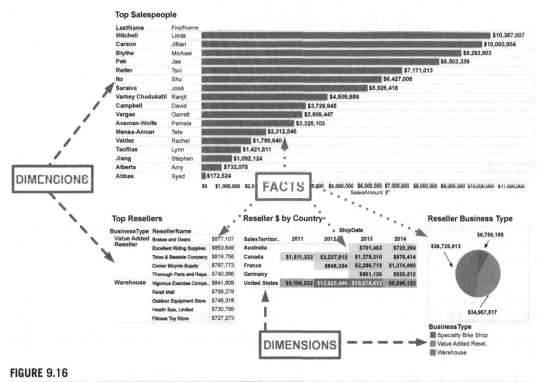

FIGURE 9.16

Mapping to a business report.

MAPPING TO AN OLAP ANALYSIS OR SPREADSHEET

Figure 9.17 provides a view that a business user would see with a data discovery tool, OLAP cube, or spreadsheet pivot table. Dimensions are displayed as labels and headers in this type of interface. In the example, the dimensions are the sales territories, product categories, product subcategories, and time (fiscal year). The main body of the report shows the actual sales revenue numbers. The example also shows, on the left under the measure group, the measures or facts listed, and under

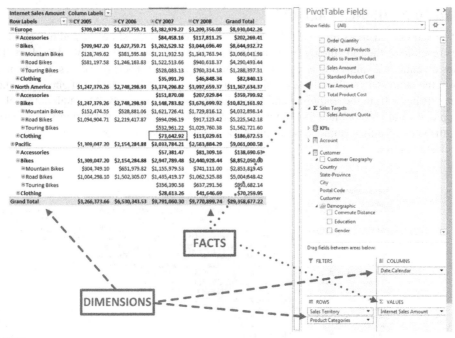

FIGURE 9.17

Mapping to an OLAP analysis.

that the dimensions such as customer, date, employee, product, and sales territory. The visual aspects of the spreadsheet, pivot table, or OLAP cube are set up specifically to leverage the dimensional model.

FACT TABLES

There are three types of fact tables in dimensional modeling: transaction, periodic, and accumulating fact.

- **Transaction fact tables** are the most common in dimensional modeling. They record a business event or transaction, one record at a time, with all the data associated with the event. An example is a sales transaction, such as the purchase of a book on Amazon. The purchase is recorded in the transaction fact table for sales.
- **Periodic fact tables** record snapshots of data for specific time, such as inventory levels at the end of a quarter or account balances at the end of the month. Each row represents a fact at a specific point in time.
- **Accumulating fact tables** store a record for the entire lifetime of the event, showing the activity as it progresses. An example of this, using an internet sales order, is where you record the first event, the order, then you record subsequent dates and events such as when the order was placed,

when a credit card transaction was processed, when the order was shipped, various states during the shipping, then finally when it is delivered to the customer. These are called role-playing date dimensions with events referred to in our example as the order date, ship date, and delivered date.

Table 9.2 shows that each of these types of facts has different properties or characteristics.

Grain: The granularity of each table highlights the first difference. The most detailed grain is stored in a transaction table, where you get a row for every business event related to that fact. Periodic has less detail, with one row covering an entire time period. For example, rather than showing every transaction in your banking account, it shows one row related to the end of month or end of period balance. Finally, the least-detailed grain and fewest rows is the one where you're accumulating facts. For example, you placed an order, and all the dates related to the order data are requested, filled, shipped, etc., and all placed on the same record. That record is updated and in place.

Date dimension: The date dimension for these three facts shows a similar decrease in the level of granularity as it progresses from the transaction table to the accumulating table. For example, the transaction table might show the date of a sale, the periodic table might show Q1 sales because it's just the end of the period, and finally the accumulating fact table might show all the dates of the various stages of a sales cycle for example.

Number of dimensions: The number of dimensions is the least in the transaction, the most in the accumulating, and in between in the periodic.

Facts: The difference in the facts, similarly, is that they are based on individual transactions (you made a deposit to your checking account), entire periods of time (your monthly balance), or numerous events over the lifetime of an event (the many steps involved when applying for a mortgage with a bank).

Measurement: In the transaction table, the numbers are always additive   you can add up all of the deposits you made to your checking account. In periodic, they're semiadditive, or an average number. So, the bank can find the average of your 12 monthly balances. In the accumulating table, the numbers have to be derived. For example, it would derive the difference in time between the date you first contacted the bank about applying for a mortgage and when you signed the final paperwork.

Conforming dimensions and facts, and database size: All three types of fact tables have conformed dimensions and conformed facts. The database size is the largest for a transaction table, since it needs to store a huge volume of transactions; the size is smallest for accumulating, and in between for a periodic table.

Table 9.2 Comparison of Fact Tables Types			
Property	**Transaction**	**Periodic**	**Accumulating**
Grain	One row per transaction	One row per time period	One row per lifetime of an event
Date dimension	Lowest level of granularity	End-of-period granularity	Multiple per row
Number of dimensions	Least	Average	Most
Facts	Transaction related	Period related	Numerous events over lifetime
Measurement	Additive	Not additive, average	Need to derive
Conforming dimensions	Yes	Yes	Yes
Conforming facts	Yes	Yes	Yes
Database size	Largest	Smaller	Smallest

ACHIEVING CONSISTENCY

Keeping data consistent is a recurring theme in DW and BI. Businesses that make decisions based on inconsistent data tend to make expensive mistakes. Data consistency leads us to one of the key differences between operational and DW/BI systems: that the operational system only has to keep data consistent within itself. On the other hand, a DW or BI environment needs to make the data consistent across multiple operational systems, and also, sometimes, external to the enterprise.

CONFORMING DIMENSIONS

This need for consistency brings us to conforming dimensions—dimensions that are consistent and conformed across the enterprise. This ensures that any fact that links, for example, to the customer dimension, will get consistent customer information; all reporting and analytics is consistent because of these conformed dimensions.

There are several dimension-related terms used in the industry today:

- Master data management (MDM)
- Customer data integration (CDI)
- Product information management (PIM)

There are other buzzwords used as well. All of them center on the idea of creating a master list of customers, products, suppliers, organizations, locations, and time. All of these are dimensions, and all fall into the category of conforming the dimensions to be able to do reporting and analytics.

You always define the dimensions at the most granular or detailed level possible. Sometimes that's referred to as the atomic level. And each conformed dimension has a surrogate key as the primary key, and every row in the dimension is unique. When you conform or make them consistent, you can get consistent reporting.

CONFORMING FACTS

Accompanying conformed dimensions is conformed facts. Conforming in this context also means standardizing—defining standard definitions for facts, measures, or key performance indicators (KPIs). Defining a fact, measure, or KPI means defining the business rules, formulas or algorithms, allocations, filters, and whatever else is necessary to transform a piece of data into a piece of information that's useful for the business. The examples include calculating revenue, profit, standard cost, price, margin, and so on. All of these calculations are done in businesses on a daily basis.

There are two traps to avoid when it comes to standardizing facts: "single version of the truth" and politics.

First, you've likely heard of the phrase "single version of the truth" when learning about enterprise resource planning (ERP) systems and data warehousing. It's simplistic to think of one interpretation of a fact or measure or KPI. At an operational level, which means at the most detailed level of running a business, there are different interpretations or definitions of facts based on the business context. This is not to be confused with making numbers up or having different interpretations because you don't understand them. There can be different numbers for revenue and profit if they are calculated differently at various parts of a business chain, based on different sets of business processes, and created for different business groups. The sales force, marketing group, and manufacturing group all sell, market, or build the same products, but based on where you are in the business cycle within the company, you would look at the revenue or profit calculations differently, because that's how it would be assigned or allocated to your business group.

This means you're not going to get a single definition of a profit margin; you're going to get different definitions of profit margin for many different processes. However, each process needs to have the same measures across that process, which is where the consistency comes in.

The second trap to avoid is thinking that numbers are detached from politics. Often, technical people think that all they need to know about business rules, formulas, and algorithms is getting the numbers and writing them up. The reality, however, is that there is a time-consuming process of getting everyone to agree on what those measures across the enterprise are. If the numbers have historically been manually calculated in spreadsheets, then the business rules and relationships need to be documented and used in designing the data model. Once a number is in a data model and shared, it's visible, it's transparent, and it has to be agreed upon. Take the time to get the right measurements documented within your data model.

ADVANCED DIMENSIONS AND FACTS

Dimensional modeling uses many concepts, relationships, and approaches in constructing some very sophisticated business models that support business processes. Some of the terms used in dimensional modeling, like "degenerative," can sound esoteric and obscure. As you learn more about advanced dimensional modeling and need to implement it in the real world, however, you'll see how important it is to understand these terms and how they apply. It's important to realize these aren't just esoteric concepts, but are actually very useful in representing the business and supporting the reporting and analytics.

DATE (OR CALENDAR) DIMENSION

Date dimensions are not only a best practice, but also a workhorse in dimensional modeling because almost every fact has at least one date and most queries are examining a date-related measure. In spite of this, many people do not understand the need for a date dimension. Let's start with why this type of dimension was created.

Dates are not as easy as they look because there is a lot more going on behind the scenes than one thinks. When business people look at the date of a sales transaction they immediately know what the year, quarter, and month of that sale. They will also know if the sale occurred in the period that they wish to analyze, for example last month, last quarter, or comparing this month to the comparable month last year. The business person is performing date substring manipulation and data arithmetic without being aware of it.

Almost every fact table has at least one attribute that is a date. That attribute may be stored as a DATE data type "2004-10-27," more commonly as a DATETIME data type in the format "2004-10-27 23:40:01.918" or infrequently as an alphanumeric character string.

The following are just some of the potential date substring manipulations, calculations, or business rules that need to be applied to every date on every row for almost every query or analysis performed in BI:

- **Selecting dates for specific calendar periods such as a month, quarter, or year.** This requires a function to extract the specific DATE substring being filtered on for every applicable date on every row in the fact table(s) being examined to determine if there is a match. And if the period is more detailed than a year, then every level in the hierarchy (year-quarter-month-day) above the period needs to be included in the substring comparison.
- **Selecting or comparing dates with DATETIME data type is not same as comparing dates with DATE data type.** Many dates in a DW have a DATETIME data type because the transaction system recorded that level of detail when the transaction occurred, and that detail is brought into the DW. However, much of the analysis an enterprise conducts is DATE-based. SQL converts the date of "2004-10-27" to the default time of "2004-10-27 00:00:00.000" before it can compare it with a DATETIME data type. It does this so they can match; they must have the same data type. So, an event "2004-10-27 23:40:01.918" would not be selected at all, which then makes the data erroneous if the business analysis was selecting items by DATE. Therefore, every time a date with a DATETIME data type is compared, it needs to be converted to a DATE data type.
- **Switching between standard and fiscal calendar dates if they are different from each other.** There are formulas based on governmental rules that convert standard calendars dates to the fiscal calendar that an enterprise is using.
- **Assigning holidays or time periods** that have a significance to an enterprise is typically determined by creating look-up tables or manually coding the list of dates in reports or spreadsheets.
- **Selecting calendar periods that are calculated by date functions** such as quarter, week in year and day in year.

Before the introduction of a date dimension concept in dimensional modeling, every BI application had to perform these date operations every time a query was performed.

Designing a Date Dimension

Figure 9.18 depicts a fact table (*Fact_Store_Sales*) with a foreign key (*Date_SK*) linking to a calendar date dimension (*Dim_Date*). Although the composition of a data dimension varies between enterprises based on filters and date headings for reports used by business people, the designs follow specific design standards and conventions.

The two columns that are mandatory in a date dimension are the primary key and a full date value. In our example, these are *Date_SK* the primary (and surrogate) key, and *Date_Value* full date value.

For the first mandatory column, primary key, the date dimension is the one exception to the dimensional modeling rule that a dimensional table's surrogate key should be a meaningless integer. The best practice is that the date's surrogate key is an integer in the form of YYYYMMDD with YYYY = four-digit year (1991), MM = two-digit month (03), and DD two-digit day (03) yielding 19910303 in this example.

If a meaningless surrogate key such as a database IDENTITY data type is used, then the key assigned to any date would vary based on the starting date assigned to the dimension. This means that different

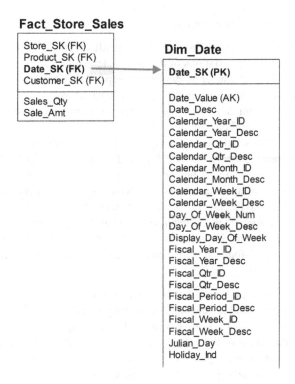

Fact_Store_Sales

Store_SK (FK)
Product_SK (FK)
Date_SK (FK)
Customer_SK (FK)

Sales_Qty
Sale_Amt

Dim_Date

Date_SK (PK)

Date_Value (AK)
Date_Desc
Calendar_Year_ID
Calendar_Year_Desc
Calendar_Qtr_ID
Calendar_Qtr_Desc
Calendar_Month_ID
Calendar_Month_Desc
Calendar_Week_ID
Calendar_Week_Desc
Day_Of_Week_Num
Day_Of_Week_Desc
Display_Day_Of_Week
Fiscal_Year_ID
Fiscal_Year_Desc
Fiscal_Qtr_ID
Fiscal_Qtr_Desc
Fiscal_Period_ID
Fiscal_Period_Desc
Fiscal_Week_ID
Fiscal_Week_Desc
Julian_Day
Holiday_Ind

FIGURE 9.18

Date dimension.

dimensional tables have different values assigned to a date, resulting in inconsistency. In contrast, using the convention of YYYMMDD guarantees that a specific date has the same value in every date dimension table. For example, March 3, 1991, would be 19910303 on every date dimension table no matter when it was generated or by whom.

There are several advantages to using this smart key:

- It is universally understood
- It conforms to ISO 8601 date and time international exchange standard.
- Most importantly, this convention establishes date dimension consistency, which helps enable data sharing in an enterprise.

The second mandatory column, which has the full date value typically stored on a DATE data type column, is essential because it is used as the look-up column in the ETL processes that assign the fact table date foreign keys. In our example, the ETL process matches the sales date from the source system sales data with the corresponding row from the date dimension (*Dim_Date*) and then assigns the foreign key (*Date_SK*) value to the sales fact table (*Fact_Store_Sales*).

In addition to the two mandatory columns, various columns are populated to enable filtering, aggregating, grouping, and labeling dates in reporting and analytics. These columns may be numeric or alphanumeric based on business needs.

Some of the common date attributes include:

- Calendar periods derived from date substring: year, month, and day.
- Multiple columns representing variations of the same calendar period, such as a full name of a month "September," a three-character abbreviation "Sep," Polish translation "Wrzesień," numeric 9, character equivalent of month number "09" and other variations.
- Calendar periods derived from date functions: quarter, week number in year, day number in year, day number in month, day number in week, etc.
- Columns that are used as flags indicating if a day is a week day, weekend day, holiday, etc. These flags will vary by enterprise, country, business line, and even across years for "floating" holidays. This might result in country-specific or business-specific date dimensions used when the data is analyzed. Note that the use of these specific date dimensions in the BI environment has no impact on extract, transform and load (ETL) processes that load fact tables or the underlying fact table designs.
- Seasonal periods that are specific to the enterprise may also be flagged. For example, a greeting card company may flag key card-buying seasons such as the period of time leading up to Mother's Day, whereas an agricultural-focused firm such as a farm equipment or a fertilizer manufacturer would have growing seasons.

Enterprises may have two calendars: a standard and a fiscal calendar. The standard calendar would begin on the first day of the applicable year, such as January 1 in the United States. The fiscal calendar is set up for governmental and tax reporting purposes. There are specific rules that define the specific parameters such as beginning date of the year, each quarter's start date, and the length of each quarter. When the standard and fiscal calendars are different, then date dimensions will have both the standard and fiscal equivalents of the calendar periods for each date row.

Benefits

Using a date dimension in your BI architecture allows simplification and consolidation. For example, using the date dimension means the following need to take place only once:

- A date surrogate foreign key is assigned to every date field when it is loaded from source systems.
- Data substring and data calculations are performed when the date dimension is loaded.
- Standard and fiscal calendar conversions are created when the date dimension is loaded.
- All business-specific calendar identifiers such as holidays are input into the date dimension as the singular look-up table.

Contrast this with BI reports or business analysis without the date dimension. They need to perform these same date operations on each date field on each row in a query every time they are performed. These date operations might be repeated thousands or millions of times for each report or analysis and countless amount of times across an enterprise!

The benefits of using the date dimension also include the following:

- **Query speed** is faster because you're performing the date operations once when loading the date dimensions versus countless times, as discussed above. Although each date operation takes a minimal amount of time, it adds up to be more significant than one would think.
- **Productivity** is increased for both the business people and information technology staff who do not have to repeatedly and redundantly code these date operations manually into every BI dashboard, report, query, or spreadsheet.

- **Consistency** is increased because the date is defined once and used across the enterprise without different interpretations or chance of errors.
- **Analytics** are enhanced because of all the prebuilt date dimension attributes that will be immediately available to every BI application for business people to use in filtering, aggregating, grouping and labeling calendar periods.

It seems like such a simple concept, but a date dimension is one of the bedrock ideas in dimensional modeling yielding significant business and technology benefits.

TIME DIMENSION

Much of the business analysis conducted in an enterprise, such as period-over-period, year-to-date, or quarter-to-date analysis involves only the date portion of the DATETIME data type. The actual time of day that a sale occurred, for example, is typically not needed because most enterprise performance metrics are summarized by day, week, quarter, or year. Examples of performance analysis that use time of day include capacity planning and labor utilization, but typically time-of-day data is not pertinent and can actually be confusing and misleading.

This has led to two approaches on how to handle time of day.

Time-of-Day as a Fact

First, if time-of-day analysis is irrelevant or is only done on a limited basis in your enterprise then **time is treated as a fact**. For every date in a fact table, create two columns. The first column should have a foreign key linked to the calendar date dimension that would be used in business analysis when time of day is irrelevant. The second column should contain both the date and time. There are several pragmatic reasons to retain the time of day even if there does not appear to be a business analytical need:

- Enable reconciliation of the fact's date with the transactional system's date.
- Enable the occasional time-of-day analysis by directly using the fact column with the full DATETIME. Because this type of analysis is seldom done there is no need to accommodate it with a time dimension (the other approach to handling time of day).
- If conditions change and time-of-day analysis becomes a business requirement, then having the fact attributes with DATETIME allows this type of analysis to be retrofitted by using the second approach below.

The example depicted in Figure 9.19 shows the *FactStoreSales* table with both of these columns. First, foreign key *OrderDateKey* that links to the date dimension *DimOrderDate*. Second, the *OrderDate* column containing the full DATETIME data.

Time-of-Day as a Dimension

With the second approach, **time is managed as a dimension** because there is a need for the business to analyze performance measure by the time of day. This approach stores three columns in the fact table for every date that needs to be analyzed by the business. The two columns discussed in the other time-of-day approach—foreign key linked to the data dimension and a column storing the full DATETIME—are included in this approach. The third column is a foreign key to a time dimension, as shown in Figure 9.20, which expands the previous example by adding the *Order_TimeKey* (foreign key) linked to *Dim_Time* (time dimension.)

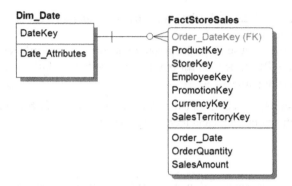

FIGURE 9.19

Time as a fact.

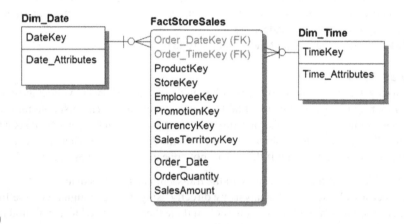

FIGURE 9.20

Time as a dimension.

The initial question when designing the time dimension is what level of grain is needed for the time-of-day analysis: hours, minutes, seconds, or hundredths of seconds? The number of rows grows significantly as the level of detail increases: for hours is 24, minutes is 1440, and seconds is 86,400. The grain of the time dimension should be whatever is required for time-of-day analysis and no more. It is not that the database or BI tools will get overwhelmed by keeping data to the second, but that the visualizations and interactions with the BI tool get more cumbersome if the level of detail goes beyond the business need.

The time dimension's primary key is a surrogate key, typically starting at zero (0). It also includes a column containing the time of day with a time data type or the equivalent based on the database being used. Additional columns would be used for filtering and descriptive purposes in analysis. Figure 9.21 illustrates a sample time dimension with a grain of an hour. *Time_SK* is the surrogate key, *Time_Value* is the time-of-day valued column and the remaining columns examples are 12 hour time; military time; am or pm; and a sample textual description. The selection of the descriptive columns is based on business analytical requirements.

Time_SK	12_hr	24_hr	am_pm	Time_Value	Time_Desc	Time_Periods
0	12	0	am	12:00:00 AM	Midnight	Late Night
1	1	1	am	1:00:00 AM	1 am	Late Night
2	2	2	am	2:00:00 AM	2 am	Late Night
3	3	3	am	3:00:00 AM	3 am	Late Night
4	4	4	am	4:00:00 AM	4 am	Early Morning
5	5	5	am	5:00:00 AM	5 am	Early Morning
6	6	6	am	6:00:00 AM	6 am	Morning
7	7	7	am	7:00:00 AM	7 am	Morning
8	8	8	am	8:00:00 AM	8 am	Morning
9	9	9	am	9:00:00 AM	9 am	Morning
10	10	10	am	10:00:00 AM	10 am	Morning
11	11	11	am	11:00:00 AM	11 am	Morning
12	12	12	pm	12:00:00 PM	Noon	Lunch Time
13	1	13	pm	1:00:00 PM	1 pm	Lunch Time
14	2	14	pm	2:00:00 PM	2 pm	Afternoon
15	3	15	pm	3:00:00 PM	3 pm	Afternoon
16	4	16	pm	4:00:00 PM	4 pm	Afternoon
17	5	17	pm	5:00:00 PM	5 pm	Afternoon
18	6	18	pm	6:00:00 PM	6 pm	Evening
19	7	19	pm	7:00:00 PM	7 pm	Evening
20	8	20	pm	8:00:00 PM	8 pm	Evening
21	9	21	pm	9:00:00 PM	9 pm	Night
22	10	22	pm	10:00:00 PM	10 pm	Night
23	11	23	pm	11:00:00 PM	11 pm	Night

FIGURE 9.21

Time dimension—hour grain.

Figure 9.22 illustrates a time dimension with a grain of a minute. In the example, the time dimension has the required surrogate key *Time_SK* and time-of-day value stored in *Time_Value*. The example has a list of filter and descriptive columns, but an enterprise needs to build the columns necessary to support their required time-of-day business analysis.

Time Periods

Time-of-day analysis is performed in industries such as retail (online and at stores), restaurants, utilities, telecommunication, and media (online, cable, and radio) when examining consumer behavior. Examples include examining existing performance metrics and campaign impact using time of day.

Often this time-of-day analysis is conducted on time periods based on banded ranges of time. For example, as illustrated in Figure 9.23, a food chain or media company has created a schema to analyze the time of day in these time bands: morning commute is 6:00–9:00 am, late morning is 9:00–11:30 am, lunch is 11:30–2:30 pm, school release is 2:30–4:00 pm and afternoon commute is 4:00–7:00 pm. Although the fact tables and time dimension contain a grain to the minute of the day detail, the time-of-day grain is the time periods. The businesses in these scenarios are not concerned with what happens exactly at 6:16 AM because that level of detail is "noise" and is not something the business needs to act on.

There are two approaches to supporting time-of-day analysis using time bands. First, if using time as a dimension, add more columns to the time dimension with the appropriate time band descriptions

Time_SK	12_hr	24_hr	am_pm	Minute_in_Hour	Time_Value
0	12	0	am	0	12:00 AM
1	12	0	am	1	12:01 AM
2	12	0	am	2	12:02 AM
3	12	0	am	3	12:03 AM
4	12	0	am	4	12:04 AM
5	12	0	am	5	12:05 AM
59	12	0	am	59	12:59 AM
60	1	1	am	1	1:00 AM
719	1	12	am	59	11:59 AM
720	2	13	pm	0	12:00 PM
1439	11	23	pm	59	11:59 PM

FIGURE 9.22

Time dimension—minute grain.

Time_SK	12_hr	24_hr	am_pm	Minute	Time_Value	Time_Period
360	6	6	am	0	6:00 AM	Morning Commute
465	7	7	am	45	7:45 AM	Morning Commute
690	11	11	am	30	11:30 AM	Lunch
900	3	15	pm	0	3:00 PM	School Release
1020	5	17	pm	0	5:00 PM	Afternoon Commute

FIGURE 9.23

Time dimension with time bands.

as illustrated in Figure 9.23. From a pragmatic perspective, it is unlikely that the time bands will stay static or that there will be only one way to group time periods into bands, but a dimensional table enables an enterprise to add as many additional columns as necessary.

Use the second approach when implementing time in fact tables without a time dimension. With this approach create a value-band dimension to define the association with time and time-of-day periods.

Either approach is preferable to manually coding time periods into each BI application or SQL query performed on these data because the manual coding is redundant, may be inconsistent, is not likely to be documented, and is not as easily modified.

DATE AND TIME DIMENSIONS ACROSS TIME ZONES

If an enterprise's operations span multiple time zones, it is a best practice to record time in two fact tables with two different time zones. The first time tracked is in the local time zone where the fact occurs, such as where a call center is located or where a package is shipped from. The second time zone corresponds to a global standard time that is used as a baseline to calculate offsets. An example of this schema is depicted in Figure 9.24.

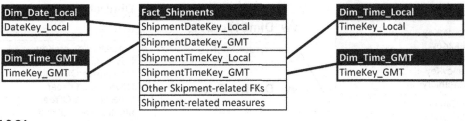

FIGURE 9.24

Time zones.

Typically, you choose one of two global standards: Greenwich Mean Time (GMT) or the enterprise headquarters' local time zone. If the headquarters is in Hong Kong, for example, the company could pick that up as the local time, making it their global standard as an alternative to GMT. As long as everything is standardized, it won't matter what time zones the various manufacturing plants, branches, or offices are located in. The system will record the local and global time of events, so the business can coordinate its view of when things occurred.

The business reasons for expressing the time in two time zones is because of the two types of time-of-day analysis that is performed:

- The business groups, which could be call centers and shipping warehouses in this example, will examine their performance metrics such as response time and workforce resource-balancing analysis in the context of their local time zone.
- Enterprise senior management and global business groups such as logistics and sales will examine performance metrics over 24-hour periods using a global standard time zone as a baseline for meaningful analysis.

Alternative approaches, such as storing a time zone indicator or hour offset from a baseline such as GMT, would rely on manual coding date calculations in BI applications and spreadsheets to enable the analysis. Manual coding has many disadvantages compared to using dimensional filtering; these include a longer time to code attributes, higher maintenance costs, and inconsistencies in the analysis.

ROLE PLAYING DIMENSIONS

There are instances when a fact table references a dimension multiple times as a foreign key. Examples of this are:

- Multiple dates associated with different events such as order, shipment, and delivery are captured in an accumulating fact table.
- Multiple address-related columns identifying different address such as shipping and billing locations.
- Multiple persons such as a customer and sales person related to a sales fact or an employee and her manager in workforce-related analysis.

Each of these foreign keys linked the same dimension to signify a different role for that dimension. For example, the date could signify an order, shipment, or delivery date. The term "role-playing" describes a physical dimension being used in different business contexts.

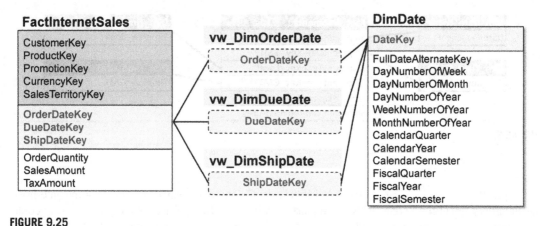

FIGURE 9.25

Role-playing dimension approaches.

Although this concept is easy to understand, it is a different matter for relational databases; although a fact table can have multiple columns with foreign keys linked back to the same dimension, these columns cannot be used in the same query. For example, you would not be able query the date dimension from a sales table by filtering a ship date and delivery date.

To support role-playing dimensions, there needs to be a database entity associated with each role. There are two different approaches to creating role-playing dimensional entities:

- Create separate tables for each role
- Create views for each role using a single dimension

  Creating views for each role is clearly the best practice. For example, see the elements in Figure 9.25.

- Date dimension, *Dim_Date*. You'd store it once, and it would create views for every role to which it applies.
- Internet sales fact, *FactInternetSales*. This has three different role dates reporting originally back to *Dim_Date*. The views defined for each of those date roles are:
  - dimension order date view, *vDimOrderDate*
  - dimension due date view, *vDimDueDate*
  - dimension ship date view, *vDimShipDate*
- To sum up, we only store *Dim_Date* once, we create a view for each role, and the fact tables and foreign key go back to *vDimOrderDate*, *vDimDueDate*, and *vDimShipDate* versus the original *Dim_Date*.

Creating views eliminates maintaining and updating multiple physical tables, saves space, and enables the multiple-way join that is required for business analysis.

DEGENERATIVE DIMENSIONS

Operational systems track transactions and business events by using business process documents such as a purchase order, invoice, travel reservation, or concert ticket. All of these process documents have

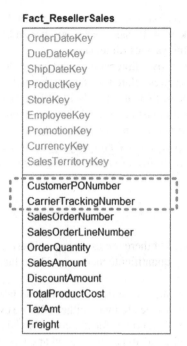

Fact_ResellerSales

OrderDateKey
DueDateKey
ShipDateKey
ProductKey
StoreKey
EmployeeKey
PromotionKey
CurrencyKey
SalesTerritoryKey
CustomerPONumber
CarrierTrackingNumber
SalesOrderNumber
SalesOrderLineNumber
OrderQuantity
SalesAmount
DiscountAmount
TotalProductCost
TaxAmt
Freight

FIGURE 9.26

Degenerative dimension example.

reference identifiers such as order, invoice, and reservation numbers that are unique and used as primary keys to entities in their supporting operational schemas.

Figure 9.26 illustrates a reseller sales fact listing the foreign keys linking to store (*StoreKey*), employee (*EmployeeKey*), order date (*OrderDateKey*), and the other dimensions that uniquely identify the transaction. There are several measures such as order quantity and sales amount. There are two attributes *CustomerPONumber* and *CarrierTrackingNumber* that represent the unique identifiers for the customer purchase order and carrier tracking number for the sale. In the operation system, these attributes would be foreign keys to operational-related entities, but in a dimensional model they would not be linked to any dimension. In the dimensional model, there would not be any requirements for these dimensions because the attributes associated with these entities in the operation system are already stored in other dimensions. For example, the purchase order would have customer-created attributes that would be stored in customer and address-related dimensions.

These attributes are essentially foreign keys that do not link to any dimensions and are referred to as degenerative dimensions. This concept often causes confusion, but it's really just a dimension whose attributes exist elsewhere. Although it is tempting to create dimensions for each of these attributes, this information would be redundant with other dimensions. Separating out, for example, the carrier tracking number or customer purchase order number in our example illustrates the duplication, because the same attributes would be stored in the reseller sales fact and in a purchase order dimension.

So is there any case in which you would replicate that data? The answer is you wouldn't. The best practice is to not make this a separate dimension, to place it in the transaction table after the dimension foreign keys, and before the numeric attributes. The example of *Fact_ResellerSales* shows the two foreign keys that are the primary key of the sales order number and line item number; we then have a series of foreign keys pointing to the various dimensions.

The example shows two degenerative dimensions—the carrier tracking number and customer PO number—followed by the real measures related to the internet sales. Realize that these degenerative dimensions are not additive numbers; they are merely identifiers that are used for a business process that we are not tracking within this dimensional model. But, we retain these numbers because it's a link back to the operational system, and if we want to audit our results or tie it back, we need to have these numbers. And, some business people, rather than querying off, for example, the sales order number, may actually be querying off the customer PO number. Degenerative dimensions enable that kind of querying.

EVENT TABLES

Facts almost always have measures, but there are exceptions. These exceptions occur when a business event does not create or monitor any quantifiable measures. These facts are either called factless fact or event tables.

Examples of factless facts or events are students attending a class or patients visiting a doctor. In both cases, there's no direct measure associated with either of those events. There is tuition paid for the student to attend that class and a bill generated for the doctor's visit, but both of these are associated with other facts and are based on other attributes such as what courses the student is registered for and what procedures the doctor performs. And bills will be generated whether the student attends a class or the patient skips an appointment.

Just because there is no direct measure associated with a factless fact it does not mean that the event is not worth tracking. For example, a teacher may take attendance in class and place an X next to a student's name.

The approach to tracking these factless facts is depicted in Figure 9.27. The example illustrates that an attribute is created as a dummy counter fact set to 1 or 0; 1 means it happened, the student showed up to class. This enables the connectivity between the fact table and a dimension—the counting of these

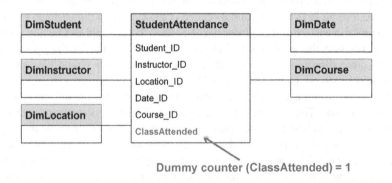

FIGURE 9.27

Event table example.

events. This factless fact table is the best practice for capturing events that have no natural numeric measurements.

The example shows an event or factless fact table:

- It has a *StudentAttendance* fact with foreign keys to the student, the instructor, the class location, the date of the class, and the course itself.
- In the *StudentAttendance* fact are all those foreign keys listed, then the last item, the class attended, is the dummy counter, set to 1 or 0.
- If the student shows up, all those foreign keys are populated with a 1.
- If you're also keeping track, you could put zeroes down if a student didn't show up.
- With a list of each student from every class session, you could sum up for that particular date how many students showed up by summing on the class attended.
- You could filter on the 0 values to determine who didn't attend the class.
- Then you could aggregate by filtering on the 1s to perform trend analysis

Implementing a dummy counter attribute in the factless fact table enables business analysis of events even though these business events do not naturally have a numeric measurement associated with them.

CONSOLIDATED FACT TABLES

As we have discussed, fact tables store data about transactions or business events representing specific business processes. Fact tables are normalized and are correlated to business entities in the operational systems' ER data models. This is exactly how a data warehouse schema should be designed if best practices are followed; however, when the data is transformed into a schema supporting data marts or cubes there may be exceptions to these rules that are called consolidated facts.

Consolidated fact tables are fact tables that are separate and distinct in operational systems, business processes, and data warehouses that are consolidated or combined to facilitate reporting and analysis. The example in Figure 9.28 illustrates a fact table (*Fact_SalesPerformance*) combining the sales measure (*ActualSales*), forecasted sales (*ForecastedSales*), a calculated variance (*ForecastVariance*), and

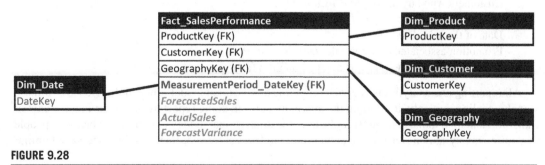

FIGURE 9.28

Consolidated facts example.

the foreign keys to several conformed dimensions—product, customer, geography, and measurement period.

Another common use for consolidated fact tables is budget-to-actual expense performance analysis.

The origins of consolidating these facts stems from the type of business analysis performed and the capabilities of the reporting tools (especially from the early days of BI) and spreadsheets used by a business. Comparing budgets or forecasts to actual performance is quite a common type of business analysis, so there is a very strong need to facilitate that analysis. The easiest method available to many reporting tools and spreadsheets is to simply consolidate these facts into one table (i.e., denormalized or flattened tables).

The two key considerations when consolidating fact tables are that the facts share conformed dimensions and they have the same grain. Obtaining the same level of detail or grain typically requires aggregating one of the underlying fact tables. For example, budgeting or forecasting sales or expenses may be at the weekly or monthly grain, whereas sales might be recorded in real time and expenses may be logged on a daily basis. If one of the facts in the consolidated fact table is aggregated, then the underlying detail is not available to anyone using the consolidated fact table for analysis.

It is a best practice to maintain separate fact tables in the DW schema and only consolidate the fact tables in BI-related data stores such as data marts and cubes.

DIMENSIONAL MODELING RECAP

Dimensional models are a set of two entities:

- **Facts**, which record the measures of business events (such as sales) occurring in an enterprise
- **Dimensions**, which represent the who, what, where, and when of these business events

The example in Figure 9.29 sums up what you've learned in this chapter by showing everything about an internet sale:

- *FactInternetSales* is the fact/business event, which is associated with some dimensions:
  - Products that are sold, *DimProduct*
  - Customers who buy them, *DimCustomer*
  - Currency the customers use, *DimCurrency*
  - Date of the sale, *DimDate*
  - Promotion associated with the sale, *DimPromotion*
  - Territory in which the sale was made, *DimSalesTerritory*

All reporting and analytics is geared toward this dimensional model. The whole science of dimensional modeling, not only developing the model, but also in doing reporting and querying, the extract transform and load tools, and the BI tools, uses the dimensional model. Although the business people in your company may never see the actual data models you create, they will become very familiar

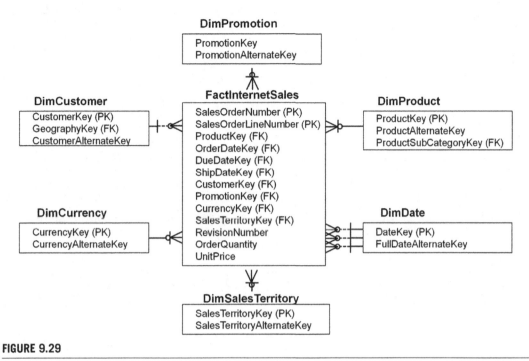

FIGURE 9.29

Dimensional modeling recap.

with the reports and dashboards they help generate. Unless those models can generate clear, effective reporting and analysis, they won't help the business view the data and use it to make informed decisions that affect operations. Dimensional modeling is the key to generating this critical business information.

BUSINESS INTELLIGENCE DIMENSIONAL MODELING

10

INFORMATION IN THIS CHAPTER:

- Hierarchies (balanced, ragged, unbalanced and variable-depth)
- Outrigger tables
- Slowly changing dimensions
- Causal dimensions
- Multivalued dimensions
- Junk dimensions
- Value band reporting
- Heterogeneous products
- Hot swappable and custom dimension groups

INTRODUCTION

This chapter on advanced dimensional modeling is based on pragmatic experience, covering various aspects of data modeling that have evolved over the years as it has been used in various industries for a wide range of business processes. Best practices have emerged in response to what business intelligence (BI) practitioners have learned along the way about the best way to meet the enterprise's need for information.

The terms covered here may seem more and more obscure, but keep in mind these are actual concepts and approaches that anyone who is going to be involved in data modeling or dimensional modeling is going to use when building applications.

The aspects of dimensional modeling will include: hierarchies, slowly changing dimensions (SCD), rapidly changing dimensions, causal dimensions, multivalue dimensions, and junk dimensions. The chapter will also take a closer look at snowflakes as well as concepts such as value band reporting, heterogeneous products, and hot swappable dimensions. The goal is to arm you with a strong understanding of how to develop a dimensional model and how dimensional modeling fits in your enterprise.

See the book's Website www.BIguidebook.com for data modeling templates.

HIERARCHIES

Many dimensions are hierarchical. Figure 10.1 shows some examples:

- **Calendar date**, which goes from year to a quarter, to month, and ending with day.
- **Product**, which goes from product category, breaking out into product subcategory, and ending with product.
- **Geography**, which goes from continent, to country, state, city, and ending with postal code.

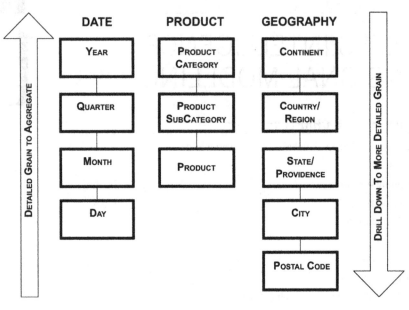

FIGURE 10.1

Hierarchies.

As the figure illustrates, data is aggregated from the most detailed level of data (i.e., the lowest level in the hierarchy up to the highest level). Typically, dashboards and reports initially display aggregated data, and business people drill down to greater levels of detail. Drilling up and down is moving along the hierarchies to examine the level of detail needed for the business analysis.

From a data modeling perspective, hierarchies are cascading series of many-to-one relationships at different levels. Each level corresponds to a dimension attribute. The hierarchies document relationships across levels. In an entity relationship (ER) model, each of these attributes would be an entity unto itself.

Dimensional models have three types of hierarchies: balanced, ragged, and unbalanced. It's important to understand the differences and how to approach them in a dimensional model.

BALANCED HIERARCHIES

The balanced hierarchy is the simplest of these three hierarchies. (It is sometimes called a fixed hierarchy.) In it, all dimensional branches have the same number of levels—the same consistent depth with a consistent parent–child relationship. Enterprises create a balanced hierarchy to group and aggregate data within dimensions. It's not unusual to have more than one balanced hierarchy within a dimension.

Figure 10.2 illustrates a balanced hierarchy. In this example, a year breaks down to a quarter, breaking down to months. An actual date would be the highest level of detail and lowest level in the hierarchy. The date dimension in Figure 10.3 illustrates a dimension with multiple hierarchies. In this example, an enterprise has a fiscal calendar that begins on July 1 and has a 4-4-5-quarter (4 weeks for fiscal months 1 and 2, and 5 weeks assigned to fiscal month 3.) This type of fiscal calendar enables an

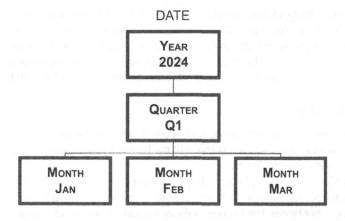

FIGURE 10.2

Date dimension.

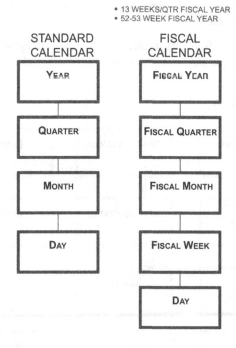

FIGURE 10.3

Standard and fiscal calendar hierarchies.

enterprise such as a retailer to analyze current versus previous periods in a more meaningful way for its business. Because the fiscal weeks are aligned with fiscal months, the fiscal hierarchy will include the fiscal week level that cannot be included in the standard calendar hierarchy because weeks do not align with standard weeks. Both of these hierarchies could be represented in the same dimension (as covered in the section on calendar dimensions in Chapter 9) with the lowest grain for both being a date.

RAGGED HIERARCHIES

A ragged hierarchy has the parent member of at least one member in the hierarchy that is not in the level immediately above it. In short, levels are skipped in the hierarchy. Both ragged and unbalanced hierarchies have branches with varying depths.

A typical example, as shown in Figure 10.4, is a geography or sales territory dimension. In the example, one branch has the continent of North America, country of United States, state of Illinois, and city of Chicago. The other branch has Europe as the continent, Greece as the country, and Athens as the city, but there is no state that is applicable to this dimension. In this example, each branch has a different depth and one branch has a gap, making this a ragged hierarchy.

If there is a limited number of levels and gaps in a hierarchy, then the pragmatic approach to handling aggregating data is to treat it as a balanced hierarchy. Depending on how the business wishes to handle the missing values, there are two options for what to populate in the missing attributes, just be sure to not use NULL in either case:

- An agreed-upon default value. In this example, that could be "not applicable" or "no state."
- The value of the level above the gap. In this example, "Greece" would be used as the State attribute.

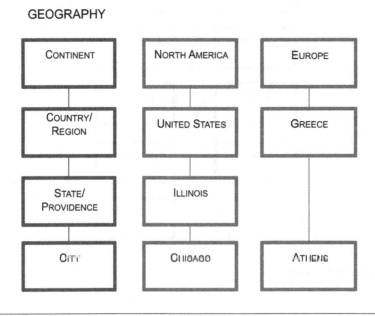

FIGURE 10.4

Ragged hierarchies.

Both approaches allow the business to perform analyses with the same hierarchy for all the data examined. It's the classic and easiest way to handle it.

If the hierarchy has many levels and gaps then use the approach discussed in handling variable depth hierarchies.

UNBALANCED HIERARCHIES

Unbalanced hierarchies occur when the dimensional branches have varying numbers of levels—inconsistent depths while still having a consistent parent-child relationship.

The classic example, as shown in Figure 10.5, is an organizational chart. In the example, as we traverse through a senior vice president's organization, the reporting relationships among employees vary widely. The organizational structure is unbalanced, with some branches in the hierarchy having more levels than others, the number of employees at each level varies, and employee titles are not uniform across a level. But there is always a parent–child relationship until the branch encounters a leaf node, such as an employee without anyone reporting to him or her. Obviously, an enterprise organizational chart would be much bigger than this, but it would still show a large amount of variation in the levels of the organization.

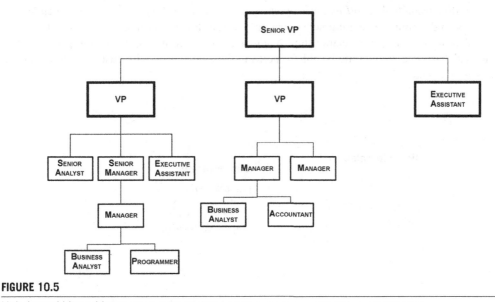

FIGURE 10.5

Unbalanced hierarchies.

WORKING WITH VARIABLE-DEPTH HIERARCHIES

The term variable-depth hierarchy refers to both unbalanced and ragged hierarchies. From a visual point of view, it is easy to see that the hierarchy is unbalanced or ragged. But it's a little more complicated from the data modeling and processing points of view, either with SQL, ETL, or a BI tool.

For accurate results, you need to understand and implement your approach to handling these various levels and not simply leave it up to the BI tool to aggregate and drill down by using the hierarchy levels.

The two approaches to handling unbalanced and ragged hierarchies are recursive pointer and bridge table.

Recursive Pointer

A recursive pointer is frequently used for handling a variable-depth hierarchy in dimensional modeling, but it has some serious drawbacks. This approach embeds a parent–child relationship in the dimension itself. The example in Figure 10.6 shows the dimension *DimEmployee*. The *EmployeeKey* is the primary key and child in the parent–child relationship, whereas the *ManagerKey* is the parent in the relationship and links back to the dimensional key itself. In a business context, the employee *EmployeeKey* points to the manager *ManagerKey*. The intent of this parent–child relationship is to recreate the organization chart in Figure 10.5.

A big drawback of the recursive pointer approach is that without custom coding, neither BI tools nor standard SQL can navigate from the top to bottom or vice versa in the hierarchy. And, if a ragged hierarchy is combined with an unbalanced hierarchy, which is common in financial charts of accounts, the added complexity of dealing with missing levels overwhelms these tools.

Figure 10.6 also illustrates how the fact tables, *FactRellerSales* and *FactSalesQuota*, are linked to the employee dimension table *DimEmployee* by using the foreign key *EmployeeKey*. The intent of the relationship is to determine which employee was responsible for a sale along with his or her sales quota, and then use the recursive relationship to aggregate the measures up to the top person in the organizational chart. You would only be able to perform the aggregation with custom coding and not with BI tools or standard SQL.

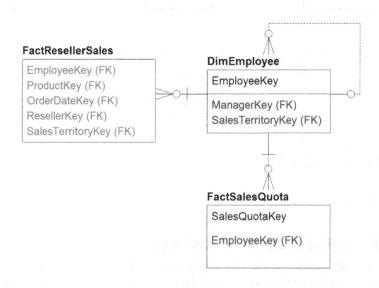

FIGURE 10.6

Employee recursive example.

Bridge Table

The second approach to handling variable depth hierarchies, which happens to be the best practice, is to create a bridge table that enables the relationships between the dimension and facts. A bridge table template design is depicted in Figure 10.7. The bridge table's columns are:

- *SK_Parent_Employee_ID*—This is the parent identifier. It is paired with *SK_Child_Employee_ID* as a combination primary key.
- *SK_Child_Employee_ID*—This is the child identifier. It is paired with *SK_Parent_Employee_ID* as a combination primary key.
- *Number_of_Levels*—This is the number of levels from the parent (top level)
- *Top_Level_Indicator*—This is a flag indicating if this is the top level.
- *Bottom_Level_Indicator*—This is a flag indicating if this is the bottom level.

The issue with this approach is that it adds complexity to the model; it's generally too complex for business people to manipulate directly. But the reality is that complexity is added because it's needed. Sometimes dimensional modeling constructs are not easily completed using Microsoft Excel or some other business end-user tool. That's why BI and online analytical processing (OLAP) tools, which understand relationships, are used in these more complex cases.

Tbl_Employee_Bridge

Column	Key
SK_Parent_Employee_ID	PK
SK_Child_Employee_ID	PK
Number_of_Levels	
Top_Level_Indicator	
Bottom_Level_Indicator	

FIGURE 10.7

Bridge table example.

When implementing a bridge table for an unbalanced hierarchy, it's important to look at how to use it to navigate between the fact and the dimension. There are two ways to navigate:

- Traversing down from the top level numbers to the detailed numbers.
- Traversing up from the detailed data to more summarized data.

Traversing down using the example in Figure 10.8, would look like this:

- Start with *FactResellerSales*.
- Record *SalesEmployeeKey*, which is the salesperson's employee identification.
- Next is the dimension *DimEmployee*, which lists all the employees in the company, their first name, last name, title, department number, and all their attributes as well as the sales territory key and the salesperson flag indicating they are salespeople.
- In the middle is the sales hierarchy bridge, which gives the parent employee key *SK_Parent_Employee_ID*, and the child employee key, *SK_Child_Employee_ID*, along with the total number of levels. There is a top level indicator, typically yes or no, and a bottom level indicator, also typically yes or no.

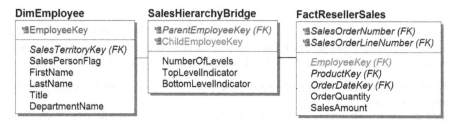

FIGURE 10.8

Bridge table navigation.

- When you're going down in aggregation, the fact joins the parent key level (remember, the data has already been aggregated). Then the dimension joins the child key row; then you move down into the lower level of detail.

    Traversing up in the detailed data using the same example would look like this:

- The level of grain is the sale transaction, which includes the employee who made the sale.
- *FactResellerSales* joins the hierarchy of the child key row with foreign key *SK_Child_Employee_ID*.
- Then the dimension *Dim_Employee* joins the parent key *SK_Parent_Employee_ID* of the sales hierarchy bridge.
- That gets us the salesperson's manager.
- So, the salesperson is the child, the manager is the parent. Then you can do a tree walk up the employee levels.

OUTRIGGER TABLES

The classic star schema has facts linked to dimensions without any relationship between dimensions themselves. Modeling an enterprise, however, is never that clear-cut and there are several conditions when dimensions link to other dimensions. We have discussed two of these conditions: snowflakes and bridges; the third condition is outriggers.

Outriggers are used when a dimension is referenced within another dimension. When a dimension is being designed, often all the attributes that are related to each other are gathered into that dimension. Further inspection reveals groups of attributes that are populated by different sources, at different times and for different purposes. In an ER model, they would be different entities.

Figure 10.9 depicts an *employee* dimension that is linked to three outriggers: *geography, hire date,* and *organization* dimensions. In the initial design of the employee dimension, some of the outriggers' attributes may have been part of that dimension until more detailed review uncovered that these attributes should remain in their respective dimensions to be referenced by the *employee* dimension.

Using outriggers eliminates the need to redundantly store and update dimensional attributes in multiple locations. An example of this would have occurred if the attributes, such as a department's name, manager, and size, were placed in the *employee* dimension rather accessing them in the *organization* dimension via a foreign key.

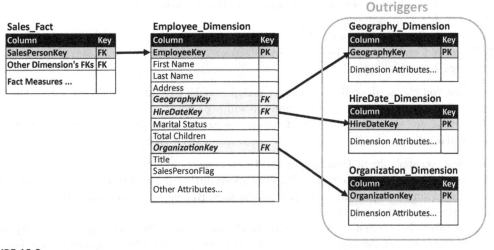

FIGURE 10.9

Dimension outriggers.

SLOWLY CHANGING DIMENSIONS

Dimensions have attributes that change over time. Products change price, cost, and composition. Employees are promoted, fired, change departments, and get new titles. Customers change addresses and names, get married or divorced, and move into different income brackets. These changes occur infrequently and unpredictably.

A business's operational and transaction processing applications keep dimensional tables updated to the most current values to support ongoing business processes. Operational applications do not track changes to dimensional values because transactions only need the most current values. In addition, operational reporting uses data from the point in time that the transaction occurred, which is referred to as either "as was" or "as transacted."

As you shift from operational to management analysis, however, the business needs to examine the facts (transactions and business events), not only in the context of the dimensional values at that point in time ("as was"), but also in the context of what the fact would look like if it occurred now with the current values of dimensions ("as is"). The capability to use either the "as was" or "as is" context is critical in business analysis such as examining trends, comparing period-versus-period performance and creating predictive models.

In the past, without formal techniques to track dimensional value changes, enterprises either ignored tracking (and lost any possibility to perform "as is" analysis) or they restated their facts by overwriting "as was" dimensional values with current values creating an "as is" state. Restating numbers was a time-consuming and messy technique that made it impossible to analyze facts "as was." Losing the visibility to examine "as was" values made this approach a nonstarter.

Based on the need for a business to analyze both "as was" and "as is" states, several techniques referred to as types were created in dimensional modeling to record these changes and manage SCD:

- SCD type 0: Keep original
- SCD type 1: Overwrite existing data (row) with new data
- SCD type 2: Create a new row for new values

- SCD type 3: Track changes using separate columns but overwrite rest
- SCD type 4: Add mini-dimension
- SCD type 5: Combine types $4+1$
- SCD type 6: Combines types $1+2+3$ (=6)
- SCD type 7: Use both types $1+2$

The type you choose depends on business analytic needs. Consider if and how you capture the dimensional changes to help decide what approach will work best.

There are several implementation considerations you need to make when selecting SCD techniques that you will use:

- First, will you apply the SCD techniques to all your dimensions equally or just to some of the dimensions? If you choose to treat certain dimensions differently, then you need to make sure that data integration developers, BI developers and business BI consumers are aware of and handle the difference when performing their work.
- Second, although it is often convenient to handle all dimensions in the same way, you typically can't do this with individual dimensional attributes because they are definitely not created equally. For example, you might need to track historical values of the attributes for people (customer, prospect, or employee) or business demographics despite the current value being sufficient for many other attributes. No matter what SCD type you have chosen for the dimensions themselves, you should only apply those techniques to the attributes where there is business value in doing so; the remaining attributes only need to be updated as their value changes, and don't need historical tracking.
- Finally, if you are tracking historical changes, you should only deploy those historical values to the business analytical processes that need it; the remaining analytical processes should get only the current view of the dimensions. This rule of thumb avoids adding complexity, confusion and processing overhead to the analytical processes that don't need historical tracking.

SCD TYPE 0: KEEP ORIGINAL

The type 0 technique writes the original dimension record but then never updates it, regardless of any changes to dimensional attributes. This is the least likely technique to be used because businesses require, at a minimum, the most current dimension values, such as data about their customers, products, and employees.

SCD TYPE 1: OVERWRITE EXISTING DATA

The type 1 technique is to overwrite historical values of dimensional attributes with the most current values. This technique keeps the dimensional values current, but disregards previous values. It is relatively straightforward to implement.

The example in Figure 10.10 shows the initial and current states of a row in the employee dimension listing the attributes for Guy Gilbert: his hire date of August 1, 2007, his title, base pay rate, and marital status. When the row was initially entered, Gilbert was a production technician, single, and paid $12.45 per hour. The current values in the row show that he is still single, paid $25.00 per hour, and is a production supervisor.

Initial Row

Employee Key	First Name	Last Name	Title	HireDate	Marital Status	Base Rate	Row Created	Row Modified
12345	Guy	Gilbert	Prod Technician	08/01/07	S	$12.45	08/01/07	

Current Row

Employee Key	First Name	Last Name	Title	HireDate	Marital Status	Base Rate	Row Created	Row Modified
12345	Guy	Gilbert	Prod Supervisor	08/01/07	S	$25.00	08/01/07	01/02/14

FIGURE 10.10

Employee dimension—SCD type 1.

SCD Type 1

Column	Key
Dimension_Durable_SK	PK
Dimension_NK	NK
SOR_SK	FK
Other Dimension Attributes	

FIGURE 10.11

SCD type 1 schema template.

There are two shortcomings to this technique:

- First, although we get the latest version of the dimensions, we lose the ability to track the history of the attributes. So we have no idea when the employee was promoted, when he was married or divorced, or when his base rate pay increased. In fact, his salary could easily have gone up multiple times, maybe even annually, but with this technique we don't see any of that information.
- Second, if we have aggregated the data in summary tables or in OLAP cubes, we will have to reaggregate it because the underlying detailed data of the aggregation has changed.

This technique, particularly in the early years of data warehousing, was the most common way to deploy SCD. Reporting was limited to "as is" analysis, but at that time that was sufficient for many businesses because data warehousing was giving them the first effective approach to analyze their enterprise's data outside application silos.

Type 1 Schema

Figure 10.11 depicts a template schema supporting the SCD type 1 technique. The template columns show:

- *Dimension_Durable_SK*: This is the surrogate key used as the primary key for this dimension. This column is referred to as the durable, supernatural, or durable supernatural key. The term durable is used because the key values that are assigned to a dimension will continue to be used regardless of any changes in the values in the systems of record (SOR). The term supernatural is used to distinguish the key as independent from the SOR natural key.

- *Dimension_NK*: This is the natural key from the SOR. This column has the data type of the SOR if there is only one SOR or if all the SORs have the same data type. If there are multiple source systems with different data types, then use a data type such as a character string that can store all the natural keys' values.
- *SOR_SK*: If the dimension has multiple SORs, such as a product dimension obtaining product lists from multiple source systems, then the SOR_SK is the foreign key linking to the SOR dimension depicted in Figure 10.11.
- *Dimension attributes*: There are one or more columns providing the values of all the attributes that the business needs to track.

Although we have differentiated dimensions' surrogate keys from the source systems' natural keys, there is an exception to this rule. This exception occurs when there is a single SOR for the dimension and that SOR generates a surrogate key as its primary key for that dimension. In this instance, the *Dimension_Durable_SK* should be the same as the *Dimension_NK*, eliminating the need to have the three key columns from the template in the dimension.

A word of caution: if the enterprise adds more SORs in the future (e.g., if a merger or acquisition occurs), then use the dimension template in Figure 10.10.

In the type 1 technique, fact tables linked to a dimension table use the foreign key. For example, see *Dimension_Durable_SK* in Figure 10.12.

SOR Dimension

Figure 10.13 depicts a template for a system of record dimension that lists information regarding the source systems used to populate dimensions. The template columns show:

- *SOR_SK*: The surrogate key identifying the source system.
- *SOR_Name*: A name identifying the source system, typically an application name.

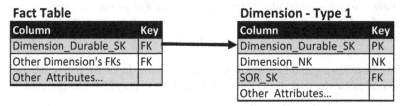

Fact Table

Column	Key
Dimension_Durable_SK	FK
Other Dimension's FKs	FK
Other Attributes...	

Dimension - Type 1

Column	Key
Dimension_Durable_SK	PK
Dimension_NK	NK
SOR_SK	FK
Other Attributes...	

FIGURE 10.12

Fact table links to SCD type 1 dimension.

Column	Key
SOR_SK	PK
SOR_Name	
SOR_Module	
SOR_Table	
Other SOR attributes	

FIGURE 10.13

SOR dimension.

- *SOR_Module* and *SOR_Table*: If there is a need to identify SOR granularity greater than *SOR_Name*, then add these two columns to the dimension. For example, the *SOR_Name* identifies an application, the *SOR_Module* identifies a module within the application, and the *SOR_Table* lists the table the data is obtained from.
- *SOR_Attributes*: There are one or more columns providing the values of all the attributes that the enterprise needs to track.

SCD TYPE 2: CREATE NEW ROW

The type 2 technique creates a new row in the dimension table every time a change occurs in an attribute that we wish to track. Unlike type 1, it enables you to track history accurately, so you see every time an attribute changes in that row and for that employee, as shown in Figure 10.14. It enables both "as is" and "as was" analysis.

This technique keeps track of all the historical changes in the dimension, allowing you to use the values of the dimension attributes at any point in time and examine the impact of those changes on the relevant fact tables. For example, if you're looking at sales of specific products, you can look at what their retail price or production cost was at the point of sale and examine the impact of price or cost changes that occurred since.

This "as is" and "as was" analysis allows you to support trending analysis and period-over-period analysis. The only way you can look at trends, or be able to do year-over-year or quarter-over-quarter analysis, is to really look at apples versus apples, not apples versus oranges.

For example, suppose that the sales organization has reorganized, or a product has been regrouped into different categories and you then need to project sales trends of product sales by sale group. You would want to use the sales organization and product dimensions with their current values "as is" rather than what they were at the point of sale ("as was"). If you're examining sales for financial performance analysis, however, you would keep the dimensional values at the time of sale "as was." The type 2 technique enables the business to switch the dimensional values based on the type of analysis being performed.

Choosing whether or not to recast history (meaning, do you want to reshape the way you look at history based on as it is now or not?) will be a business decision. Often, if you keep the details in the type 2 dimension, this applies to your aggregations, so you need to decide if you want to recast your aggregations the way things are now or leave them the way they were before.

Last Name	Title	Hire Date	Marital Status	Base Rate	Effective Date	Ineffective Date	Status
Gilbert	Prod Technician	08/01/07	S	$12.45	08/01/07		Current

Last Name	Title	Hire Date	Marital Status	Base Rate	Effective Date	Ineffective Date	Status
Gilbert	Prod Technician	08/01/07	S	$12.45	08/01/07	06/11/08	Expired
Gilbert	Prod Technician	08/01/07	M	$12.45	06/12/08	01/31/10	Expired
Gilbert	Prod Technician	08/01/07	M	$17.50	02/01/10	01/01/14	Expired
Gilbert	Prod Supervisor	08/01/07	S	$25.00	01/02/14		Current

FIGURE 10.14

Create new row.

Type 2 Schema

Figure 10.15 depicts a template schema supporting the SCD type 1 technique and Figure 10.16 provides example values. The template columns show:

- *Dimension_Table_SK*: This is the surrogate key used as the primary key for this dimension. Create a new row every time any of the dimensions have attributes that change. This key cannot be used to identify a specific dimension, such as a particular product or customer.
- *Dimension_Durable_SK*: This is the durable key for the dimension, such as a product or customer that uniquely identifies that dimension but does not provide uniqueness in this type 2 table if there have been changes to the dimension's attribute.
- *Dimension_NK*: As with SCD type 1, this is the natural key from the SOR. This column has the data type of the SOR if there is only one SOR or if all the SORs have the same data type. If there are multiple source systems with different data types, then use a data type such as a character string that can store all the natural keys' values.
- *SOR_SK*: As with SCD type 1, if the dimension has multiple SORs, such as a product dimension obtaining product lists from multiple source systems, then the *SOR_SK* is the foreign key linking to the SOR dimension depicted in Figure 10.11.
- *Effective Date*: This is the date that this row became effective and is used as the attribute value.
- *Ineffective Date*: This is the date this row's attribute values become ineffective. If this is the row that contains the current attribute values but the ineffective date is unknown (i.e., this row is active until an attribute values changes), then some people use a NULL in this

SCD Type 2

Column	Key
Dimension_Table_SK	PK
Dimension_Durable_SK	FK
Dimension_NK	NK
SOR_SK	FK
Effective Date	
Ineffective Date	
Current Indicator	
Other Dimension Attributes	

FIGURE 10.15

SCD type 2 template.

Dimension Table SK	Dimension Durable SK	Dimension NK	SOR SK	Effective Date	Ineffective Date	Current Indicator	Dimension Attributes
20123	12345	ABC123	2	1/2/2007	2/3/2009	N	
21357	12345	ABC123	2	2/4/2009	6/22/2012	N	
23488	12345	ABC123	2	6/23/2012	1/1/2014	N	
24719	12345	ABC123	2	1/2/2014	12/31/9999	Y	

FIGURE 10.16

SCD type 2 schema template example.

column; however, the best practice is to input a specific date far in the future, such as 12/31/9999, to avoid queries using a NULL in the selection criteria.

- *Current Indicator*: This is a flag indicating this is the current version of the attribute values for a particular dimension. Typically, the current flag is the first value from one of these Boolean pairs: Y/N, 1/0, or T/F. Although some people use NULL for the values that are not current, it is best practice to use the second value in the Boolean pair examples to avoid queries using a NULL in the selection criteria.
- *Dimension Attributes*: As with SCD type 1, there are one or more columns providing the values of all the attributes that the business needs to track.

In the type 2 technique, fact tables linked to a dimension table include two foreign keys: *Dimension_Table_SK* and *Dimension_Durable_SK* as depicted in Figure 10.17. This enables business analysis to select the dimensional values for the following different timeframes:

- **To get the values at the point of time that the fact occurred** "as was," select the row based on *Dimension_Table_SK*.
- **To get the current values**, select the row based on *Dimension_Durable_SK* and where the Currrent_Indicator = "Y" (or whatever flag was used to indicate it is the current row).
- **To get the value at any particular point in time**, select the row based on *Dimension_Table_SK* with the date of interest being between the *effective date* and *ineffective date*.

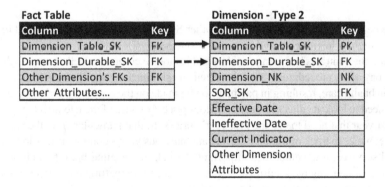

FIGURE 10.17

Fact table links to SCD type 2 dimension.

Another useful analysis that can be performed regarding timeframes is the future or "what will be." There are instances when an enterprise may know future costs they will incur because of contracts they have negotiated with suppliers or create product prices that will take effect in the future. In those circumstances, the attributes can be input into their respective dimensions with future effective date, and the business can perform what-if analysis using the future dates.

SCD TYPE 3: TRACK CHANGES USING SEPARATE COLUMNS BUT OVERWRITE THE REST

With the SCD type 3 technique, you continue to overwrite the rows as in type 1, but you add a new attribute in the row for a particular attribute that's important for the business to track. Generally, you keep track of the new or current value of that particular attribute as well as the original or the previous value in separate fields at the time of change.

The example in Figure 10.18 shows the same employee as previous examples. We want to track the employee's current title and his original title when hired. The initial row shows the employee attributes at the time of hire. The current row has the current values of the employee attributes but, just as with type 1, we have no visibility to what attributes have changed with the exception of the attributes that were added to support type 3. In our example, we selected the title as the attribute we're tracking, so we have both the current title, production supervisor, as well as the original title, production technician.

Initial Row

Employee Key	First Name	Last Name	Title	Original Title	HireDate	Marital Status	Base Rate	Effective Date	Ineffective Date
12345	Guy	Gilbert	Prod Technician	Prod Technician	08/01/07	S	$12.45	08/01/07	12/31/99

Current Row

Employee Key	First Name	Last Name	Title	Original Title	HireDate	Marital Status	Base Rate	Effective Date	Ineffective Date
12345	Guy	Gilbert	Prod Supervisor	Prod Technician	08/01/07	S	$25.00	01/02/14	12/31/99

FIGURE 10.18

Employee dimension—SCD type 3.

Although type 3 is not as commonly used as other SCD techniques, it is very useful in specific business conditions such as health care and financial services:

In health care, the contracts between providers and insurance companies reflect annual changes to prices insurers will pay for procedures. There's often a significant lag, however, in processing and paying claims in health care, resulting in payments being made on the previous year's contract. So, payment processes may need to look at either current or previous prices because of the late-arriving facts—claims that come in for past year that need to use the past year's prices. In that particular case, the attribute that we're tracking is price; we keep track of both the current and previous year's contract prices in type 3 attributes.

In financial services, it is sometimes important to track the original bank branch or account representative that a customer engaged with when opening an account, getting a mortgage or securing a loan rather than the current branch or account representative.

When comparing the SCD type 2 and 3 techniques, consider what happens if the intermediate values are lost and you cannot accurately track history. You can look at some attributes and do some comparisons, but in general, you're in the same position as you are with type 1: you can't perform both "as is" or "as was" analysis.

Type 3 Schema

Figure 10.19 depicts a template schema supporting the SCD type 3. The template columns:

- *Dimension_Durable_SK*: as with type 1, this is the surrogate key used as the primary key for this dimension. This column is referred to as the durable, supernatural, or durable supernatural key. The term durable is used because the key values that are assigned to a dimension will continue to be used regardless of any changes in the values in the SOR. The term supernatural is used to distinguish the key as independent from the SOR natural key.

- *Dimension_NK*: as with SCD type 1, this is the natural key from the SOR. This column has the data type of the SOR if there is only one SOR or if all the SORs have the same data type. If there are multiple source systems with different data types, then use a data type such as a character string that can store all the natural keys' values.
- *SOR_SK*: as with SCD type 1, if the dimension has multiple SORs, such as a product dimension obtaining product lists from multiple source systems, then the *SOR_SK* is the foreign key linking to the SOR dimension depicted in Figure 10.11.
- *Current_Value*: The current values of the attribute using the type 3 technique.
- *Original_Value* or *Previous_Value*: Either the original or previous value of the attribute using the type 3 technique.
- *Other Dimension Attributes*: as with SCD type 1, there are one or more columns providing the values of all the attributes that the business needs to track.

With the type 3 technique, fact tables linked to a dimension table use the foreign key. For example see *Dimension_Durable_SK* in Figure 10.20.

SCD Type 3

Column	Key
Dimension_Durable_SK	PK
Dimension_NK	NK
SOR_SK	FK
Current_Value	
Original_Value or Previous_Value	
Other Dimension Attributes	

FIGURE 10.19

SCD type 3 template.

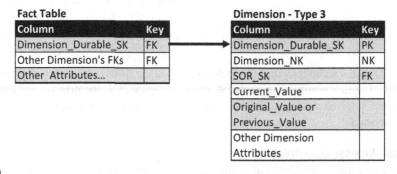

Fact Table

Column	Key
Dimension_Durable_SK	FK
Other Dimension's FKs	FK
Other Attributes...	

Dimension - Type 3

Column	Key
Dimension_Durable_SK	PK
Dimension_NK	NK
SOR_SK	FK
Current_Value	
Original_Value or Previous_Value	
Other Dimension Attributes	

FIGURE 10.20

Fact table links to SCD type 3 dimension.

SCD TYPE 4: ADD MINI-DIMENSION

Although we characterize dimensional attributes as changing slowly over time, there are instances when they change more frequently. These attributes are referred to as rapidly- or volatile changing dimensions. When rapidly changing dimensions are encountered and dimensional tables are relatively large in respect to the total number of rows, then these attributes may adversely affect both loading data and BI query performance.

The example in Figure 10.21 shows a customer dimension that has both slowly and rapidly changing attributes. The slowly changing attributes are:

- First and last name
- Address
- Marital status
- Birthday (should not change but may be corrected or filled in when initially NULL)
- Number of children

    The more rapidly changing attributes are:

- Account status
- Account loyalty level
- Various credit scores
- Income level

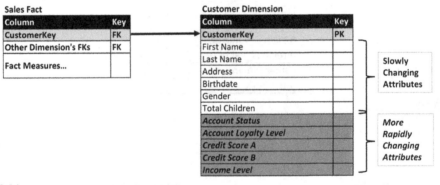

FIGURE 10.21

Customer dimension with both slowly and rapidly changing attributes.

With the SCD type 4 technique, the approach is to divide the slowly and rapidly changing attributes into two groups. The first group contains the SCD and is regarded as the primary or base dimension. The second group, referred to as a profile, contains the more rapidly changing dimensions that are put into a mini-dimension.

Multiple Mini-Dimension Approaches

As with many dimensional modeling techniques, there are mini-dimension variations used to address specific business processes or analytical scenarios. These approaches are split, multiple, and banded-value, as described below:

Split approach—single mini-dimension. The most common approach is to simply put the dimensions into primary and mini-dimension tables. Any fact tables that link to the split dimension would have foreign keys linked to these two tables.

Figure 10.22 depicts the customer dimension shown in Figure 10.21 split into two tables: *Customer dimension* and *Customer profile dimension* (mini-dimension.) We have retained the original foreign key, *CustomerKey*, in the *Sales Fact*, but now have the primary key from the mini-dimension, *CustomerProfileKey*, as an additional foreign key.

Multiple approach—multiple mini-dimensions. There are circumstances in which there are subgroups of rapidly changing attributes that behave in a similar manner. The subgroups may be updated at similar frequencies and times, or by common business processes. Under these circumstances, it is often beneficial from a processing perspective to split each subgroup into its own mini-dimension as portrayed in Figure 10.23. The relevant fact tables have foreign keys to the primary dimension table and all the mini-dimensions.

Banded-value approach. This technique with mini-dimensions is useful when the rapidly changing attributes in the customer dimension are numeric values such as credit scores, account loyalty levels and income levels. Under these conditions, you define segmentation bands that group a range of values together. This reduces the amount and frequency of changes in the segmentation bands. Figure 10.24 depicts our customer mini-dimension example that has been altered to store banded values, such as age, account loyalty, credit score, and income rather than the underlying numeric values. This is a way to avoid frequent changes because, for example, you have an income range instead of specific income numbers. You only have to update the record if the person goes above or below the threshold for that band. The primary risk with this approach is that once you lose the detail you are forced to stay with this segmentation even if business conditions or analytical needs change. There is a discussion of value-band dimensions later in this chapter.

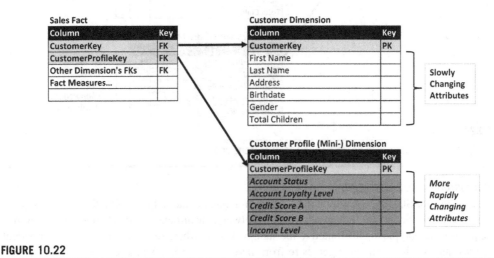

FIGURE 10.22

Customer dimension example split into primary and mini-dimensions.

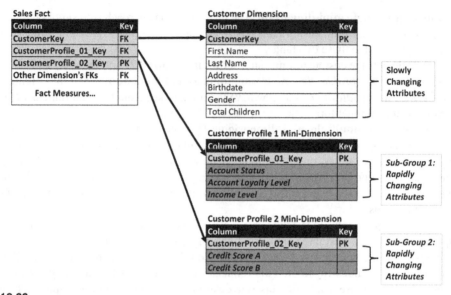

FIGURE 10.23

Customer dimension example with multiple mini-dimensions.

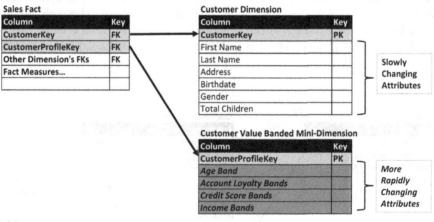

FIGURE 10.24

Customer dimension example with value-banded mini-dimensions.

Mini-Dimensions Need Outrigger

The classic design for SCD type 4 with a mini-dimension has the fact table storing the foreign keys to the primary and mini-dimensions, but no relationship between the dimensions themselves. That reminds me of the phrase, stereotypically attributed to the state of Maine, where the traveler asks a local resident for directions and is told "You can't get there from here." (Or, with a Maine accent: "You can't get theyah from heah.") That answer is no more helpful to the traveler than it is to the BI consumers.

With the classic design, your only way to relate the primary and mini-dimensions is through a fact table as an intermediary, which has the following drawbacks:

- Slow query performance both in updating dimensions and BI queries.
- Redundant combinations are returned in join queries based on how many times the dimension tables are referenced in the fact table.
- Gaps will exist where a primary dimension will not be able to connect with its associated mini-dimension because neither is referenced in a fact table.

The best practice is to place a foreign key to the mini-dimension in the primary dimension as depicted in Figure 10.25 where *CustomerProfileKey* links the customer dimension to the customer profile mini-dimension.

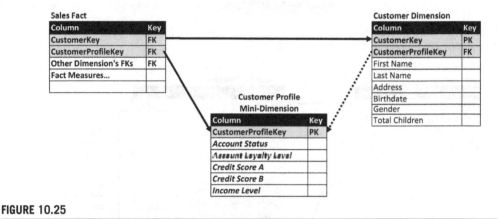

FIGURE 10.25

Mini-dimension as outrigger.

SCD TYPE 5: COMBINE TYPES 4+1

The SCD type 5 technique builds upon the type 4 technique by splitting the dimension into a primary dimension with the slowly changing attributes and a mini-dimension with the rapidly changing attributes. It then grafts the type 1 technique of storing a current copy of the mini-dimension attributes. The technique is referred to as type 5 because it is the combination of types 4+1.

There are several approaches to implementing type 5:

- Create a separate mini-dimension that contains the current values of the rapidly changing attributes as depicted in Figure 10.26. The primary dimension, *Customer Dimension*, contains the foreign key, *CustomerCurrentProfileKey*, to the second mini-dimension, *Customer Current Profile Mini-Dimension.*
- The second mini-dimension, *Customer Current Profile Mini-Dimension* in our example, is actually a view created from the first mini-dimension, *Customer Profile Mini-Dimension* using a *Current_Indicator* attribute that is present in type 2 dimensions (which both the primary and first mini-dimensions are.)

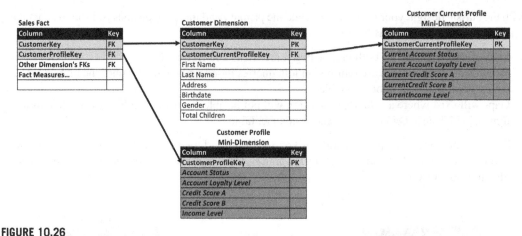

FIGURE 10.26

Customer example type 5 with second mini-dimension.

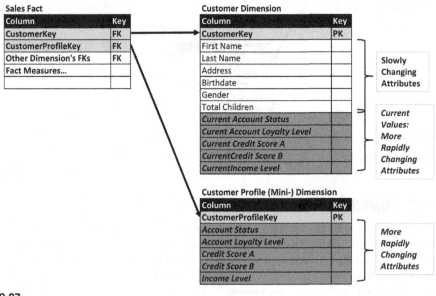

FIGURE 10.27

Customer dimension example with hybrid mini-dimensions.

In the third approach, place the current values of each of the rapidly changing attributes in the primary dimension table. Figure 10.27 depicts the customer dimension with each attribute in the mini-dimension (account status, account loyalty level, etc.) having corresponding attributes in the primary dimension with the current values (current account status, current account loyalty level, etc.).

Use this approach when most of the business analysis with this dimension is going to use the current value in "as is" reporting. The primary dimension contains all the current values of the attributes supporting "as is" queries, whereas "as was" queries, assumed to be infrequent, use the mini-dimension that tracks the historical values.

SCD TYPE 6: COMBINE TYPES 1 + 2 + 3 (=6)

The SCD type 6 technique blends portions of SCD types 2, 1, and 3. Similar to type 2, a type 6 schema creates a new record with every change in attribute values that are being tracked. The current value (type 1) of a specific attribute is added as a column (type 3) onto every row. This allows rows to be filtered or grouped by either the current or historical value of the type 3 column. The type 2 portion of this technique enables "as is" and "as was" analysis.

Figure 10.28 depicts an employee dimension using the type 6 technique. The example shows three different states of the dimension's rows for a specific employee: original row when the employee is hired, the first time the employee's attributes are changed—he or she got married, received a promotion and salary increase, and the current state of his or her employee records listing all the changes in title, marital status and salary. As with the type 2 technique, the effective and ineffective dates of each row are recorded along with a current status indicator. The *Historical Title* column lists his or her title during the effective time period, whereas the *Current Title* is always updated to reflect the current title.

Original Row

Employee Key	First Name	Last Name	Current Title	Historical Title	Hire Date	Marital Status	Base Rate	Effective Date	Ineffective Date	Status
12345	Guy	Gilbert	Prod Technician	Prod Technician	08/01/07	S	$12.45	8/1/2007	12/31/9999	Current

1st Change in Values

Employee Key	First Name	Last Name	Current Title	Historical Title	Hire Date	Marital Status	Base Rate	Effective Date	Ineffective Date	Status
12345	Guy	Gilbert	Senior Prod Technician	Prod Technician	08/01/07	S	$12.45	8/1/2007	6/11/2008	Expired
12345	Guy	Gilbert	Senior Prod Technician	Senior Prod Technician	08/01/07	M	$15.25	6/12/2008	12/31/9999	Current

Current State of Rows

Employee Key	First Name	Last Name	Current Title	Historical Title	Hire Date	Marital Status	Base Rate	Effective Date	Ineffective Date	Status
12345	Guy	Gilbert	Production Manager	Prod Technician	08/01/07	S	$12.45	8/1/2007	6/11/2008	Expired
12345	Guy	Gilbert	Production Manager	Senior Prod Technician	08/01/07	M	$15.25	6/12/2008	1/31/2010	Expired
12345	Guy	Gilbert	Production Manager	Prod Supervisor	08/01/07	M	$17.50	2/1/2010	1/1/2014	Expired
12345	Guy	Gilbert	Production Manager	Production Manager	08/01/07	S	$25.00	1/2/2014	12/31/9999	Current

FIGURE 10.28

Employee example SCD type 6.

Type 6 Schema

Figure 10.29 depicts a template schema supporting the SCD type 6 technique. See the descriptions for the SCD type 2 columns in the section "Type 2 schema" earlier in this chapter, as they are the same in this schema:

- *Dimension_Table_SK*
- *Dimension_Durable_SK*
- *Dimension_NK*
- *SOR_SK*
- *Effective Date*
- *Ineffective Date*
- *Current Indicator*
- *Dimension Attributes*

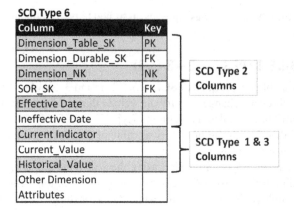

FIGURE 10.29

SCD type 6 schema.

The blended SCD types 3 and 1 techniques are provided by the following columns:

- *Current_Value*: The current value of the attribute being tracked. This value is applied to this column in all rows associated with the durable key.
- *Historical_Value*: The value of the attribute being tracked at the point in time that the row was initially created. This value does not change once it has been input into its row.

SCD TYPE 7: USE BOTH TYPES 1+2

SCD type 7 technique creates both type 1 and type 2 versions of a dimension. From a data perspective, with this technique you accurately track all the historical changes to dimensional attributes that the business requires. From a business analysis perspective, you have the option to either expose the historical values in the type 2 dimension for both "as was" and "as is" analysis or provide current values from the type 1 dimension for "as is" analysis. The benefit of offering both is that when only "as is" is needed query performance and business productivity are greatly increased. Because a considerable portion of business analysis will be "as is," these benefits will occur often.

Most businesses need to have historically accurate dimensional data. They want to be able to track history, perform "as is" and "as was" reporting, and meet industry and governmental regulatory requirements. Most common business queries, analytics, and reports, however, only require current values. The vast majority of reports that people create on a daily basis are just looking at "as is" conditions. How many customers do I have? What are my sales? What are my costs related to the state of the dimensions at that particular time? This is type 1 data, and query performance is fast because you only have one unique row in each dimension.

It gets more complicated, however, when you have type 2 data. Rather than one row for an employee or product in a dimension, you have many rows tracking all the changes over time. Now the queries are very complex, and it's time-consuming to actually select the rows within the dimensions because you have to specify time periods, the durable keys, and any other attributes by which you need to filter. And, you may have dozens of dimensions that you want to select and join with the fact table. Each of these queries has to use ineffective and effective dates in order to accomplish and pick out the right dates.

This problem required a solution that would let you get the best of both worlds: track historical data in type 2 processing *and* get type 1 query performance. The hybrid approach tracks the dimensions in type 2, slowly changing dimension processes within the data warehouse, and then exposes a type 1 view of that as a source of most queries, reports, and analysis. That view is available in data marts and OLAP cubes. You can also implement it either as a table that just has the type 1 version of the type 2 dimension or you can use some database constructs like materialized views, indexed partitions, or simple database views in order to create the type 1 view of the type 2 data—in which case, any queries that just need "as is" reporting would not have to look at the effective and ineffective dates for the current flags.

I recommend the SCD type 7 technique as the best pragmatic approach to capturing historical values and then matching the appropriate schema for the business analysis that is going to be performed. You only need to provide current values (type 1). It greatly simplifies querying, lessens the chance for errors, and improves understanding. As an aside, this technique is used by some of the Master Data Management vendors.

The SCD type 7 technique goes by many other names:

- SCD type 4—this was its first name until the numbers were shuffled around
- SCD hybrid approach
- Current and history table approach

Type 7 Schema

Figure 10.30 depicts a schema supporting the SCD type 7 technique. There are three types of tables involved: *fact*, *current* (type 1), and *history* (type 2).

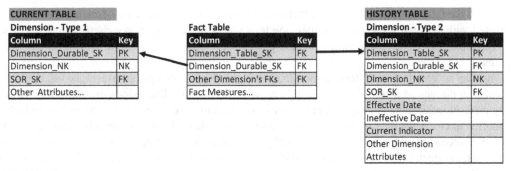

FIGURE 10.30

SCD type 7 schema.

The history table includes the SCD type 2 columns (see "Type 2 Schema" earlier in this chapter) and contains all the entire history of attribute changes for the dimension. As with type 2, the schema has these columns:

- *Dimension_Table_SK*
- *Dimension_Durable_SK*
- *Dimension_NK*

- *SOR_SK*
- *Effective Date*
- *Ineffective Date*
- *Current Indicator*
- *Dimension Attributes*

The current table also includes the SCD type 1 columns (see "Type 1 schema" earlier in this chapter) and only contains the most current rows of the dimension's attributes. The standard convention is to prefix the names of the attribute columns from the history table with the string of "current_" to differentiate the current and history attributes. The schema includes:

- *Dimension_Durable_SK*
- *Dimension_NK*
- *SOR_SK*
- *Dimension Attributes*

Some people will add the SCD type 2 attributes—*Dimension_Table_SK, Effective_Date*, and *Ineffective_Date*—but if it is not needed for the business analysis, then that goes against the reason why the current table is being used.

There are two alternatives: (1) creating and updating two tables—history and current—by using data integration, or (2) using the database to create a view or a materialized view.

CAUSAL DIMENSION

Facts have obvious attributes such as product, customer, geography, and time. This is the "who, what, where" of the fact. But facts also have a "why" component. This is the causal dimension. (Not to be confused with "casual.") The causal dimension tells you why a customer bought or returned a product. Examples of causal relationships include promotions, campaigns, and the reason for sales and returns.

This can be very important information, but often these relationships are overlooked in the initial design of a dimensional model; they are looked at as degenerate dimensions, meaning they're just some piece of information about the fact that we don't need to store. They tend to be overlooked when promotion or campaign data is being stored somewhere outside of the enterprise application that is the primary source system feeding the dimensional model, such as in a campaign tool or a separate database. This, in effect, hides the attributes and dimensions from the source system you're actually pulling data from.

Likewise, reason codes—reasons why people buy, exchange or return products—typically aren't in the initial source system either, causing them to be overlooked. These reason codes can be essential for sales and marketing analytics on customers behavior, so bringing this data into view is very important.

Figure 10.31 shows two casual dimensions: *DimPromotion* and *DimSalesReason*.

On the left side, the fact table *FactInternetSales* with the foreign key *PromotionKey*, links to the casual dimension *DimPromotion*, which has attributes such as promotion name, item discount amount, promotion type, category, start and end dates, and quantities for that promotion. With this promotion dimension, the business can track the effectiveness of the promotion, view trends for different types of promotions, and undertake related analytics.

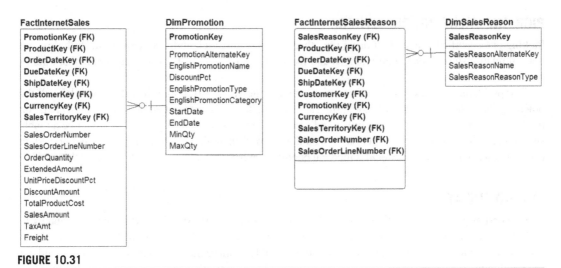

FIGURE 10.31

Causal dimension examples.

The fact table *FactSalesReason* has the foreign key *SalesReasonKey* that links to the casual dimension *DimSalesReason*, which has the attributes for why somebody bought or returned a product. These reasons might be captured by a call center worker, by a salesperson, or online in a survey. The information provided by the causal dimensions is invaluable to the marketing and sales analytics.

MULTIVALUED DIMENSIONS

When you start to encounter more complicated data situations that require advanced data modeling techniques, you may need to use a multivalued dimension situation. These kinds of situations arise when a fact measurement is associated with multiple values in a dimensional table. This is opposed to the more typical scenario, in which a fact measurement is associated with one value in a dimension, allowing a normal fact and dimensional star schema.

Health care is a common real-world example of multivalued dimensions. A patient arrives at the emergency room after a vertigo episode caused him to fall and break his arm. He will have at least two diagnoses—vertigo and broken arm—and will require several types of treatments for the vertigo and setting the broken bone. The hospital has diagnostic codes for each ailment and procedure codes for each treatment. The hospital must track all of the codes for this patient's visit and any subsequent visits.

Insurance and financial accounts provide another example. It is common for financial accounts and certain types of insurance policies to be associated with two account owners or policy holders. One account will have multiple types of products or accounts associated with the owners, such as checking, savings, a mortgage, and a credit card. It's a many-to-many relationship between the account owners and the products in their account.

There are three typical approaches to handling these complicated data situations:

- Pick one value, ignore others
- Extend the attributes
- Create a bridge table

PICK ONE VALUE, IGNORE OTHERS

Picking one specific value and ignoring the other values is the quick and dirty approach. With this, our normal relationships between dimensions and facts stay intact and our BI tools can handle that kind of construct.

The problem, of course, is that if you pick one specific value and ignore the others, you lose all the other details. If the details aren't needed, such as if you're just looking to get an insurance claim paid, you might have a business rule that you only need one value upon which to get paid. This would be a viable situation. But a hospital, on the other hand, would need to track all the different diagnostic and procedure codes that went along with a patient's medical condition, whether the claim is paid for one value or not.

EXTEND THE ATTRIBUTES

The second approach, which I've seen many times, is to actually extend the dimension attributes to include a fixed number of multivalue dimensions. In essence, this creates a list within the dimensional row. For example, the hospital could assume no one will have more than 10 diagnoses, so you would put in 10 columns, one for each code (or make it 20 to add a buffer). It's a quick way to solve the problem when you can assume that there is an upper bound to the number of times that an attribute can occur.

The problem with this approach is that it's limited by the context of the upper bound, and, more importantly, that you're imposing a repeating group into your dimensional row. That causes problems when you want to look at the total number of diagnostic codes, for example, and how many instances there are of a particular diagnostic code.

BRIDGE TABLE

The third solution, building a bridge table, is the most sophisticated approach for multivalued dimensions and produces the most complete results. As the name implies, it bridges the gap between the fact and dimension tables.

The bridge table needs to support the many-to-many relationships between a fact table and associated dimensions. The example in Figure 10.32 depicts:

- **Fact table:** *FactBillingLineItem* with information about the patient, about the provider (doctor), treatment date, what organization the doctor is from, other key information such as treatment and location. It contains the foreign key *DiagnosisGroupKey* that links to the bridge table.

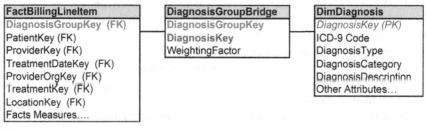

FIGURE 10.32

Bridge table approach.

- **Bridge table:** *DiagnosisGroupBridge* with the *DiagnosisGroupKey* that is used to group the set of diagnoses that a patient encountered in a visit to a provider (i.e., a row in the fact table), the foreign key *DiagnosisKey* linking to the dimension table, and a weighting factor (discussed in the following section).
- **Dimension table:** *DimDiagnosis* with a primary key of *DiagnosisKey* and several types of medical terms or categorizations that are applicable to that diagnosis.

A bridge table has a weighting factor if all the members of the *DiagnosisGroupKey* are not considered equal and are determined by a predefined weighting. The weighting factor allocates numeric additive facts. In this example, the weighting factor is the method to sum up the additive attributes associated with specific diagnosis. Typically the weighting factor adds up to one. In the example, this relates to one visit to the doctor. There is a certain percentage weighting factor adding up to one for one to N number of rows for the different diagnostic keys. Sometimes these weighting factors will be described in medical health care provider situations, there are formulas they use for other cases where this is marketing or sales, when they come up with the weighting or allocations.

There are two types of queries with a bridge table:

- **Queries with a weighting factor to allocate the values**. For example, based on a health care insurers' contract, a health care provider, such as the doctor, will use the weighting factors when "scoring" (i.e., aggregating attributes from the diagnosis dimension).
- **Queries without a weighting factor to allocate the values**. In this scenario, the health care provider treats each diagnosis equally and aggregates the diagnosis dimension's attributes without applying any weighting factor. There is no weighting factor to determine the total number of occurrences of a diagnosis regardless of how many diagnoses for the patient. Suppose you want to know how many times, for example, swine flu was diagnosed. That would be one occurrence in multiple group keys. So you ignore the weighting factor; in this case, you're just trying to get the total number of diagnosis keys.

Using the bridge allows you to perform analysis of facts and dimensions with a many-to-many relationship. It also enables the ability to treat the relationships equally or, as so often happens because the relationships are not all equal, to use a weighting factor based on business rules.

JUNK DIMENSIONS

Perhaps you have a junk drawer in your kitchen where you put miscellaneous things that you know you'll need some day, but you're not sure where else to put them. Dimensional modeling has a junk drawer too, and it also manages clutter and helps make things more productive. Junk dimensions are a way to handle the multitude of low-cardinality transactions, system codes, flags, identifiers, and text attributes by putting them into one table so you can better manage them.

It is typical for these miscellaneous flags to have 2–10 possible values. Sometimes they are yes or no attributes, whereas other times they are a short list of options to complete a business transaction.

JUNK, GARBAGE, CROSS-REFERENCE

Many information technology people hate the name junk (or garbage) dimension because they do not want to tell their business people that they are creating junk. These are also called "cross-reference dimensions"—this is the term I prefer to use with clients. The term junk dimension, however, is well-recognized in the industry, so we use it here to avoid confusion.

Table 10.1　Junk Dimension Alternatives That Don't Work Well

Alternatives	Results
Put them into an existing dimension	Does not fit because attributes have different grain. Creates Cartesian product
Leave them in the fact table	Too cluttered, row size too large, affects speed, cannot be conformed
Make them into separate dimensions	Overly complex with too many tables, affects speed and maintenance
Eliminate them	Cannot eliminate if used by business group and needed in analytics

MISGUIDED ATTEMPTS

As shown in Table 10.1, there are four misguided ways people attempt to approach the problem of these miscellaneous flags:

- First, they put them into an existing dimension. Force-fitting doesn't work when the attributes are different grains or if it creates a Cartesian product and makes the dimension too large.
- Second, leave them in a fact table. This common, misguided approach makes the fact table cluttered and the row sizes very large; it also slows down performance and makes it so the dimensions cannot be conformed.
- Third is to make them into separate dimensions. It takes out code fields and puts the attributes into their own dimension tables. Although this is much better than the first two approaches, it creates many, many tables with a small number of rows, 10 rows for example. This negatively affects speed because you're always doing queries and joins to these many small tables. It increases maintenance because there are so many tables to maintain. It is much better, however, than hand-coding the flags in your applications because it makes them visible and documented.
- Fourth, is to just eliminate them. Then they can't be used by the business, which is a problem if they are needed for analytics.

RECOMMENDED SOLUTION

The solution to these numerous miscellaneous flags, codes, or indicator fields from the transactional systems is to create a junk dimension, and then to use views similar to role-playing dimensions when necessary. In essence, it takes the third option mentioned previously, which is generating numerous tables to have these values, and putting together or collapsing them into one junk dimension.

Junk_ID	Group_Name	Code	Code_Description	SOR_Table_Name	SOR_Field_Name
201	Promotion Status	A	Approved	imm_promo_header	status
202	Promotion Status	C	Cancelled	imm_promo_header	status
203	Promotion Status	D	Deleted	imm_promo_header	status
204	Promotion Status	F	Pending Promo	imm_promo_header	status
205	Promotion Status	N	Running	imm_promo_header	status
206	Promotion Status	R	Released	imm_promo_header	status
207	Promotion Status	X	Expired	imm_promo_header	status
208	Promotion Status	Z	Frozen	imm_promo_header	status
401	Order Status	A	Tech-Approved	imm_item_order_wkbk	order_status_code
402	Order Status	E	Estimated	imm_item_order_wkbk	order_status_code
403	Order Status	H	On Hold	imm_item_order_wkbk	order_status_code
404	Order Status	N	Not Reviewed	imm_item_order_wkbk	order_status_code
405	Order Status	P	Pending	imm_item_order_wkbk	order_status_code
406	Order Status	R	Released	imm_item_order_wkbk	order_status_code
407	Order Status	S	Skipped	imm_item_order_wkbk	order_status_code
501	Price Type	C	Cost Base	bn_item	price_type_code
502	Price Type	F	Freight Pass Thru	bn_item	price_type_code
503	Price Type	N	Net Price	bn_item	price_type_code
504	Price Type	R	Retail	bn_item	price_type_code

FIGURE 10.33

Junk dimension example.

The dimension consists of low-cardinality columns, such as flags, codes, indicators, and text attributes, meaning there are not too many values. These values rarely change, but there may be no correlation between the groups of these attributes within the junk dimension.

This is a pragmatic approach because it takes the best attributes of the large number of tables and puts them into one location to be managed, updated, and queried upon. The primary function of this junk table is to enable filtering reporting. It prevents these attributes from being embedded in the report code, and it enables a much better documentation of the system.

In the example in Figure 10.33, code fields and their descriptions are grouped together based on common usage and input into a junk dimension. The columns in this example are:

- *Junk_ID*—surrogate key
- *Group_Name*—a set of common code fields
- *Code*—list of code fields
- *Code_Descriptions*—textual description displayed for the codes
- *SOR_Table_Name*—table from source system from which these codes are obtained
- *SOR_Field_Name*—field in table from which these codes are obtained

These code fields are often used for filtering and grouping data in reporting. A BI application such as a dashboard or interactive report might provide pick lists or pull-down menus using the groupings and codes as the options presented. Creating a junk dimension replaces hard-coded options in applications, makes it easier to maintain and change these codes, and increases the ability to reuse and share because these codes are in tables rather than embedded in code or personal spreadsheets.

VALUE BAND REPORTING

It is common in reporting and analytics to group data together. You group the facts by a particular dimension or fact measurement. When grouping by a dimension, you may have a hierarchy, which is a natural group. When grouping a product that has a subcategory and a category together, you could aggregate on each of those levels.

But grouping fact measures, especially numbers, is not so easy or efficient. Often the range of numbers is hard-coded into a report, making it impossible to make changes to that band or even document what that band is. So the best practice is to create value band groupings for particular fact measures.

The two examples in Figure 10.34 are for income and age. The income column includes bands from the US Census Bureau: super rich, rich, upper middle class, lower middle class, working class, and poor. (That is the Census Bureau's wording, not mine!) The age column has bands for age groups: infant, elementary, high school, college, young adult, 30s, 40s, 60s, and really old. Both have a lower and upper band.

The examples show that two different groups or kinds of analysis might need to group income levels differently. They might have more groups of income levels, smaller groups of income levels, and based on international settings, have different numbers based on whether it's Canada, the United States, or Europe. The same applies to the age groupings. If you're selling toys, you might have a fine-grained age band for younger people and may not care about anyone over the age of 12.

If you're looking at social security and retirement benefits, you might have everybody grouped under 30 in one band, and more do fine-grained tuning of people over 60. There is a lot of room for variation in these group bands, so it's best practice to put these bands into tables, rather than hard coding them into reports.

Rather than hard-code value bands in reports, you should use a value band table for analysis. Figure 10.35 depicts an example where a fact table, *Fact_Account_Balances*, uses the value band dimension, *Value_Band_Dimension*, to group accounts by ranges of account balances. The value band dimension contains the following:

- *ValueBandGroup*: Primary key
- *ValueBandName*: Name used to describe the band, such as super rich and poor in the previous example. This column would be used for filtering, sorting, and grouping accounts in reports.

Group	Lower Band	Upper Band
Super Rich	$1,000,000	$10,000,000
One Percenters	$250,000	$999,999
Upper Middle Class	$100,000	$249,999
Lower Middle Class	$35,000	$99,999
Working Class	$18,000	$34,999
Poor	$0	$17,999

Group	Lower Band	Upper Band
Infant	0	4
Elementary	5	13
High School	14	17
College	18	21
Young Adult	22	29
30s	30	39
40s	40	49
30s	30	33
60s	60	69
Really Old	70	99

FIGURE 10.34

Value band reporting.

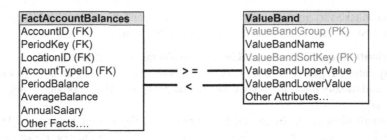

FIGURE 10.35

Value band reporting approaches.

- *ValueBandSortKey*: Often the *ValueBandName* does not sort in the order that business people prefer, so this numeric column would be used to obtain the preferred order.
- *ValueBandUpperValue*: The upper bound of the range in this value band.
- *ValueBandLowerValue*: The lower bound of the range in this value band.

When assigning accounts to value bands, the account's *PeriodBalance*, for example, is compared with the value band upper and lower values.

This example allows numerous value bands for age and income depending on who wants to look at the numbers. It lets you change the bands without having to change the fact table.

It's also possible to take a hybrid approach, where you follow the first approach, which is to create the value band table and put the foreign key in the fact table, but then keep the original fact measure in the balance table so you can do numeric calculations directly on the detail. You can do either direct numeric analysis or the value band analysis in your dimensional model.

HETEROGENEOUS PRODUCTS

Heterogeneous products and services can present some challenges with dimensional models. When you have diverse sets of products and customers, you can simply have multiple facts and dimensions. For example, General Electric sells light bulbs to customers, jet engines to the airline industry, and gas turbines to utilities. It's not a common set of customers; it's a diverse set of customers and diverse products.

It's more complicated, however, when a company sells diverse products to a common set of customers. How do you represent these diverse products and services as one fact in situations like the following:

- Multiline insurance companies sell distinct products—life, auto, property, and casualty insurance to the same customer.
- Financial services companies have retail banks, commercial banking, credit cards, mutual funds, 401k plans, and many other financial instruments, all targeted to the same customer. These products have facts and dimensions that are very different from one another.
- High-tech companies sell hardware, software, training, maintenance, and services to a common customer base, but they have different facts with very different measures and attributes.

Enterprises can take various approaches to handle heterogeneous products sold to a common set of customers. The first one, however, is something you should avoid:

- **Merge attributes into a single fact table**. This results in large fact tables with rows that have many empty values. It gets to be a very complex fact table that's being updated by multiple lines of business and usually there are many coordination problems. This approach is not recommended.
- **Create separate dimensions in fact tables representing the diverse businesses**. This is viable if they are totally separate businesses. That, however, is typically not the case if they are trying to sell to a common base of customers. Even if you have separate dimensions in the fact tables, you still need some set of financial consolidation in the company because you have to report to the government, and you need to look at your overall enterprise financials. This approach may not be applicable.
- **Create a single dimension and a single fact table representing a set of core attributes or measures**. This approach works when there are common measures such as financial data used in corporate finance, regulatory reporting, and senior management looking at the performance metrics of the enterprise. It uses fact and dimension tables that are specific to the diverse products or businesses that can then be linked to the core tables. This recommended approach is a hybrid solution that, from a pragmatic point of view, has been highly effective in representing heterogeneous products.

ALTERNATE DIMENSIONS

The classic assumption is that facts are connected to a set of conformed dimensions, meaning that all business analysis uses the same definition and hierarchy of a specific dimension. That implies that there is only one way to group customers or products, for example. But this attempt to create conformity inhibits the ability to create customized views of dimensions to match the analytical requirements of business functions and processes. Finance, marketing, sales, and manufacturing may have legitimate business needs to group customers and products differently.

When one standard dimension is available for business analysis, then the burden is shifted to business people to create the alternative views of the dimensions. This is typically done by extracting data to spreadsheets to enable analysis using alternative versions of dimensions that were created manually by business people. Not only is this a productivity drain, but there is no documentation, sharing is haphazard, and the potential for inconsistency is high.

Dimensional models need to accommodate alternative views of dimensions to support business needs, improve productivity, and provide consistency. There are two basic approaches:

- Hot swappable dimensions (also called profile tables)
- Custom dimension groups

HOT SWAPPABLE DIMENSION

Hot swappable dimensions are switched at query-time based on business needs. They got their name because someone thought it was analogous to hot swappable hardware components that are switched in real time.

Hot swappable dimensions are implemented by connecting a fact table with alternate versions of a dimension, then using one alternative for analysis at query time. The alternative is either selected by the business person explicitly or automatically by the BI application based on specific business rules. Figure 10.36 depicts an example of hot swappable dimensions used for both the product and geography dimensions. The product and geography dimensions in this example are each considered to be conformed dimensions. Each of the alternatives is a variation based on:

- Having a subset of the conformed dimension attributes
- Filtering the rows from the conformed dimensions
- Creating a different hierarchy or grouping of the dimensions

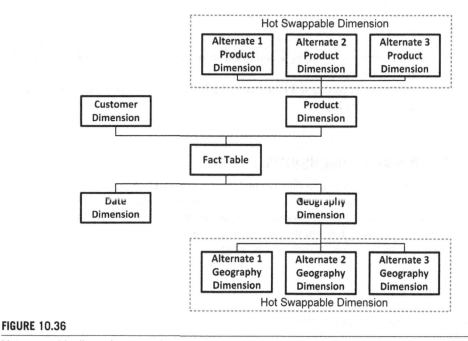

FIGURE 10.36

Hot swappable dimension example.

If hot swappable dimensions are a subset of the rows and columns in the conformed dimensions but do not provide alternate hierarchies, then they can be implemented as either tables or views. However, with alternate hierarchies, physical tables are required.

CUSTOM DIMENSION GROUPS

The second approach to creating alternative dimensions is to enhance the dimension's schema to accommodate different dimensional groups.

As depicted in Figure 10.37, an additional dimension is created, *Custom_Dimension_Groups* that has a row for each alternate grouping with descriptive attributes. The new dimension could be used as a filter to select alternates during query time or to create views that would be made available to specific groups of business people. The foreign key *Dimension_Group_SK* is added to the dimension table.

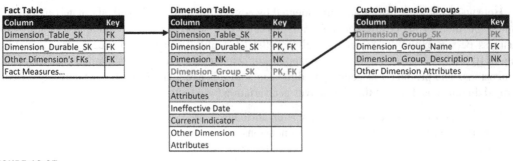

FIGURE 10.37

Alternate dimension groups.

The primary key for the dimension table is a combination of *Dimension_Table_SK*, *Dimension_Durable_SK*, and *Dimension_Group_SK*.

Fact tables are not modified, however, and continue to be linked to the dimension table using the *Dimension_Table_SK* as the foreign key.

TOO FEW OR TOO MANY DIMENSIONS

When you complete your first iteration of a dimensional model, you might find that you have too few or too many dimensions. It is common to have 6–18 dimensions to model a business process. Although there will be common or conformed dimensions across business processes, it is likely that as the number of processes modeled grows, so too will the number of dimensions.

If you have too few, consider if any of these are missing:

- Outriggers
- Role-playing dimensions
- Causal dimensions
- Multivalued dimensions and bridge tables
- Value band tables

It's possible to add any of these after you enter into the production phase of your dimensional model because they don't affect the existing primary and foreign keys in your dimensional model. Keep in mind, however, that striving to develop a comprehensive a model early will improve productivity and analytical capabilities.

If you end up with far too many dimensions, such as hundreds, for example, then you need to determine if you have any of these issues:

- Some of the dimensions are dependent on each other and need to be combined. If there is a one-to-one mapping they definitely need to be combined.
- There are degenerate dimensions, which need to be collapsed as talked about in Chapter 9.
- Many of the dimensions are really an accumulation of junk dimensions that could be put into one table to improve management and productivity.

DATA INTEGRATION DESIGN V

DATA INTEGRATION DESIGN AND DEVELOPMENT

11

INFORMATION IN THIS CHAPTER:

- Data integration design and development
- Data integration justification
- Data integration architecture
- Prerequisites and requirements for data integration
- Data integration design
- Data integration workflow
- Project and DI development standards
- Reusable components
- Historical data
- Prototyping
- Testing

GETTING STARTED WITH DATA INTEGRATION

One of the key deliverables in business intelligence (BI) is providing consistent, comprehensive, clean, conformed, and current information for business people to enable analysis and decision making. Delivering the five C's is not achieved by BI tools simply accessing disparate data, but rather through data integration. Data integration combines data from different sources and brings it together to ultimately provide a unified view.

Data integration is like an iceberg. BI gets all the attention, just like the part of the iceberg that is visible as it is floating in the ocean. But the vast majority of the iceberg is below the waterline, just as the vast majority of the work in a BI project is in designing and developing data integration processes. As much as three quarters of the BI project's time is devoted to data integration when new data sources are added to the data architecture.

With so much of the project's time devoted to this one area, it is critical to adopt best practices to design robust, scalable, and cost-effective data integration processes.

HOLISTIC APPROACH

BI projects are generally undertaken tactically, independent of other projects. Creating discrete projects that can be scoped and completed is a proven project management approach. However, the danger is that discrete becomes disjointed. Separate projects can either perform redundant tasks or, even worse, contradictory work.

See the book Web site www.BI guidebook.com for requirements and design templates.

Each project looks at its needs and then builds accordingly. Years ago, telecommunication systems—phones, networking, and e–mail—were often purchased and deployed by multiple groups within an enterprise, sometimes in the same building. At some point, people realized these systems should be part of an enterprise backbone that needed an overall architecture and then deployed to support both enterprise-wide and group-specific needs. Without this holistic view, enterprises were generally paying too much in cost, time, and resources deploying overlapping and sometimes incompatible systems.

Likewise, data integration needs to be architected in a holistic manner, enabling an enterprise-wide solution that supports both enterprise and specific business groups' needs without costly overlaps and inconsistencies. Data integration needs to be architected in a top-down fashion, supporting its information, data, technology, and product components while being implemented in a bottom-up fashion, i.e., project by project.

INCREMENTAL AND ITERATIVE APPROACHES

Although it is imperative to take a holistic approach in designing an overall architecture, the potential trap is viewing that architecture as the end goal. The real goal is to transform data into business information, but sometimes technically oriented folks lose sight of that. The architecture is a means to an end, not the end itself.

Data integration processes should be:
- **Holistic**—avoid costly overlaps and inconsistencies.
- **Incremental**—more manageable and practical.
- **Iterative**—discover and learn from each individual project.
- **Reusable**—ensure consistency.
- **Documented**—identify data for reuse, and create leverage for future projects.
- **Auditable**—necessary for government regulations and industry standards.

Building the architecture blueprint and implementing an enterprise data integration solution should be both incremental and iterative.

Incremental: do not attempt to "boil the ocean." Most enterprises do not have the time, money, or resources to build out an enterprise integration solution in one grandiose project. Instead, incrementally building out the architecture one project at a time allows a more manageable and practical method to achieve the architecture. The individual projects should be viewed as incrementally building the enterprise data integration portfolio. When you have an overall architecture, you can design each tactical project to fill in more pieces of that portfolio in an orchestrated fashion, rather than just hoping it happens by itself.

Iterative: building out the architecture iteratively offers the opportunity to discover and learn from each individual project. Neither the business nor IT will begin with complete knowledge of current or future information needs as you start your integration efforts. The architecture and implemented solutions need to evolve iteratively to incorporate discovery and learning, along with adapting to changing business needs. Thinking that you know everything or being inflexible are traps that will sink your data integration investments.

PRODUCTIVE, EFFICIENT METHODS

Data integration is most successful when you use productive, efficient methods. Three of these methods are reuse, document, and make it auditable.

Reuse: reusing data definitions and transformations is not only the most productive method to build an enterprise-wide solution, but also the surest method to ensure consistency. Why reinvent the wheel with every integration project when you can leverage past work and ensure consistency? This seems like a no-brainer, but only if the definitions and transformations from projects are readily available.

Document: documentation enables the identification of data that has been defined before and is a candidate for reuse. This documentation needs to be created and maintained for all data integration projects. It needs to be stored along with data integration application source code. Fortunately, most data integration tools generate application documentation, making your job easier. However you document the project, it should include detailed listings of source and targets and, ideally, graphical visualizations of the data integration workflows. Each project needs to be able to leverage other projects' learnings, and should make its own shareable as well.

Auditable: with the rise of various government regulations and industry standards, such as Sarbanes-Oxley and Health Insurance Portability and Accountability Act (HIPPA), being able to audit your data integration is not just a "nice to have," but a business necessity. The audit capabilities to examine data lineage and perform impact analysis provide a better understanding of the data integration processes, improve maintainability, and lowers its total cost of ownership (TCO).

DATA INTEGRATION ARCHITECTURE

The data integration architecture represents the workflow of data from multiple systems of record (SOR) through a series of transformations used to create consistent, conformed, comprehensive, clean, and current information for business analysis and decision making. Although an enterprise may just start with an enterprise data warehouse (EDW) to enable its BI applications, the data integration architecture needs to be designed to accommodate the workflow. See Figure 11.1, which illustrates the most advanced data architecture discussed in Chapter 6. Each data store in the diagram represents a specific data integration state needed to transform data into information. An enterprise has various alternatives in implementing the data stores; these range from each being an individual database distributed across the enterprise to a single database with each data store representing a schema or collection of tables. The number of tables in this architecture could range from dozens to thousands, depending on the size and complexity of an enterprise's business.

As data advances from the SORs loading successive data stores, each of those transformations, as depicted in Figure 11.2, requires a set of data integration processes. Each breakpoint in the diagram represents an iterative stage in the development of the data integration workflow. Each stage needs the previous stage's data in order to perform its integration.

The list of stages in the order of development are depicted in Table 11.1.

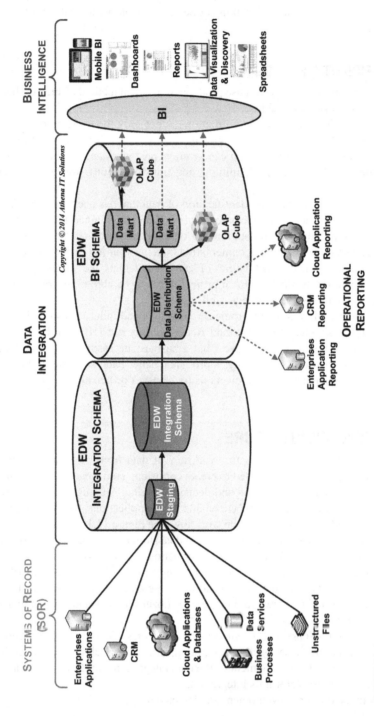

FIGURE 11.1

DI workflow.

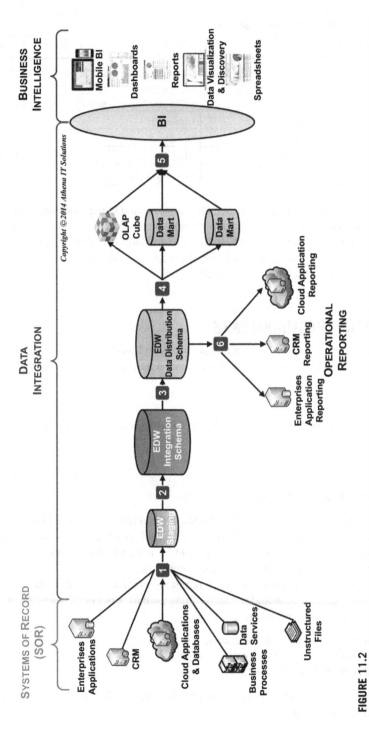

FIGURE 11.2

DI workflow integration breakpoints.

Table 11.1 Data Integration Workflow Stages			
Stage	**Source**	**Target**	**DI Phase**
1	SOR	Staging	Data preparation
2	Staging	EDW integration schema	Data preparation
3	EDW integration schema	EDW distribution schema	Data distribution
4A	EDW distribution schema	Data mart	Data distribution
4B	EDW distribution schema	OLAP cube	Data distribution
5	Data mart, OLAP cube	BI application	Data distribution
6	EDW distribution schema	Data distribution	Data distribution

As discussed in Chapter 6, the data stores actually implemented in the workflow may vary from the logical design depicted in Figure 11.1. The simplest implementations will contain an enterprise DW and data mart, while the more complex will have all the data stores depicted in the diagram plus many business-specific data marts or cubes. Regardless if these are just two data integration stages or many more, use the same design methodology and principles.

DATA INTEGRATION REQUIREMENTS

Designing the data integration architecture with its processes and workflow requires detailed information about all data sources and targets, along with the transformations required to deliver the information five C's.

PREREQUISITES

The prerequisite project deliverables needed to design data integration processes are:

- Data architecture
- Data requirements
- Source systems analysis
- Data models for each target data schema

The data architecture, such as Figure 11.2, includes the data stores that the BI team has determined are necessary to support its business requirements. This establishes the framework to design the data integration processes. Data integration designers should examine the data architecture and work with the BI team's architect(s) to design a data integration workflow.

In Chapter 3, we discussed the process to define requirements. The data requirements portion of that process, as depicted in Figure 11.3, includes data profiling used to perform the source systems analysis. This analysis will document the following:

- Data sources such as applications or databases.
- Source systems' tables and columns (or files in fields).
- Detailed attributes of all these objects.

Chapter 12 reviews the detailed output provided by the data profiling tools that will be used as the source systems analysis deliverable.

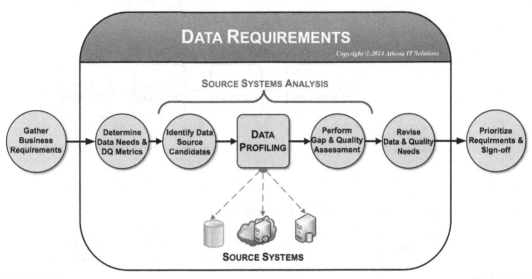

FIGURE 11.3

Gathering data requirements.

If the data integration designers were involved in gathering the data requirements and performing the source system analysis, then they will have known it was necessary to document that process. If they did not perform these tasks, then they need to review the documents with the people who did. There may be follow-up meetings with source systems' subject matter experts (SMEs) if more details or clarifications are necessary. In addition, there may be follow-up meetings with the BI team's business analysts and business people to examine business transformations (business rules, algorithms, and metrics) needed for data marts or online analytical processing (OLAP) cubes in more detail after the data source integration has been designed.

The following table- or file-related metadata needs to be provided for data integration design:

- **Table schema:** columns names, data types, keys, constraints, range of values, minimum and maximum values (if applicable), if nulls are allowed, percentage of column that are null (if applicable).
- **Data load cycle:** how often each table will be updated in BI environment.
- **Data volumes:** total rows and size, load cycle volumes (average, minimum, maximum, and growth rate).
- **Historical data:** earliest date that data is available, earliest date that data will be extracted into BI environment, list of differences in schema or processing for historical data providing applicable date ranges.
- **Transformation logic:** transformations applied to data as it is loaded from data sources. Note: this is different from transformations applied to data for analytical purposes when data is moved from EDW to data marts.
- **Data dependencies:** tables that need to be loaded prior to this table. The dependencies may be related to business rules for business processing or referential integrity constraints.
- **Systems dependencies:** enterprise systems interactions or prerequisites for data integration processes.

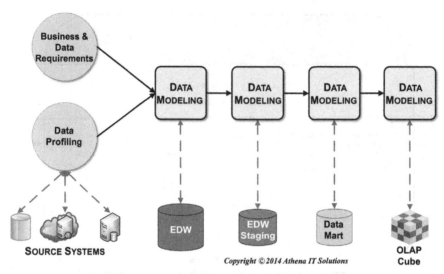

FIGURE 11.4

The order of designing data models.

Whereas data profiling provides a detailed schema and structural analysis of the source systems, data models are necessary to describe the target schemas. There is a temptation to begin designing the analytical-related data models, such as the data mart or OLAP cube, rather than the EDW and staging areas since that is what the business people are excited about. However, you should actually design the data models in the reverse order. Designing the data models in the sequence illustrated in Figure 11.4 is a best practice because it ensures all sources are designed and understood prior to designing target schemas, and, as an aside, it creates a project with the best utilization of resources.

The data integration designers and developers need to have design walk-throughs of each of the target data stores' physical data models with those models' designers. After designing, developing, and testing data integration processes, it is common for the data integration developers to meet with the data modeler(s) to discuss model revisions based on knowledge gained. Data models are also likely to be revised based on knowledge gained from BI application development and subsequent business user feedback when using the BI applications.

BUSINESS REQUIREMENTS

In addition to taking care of the prerequisites, discuss data integration requirements with the business and obtain agreement. Some of these requirements will be applicable to all data integration processes, while many will be applicable to specific data subjects, tables, or columns.

The data integration business requirements include:

- **Data velocity or latency:** data velocity or latency refers to how up-to-date the data needs to be in relation to the source systems. Many enterprises have standardized on daily update cycles based on business analytical needs, but there are certainly instances of business analysis for particular industries, companies, or processes that need real time or near real time updates. The latter will require different data transport services than the standard extract, transform and load (ETL) (see Chapter 12) and may require different rules regarding data conformance and standardization. Even when an enterprise needs real time updates, it is not likely to need it universally. Data velocity requirements should be listed to the granularity of data sources and associated tables.

- **Tracking changes to data:** the dimensional modeling term used to refer to keeping track of changes in data is slowly changing dimensions (SCD). However, since the business people are not going to know what the SCD requirements are, it is probably best to ask if they need to track changes in reference data, including business hierarchies. In addition, the requirement should include whether the business will perform "as is" analysis, "as was" analysis, or both types of analysis. These requirements should be listed by table.
- **Historical and archiving requirements:** the business needs to determine how far back in time historical data should be stored for business analysis, and at what age data should be archived off-line (but where it could be reloaded for an unanticipated requirement). It is typical for an EDW to have years of historical data available; however, if every data mart does not need all the historical data, you can improve query performance by limiting historical values, such as just to the past two years. When discussing historical data requirements you need to consider two things:
  - Do all the source systems have leveled history that is needed and, at some point in time, did the structure of the historical data change?
  - Has the data quality deteriorated too significantly for it to be of use?

Historical data requirements are typically in the granularity of either data subject or source system.

- **Security and Privacy:** with the pervasiveness of data across our business and private lives, sensitivity to privacy and security is ever increasing. With a wide variety of infrastructure, applications, and physical locations in an enterprise, security has always presented challenges to any application, such as a BI environment, whose mission is to provide widespread access to data. And with data integration being the actual engine that gathers, transforms, and delivers data, it needs to be built to comply with whatever security and privacy levels are required of the enterprise. Security and privacy requirements will likely extend to business subject areas, applications, tables, and even columns. The requirements may be role-based or person-specific. The BI team needs to work with any security or privacy group within the enterprise, as well as the data governance program if it exists. It is likely that security will need to be implemented using mechanisms in networks, applications, and databases.
- **Regulatory compliance:** certainly, industry or government regulations need to be complied with. Multinational corporations will have regulations that vary by geopolitical boundaries. Typically, an enterprise will have a regulatory compliance group with which you need to consult to provide the regulatory requirements. In some companies, the HR group or a single executive performs this function, signing off both on the regulatory requirements to be implemented in the BI environment and its compliance when operating.

- **Information delivery to BI applications:** key goals of the data integration architecture are to enable the information 5 C's while lowering enterprise BI TCO, decreasing time to analysis, and increasing productivity. These may be lofty goals, but they are attainable if the enterprise has shifted its many data and business transformations, which are typically coded repetitively (and redundantly and differently) in countless spreadsheets and BI applications, to data integration processes and then loaded them into data marts and OLAP cubes. This "do once and use many times" approach is the cornerstone of this architecture.

To design the processes that load the EDW (data preparation) and the data marts (data franchising), it is essential to separate the data sourcing business rules from those that are used to load business process-specific analytical processes used in data marts.

DATA SOURCING SYSTEM REQUIREMENTS

In addition to the details about the data source tables and columns, the following system-related requirements need to be agreed upon:

- Extraction strategy for each source system
  - How will the data from each source system be accessed?
  - Will the data extraction be a push from the data source or a pull from the data integration tool?
  - Will the extraction be in the form of a file extract or a data stream?
  - Will the source system's application team create a data extract that will be put into a staging area, or will the data integration team be responsible for the extraction regardless of how it is implemented?
- Systems availability
  - At what times during the day is each source system available for extractions?
  - Is there a time limit or row count limit for any extraction process from any source system?
  - Are there specific times that data updates from specific source systems need to be completed and available to business people?
- Staging areas
  - Will all, none, or some of data source extracts use a staging area?
  - How will each source system extraction process use a staging area?
  - Will staging be persistent, transient, or archived?
  - Will the staging area contain file extracts or be relationally based? If relational, will staging tables be identical to source system extractions?
  - Will the staging area be used for auditing?
- Database strategies (assuming relational)
  - Will indexes be treated when loading data? For example, will they be dropped and rebuilt?
  - How will partitioning be used when loading data?
  - Will surrogate keys be built using database or ETL functionality?
  - Can you assume that referential integrity will be handled by ETL processing rather than database constraints? (Confirm this with the DBAs so they are not surprised.)

DATA INTEGRATION DESIGN

Data integration design starts at the first stage in Figure 11.2 that gathers data from the SORs and proceeds incrementally until you design the final stages that load the data marts. Each stage can be designed as its prerequisites (data architecture, data requirements, and data models for the sources and targets) become available. In this manner, the design can start before all the prerequisites for the entire architecture are completed. This supports the project approach we discuss in Chapter 18.

The steps involved in designing the data integration processes are to:

- Create a stage-related conceptual data integration process model.
- Create a stage-related logical data integration process model.
- Design a stage-related physical data integration process model.
- Design stage-related source to target mappings.
- Design overall data integration workflow.

The design specifications include:

- Conceptual, logical, and physical data integration process models.
- Logical and physical data models for sources and targets.
- Source to target mappings.

There are two approaches to developing the design deliverables that are listed below.

One approach is to develop the design specifications using process modeling tools and to fill in source to target templates. This approach works well when the data integration processing is complex and a senior designer is preparing the specifications for developers to build.

The other approach is to create the conceptual and logical process models with diagramming software and then develop the remaining specifications (physical process model and source to target mappings) by prototyping the data integration processes. And, of course, then using the data integration tool's documentation capabilities to create the models and mappings. This approach works well when the same people do design and development, so there is not a hand-off of specifications from designer to developer. Creating documentation will likely be faster than using a process modeling tool when the developers are familiar with the data integration tool. However, the benefit of using prototyping when the developers are new to the tool is that it provides a learning opportunity for them, even if the documentation takes longer. The greatest risk in this approach is that the code will be created, and the developer will not create the supporting documentation. A best practice when using this approach is to have the developer conduct a design walk-through with the appropriate members of the BI team.

CREATE STAGE-RELATED CONCEPTUAL DATA INTEGRATION MODEL

A conceptual data integration process model illustrates the sources and targets for each data integration stage. The model's granularity is the enterprise applications or databases used as sources or targets. Figure 11.5 provides a generic example. The conceptual model is a visual tool to confirm all the data sources used throughout the data integration workflow; it is also helpful for discussions between the BI team, source system SMEs, and business people.

Because prerequisites to the design stage include identifying source systems and performing data profiling, the conceptual model for the stage that loads the source systems should be fairly straightforward.

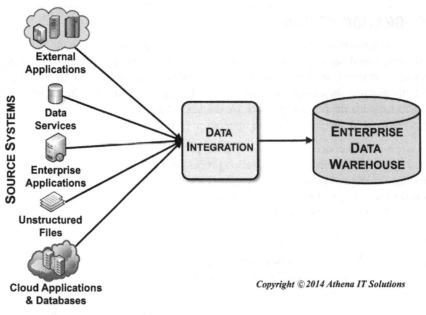

FIGURE 11.5

Conceptual data integration model—data sourcing.

CREATE STAGE-RELATED LOGICAL DATA INTEGRATION MODEL

The next step in designing the data integration stage-specific processes is to create a logical model. The logical model, as depicted in Figure 11.6, illustrates the sources and targets at the table or file level of granularity.

Each source and target object illustrated represents a component in the data integration toolkit that gets input data, fetches look-up data, or writes data to an output. Each of these components will be specific to the data store, such as a particular database, file structure (spreadsheet, CSV, XML, etc.), or business application. Sourcing, look-up, and target components typically allow filtering rows and columns, data type conversions, calculations, and custom SQL code or the tool's own scripting language. The ability of data integration toolkit components to write to targets varies considerably by product. At a minimum, these components will simply write the output data to the targets, but more sophisticated components may provide such functions as truncating the table before loading, creating target tables if they do not exist, or automatically determining which rows should be inserted or updated.

There is a group of data integration components that gathers data from sources, transforms it in some fashion, and then outputs the data to one or more targets. Examples of the functions that these components perform are:

- Join tables.
- Map multiple sources to potentially multiple targets. This function provides expanded join functionality.
- Split table.

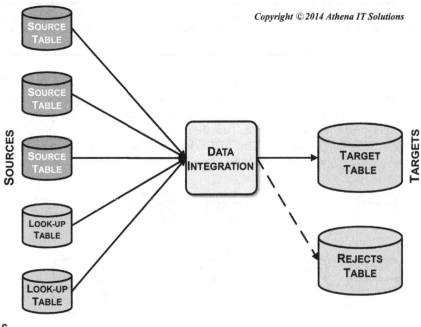

FIGURE 11.6

Logical data integration modeling

- Join one or more tables.
- Aggregate tables.
- Update data based on one or more types of SCDs.
- Update data based on prebuilt change data capture (CDC) rules.

It is typical for these components to have one or more "success" paths for data, depending on the type of function being deployed, and to also have a "reject" (or failure) path to direct data that has either not met integration criteria or encounters an error condition. Figure 11.6 is an example of a mapping component with success and reject paths. It is a best practice to always have success and reject paths for each data transformation throughout the data integration workflow.

CREATE STAGE-RELATED PHYSICAL DATA INTEGRATION MODEL

The next step in designing the data integration stage-specific processes is to create a physical process model. This model includes:

- All data used in this stage: sources, targets, and look-ups. No data should be used in any data integration component without being accounted for in this model. Even if custom code or SQL is used in this stage, the data that is used in that code needs to be documented.
- The product-specific data integration components used.
- The product-specific workflow with all data and data integration components documented.

Both Figures 11.6 and 11.7 may perform the same data transformations, but because of the differences between product component functionality, the first tool only needs one component, while the other tool requires that you execute a series of components to complete the same task.

One approach to document the physical model is to use a diagram such as Figure 11.7 with the specific tables and data components named (rather than the generic names used in this example), accompanied by a spreadsheet or document explaining the workflow processing details. The other approach is to prototype the physical model and use the data integration tool's functionality to produce the documentation. With sample data available to develop the prototype, this is an excellent and very productive technique to design and document the physical model.

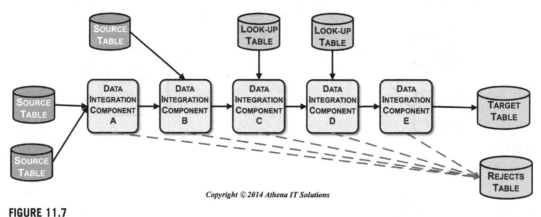

FIGURE 11.7

Data Integration physical model.

DESIGN STAGE-RELATED SOURCE TO TARGET MAPPINGS

An oversimplification in regards to source to target mappings, particularly when loading source systems' data, is that there is a simple one-to-one mapping between a source table and the target table. Although it is possible to map them one-to-one, it is more common to use multiple source tables because of these typical scenarios:

- A fact table has attribute data spread across multiple source tables, such as a sales order that has separate order header and order line item tables.
- A fact or dimension table has multiple source systems supplying the data, such as when a company has separate order processing systems in different geographies or sales channels.
- A dimension table's attributes are gathered from multiple source system tables and denormalized, such as when customer-related data is managed in many tables in the source systems.
- A fact table has its foreign keys generated by table look-ups into associated dimension tables.
- A fact table's measures require calculations using tables other than what was used to get its other attributes.

The source to target mapping must include the target data and all the data used to derive it. The most common documentation tool used is a spreadsheet, but, as previously mentioned, documentation created by the data integration tool from a prototype is an alternative if the prototype represents the complete set of data and components for this stage.

Source to target mappings require the following:

- Target tables.
  - Table name.
  - Table schema type, such as dimension, fact, or bridge. It is also useful to categorize the type of dimension or fact.
  - Table location, such database and schema.
  - Column name.
  - Column attributes, such as data type, if it is an identity type, if nulls are allowed, and default value and constraints, if applicable.
  - List of transformations applied to this column.
  - Content SME, who may be a business person or an application expert.
  - Target data store SME, who may be a data modeler, an architect, or a business analyst from the BI team.
- Source tables.
  - Table name.
  - Table location, such as database and schema.
  - Column name.
  - Column attributes, such as data type, if it is an identity type, if nulls are allowed, and default value and constraints, if applicable.
  - Mapping rules applied to this column.
  - Relationships or dependencies with other columns.
  - SME, who may be a business person or an application expert.
  - Source data store SME, who may be a DBA or an application developer.
- Mappings.
  - List all mapping connections between source and target columns. This may be as simple as aligning rows in a spreadsheet, but if many-to-many relationships are involved, then diagrams will be needed.
  - List all joins, splits, unions, aggregations, or other data integration functions with the columns or variables used to perform these functions.
  - List all columns and variables used for data transformations or metrics calculated.

DESIGN OVERALL DATA INTEGRATION WORKFLOW

The source to target mappings and data integration process models are the building blocks of the overall data integration architecture. The data integration team needs to design a data integration architecture with a workflow that controls all the data integration processes used throughout the enterprise. The high-level logical view of that workflow is depicted in Figure 11.2, where the completion of each successive data integration stage triggers the start of the next stage. In an enterprise, there are many interactions and dependencies across source systems and tables within the data architecture that influence the design of the data integration architecture; this often creates the need for multiple workflows handling different segments of the enterprise's data.

There are two things to watch for with these workflows:

- First, you have to synchronize source systems across an enterprise. (If the source systems are large or diverse, however, this task may not be possible until later.) For this synchronization, you will need to design data integration workflows to not only perform the data integration processes, but also to do so in a sequence dependent on the source systems availability and interactions. The EDW will be updated at different times of the day based on the schedules of the different workflows.
- Second, the dependencies in the dimensional model between different table types for related data may also necessitate the design of multiple workflows. For related data, such as accounting or marketing data, load the dimensional table types in the following order: subdimensions, dimensions, and facts. Each data subject may be handled in an independent workflow if there are no data dependencies.

DATA INTEGRATION STANDARDS

One of the key drivers to developing a cost- and resource-effective data integration architecture is creating and using a broad set of design, development, and deployment standards. These standards include principles, procedures, use cases, templates, and reusable code that is applied to specific combinations of data, data integration processes, and requirements.

Although a business case can easily be made for these standards, we should address the "elephant in the room," which is that most BI teams are so pressed for time that standards always seem like a "nice-to-have" that they will get to later. This lack of urgency is understandable, because the business people who drive the requirements and the budget do not have data integration standards anywhere on their list of priorities or even on their radar.

FOR STANDARDS, ADOPT A SOFTWARE DEVELOPMENT MINDSET

Before I got into consulting, I worked in software engineering for a company that sold software, and then I joined a Fortune 100 company's IT group. I was very surprised by the differences in attitudes regarding software development and standards when I moved into IT. In the software firm, design, development, and deployment standards were necessities, not "nice-to-haves." In fact, they were given the same priority as coding.

How is creating an application in a software company so different from an application in an IT department? First, the software product is sold and installed in many companies, but the BI application is built and installed in one company. The software product has, if successful, many versions and releases that may be supported simultaneously, but the BI application has one version supported in one company. A company may have BI users spread across many business units, subsidiaries, and geographies, but it can still keep them all on a single production version of its application.

Second, the software product has formal documentation and training for both technical and business people. You cannot sell a product without them. Although BI applications may have a limited set of documentation and training, it certainly is not as extensive or thorough as what a software company would have.

Third, software firms have people dedicated to building, maintaining, supporting, and selling their products. IT not only creates and maintains BI applications, but it is responsible for many other applications and technologies. Software firms judge their developers by what they produce, while IT staff are judged by how fast they respond to "fire drills" and how much they cost.

Finally, the software we created at the software firm was the firm's product— its asset. For the Fortune 100 company where I worked in IT, the software was an application used to measure company performance; it was not what the company sold to produce revenue. With this background in mind, it is easier to understand why the software applications in these two cases were treated quite differently. The software company's product created revenue, and the BI application created costs (disregarding ROI).

In order to be a viable product in the marketplace, the software product needed to have release management, version control, business and technical documentation, programming standards, and adherence to industry standards to work in diverse environments. The BI project, on the other hand, did not need those standards and procedures, or the staff felt that their users did not want to pay for it.

Why do BI applications take so long to modify and maintain? Why are they full of nasty surprises? The short answer is that IT does not adhere to standards during their creation and maintenance. Sure, you can cut corners by not following standards and still create the report that the business people want; however, the IT group will pay for it in the long run with higher IT costs and a whopping loss in responsiveness when they struggle to rediscover the application every time they touch it.

Enforcing standards for building and maintaining BI applications from the start delivers long-term benefits. It takes an investment to implement the standards retroactively; it's always more expensive to retrofit your applications, but the ROI justifies it.

DEVELOPMENT PROJECT STANDARDS

Regardless of whether you are creating a software product, a data warehouse, or a BI application, basic standards are needed to manage the development project and its application. The following key standards apply to the entire project:

Use and enforce source code and version controls: you cannot fix a bug if you cannot find the correct version of the source code or reproduce the problem. Software firms use source code control (software is their asset) but IT groups tend to be much more lax. Lack of code control slows application development and enhancement, and makes it much more costly to maintain. BI applications should be managed like valuable company assets. In more than two decades in the IT industry, I have noticed that it is it uncommon for IT groups to implement and enforce code management controls for the entire application, including data models, data integration code (both tool-generated and manually built), BI applications, and the custom SQL code used for all aspects of the project.

Document your business requirements: document all the business and technical requirements, and keep track as you change the application. The documentation can be used for change management, as well as the business and technical documentation. This used to be a very tedious task with documents that were put into folders no one ever looked at but that has changed. With cloud and mobile collaborative applications that support all aspects of the application development lifecycle (from design to support), all BI stakeholders are able to access and contribute to the requirements, along with providing feedback throughout the project. Regardless of whether the BI team is following a waterfall, agile, or hybrid methodology, these collaborative applications enable business interaction and validation.

Document your application: this is the corollary to source code and version control, as documentation needs to be created and saved whenever a new version of the application is released. This documentation includes BI applications, data integration code, and data models. If the development team is using BI, data integration, and data modeling tools, then they can use those tools to generate the documentation. Manually created code also needs to be documented, and the development team needs to understand that creating that documentation is part of the time and cost of doing it manually. Even with tools, there are still details that need to be created by the development team, such as documenting the code with comments and descriptions. In addition, the data fields accessed by the application need to have data definitions in both business and technical terms; BI, ETL, and database tools make it easy. Document all of your data—database schema, file layouts, reference data—along with the corresponding code.

Develop and implement testing plans: test code with sample data not only in the individual units, but also in the complete application. Allow business people to test the analytical and reporting functionality with samples of real data. If possible, test with full data volumes. Test the ETL functionality with actual data from each of the source systems that will feed the data warehouse or data marts. Too often, the development team is surprised when they learn at the end of the project that the source systems had dirty data. Source systems always contain dirty data; your ETL code must be able to handle it somehow. Before the system goes into production, IT and the business need to agree on how to handle dirty data: pass it on, flag it, suspend it, or delete it.

Document how to use your application: document the use and operation of your application from both the technical and business perspectives. The IT staff may not need to develop the formal user guides, installation notes, and tutorials of a software product, but they should create a simple application guide. Too often, I see application developers trying to figure out which disks and directories contain their programs, scripts, log files, and data. This should all be documented for easy maintenance.

Naming conventions: boring, yes, but absolutely necessary. Consistency should be the driving principle for creating the naming conventions, rather than elegance. It is not worth the time to be elegant or overthink them. Just create the standards and move on. Of course, the team needs to enforce their use. Naming standards apply to data schema, data integration code, and BI applications.

Deliverable reviews: these include technical reviews within the BI team on data models and applications or stakeholder reviews on requirements, testing, user feedback, and project status. Although meetings with people in the same room is optimal, you can also use collaboration tools that enable presentations, remote application access, desktop displays, and interactive document development, along with audio and video conferencing. With all of these choices, there is no excuse to not getting the appropriate stakeholders involved.

DATA INTEGRATION REUSABLE COMPONENTS

"Write once, use many times" is the driving principle for designing and deploying a common set of reusable data integration components. The benefits are consistency and productivity.

The data integration team should examine the data architecture and data integration processes to determine how to break up the processes into a common set of reusable data integration components. Processes that are candidates to be split and used as components are:

- Change data capture (CDC)
- Each of the applicable SCD types

- Error handling
- Auditing
- Fact table processing
- Dimension table processing
- Hierarchy handling
- Special purpose dimensions processing
- Data quality processes
- Building aggregations

The most effective components are loosely coupled and highly cohesive. Loose coupling means the components are modular with little to no dependencies on other components. This type of modularity makes it easier to maintain, test, execute in parallel, and recover. Highly cohesive components focus on performing specific tasks and interact well with other components.

There are several sources for a common set of reusable data integration components:

- A data integration product's prebuilt components.
- DI team custom-designed components.
- DI team-designed templates used to develop components.
- DI team agreed-upon guidelines used to develop components.

The best scenario is when the data integration product being used has prebuilt components that perform well-defined processes matching your enterprise's needs. These components will be documented, known by developers who have experience with a product, and maintained by the product vendor.

If prebuilt product components are not available, then the development team needs to determine whether it is better to build custom-designed components, design templates for designing components, or agree on a set of guidelines for designing components. These options are presented in the order of declining productivity gains. The choice of which path to follow depends on the flexibility of the data integration product being used and the software engineering skills of the data integration team.

The pragmatic approach to DI reusable components is to agree on the components that are needed, and then develop them on an as-needed basis, rather than developing them all up front. It is highly likely that the components that the enterprise will actually need and how they will function will evolve over time. The best way to determine this is by getting the components in use as soon as possible.

DATA INTEGRATION DEVELOPMENT STANDARDS

The following is a minimum set of standards that should be agreed upon for the design, development, and execution of data integration processes:

- Assume all dimension tables have surrogate keys that function as their primary keys.
- Decide whether fact tables will use surrogate keys as their primary key. The convention in dimensional modeling is to use the set of foreign keys that, when combined in a multipart key, guarantees uniqueness. If there is not a set of foreign keys that will guarantee uniqueness, you must generate the surrogate key as the primary key. Another reason for using a surrogate key as the primary key is when it is the enterprise database standard to do so.
- Decide if surrogate keys are built using a database function, such as an identity data type, or if they will be generated by a data integration component.

- Decide what data type will be used for surrogate keys. The assumption is that this is typically an integer, but if the table in which it is being used will eventually have more than two billion rows, then another data type will be needed to handle that number of rows.
- Implement a SOR dimension listing the SORs used in data integration processes, as depicted in Figure 11.8 and explained in Chapter 10.
- Retain the primary key from the SOR as a natural key in the BI data store tables and point a foreign key to the SOR dimension if more than one SOR is used to populate the tables, as depicted in Figure 11.9.
- Add three columns to each table's schema for operational and audit purposes, as depicted in Figure 11.10. *DI_Job_ID* uniquely identifies a data integration processing job and, possibly, is a processing ID generated by the data integration tool that can be linked to the processing metadata. The remaining columns track the time a row was created and last time it was modified.
- Ensure that each dimension that supports an SCD type that tracks changes to rows has three columns to determine the time period the row applies to, as depicted in Figure 11.11. There is a

Column	Key	Description
SOR_SK	PK	SOR Surrogate Key
SOR_Name		SOR Application Name
SOR_Module		SOR Application Module Name
SOR_Table		SOR Table Name
Other columns...		

FIGURE 11.8

Systems of record (SOR) dimension.

Column	Key	Description
Table_SK	PK	Table's surrogate key
SOR_NK	NK	SOR's Natural Key
SOR_SK	FK	Foreign key to SOR Table
Other columns...		

FIGURE 11.9

Natural key standard.

Column	Data Type	Key	Description
Table_sk		PK	Table surrogate key
Other columns...			
DI_Job_ID	Integer	FK	Data Integration Job Identifier
DI_Create_Date	DateTime		Date & time row was created
DI_Modified_Date	DateTime		Date & time row was last modified

FIGURE 11.10

Audit column standard.

Column	Key	Description
Table_SK	PK	Table's surrogate key
Other columns...		
Effective Date		Date row becomes effective
Ineffective Date		Date row becomes ineffective
Current Indicator		Indicator current row

FIGURE 11.11

Slowly changing dimensions effective date standard.

Table_sk	Description
-1	Unknown
-2	Missing
-3	Invalid

FIGURE 11.12

Dimension table with rows indicating null values.

date pair that has the effective and ineffective dates (date range row applies), as well as a current indicator.

- Assume foreign keys cannot be null.
- Determine the default value used if a foreign key is null when being loaded from a source system. A typical value is a negative number, such as −1, since the surrogate keys are positive integers. The row in the dimension table with the null value indicator should have a description such as "unknown." There are cases where there may be more than one business condition that results in a null value in the foreign key, such as unknown, missing, or invalid. In those cases, the dimension table would have multiple rows replacing nulls with negative key values and descriptions as depicted in Figure 11.12.
- Determine the SCD type to use for each dimension table and use the appropriate reusable component.
- Determine the SCD type to use when updating an accumulating snapshot table and use the appropriate reusable component.
- Determine how each type of hierarchy will be managed and use the appropriate reusable component.
- Identify each error use case, determine how to process that error, and use the appropriate reusable component.
- Determine how to handle late-arriving dimensions or facts and use the appropriate reusable component.

LOADING HISTORICAL DATA

Data integration design efforts focus on the current state of the enterprise in developing ongoing, incremental processes; however, there may be a need to load historical data in a different manner or to perform historical data conversions. Loading historical data is similar to data migration projects in that it must be repeatable, auditable, and documented, but it does not need the same operational processes as ongoing, incremental processes.

SAME AS THE OLD

If an SOR has remained consistent over time from a schema and business processing perspective, then the ongoing, incremental data integration processes that are being designed can be applied to all the historical data in that SOR. These conditions occur when, for example, an enterprise recently migrated to a new ERP system, or when the business group adopted an application to support their business processes and now want to bring that data into the enterprise BI environment.

Under these circumstances, loading data from the SOR begins with the oldest data and progresses until it gets to the current data. Depending on the volume of data, particularly with fact tables, the development team may process the data in incremental batches rather than all at one time. The team may also leverage alternative methods to speed up processing, such as:

- Dropping indexes during the load and rebuilding them afterwards.
- Using database partitions to load specific date ranges of data.
- Using bulk loading of data.
- Using file extracts from the SOR and then presorting the data prior to the data load.

If there have been no changes to the schema or business processing rules in the SOR, then one set of data integration processes will handle both historical and ongoing, incremental data updates.

Typically, these processes assume that only data that has been inserted or updated since the last load cycle will be processed. This is based on the assumption that all loads process correctly; that data feeds from source systems, including those from external vendors, partners, or suppliers never have to be reprocessed (maybe due to their errors); that there is no need to load historical data since it has already been processed; and that no source systems that have historical data will be added to the BI environment in the future. It is a best practice to plan for one or more of these assumptions to be violated.

Design the ongoing, incremental processes to load data based on a range of dates. In the first and most common case, the beginning date of the data to be loaded is the last successful data load time, and the ending date is the time and current load. This use case is identical to a typical ongoing, incremental process.

In the second use case, the beginning and ending dates of the data to be loaded are passed as a set of parameters to the data integration processes. If data in target tables involved can be updated from multiple source systems, then add an SOR identifier from the SOR dimension as an additional parameter. The data in the target tables that represent inserts or updates that have been previously processed for the beginning and ending dates needs to be "backed out" from these tables. The processing for fact tables is straightforward, as the rows in those tables that are within the date range should be deleted. Dimension tables are more complicated than fact tables because of their SCD update processing. Dimension table rows that are within the beginning and ending date needed be deleted just as with fact tables; however, an additional step is necessary to adjust effective and ineffective dates on the remaining rows. The adjustments are necessary to ensure that there are no gaps between the effective and ineffective dates throughout the table.

After adjusting the rows that fall within the beginning and ending dates, process the inserts and updates. Fact table processing is straightforward, as rows are simply inserted as they normally are.

Inserting or updating dimension table rows within beginning and ending dates of this load will require adjustments to any existing rows that overlap their effective and ineffective dates.

HISTORICAL DATA IS DIFFERENT OR DIRTY

When the SOR schema or business rules have changed in the past or when historical data has data quality problems, then you need to create a historical data integration process that operates independently from the ongoing, incremental process. Although there may be a set of data integration components that are shared across both processes, historical processing is different enough to warrant the split. Under these circumstances, historical data processing should be considered equal to the data migration project.

Schema or business rule changes are the result of business or technology events that occurred in the past. Business events may have been triggered by a merger or acquisition, adding new lines of products or services, adding new sales channels, adding new regulations, or expanding into new geopolitical areas. Technology events are typically related to the replacing, upgrading, or adding of enterprise applications. Besides these major events, the farther back in the past that source data exists, the more likely that numerous small changes have been made to the schema or business rules that, when viewed in total, have created significant changes. A big risk with loading historical data is that small changes are often not documented or have been forgotten, thereby surprising the development team. You can significantly reduce the risk, however, if you perform data profiling, as previously recommended.

The following steps are needed:

- **Assess historical data conversions:** once the development team has determined if and when changes have occurred in historical data, they need to assess what is needed to convert the historical data and migrate it to existing schemas. This assessment needs to be not only what needs to be done, but also how long it will take, what resources will be involved, and the estimated cost.
- **Obtain business sign off on historical data conversion:** although the business has requested this historical data, the business sponsors need to examine the impact of the historical conversion on the project timeline, costs, and functionality. Based on this impact, the business may decide to convert all the historical data or alter its requirements and only convert a portion of the historical data. And for the portion of the historical data that is not converted, the business choices are to completely ignore that data or to migrate it unchanged into operational data store (ODS) tables that are available for stand-alone historical data analysis.

If historical data conversions or migrations are required make the appropriate adjustments to the project timeline and costs.

- **Design and develop historical data conversions:** this follows the standard design and development steps for data integration. Map the historical data sources to their respective target by time frame, design the data integration workflows, and then build and test the data integration processes.
- **Load converted historical data:** although many refer to this as a one-time process, the reality, just like in the data migration project, is that it will likely take multiple attempts at loading the data before it meets acceptance criteria. Each time the data is loaded, you will need to analyze it to determine if there are any gaps between its quality and the acceptance criteria. If the data is not

acceptable, you will need to make the revisions in the data integration processes and then reload the data. This cycle continues until the data meets its acceptance criteria. Until the historical data meets this criteria, it should be loaded into tables separate from the existing current data tables. This enables the loading, testing, and reloading to occur without impacting current processes. When historical data conversion has reached acceptance levels, then it can be loaded with current data.

DATA INTEGRATION PROTOTYPING

In Chapter 18 we recommend an iterative and incremental project methodology that uses a more traditional waterfall approach to design the overall BI framework and architecture while blending an agile approach to develop the architecture's components. Data integration is a perfect example of designing the architecture and overall workflow using the traditional approach and then developing data integration components using an agile approach (specifically prototyping).

Although the initial requirements for data integration components can be defined, the final design is typically developed through a discovery process. It is not until the component works with the actual source data that you discover the nuances of that data and its interaction with other data. You need to validate and change data in business rules during the development process. Prototyping is a best practice approach toward enabling this discovery process.

The prototyping tasks include:

- **Defining the scope of the prototype:** determine the source and target data, along with the transformation logic involved.
- **Establish the prototyping environment:** ensure that the development environment, data integration tools, and sample data are available for prototyping.
- **Create a data integration component prototype:** develop the component by mapping source to target data with transformation logic.
- **Perform tests:** execute the prototype and examine results. If changes are required, then revise and reload.
- **Review results:** validate results with a SME, who may be a business person or an application developer.
- **Revise as necessary:** if the prototype does not pass SME validation, then revise and repeat the prototype.
- **Prototype signoff:** SME validates and signs off on results.

DATA INTEGRATION TESTING

Data integration testing is another set of tasks that should be performed iteratively and incrementally, as advocated in the project methodology that is discussed in Chapter 18. Testing complements prototyping in the requirements discovery process by identifying differences in source system data and business rules.

Test each data integration component to ensure it gathered source data completely and correctly, then proceed to transforming that data and loading it into its targets. The initial sourcing of data from the SOR will need to perform specific checks to validate correctness. The first check will be that the extracted rows match the SOR. Often, row counts and checksums are used as verification. The second check will involve verifying the results of any filters and transformations on those extracted rows. The filters and transformations may result in the source and target rows not matching from a row count and checksums perspective. Testing this process must verify that any differences that exist are the result of the correct processing of those filters and transformations.

The following types of testing need to be performed:

- **Unit testing:** this involves testing each data integration component to validate that it performs properly.
- **Integration testing:** this involves testing a workflow with its individual components to validate that they work together cohesively and correctly.
- **User acceptance testing:** this involves business people validating the data by analyzing it within the various BI applications, such as dashboards and reports that they have access to.
- **System testing and performance testing:** this involves testing the entire data integration workflow, gathering data from all data sources, and loading into all their target tables. This test not only involves validating data, but also examining the performance of the data integration processes, databases, and BI applications.

A testing plan listing test cases with acceptance success criteria needs to be developed, documented, and signed off by the appropriate responsible party. Each component should have the ability to handle both success and reject rows. After the tests have been conducted, the results need to be documented and reviewed. These results should include processing metadata, such as the time for the components to complete and any inflow or outflow of data through these components.

DATA INTEGRATION PROCESSES

INFORMATION IN THIS CHAPTER:

- Manual coding versus data integration tools
- Data integration services
- Selecting the right tools
- Access and delivery (extract and load)
- Data ingestion
- Data profiling
- Data transformation
- Data quality
- Process management
- Operations management
- Data transport

INTRODUCTION: MANUAL CODING VERSUS TOOL-BASED DATA INTEGRATION

Data integration (DI) activities are the most time- and resource-consuming portion of building an enterprise business intelligence (BI) environment. Industry analysts estimate that upwards of 70% of the time spent on a BI project is devoted to these tasks. Using data integration tools, in particular extract, transform, and load (ETL) tools as depicted in Figure 12.1, has been the best practice in BI for more than a decade, but a dirty secret in the BI world is that manually coded extracts are the mainstay of the industry. Also known as hand-coded extracts, these are prevalent in small- to medium-size businesses (SMB), but even large enterprises that adopted data integration tools as their best practice to load their enterprise data warehouses typically resort to manually coded extracts to feed their BI data stores such as data marts, online analytical processing (OLAP) cubes, reporting data-bases, and spreadsheets.

How have manually coded extracts become so prevalent? It is not as if there are not enough data integration tools around, including ETL tools. Manually coded extracts are the IT equivalent to business-created data shadow systems we discuss in Chapter 16. Both grow haphazardly and are seldom documented, which practically guarantees that they will become an enterprise nightmare by increasing data silos and costs while adversely affecting the goal of the information five C's (clean, consistent, conformed, current, and comprehensive).

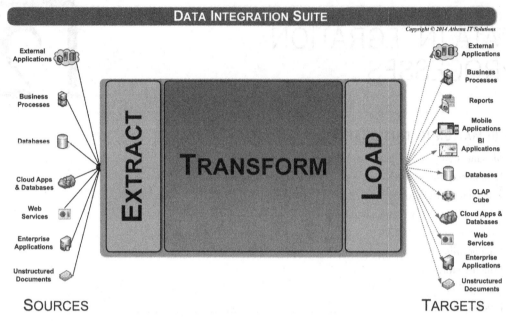

FIGURE 12.1

Extract, transform, and load tools.

WHY WE HAND CODE

IT groups provide many reasons for why they manually code instead of using tools, the approach that is considered a best practice. The reasons, however, are usually misconceptions or bad reasons that are used to rationalize their old habits:

Bad reason 1: Tools are too expensive. The top tier tools are indeed expensive. They are out of reach for SMBs and can even be too expensive for large enterprises to expand their use from loading their enterprise data warehouse (EDW) to BI data stores such as data marts and cubes. Even those large corporations that could afford the top-end tools have found that getting the throughput and performance out of these tools has required significant investments beyond software licensing costs. These investments have been in purchasing hardware and memory along with the expertise to tune the servers, storage, networks, and databases. Enterprises often spend hundreds of thousands of dollars on software and infrastructure when using these top-tier tools. Annual maintenance fees and upgrades, beyond labor costs, create a heavy ongoing expense.

It is a misconception to say that all tools are too expensive. It would be true if the top-tiered tools were the only options in the market. However, the reality is that there are many data integration products that can be acquired by more cost-sensitive budgets. These options include a wide range of products: open source software, software bundled (free) with a database or BI tool, cloud-based software with a subscription model rather than an upfront purchase, and other tools that are priced more economically. In addition, as we discussed in Chapter 7, many of the data integration products have shifted from an ETL architecture that often requires dedicated infrastructure to an extract load transform (ELT) architecture that does not. This architectural shift has significantly reduced the infrastructure investments beyond licensing that large enterprises were encountering while loading their EDWs.

Bad reason 2: Expertise is scarce. In large enterprises, the centralized data warehouse team likely has deep data integration tool experience, but their backlog of work means that people creating BI data stores are left on their own. Therefore, they end up hand coding. In SMB firms, the IT staffs are too small to dedicate anyone to data integration, so no one is an expert in what is available; therefore the de facto tool becomes hand coding.

The top-tiered tools require deep expertise primarily due to their complexity, however, the truth is that the other products mentioned above are not that hard to learn. As an aside, many of these tools have online training, tutorials, and samples enabling IT developers to learn them quickly. The skills gap can be easily overcome.

Bad reason 3: You do not know what you do not know. Even when enterprises use data integration tools, they often do not use them well. The biggest reason why people misuse these tools is that they do not have a firm grasp of the concepts of data integration processes and advanced dimensional modeling. Tools are easy; concepts are harder. Anyone can start coding; it is a lot harder to actually architect and design.

So, here is what happens: instead of using data integration best practices, people design the data integration processes the same way they would create a sequential series of SQL scripts to integrate data. In fact, many an ETL process simply executes stored procedures or SQL scripts. Why use the tool at all if you are not going to use its capabilities? When this happens, IT figures it was a waste of time to use the ETL tool to begin with, and the ETL tool investment had no return on investment (ROI). This becomes a self-reinforcing loop, enabling IT to justify (or rationalize) manual coding.

Bad reason 4: Data never sleeps. Regardless of the state of data integration expertise and investment at an enterprise, business people still have to run and manage the business. This requires data. If the data has not been integrated for them, they will figure out some other way to get it—even if it means cutting and pasting data from spreadsheet queries or getting IT to "crank out" SQL scripts. This is why data shadow systems or spreadmarts are started and then become so prevalent. Moreover, if an IT person needs to get data and they do not have experience with data integration tools, then the go-to solution is hand coding.

Bad reason 5: Not seeing the forest for the trees. IT has generally treated data integration projects tactically, thereby failing to recognize the need for and benefits of common and reusable data integration processes. They hand code each project just enough to move the data from source to target, but do not take the time or have the ability to get beyond the bare essentials. This creates overlapping and redundant efforts as depicted in Figure 12.2, which leads to data silos, overly expensive projects, and a diminished ability to respond to business needs.

Bad reason 6: Limiting data integration to batch-driven ETL. IT has too narrowly viewed data integration as simply ETL. Building a data warehouse using batch-driven ETL has defined, from an IT perspective, what data integration can do, but many data integration vendors support real-time updates using such techniques as messaging and enterprise information integration (EII) and through services via service oriented architecture (SOA). With the limited viewpoint that data integration is only ETL, many integration projects were done by hand coding or by introducing narrowly focused tools rather than a full-faceted data integration tool. This has driven up the cost of integration, strained resources, and created yet more data silos.

Bad reason 7: Coding is easier than thinking. There is an inherit bias for the IT staff to generate SQL code. They know it (just like the business person knows spreadsheets), they can crank something

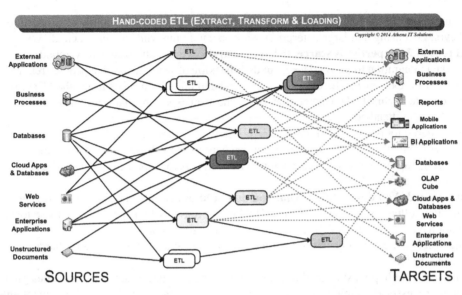

FIGURE 12.2

Hand-coded extract, transform, and load.

out quickly, and it does not cost anything extra. The typical scenario is that the IT person creates a SQL script or a stored procedure to pull data from one source and things are fine. But then several hundred SQL scripts or stored procedures later, the hodgepodge and undocumented accumulation of pseudo ETL processes becomes the recurring method to load the data warehouse or BI data stores. Each change to that set of code takes longer and longer. It consumes more and more resource time just to maintain it. When new data needs to be integrated, another IT person starts the next hodgepodge of undocumented code with yet another simple SQL script.

WHY WE USE TOOLS

Historically, for all the reasons mentioned above, hand coding extracts has become the de facto method to develop data integration processes for most projects. This has been a tale of the rich versus the rest. Large corporations with significant budgetary and resource means have adopted tool-based development as a best practice, while everyone else, including other projects in the same companies, have opted for hand coding.

The benefits of tool-based development versus hand coding include:

- **Reusable dimensional processes.** Data integration tools offer many prebuilt functions or transformations used in data integration processes. These functions and transformations are based on best practices, such as slowly changing dimensions and hierarchy management that are used repeatedly in data warehousing, business intelligence, and data migration applications. Not only does hand coding require these to be built from scratch (delaying the project and potentially introducing errors) but the hand coders may not even be aware of the best practices for those functions.

- **Robust data quality processes.** Many data integration tools have data cleansing, data conforming, and data standardization processes that are critical to data quality but are often too complex to be implemented using hand-coded SQL.
- **Workflow, error handling, and restart/recovery functionality.** These tools manage operational processing, enabling not only recovery and status notifications but also the ability to analyze performance to identify bottlenecks and interactions with other applications. With hand coding, all this has to be coded in addition to the basic data integration processing, incurring a heavy cost in time and resources. More often than not there is no time to hand code this functionality.
- **Impact analysis and where-used (lineage) functionality.** This enables change management, improves productivity, and reduces error surprises. With hand-coded applications, it is often a guessing game as developers have to search through pages of code and hope that they are even accessing all the code that is being used.
- **Self-documentation of processes and entire workflow.** The documentation (if it is even created) associated with hand coding is generally incomplete and out of date. Documentation provides auditing and fosters understanding of the data both for the business person and the IT developer.
- **Enables data governance.** Data integration tools that provide repositories and semantic dictionaries enable the reuse and easy maintenance of business and technical definitions, often referred to as metadata. Although this functionality may be "hidden under the covers," it provides the significant benefit of helping each subsequent data integration project leverage existing work, thus speeding up development time (time to market) and reducing business errors.
- **Productivity gains.** With all the functionality already prebuilt in data integration tools, why would an IT organization, even if it had the time and money, reinvent it? Not only does IT become more productive because the functionality is already built in, but because the tool follows industry best practices, the IT group can avoid the costly errors that would happen without that knowledge.

Although an enterprise's initial data integration projects will not necessarily be faster with a tool-based approach, the deliverables will be more robust and sustainable, enabling a BI environment to provide the information five C's. As depicted in Figure 12.3, the costs per project decline and the long-term total cost of ownership (TCO) is significantly superior for a tool-based versus a hand-coded data integration approach.

The fact that projects with sufficient resources, i.e., budget and skills, almost always use data integration tools indicates their usefulness. The good news for everyone who has felt they could only afford a hand-coded solution is that there are data integration products whose cost and skill requirements will easily be justified in terms of business and IT gains.

SELECTING A TOOL

IT groups create their short list of data integration vendors based on either the current market leaders or on industry analyst groups' top-ranked vendors. But no short list comes into play with hand coding, which is the predominant method used for data integration. It appears that there is a major disconnect between the current short-listed vendors and the needs of many enterprises.

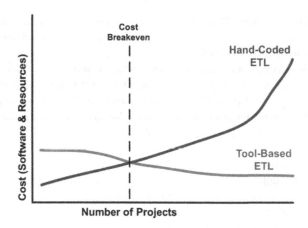

FIGURE 12.3

Cost comparison: hand-coded versus tool-based extract, transform, and load (ETL).

The criteria to use when selecting a data integration tool include:

- Best fit
- Supports programs not just projects
- Data governance
- Scalable, expandable, and pervasive
- Role-based development
- Cost and resource effective
- Business ROI

Best Fit

If we used the same logic in selecting and purchasing a calculator as IT groups do for ETL tools, then all of us would walk out of the office supplies store with a scientific, graphing calculator. Why? Because those calculators have the most features and therefore are the "best." But most of us would not know how to use the bulk of its functionality; we should not be forced to buy something we will not use. Almost all of us purchase a simple calculator that can do the basic calculations for balancing our checkbook or calculating taxes and tips. We buy the best fit for us, not what is the "best," i.e., most feature-laden, calculator.

The "best" ETL products are great, but they are generally expensive, complex, and require a greater investment (time, money, and skills) than other products, which also may do everything you want but at a potentially significantly lower TCO.

When an enterprise selects a data integration tool, it has to determine what it needs, how much it is willing to spend, and what skills it has to implement the software. Getting a product that is too complex for your staff or the tasks that need to be done means the product will likely sit around unused (shelf-ware). Match your integration needs, skills, and budget to the tool, not the other way around.

The term "good enough" is often used in product selection, but that sounds too critical of the products and gives the impression that you are settling for something less just because of price. There is a wide variety of data integration tools that can handle most, if not all, the data integration requirements for enterprises of all sizes and across industries. It is fine if your enterprise needs the top tier (and most expensive product) for its workloads, or if it simply wants and can afford the luxury brand. The rest of us, however, can likely get it done with less. Also, keep in mind that many of the rest of us should really be comparing hand coding with the affordable tools, because that would be what we use, not the top-tier tools.

A good test of the best fit is to run a proof of concept or prototype with your selected data integration tool using your own data. That gets you familiar with both the tool's capabilities and the skills you will need to use it.

Supports a Data Integration Program, Not Just Tactical Projects

A data integration tool that supports multiple projects and developers spread out over a data integration program delivers significant business and IT benefits. This capability facilitates the reuse of data definitions and transformations amongst projects and collaboration between developers.

From a business perspective, this also improves data consistency and reduces the likelihood of creating data silos. From an IT perspective, reuse and collaboration boosts productivity and makes it easier to bring additional people onto each project because knowledge is not locked into a programmer's "proprietary" custom code.

Data integration tools foster sustainable software development and maintenance practices such as source control, revision management, and functional sharing. With the importance of data and its integration to an enterprise, it is often too risky to rely on manually creating, documenting, and managing custom code, not to mention that it is more costly, time consuming and error prone.

Supports Data Governance

As discussed in Chapter 17, a successful data governance program obtains business ownership of the data definitions and transformations, which is vital to implementing consistent information throughout an enterprise. It is important to have a data integration tool that can then support those definitions and transformations so that the processes do not just become a paper exercise that is not implemented in the integration processes. Role-based support of various data governance activities improves responsiveness to business needs and the demands placed on changes in the business. In addition, data lineage, input analysis, auditing, and metadata management support aids data governance.

Scalable, Expandable, and Pervasive

Enterprises, from Fortune 1000 to SMBs, typically need to integrate many varied data sources. These sources are spread across many platforms, stored in structured and semistructured data types, have different update cycles, are interconnected and codependent, and need batch or real-time processing. In short, most enterprise data integration needs are diversified and challenging. The data integration tool you select must be able to handle this diversity.

In addition to supporting varied data sources, it is highly desirable for a data integration tool to be able to optimize data processing, particularly with parallel capabilities. This functionality leverages whatever size infrastructure footprint is used for data integration by maximizing data throughput. This optimization saves money by reducing the infrastructure investments that would otherwise be required and helps those committed to green computing (with a reduced environmental impact). In addition, optimization results in shorter integration processing, always a plus in today's business climate.

Historically, integration efforts have been siloed across an enterprise because of the varied requirements discussed above. Because ETL products often supported only batch-driven processes primarily accessing relational databases and flat files, their focus was generally data warehousing and business intelligence. With these diverse integration needs, select a data integration product that goes beyond data warehouse (DW) or BI and that enables data migration, data synchronization, SOA, data quality, enterprise data access, complex data exchange and master data management (MDM). An enterprise's initial integration efforts may be focused on DW and BI, but many of these other areas will arise in the future, and it will be desirable to simply expand your data integration platform rather than building a whole new, and likely overlapping, integration platform.

To make sure your data integration tool is widely used in the enterprise, be sure to choose one that supports diverse sources, data processing models, and applications.

Cost and Resource Effective

Data integration tool-based development has historically been viewed as too expensive and hard to learn, as well as taking too much time on each project to develop the integration processes. The market "leaders" started as batch-only tools for DW development. Expanding this functionality required incorporating software from acquisitions or altering existing architectures with the new functionality while trying not to disrupt current customer implementations. As a result, customers deployed these complex products for uses that did not require complexity. And, they were still paying mainframe-level prices—a big blow to their ROI.

The good news is that times have changed. Newer data integration tools have been architected from the ground up to support a diversity of data source and integration styles. This means that a development team should be more productive sooner and be able to reuse these tools in various situations.

In addition, newer pricing models bring these tools within most enterprises' reach. In many cases, more expensive products are not necessarily the best choice for an enterprise. Many enterprises in the past have "blown their budget" on the ETL tool and then had no budget to finish the project. Make sure that the product you select is affordable and provides the functionality needed by your enterprise.

Business ROI

No matter how successful your integration efforts appear, it is important to determine the business ROI that your data integration efforts have achieved. The business benefits will be both quantitative and qualitative.

Qualitative benefits abound from data integration projects. Being able to access clean, consistent, conformed, current, and comprehensive information reduces guesswork, enables better analysis, and improves decision making. Business productivity improves by shifting employees' time from gathering data to analyzing and acting on that data. IT productivity gains by placing the right tools to create the integration processes. It also helps the business meet various government and industry regulations. All are enabled by an enterprise's data integration program.

Sometimes it is more difficult for the business to quantify business benefits. The business benefits of data integration enable improved decision making, leading to increased sales, improved customer service, increased profitability, or reduced costs—but there are other processes involved. Data may be the key ingredient to performance management systems, but there have to be business processes in place to leverage that knowledge that, in turn, produced the business benefit. The trick is to not claim that data integration alone created this business benefit, but that the data-enabled solution did. With this mind-set, one should be able to quantify the benefits from the various data-enabled solutions deployed in the enterprise.

TWO TOOLS MAY BE BETTER THAN ONE

If your enterprise is already using a data integration tool exclusively to load the EDW while other projects load data marts and OLAP cubes with hand-coded extracts, then you should validate the reasons why it is being used in this manner. There are two scenarios for this situation.

In the first scenario, the enterprise has simply not adopted the tool-based approach for all data integration projects. This is typical when data integration projects are treated tactically and not viewed within an enterprise-wide perspective. The best practice is to initiate a data integration program, train data integration resources in concepts and tools, and declare the tool-based approach as the de facto standard.

In the second scenario, which is very common for large enterprises that were early adopters, the IT group is using a top-tier ETL tool to load the EDW, but has encountered resource constraints—skills, budget, infrastructure, and licensing—beyond that use. Assuming that the existing data integration tool is successfully loading the EDW, then the question is: Will the enterprise make the investment to eliminate hand-coded extract projects? Although there is a bias for an enterprise to select one tool to do a particular task, the reality with data integration is that it is viable to use two data integration tools in an enterprise:

- The first data integration tool would be the top-tiered tool to load the EDW because its capabilities are needed, but it has significant investments to enable those capabilities.
- The second tool would be used to load data marts and OLAP cubes because the tool used to load the EDW is too expensive to use for data marts and cubes. The objection by the IT staff in this scenario is always that the second tool is not as powerful as their top-tiered tool, and they always declare one tool as a standard. However, the reality is that they have already declared hand coding extracts to be the second standard. So the second tool should be compared to hand coding extracts rather than the top-tiered tool, since it is not being used for these projects.

Although a single standard tool is theoretically the best course, if an enterprise has declared two standards—top-tiered tool and hand coding—then two data integration tools are better than one. The second may not be a standalone tool, but may be embedded in a BI tool or part of a tool that builds a complete BI application including data marts.

DATA INTEGRATION SERVICES

In order to support the explosion of data and the increasing demands of business intelligence, data integration tools have become more complex and sophisticated. The first generation of ETL tools, as depicted in Figure 12.1, were simple code generators that were expensive and had limited functionality. Many companies that evaluated them found it more effective to develop their own custom integration code.

The second-generation ETL products, as depicted in Figure 12.4, offered more functionality, particularly in managing operational processes and software development. These tools, however, were still primarily batch oriented, required extensive skills to use, and needed an additional infrastructure investment to perform well. Based on those two sets of tools, many people in IT were left with the feeling that ETL software was not worth the effort to learn and would not be able to meet their performance needs.

> Manually coding may be the best choice for data exploration and prototyping, but when the DI is a recurring process it should be shifted to an automated DI tool.

The current generation of tools consists of full-fledged data integration suites that include ETL, real-time integration, message streaming, Web services, complex event processing, and data

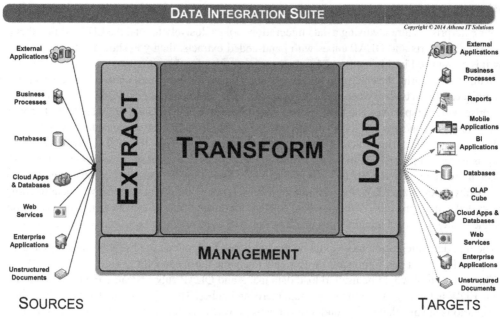

FIGURE 12.4

Extract, transform, load, and manage.

virtualization functionality. The suites can support data integration processes in traditional batch mode, near real time and in real time if the right connectivity is in place to support it. In addition, many suites offer extensions for data quality, data cleansing, data profiling, and MDM functionality.

Data integration suites can access and deliver a wide variety of data spanning structured, semistructured, and unstructured formats. Data exchanges can occur with databases, files, processes, business applications, or analytics tools.

In addition, the plethora of services provided by these data integration suites are built based on the best practices that we have discussed in data architecture, data modeling, and data integration. These best practice services help deliver the information five C's, provide a robust development and production platform, improve enterprise productivity, and increase BI ROI.

The data integration categories of services as depicted in Figure 12.5 are:

- Access (extract)
- Delivery (load)
- Data profiling
- Data ingestion
- Data transformation
- Data quality
- Process management
- Operations management
- Data transport

Figure 12.6 depicts a more detailed list of services provided in each data integration category.

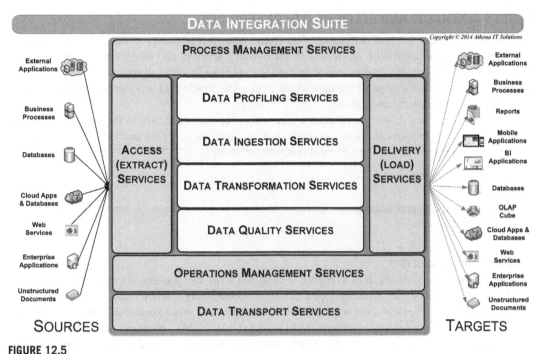

FIGURE 12.5

Data integration suite—services.

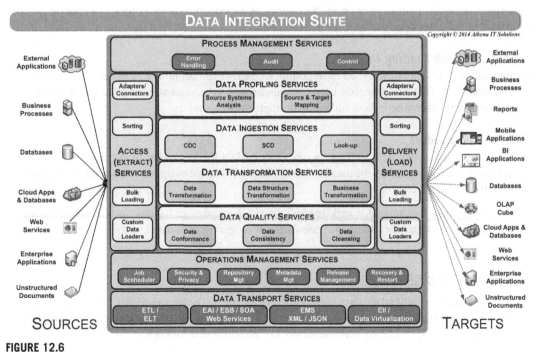

FIGURE 12.6

Data integration suite—services breakdown.

ACCESS (EXTRACT) AND DELIVERY (LOAD) SERVICES

The purpose of access services is to gather data from one or more sources so that it can then be consumed by other data integration services with the delivery services and then loading that data to its targets. Although much attention is paid to gathering data from systems of record (SOR), access and delivery services are used with all the data stores in an enterprise's data architecture such as staging, data warehouse, data marts, and cubes.

Although access and delivery services are pictured as separate bookends to the other data integration processes, they fundamentally use a common set of functions that read and write data throughout the data integration workflow. The common functions include:

- Adopters and connectors
- Sorting utilities
- Bulk import and export loading
- Custom data loaders

Adopters and Connectors

There are adopters and connectors available to read and write to a variety of structured, semistructured, and unstructured data sources. Open database connectivity (ODBC) and Java database connectivity (JDBC) are heavily used with relational databases and other structured sources. There are also application programming interfaces (APIs) to flat files, XML, business applications, OLAP cubes, HL7, statistical databases, Big Data databases, representational state transfer (REST), enterprise service bus (ESB), cloud applications, and many other sources. The list of APIs continually expands as new data sources emerge and the demand to access those rises. Most data integration suites also allow custom web or data services to be created to access and deliver to data sources that have not been prebuilt in their product.

Sorting and Bulk Loading Utilities

Sorting and bulk loading utilities are most common in either the beginning or the end of the data integration workflow. They are primarily used for sources with large data volumes that are processed in a batch-oriented manner where these utilities will improve performance.

Custom Data Loaders

There are instances when data sources require custom data loaders rather than callable APIs or data services that can be invoked by the data integration suite. There are two common scenarios where these custom data loaders are used:

- Proprietary data structures that require specialized schema design loading such as OLAP cubes.
- Business applications that do not provide APIs for accessing or loading.

DATA INGESTION SERVICES

After access services gather data, data ingestion services update the targets with the latest data based on business rules for tracking data as it is created and modified. The processes involved are change data capture (CDC), slowly changing dimensions (SCD), and reference lookups.

Change Data Capture

The CDC process needs to determine what data to access from data sources and updates its targets while typically retaining historical values. Unless all the data from the data sources is gathered and then indiscriminately loaded into the targets, for example, the targets are truncated to avoid duplicates and then all data is inserted, then CDC needs to:

- Gather the data that has been changed—inserted, modified, or deleted—in the data sources since the last time CDC process has been run.
- Insert, modify, or delete data in the targets based on what data was gathered from the sources and what data exists in the targets.

Sometimes the CDC process of gathering data from the data sources cannot be precise enough to discern only the records that have been changed since it was last executed. In these cases, the approach is to overcompensate by making sure that you will get all the records that were changed—even if it means bringing some records that were not changed. This approach necessitates that the CDC processes that determine what needs to be updated and the target systems have to be able to differentiate which worker records were changed since the last CDC.

The CDC techniques used to determine what data has changed in the source systems from the last CDC execution are:

- Audit columns
- Timed extracts
- Row difference comparisons
- Log or message queue scanners
- Event triggers

The CDC techniques employ push, pull, or a combination of both of these operations. Key criteria used in determining push versus pull are the impact on the source systems in terms of performance and the enterprise rules regarding source system access, which may override performance considerations.

A CDC approach employing push operations is common when the data source is a transactional system with high performance demands, or when it is a system that does not allow external applications, i.e., the data integration suite, to directly access it. In these cases, the BI system's data integration suite would not be involved in performing the initial gathering of data from the data source. Under these conditions, the source system may use its own CDC capabilities with one of the techniques described above, or custom coding will be needed. It is very common for source systems applications staff to write the custom code that will create a flat extract that will be pushed to the BI systems staging area, which then triggers its data integration suite to initiate its own CDC processing using a staging area as its data source.

Audit Columns

This technique uses audit columns, which record the date and time that a record was inserted or modified. The most effective schema is to have two date columns in both the source table and associated target table as depicted in Figure 12.7.

The CDC logic for the technique using Figure 12.7 is:

1. Get the maximum value of both the *TGT_Create_DateTime* and *TGT_Modified_DateTime* columns.
2. Select all the rows from the data source with *SRC_Create_DateTime* greater than (>) *TGT_Create_DateTime*, which are all the newly created rows since the last CDC process was executed.

Source_Table

Column	Data Type	Key
SourceKey		FK
Attributes		
SRC_Create_DateTime	DataTime	
SRC_Modified_DateTime	DataTime	

Target_Table

Column	Data Type	Key
SourceKey		FK
Attributes		
TGT_Create_DateTime	DataTime	
TGT_Modified_DateTime	DataTime	

FIGURE 12.7

Change data capture—two audit columns.

Source_Table

Column	Data Type	Key
SourceKey		FK
Attributes		
SRC_Modified_DateTime	DataTime	

Target_Table

Column	Data Type	Key
SourceKey		FK
Attributes		
TGT_Modified_DateTime	DataTime	

FIGURE 12.8

Change data capture—single audit column.

3. Select all rows that have a *SRC_Modified_DateTime* greater than (>) *TGT_Modified_DateTime* but less than (<) *TGT_Create_DateTime*. The reason for the exclusion of rows less than the maximum target create date is that they were included in step 2.
4. Insert new rows from step 2 or modify existing rows from step 3 in the target based on the SCD logic (below) that is being used for that specific table.

The CDC logic for the technique using Figure 12.8 is:

1. Get the maximum value of the *TGT_Modified_DateTime* column.
2. Select all rows that have a *SRC_Modified_DateTime* greater than (>) *TGT_Modified_DateTime*.
3. Determine which of the rows from step 2 need to be inserted and which require existing rows to be modified.
4. Based on the determination in step 3, insert new rows or modify existing rows in the target based on the SCD logic (below) that is being used for that specific table.

Timed Extracts

This CDC approach involves:

1. Selecting all the data that was created or modified in the source during a preset interval of time such as a day. The most common time interval is to load all of yesterday's created or modified rows.
2. Determine which of the rows from step 2 need to be inserted and which require existing rows to be modified.
3. Based on the determination in step 3, insert new rows or modify existing rows in the target based on the SCD logic (below) that is being used for that specific table.

This was a very common technique in the early days of data warehousing and continues to be an approached favored by IT people who are new to BI.

Although at first blush this would seem to be a very straightforward approach to CDC, there are risks associated with this technique. The most significant risk is duplicate processing if there are any failures and restarts that occur during CDC processing. There is also the risk that if a specific time interval is skipped due to an operational problem, it (the time interval) may never be processed. As the data volumes involved in CDC processing and the time to complete overall ETL loads increase, this method becomes less reliable.

Because of these potential risks and reliability issues, this CDC technique is generally discouraged.

Database Log or Message Queue Scanners

This CDC technique takes a snapshot at a predefined point in time of either the data source's database log or message queue, searches that snapshot for any transactions that indicate changes in data, and then updates the targets reflecting these changes.

The advantages with using this technique are that it:

- Creates minimal impact on the data source's database or message queue
- Eliminates the need to change the data source's schema to flag changes in data.

There are, however, several significant challenges to using this technique:

- There are no standards related to the structure or process flow, so every database or message queue will require a different CDC application.
- Most database management systems and message queues do not document the internal format of the logs or queues. This will require the purchase of a separate CDC product that handles the specific databases or message queues that need to be accessed.
- Often the level of detail needed and the database log or message queue to support CDC decreases the performance of the underlying application and increases the size of the log, significantly degrading performance.
- A common occurrence when the logs or queues become too big is for the database administrators (DBAs) to truncate them, which then eliminates the ability to perform CDC.

Because of its challenges, this CDC technique is typically used when it is the only method able to capture data changes.

Table or Event Triggers

This CDC technique uses triggers that are either set up in the database or coded in the data source's application to record all changes in the data source by writing them out to a separate table or file to be used as a CDC queue to update the targets when requested. It's best to avoid this technique because it adversely impacts the source systems performance by requiring multiple writes to a database every time a row is inserted or modified.

Row Difference Comparisons

With this CDC technique, a full snapshot of the data sources is taken every time the CDC process is run. The current snapshot is compared to the previous snapshot to determine all the changes that occurred in the data source since the last CDC run. The full comparison of the differences between the two snapshots on a row-by-row basis produces a thorough and accurate accounting for all changes including inserts, modifications, and deletions. The snapshots of the data sources can be stored as separate tables or files in the BI environment's staging area.

While this is the most reliable of all CDC techniques, it is typically avoided whenever the number of data sources and data volumes is high because:

- Row-by-row comparisons across tables is very time consuming
- Demand for storage significantly increases because you need three copies of the data sources that are being used in this technique: the original data, previous snapshot, and current snapshot.

Slowly Changing Dimensions

The CDC service determines what source data has been changed—inserted or modified—while the SCD service updates the target data based on the rules specified in the SCD type that has been selected for a particular target. The best practice is to use the database to generate surrogate keys when possible, otherwise this service is responsible for generating surrogate keys. Some data integration suites have prebuilt functions that can be used to generate the surrogate keys, but when not available the process needs to be created and embedded in this service.

This service is applied to both fact and dimension tables even though its name would imply otherwise. The description of these rules and supporting schema was discussed in Chapter 10. For transactional and snapshot fact tables, rows are always inserted and never updated so that SCD type 0 applies. The SCD type needs to be selected for accumulating snapshot fact tables and all dimensions, as there are no default types. See Table 12.1.

Table 12.1 List of Slowly Changing Dimension (SCD) Types	
SCD Type	**Description**
0	Keep original
1	Overwrite existing data (row) with new data
2	Create a new row for new values
3	Track changes using separate columns but overwrite rest
4	Add minidimension
5	Combine types 4 and 1
6	Combine types 1, 2, and 3 (= 6)
7	Use both types 1 and 2

Reference Lookups

The data ingestion service supports reference lookups throughout the data integration workflow. These lookups are used for such tasks as:

- Data validation
- Cross-reference mapping and substitution
- Adding the foreign keys to fact tables that link back to dimension tables' surrogate keys
- Adding the date dimension's surrogate key to a fact table for every occurrence of a date that will be queried in the BI environment

The reference lookup service may be needed by many tables and repeatedly performed for each row processed in the table. There are several best practices to improve lookup performance. First, when querying the lookup table, only select the columns used to match the rows, and then substitute the replacement values on the target table. Second, many data integration suites allow lookup tables to either be cached to local files or to be stored in memory rather than repeatedly querying the source system. Using either a file or memory cache will significantly improve data integration processing.

DATA PROFILING SERVICES

Data profiling, often called source system analysis, is a process of examining the structure and content of data sources. This can be a very time-consuming task based on the variety and complexity of the source systems, but the resource commitment to perform it is typically underestimated because people assume that they know the state of the data in the source systems. After all, enterprises have applications that run their business on a daily basis and may have been successfully operating for years, so the assumption is that these applications and the data inside them are well understood and documented.

But this is when the data monster rears its head in BI projects. After all the data has been loaded and the BI applications are in operation, business people start seeing "funny" data values. Their business analysis is then inaccurate, or they cannot complete it. This immediately results in a fire drill to find the data problem and get around it, but then other anomalies appear. Next, the business people feel there is a severe data quality problem and the BI application stops being used. What happened?

Many BI projects fail simply because the project team was surprised by the data—specifically, they were surprised by data anomalies lurking in the source systems. Sometimes the problems can be blamed on data quality, but often there is no problem with the correctness of data. Rather, the problems lie with the data's completeness or the way specific fields are being used. A field might be used for multiple purposes depending on the business process or division that updated it, but those multiple uses are not documented, so it ends up looking wrong.

Why do teams get caught off guard? You would think that if the project managers did source systems analysis, you would not have any surprises. To understand how this happens, let us look at the usual approach a manager takes. The team gathers the business requirements, determines the data needed to fulfill those requirements, and determines the SOR needed to source the data. After that, the team assesses the SOR by obtaining field layouts, talking to the IT staff supporting the SOR, and finally writing queries to fetch information about the SOR contents. The next step is to write the ETL code, test it, and finally start loading the data warehouse. So far, so good. The data starts getting loaded and the BI portion of the project—reports, cubes, dashboards, etc.—gets built. Then, when the business people use the BI environment, the numbers do not seem to match what they are reporting on and some "funny" results appear.

The problem is not that source system analysis was not undertaken. The problem is that it was neither comprehensive nor complete. Examining the source systems for data anomalies is a process that most of us do not have much experience with. Also, most of us are not allowed enough time in the project to build all the SQL scripts needed to examine the data thoroughly and systematically.

Data profiling is the answer to this problem. To profile data effectively, you have to understand the source system data—how it is defined, its condition, and how it is stored and formatted. When all the source systems were back-office, custom, legacy systems, this was a huge task requiring a lot of people and time. Widespread enterprise resource planning (ERP) system deployments replaced many of the customized legacy systems, resulting in a better understanding of data sources. With ERP implementations, you either have documented data or implementation resources people who are familiar with the data. However, what if your company lacks knowledge or documentation of your source systems? That is when you need data profiling software so you can examine and document data sources, rather than use a people-intensive investigation of these sources.

Data profiling tools automate a methodology and set of algorithms that examine your source systems. These tools generate many more data queries than your staff could perform to examine data values, data ranges, frequency distribution, broken relationships, and many other characteristics that are indicative of potential data anomalies. These tools encode the experience that your staff probably lacks when it comes to deeply examining data for problems. These tools assist your staff in truly understanding not just the definitions of what the data is supposed to represent, but more importantly, the real content of that data.

Data profiling should be established as a best practice for every data warehouse, BI, and data migration project. Data profiling is essential to establishing a data quality process. In addition to performing data profiling during your project, it should be an ongoing activity to ensure that you maintain data quality levels.

Early detection is best, and the further in the process you are, the more expensive the errors are to correct. Certainly, too many BI and DW projects have missed their deadlines or budget because of data quality surprises late in the project. Data profiling activities benefit these projects by improving project planning and its financial performance. It should be a requirement early in the project, just as systems testing and user acceptance testing occur toward the project's completion.

Source Systems Analysis

The use of data profiling tools to automate the source systems analysis process should be a fundamental requirement within data integration services. These tools enable the BI team to comprehensively examine the structure and content of the source systems to validate business requirements, quantify the state of data quality, and assist in the design of the data integration workflow.

Data profiling services, as depicted in Figure 12.9, perform the following functions:

- Accessing source system
- Structure and content analysis
- Recording results in a profiling repository
- Providing data profiling reporting

The structure and content analysis of source systems involves:

- Table analysis
- Column analysis
- Relationship analysis
- Primary key analysis
- Cross-table analysis

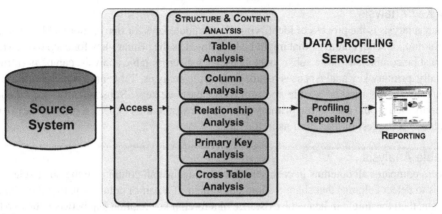

FIGURE 12.9

Source systems analysis.

Table Analysis

This process examines data selected from the data values for all columns of a table in order to compute the functional dependencies for the table. Table analysis finds associations between different columns in the same table.

When reviewing all function dependencies, you decide whether or not to exclude a functional dependency from further analysis. Proper inclusion of functional dependencies is important because it supports the later identification of primary keys, relationships, and normalization of a table.

Column Analysis

This process examines all values for the same column to infer the column's definition and other properties such as domain values, statistical measures, minimum/maximum values, etc. During column analysis, each available column of each table of source data is individually examined in depth. Many properties of the data are observed and recorded; some examples are:

- Minimum, maximum, and average length
- Precision and scale for numeric values
- Basic data types encountered, including different date/time formats
- Minimum, maximum, and average numeric values
- Count of empty values, *null* values, and non-*null*/empty values
- Count of distinct values or cardinality

Additionally, column analysis makes certain inferences about the column's data such as:

- Data type, precision, and scale
- Whether or not *nulls* are permitted
- Whether or not the column contains a constant value
- Whether or not the column values are unique

Primary Key Analysis

Primary key analysis is the process of identifying all candidate keys for one or more tables. The goal is to detect a column, or set of columns, that might be best suited as the primary key for each table. This analysis step must be completed before subsequent steps, such as cross-table analysis, can be performed.

Normally, primary key analysis uses results from table analysis. Table analysis identifies the dependencies among the columns of a table and proposes candidate keys. Subsequently, one candidate key must be confirmed by the user as the primary key. As you would then expect, a primary key determines all the values for the rest of the columns in the table.

Cross-Table Analysis

This process compares all columns in each selected table against all columns in the other selected tables. The goal is to detect columns that share a common domain. If a pair of columns is found to share a common domain, then this might indicate the existence of a foreign key relationship between the two tables, or simply redundant data. These possibilities are examined during the subsequent relationship analysis step.

Relationship Analysis

This is the process of identifying relationships between tables. This process uses information gleaned during execution and review of primary key analysis and cross-table analysis. Primary key analysis produces the primary key for each table, and cross-table analysis identifies columns in different tables that share common domains. The existence of a common domain may be indicative of a relationship between two tables, since columns in two tables that are related will often share a common domain.

Source-to-Target Mapping

During the design, development, and testing of data integration applications, the source-to-target mapping service enables the developer to see the structural content of the sources and targets. In addition, sampling of data and row counts are available to aid in design.

DATA TRANSFORMATION SERVICES

As depicted in Figure 12.10, the data integration processes access and deliver data with various data stores and their schemas such as staging, DW, and data marts. The data transformation services build and populate the schema—tables, columns, and relationships—of each of these data stores.

The key data transformation services are:

- Data conversion
- Business transformation—rules and metrics
- Data structure transformation

Data Conversion Services

Data conversions are typically straightforward and can be implemented either as an ETL transform or within its source-to-target mapping application. Most of the data conversions are performed as data is gathered from source systems and loaded into a DW. The following are examples of when data conversions are needed:

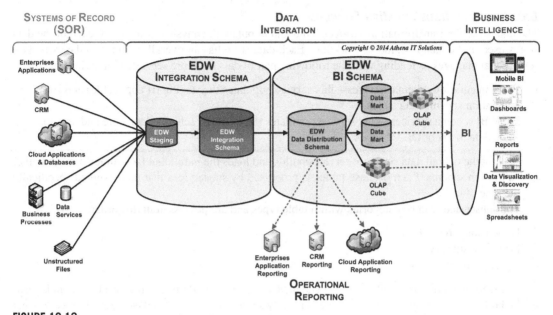

FIGURE 12.10

Data integration workflow.

- Source system data types are incompatible with the target database.
- Multiple data sources with different data types may be populating a particular column.
- A data source column may contain multiple codes combined into an "intelligent" key and needs to be broken into its separate components.
- BI environment has adopted column standards in regard to data types that must be followed.

Business Transformation Services

Business transformations involve applying business rules, algorithms, and filters to create business measures, metrics, and key performance indicators (KPIs) for use in specific business processes and business groups. DW fact tables contain measures such as sales quantity and revenue, but these measures are typically business neutral. Business transformations, on the other hand, may only apply to corporate finance or the supply chain management, for example.

The best practice is to perform the business transformations applicable to a business process or group within the data marts or OLAP cubes that the business people use. Keeping these business transforms out of the DW allows it to keep its focus as the general purpose enterprise data hub that can be used by all groups (or at least as feeds into their business-specific data marts). We have seen too many DWs labeled as the finance or sales DW because those groups' business transformations were created there and all the other enterprise groups felt that the DW did not apply to them. Another practical aspect of implementing the business transformation in business-specific data marts is that it means only the business people who use that transformation need to define it. Otherwise, each business transform needs to be reviewed and approved by groups with no interest in or contrary views of that transformation.

Data Structure Transformation Services

The data structure transformation services build and populate the physical schema for each of the data stores used in the data integration workflow. Each data store has an overall (or master) data structure service that manages its loading with the following pair of data structure services that orchestrate them:

- EDW integration schema services—this service populates the staging (if applicable) and EDW integration schema data stores.
- EDW BI schema services—this service populates the EDW BI schema data store and any applicable data marts or OLAP cubes.

Each of the overall data structure services builds and loads the individual fact, dimension, and other tables in each schema. Each of these tables is processed by subservices that are designed specifically for the type of table.

The subservices can be categories within table types and are processed in this order:

1. Dimension table subservice
2. Fact table subservice
3. Aggregation subservice

The workflow order is based on the dependencies of each subsystem. Aggregates, for example, cannot be built unless the underlying fact tables that they summarize exist. Likewise, fact tables cannot get assigned the foreign keys to dimension tables until they are built. In addition to the dimensional model structural dependencies, each table will have to depend on the data in source systems or other tables in the BI schema. It is critical to have the dependencies mapped out to ensure the proper construction and population of the BI environment.

Dimension Table Subservice

This subservice populates dimension tables. As depicted in Figure 12.11 the dimension table subservice gathers one or more source tables from the source schema, structures the attributes based on the target dimension table type, and, if applicable, will also populate any required subdimension tables

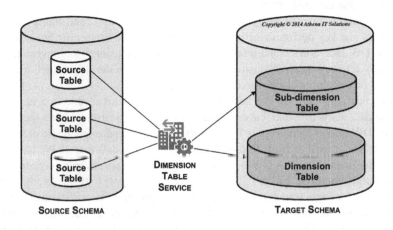

FIGURE 12.11

Dimension table service.

such as minidimension or bridge table. The order in which the tables are populated is: subdimension, dimension, and bridge.

This subservice populates all dimensional table types and their building blocks, including:

- Flattened dimension
- Snowflake dimension
- Miniprofile dimension
- Hierarchy manager
- Bridge table
- Date dimension
- Time dimension
- Junk dimension
- Dimensional role manager

Fact Table Subservice

This subservice populates fact tables after all the dimension tables it is dependent upon are populated. As depicted in Figure 12.12, the fact table subservice gathers one or more tables from the source, assembles them into the fact table structure, performs lookups to input foreign keys to the dimension tables it references, and then populates the fact table.

This subservice populates all fact table types and their building blocks, including:

- Transaction facts
- Periodic snapshot facts
- Accumulating snapshot facts

Aggregation Subservice

This subservice populates the following aggregation-related tables:

- Shrunken dimension table
- Aggregation (fact) table

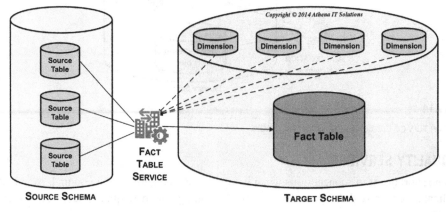

FIGURE 12.12

Fact table service.

As depicted in Figure 12.13, you create shrunken dimension tables from a dimension table that has more detailed grain. Examples are monthly and quarterly shrunken dimension tables created from a date dimension table.

As depicted in Figure 12.14, you create aggregation fact tables by aggregating metrics from a fact table, which you do by referencing a dimension table to determine the level in the hierarchy to which you need to summarize. You may use a shrunken dimension table, if it is available, as the reference rather than the more detailed dimension table. An example is summarizing monthly sales or expenses. There are some BI tools or OLAP cubes that create their own aggregations on the fly and do not require aggregate fact tables to be prebuilt.

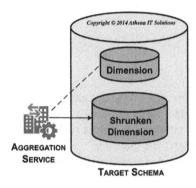

FIGURE 12.13

Aggregation service creates shrunken dimension.

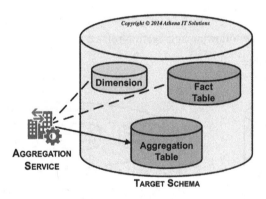

FIGURE 12.14

Aggregation service creates aggregation fact table.

DATA QUALITY SERVICES

There is no shortage of misconceptions when it comes to data quality. Once you understand what they are and how to recognize them, you can move on to building your data quality service and then putting it in action.

Misconceptions about Data Quality

There are several misconceptions people have concerning data quality that thwart efforts to establish the information five C's in an enterprise BI environment:

- The DW has a data quality problem
- Data quality is the result of errors in data entry or data acquisition
- The data quality in our source systems is excellent.
- The DW is a read-only operation and never alters data
- Data cleansing tools will fix data quality problems

The DW Has a Data Quality Problem

If data warehouses could talk, they might say, "Don't shoot me, I am just the messenger!"

When business people encounter data quality issues using BI applications, they tend to immediately blame the DW. After all, they have been using the data from these source systems for years, either through application reports or spreadsheets with extracted data, and they never encountered these problems before.

There is certainly a chance that there were bugs in the ETL loads or BI applications that slipped through testing, but those errors can be identified and corrected. And they are likely to be exceptions. What we are referring to are data quality problems that appear even when the data in the DW matches the source systems exactly.

Since the DW is often the only place where business people have an enterprise-wide view of their data, the DW is often the "canary in the coal mine." Most of the reports and spreadsheets that the business person uses gathered data from a single source system. Because of this, they have never truly seen the data sourced from its many data silos with its potential data inconsistency problems. In addition, they might also be unaware of how the source system application reports or spreadsheets may have masked data quality issues within that source system.

Data Quality is the Result of Errors in Data Entry or Data Acquisition

Data entry or data acquisition in operational (source) systems is often blamed for data quality problems. Although incorrectly entered or missing data may cause problems, most source systems today have very robust validation screens or processes ensuring that data was entered correctly, so this type of error is typically minor in scope.

Although it is easy to blame data quality problems on the systems where the data was created or acquired, the majority of the quality issues relate to consistency, completeness, relevancy, and timeliness of the data. If two divisions are using different customer identifiers or product numbers, does it mean that one of them has the wrong numbers? Or is consistency the problem between the divisions? If the problem is consistency, then it is an enterprise issue, not a divisional issue. The long-term solution may be for all divisions to use the same codes, but that has to be a high-level enterprise decision.

The larger issue is that you need to manage data from its creation all the way to information consumption. You need to be able to trace its flow from data entry, transactional systems, data warehouse, data marts, and cubes all the way to the report or spreadsheet used for the business analysis. Data quality requires tracking, checking, and monitoring data throughout the entire information ecosystem. To make this happen, you need data responsibility (people), data metrics (processes), and metadata management (technology).

The Data Quality in Our Source Systems is Excellent

This is the answer given by many business and IT groups and, in particular, the source system application owners. This opinion is reinforced by the fact that often the source systems have been running for years, supporting enterprise operations without data problems. And business people have trusted the data from reports and spreadsheets to make business decisions during that entire period.

Do not fall into these traps. Do not assume anything about the state of the data. The areas where data quality and inconsistency problems lurk include:

- Data quality within SOR applications may be "masked" by corrections made within reports or spreadsheets created from this data. The people who told you the data is fine might not even be aware of these "adjustments."
- Data does not age well. Although data quality may be fine now, there is always the chance that you will have problems or inconsistencies with the historical data. The problems can also arise when applications like predicative analytics need to use historical data.
- Data quality may be fine within each SOR application, but may be very inconsistent across applications. Many companies have master data inconsistency problems with product, customer, and other dimensions that will not be apparent until the data is loaded into the enterprise DW.

You Cannot Blame the DW because It Is a Read-Only Operation and Never Alters Data

Although the BI program cannot be blamed for creating the data quality problems, it can be blamed for not identifying and addressing the problems. The unfortunate events are that data quality and inconsistency problems will become evident in the enterprise DW and it will be blamed. Even if the DW program can prove the problems reside in the SORs, it still will be blamed for being surprised and not proactively dealing with it. The worst case is that the DW program's credibility will be dealt a blow from which it cannot recover.

The first widely publicized definition of a data warehouse was that it was subject oriented, integrated, time variant, and nonvolatile. This established that the data warehouse was read-only and should not alter data—it is what it is. The DW mantra was that if the data is broken, fix it at its source. That was reinforced by the overall quality control mandate that you fix a problem at its source or as close as you can to it.

But if most data quality problems today are the result of data being inconstant due to data silos, then where is the root cause? No one source system owns the problem, so who becomes responsible? The pragmatic answer is that the enterprise BI and MDM programs own the problems. Maybe they cannot, realistically, fix them at their root since that is more in the people, process, and politics domain, so they should establish the information five C's as best as they possibly can.

Data Cleansing Tools Will Fix Data Quality Problems

If only it were true that data cleansing tools fixed data quality problems. There are two main reasons why it is not.

First, data cleansing tools, although highly beneficial in certain use cases, do not address the primary data quality issues most enterprises face—data inconsistency and incompleteness. Much of the data cleansing tools are oriented toward cleaning up an enterprise's people- and businesses-related attributes such as names and addresses. These attributes may apply to customers, prospects, suppliers, partners, employees, or patients. The locations could be homes or businesses. Much of this data is textual or location oriented, which means there is a high probability that these attributes will vary between data sources or interactions with people. The data cleansing software does parsing, matching, standardization, enrichment, and other functions that create one list of things such as customers, businesses, or products. Much of this data cleansing falls under the MDM umbrella. Although these tools do address particular data inconsistency use cases, even a large enterprise with significant investments in MDM will still need to deal with data inconsistency and incompleteness arising from its many silos. And SMBs will not likely make the MDM investments, so they will have to deal with these data issues without the benefit of these tools.

Second, technology is not a cure-all for data quality, especially since the root of the problems arise from people, processes, and procedures. As we discuss in Chapter 17, an enterprise needs to recognize that data is an enterprise asset and establish a data governance program to help manage that data on an ongoing basis.

Build the Data Quality Services

Once it identifies and resolves the misconceptions, the BI team needs to proactively build and deploy data quality services. The steps the BI team needs to undertake are:

- Obtain data quality and consistency estimates and assumed metrics as part of a service level agreement (SLA) when gathering the business and data requirements from the business and SOR application owners.
- Perform a data profiling and source systems analysis to determine the current state of data quality and consistency within and across SORs.
- Create a gap analysis between current state and desired state, i.e., data quality metrics in SLA.
- Propose data integration tasks that are needed to bridge that gap. This should include timeline, tasks, resources, and costs to implement and maintain an ongoing set of data quality processes.
- Negotiate with business and SOR application owners if effort or costs are too high to lower metrics within SLA.
- Once the BI team has the agreed-upon data quality metrics, they can define them, determine how to monitor them, and then design the data quality reporting or alerting application.

There are three categories of data quality measures that the BI team needs to define, develop, and deploy within the data quality services:

- **Structural.** This verifies that the relationship between tables and columns is correct. This involves checking referential integrity, hierarchies, multivalue relationships, and the integrity of subdimensions. There may also be groups of columns that are related that need to be verified.
- **Attributes.** This verifies that the attribute content adheres to property definition and constraints (but not that the actual attribute value is correct). These properties include:
  - Whether or not it can be null
  - Numeric value within allowable range, if applicable
  - A member of a list of values
  - Matches allowable character patterns, if applicable
  - Valid data types
- **Business rules.** This verification could span a wide variety of business context checks or business algorithms. The data needed to perform these verifications may be sourced from a variety of data sources. This may be quite complex. The business rules need to be signed off on by a responsible business person as part of the business and data requirements.

Implementing Data Quality Services

The three data quality services are:

- Data conformance
- Data consistency
- Data cleansing

Data conformance involves creating and populating a conformed dimension when there are multiple data sources for a particular dimension. The most common examples are creating a single customer list or product lists. Data profiling determines the extent of the nonconformance in business rules. You will need to define this with the business people when designing this service.

Data consistency involves making sure that there are standard measures on fact tables when there are multiple variations of that measure. Similar to data conformance, data profiling determines the extent of the nonstandardization in business rules and requires working closely with the business to define what is needed.

Data cleansing is the term used for the off-the-shelf data quality products (discussed earlier in this chapter). These tools include features such as parsing, matching, enrichment, survivorship, and householding. Because of their expense and specific use cases, typically only a limited number of the largest firms use them.

Each of the data quality services will monitor one or more of the data quality measures in regard to structure, attributes, or business rules. Process management services will record the results through its audit subservice and will process errors through its error handling subservice.

PROCESS MANAGEMENT SERVICES

The process management services are the command-and-control center for the data integration jobs. Depending on what data integration product is being used, jobs may also be referred to as sessions, workflows, flows, job sequences, or packages. These services include:

- Job control—manages the workflow of data integration jobs.
- Audit—records processing metadata of the data integration jobs.
- Error handling—processes errors according to predefined rules and records error events.

Each of these services generates process metadata that tracks data integration operations. Although all data integration tools perform these services, there is a wide variety in the prebuilt functionality and the extent of the process metadata that is tracked. Although one would be correct in assuming that the most expensive data integration tools have extensive command-and-control capabilities, it is interesting to note that some of the more economical tool offerings in terms of licensing costs also have robust capabilities.

Job Control Services

As data is gathered, transformed, and delivered as information, there will be many data integration services that are invoked in a complex workflow. Related services are bundled together in jobs that gather data, transform it, and then load it into a target data store. These jobs operate successively, as depicted in Figure 12.15, moving data from SORs to its eventual consumption in BI applications.

Data integration jobs are bundled together in parent jobs with the job control service managing their interactions, dependencies, and workflow with other jobs. The job control service will interact with both the error handling and audit services.

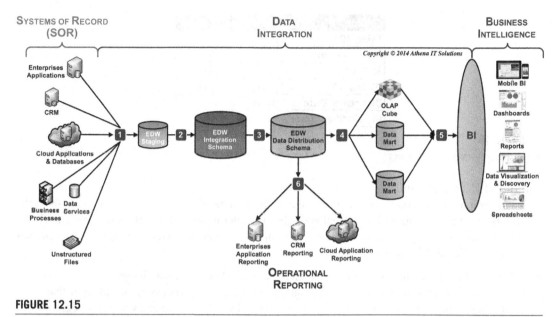

FIGURE 12.15

Data integration jobs workflow.

Audit Services

The purpose of audit services is to track the processing actions that occur for all tables and columns in the BI data architecture. The audit services track the following three areas:

- Data integration jobs
- Table and row updates
- Data quality metrics

Data Integration Jobs

The data integration products offer a wide variety of audit services for job-processing metadata. The base level of job audit data should be as follows:

1. Job ID—unique processing identifier for a data integration job.
2. Job hierarchy with each *Parent Job ID* that invokes a *Child Job ID*. There ultimately would be a *Master Job ID* for the top level job in the workflow.
3. Start time, completion time, and duration for each job.
4. Completion status such as success, warning (error), or failure (job stopped).
5. List of source, target, and lookup tables along with number of rows accessed, successfully processed, and rejected.
6. The most complete job audit services will also provide the data for 3–5 above to the grain of the individual data integration functions performed within the job.

Job audit data enables the data integration team to monitor processing and improve performance by identifying bottlenecks or adverse trends that need to be addressed.

Column	Data Type	Key
Table_ID		PK
Other columns...		
SOR_ID	Integer	FK
DI_Job_ID	Integer	FK
DI_Create_Date	DateTime	
DI_Modified_Date	DateTime	

FIGURE 12.16

Data integration table—job audit columns.

Table and Row Updates

Data integration job audit data tracks the flow of data through the BI data architecture at the grain of the table. It is a best practice to track row level audit data to better manage it, enable data lineage analysis, and assist in improving system performance. The template schema as depicted in Figure 12.16 enables this type of audit data. The schema includes:

- *DI_Job_ID*—the data integration job identifier is the job ID that the data integration tool generated. This identifier is a foreign key to the data integration tool's processing metadata. If that metadata is available, then this link provides a powerful mechanism to analyze data integration processing and performance down to the level of a table's row.
- *SOR_ID*—This is the SOR identifier that will tie this row to a particular SOR. Use this when the table the row is sourced from multiple systems of records and enables the row to be tied to the specific SOR.
- *DI_Create_Date*—This is the date and time that this row was originally created in this table. Often a database trigger is used to insert the current time, but the data integration job could also insert the current time directly.
- *DI_Modified_Date*—This is the most recent date and time that this row has been modified in this table. Often a database trigger is used to insert the current time, but the data integration job could also insert the current time directly. It is often a standard practice to populate this column with an initial value far in the future such as "9999-12-31" rather than leaving it a NULL to avoid queries with NULLs when analyzing this column.

Data Quality Metrics

This is a best practice when data quality metrics have been designed and deployed for specific fact tables in the BI data architecture. There are two tables defined:

- Data quality metrics—this contains the list of each of the data quality metrics that are tracked and the tables to which they apply.
- Data quality audit—this table has a row for every data quality metric that was violated, its data source, and its target table. In addition, it includes the job audit columns.

Error Handling Services

When an error occurs in a data integration job, the possible options are:

1. Stop processing

2. Treat as a warning and continue processing
3. Do something and then resume processing at a designated point in the workflow

Although there are always errors that the data integration team cannot anticipate, the best practice is to manage the error processing as in option (3).

The data integration team needs to perform the following tasks:

- Identify where in the data integration job processing workflow errors may occur and what they would be.
- Determine the actions to be performed for each identified error and workflow location.
- Determine the point in the workflow that processing will resume.
- Design and implement the error handling actions in the data integration jobs, including recording the error audit metadata.

Fortunately, most data integration products have, prebuilt into every data integration function that processes data, the ability to divert the actual error data to a table or file that is designated to store it.

You can use several tables to implement this functionality:

- Error conditions—This contains the list of all of the error conditions that are tracked and what tables to which they apply.
- Error audit—This table has a row for every error condition that was encountered, its data source, and its target table. In addition, it includes the job audit columns.
- Error data—This table contains each of the error rows encountered, a foreign key linking the row to the error audit table, and the job audit columns.

OPERATIONS MANAGEMENT SERVICES

You can use operation management services to monitor and manage the design, development, and running of data integration services. These services need to make the data integration environment efficient in terms of utilizing resources and effective in terms of achieving business and technical objectives. Those objectives should have reliability and responsiveness as key success criteria. When possible, it is a best practice to agree to and then meet SLAs regarding those criteria.

The list of operational management services include:

- **Scheduling.** This service allows you to schedule data integration services, execute that schedule, monitor services, trigger status alerts, and provide operational reporting. Invoke the services based on a time schedule or event triggers such as the completion or failure of other services. In addition to having independent scheduling services, it is common for data integration tools to support interaction with an enterprise's independent job scheduling applications.
- **Restart and recovery.** The service enables you to suspend or stop the execution of other services. It also provides the ability to recover from and restart services that were either stopped manually or through system error. This service will need to leverage the commit and rollback functionality of the target data stores such as databases or file systems. Ensure that error handling can interact with the service when specific severe error conditions are encountered. It is a best practice to design each data integration service with the ability to restart and recover independent of other services.

- **Security and privacy.** This service provides account and role-based security both during the creation and execution of data integration services. Overall enterprise data security and privacy, however, will be a combination of network and database mechanisms rather than what the data integration service will provide. It is essential that you develop and enforce security policies and procedures for operating data integration services because they are likely to access confidential or sensitive data in an enterprise.
- **Documentation.** This service provides documentation of individual data integration services as well as the workflow and dependencies between them. This documentation should include descriptions of services, the metadata explaining the service (such as the source and target mapping), and graphical representation of the workflows. Make sure this documentation can be saved with its associated code in the release management system. In addition, make sure the service can provide data lineage and "where used" functionality to enable analysis of where (source and targets), when (in what specific data integration services), and how data is transformed throughout the data integration services.
- **Software management system.** This system manages the entire software lifecycle including design, development, testing, deployment, operations, maintenance, and releases. This includes the software code and its associated documentation across software releases or versions. This system may interact with an external software code management application from a check-in and checkout perspective.
- **Repository management.** This service manages the business, technical, and processing metadata in the data integration suite's repository. It creates and updates this metadata during the design, development, and operation of data integration services. This service provides import, export, and backup of the metadata.
- **Operations reporting.** This service provides monitoring, reporting, and analytical functionality on management services. This also includes the ability to send alerts based on development or processing events. It is a best practice to provide operational metric dashboards, reporting, and trending on an ongoing basis for both business sponsors and the enterprise's infrastructure group. If SLAs are in place, this is an effective method to monitor those criteria.

DATA TRANSPORT SERVICES

Business intelligence systems are built to create the information five C's and break down the data silos that enterprises have been building for decades. Just as they have built data silos, enterprises have also been building integration silos using a wide variety of integration technologies that address specific integration use cases. Whereas data integration has become identified with ETL or ELT technologies, the other integration uses have fallen under the umbrella of application integration.

The more sophisticated data integration vendors recognized that there was a significant amount of overlap in the uses of data and application integration technologies. In many uses, any of the integration technologies handle the following three fundamental operations:

1. Access data
2. Transform data
3. Deliver data

These fundamental operations are what data integration tools have been doing for years. These data integration vendors have integrated a wide variety of integration technologies into their tools. The integration technologies we have labeled as data transport services enable data integration to be performed across a variety of integration platforms.

This list of data transport services includes:

- ETL and ELT
- Enterprise application integration including ESB, SOA, and Web (or data) services
- Enterprise message services including XML and JSON
- EII including data virtualization and data federation

BUSINESS INTELLIGENCE DESIGN

VI

BUSINESS INTELLIGENCE APPLICATIONS

INFORMATION IN THIS CHAPTER

- Creating BI content specifications
- Choosing the BI application
- Creating personas
- Best practices for BI design layout
- Data design for self-service BI
- Matching visualization and analysis types

BI CONTENT SPECIFICATIONS

> *A quick note on terminology before you read this chapter*: this book uses *BI application* as the all-encompassing term to represent any BI project deliverable that the BI team develops for business people to use in their analysis. This can be a dashboard, scorecard, report, data visualization, ad hoc query, OLAP cube, predictive model, or data model. Others may use the terms *report*, *BI object,* or *BI artifact* instead, but I find that these are either misleading or too obscure. (Not to be confused with BI tool, which is software a vendor sells to help you develop the BI application.)

The project team needs to develop BI content specifications in order to design and document the BI applications they are going to build. The requirements gathering processes discussed in Chapter 3 will have collected the preliminary content for the specifications, but more details are needed, and the input from the requirements must be organized in the context of the BI applications.

The BI project should use an iterative and incremental methodology that includes a mix of waterfall and agile for specific portions of the project. (You will find these concepts covered in Chapter 18.) Developing the specification is not an end unto itself. Rather, it is a tool to help in the design, development, and maintenance of each BI application. The specification is a living document that will be updated and modified at various points in the project as designers, developers, and business people (its consumers) discover different aspects of the BI application or the data that it analyzes throughout the project lifecycle.

The amount of time and resources required to develop the BI content specifications will vary considerably based on the complexity of the BI application and its underlying data, as well as whether the project needs to source and integrate new data into the BI environment.

Is the data that the BI application needs already in the BI environment? And is it documented either in the enterprise data warehouse or in an operational application (assuming it supports operational BI)? If so, the BI application can be moved along a faster path, because data discovery, profiling, and integration will not be necessary. Under these circumstances, the project team should consider using either

337

prototyping or an agile project methodology to design and develop the BI application. When BI vendors discuss how quickly a dashboard can be built, they are really referring to this serendipitous set of circumstances. If they were more forthcoming, they would have a legal disclaimer that says, "you can quickly develop a dashboard *provided the data exists and is documented.*"

The BI application content specification includes the following:

- **Identifier:** A unique identifier. It is useful to create a naming convention for this identifier, similar to what is being used for table and column naming.
- **Name:** A brief, descriptive name. This may be used as the display name in portals, menus, or in title fields. Stick to a naming convention. It is common for this field to be modified later in the project as you get business feedback.
- **Description:** A brief description of its business purpose. This should be descriptive enough that a business person can decide if this application will be useful.
- **Category:** A functional grouping of BI applications, such as customer profitability, sales performance, or expense tracking.
- **Business processes:** A list of the one or more business processes supported by this BI application.
- **Data:** Lists of the data used by the BI application. The granularity will be at the column or field level and includes the following attributes:
  - **Data sources**. List the data sources that the BI application directly queries. A partial list of sources are the enterprise data warehouse (EDW), a data mart, an online analytical processing (OLAP) cube, a spreadsheet, or an operational system.
  - **Data source structures**. List the data structure of the data sources, such as relational, columnar, comma separated value (CSV), XML, OLAP cube, Hadoop, or NoSQL.
  - **Table names**. List the names of the tables or files used from the BI data sources.
  - **Column names**. List the names of the columns or fields from the BI data sources.
  - **Column data type**. List the column or field data type. *Note*: column attributes, such as whether it can contain nulls, its default value (if any), and the possible values are not necessary for the data content, but they will be useful for the functional content design.
  - **Status in the data source**. The options are:
    - It already exists in the BI data source and just needs to be queried when the application is executed.
    - The underlying data exists in the data source, but a business transformation, business rules, or an algorithm needs to be created to make this data available to the BI application. An example is a new measure, metric, or key performance indicator (KPI) that needs to be created from data that already exists.
    - The data does not exist in the BI data source, but needs to be obtained from one or more systems of record (SORs). The details of this are in the data integration specifications.
  - **SOR**. List the originating source system for this data. The details will be in the data integration specifications and data profiling reports.
- **Business transformations for incoming data**: List the filters, business rules, and algorithms used as data is retrieved from the BI data store. *Note*: this is not the business or data transformation performed on the SORs by the data integration processes, but what needs to happen in this BI application.

- **Business transformations for analysis**: Calculate measures and KPIs.
- **Analytical style**: List the BI analytical styles that this application will use to present the data for analysis. These styles include reports, dashboards, scorecards, OLAP cubes, pivot tables, ad hoc queries, data discovery, data visualization, triggers or alerts, and others. *Note*: this is not the functional specification, so this does not include such items as visual layouts and charts.
- **Business people**: List the potential business people who will use the application along with their level of data and analytical skills. Although later you will need their actual names, at this point it is just essential to categorize them by their data and analytics skill levels. Also, if actual names are not provided, then provide an estimate of how many people are in each of these categories.
- **Business owner**: List the business owners of this application.
- **Business contact**: List the business person who is the contact for discussions on the content and functioning of this application if the business owner is delegating this responsibility.
- **BI owner**: List the BI team member responsible for the project delivery of the BI application.
- **BI developer**: List the BI developer responsible for the development of the BI application.
- **Business priority**: List the business priority or value assigned to this BI application relative to the other BI applications on the BI program or project lists.
- **Technical level of effort**: Estimate the time, resources, and degree of difficulty of building this BI application.
- **Risks**: List risks, complexities, or dependencies of this BI application.
- **Comments**: List overall comments provided by business and technical staff.

> A typical method to document this specification is a spreadsheet. As an alternative, you can use a collaborative service, including one that is cloud-based. Spreadsheets work well because they are available, familiar, and enable both sorting and filtering. You can easily set up a spreadsheet to be accessible by team members for collaborative access and updates.
>
> See the book's Web site www.BIguidebook.com for a template you can fill in and use for the BI application content specifications.

REVISE BI APPLICATIONS LIST

Create the initial list of BI applications by reviewing the data and business requirements gathered earlier in the project. The BI content specification process will help you create a revised and agreed-upon list of BI application deliverables. The revisions will evolve during the following steps:

- Assessing scope
- Consolidating BI applications
- Reviewing specifications
- Creating an agreed-upon BI deliverables list

Assessing scope. Defining the BI content specifications involves categorizing the BI applications, getting the business to set priorities, and estimating the level of effort to create them. The BI team members developing the specifications will need to coordinate with data modeling and data integration efforts. Review any data schemas that will be used by the BI applications. BI application design (especially if prototyping is involved) and BI development efforts will need to have BI data stores populated with data, even if it is just sample or test data to begin with. Identify and document project dependencies and risks in the BI application specifications.

Consolidating BI applications. Refine the initial list of BI applications to be delivered during the BI content specification process. Examine each of the individual BI applications in the context of the entire list. First, there are often overlapping requirements across multiple BI applications that can be consolidated into a single BI application with the use of filtering or parameters. Second, the use of more self-service oriented BI analytical styles, such as data discovery, OLAP, and in-memory columnar analytics, enable what appeared to be separate BI applications to be viewed on a dashboard. Both of these scenarios are very common when legacy reports are included in the mix of BI deliverables. Do not be intimidated if there are hundreds or even thousands of legacy reports to be migrated; I have been in projects where the consolidation ratio was 10 to 1. This is likely to be the only time during the BI project where BI deliverables will be reduced rather than expanded.

Reviewing specifications. The consolidated list of BI applications with their content specifications needs to be reviewed by the business stakeholders and reporting subject matter experts (SMEs) to provide feedback and confirm or refine deliverables. In addition, the project dependencies and risks must be reviewed within the context of business priorities to determine if any adjustments need to be made to the list of deliverables, the schedule, or project resources.

Creating an agreed-upon BI deliverables list. This milestone reflects the exit criteria for the BI content specification process and, more importantly, BI scoping. With the agreed-upon list in place you can proceed with the tasks of data modeling, data integration, and BI development.

See the book's Web site www.BIguidebook.com for a template you can use for revising the BI application list.

As with the BI content specifications list, you should make sure team members can collaborate on whatever tool you use to track the BI applications list. If you do choose to use a spreadsheet, be sure it is set up so the team can share information, solicit feedback, and track revisions. This collaboration can range from the use of file sharing with document revisions turned on to a more comprehensive project-oriented collaboration tool. Using collaboration technology will increase business stakeholder involvement, increase visibility and transparency, and improve overall productivity. It shifts the work away from writing elaborate documents and allows the team to focus on gathering information from people in a much more fluid and agile process.

BI PERSONAS

In almost every industry, marketing groups perform customer segmentation analysis for their companies to sell products or services targeted at specific segments. They target restaurants, hotels/motels, vehicles, cameras, and beer to different customer segments based on needs, perceived value (by customers), income, and many other factors.

Customer segmentation is marketing 101, but for some reason the high tech industry does not seem to get it. In fact, their strategy is often one-size-fits-all. In the business intelligence market, product vendors and industry analysts have been targeting one narrow segmentation over the years: the business power user. Power users are business people who are enamored by technology and typically prefer that to their business role. Many successful business managers have a power user on their staff to whom they can off-load any analytical chore. Most industry analysts estimate the power users are just five percent of the total business population, yet it seems every BI tool is pitched to the power user.

Fortunately, there is a wide variety of BI analytical styles available to implement BI applications. The key to success, just like in marketing, is to target the BI application to the correct customer segmentation. We refer to the characteristics of a segmentation of business people as a persona. Product vendors and IT personnel have been frustrated for years that they have not been able to get BI to be pervasive throughout an enterprise. The key to making it pervasive is to identify the BI personas, determine what tools support them, and then structure BI applications for them.

The business personas are:

- Casual consumers
- Analysts
- Power users
- Data scientists

Although the personas very greatly in their data and technology skills, it is a mistake to associate competence with how data- or technology-savvy a person is. BI applications are merely an enabling tool for a business person. Although power users love using technology for its own sake, the typical business person just sees it as a means to an end. Only a small segment of the population includes car geeks, the equivalent of the BI power user, yet the auto industry sells a wide variety of cars to all sorts of auto personas. If BI is to truly become pervasive and enterprises leverage the potential return on investment (ROI) from BI, then the industry needs to recognize different BI personas, and the BI development team needs to create BI applications for all BI personas.

CASUAL CONSUMERS

Many, if not most, of the people in an enterprise are casual consumers of analytics. These business people will use reports and dashboards to obtain information they need to perform their jobs and will not loiter in the BI applications. They wish to have their report or dashboard filled in with the data they need when they view it. If filters or parameters need to be input in order to obtain their specific data, then they would prefer to save the settings so they do not have to remember them for the next time.

Casual consumers may range from operations staff to executives. Operations staff access real time or near real time data from specific operations systems, and they often use embedded BI in those systems. Executives access prebuilt and populated scorecards and dashboards that track enterprise KPIs they are using to monitor and manage. IT will have created at least some of the BI applications the executives use, but it is likely that power users on their staff will have created very tailored BI applications to meet current and emerging analytical requirements.

There are certainly operations staff and executives who are more data-savvy and analytical-savvy, but in general, an operations person is not being paid to spend his time working on dashboards, and an executive will delegate any analytical workload onto her staff.

ANALYSTS

The analyst persona includes people in an enterprise who regularly use BI applications to gather and explore data they need to perform their jobs. Data analysis is in their job descriptions. The job titles may include the word "analyst" (business analyst, financial analyst, sales analyst, operations analyst, etc.) but many other managerial or staff jobs also apply.

Analysts will leverage their business knowledge to explore and analyze data using spreadsheets and BI applications. They are quite comfortable using pivot tables, so BI applications that present data in that context are easy for them to use. A wide range of BI styles present data in this context, including OLAP cubes, in-memory columnar data, discovery, data visualization, dashboard, scorecard, and report tools.

Analysts typically use a dashboard or report template rather than building it from scratch. They will drag the dimensions and measures presented in the power pivot palette onto the templates to perform their analysis. Analysts will also typically use existing data models, but may augment those by adding calculated measures or augmenting the data with something from a spreadsheet.

Analysts offer the most significant opportunity for the BI application to expand and increase its overall business ROI because they are underserved in most enterprises, yet their job role means they would benefit from becoming BI application consumers.

POWER USERS

Power users have always been the sweet spot for BI sales, as they have the business needs of the analyst persona, but they also love technology. These people are the departmental experts in the BI tools that have been bought, and they are their core enterprise customers. Over time, their peers and managers will anoint them as the "go to" people in the business group whenever they need new or enhanced analytics. In fact, their job role and time spent shifts to using BI applications. Whenever BI evaluations are conducted or prototypes developed, they are at the forefront. Because their efforts to build and enhance BI applications gives them a pseudo IT role, they take the time to learn all the BI tools' features and keep asking for more.

Although power users are the core of an enterprise's BI efforts, they present risks to those efforts:

- First, their skills and enthusiasm for BI tools does not represent those of the other business people. The others may enjoy using BI applications because of the results they get, but they are not feature addicts. BI vendors and IT departments need to position BI applications to support the power users but, more importantly, support the rest of the business community.
- Second, power users are the people who have been creating data shadow systems for years. These systems provide them with their gravitas with their peers and managers—something they are not likely to give up easily. Keep in mind that power users may build their next data shadow system with the BI tools rather than a spreadsheet. With that in mind, make sure that migration of legacy reporting and data shadow systems are part of the deliverables for BI projects.

DATA SCIENTISTS

These are the data and statistical geeks! I have an undergraduate engineering degree, so I use the terms geeks and nerds with pride and respect. Data scientists work with predictive analytics.

Predictive analytics moves BI from merely analyzing the past and present to leveraging that knowledge to predict outcomes. The predictions are just that—predictions, as they present probabilities not absolutes. When done well, however, predictive analytics improves business outcomes. Data scientists know statistics and math, but what is often overlooked is their expertise in their enterprise's business and industry. They may also have expertise in psychology, economics, or other disciplines that help build predictive models.

The size of the data scientist population in most enterprises is small, but their business impact may be significant. This book covers predictive analytics and how to build BI applications for the data scientist persona in Chapter 15.

BI DESIGN LAYOUT—BEST PRACTICES

BI is an enabling technology. It is the business person who performs the analysis, gains insights, and takes actions based on those insights. BI applications have no value unless they are used and they assist business people in their jobs. The BI developer is not creating a work of art, but rather a functional tool. This section discusses how to design the applications so they are intuitive and functional.

FOCUS ON THE PURPOSE

The BI team identifies the who, what, where, and how of each BI application in the BI content specifications and establishes its specific purpose. Designing the application should begin with finding the area focus up front and then ensuring that it will be adhered to. The business person will inevitably ask for more, tempting the BI developer to expand the focus, but that should be avoided at all costs. If new purposes arise, then the BI team needs to determine if it needs to develop new BI applications to fulfill those requirements.

BI design techniques, such as wireframes, mockups, and prototyping, are extremely useful in getting business feedback and in maintaining focus on the purpose of the application.

DESIGN LAYOUT

Follow these basic design layout practices when developing BI applications:

Consistency beats elegance. The BI team should develop a template layout for each BI style deployed in BI applications. The layouts should be as consistent as the variation in BI styles allows. The template should include standard positioning for titles, legends, navigation tools, help, and visual elements, such as icons and text styles. There should also be a standard background and branding such as a company or product logo. Business people should feel that each BI application is familiar in both layout and navigation, which improves their productivity and allows them to concentrate on the analysis rather than on the application. Effective Web sites have been using this technique of standardizing layouts for years. In addition, developing templates improves the productivity of the BI team, speeds up BI delivery, and decreases maintenance costs.

Figure 13.1 depicts a standard template designed by a BI team for a product marketing group. Design elements that are standardized in this example include:

- Filters located on the upper left corner of the display.
- Comparison and contribution analysis presented in two left-hand quadrants. Data is aggregated and drillable when there is a dimensional hierarchy.
- Trending analysis presented as a line chart in the upper right quadrant.
- Sales data presented in tabular form in the lower right quadrant.

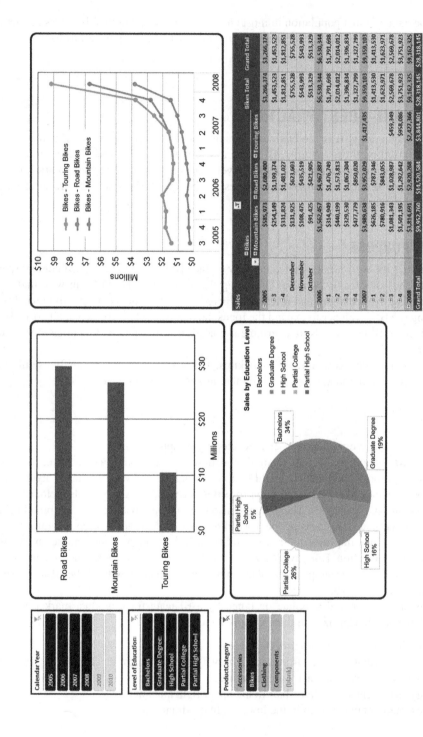

FIGURE 13.1

Dashboard example 1.

See the book Web site www.BIguidebook.com for more design layout examples.

Keep it simple. There is a temptation to try to cram too much information or too many visual elements onto a BI application's display. Creating too much visual clutter makes it more difficult or sometimes impossible to work effectively. Do not be afraid of white space, as it is not a sign of weakness; rather, it shows restraint. The term data-ink ratio identifies the relationship between data and white space. Business people should be able to determine at a glance what elements on the layout they are going to work with.

Location, location, location. Place the most important data at the top of the dashboard, in particular the upper left-hand corner, which is where a person's eyes travel first. If visualizations are linked together to support a particular business analysis, then the workflow should be from top to bottom and from left to right. This workflow places the last visualization at the bottom or bottom right of the layout.

Use colors judiciously. Colors can be used very effectively to enhance the understanding of data, but they can also become a distraction or even a hindrance. It is very common to encode or associate colors with specific values of something, such as a different color for each product category displayed on a line chart. In addition, making a color hue darker or increasing the size of an object on a chart can portray increasing values, such as sales or income. Always keep in mind that the layout needs to be understandable even if only seen in grayscale in order to accommodate people who are color blind, or when the display has been printed (or saved to a PDF document) without color. There are several guidelines:

- Use a limited number of colors, as too many colors makes it impossible to discern how the data has been encoded. Also limit the number of color palettes in the layout to no more than two.
- Color gradients are effective in displaying differences in measures' sizes or rankings. This technique can reduce the total number of visualizations necessary to convey information and can also reduce the number of colors needed.
- Use contrasting colors rather than colors with slightly different hues, as it will be difficult to distinguish between the colors.
- Color schemes should represent distinct things on the single display. Overlapping color schemes on different views creates confusion because the same color is used to represent two different things.
- Use colors conventionally whenever possible. The best example is to use the color green for positive values such as business profits and the color red for negative values such as business losses. This enables the business person to mentally encode the visualization without the need for any legend or other visual cue.

It looked great on my monitor. Many data visualization tools enable the dashboard to be designed once and deployed on many platforms, such as PC, tablet, and smartphone. These devices range in size from huge wide-screen monitors to handheld phones and will also vary in display quality. Dashboards designed on a huge wide-screen monitor may look very compelling, but may be too cluttered on the typical notebook's screen and impossible to use on a tablet. If the BI applications are planned to be deployed on multiple platforms, then the developer needs to prototype the layout on each of those platforms from screen size and display quality perspectives. It is quite possible that, similar to Web sites, there needs to be different versions of the BI application display for different target devices. And even if the BI application will only be displayed on PCs, notebooks, and monitors, the BI developers cannot assume everyone will have their size monitor.

Limit the visualizations on a single layout. The classic dashboard has four visualizations or charts that are related to each other in a business context. If the layout starts adding more than four visualizations, it gets cluttered, the data-ink ratio goes astray, visualizations get smaller, and the overall usefulness of the BI application decreases. If additional visualizations are linked to one of the four selected for the BI applications layout, you should place those visualizations on another dashboard or report.

Figure 13.2 depicts a different standard template designed by a BI team for a product marketing group. This template uses a:

- Bar chart for ranking analysis.
- Geomap for sales.
- Scatter graph for correlation analysis.
- Heat map for contribution analysis.

Leverage filters and slicers. Filters enable business people to customize their data discovery and exploration within a BI application. They allow business people to reduce the data set into more detail. There are several guidelines:

- It is best to apply filters to all visualizations in a layout. This avoids different visualizations using different filters, which would be misleading. For example, if there is a product category filter, then all the visualizations with the product category should only display those filtered product categories.
- Filters are typically implemented by selecting from a list of values; however, deep and numeric values are best displayed by using a sliding bar filter.
- Visibly display filters that are in use so that the business person knows what they are saying in the visualizations. In addition, dynamic titles that include filters that were applied are often useful if the number of values is limited.
- If attributes being used in filters have hierarchies, then the filters should be displayed in hierarchical order from highest to lowest. Filter values applied in a hierarchy should cascade to all levels of the hierarchy.
- If a filter value list is lengthy, it may be useful to include all or none options in the filter list.

Use legends judiciously. Legends are another visualization that can lead to clutter if overused. Only use legends when needed to understand a visualization such as when colors aren't labeled. Also, many times visualizations that are related to each other may be able to share the same legend. When using a common legend for multiple visualizations, make sure it is visible everywhere it is needed.

Outliers should be flagged. Assuming that outliers are the exception rather than the rule on the display, then there should be a visual cue indicating that it is an outlier. These cues may involve using color, size, boldness, highlighting, or icons. The outliers may represent the best and/or worst measure values, depending on what the business is interested in tracking.

Make it easy to read labels. Horizontal labels are much easier to read than vertical labels. Consistent text style, fonts, and size also adds to readability.

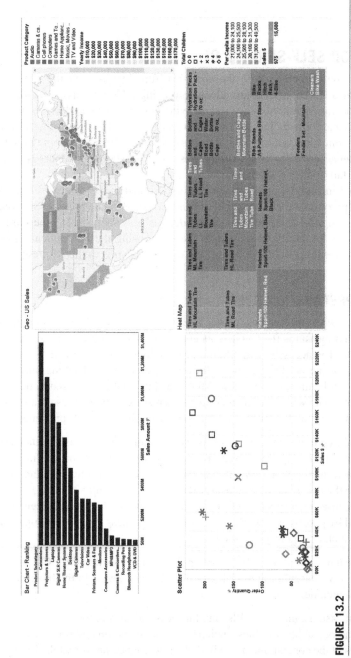

FIGURE 13.2

Dashboard example 2.

Scrollbars. Typically it is best to avoid scrollbars because it is difficult to ascertain the full context of the data being presented. If the business person does need to see a tabular data grid, then consider linking to a stand-alone grid from the initial dashboard.

DATA DESIGN FOR SELF-SERVICE BI

BI designers need to be concerned with the analytical functionality and the visual layout of their BI applications. Both of these aspects are adequately being addressed as BI vendors enhance their products with ever-increasing functionality and evolving best practices to design effective BI application layouts. Function and form are just as critical in regards to the data that is presented to the business person using the BI application, but too often this gets overlooked because people keep thinking that as long as the BI tool can access data, then everything is fine. This shortsightedness is why so many self-service BI initiatives fail to meet expectations.

The data presented in each BI application must be designed in the context of the ease-of-use and functionality that is appropriate for its intended use and audience. In the previous section, you read that cluttered and poorly designed visual layouts can hinder business analysis. It's the same with data layouts. When the data model that business people see when using the BI application is cluttered and poorly designed, it makes it much harder to use. We will refer to this as the BI presentation model.

THE LAST DATA PREPARATION STEP

Most BI tools present data to the business people in the context of a dimensional model, displaying the data as dimensions and measures (or facts). This context exists regardless of the data structure of the data sources the BI tool is accessing. In addition, hierarchies can be created by linking dimensions together, new measures can be derived by performing functions on other measures, entities can be renamed, and things can be hidden from view. All of this information is stored in the BI tool's repository. The dimensional model with all of its modifications results in the BI presentation model that business people see when using the BI applications. Two approaches for the BI presentation model are:

- **Vertical**—it is tailored to meet the needs of its BI application just like the visualizations and analytical functionality. It is geared toward a specific business group and the functions that they perform. This is a vertical orientation with the same people performing different functions. Examples include the accounts receivables (A/R) or the sales group.
- **Horizontal**—it focuses on a specific business process. This is a horizontal orientation with one process supported by people who work across different business groups. Examples include supply chain management and budgetary planning.

Assuming that the data sources used by the BI application conform to the 5 C's, then the key design principle is to create a BI presentation model with data that is relevant to the business people using it. For example, it could include:

- Facts, including measures, metrics, KPIs, and business transformations.
- Dimensions and associated hierarchies, such as sales organization and product hierarchy.
- Filters and subsets of the content, including both the rows and columns that the business people need.

Too often, business people get information overload when presented with the BI presentation model for their particular analysis. Just as a dashboard overloaded with irrelevant or inappropriate visualizations is distracting, an overloaded BI presentation model is also a hindrance. The project team can build relevancy into the BI presentation model by:

- **Eliminating clutter.** When a business person is performing analysis, it is best to have available relevant dimensions or measures rather than have to sort through dozens of irrelevant choices. For example, if the business person is interested in sales data, then manufacturing measures will not be useful.
- **Using business terminology.** The dimensions and measures should use the names and terminology of the people who will be using it. Although the BI team or source system applications may have well-thought-out data-naming conventions, what the business people see is not the database column name, but the name they use.
- **Prebuilding hierarchies and business-specific measures.** During data discovery, the project team should have uncovered the hierarchies and business-specific measures that are being used in the business process or analysis being supported.

WHEN INCONSISTENCY IS REINTRODUCED

BI applications can be built to access a wide variety of data sources as depicted in Figure 13.3. One group of data sources is the BI environment that may include operational data stores (ODS), EDW, data marts, and OLAP cubes. Each of these data stores was created using data integration processes that generated the information 5 C's, so along with the steps we just discussed the business people will have consistent and relevant data.

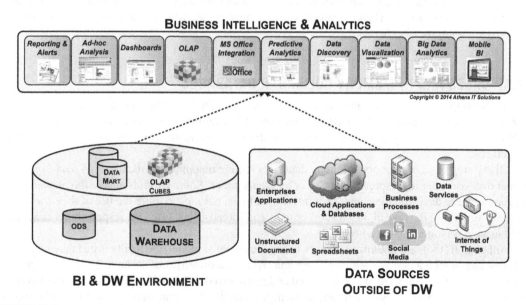

FIGURE 13.3

BI data sources.

The other group of data sources comes from the operational environment with enterprise applications, cloud applications, unstructured data, spreadsheets, databases, or files. These data sources may be terrific for operational reporting, but when used together, may result in inconsistent or incompatible data.

The best practice is to work with the business people who are going to be involved with self-service BI and discuss what data sources from the operational and BI environments they plan to intermix. The BI team should perform data profiling and data discovery on the operational data sources, if they have not done so already, when building the BI environment. From the data profiling and discovery activities you can classify the operational data in the following categories:

- **Data augmentation.** The operational data sources do not overlap any existing BI data source and expand the amount of data that can be used for analysis while retaining consistency.
- **Data consistent but semantically different.** The operational data source does augment the BI environment; however, due to naming or other metadata differences, it may be difficult for the business people to conduct their analysis. In this case, the BI team should assist the business people by creating consistent semantics within the BI presentation model.
- **Data consistent but not able to link together.** The operational data sources have relevant data but it does not have the form or relationships to support the dimensions and measures presented in the BI application. In this case, the BI team may expand an ODS, EDW, or data mart, depending on the scope of the data involved, to integrate the data into a dimensional model.
- **Data is inconsistent.** Sometimes the operational data and BI data sources are not consistent or compatible. Under these circumstances, the BI team and business people using the BI application must discuss the issues. Then the business people must decide which data is more valid for their business analysis.

OLAP CUBES AND IN-MEMORY COLUMNAR DATABASES

BI tools support various BI analytical styles that use OLAP cubes or in-memory columnar databases as one or more of their BI data sources. Both require building a logical data model to present the data to business consumers, even though they have different underlying physical structures.

OLAP cubes and in-memory columnar databases require mapping and then loading data from relational databases, flat files, spreadsheets, or other data sources. Some BI tools enable the mapping and loading of these data structures with data integration tools, but most require the use of their own tool-specific utilities. In the case of data discovery tools and spreadsheets, often the responsibility rests with the business person using the BI tool.

Although BI tools are optimized to work with a dimensional model, the reality is that they will work without one or with a poorly constructed schema. Without a dimensional schema, business people are basically using the equivalent of a series of flat or denormalized tables, which limits the tool's effectiveness for their business analysis and lessens their productivity. Unfortunately, many proofs of concept and pilots use a limited number of data sources and do not expose the problem of a poorly designed schema.

The best practice is to designate a BI team member to be responsible to define and create the dimensional models that will then be loaded into the OLAP cubes or in-memory columnar databases. The BI team should work with the business people using the BI application to then fine-tune the BI presentation model for effective business analysis.

MATCHING TYPES OF ANALYSIS TO VISUALIZATIONS

When designing the BI application, keep in mind the type of analysis that the business person needs it to perform. This will help you choose the best type of chart to optimize visualization. The most common types of analysis performed include:

- Comparative
- Time-series or trending
- Contribution
- Correlation
- Geographic data
- Distribution

COMPARATIVE ANALYSIS

People frequently compare and rank data. An enterprise, for example, will compare sales by categories of product and then rank those sales by the top products, as depicted in Figure 13.4. Bar charts, as illustrated in the example, are very effective for comparative analysis because the lengths of the bars represent quantitative measures that can be compared quite easily. When ranking is important, sorting bars by the measure's value enables a person to quickly discern the ranking order.

It is best to use one color for the bars rather than multiple colors, because it is easier to estimate the different bar sizes. Horizontal bars work well for any number of items. Vertical bars work well with fewer than a dozen items.

TIME-SERIES OR TRENDING ANALYSIS

Examining trends over time, such as tracking sales or the changing of people's opinion, is a very frequent analytical activity. Often the data tracked is broken down by some form of segmentation, such as product categories or by a person's income level. The best visualizations for time-series analysis are line, area, and bar charts.

Line charts are very effective at displaying segmented data as it changes over time, as depicted in Figure 13.5. Both the trends and relative differences in each of the segments are easy to discern. Different colors or line types often enhance usability.

Line charts are better than bar charts if the person using the chart is interested in examining the trends, not only of the individual segments, but also their totals. Figure 13.6 illustrates how the segments and their total are highlighted using an area chart.

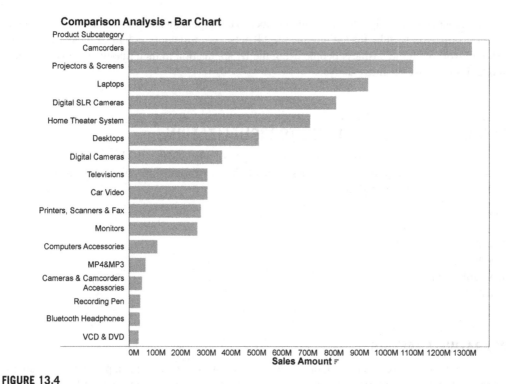

FIGURE 13.4

Comparison analysis—bar chart.

Bar charts, as depicted in Figure 13.7, are effective when there are only a few segments to be tracked or when each time period is discrete and people are not interested in seeing the trend, such as in a line chart.

The convention for the trending charts is for time to be displayed horizontally on the X-axis while the measure is displayed on the Y-axis.

CONTRIBUTION ANALYSIS

In this analysis, the contribution that each segment of something makes in relationship to the whole is typically represented by a percentage. The most common visualization used for this purpose is a pie chart, but it really is only effective when there are only a few elements to display, such as three or four. When there are too many slices it is very difficult to compare the slices relative to each other, especially when they are nonadjacent. As the number of slices gets larger, use other visualizations. Bar charts where each bar is the same length and segments are sized by percentages support a larger number of segments than pie charts, but they still encounter an upper bound fairly quickly. As shown in Figure 13.8, the preferred contribution analysis visualization is the heat map, as it can accommodate a large number of slices, especially when a color gradient is used to enhance its usefulness.

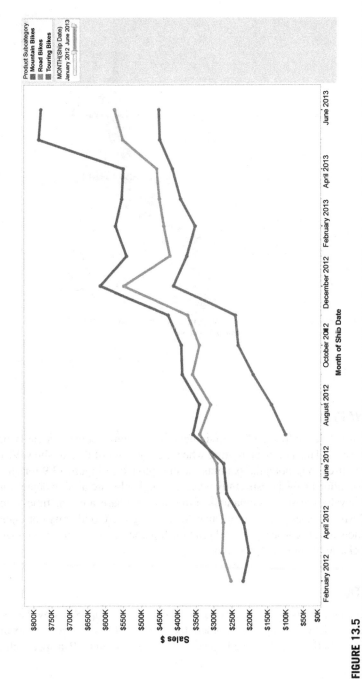

FIGURE 13.5

Trend analysis with line graph.

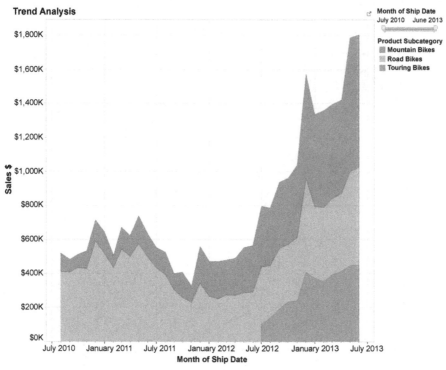

FIGURE 13.6

Trend analysis—area chart.

CORRELATION ANALYSIS

Visualizations are more effective than tables of numbers for enabling people to identify potential relationships among measures. This is especially true when there is a lot of data to show. Visually, people have become adept at discerning potential patterns. Scatter plots (see Figure 13.9 for an example) are very effective for correlation analysis, especially when size and color are used to depict variation in the measure's quantitative values. Also, combinations of line and bar charts are sometimes effective to support correlation analysis, especially when trend analysis is being used to identify correlations.

But be cautious, however, because a potential relationship does not guarantee a correlation. Validate causation prior to declaring there is a correlation.

GEOGRAPHIC DATA

The most effective method to visualize data by location is to use a map. Sales by the location of the retail store where the product was bought or by where the customer lives are excellent examples of how a map can show the distribution of sales. See Figure 13.10 for an example. Pairing an additional chart,

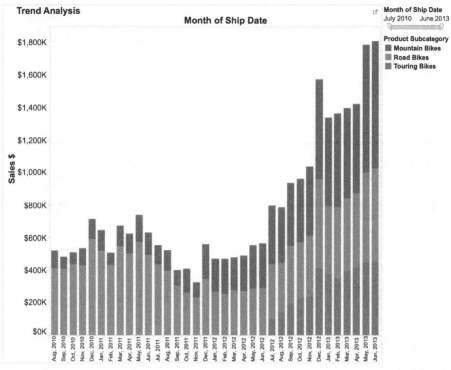

FIGURE 13.7

Trend analysis—bar chart.

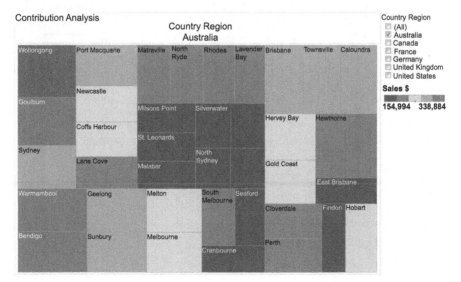

FIGURE 13.8

Contribution analysis—heat map.

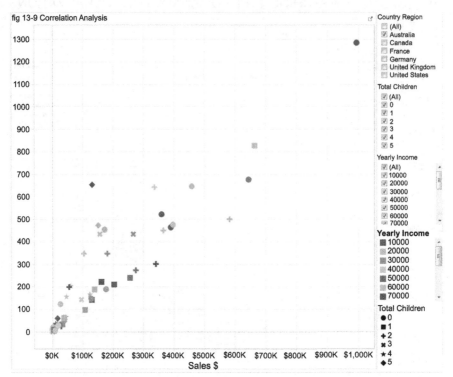

FIGURE 13.9

Correlation analysis—scatter plot.

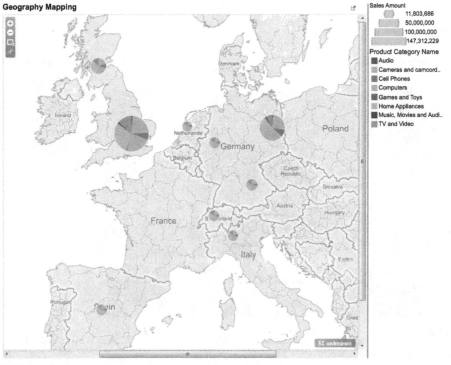

FIGURE 13.10

Geography mapping.

such as a line chart showing trends or a data table providing the underlying detail with the map, is often very useful in enhancing the information conveyed.

DISTRIBUTION ANALYSIS

This type of analysis displays the distribution of values across your full quantitative range. For example, call center talk time is examined by the length of call with its average, minimum, and maximum for different types of support calls. The two visualization techniques used to support distribution analysis are box plots and histogram. Figure 13.11 provides an example.

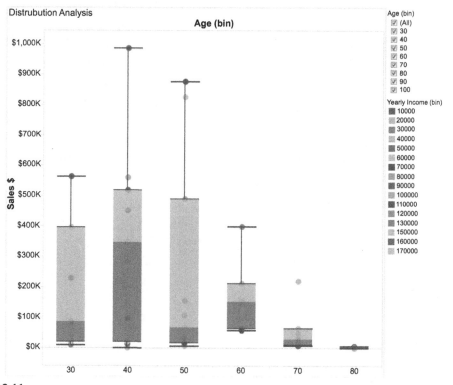

FIGURE 13.11

Distribution analysis—box plot.

BI DESIGN AND DEVELOPMENT

INFORMATION IN THIS CHAPTER:

- BI design
- BI user interface
- Privacy, security, access standards
- Design methods
- Prototyping lifecycle
- Application development tasks
- BI application testing

BI DESIGN

The business intelligence (BI) content specifications document all the data processes in the BI application—access, integration, transformation, and analysis. The next step is to design the BI application's visual layout and how interacts with its users. This includes creating and adhering to standards for the user interface, and standards for how information is accessed from the perspectives of privacy and security.

> Data visualization is a related topic because it also concerns the pictorial presentation information. As it is closely tied to analytics, it is covered in Chapter 15.

BI USER INTERFACE (UI) STANDARDS

Websites are designed with UI standards that make the layout, navigation, and functionality consistent across all pages. This consistency makes us more productive; we can immediately use the Website for its intended purpose without having to figure out how it works. Likewise, it is critical for the BI team to implement UI standards for all BI applications so people using them can focus on what they need to accomplish.

In keeping with the Website analogy, the Web and BI development communities face similar challenges as depicted in Table 14.1.

Although they face similar challenges, there is a significant difference in results. The Web developer can create a Website that can be deployed on any Web browser, perform various functions, and be delivered on different platforms, yet still be consistent. But that consistency typically eludes BI developers.

Table 14.1 Web and Business Intelligence (BI) Development Challenges

Areas Affecting User Interface	Web	BI
Consumer interactions	Different Web browsers such as Chrome, Firefox, Internet Explorer, etc.	Different BI styles such as reports, dashboards, pivot tables, etc.
Application functions	Read, search, shop, social media interactions, etc.	Different types of analysis such as sales figures, future customer behavior, profitability, etc.
Delivery platforms	Web browsers, different-size monitors, tablets, smartphones, print, PDF, etc.	Same as Web

The Web community's response to the various challenges it faced was to participate in an international standards consortium, World Wide Web Consortium, to develop UI standards covering customer-facing applications, application functionality, and delivery platforms. These standards include HTML (hypertext markup language), DHTML (dynamic HTML), cascading style sheets (CSS), extensible markup language (XML), asynchronous JavaScript and XML (AJAX), portable network graphics (PNG), scalable vector graphics (SVG), and many others. These standards, because product vendors adhere to them, ensure that the consumer has a consistent UI and the developers can concentrate on content rather than on all the differences in UI across the platforms, functions, and customer interactions.

On the other hand, the BI community still faces significant differences between vendors' products and BI styles. Although they follow a few standards, such as the database language and access protocols along with the Web standards just mentioned, those were agreed to by communities outside of BI. When it comes to customer interactions and application functions, rather than collaborating on industry standards, the BI product vendors continue to either view the differences as their edge over the competition or see standards as actually being harmful by commoditizing their products. This has resulted in differences between the various BI styles, how various product vendors implement the same BI style, and how the various analytical functions or charts are implemented. Because many BI product suites were created through product acquisitions, there is even an inconsistency in UI between the different tools within the suites.

The competition in the BI market has prevented the type of collaboration that is seen in the Web community, placing a burden on BI project teams to develop a group of UI standards to ensure a consistent UI experience for their customers. The BI UI standards need to cover the following areas:

- **Layout standards specific for each BI style** such as a report, dashboard, scorecard, or pivot table that is planned to be used. Each of these BI styles has unique layout and functional characteristics that need to be standardized every time they are used within the enterprise's BI applications. Examples of standardized that need to be addressed include:
  - Dashboards and scorecards—the minimum and maximum number of panels that can be used, the sizing and orientation of those panels, to the position of filters in, and the workflow between panels and other dashboards.
  - Pivot tables—how dimensions and measures are displayed and selected
  - Reports—whether production reports be pixel-perfect and static, what interaction people will have with the reports, how they will be delivered, and if people will be able to print or save reports as specific formats.

- **Common layout standards** need to be defined across all BI styles and delivery platform.
  - Layout—backgrounds, BI applications' branding, and logos.
  - Text—fonts and styles for title, subtitles, labels, etc.
  - Color—color scheme for backgrounds, panels, labels, and chart types.
  - Filters, parameters, and slicers—how they are displayed, function, and are related to each other.
- **Delivery platform standards** need to be defined for each medium in which the BI application will be used (e.g., Web browser, notebook, tablet, smartphone, print, PDF). This also includes determining how to handle the differences in wide-screen monitors and notebooks, each of which is being viewed on a Web browser but with size differences drastically affecting what a person can see and interact with on the screen.
- **Chart type standards** need to be defined to match each type of analysis with the chart types that best supports it.

Many UI standards need to be developed for BI applications. It's a good idea to develop these standards on an as-needed basis rather than dedicating a significant a front portion of the project to defining them. Developing UI standards on an as-needed basis has these advantages:

- Supports an iterative and incremental approach, as advocated in Chapter 18, which in the long run will be faster than a waterfall methodology where all of the standards are defined up front, delaying when BI application deliverables reach the business people.
- Defining the UI standards when they are needed provides the context of immediately available use cases.

See the book's Website www.BIguidebook.com for a UI template.

Although some BI teams will create UI standards solely using text, it's best to supplement text with one of the following visual techniques: sketches, wireframes, storyboards, or mockups to better depict what the UI will look like. The old saying a picture is worth 1000 words is absolutely correct in this instance. And if time and resources permit, use a proof of concept, pilot, or prototype to implement the proposed UI standards in selected BI applications to obtain both developer and user feedback to better refine and validate standards.

The UI standards need to be built into templates for each BI tool, BI style, and delivery platform that will be used. Templates ensure consistency and improve productivity for both the business people and developers.

CREATE PRIVACY, SECURITY AND ACCESS STANDARDS

Although privacy, security, and access are often intermixed, it is import to examine and establish standards for each.

First, establish standards for data that should not be disseminated because of regulations or a code of conduct. This can include data on customers, prospects, suppliers, employees, and more. In this age of Big Data and the Internet of Things, where the collection and analysis of data about people, places, and things is rapidly increasing, a BI team must work with the business to define standards and enforce them. This enforcement will extend to both business and IT.

Second, create security standards on how to determine what data needs to be secured and how that will be implemented in the BI applications. The implementation may involve establishing a data schema with the name and pertinent attributes to resolve security access. Enterprise security regarding the BI applications and the data that they access will involve business and IT staff beyond the immediate BI team and stakeholders. Networking, server, storage, database, and file access are all part of the security framework. BI security standards establish what the BI applications need to do to contribute to the overall enterprise security.

Finally, with privacy and security standards in place, a BI team can work with the business to define access standards. These standards are not about declining someone's access for security or privacy reasons, but rather because it just makes them more productive. Typically, access standards specify BI consumers' attributes that will determine their access right. For example, someone's business group combined with their title, role, and location forms a set of attributes that many enterprises use to define access rights. The BI application using these access standards may expose data along product lines or geographies based on these attributes.

DESIGNING EACH BI APPLICATION

Using the BI content specifications and UI standards, the BI designers should design the visual layout and workflow of each BI application. The deliverable of this design task is either a written specification or working prototype.

Historically, when the BI style was exclusively a printed report, the written specification would be straightforward and likely entirely in text. They would include a report header and footer, and a table grid in the report body. Since that time, many different BI styles have emerged that support a wide variety of visualizations. Dashboards started the trend of a BI application being a mashup of other BI applications. For example, a dashboard will contain multiple charts, each of which could be considered its own BI application. In addition, the mashup of BI applications will contain a workflow between them and may be interrelated, sharing filters, and drill-down or drill-across paths.

Just as with developing UI standards, using visual design methods improves the understanding of what is being proposed and encourages business people to provide feedback. The various techniques that BI designers use in creating BI application specifications are depicted in Figure 14.1. The methods are displayed in the order from left to right of increasing visual detail. A guiding principle for selecting and using one or more of these visual design methods is that they should be done quickly and not become projects unto themselves. The deliverables from these methods are design needs, not masterpieces of art.

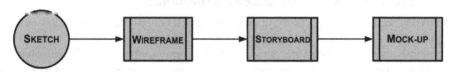

FIGURE 14.1

Business intelligence (BI) visual design methods.

A working prototype may be used as a follow-on to any of the visual design methods or to replace these methods altogether. To develop a working prototype the following conditions must be met:

- Target schema with sample data must be available
- BI tool must be installed
- Prototyping environment must be available
- Team must have some level of development experience with a BI tool

We will discuss these prototypes for design and development later in this chapter.

Sketches

Most visual designs will start off as a sketch as depicted in Figure 14.2. Using a whiteboard or paper is a quick, easy, and inexpensive way to draw the initial sketches and begin discussions. A drawback of using a whiteboard or paper is that it is difficult to get it into the specification document and share with others. With that in mind, there are drawing applications that can save the output into various formats, and collaborative applications that enable sharing by providing a virtual whiteboard. Another benefit of these applications is that you can use prebuilt shapes, making the sketches faster to draw, but more importantly, much neater. (From my diagram, you can see I need help drawing straight lines!)

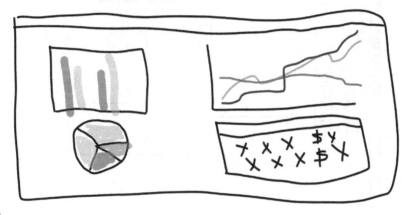

FIGURE 14.2

Whiteboard sketch.

Sketches enable brainstorming and participation since the process of creating them is quick, fluid, and disposable. Even though sketches are minimally detailed, they visually portray the structure of the BI application that text alone would not. Sketches are an excellent method to discuss and communicate the intent and content of the BI application from a conceptual view with the BI stakeholders.

Sketches are a starting point for the visual design of BI applications, but they are still ambiguous and you need to add more detail using other visual design techniques.

Wireframes

Designing applications using wireframes is a technique that is used extensively in Web design. A wireframe, as depicted in Figure 14.3, is a much more detailed representation of the visual design than a sketch; however, the technique deliberately does not attempt to provide detailed visual design.

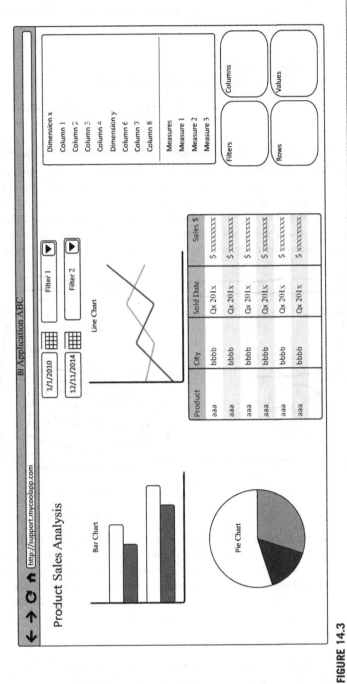

FIGURE 14.3

Business intelligence (BI) application wireframe.

A wireframe is referred to as a low fidelity representation of the design. A wireframe is similar to a blueprint (low fidelity) of a house rather than a three-dimensional CAD/CAM picture (high fidelity). A convention for wireframes is that they are drawn in black, shades of gray, and white rather than in color. This convention is used to constrain the scope of the wireframe and focus its purpose.

A wireframe portrays the visual structure of the BI application and provides the next level of detail beyond sketches.

The wireframe drawing contains:

- Each data content group.
- Content location in a layout.
- A representation of the visualizations as a chart or table. Some wireframe tools have prebuilt visualizations such as bar, line, and pie charts, but if your tools do not or the particular visualization that will be used is not a prebuilt icon, then use a box as a placeholder.
- Description and placement of filters, sliders, titles, subtitle, text fields, logos, and any other layout item. Placeholder boxes are typical in those cases because this is a low fidelity design, and you want to do it quickly.

There are many inexpensive and easy-to-use wireframe tools. In addition, spreadsheets and presentation applications are commonly used because they are available and people already know how to use them. The wireframe design process should be quick and inexpensive, without requiring sophisticated technical abilities.

A wireframe focuses on how the BI application screen layout will look rather than the navigation or the functionality involved, which is addressed by mock-ups, storyboards, and prototypes.

Storyboards

The storyboarding technique is used extensively in the film industry to design both live-action and animated movies. Sketches are created to represent scenes in the movie; they are then laid out in scene sequence, illustrating all the major changes in action. Similarly, the BI storyboard lays out all the major actions that occur when business people are performing analysis in the BI application. The scenes that are used in the BI storyboard are each analytical process the business person performs in the BI application.

BI storyboards focus on the business user interaction of the analytical processes within the BI application. Storyboarding recognizes how business people actually work with BI applications such as a dashboard in order to gain insight into the business. Business people will typically perform several analyses, some of which are dependent on each other, to determine if they need to perform some action and what that action is. The storyboarding technique enables the BI designer gain a better perspective on how each type of analysis is related and enables the development of a more effective layout.

In the BI application depicted in Figure 14.3, the analytical processes or scenes are the comparison analysis (column chart), contribution analysis (pie chart), trend analysis (line chart), and detailed drill-down of the trend analysis (tabular grid). Figure 14.4 illustrates the workflow between each of these analysis processes laid out in sequence.

Storyboards are the most complete representation of visualization and workflow that a BI team can develop without constructing a working prototype.

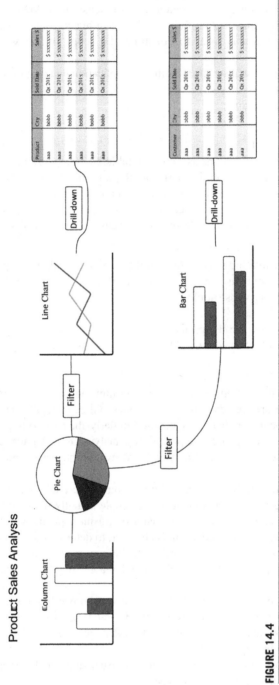

FIGURE 14.4

Business intelligence (BI) storyboard example.

Mock-ups

Mock-ups are the medium- to high-fidelity representations of the BI application's layout. Returning to our analogy of the architectural drawings, the mockup is the three-dimensional CAD/CAM drawing of the house. The mockup is a static visualization of what the BI application will look like to the business person, including the colors, icons, buttons, text, and charts that will be used. It is a static representation so that business people cannot actually interact with it, but will be able to see what they will work with once it has been developed. Figure 14.5 depicts a mockup of the wireframe in Figure 14.3.

Mockups are most often used in creating multimedia items that are very expensive to create and produce. In those cases, they save time and money by working out the visual details beforehand. This is not a typical situation in most BI projects because the BI tools can create a prototype of the actual BI application's layout much more quickly than a mockup tool. In addition, the BI prototype can then be used to template. For these reasons, mockups are typically not used unless the BI tool creates them along with the prototype.

BI DEVELOPMENT

Chapter 18 recommends a hybrid iterative and incremental project methodology. This hybrid methodology uses the traditional waterfall approach to design the overall BI framework and architecture while using an agile approach to develop the architecture's underlying components, such as the BI applications. Although I advocate an agile approach, this book is agnostic as to whether a formal agile project methodology needs to be used by the BI project manager. There are other alternatives that can be used to achieve the same results, as discussed in Chapter 18. From a development perspective, the BI team needs to build the BI applications incrementally and iteratively by using prototyping (described later).

> Note that this book uses the term *BI application* to mean the application that business people interact with to perform their reporting and analysis. The BI application may be built with any BI style such as reports, dashboards, scorecards, online analytical processing (OLAP) cubes, data discovery, predictive analytics, or advanced data visualizations. The assumption is that the data that the BI application uses is already available for the development team, but if not, then those data integration tasks discussed in the data integration section of this book will need to be done.

Business people are always getting surprised when BI applications are implemented. They will say that the application doesn't do what they asked for, is providing results different than expected or they need to add something they forgot to ask for. This scenario plays out time and time again. It is exacerbated when teams use a waterfall project methodology in which business people are engaged to gather requirements in the early stages of a project. Then, weeks or months later, when business people are reengaged to test the completed BI application, they notice different things. Although it's still a good idea to do the requirements early in the project to define scope, ensure that the overall framework is built, and to get the data in place for BI application development, switch to prototyping mode when you get to the BI application development phase. This gets people actively involved in a feedback loop and avoids the implementation surprises that plague so many BI projects.

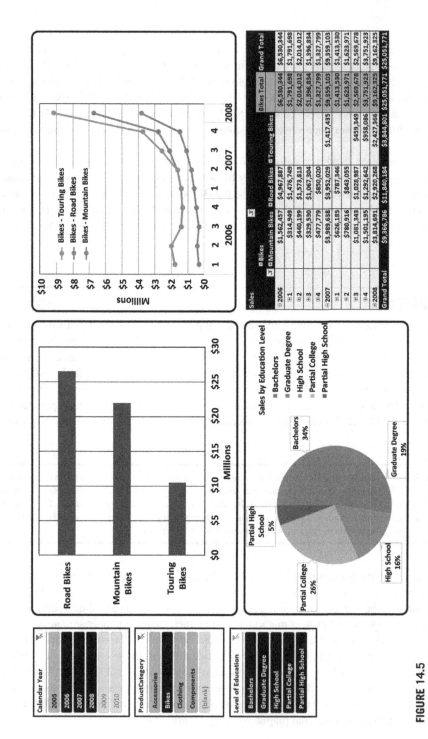

FIGURE 14.5

Business intelligence (BI) mockup example.

PROTOTYPING LIFECYCLE

Software prototyping is a technique to build specific portions of an application to investigate certain aspects such as functionality, feasibility, efficiency, performance, or how well it meets requirements. There are two primary objectives for BI prototypes:

- Obtain feedback from its intended users.
- Enable developers to build BI applications in an incremental manner.

There are several critical success factors in the BI prototyping efforts:

- **Dedicate time and effort**. Business people who will be using the BI applications in their jobs need to be actively involved in working with the BI prototypes and providing feedback to the BI developers. Business management needs to make a commitment that these people will have dedicated time assigned to these prototyping tasks. The BI team should create a schedule with times and tasks for these business people to participate in prototyping.
- **Work incrementally**. Although there are software prototypes that are either throwaway or only work on part of an application, you're better off using a BI prototype that incrementally builds the entire BI application. This type of prototyping may be referred to as incremental, evolutionary, or extreme.
- **Time-box it**. The prototypes are rapid and time-boxed. This approach keeps both the developers and business people focused and better able to manage their time (the business people will have their "regular" jobs to complete besides the prototypes). Building the BI application in small and discrete increments enables a more thorough examination and validation when the prototyping is completed. Using this approach, you can develop and test incremental prototypes within hours.

The BI prototyping lifecycle as depicted in Figure 14.6 consists of the following tasks and feedback loops:

- **Define the prototype scope**. Determine the component that will be developed. Identify the participants (developers, reviewers, and manager). Define the objectives, deliverables sign-off criteria (success criteria), and the timeline. If the team is using a rapid prototyping or agile approach then this step may be completed in a single meeting.
- **Create BI application prototype**. Build the assigned component of the BI application. The assumption is that it will be built with the BI tool selected to deploy the BI application. The prerequisites are that a development environment exists and, at a minimum, sample data from the BI schema is available.

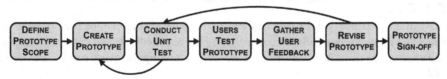

FIGURE 14.6

Business intelligence (BI) prototyping.

- **Conduct unit tests**. The developer runs the prototype and examines test results. If changes are required, then revisions are made and the test is rerun. The prototype should only be passed along to the business people to conduct their own tests if it has passed the unit tests. If not, the developer informs the business people of any outstanding issues.
- **Users test prototype**. The business people test and assess the prototype. Over the course of the incremental prototypes, business people will test the data, UI, and types of analytics offered.
- **Gather user feedback**. The intent is to more actively involve business people in the development process to solicit their feedback and improve the overall BI application.
- **Revise as necessary**. If the prototype has serious flaws or shortcomings, then it should be revised and that prototyping lifecycle repeated. If the issues are minor or need to be investigated further, then implement any changes and test them in the final prototyping step that involves the overall BI application.
- **Prototype signoff**. For the individual components that are prototyped, a signoff indicates the next prototype can proceed. For the final prototype, the signoff indicates that the overall BI application has been validated and can proceed to the BI application testing lifecycle.

BI APPLICATION DEVELOPMENT TASKS

BI prototyping is used for one or more of the following reasons:

1. Validate, expand, or gather business, data, and technical requirements
2. Determine feasibility of specific functionality
3. Examine effectiveness of components built
4. Engage business people to work with and provide feedback

The BI team may use prototyping to flush out the requirements (reason 1 listed previously) for the BI design. Prototyping may be used to determine either the BI content or the types of analytics that will be used in the BI application UI. If prototyping is used for design purposes, the BI team needs to document the design by using the BI tool's documentation capabilities. The prototype itself should be saved as part of the documentation.

BI prototyping is the best practice technique to develop BI applications (reasons 2-4 listed previously). The BI application will be divided into the following three components:

- Create data content
- Create data chart or visualizations for analysis
- Create overall BI application

The BI prototyping lifecycle is depicted in Figure 14.7.

Create Data Content

The objective of this task is to get the data required for the analysis that will be performed using the BI application. At a minimum, this includes connecting to the required data sources, executing queries to gather the data, creating the schema used by the BI tool, examining the query results, and testing if the data is valid.

If the data sources are relational databases, then use open database connectivity (ODBC), java database connectivity (JDBC), or direct database connections. Nonrelational sources will require

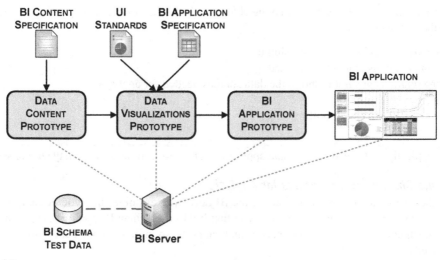

FIGURE 14.7

Business intelligence (BI) application development lifecycle.

connection information filled into source-specific application programming interfaces (APIs). BI tools typically provide all the prebuilt connection APIs that a BI developer would need, but there are ways to supplement those if necessary.

Typically, BI developers have several options for querying the data:

- Specify the data sources, often tables or files, and use the default setting of getting all the available columns or fields from that source.
- Specify the data sources and filter the columns (and any rows) that are retrieved.
- Write a custom-coded SQL statement (or whatever the equivalent is in the data source you are accessing) to get the rows and columns required.

When pulling data from more than one source table or file, use joins to gather the correct information. The typical options provided by the BI tool are as follows:

- The BI tool will join tables either by assuming that identical names in different tables imply a primary and foreign key relationship, or by querying the source database's metadata to identify columns designated as primary and foreign keys.
- The BI tool provides a visual application or a scripting language for the BI developer to designate primary and foreign keys. This may be the primary means to assign these keys or it may be how a BI developer would override assumptions that the BI tool had made regarding the key relationships.
- Write a custom-coded SQL statement (or whatever the equivalent is in the data source you are accessing) to join the appropriate tables.

The scope of creating and modifying the schema used by the BI tool, often called a repository, will depend on whether the business person accesses the schema to perform analysis or relies on prebuilt filters and drop-down lists to select data. Self-service BI applications such as data discovery, OLAP cubes, and pivot tables are the type of application requiring the business person to access the schema.

When this happens, the BI developer may need to modify the BI tool schema to make it easier to use by doing the following:

- Creating user-friendly names for columns
- Removing columns that are never used
- Creating relationships not found in the data sources needed for analysis
- Creating new measures
- Implementing business algorithms
- Creating aggregations

This is typically performed using visual applications; however, some BI tools may require scripting.

Create Data Chart or Visualizations for Analysis

To select the best data chart or visualization, the BI developer examines the type of analysis that the business person is going to perform and the data that it will use. Many BI applications, such as dashboards, will support multiple types of analysis and data sets, so more than one data chart or visualization will need to be selected.

After the data content has been loaded, the BI developer creates each data chart individually and tests how well it meets business requirements. After these tests, business people should get a chance to provide feedback on each of these data charts. This is not a formal user acceptance test (UAT), but rather one of several checkpoints in the development lifecycle to get feedback as the BI application is being incrementally built.

Create Overall BI Application

Once all the data sources have been set up and each data chart has been built it is time to create the overall BI application. This means putting all the individual components into the overall BI application layout, establishing the navigation capabilities, implementing the UI standards and interconnecting the components as needed to support business requirements.

Once the overall BI application has gone through its prototyping tasks, then it will proceed into the BI application testing lifecycle discussed in the following section.

BI APPLICATION TESTING

It is best to conduct BI application testing iteratively and incrementally as discussed in Chapter 18. BI testing is a collaborative effort between BI developers and business people whose involvement in working hands-on with the BI applications started with the BI prototyping tasks. As depicted in Figure 14.8, there are three testing phases: unit, BI applications, and BI systems.

The following tasks need to be performed:

- **Developer unit tests**. BI developers test each BI application after it has been built. The developers verify that the BI application operates in accordance with the BI specifications as they interpret them. This is a technical test of the application. If the developers discover any issues that would hinder business people from testing the application, then they should notify them and try to fix whatever is preventing the application from moving forward.

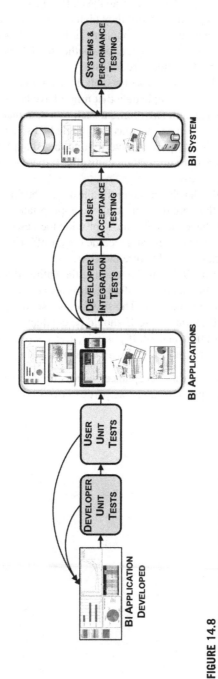

FIGURE 14.8

Business intelligence (BI) application testing.

- **User unit tests**. Business people test each BI application to verify that the application accesses the right data and performs the requested type of analysis. Business people will check that the UI's navigation and workflow support the work they plan to perform using this application. Also, business people should present any feedback, concerns, or issues they have with using the BI application. They and the developer should agree on whether the BI application is set to move on to the next phase or if fixes or modifications are necessary.
- **Developer integration tests**. BI developers will test all the BI applications that are planned to be released using "real" data rather than sample data that might have been used in unit tests. The real data should either be from a production environment such as a data mart, OLAP cube, or data warehouse, or from a testing environment that has the planned BI schema along with a representative subset of production data. The purpose is to verify that the BI applications can handle the real data and that the application functions correctly technically. If these conditions are met then UAT can commence.
- **UAT**. Using the same data as the developer integration tests, the business participants will validate that all BI applications access the right data, perform the appropriate analysis, and have UIs that are sound. The business people have the authority to provide the yes/no decision regarding the release of the BI applications. The business and technical sign-off criteria should have been established for the data, analytics, and UI before the UAT.
- **System and performance testing**. This involves testing the entire BI system including databases, data integration, and BI. The entire analytical lifecycle needs to be tested: sourcing, integrating, accessing, analyzing, and delivering the data. The system tests should involve several data-loading and business–analysis cycles. Performance tests should be conducted on the entire BI system including databases, data integration, and BI. If possible, create stress tests to simulate current estimated peak load and anticipated peak levels over the next 2 years.

A BI testing plan listing test cases with acceptance success criteria needs to be developed, documented, and signed off by the appropriate responsible parties prior initiating the BI test lifecycle.

ADVANCED ANALYTICS

15

INFORMATION IN THIS CHAPTER:

- Advanced analytics definition
- Predictive analytics & data mining
- Analytical sandbox
- Analytical hub
- Big Data analytics
- Data visualization

ADVANCED ANALYTICS OVERVIEW AND BACKGROUND

Enterprises are deluged with data about their customers, prospects, business processes, suppliers, partners, and competitors. They come from traditional internal business systems, cloud applications, social networking, and mobile communications. With the flood of new data and analytical techniques comes the opportunity for business people to perform new types of analyses to gain greater insight into their business and customers.

Business intelligence (BI) historically has enabled monitoring of what has occurred, analyzing why it happened, and then acting on that analysis. Over the years, organizations have been able to monitor, analyze, and act on greater data volumes and more diverse data sources more efficiently. The current marketing catch-phrase used to characterize Big Data is "increasing data volumes, varieties and velocity"—referred to as the 3 Vs. Although many believe that the 3 Vs are a recent phenomenon, it is really just a data evolution that organizations have been experiencing for years.

BI started out as providing tabular, printed reports, often many pages that business people would search through until they found the information they were looking for. BI has progressed, and now people can query and interact with a variety of data they analyze and then display in a variety of presentations such as scorecards, mash-ups, online analytical processing (OLAP) cubes, pivot tables, business graphics, and data visualizations. All of these presentations are usually packaged in dashboards geared for specific business groups and analysis.

> Advanced analytics focuses on gauging the future and allowing what-if analysis. The terms "advanced analytics," "predictive analytics," and "data mining" are often used interchangeably, but most agree that advanced analytics is the umbrella term, and predictive analytics and data mining are the processes by which one undertakes advanced analytics.

THE WINDOW TO THE FUTURE

With all the capabilities added to BI and gains in the data 3 Vs, business people were still monitoring, analyzing, and acting on past events. Knowing what already happened is still useful, but at times when their business, customers, and competitors are changing, it is a little like driving by watching your rearview mirror. Advanced analytics represents a second BI wave where business people are just not reacting to the past, looking in the rearview mirror, but also trying to gauge the future and act on those predictions.

The opportunity, however, comes with new challenges. Performing business analytics used to mean defining business requirements and then using predefined reports. But now, with the flood of data and constantly changing business environment, people do not always know what they need ahead of time, so predefined reports and dashboards are not always relevant to what a business person needs in a specific situation. Instead, people need to conduct new analysis using different data that they may be using in their current dashboards based on what is happening right here, right now. As a result, business analytics has to be "situational;" that is, it needs to respond to rapid changes in the business, economic, and competitive environment.

Advanced analytics is an organization's window to the future. Where BI looks at historical information to learn what has happened by measuring and monitoring it, advanced analytics help you make predictions and forecasts based on examining that historical data in new ways. With advanced analytics, an organization can identify meaningful patterns and relationships in data to help predict future events and determine the best course of action. These predictions are not foolproof but can be very reliable based on the modeler's skills and the quality of the model that she develops.

For example, you can use it to predict customer behavior, identify fraud before approving a credit card transaction, or, as Google has been known to do, show where flu outbreaks are occurring across the country. It is also used for national security (although controversial), when governments use it to discern patterns in phone records that identify potential terrorist activity.

DON'T IGNORE THE PAST

A common misconception is that predictive analytics frees an enterprise from having to capture, integrate, and cleanse historical data. This misnomer is based on the often-used marketing pitch that BI is about the past and predictive analytics is about the future. Although the pitch is true from the perspective of what the business person sees on her advanced analytics presentations, it fails to appreciate that in order to get those predictions the statistical database or predictive models had to analyze historical data. If historical data was not used for predictions, then there would not be predictive models but merely guesses as to what will happen.

Often, new waves of technology are ushered in with the impression that things are completely different this time and a revolution has occurred. Advanced analytics, along with Big Data hype, is being ushered in with the feeling that an enterprise can escape the hard work of data integration that has accompanied BI and data warehouse (DW) efforts and just skip ahead to advanced analytics. If only that were true! The reality is that the need for greater amounts of the 3 Vs and accompanying data integration significantly increases with advanced analytics.

ADVANCED ANALYTICS IN ACTION

The industries that pioneered the use of advanced analytics software are insurance, financial services, consumer products, and retail. Companies in those industries share the need to understand who their customers and prospects are, how to up-sell and cross-sell products and services, and how to predict customer behavior (including bad behavior through processes such as fraud detection). Advanced analytics tools can help in all of those areas. Many companies also need to examine economic and competitive factors affecting their business, while more-specific needs may include data on weather, life expectancy, and component prices. Other industries that have benefited from advanced analytics include telecommunications, travel, health care, and pharmaceuticals.

Advanced analytics has even been a driving force in political campaigns to determine who might be persuaded to vote for a candidate. A recent presidential campaign broke new ground in data mining social media by scouring the Facebook friend lists of its supporters (who had "liked" its page) for names that matched those of potential or undecided voters; determined which ones were "real" friends, in part by examining who was tagged in photos with whom; and thus winnowed the list down to 15 million people to target in swing states. They then matched this list of people with data from their TV set-top boxes, which showed exactly what programs they watched and when. This enabled precise TV ad placements on cable channels, costing far less money than blasting ads in prime time on the major networks [1].

Marketing and sales campaigns across all industries will be increasingly driven by advanced analytics. The most successful marketing and sales organizations have always incorporated a way to measure the effectiveness of their campaigns, which dovetails measuring the effectiveness of their predictive models. This feedback loop is essential for building and refining effective predictive models (see process next).

PREDICTIVE ANALYTICS AND DATA MINING

Predictive analytics and data mining are the processes by which you perform advanced analytics for forecasting and modeling. While BI has become widely used, even to the point of being pervasive in many organizations, far fewer organizations use advanced analytics tools.

In addition, whereas information technology (IT) groups typically develop BI dashboards and reports for business users, predictive analytics and data mining models usually are created by a handful of highly skilled end users. It can be an eye-opening experience for IT workers to realize that the people who build these models are more data savvy and technically oriented than they are. (In fact, predictive model builders often view the IT staff merely as data gatherers whose purpose is to feed their data-hungry models.)

Predictive model builders are often called data scientists, but unfortunately, as with many popular terms in our industry, this job title is increasingly being used to describe any person who is involved in a Big Data or advanced analytics projects. We take a much narrower view of who should have this job title. A data scientist is a predictive model builder who has expertise in data and statistics, as well as understanding the organization's business model, its industry dynamics, and the economic climate. (Roles and responsibilities are covered later in this chapter.)

SETTING UP A PREDICTIVE ANALYTICS OR DATA MINING PROGRAM

Across industries, there are common approaches that organizations can take to build the required predictive models, select technology, and staff for successful predictive analytics projects.

Building predictive models is a combination of science and art. It is an iterative process in which you create a model from an initial hypothesis and then refine it until it produces a valuable business outcome—or discard it in favor of another model with more potential (see Figure 15.1).

With a typical BI project, business users define their report requirements to the IT or BI group, which then identifies the required data, creates the reports and hands them off to the users. Similarly, in

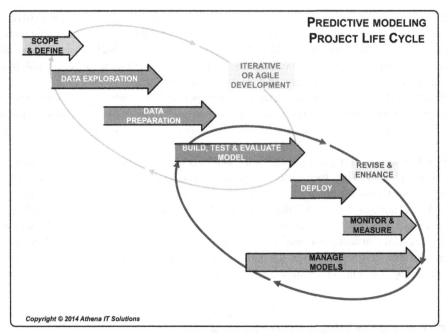

FIGURE 15.1

Predictive modeling project methodology.

predictive analytics and data mining deployments, a joint business–IT team must scope and define the project, after which IT assesses, cleanses and integrates the required data. At this point, though, advanced analytics projects deviate from conventional BI projects because it is the users—for example, statisticians, mathematicians, and quantitative analysts—who take over the process of building the predictive models.

The IT or BI group reenters the picture after the models have been developed and start being used by business and data analysts. For example, IT or BI teams might incorporate the predictive analytics results into dashboards or reports for more pervasive BI use within their organizations. They might also take over the physical management of predictive models and their associated technology infrastructure.

To run predictive models, companies require statistical analysis, data mining, or data visualization tools. Typically, predictive analytics software and other types of advanced data analytics tools are used by experienced analytics practitioners who are well versed in statistical techniques such as multivariate linear regression and survival analysis.

TASKS FOR DEVELOPING AND USING MODELS

Developing and then using predictive models involve the following tasks:

1. **Scope and define the predictive analytics project**.
   Although important in any BI project, it is especially crucial in predictive modeling projects to target what is being addressed rather than having a "fishing expedition." Far too many projects get

sidetracked, wasting time and money, without generating any business benefits because of inadequately defined scope. Answer the following questions:

- What business outcomes are you trying to effect?
- What business processes, external events, and factors, such as economic or demographics, will you analyze as part of the initiative?
- Who (people) and how (business processes) will the predictive models be used?

2. **Explore and profile your data**.

Because predictive analytics is a data-intensive application, considerable effort is required to determine the data that is needed for the project, where it is stored, whether it is readily accessible, and its current state, especially in regard to completeness and quality. A major difference with typical DW projects is that it is common to use data that is incomplete or has quality issues simply because it is the best that can be obtained. The data scientist needs to understand the state of the data and determine the impact and then may need to adjust the models to compensate for the data quality.

3. **Gather, cleanse, and integrate the data.**

Once the necessary data is located and evaluated, work often needs to be done to turn it into a clean, consistent and comprehensive set of information that is ready to be analyzed. That process may be minimized if you leverage an enterprise data warehouse as the primary data source. But if you augment the warehoused information with external and unstructured data, it will add to the data integration and cleansing work you need to do.

Another difference from DW projects is that sometimes data need to be synthesized or created to be used as input to the predictive models. Two examples follow:

- Incomplete data on consumer use or behavior in regard to competitive offerings
- Economic forecasts that are too high and may not adequately reflect effects on your targeted customers and prospects

In both of these examples, the data scientist may need to create separate predictive models for each just to generate the input data needed for the primary predictive model. Creating predictive models as input to other predictive models is sometimes referred to as synthesizing data. This adds to the complexity and time to build the predictive models, but it is essential to creating truly predictive models.

4. **Build the predictive models.**

The model builders take over here, creating models and testing their underlying hypotheses through steps such as including and ruling out different variables and factors, back-testing the models against historical data, and determining the potential business value of the analytical results produced by the models. This is a highly iterative process of examining dozens or hundreds of variables and correlations. In the process of creating and testing models, the modeler may uncover the need for additional data and data integration to develop a more robust model.

5. **Incorporate analytics into business processes.**

Predictive analytics tools and models are of no business value unless they are incorporated into business processes so that they can be used to help manage (and hopefully grow) business operations. Fraud detection is an example of a predictive model that can be integrated and automated into a business process. Other predictive models may assist sales people in identifying prospects or support personnel in offering cross-sell and up-sell opportunities with existing customers with whom they are talking or chatting.

6. **Monitor the models and measure their business results.**
   Predictive models need to adapt to changing business conditions and data. And the results they are producing need to be tracked so that you know which models are providing the most value to your organization and can alert the business if a model's value starts to decline. With increasing data sources and volume, predictive model performance data, and additional business insights, new or modified models are likely to emerge.

7. **Manage the models.**
   Too often, enterprises think model management is simply managing the modeling code. Although code management should be a basic process, model management best practices involve business value management. An enterprise needs to prune the models with little business value, improve the ones that may not yet be delivering on their expected outcome but still have potential, and tune the ones that are producing valuable results to further improve them. The goal is to improve business return on investment from modeling.

SELECTING TOOLS

Most BI vendors sell integrated product suites that include query tools, dashboards, and reporting software. But if they offer predictive analytics software, it tends to be sold as a separate and distinct product. While that is starting to change, the predictive analytics tools now being used primarily come from vendors that specialize in statistical analysis, data mining, or other advanced analytics.

> See the book Website www.BIguidebook.com for discussions of vendors and products.

Compared with a typical BI software evaluation, where the IT or BI group drives the software selection process while soliciting input and feedback from business users, an evaluation of predictive analytics and data mining tools is turned upside down—or at least it should be. Ideally, the data scientists, statisticians, and other users who build the predictive models should take the lead in evaluating the predictive analysis tools being considered, with IT providing input on the software's potential impact on the organization's technology infrastructure. In this case, the users are likely to be the only ones who understand the statistical or data mining techniques they need and whether the various tools can support those requirements.

ARCHITECTURE FOR PREDICTIVE ANALYTICS AND DATA MINING

In a typical BI architecture, the business person is at the end of the information workflow (that is why they are referred to as end users) with IT handling the workflow from data creation, data integration, and distribution until consumption. In advanced analytics, however, the business people that create predictive models participate in the entire data workflow plus they use the predictive models (since they still are the end users).

In Figure 15.2, the predictive modeler will use the analytical data mart to create her models, and the end users consume those models in the usual BI environment. The section on "Analytical Hubs" will discuss the architectural approaches that support advanced analytics.

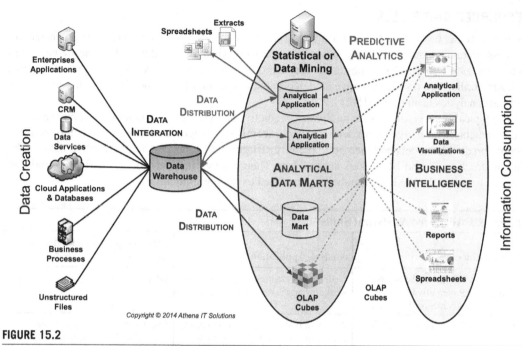

FIGURE 15.2

Example of advanced analytical architecture

TECHNIQUES FOR PREDICTIVE ANALYTICS AND DATA MINING

Advanced analytics comprises several techniques for analyzing current and historical data to make predictions about unknown events (Table 15.1).

Table 15.1 Advanced Analytics Techniques and Examples	
Technique	**Example**
Statistics	Use for customer segmentation.
Predictive modeling	Create fraud detection models for credit cards.
Forecasting	Create sales forecasts for each product category and country including seasonality and weather.
Data mining	Determine college freshmen retention rates based on demographic and academic attributes.
Descriptive modeling	Split customers into categories by their product preferences and stage of life (age, children, marital status, working, etc.)
Econometrics	Determine impact of economy and US Federal Reserve's bond buying policy on job postings and hires.
Operations research	Determine the flow of raw materials in supply chain using variability of demand and supply.
Optimization	Determine the best routes for delivery trucks.
Simulation	Determine what the impact is to customers' loyalty and market share from pricing changes.
Textual analytics	Perform a sentiment analysis on the introduction of product line extensions and new categories.

RESOURCES AND SKILLS

Predictive model builders and users must have a strong knowledge of data, statistics, an organization's business operations and the industry in which it competes. They also need to understand statistical and data visualization tools. Companies, even very large ones, often have only a small number of people with such skills. As a result, predictive modelers and analysts are likely to be viewed as the star players on a data analytics team (Table 15.2).

The typical organizational structure places predictive analytics experts in individual business units or departments. The analysts work with business executives to determine the business requirements for specific predictive models and then go to the IT or BI group to get access to the required data. In this kind of structure, IT and BI workers are enablers: Their primary tasks are to gather, cleanse, and integrate the data that the predictive analytics gurus need to run their models.

Table 15.2 Advanced Analytical Skills		
Model Builders	**Analytic Application Builders**	**Data Preparation and Integration Developers**
Excellent knowledge of the business and industry. Potentially understands economics and consumer behavior.	Understands business processes and workflow application development.	Deep data knowledge.
Knowledge of data and relationships.	Ability to build BI and data visualization applications for consumers of predictive models.	Experts in data integration, data cleansing, data profiling.
Experts in statistical and data visualization tools.		

ROADBLOCKS TO SUCCESS

With all the press regarding the business value of advanced analytics and the accompanying product hype proclaiming analytics nirvana, advanced analytics projects are particularly vulnerable to the following roadblocks:

- **Data overload:** Who would have ever thought this would be a problem? With the significant increase of the 3Vs it is up to the predictive model builder to determine what data is relevant and what is simply noise or even misleading. Finding that needle in a haystack is an apt analogy, since the modeler will likely examine dozens or hundreds of attributes to determine which ones actually are relevant to making a successful model.
- **Dirty, disparate, and incomplete data:** The expression GIGO (garbage in, garbage out) is especially pertinent to building models. Data needs to be clean, accurate, complete, and easily accessible to be useful in models.
- **Data silo:** Enterprises have been building business, application, and data silos over the years. Multiple silos means multiple versions of the data, raising the issue of whether the version of the data is the correct one.
- **Confusion:** Predictive analytics and data mining can be difficult concepts to explain in simple terms. This confusion can lead to unrealistic expectations regarding time and resources to build predictive models. In addition, inflated business expectations can derail future projects.

- **Expertise:** There is a major skills gap for people who can build effective predictive models. The combination of technical and business knowledge necessary is often shortchanged as an enterprise thinks that programming or statistical tools expertise is sufficient by itself to build a business relevant model.
- **Silver bullet solutions:** As with any emerging technology application, product hype often shortchanges the amount of time and skills necessary to be successful. Good technology can make your modeler more productive, but without the expertise and business knowledge it is unlikely to result in business success.
- **Synthesizing data:** It is very common to need to create or synthesize data to build predictive models, but often this is a very time-consuming process that IT would prefer to avoid. It is necessary to explain the purpose and business value of creating this data to overcome this hurdle.
- **Creative destruction:** Building successful predictive models means being able to learn from their use to modify or replace existing models to improve business return on investment. The world changes, and with it often so do the factors influencing a model's business performance, meaning a modeler cannot stand pat on what he built but needs to be willing to modify or replace it.

The critical success factors for successful deployments of predictive analytics tools include having the right expertise (i.e., predictive modelers with a statistical pedigree); delivering a comprehensive and consistent set of data for predictive analytics uses; and properly incorporating the predictive models into business processes so that they can be used help to improve business results.

ANALYTICAL SANDBOXES AND HUBS

When business people cannot easily get the data they need they take matters in their own hands and create data shadow systems. In order to avoid this, IT needs to build self-service data environments for the business. This implies a fundamental shift from today's enterprise BI systems, where IT provides the data and creates all the BI dashboards and reports. The new approach means IT concentrates on building the data backbone and shifts BI responsibility for discovery analytics to business people in a self-service environment. (IT still provides the recurring, preplanned reports, and dashboards in a production environment.)

The self-service data environment will include physically integrated data stores, such as data marts and OLAP cubes, but more importantly data virtualization to enable business people to be able to tap data that have not been physically integrated or data specific to their business analysis that may not (or should not) be shared in a data warehouse.

Best-in-class enterprises need two distinct types of self-service data environments based on different business analytical requirements:

- Analytical sandboxes
- Analytical hubs

ANALYTICAL SANDBOXES

Business analysts and business "power" users perform much of the discovery analysis. These business people often leverage an enterprise's data warehouse as a starting point for their analysis but need additional data and metric calculations. Some of these special needs can be anticipated and built into a data mart, often called an exploratory data mart or OLAP cube, but even with this there is a significant data gap.

An exploratory data mart may be terrific, but IT also needs to create an analytical sandbox environment enabling business users to be able to add data and derive metrics. Without the ability to expand their data footprint, business people will be forced back to their spreadsheets and data shadow systems to perform the analysis needed to do their jobs.

The key components (see Figure 15.3) of the analytical sandbox environment are:

- **Business analytics**—contains the self-service BI tools used for discovery and situational analysis by business people
- **Analytical sandbox platform**—provides the processing, storage, and networking capabilities for analytical and query processing
- **Data access and delivery**—enable the gathering and integration, physical or virtual, of data from a variety of data sources and data types
- **Data sources**—sourced from within and outside the enterprise, it can be Big Data (unstructured) and transactional data (structured); e.g., extracts, feeds, messages, spreadsheets, and documents

Many business analysts start out with data from an enterprise data warehouse and specific business applications; they often need to augment it with data from other sources such as spreadsheets or even data from outside the enterprise.

Today, those data sources can be physically local, virtual, or in the cloud. Earlier attempts to source data from these types of environments required exploratory data marts or OLAP cubes but were thwarted by Big Data integration and BI backlogs, so people were forced to create data shadow systems. Many business analysts spend significant time creating these systems and manually importing data from a variety of sources.

Data virtualization empowers business people in a couple of ways. First, it enables them to expand the data used in their analysis without requiring that it be physically integrated. Second, they do not have to get IT involved (via business requirements, data modeling, ETL and BI design) every time data needs to be added. This iterative and agile approach supports data discovery more productively for both business and IT.

Data virtualization eliminates the undocumented, overlapping and time-consuming point-to-point direct access connections that business people got stuck doing in the past with their data shadow systems. With data virtualization, IT and business people can add data sources into a repository that will document them, identify relationships between sources and uses, and encourage reuse. To the business analyst, the virtualization repository provides an information catalog to the relevant data needed for their analysis.

ANALYTICAL HUBS

Advanced analytics, such as predictive analytics, involves more extensive and intensive data gathering and analysis than what would be performed within an analytical sandbox. Typically, a data scientist, statistician, or someone with a similar background will be developing business models using a combination of statistical and data visualization tools consuming large quantities of data. This is an advanced analytical development environment referred to as an analytical hub. The analytical sandbox and hub have similarities, but the hub is a more advanced architecture created for more advanced users and uses. (Figure 15.4.)

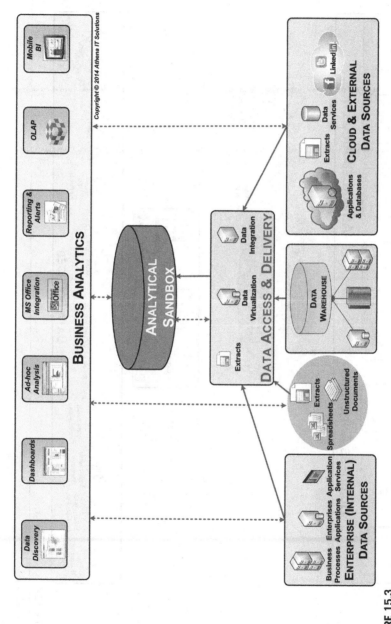

FIGURE 15.3

Analytical sandbox.

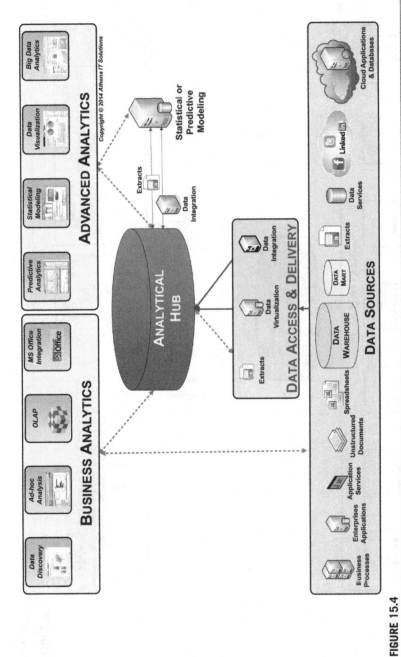

FIGURE 15.4

Analytical hub.

The key components of the analytical development environment are:

- **Business analytics**—contains the self-service BI tools used for discovery and situational analysis
- **Advanced analytics**—contains analytical tools used for statistical analysis, predictive modeling, data mining, and data visualization
- **Analytical hub platform**—provides the processing, storage, and networking capabilities
- **Predictive modeling**—analytical servers, e.g., statistical databases and predictive modeling engines
- **Data access and delivery**—enables accessing and/or integrating a variety of data sources and types
- **Data sources**—sourced from within and outside the enterprise, it can be Big Data (unstructured) and transactional data (structured), e.g., extracts, feeds, messages, spreadsheets, and documents

Developing predictive models requires iteratively testing various hypotheses by varying data, variables, and relationships. Often, the gating factor to data scientists has been getting the data they need. Generally, they spend much of their time gathering and loading data before they can even build the models. By adding data virtualization into the mix, data scientists can find data more quickly and not have to load all the data they need into their own environment before they start analysis. This greatly speeds up designing, validating, and refining the predictive models.

Data commonly comes from an enterprise data warehouse and various business applications; however, that is rarely sufficient for advanced analytics. Syndicated data feeds, data publically on the Web, Big Data sources, unstructured data, and spreadsheets are typically used to supplement traditional enterprise BI data sources. The analytical hub provides data scientists with the ability to gather and, either physically or virtually, integrate data from these diverse data sources. Contrary to the traditional IT managed data environment, data scientists need the flexibility to gather data regardless of, and sometime despite, its quality in order to perform analysis.

HUB AND SANDBOX DESIGN PRINCIPLES

When creating analytical hubs and sandboxes, follow these design principles to provide the right enterprise environment:

- **Data from everywhere needs to be accessible and integrated in a timely fashion**—Expanding beyond traditional internal BI sources is necessary as data scientists examine areas such as the behavior of a company's customers and prospects; exchange data with partners, suppliers and governments; gather machine data; acquire attitudinal survey data; and examine econometric data. Unlike internal systems that IT can use to manage data quality, many of these new data sources are incomplete and inconsistent, forcing data scientists to leverage the analytical hub or sandbox to clean the data or synthesize it for analysis.Advanced analytics has been inhibited by the difficulty in accessing data and by the length of time it takes for traditional IT approaches to physically integrate it. The analytical hub needs to enable data scientists to get the data they need in a timely fashion, either physical integrating it or accessing virtually integrated data. Data virtualization speeds time-to-analysis and avoids the productivity and error-prone trap of physically integrating data.
- **Building solutions must be fast, iterative, and repeatable**—Today's competitive business environment and fluctuating economy are putting the pressure on businesses to make fast, smart decisions.

Predictive modeling and advanced analytics enable those decisions to be informed. Data scientists need to get data and create tentative models fast, change variables and data to refine the models, and do it all over again as behavior, attitudes, products, competition, and the economy change. The analytical hub and sandbox need to be architected to ensure that solutions can be built to be fast, iterative, and repeatable. The analytical hub needs to support managing predictive models and the data sets used to build, test, and revise them.

- **The advanced analytics elite needs "run the show"**—IT has traditionally managed the data and application environments. In this custodial role, IT has controlled access and has gone through a rigorous process to ensure that data is managed and integrated as an enterprise asset. The enterprise needs to entrust data scientists with the responsibility to understand and appropriately use data of varying quality in creating their analytical solutions. Data is often imperfect, but data scientists are the business's trusted advisors who have the knowledge required to be the decision-makers in this regard.
- **Solutions' models must be integrated back into business processes**—When predictive models are built, they often need to be integrated into business processes to enable more informed decision-making. After the data scientists build the models, there is a hand-off to IT to perform the necessary integration and support their ongoing operation. IT will also need to gather data from these processes for the data scientists to monitor the performance and effectiveness of these processes.
- **Sufficient infrastructure must be available for conducting advanced analytics**—This infrastructure must be scalable and expandable as the data volumes, integration needs, and analytical complexities naturally increase. Insufficient infrastructure has historically limited the depth, breadth, and timeliness of advanced analytics as data scientists often used makeshift environments.

HUB AND SANDBOX ARCHITECTURE OPTIONS

See Figures 15.5 and 15.6 for the architecture layers of hubs and sandboxes, respectively. They show the following components: business analytics, advanced analytics, hub platform, predictive analytics, and data access to a variety of data sources. Architectural options are outlined for each layer using the design principles cited.

Business Analytics and Advanced Analytics Layers

In both the hub and the sandbox, the goal of the *business analytics layer* is to provide the analytical tools to support self-service BI. The technology selected in this layer needs to support business analysts and data scientists who are conducting their own analytics rather than relying on IT to design reports or dashboards. Their analytical styles and the BI platforms are important considerations. This layer is often used in the initial steps of the analysis to determine data availability.

The goal of the *advanced analytics layer* in the hub is to provide the "front-end" advanced analytical tools for data scientists; the companion "back-end" or server-based technology is in the predictive analytics layer. This layer is used to perform the advanced analytics' processes and to develop predictive models.

Some important considerations when you are designing both the analytical hub and sandbox include:

- **Multiple BI analytical styles**—Data scientists use different analytical styles depending on the type of analysis they are performing, the data volume and the data variety. Business analytical styles

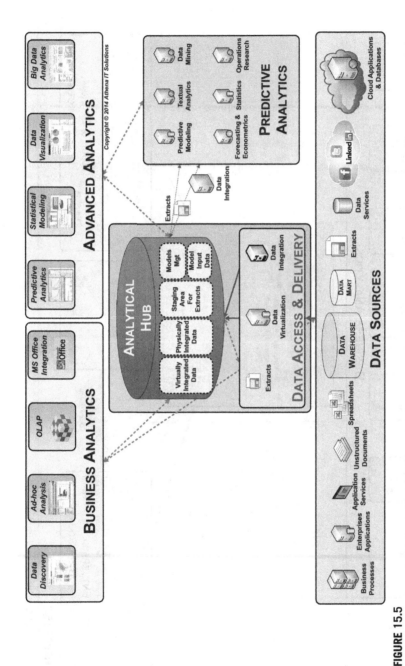

FIGURE 15.5

Analytical hub—architecture.

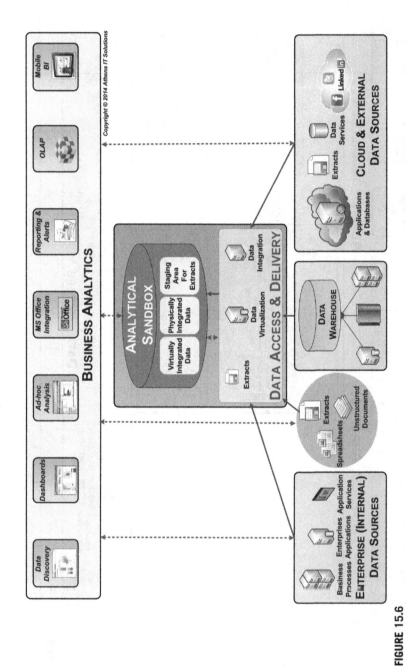

FIGURE 15.6

Analytical sandbox—architecture.

include data discovery, OLAP, ad-hoc, dashboards, scorecards, and reporting. Advanced analytics styles for hubs include: predictive analytics, statistical modeling, data visualization, and Big Data analytics. It is important to provide the many analytical styles that are needed by data scientists and enable them to use these tools in a self-service mode.

One of the topics widely discussed in regards to providing multiple styles is whether it is best to get all the tools from a single vendor in a BI suite or use the "best-of-breed approach" acquiring the best fit regardless of whether they are from different vendors. With the vendor and product landscape constantly changing, along with enterprise preferences in regards to vendor selection, an enterprise should make this choice based on the tool that is the best fit to deliver that functionality to its users.

- **Multiple BI delivery and access platforms**—The analytical hub and sandbox need to provide access from and delivery to analytics performed on the desktop, in the cloud, on mobile devices (tablets and smartphones), and Microsoft Office applications. This enables data scientists to perform their analysis on the most appropriate platform for their needs. In contrast to business analysis that is typically read-only, advanced analytical tools will be performing read and write operations on data hosted in the hub platform, particularly when developing predictive or statistical models. Data scientists need these write operations to be self-service, which requires write access to databases typically not provided to business people.

Analytical Hub and Sandbox Platforms

The analytical hub platform is the back-end or server-based development environment for data scientists. Whereas the analytical sandbox supports ad-hoc analysis exclusively, the analytical hub supports ad-hoc analysis along with the recurring creation and refinement of models. The hub development environment needs to support the following data management functions:

- **Gathering data**
  - Staging area for extracts
  - Model input data
- **Data integration**
  - Physically integrating data
  - Virtually integrating data
- **Model management**

The predictive analytics layer is depicted logically as a separate layer in Figure 15.5, however, it's necessary to examine important architectural alternatives to determine if that layer should physically be hosted on the hub platform.

There are many architectural choices for hosting processing and storage capabilities. Architectural options exist for:

- Analytical processing
- In-memory business analytics
- Database

These are explained next.

Analytical Processing

The two architectural considerations are:

- **BI appliances versus traditional distributed servers**—Analytical hubs and sandboxes typically start on traditional distributed servers that IT manages and supports. Enterprises often deploy in this type of environment because it meets initial data and processing needs, and because of their experience with these platforms. Depending on the analytical sophistication and data volumes, a BI platform dedicated to deploying analytical hubs and sandboxes may be the only platform capable of meeting these needs. Many of the advances in servers, storage, database, BI, and data-integration processing have been used in the design of the BI appliances. There is a wide variation in the underlying architectures, and an enterprise needs to evaluate what best fits their need and budget.
- **On-premise versus cloud infrastructure**—Another architectural consideration is whether all the components of an analytical hub or sandbox should be on the traditional on-premise platform, or if some or all can be moved onto the cloud. Historically, the cloud options have been limited, but that has dramatically changed. Often, cloud components are seen as a cost- and resource-effective solution that speeds up time-to-solution.

In-Memory (or in-Database) Business Analytics

A significant advancement that has enabled more in-depth and speedier analytics has been leveraging the advances in memory of the devices on which BI and predictive analytics are performed, and on the BI appliance if it is part of the architecture. In-memory analytics architectural options include in-memory analytics in the BI tools, as part of the database or on the BI appliance platform.

Database Options

The traditional database deployment option for BI solutions has been relational databases, but there are more options available based on advances in technology and increased data variety. Options include:

- Relational versus columnar versus others
- Structured versus unstructured (particularly Big Data)
- Hybrid mix of above

Predictive Modeling With the Analytical Hub

The purpose of the predictive modeling layer is to provide the analytical engines, such as statistical databases and predictive analytics, for data scientists to develop the forward-looking models, such as predicting customer behavior or fraud detection. This layer may need to support a combination of the following analytical methods:

- Statistical modeling
- Predictive modeling
- Forecasting
- Data mining
- Descriptive modeling
- Econometrics
- Operations research
- Optimization

- Simulation
- Textual analytics

IT retains its traditional role of managing these various analytical engines and associated infrastructure (if on-premise versus a hosted cloud service); however, unlike other enterprise applications, the data scientist owns and manages its content. This change in roles is crucial to success, particularly to time-to-solution.

There can be various architectural alternatives for this layer. Each analytical engine, if more than one is used, will have its own infrastructure requirements, potentially making for a complex environment. Besides being its own physical environment, predictive modeling may be a logical layer that is incorporated into the analytical hub platform or deployed as a set of services in the cloud.

Data Access and Integration with the Hub or Sandbox

Business people typically perform data access and integration by accessing an application (silos) directly, using a data warehouse, or with a combination, where they likely will use spreadsheets as the superglue creating a data shadow system. The analytical hub needs to provide business people with the ability to access, filter, augment, and combine data from many sources and in many varieties from within and outside their enterprise.

With self-service BI, the goal was truly shifting the analytical workload to the business. With data access and integration, however, the goal is not self-service data integration, but rather *empowerment*. Typically, data integration has emphasized physically integrating the data into a DW or another application. This has proved to be very time-consuming, resulting in significant backlogs and limiting business analytics. In addition, business people have often been granted limited access to nonintegrated data to protect them from potential inconsistencies.

The data access and integration layer needs to empower the business people to get the data they need as quickly as possible, recognizing that getting the best available data, even if not perfect, is better than making a decision with incomplete data or by using a data shadow system.

There are several considerations for the architectural options of this layer:

- **Data access**—The access options, provided that security and privacy requirements are met, include query sources directly, data services, using local files, and data virtualization. The first three alternatives are all point-to-point access where the data scientist must know about the source, secure access and then navigate the source. Data virtualization (next) is an architectural option that creates a data source catalog that can be saved, shared, and documented for business analysts and augmented by the IT staff.
- **Self-service data integration**—Today, data scientists rely on IT-built reporting or custom extracts fed by data-integration tools, and then use spreadsheets to fill the gaps. Gathering requirements and designing and building the IT-built extracts severely slows down the time-to-solution. The analytical hub leverages analytics tools, such as data discovery or data virtualization, to enable the business analyst to perform this functionality. In addition, there is a new generation of data integration tools, such as extract, load, and transform (ELT) that are easy enough to use by the data-savvy data scientists. This wave of self-service data integration tools often can work in batch, real-time, and through services, as well as being able to integrate structured, unstructured, and Big Data.
- **Augmenting enterprise data sources**—Often, critical data to classify, filter, and analyze is not available from enterprise sources but may require an external data feed or an import from another business group. The hub needs to provide the storage and ability to extract that data and then import it into the environment.

- **Data virtualization versus ETL data integration**—Data integration, data management, and building a consistent, clean and conformed data warehouse will continue to be the responsibility of the IT group. The data-integration capability will expand beyond traditional ETL to include data virtualization.

  Data virtualization empowers business people in a couple of ways. First, it enables them to expand the data used in their analysis without requiring that it be physically integrated. Second, they do not have to get IT involved (via business requirements, data modeling, ETL and BI design) every time data needs to be added. This iterative and agile approach supports data discovery more productively for both business and IT.

  Data virtualization eliminates the undocumented, overlapping and time-consuming point-to-point direct access connections that business people got stuck doing in the past with their data shadow systems. With data virtualization, IT and business people can add data sources into a repository that will document them, identify relationships between sources and uses, and encourage reuse. To the business analyst, the virtualization repository provides an information catalog to the relevant data needed for their analysis.

ADVICE FOR HUBS AND SANDBOXES

The following advice applies to designing and operating analytical sandboxes and hubs that will enable the analytical elite to conduct their situational analysis quickly and then act on their insights:

- **Build for the advanced analytical elites, not the masses**—The advanced analytical elite, that is, data scientists and "power" users, are the people who build predictive models and create forward-looking analytics. They are the advanced members of the analytical elite who often have a statistical background and are typically more data-savvy than IT. They do not need IT to create BI solutions for them, but rather create the analytical hub for them to develop the analytical solutions. Trust them. Create the analytical hub. And then get out of their way!
- **Create an enterprise information backbone and integration pipeline**—Predictive models are data hungry, needing ever-increasing volumes and variety at an ever faster pace. IT needs to continue to manage enterprise applications and extend BI solutions as the trusted enterprise information backbone for all types of business people to use. In addition, IT needs to establish an enterprise information pipeline for data scientists and others who need to go beyond the information backbone.

  Embrace data virtualization and a hybrid data view mixing physically and virtually integrated data. Virtualization enables business relationships and metrics to be built into the data view without having to go through the lengthy ETL integration process. In addition, it enables you to include various data types and data sources that should not be physically integrated.
- **Do not be afraid to try something new**—the technologies and design approaches for advanced analytics, predictive modeling and data integration are continually evolving in terms of capabilities, scale, and total cost of ownership. Also, the vendor landscape has been vibrant with startups bringing new technologies to the market, while mergers and acquisitions consolidate and expand existing product capabilities. To meet the demands of data scientists, analytical hubs need to be designed differently than the standard production BI solution. Do

not be afraid to try new database, in-memory, virtualization, and integration technologies from new vendors. Meeting the needs of forward-looking analytics is going to mean thinking "out of the box."

- **Establish separate but complementary business and IT roles**—Historically, IT has built the entire analytical solution. When that solution did not have the data that the business needed or could not deliver it quickly enough, the analytical elites were forced to build their own data shadow systems that included BI and data integration.

  It is time to tu rn BI and analytics over to the analytical elites and let IT concentrate on data integration and delivery. The first ingredient for successful self-service BI is an analyst with business knowledge and analytical expertise. The second ingredient is IT that can enable self-service data to feed the analyst.

- **Data may be dirty, inconsistent, or incomplete**—IT's charter is to provide cleansed and consistent data, which is the correct goal for the typical BI solution, but data scientists often need raw data that may be be dirty, inconsistent, or incomplete. Data scientists often need to tap dirty data because that is the best that is available at the time for them to develop their model. Much of the behavioral and attitudinal data that is used in models is outside the control of the enterprise and will never be clean.

  Trust that data scientists understand how to use both the clean and dirty data. Their modeling techniques takes into account the shortcomings of the data that is available, which is why they often use many sources to improve the accuracy of their models.

BIG DATA ANALYTICS

When working with Big Data, companies need to understand what it is, how to manage it effectively, and how to get a business return on investment from their investments to leverage it.

Before starting a Big Data analytics project you need to determine the project scope, how to manage the project, what kind of architecture you are going to deploy, and what resources you need.

But, first, because working with Big Data often means working with unstructured data, Table 15.3 provides a reminder of the difference.

Table 15.3 Comparison of Structured versus Unstructured Data	
Structured Data	**Unstructured Data**
Organized	Unorganized, raw
Exists in a structure, e.g., database. Each field is named, relationships are defined	Usually not stored in a relational database or any identifiable structure
Has a structured access method; you can parse it	Requires further parsing before you can use it in modeling
Date, time, sender, and recipient of an email	Body of an email. Also: videos, sound files, articles, tweets, blog posts, etc.

SCOPE

Big Data projects are often starting off like the first generation of DW, reporting, OLAP, and dashboard projects (i.e., "if we built it they will come"). Whenever a new technology wave is hyped so extensively, there is a tendency for enterprises to buy into that hype and assume that the new technology solves all. The result of this initial wave is often expensive projects failing to meet expectations and setting back efforts to invest in this new technology in the future.

The key to planning a successful Big Data project is to determine the why, where, what, and how of the project.

Why Is the Business Interested in Big Data?

What are the long-term business objectives for implementing Big Data analytics applications? Is it, for example, to track what is trending on social networks? Increase the effectiveness of marketing campaigns? Improve supply chain performance? Knowing the "why" is essential to establishing the business scope and determining the expected ROI for these projects.

Where in the Organization Is Big Data Going to Be Used?

Once you know why you are building a Big Data analytics system, you need to catalog the business processes, applications, and data sources that will be involved. That information is essential to assessing the impact not just from a technology perspective, but also from the standpoint of people, processes, and the corporate culture so you can develop a change management plan upfront. Not doing so can imperil efforts to unlock the business value of Big Data.

What Data and Business Analytics Need to Be Included in Your Big Data Project?

Discussions about Big Data often concentrate on data from social media sites such as Facebook, LinkedIn, and Twitter, but that oversimplifies what an enterprise may need. Big Data also includes Web logs, sensor data, clickstream data, call detail records, XML, audio, video, streaming data, application logs, and much more. Organizations need to determine which of the various types of data that could be captured are wanted for analysis by business people. Answering that question will also help identify applicable Big Data applications designed to handle specific data types.

Do not make the mistake of ignoring non–Big Data needs that should be included in the overall architecture. It is terrific, for example, to use Big Data to determine how well your sales campaigns perform, but even greater business value is derived when an enterprise can determine not only who became customers but also how valuable those prospects were (i.e., how much they bought, the profit margins, whether they were repeat customers, and how much it cost to retain them as customers). Big Data projects have the potential to become Big Data silos if designed solely for implementing Big Data technology for its own sake.

How Big Should It Be?

Once the required data types have been identified, the anticipated data volumes and update frequency—that is, velocity—need to be factored into your planning. Those two characteristics are often coupled with data variety and referred to as the 3 Vs of Big Data. Although rapid updates and significant data volumes are commonly assumed, the reality is that the needs of companies vary widely based on size and the intensity of information usage. Accurately assessing your organization's requirements will help you determine the architecture and the technology investments needed to effectively capture, manage, and analyze Big Data.

It is tempting to believe that Big Data analytics success is within your grasp provided you buy the right technology and commit enough resources to the project. In reality, a Big Data deployment typically requires significant systems and data integration work; introduces new tools and analytics techniques; and calls for new skills on both the systems management and analytics sides. Trying to boil the ocean will result only in doing too much, too fast—a recipe for frustration and failure.

THE PROGRAM

Plan to build your organization's Big Data environment incrementally and iteratively. If you already have a business analytics or BI program then Big Data projects should be incorporated to expand the overall BI strategy. An incremental program is the most cost- and resource-effective approach; it also reduces risks compared with an all-at-once project, and it enables the organization to grow its skills and experience levels and then apply the new capabilities to the next part of the overall project.

Establish an architectural framework early on to help guide the plans for individual elements of a Big Data program. But because the initial Big Data efforts likely will be a learning experience, and because technology is rapidly advancing and business requirements are all but sure to change, the architectural framework will need to be adaptive.

With an overall program plan and architectural blueprint, an enterprise can create a roadmap to incrementally build and deploy Big Data solutions. The roadmap can be used to establish the sequence of projects in respect to technologies, data, and analytics. The individual projects will then be more focused in scope, keeping them as simple and small as practical to introduce new technology and skills.

HYBRID ARCHITECTURE

Companies initially developed Hadoop, MapReduce, NoSQL databases, and other Big Data technologies so they could store and analyze large amounts of unstructured and semistructured data that wasn't a good fit for mainstream relational databases. (Google and Yahoo are two examples.) They, along with other early adopters, successfully used open source technologies, and they're now widely available in commercial versions supported by Big Data software vendors. But a key issue to consider in designing a Big Data architecture is how much of your data analysis needs can be met by Hadoop and its cohorts on their own.

Combining the Big Data (unstructured) with structured transaction data provides the most complete view of your business operations, enabling you to use analytics applications that can yield valuable insights to aid in improving business processes and increasing revenue. This data integration requirement drives the need to create an enterprise-wide architecture that includes both types of data. The architectural options include:

- All data on Big Data platform
- All data on transactional (relational database) platform
- Hybrid architecture tying together both kinds of systems

There are fundamental differences between unstructured and structured data. Relational databases have been used for decades for structured data while Hadoop and NoSQL databases have been built to handle unstructured data. It does not make sense to host both types of data on either of these different platforms, since relational cannot scale to handle unstructured data and there is too much business value lost (and too great a cost) to migrate transactional data to a Big Data database.

The best approach is a hybrid architecture that could also include data marts and specialized analytical data bases, such as columnar systems. Choosing the hybrid option creates a logical infrastructure that leverages existing IT investments in data warehouses and relational databases while enabling orga-nizations to channel data processing and analytics workloads to the most appropriate platforms.

The hybrid data architecture targets Big Data database technologies for unstructured data while leveraging the existing IT investments in relational databases for enterprise applications and DW and BI solutions (Table 15.4). You can implement these platforms on traditional servers, but BI appliances may offer a cost-effective alternative. The appliances can be a mix of hardware and software with vary-ing components such as database technologies (Hadoop, NoSQL, relational, columnar or other), MPP architecture, in-memory BI, or in-memory database analytics. The appliance is quicker to implement, reduces risk, and has an easier learning curve. Another advantage of BI platforms is that although cur-rently Big Data technologies, techniques, and processes are immature, product vendors are helping to rapidly advance these products and provide needed support.

Data integration technologies and products have added significant capabilities to extract data from Big Data environments and enable integration into existing DW and enterprise applications, replacing the previous need for an extensive amount of custom coding.

To produce sustainable business value, Big Data projects must be disciplined. Implementing a hybrid data architecture makes it more likely for Big Data projects to leverage the best practices for data management, data governance, data integration, data cleansing, security, and privacy.

Table 15.4 Recommended Hybrid Data Architecture Components

Big Data platform	Capture, management and analysis of Big Data
Relational databases	Capture and management of transaction processing in enterprise applications
Data warehouse	Store physically integrated data
Data virtualization	Extend DW by virtually integrating data from all platforms
Data integration	ETL and other integration technologies that can gather both structured and unstructured data to be delivered to a DW and BI environments
Business intelligence (BI)	Potential mix of BI technologies that can analyze data across platforms

THE BIG DATA TEAM

Having people with the right skills and experience to leverage Big Data analytics tools will make all the difference in your project. Knowledge of new or emerging Big Data technologies, such as Hadoop, is often required, especially if a project involves unstructured or semi-structured data. But even in such cases, Hadoop know-how is only a small portion of the overall staffing requirements; you also need skills in areas such as BI, data integration and data warehousing. Business and industry expertise is another must-have for a successful Big Data analytics program, and many organizations also require advanced analytics skills, such as predictive analytics and data mining capabilities

Table 15.5 shows the key skill sets and roles that should be part of Big Data analytics deployments. You can bundle together the required roles and responsibilities in various ways based on the capabilities and experience levels of their existing workforce and new employees that you hire.

It can be exciting to tackle a Big Data analytics project and to acquire new technologies to support the analytics process. But don't be lulled into thinking that tools alone spell Big Data success. The real

Table 15.5 Advanced Analytical Skills

Title and/or Skill Set	Description
Business knowledge	The team needs a member with knowledge of a company's own business strategy and operations as well as its competitors, current industry conditions and emerging trends, customer demographics and both macroeconomic and microeconomic factors. Much of the business value derived from Big Data analytics comes not from textbook key performance indicators, but rather from insights and metrics gleaned as part of the analytics process. That process is part science (i.e., statistics) and part art, with users doing what-if analysis to gain actionable information about an organization's business operations. Such findings are only possible with the participation of business managers and workers who have first-hand knowledge of business strategies and issues.
Business analysts	These people help your organizations understand the business ramifications of Big Data. In addition to doing analytics themselves, business analysts can gather business and data requirements for a project, help design dashboards, reports, and data visualizations for presenting analytical findings to business users and assist in measuring the business value of the analytics program.
BI developers	These people work with the business analysts to build the required dashboards, reports and visualizations for business users. In addition, depending on internal needs and the BI tools that an organization is using, they can enable self-service BI capabilities by preparing the data and the required BI templates for use by business executives and workers.
Predictive model builders	Deep statistical skills are essential to creating good models, which are generally custom-built. Knowledge of mathematical principles is needed, not just experience with statistical tools. Predictive modelers also need some business knowledge and an understanding of how to gather and integrate data into models, although in both cases they can leverage other people's more extensive expertise in creating and refining models. Modelers also need the ability to assess how comprehensive, clean and current the available data is before building models, in order to close inevitable data gaps.
Data architects	A Big Data analytics project needs someone to design the data architecture and guide its development. Typically, data architects will need to incorporate various data structures into an architecture, along with processes for capturing and storing data and making it available for analysis. This role involves traditional IT skills such as data modeling, data profiling, data quality, data integration, and data governance.
Data integration developers	Data integration is important enough to require its own developers. They design and develop-integration processes to handle the full spectrum of data structures in a Big Data environment, ideally as part of a comprehensive data architecture, as opposed to being done in silos. It is also best to use packaged data-integration tools that support multiple forms of data, including structured, unstructured, and semistructured sources. Avoid the temptation to develop custom code to handle ETL operations on pools of Big Data; hand coding can increase a project's overall costs—not to mention the likelihood of an organization being saddled with undocumented data-integration processes that can't scale up as data volumes continue to grow.
Technology architects	This role involves designing the underlying IT infrastructure that will support a Big Data analytics initiative. In addition to understanding the principles of designing traditional DW and BI systems, technology architects need to have expertise in the new technologies that often are used in Big Data projects. If you plan to implement open source tools, such as Hadoop, the architects need to understand how to configure, design, develop, and deploy them.

key to success is ensuring that your organization has the skills it needs to effectively manage large and varied data sets as well as the analytics that will be used to derive business value from the available data.

BIG DATA ANALYTICS WORST PRACTICES

There are many reasons why Big Data analytics projects fall short of their goals and expectations. You can find lots of advice on Big Data analytics best practices; the following are some worst practices for Big Data analytics programs so you know what to avoid.

- **"If we build, it they will come"**—Don't get sold on the technology hype and forget that business value is your first priority; data analysis technology is simply a tool used to generate that value. Determine the business purposes that would be served by the technology in order to establish a business case—and then choose and implement the right analytics tools for the job at hand. Without a solid understanding of business requirements, the danger is that project teams will end up creating a Big Data disk farm that really isn't useful.
- **Assuming that the software will have all the answers**—Building an analytics system, especially one involving Big Data, can be complex and resource-intensive. As a result, many organizations hope the software they deploy will be a silver bullet that magically does it all for them. Software does help, sometimes dramatically. But Big Data analytics is only as good as the data being analyzed and the analytical skills of those using the tools.
- **Not understanding that you need to think differently**—In the case of Big Data, some organizations assume that "big" just means more transactions and large data volumes. It may, but many Big Data analytics initiatives involve unstructured and semistructured information that needs to be managed and analyzed in fundamentally different ways than is the case with the structured data in enterprise applications and data warehouses. As a result, new methods and tools might be required to capture, cleanse, store, integrate, and access at least some of your Big Data.
- **Forgetting all the lessons of the past**—Sometimes enterprises go to the other extreme and think that everything is different with Big Data and they have to start from scratch. This mistake can be even more fatal to a Big Data analytics project's success than thinking that nothing is different. Just because the data you're looking to analyze is structured differently does not mean the fundamental laws of data management have been rewritten.
- **Not having the requisite business and analytical expertise**—You need more than IT staffers to implement Big Data analytics software. An effective Big Data analytics program has to incorporate extensive business and industry knowledge into both the system design stage and ongoing operations. Don't underestimate the extent of analytical skills that are needed. If Big Data analysis is only about building reports and dashboards, enterprises likely can leverage their existing BI expertise. However, Big Data analytics typically involves more advanced processes, such as data mining and predictive analytics. That requires analytics professionals with statistical, actuarial, and other sophisticated skills.
- **Treating the project like it's a science experiment**—Too often, companies measure the success of Big Data analytics programs merely by the fact that data is being collected and then analyzed. In reality, collecting and analyzing the data is just the beginning. Analytics only produces business value if it is incorporated into business processes, enabling business managers and users to act on the findings to improve organizational performance and results. To be truly effective, an analytics

program also needs to include a feedback loop for communicating the success of actions taken as a result of analytical findings, followed by a refinement of the analytical models based on the business results.

- **Promising and trying to do too much**—Many Big Data analytics projects fall into a big trap: Proponents oversell how fast they can deploy the systems and how significant the business benefits will be. Overpromising and underdelivering is the surest way to get the business to walk away from any technology, and it often sets back the use of the particular technology within an organization for a long time – even if many other enterprises are achieving success. In addition, when you set expectations that the benefits will come easily and quickly, business executives have a tendency to underestimate the required level of involvement and commitment. And when a sufficient resource commitment is not there, the expected benefits usually do not come easily or quickly—and the project is labeled as a failure.

Big Data analytics can produce significant business value for an organization, but it also can go horribly wrong if you are not careful and do not learn from the mistakes made by other companies. Do not be the next poster child for how not to manage a Big Data analytics deployment.

DATA VISUALIZATION

People are good at recognizing visual patterns and trends but not so good at remembering numbers. Yet even though people think visually, their BI reports and spreadsheets are dominated by a flood of text and numbers. Individual facts tend to be meaningless and need to be used in comparisons to be useful. They take on even more meaning when represented visually.

Pick up any major newspaper (or read it online) and you will see excellent examples of data presented visually. Even a weather map of the country that shades areas based on temperatures speaks volumes more than a chart of temperatures for each major city—and conveys the information in seconds. You will be able to know where it is hot, cold, raining, or snowing at a glance; in a similar fashion, an analyst might be able to spot business trends by looking at well-designed data visualization.

Data visualization presents information pictorially, often graphically, helping communicate it in a more intuitive way. Using data visualization techniques to mix and match data can help your business group view it in new ways and ultimately glean more insights from it. The initial wave of data visualizations for BI has become common and includes basic business graphics such as bar charts, pie charts, and sparklines. More sophisticated visualizations techniques incorporating data relationships and comparisons are increasing being used as a part of advanced analytics to better analyze information.

WHY DATA VISUALIZATION IS NEEDED

As the volume of data increases rapidly, it becomes harder and harder to turn it into information to analyze. We are data rich, but information poor—overwhelmed by data complexity and volume. As a result, we base business decisions on incomplete, inconsistent, or inaccurate data. In addition, data relationships may be unrecognized or misinterpreted if not properly visualized.

Simply accessing information in the traditional ways can fall short, such as when IT queues are long. Or the methods for getting data can be complex—geared to IT people, not the business people who need to consume the data.

To help enable better access to data, organizations can offer three things: self-service BI, data visualization, and data discovery.

- **Self-service BI**—leverages business knowledge, allowing you to use an intuitive tool to "mash-up" data, combine it across sources, and collaborate with others. Data is the focus, not the tool.
- **Data visualization**—lets you compare more diverse data in greater volumes, in greater ranges, and in different views.
- **Data discovery**—this combines analytics and data visualization to better equip business people to build data models and make predictions. Aimed at business people, it is visually oriented, interactive and iterative, and allows data to be combined and shared.

WHAT DATA VISUALIZATION IS NOT

In recent years, BI vendors have introduced dashboards, which are very visual representations of information. While data visualization tools use dashboards, a dashboard, is not automatically a good example of data visualization. As eye-catching as a dashboard can be, it does not mean that it is communicating information clearly and concisely. While attractive at first glance, dashboards can be cluttered and confusing. This clutter is often the result of the developer not having a foundation in the art of visualization and succumbing to the "techie" impulse to use every feature that a visualization tool offers.

Data visualization is not just flashy visuals; it is *effective* visuals that enhance our understanding of something.

REFERENCE

[1] Data you can believe. In: The Obama Campaign's Digital Masterminds Cash in. The New York Times; June 23, 2013. [Web].

DATA SHADOW SYSTEMS

16

INFORMATION IN THIS CHAPTER:

- Identifying and triaging data shadow systems
- The evolution of data shadow systems
- The damages caused by data shadow systems
- The benefits of data shadow systems
- Moving beyond data shadow systems
- Renovating data shadow systems
- Recommendations

THE DATA SHADOW PROBLEM

Business groups are empowered by knowledge—and knowledge comes, in part, from having access to accurate and timely information. It is generally up to IT groups to make that happen. But it does not always work out that way. Departments create their own reporting systems—data shadow systems—and these solutions can put the business at risk.

What are data shadow systems and how do they originate? Quite often, business groups take matters into their own hands because they are not getting the data they need and business decisions are affected. Perhaps their requests are too low in the IT group's project queue. Or maybe they simply have not been able to effectively collaborate with IT to create a solution that meets their needs. Worse yet, if they are not a Fortune 500 company, there might not even be any IT resources available to them. Whatever the reason, their solution is to create a departmental data shadow system.

Data shadow systems, also called spreadmarts, are a group of spreadsheets and customized, work-group databases created by business groups to gather data to enable reporting and analysis. Historically, the workgroup databases used Microsoft Access, and often still do, but more often nowadays these are relational or statistical databases that a business group controls.

Data shadow systems support many business processes such as budgeting, forecasting, pipeline analysis, profitability analysis, or other analytical tasks. They include data from enterprise applications, data warehouses, data marts, external sources, BI applications, and even PDF or printed prebuilt reports. Although data shadow systems are really business-built reporting applications, the business groups probably would not think of them as applications because they generally start as spreadsheets and later grow into data shadow systems.

Collectively, data shadow systems support many business people in an enterprise. Often, they are also using the BI and enterprise data warehousing set up by their IT group, but they do their "real" reporting and analysis from the data shadow systems.

This approach is both good and bad. Initially, it is good for the business group because they are finally getting the information they need to contribute to the health and success of the business. Getting information from a data shadow system is fast—a business analyst has the ability to make urgent requests for information a priority. Also, while techies may scoff at the use of Microsoft Excel and workgroup databases for data analysis, using these familiar tools can make business people comfortable and more independent.

The negative aspects of data shadow systems depend on how they are used and whether they are integrated into the organization's overall BI architecture—which they almost never are. One of the biggest weaknesses is if the data shadow system is a data silo, as shown in Figure 16.1. In that case it will promote the creation of data that is no longer consistent with other data being used in the enterprise. In order to achieve a high level of quality, data must be viewed from an enterprise and holistic perspective. Data may be correct within each data silo, but the information will not be consistent, relevant, or timely when viewed across the entire enterprise. To make matters worse, each report or analysis interprets the data differently, so even when the numbers start off the same in each silo, the end results will not be consistent.

WHAT IS BAD ABOUT THEM?

Here is a brief list of the problems that data shadow systems cause. All are explained later in this chapter.

- Inconsistent data across the enterprise
- Lost productivity
- Data errors during importing, calculating, and data source changes
- Stale data
- Limited scalability
- Increased risk
- Lack of discipline
- No audit trail
- No documentation

BUSINESS INTELLIGENCE (BI) SILOS

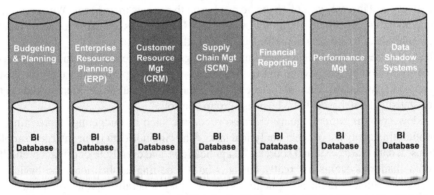

Each project develops its reporting and analytical solution, i.e. BI silo complete with BI tool & supporting databases (DW, data marts, cubes, etc.)

FIGURE 16.1

Data shadow systems are BI silos.

Too often, people using data shadow systems feel that as long as the data that their silo is using came from the same source as other silos then everything is OK. However, with the myriad data filters, business rules, data manipulation, and macros applied to each silo, it is almost guaranteed that data will not remain consistent.

Inconsistent, inaccurate data will certainly tarnish the image of a data shadow system for business people. But they will also feel the strain of creating and managing their own departmental systems. Ideally, they should focus on their "real" jobs and spend less time on the care and feeding of the data shadow system. When the people most experienced with using an undocumented shadow system move on to other jobs, those left behind have little knowledge and no documentation of the data shadow system's inner workings.

Data shadow systems are a fact of life in companies of all sizes. Whereas they do not offer an optimal solution from a technology standpoint, they have many business-oriented benefits that cannot be ignored. Keeping the needs of business people in mind, it is possible to replace or rework these shadow systems with solutions that dovetail with a company's overall DW/BI architecture.

ARE THERE DATA SHADOW SYSTEMS IN YOUR ORGANIZATION?

Does your organization have data shadow systems? The answer is probably yes, despite what IT thinks. With that in mind, the first step is to identify them so that you can then scope out the extent of the problem and determine what to do.

WHAT IS GOOD ABOUT THEM?

Here is a brief list of the benefits of data shadow systems. All are explained later in this chapter.

- Contain business knowledge
- Responsive, fast, and flexible
- Fill in IT and tool gaps
- Accessible and inexpensive
- Familiar to business people
- Effective for certain tasks

Clues that business groups are using data shadow systems are that people are finding out that numbers are inconsistent, there is a lot of debate about the differences in these numbers during meetings, and business analysts are spending time gathering and reconciling data. Each group thinks it has the most accurate numbers, and that the other groups' numbers are off the mark.

Maybe the finance group is using spreadsheets—even dozens or hundreds of them—to create reports to examine business performance. They are comparing actual revenue and expense numbers versus budget and forecast. They are figuring out what is selling, who is selling it, how much it costs to produce and deliver, and how much profit they are making. They could also be using dozens of spreadsheets or workgroup databases to extract data from enterprise resource planning (ERP), enterprise applications, and even the data warehouse to transform that data for use in their spreadsheets.

The marketing, sales, and other organizations could also be using their own workgroup databases and spreadsheets to gather data from across your organization, transform it, report on it, and analyze it. The problem could also be deeper if departments are using their own operational systems, such as a cloud application, without IT's knowledge and/or support. Collectively, these systems may informally support many independent business units, end users, and business processes across the enterprise.

Despite all the powerful BI tools available, your company is resorting to workgroup databases and spreadsheets for data integration. The biggest issue here is that each group has its own version of the numbers, and each group thinks its numbers are the "right" ones because, from their perspective, they are right. How can these business groups make informed decisions about the business when, from an enterprise perspective, no one has the right numbers?

WHAT KIND OF DATA SHADOW SYSTEMS DO YOU HAVE?

Business groups create various types of data shadow systems depending on their level of knowledge and the data they need. Rather than taking the stance that you should eliminate or replace all of them, step back and examine each shadow system to determine whether it is appropriate for its task. There are three main types of data shadow systems:

- **One-off reports (mild)**—Business people use spreadsheets to filter and transform data, create graphs, and format them into reports that they present to their management, customers, suppliers, or partners. With this type of data shadow system, people are using data they already have and the power of Excel to present it. There is no business justification—or even time—for IT to get involved.
- **Ad hoc analysis (moderate)**—Business analysts create data shadow systems for performing exploratory, ad hoc analysis for which they do not have a standard report. For instance, they may want to explore how new business conditions might affect product sales or perform what-if scenarios for potential business changes. They use the data shadow system to probe around, not even sure what they are looking for, and they often bring in supplemental data that may not be available in the data warehouse. This exploration can also be time sensitive and urgent.
- **Full-fledged analytical application (serious or very serious)**—Most data shadow systems start out as one-off reports or ad hoc analysis, then morph into full-fledged reporting or analytical applications. It is usually not the goal to create such a system, but after power users create the first one, they are asked by the business to keep producing the report, then asked to enhance it, add more data, and add more reports until, eventually, it becomes an application itself. Business processes, such as budgeting, planning, and forecasting, are often supported by data shadow systems on an ongoing basis. It is common to find these systems supporting business functions in marketing, finance, sales, HR, and operations.

The key characteristics differentiating one-off reports and ad hoc analysis from full-fledged analytical applications are scope and the ongoing nature of the analytical applications. These are listed in Table 16.1.

Table 16.1 Comparison between Types of Data Shadow Systems		
	One-Off Reports or Ad hoc Analysis	**Analytical Applications**
Data sources	Fixed and relies on "authorized" data sources	Expands as time goes on and uses a variety of data sources including departmental and external sources that may not be used by IT
Data integration	Limited—relies on data sources to have consistent data that can be easily combined in spreadsheets	May be extensive—depends on the variety of data sources used and their data consistency
Data transformation	Limited—typically limited to metrics calculated in reports	May be extensive—depends on the business needs and complexity of the business processes supported
Reporting and analytical functionality	Leverages spreadsheet capabilities so reporting may be very robust but typically limited to stand-alone reports or analysis	Leverages spreadsheet capabilities but typically must build in application functionality due to more complex analytics and/or potentially many interconnected reports

DATA SHADOW SYSTEM TRIAGE

Not all data shadow systems are created equally, so handle them differently based on scope, use, and risks. Just as paramedics or emergency room medical personnel have to triage their patients, both business and IT groups need to perform a data shadow system triage to determine where they should expend their limited time and resources, as well as how to maximize business values and ROI.

MILD AND MODERATE

First, one-off reports and ad hoc reports may actually be good candidates for data shadow systems. Maybe power users and IT could create these reports using BI tools, but if the business people are getting what they want, then it may be best to leave these shadow systems alone, especially if there is a limited number of reports or business people involved. If these reports perform limited or no data integration or data transformations, then the primary risk of data shadows systems, data inconsistency, is avoided altogether. The patient may have mild symptoms, but since none are life threating (no business risk), move onto more pressing matters.

SERIOUS

If, on the other hand, the data shadow system is a full-fledged analytical application with many reports or users but still limited in its data integration and data transformation, then IT may offer to help by augmenting it rather than replacing it. These systems are similar to patient symptoms that are serious, but still not life threatening—you deal with them, but they are still less than the "very serious" category. Potential remedies may include:

- Upgrading to the latest version of the spreadsheet and enabling the self-service BI capabilities offered in that spreadsheet ecosystem.
- Offering more extensive prebuilt data connections to the business applications and data sources being used in the data shadow systems. Maybe offering data connections to your data warehouse or data marts that have already been built for the business groups involved.

- Enabling or identifying spreadsheet integration capabilities in the current BI environment that may be used by the business users instead of expanding the data shadow system even more.

VERY SERIOUS

The category of data shadow systems that should command the highest priority—those with very serious symptoms—is those used extensively for data integration and data transformations, creating silos of data inconsistency. These systems have likely become productivity traps, as the analysts supporting them spend ever-increasing amounts of time taking care of the systems, leaving less time for their "real" jobs. The commitment of resources and the time to keep these systems supported and growing indicate their business value. These are the systems that must be either renovated or replaced.

It is important to view each category of data shadow systems as business-built self-service BI applications that have likely been very useful to the business community. IT needs to embrace and support those used for one-off and ad hoc reports, but consider renovating or replacing those used for full-fledged business reporting. This latter category causes more harm than good when they have become data and analytical silos. The remainder of the chapter deals with this category of data shadow systems.

Table 16.2 provides some guidance on the triage process.

Table 16.2 Data Shadow Systems—Triage

System Value and Usage	Action
The system has little business value.	Eliminate it.
Only a few business users make use of it.	Not worth the effort to renovate, just leave it in place.
It is used for one-off reporting or ad hoc, exploratory analysis.	Leave it in place.
There is significant business value and/or many business users.	Target the data shadow system for renovation or replacement.

THE EVOLUTION OF DATA SHADOW SYSTEMS IN AN ORGANIZATION

When determining the best way to evaluate and possibly replace data shadow systems, it is important to understand how and why they come into existence.

FILLING IN A GAP

Generally, data shadow systems are created and expand when business people find that the existing reporting applications do not supply them with all the data they need to do their jobs and operate the business. A business must be able to respond and adapt quickly. Business decisions cannot be placed on hold while IT addresses its backlog of requests from the rest of the enterprise for new capabilities, new data feeds, and custom programs. Likewise, business people may be in a rush to obtain data, and do not have the time for IT's process of collecting requirements, performing impact analysis, designing applications, and creating the BI solutions.

So, when it cannot obtain the information it needs when it needs it, a business group takes matters into its own hands. Management asks the group's business analysts and power users to gather the data and create custom reports to support the business analysis needed—however they can.

We have tried to keep this book product agnostic and avoid mentioning specific vendors and products. However, despite the growing number of cloud-based and open source spreadsheet alternatives to Microsoft Excel, the reality is that there are hundreds of millions of Microsoft Excel users, making it pervasive and the go-to spreadsheet used in data shadow systems.

Along these same lines, a second tool historically used in data shadow systems is Microsoft Access. Although Access is still prevalent, there are several alternatives:

- Databases—because of many innovations there are various database options that do not require a database analyst (DBA) and can be managed by a business group.
- Statistical tools—as more business people are becoming proficient in statistics and predictive analytics these tools are being used in conjunction with spreadsheets.
- Data discovery and other self-service BI tools—although IT is deploying these tools for BI, they are often being used as the query tool to feed spreadsheets and data shadow systems.

The analyst's typical process looks something like this:

1. Pull data from a data warehouse, data mart, or enterprise application into a spreadsheet or a local database
2. Manipulate the data a few times with database queries or Excel macros (maybe a dozen times or more)
3. Pull in some other data the business unit uses
4. Put the results into a spreadsheet or another worksheet
5. Crunch some numbers to perform final analysis
6. Maybe create pivot tables or charts
7. Prepare reports in the final worksheets or spreadsheet.

What happens next is how a "simple" spreadsheet or report explodes into a data shadow system. The analyst presents the findings with supporting spreadsheet reports and management or peers ask for more: more data from more sources; more data manipulation and calculations; more business rules; more graphs; more reports. The spreadsheet expands to include dozens upon dozens of worksheets pulling in ever-increasing data, more worksheets integrating and transforming the data, and, finally, many more worksheets used for reports.

It is typical to see either a pool of spreadsheets or one massive spreadsheet with many worksheets. (Sometimes analysts use many separate spreadsheets, wheras others may have one spreadsheet with many worksheets depending on file size and habit—but it is the same thing no matter how they implement it.)

As shown in Figure 16.2, the data shadow system performs three primary functions:

1. **Data gathering** from many sources including local and enterprise spreadsheets and databases using either (a) queries from spreadsheets, database tools, statistical tools, or BI tools, or (b) data exports from enterprise applications, DW, data marts, external sources, or other spreadsheets.

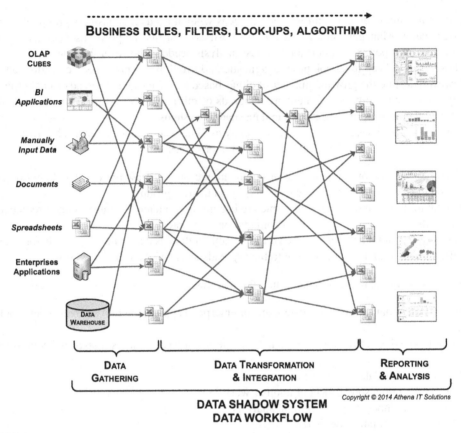

BUSINESS RULES, FILTERS, LOOK-UPS, ALGORITHMS

OLAP CUBES

BI Applications

Manually Input Data

Documents

Spreadsheets

Enterprises Applications

DATA WAREHOUSE

DATA GATHERING

DATA TRANSFORMATION & INTEGRATION

REPORTING & ANALYSIS

DATA SHADOW SYSTEM DATA WORKFLOW

Copyright © 2014 Athena IT Solutions

FIGURE 16.2

Data workflow.

2. **Data integration and transformation** using dozens of worksheets to manipulate and transform the data—filter, merge, aggregate, apply business rules, etc.—to support whatever analysis needs to be performed.
3. **Data reporting and analysis** using many more worksheets to perform the business analysis and produce the reports.

AS THEY GROW, IT IS HARDER TO TURN BACK

As we have chronicled, the initial request for a report grows from one spreadsheet into an ever-expanding data shadow system. Not only does the data shadow system expand in terms of data and reporting, but the number of business people relying on it likely expands dramatically. As soon as one data shadow system sprouts, many others will appear not only in the business group that created the first one but also across the enterprise. It is common for an enterprise to have many data shadow systems that people increasingly rely on for business analysis or examining reports. There is a tipping point, and many enterprises have long since passed this, where data shadow systems are the predominant BI solution used by the business. This may happen even if an enterprise has made significant investments in data warehousing and business intelligence.

With the rise and expansion of data shadow systems, more and more business analysts are caught up in building, expanding, and "feeding" them. This care and feeding is overwhelming and takes time away from the tasks they used to do. The new workload is initially justified because of the business value created for the analyst's management and peers. In some cases, the data shadow system work is actually part of their initial job description. Then, over time, it becomes clear that it is a problem.

As the data shadow systems become more entrenched, it is harder to turn back and involve the IT group. The power users are reluctant to adopt a new corporate reporting "standard," which they believe will limit their effectiveness. Change comes hard, especially when it means learning a new toolset and adapting to new definitions for key entities, calculations, or metrics. They are used to using Microsoft Excel, which does some things better than traditional BI tools. Executives perpetuate the problem because they do not want to pay hundreds of thousands of dollars or more to build a robust data infrastructure and deploy enterprise reporting and analysis tools to recreate the reports they already have. It is easier and faster to keep asking the power users to generate the reports.

Then, unfortunately, the business group finds itself basing its "real" decision-making on the information it receives from these localized, silo'd systems. It may seem like a fine, quick fix, but as you will see further in this chapter, it is a situation plagued with problems and risks.

IT GROUP RESPONSE TO DATA SHADOW SYSTEMS

The emergence of data shadow systems can leave IT managers scratching their heads, wondering why the business group is creating shadow systems when it already has great DW and BI tools.

Their reactions can include:

- **Hostility**—"Your system is poorly designed and was not needed in the first place. Do not expect us to support it," and "Why are you clinging to Excel when you have the best-of-breed BI tool available for your use?"
- **Peaceful coexistence**—"We know the shadow system gives you the information you need, so let us figure out how we can all work together so you continue getting your data in a way that is consistent with company IT standards."
- **Blissful ignorance**—"We have no idea what they are doing with all those spreadsheets and Access databases in Marketing, and we do not want to know," and "They are using our BI tools, so we do not think it is an issue that they are also using spreadsheets."

The most likely scenario is blissful ignorance and the least likely is peaceful coexistence.

Unfortunately, the hostility scenario can become adversarial, especially if IT tries to shut the data shadow systems down. The business reaction will be to tell IT they would not have created the shadow system if the DW and BI solution did what is was supposed to do. The reality is that data shadow systems usually have business value, otherwise no one would have created them in the first place or continue to support them. Because they have business value and the business groups are IT's customers, it is highly unlikely that IT is going to "win" in a confrontation. Actually, everyone loses in the hostile scenario.

Later we will discuss ways to work out a compromise between the groups.

DAMAGES CAUSED BY DATA SHADOW SYSTEMS

Data shadow systems may give business groups what they want, especially in the short run, but it does not mean they are happy. Business people do not want to spend so much time creating, expanding, and then maintaining these systems. Nor should they. They should be spending their time gaining a better understanding of their business, not wrestling with technology.

Data shadow systems may start off for good reason and are quite manageable. But as they change and expand over time, they tend to turn into productivity traps. The problems associated with shadow systems include:

- **Inconsistent data across the enterprise**—each business group uses its own data sources, filters, business rules, data conversions, naming conventions, and calculations to generate reports and analyses based on its view of the business. Each group may view customers, products, services, accounts, and geographic hierarchies differently. Different business units sell the same products with different names, packaging, pricing, and partner channels. The business may operate very differently in different countries or regions. Even when the same data sources are used across data shadow systems with all interpretations noted, it is unlikely that they are consistent. Although there may be valid reasons for these differences at the departmental level, they are a problem at the enterprise level. When each group manages its own data and processes, it is nearly impossible to deliver a consistent, enterprise view of customers, products, sales, and profits.
- **Lost productivity due to "analyst time sink"**—business analysts might spend half their time each month creating, loading, and maintaining data shadow systems. Instead of analyzing data, these high-priced employees act like surrogate information systems professionals, gathering, massaging, and integrating data. Many executives have initiated BI projects simply to offload these time-consuming data management tasks from analysts.
- **Lost productivity due to reconciliation**—another productivity trap is the time wasted arguing whose numbers are correct and performing the inevitable reconciliation analysis that will be needed to "validate" the numbers. This lost time is directly attributable to inconsistent data noted above. This is a more subtle time sink, but one that takes business people away from gaining insights from the data and running the business.
- **Data error #1 (import)**—with analysts getting data into the data shadow systems on their own there is a risk that the wrong data will get into the system. There are three common methods for getting data into systems: (1) manually entering data (primarily for lookup and reference data), (2) extracting data from a database or application and then importing it into the system, and (3) performing a query to import data directly into a system. Although typos are the primary risk when doing (1), processes (2) and (3) are more likely to carry the risk of the wrong data being imported due to applying incorrect filters or business rules. Since most data shadow systems are not documented, even when (2) and (3) are initially correct, business rules or filters are not changed when they should be, resulting in incorrect data.
- **Data error #2 (calculations)**—users embed logic in complex macros and hidden worksheets that are not documented and that few people other than their creator may understand. There are many cases of errors in macros that are not uncovered for long periods of time, resulting in incorrect data. Similar to the problem with filters and business rules changing in the example above, macros are not modified based on business or data changes, resulting in incorrect data. An even more

pervasive problem is when one analyst copies another analyst's spreadsheet without knowing or understanding the macros being used, potentially leading to unreliable data.

- **Data error #3 (data sources change)**—data shadow systems may generate system and data errors when they are linked to data sources, such as enterprise applications or files, that change without notice. IT generally manages changes in enterprise applications by performing a change impact analysis to avoid this risk, but data shadow systems are typically not on their radar and therefore not part of the impact study.
- **Data error #4 (stale data)**—shadow systems may be initially populated with "official" corporate data. However, once data is part of a shadow system, it may no longer reflect updates and changes from the corporate system where it originated.
- **Limited (or no) scalability**—few data shadow systems scale well either because of the limitations of the tools used or because of the skills of the analysts. The tools may not be able to keep up with increasing data volumes, update frequency, or the number of business people using it. Sometimes the issue is simply that the analyst in charge just does not have the time to expand the scale of the data shadow system.
- **Increased risk**—business people may make decisions based on faulty data, establish plans using assumptions based on incorrect analyses, and increase the possibility of fraud and theft of key corporate data assets.
- **Lack of discipline**—because dealing with technology and architectural design are not what business users do best, they cobble data shadow systems together with tools they know but without an overarching design. Each addition or modification becomes more difficult to implement and more costly to maintain, and when data management principles and disciplines are not followed, data consistency and integrity suffer. This is not so much of a problem at the onset when the analyst creates the initial spreadsheet, but develops into an increasing problem as the system expands with an accidental architecture and does not follow best practices.
- **No audit trail**—these systems are often a loose collection of spreadsheets, personal databases, extractions, filters, queries, business rules, and macros, so it is nearly impossible to trace or audit the processes that created them to ensure adequate control and compliance. It is often ironic that a finance group can pass an audit because the IT processes it uses are auditable, but the data shadow systems that they use to make decisions are not, and are ignored in an internal audit.
- **No documentation**—when the analysts who created or are responsible for an undocumented shadow system move on to other jobs, those left behind to support it have limited or no knowledge of how this now critical system works. Many a data shadow system is treated as an authoritative analytical source even though no one knows what data is being used or how it is manipulated. The dangers from this increase as the data shadow system ages.

THE BENEFITS OF DATA SHADOW SYSTEMS

Despite these problems, data shadow systems do have their advantages; otherwise the business would not have them. Based on their good points, it is often not realistic to totally eliminate all of them. Some of their advantages include:

- **Business knowledge**—because data shadow systems have been used to operate and manage business groups, they are teeming with the knowledge that drives a business. They already contain the algorithms that transform data from ERP, enterprise applications, and data warehouses, into relevant information people can use to understand their business. Combined with email, they also support the informal workflow of information and they are the informal business processes that drive decision-making for performance management.

- **Responsive**—business people often need to make timely decisions, such as close a deal, develop a new plan, monitor a key process, manage a budget or fulfill a customer requirement, regardless of the state of their existing reporting applications. Data shadow systems can give business people a short-term fix by giving them at least some of the data that they need to make a more informed decision.
- **Fast and flexible**—the senior VP must have a financial report ASAP, but IT has a weeks-long queue. Business cannot be put on hold, competitors cannot be slowed down, and shifting market-places cannot be frozen in time to accommodate the time it takes to source and integrate the data into a static data warehouse structure. Often, analysis is an iterative process with one report creating the desire for additional data and modified reports. A data shadow system enables that senior VP to keep asking the analyst to refine the latest report and make the changes rather quickly.
- **Fills in IT gaps**—some organizations may not have an IT staff or a data management infrastructure, or IT is understaffed and cannot support them quickly or inexpensively. In either case, business groups need to build their own analytics solutions.
- **Fills in tool gaps**—the organization's BI tools may not support the types of complex analysis, forecasting, or modeling that business analysts need to perform, or they may not display data in the format that executives need.
- **Accessible and inexpensive**—because data shadow systems are based on readily available desktop tools, they are cheap and quick to build. Within a day or two, a savvy business analyst can prototype, if not complete, an application that can handle the task at hand.
- **Familiar**—business users want tools that they know and understand. Their jobs are to manage and improve their business, not spend a lot of time learning how to get the most out of new and different software tools. Also, they know what information is in their systems and how to use it for analysis.
- **Effective**—data shadow systems are built for business people by business people. These systems get the job done. On the other hand, with IT-built systems, some of the business requirements may have been lost in translation or new business requirements may have missed the window to be incorporated at all. Sometimes, enterprise standards overwrite departmental standards that were actually of great value. Any data shadow system that did not get the job done would have been scrapped by now.

Despite these benefits, there is a high price to pay for data shadow systems in the long term. Many executives have recognized the dangers of data shadow systems and made significant investments to fix this problem. However, not all have succeeded. In fact, most struggle to deliver a robust data delivery environment that weans business groups off data shadow systems and delivers the consistent, timely information they need.

MOVING BEYOND DATA SHADOW SYSTEMS

You have uncovered data shadow systems in your organization, and you see the problems they cause. Now what? You might wish you could just pull the plug. But moving beyond data shadow systems is a process that requires communication, accountability, and compromise.

> **ALIGN BUSINESS AND IT**
> - Communicate and convince the business that data shadow systems need to be fixed.
> - Enlist business executive sponsorship (funding) and commitment (resources) so you have what you need to fix the problems and not recreate new data shadow systems every time there is a fire drill.
> - Get the business involved, ask questions, and make sure they are part of the renovation team.
> - Get IT involved and working in an agile manner, willing to compromise on technology for the sake of business usage and consistent data.

STOPPING THE BLAME GAME

Before anything else, the business and IT groups need to have a civilized dialogue. Rather than getting into the blame game, which will thwart any productive effort, both sides need to communicate the good, the bad, and the ugly. The business needs to communicate why it created the data shadow systems, what they see as the benefits, and the problems and risks of maintaining the status quo. IT needs to listen and not judge or be defensive. IT needs to discuss what it sees as the problems and risks associated with keeping the data shadow systems without "attacking" the business. These discussions are almost like couples therapy.

The next step in this process is for both the IT and the business groups to share the blame for the current situation and then move on to solving the problems. See Table 16.3.

If business and IT can share the blame, then it is time to determine how to move forward.

Table 16.3 How Each Group Can Share Responsibility

Business Group	IT Group
Takes responsibility for the fact that inconsistent data across the enterprise raises costs, lowers productivity, and may result in decisions based on erroneous data.	Takes responsibility for slow response times and inflexible processes. Learns to develop agile systems that adapt quickly to rapidly changing business conditions and requirements.
Learns to recognize the importance of building sustainable, scalable solutions.	Learns about the business group's goals, how they operate, even the terminology they use.
Does not blame IT for failures that the business caused by underfunding projects and overriding IT decisions, making it impossible to serve the business's needs.	Does not blame the business for creating the shadow system and realizes why they created it. Understands the business value of the shadow system and the data it provides.
Treats IT as a partner.	Treats business as a customer.

BUSINESS AND IT—IN IT TOGETHER

The next hurdle in our couple's therapy is to determine what both sides will agree on to get things done. This is a significant hurdle because it involves compromise by both sides. If both sides are not willing to compromise then any efforts regarding the data shadow systems are doomed to fail. These failed efforts are very costly in terms of time, expense, and likely a degrading relationship between business and IT.

I have seen too many IT groups propose an all-or-nothing solution—either the business users do it the "right" way or it will not get done. But no matter how great the architecture and BI are, if the solution does not offer the business value or ROI it either will not get approved or even worse it will get approved and built, but then ignored by the business. "My way or the highway" is a silly approach for IT to take because, ultimately, the business groups are its customers. Just as with any customer, you cannot force them to buy or use your product. IT needs to sell the business groups.

If new solutions are not built or used, then the business people return to the expanding data shadow system that neither side really wants. That scenario, repeated time and time again, costs companies millions of dollars and undermines business and IT productivity. In addition, the ever-increasing data silos put the business at risk by enabling decisions made from inconsistent and incomplete data.

As part of a compromise, the business and IT need to explore the following alternatives and honestly assess the outcomes. See Table 16.4.

Table 16.4 Assessing the Choices

Scenario	Action	Outcome
Rip & replace (Green field)	The IT group architects and develops the "right" solution.	Too long and expensive. While the "right" solution is being built, the business needs to make new business decisions, so it builds more data shadow systems.
Stand still	The business group continues to use and expand the data shadow system.	All the same problems persist; nothing has changed. Both IT and business are frustrated, but the business continues to build new data shadow systems.
Renovate	Together, they agree on a more cost-effective and timely solution for data shadow systems that need to be replaced and leave others alone.	New solutions better meet the business group's needs with timely and consistent data. The business does not feel a need to build new data shadow systems.

In the last alternative shown in the table, the groups use a triage approach to determine what data shadow systems should be targeted for renovation or replacement. Once they target them, the renovation team needs to determine what portions of the data shadow systems need to change or be replaced. This is significantly different from the "rip & replace" approach, which assumes everything must go. This is the time to think outside of the box and build systems quickly while IT incrementally builds out a unified data backbone that business users can access when they quickly need to get to data to make decisions.

We will examine options later, but as an example, consider building a business group-specific database, e.g., a data mart, to replace the workgroup databases and replace cobbled-together queries with more robust data integration processes. Shift the data sources to the enterprise data warehouse, if available, or the systems of record when not in the EDW. Also continue to use additional lookup tables and external data that business users incorporated in the existing data shadow system as necessary to support analytics.

CHANGING THE APPROACH

The problem with data shadow systems is not the technology used to create them. Spreadsheets and other desktop-oriented tools are an important part of any organization's technology portfolio. Problems arise when individuals use these tools as data integration tools to collect, transform, and house corporate data for decision-making, planning and process integration, and monitoring. Adding insult to injury, the data integration performed is a hodgepodge of processes that are not designed nor documented. When this happens, data silos proliferate, undermining data consistency and heightening business risk. The problem is that spreadsheets are an inappropriate tool for the data integration processes, not necessarily the wrong tool for analysis. Too often the attack from IT on data shadow systems concentrates on the overall use of spreadsheets rather than narrowing the focus to data integration.

The technical remedy for data shadow systems is to manage and store data and logic centrally in a uniform, consistent fashion and then let individuals access this data using their tools of choice. In other words, the presentation layer should be separated from the logic and data. When this is done, business people can still access and manipulate data for reporting and analysis purposes, but they do not create new data or logic for enterprise consumption. The goal is to transform data shadow systems into managed spreadsheets.

This lets IT do what it does best—collect, integrate, and validate data, and implement business rules (data integration)—and lets business analysts do what they do best—analyze data, identify trends, create plans, and recommend decisions (analytics). BI vendors are starting to offer more robust integration between their platforms and Microsoft Office tools. Today, the best integration occurs between Excel and OLAP databases, where users get all the benefits of Excel without compromising data integrity or consistency, since data and logic are stored centrally. Microsoft Excel is most likely the final BI tool used in the analysis food chain. Another BI tool may be included in the environment to pull data from the data mart, but that tool must get the data into the spreadsheet for the business users to complete their analysis.

CHANGING THE CULTURE

Applying the right mix of technology to address the data shadow system problem is the easy part. The hard part is changing habits, perceptions, behaviors, processes, and systems. People do not change on their own, especially when they have been successful with a certain set of tools and processes for analyzing data and making decisions.

Changing a data shadow system-dependent culture usually requires top executives both to communicate the importance of having unified, consistent, enterprise data and to apply incentives and penalties to drive the right behaviors. The reality is that executives are often the enablers for data shadow systems when they ask their staff to answer some questions or perform some analysis ASAP. The business people bringing back the answers quickly are likely to be rewarded regardless if they are using a data shadow system. Everyone needs to make changes from the top down. Ultimately, change takes time but the right organizational levers can speed up the process.

It helps if you can use some of the agile project methodologies described in Chapter 18. This includes keeping the project team small and making the deliverables quick, letting the business group drive the renovation project, and using a working proof of concept to present the initial deliverables.

MISGUIDED ATTEMPTS TO REPLACE DATA SHADOW SYSTEMS

Often, IT's knee-jerk response to data shadow systems is to replace them. IT views the data shadow systems as technical abominations and therefore figures that the right technical solutions will solve all. IT assumes that the business users will see the technically superior system as better than their data shadow systems and naturally flock to that new solution. This is a harsh response, and is not recommended.

There are two technical directions that IT generally uses to replace data shadow systems, and neither is very successful:

- Migrate to a best-in-class BI tool
- Create a standard set of reports meeting business needs.

MIGRATING TO BI TOOL

BI tools have evolved over the years to include reporting, analysis, dashboards, visualizations, and many more capabilities, sometimes turning into power BI product suites. Each new generation of BI tool gets expanded functionality and is heralded as business friendly. In product evaluations these tools fulfill numerous checklist items and receive high praise from the technology oriented. Vendors assume that since these BI tools have so much functionality, business people will drop the use of spreadsheets for them.

But a funny thing happens at many organizations; business people view the comparisons between spreadsheets and best-in-class BI tools differently. Business people are quite familiar with spreadsheets and have likely been using them their entire careers. Just as BI tools have gotten more powerful, so too have spreadsheets. Business people are likely to stay with spreadsheets and their data shadow systems because they provide the information they need to do their jobs. Too often, IT misreads why data shadow systems were created, not because of the reporting interface but rather because the data is not readily available.

Selecting and standardizing on a BI tool is a sensible strategy for an organization, but it should leave room for spreadsheets in the organization's BI portfolio. If IT wants to change the data shadow system landscape, then they will need to realize that a shiny new BI tool is not going to compel business people to abandon their data shadow systems.

CREATE A STANDARD SET OF REPORTS

The second misguided option that IT tries to use to replace data shadow systems is to create or expand a standard set of reports for business people. It gathers the requirements, builds the reports, and then becomes frustrated as business people continue to use and expand their data shadow systems. This approach typically results in failure because of the very nature of the one-off reports and ad hoc analysis that kick off the creation of data shadow systems—business and data requirements are not all known and, in fact, are evolving as the business itself changes. The second limitation of creating a standard set of reports is that the business person likely has limited or no ability to expand or modify these reports as he/she can in a spreadsheet. The business people often see this approach as handcuffing their ability to do their jobs.

RENOVATING DATA SHADOW SYSTEMS

The key to renovating a data shadow system is to split it into its data integration and analytical processes, and then work to understand each. This is easier said than done, however, as data shadow systems are usually built with an "accidental" architecture. They are not planned; they evolve over time.

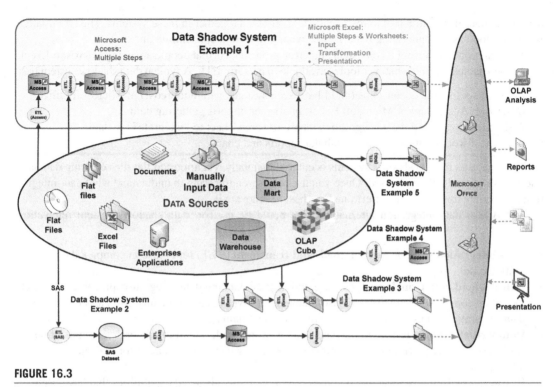

FIGURE 16.3

Data shadow system example.

Their creators use familiar, convenient tools rather than the tool that is appropriate for the task. The systems evolve haphazardly and are not typically documented. See Figure 16.3 for an example of a data shadow system accidental architecture.

To understand the shadow system's data integration and analytics capabilities requires a laborious reverse-engineering process of examining spreadsheet macros and queries, database queries, workgroup database code, and any other process used to integrate or analyze data.

The reverse-engineering process may be onerous, but it is important because these data shadow systems are where data is truly transformed from data into *business information*. This is because there is often a gap between what is in an organization's data warehouse and what the business person needs to do analysis. Reverse-engineering not only is needed for renovation but also is an excellent way for IT to understand what the business really needs in regard to data. If IT fails to close that data gap in their data warehousing environment, then the business will fill that gap with data shadow systems.

DATA INTEGRATION CONSIDERATIONS

The most significant liabilities of data shadow systems are data inconsistency and data quality. Too often IT thinks the "problem" of data shadow systems is that people are using Microsoft Excel as the front-end BI tool. When you are replacing or renovating a data shadow system your main concern should not be whether you should use Microsoft Excel as a BI front end. Rather, you should focus on using your data-integration tool to replace the ETL cobbled together in these systems. The BI initiative is only as good as the underlying data. *That* is what you should concentrate on.

The real problem causing inconsistent and error-prone data is that people are using Microsoft Excel, workgroup databases, and whatever tool is available to perform ETL. A typical data shadow system has:

- Between six to three dozen steps (and I have seen systems with hundreds!) of Microsoft Office (Microsoft Access and/or Microsoft Excel) queries or imports gathering data
- A series of steps using the workgroup database or spreadsheet to "integrate" the data
- A series of worksheets to create the tabular reports and charts.

The data used by data shadow systems is entered manually, via imported flat files or using database queries. Rarely are ETL tools used. Once you use reverse-engineering to understand what data-integration process are used, you can determine how best to renovate it.

The typical data-integration alternatives that could be used in data shadows system renovation include:

- **Data integration suite or extract, load, and transform (ELT) tool**—use in complex data-integration cases.
- **Extract, load, and transform tool**—use with less demanding data-integration processes. An ELT tool often comes bundled with database-management systems and typically costs less than data-integration suites tools (but may have less functionality).
- **Data virtualization**—use when the data shadow system pulls small to moderate amounts of data from several sources with moderate transformation, or when there is a need for real-time integration.
- **BI queries or imports**—use when you can leverage more advanced capabilities that have been built into self-service BI tools without having to use the tools above.

When designing data-integration processes, IT groups have a tendency to use the data-integration suite or ETL tool they use for loading their data warehouse. Although this can be a viable option, it sometimes contributes to the data shadow system problem because the cost of using these tools is too high or the backlog to get new data built is so long. If this is the case, then IT should consider alternatives to their standard data-integration suite, such as using ELT tools or other data-integration options.

The resistance that I generally see in these situations is: (1) IT wants to have one enterprise standard and/or (2) IT feels that their standard tool is superior to the alternative. This is a time when IT needs to compromise and consider the big picture. Even though their arguments makes sense intellectually, the reality is if they do not compromise then data shadow systems will continue to be built with a hodge-podge of undocumented integration processes. From the business group's perspective, the choices are not the enterprise standard ETL tool versus the data-integration alternative. Rather it is a choice between building the data shadow systems with Excel or not getting the data they need. Remember, this might be critical data that is needed to run the business. Compromise may be better for the business and produce more business value. This all-or-nothing scenario is often the single breaking point for many projects. If the project is too costly, it ends up being a lose/lose situation.

Your data-integration suite should have a portfolio of options to replace the ETL processes of your data shadow systems. These options include your standard ETL batch process, pushdown or ELT processes, real-time enterprise information integration, or even data-integration services (implemented as part of your service-oriented architecture strategy).

No matter what data-integration choice you make, it surely will be a significant improvement over stringing together Microsoft Office products to perform ETL.

ANALYTICAL PROCESS CONSIDERATIONS

The business is focused on getting its analysis done, not on the tool it is using. The IT group, however, will be frustrated if the business is ignoring the BI tool it selected for them and is using spreadsheets instead. Under these circumstances, IT needs to critically examine if their standard BI tool really meets business needs better than a spreadsheet. The key is to examine this from the business person's perspective rather than the technologist's. A business person may feel that the spreadsheet is good enough and it is not worth learning a new tool, even if it is technically superior. IT might not like that answer, but they need to hear it.

IT should consider a quick fix for renovating the data shadow system front end that continues to use spreadsheets, but also leverages the self-service BI capabilities that have been built into these spreadsheets. The key is that the spreadsheets are used for BI, not data integration. Another quick fix would be to enable a BI tool to supplement the spreadsheet or be an optional alternative. This does not force the business person to abandon the spreadsheet, but allows them to explore and move to the BI tool if they desire.

Often business people do not feel the need for all the functionality that is built into the best-of-breed BI tools IT selects for them. Although they look great on paper, the reality is that the BI tool only has a business value and ROI if it is used by the business. IT should evaluate alternatives to their standard BI tool if the business is not willing to use it. There are many user-friendly, cost-effective BI options in the marketplace today. Also consider the latest generation of self-service BI tools that are being adopted and used by business people. These tools might not always win the evaluation bake-off, but they win in business value because they are really being used.

THE RENOVATION APPROACH SHOULD PROVIDE:

- Consistent, comprehensive, accurate, and timely data.
- Flexibility to augment or supplement data that is not in your data warehouse.
- Minimal need for business people to gather and integrate data on their own.
- An adaptable architecture that enables rapid application development.
- Easy-to-use, flexible tools for a business user to report on and analyze data (and remember, Microsoft Excel is going to be part of your BI portfolio).
- Ability to publish reports, allow subscriptions, provide alerts, and enable workflows.
- Increased responsiveness and understanding of business needs and processes.
- Easy to use reporting and analytics, balancing responsiveness to business needs and data integrity.

BALANCED PRIORITIES

Any BI tool that you build or buy has to balance business/IT priorities, processes, and standards. For many companies that have successfully renovated their data shadow systems, it has taken a couple of attempts to satisfy business needs and get business people to use the solution. Often these companies use a replacement strategy with an application or tool that wins their evaluation bake-off and that IT feels the business will readily embrace. This approach usually receives a lukewarm reception. Enlightened enterprises then take the next step of truly reengineering the solution, separating data-integration and business intelligence processes.

ORGANIZATION VII

VII

VII ORGANIZATION

PEOPLE, PROCESS AND POLITICS

THE TECHNOLOGY TRAP

For those of us in high tech, it's easy to fall into the trap of concentrating too hard on the products, technology, and architectural aspects of a business intelligence (BI) project. We might feel more comfortable with technology because it's something we can control. It's not just IT people who feel this way; in today's society, people often assume technology is going to magically solve their problems.

However, the problem with our comfort level with products is that often the critical success factors of a solution lie with the other three P's: *people*, *policies*, and *politics*, as shown in Figure 17.1. These are three things that are a lot harder to predict and control than technology. Technology will do whatever people make it do; however, people, the processes they create, and the politics that drive them can be weak links in a project if they're not understood or handled properly.

Successful BI projects focus on business needs, not IT needs. It doesn't matter how big a data warehouse (DW) is or what features a BI tool has. What matters is if the business people get the right information to do their jobs. As we know, when they don't get what they want, they end up building data shadow systems to get the information they need, and this just causes more problems.

MEETING EXPECTATIONS

When you fall into the technology trap, you're so focused on technology that you tend to forget about peoples' expectations. And one of the biggest reasons BI/DW projects are considered failures is because they don't meet expectations.

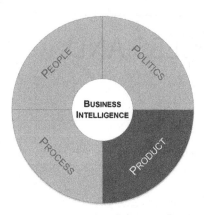

FIGURE 17.1

Four P's of Business Intelligence (BI).

The project may have proceeded exactly as the IT group, systems integrator, or software vendor said it would, but in the end, the business group is still disappointed. They didn't get what they thought they would. More specifically, they could be faced with one of these typical outcomes:

- **Unpopular solution**—Maybe the business expected that many more business people would have found the resulting BI reports/dashboard/analytics easier to use or more helpful. So the shortfall is that only a small portion of the expected business people are customers of the BI solution.
- **Difficult analytics**—Perhaps the business people expected a lot more analytics built for them rather than reports or "roll your own" analysis (self-service).
- **Information shortfall**—Or, maybe some of the critical information that the business was expecting has not become available or is not clean enough to use with the BI solution.

Who do you blame? There could be various guilty parties: the software vendors or systems integrators (SI) who were a little over zealous with their commitments, the IT people who were a little inexperienced or did not do enough due diligence with the vendor or SI promises, and the business people who were naïve enough to believe the claims proclaimed in PowerPoint slideshows from sales people. If it looks too good to be true, it probably is. BI projects would be easy if all it took was buying the right tool.

For your BI effort, do your due diligence, understand what it will realistically take to deploy what the business wants, and above all, set the proper expectations. You might have to tell business people something they don't want to hear, but the push-back in the beginning is nothing compared to the push-back at the end if the project fails to meet expectations. Remember, it does not matter how much you think has been delivered, it only matters what the business, your customer, thinks.

GETTING PEOPLE, PROCESS, AND POLITICS UNDER CONTROL

So, if you're going to launch and sustain BI programs that meet the business group's expectations, you've got to put the people, policies, and politics on your front burner. The areas to focus on include:

1. The relationship between business and IT groups
2. People's roles and responsibilities

3. Organizational structure, not just of the project team, but also the people involved in the project's use and maintenance
4. Training
5. A data governance program on the business side
6. Program and project management
7. Centers of excellence (COEs)

The rest of this chapter will focus on first five areas, with Chapter 18 discussing project management and Chapter 19 discussing COEs.

THE BUSINESS AND IT RELATIONSHIP

As with any relationship, the interactions between IT and business are vulnerable to misinterpretations, poor communication, and disagreements that can bog down a BI project. Becoming aware of these problems is the first step these groups can take to resolve them, perhaps even avoid them altogether.

USERS OR CUSTOMERS?

IT has historically created BI solutions for people working in internal business groups. While this is still the main customer base for BI projects, it's now common to have external customers such as workers in far-flung business groups, prospects, partners, suppliers, and other stakeholders. So, how do we refer to these people?

Other than the term "power user," which describes a highly-technical member of a business group, I've never liked calling people "users." When it comes to IT and BI, this is more than just semantics. Instead of thinking of business *users*, which is rather abstract, try to think of them as business *customers* and/or *partners*, or at the very least, as *people*. It implies that they are more important to you, and that satisfying their needs is more critical.

Adopting a *customer* or *partner* mindset, as opposed to a *user* one, will help drive the interaction between IT and the business group and encourage the formation of more balanced, respectful relationships.

WHO'S IN CHARGE?

In a worst-case scenario, IT and the business are completely at odds with one another. IT says they are in control of all things related to technology and don't want business groups acting without them. Business groups, on the other hand, feel they either do not need IT or cannot afford to wait for them. Should one side be in charge?

Like the parent of a young adult, IT needs to realize that control is no longer possible or desirable. IT needs to resist hovering over the business and, in the context of using technology, embrace business groups as their customers as opposed to their children. Customers come back if you provide great service, and rarely return if made to feel foolish.

The business group, on the other hand, has to understand that IT sometimes has to take a little more time on projects in order to better serve them, and the rest of the enterprise, in the long run. They may be juggling requests from many different business groups. Business groups that are being courted directly by software vendors also need to understand that although new technology can seem alluring, it's not always a quick solution to their problems.

COMMUNICATION SHORTCOMINGS

> "What we've got here is failure to communicate."
>
> **Captain in the 1967 film *Cool Hand Luke***

One of the key ingredients to setting and meeting business expectations (assuming the IT group can deliver the technology solution) is communication.

For communication to be effective, it must be with the right people and involve two-way discussions. The most common communication shortcomings in BI projects are:

- **Overreliance on business power users**. Power users are the business people most involved in using data and technology for reporting and analysis. It is natural that they are the business people with whom IT most closely works. However, they may provide a barrier to two-way feedback. Plus, they are also the people who develop the data shadow systems that are competing with the BI solution.
- **Wrong (and unmotivated) people**. The IT governance committees may not have the right people to make or influence decisions on the steering committee. It might also have the wrong people to get the tasks done in the working committee. The wrong people tend to send the wrong messages. When the committee is staffed with people who are involved and encouraged, they'll be more likely to provide honest feedback. Too often, these committees become more about process than communication.
- **A bogged-down feedback loop**. The formal processes created for providing BI feedback and enhancement requests may have become so bureaucratic or time-consuming that business people give up in frustration. If all the work goes into the request process rather than fulfilling the request, people will seek answers elsewhere, such as in data shadow systems or listening to software vendors pitch the latest prebuilt BI solution to replace the current BI efforts. If your business customers stop asking for things, then it is likely they are getting their requests satisfied elsewhere.

Tips for Communication During a BI Project

Communicate with all your customers, not just power users

Make sure committees have the right people and that they're motivated

Create a simple, easy-to-use feedback loop

Use clear, simple language, not technical jargon

Be honest

Speak up when there are snags and scope-creep

The best communication is open and frank. When a project is taking longer than expected, discuss this fact and provide clear reasons in the language that the business people understand—not technical gobbledygook. Projects can be slowed down when the data integration effort is snagged by the state of the data or when the reports the business group initially specified are a lot more involved than anticipated. These are not uncommon occurrences, but they need to be openly discussed and managed.

The business and IT groups should share the responsibility for any tradeoffs or project extensions. In addition, they should communicate and manage slow creep of little snags or changes. Many projects keep moving forward with the IT group doing a great job of handling these small issues, only to be hit with a death by a 1000 needles. The business will not know your truly Herculean efforts unless they are kept informed. It is important that communication is both verbal and written so that a history is kept for reference. If they find out afterward, when you have missed your deadlines and gone over budget, it only sounds like excuses.

Don't provide the opportunity for business people to think your BI project hasn't met expectations, or worse, is a failure. Make effective use of two-way communications to ensure you meet expectations and avoid unwelcome surprises.

ROLES AND RESPONSIBILITIES

When it comes to business and IT groups, each has its main role, and then there are areas where the roles can overlap. For the most part, IT's role is to create the infrastructure, integrate the data, and give business people what they need to perform analytics. IT handles everything in the "back office." The business group handles the "front office," that is, using the data IT provides to do business analysis. New technology and self-service BI is now blurring these distinctions—something we discuss in Chapter 14.

THE SCOOP ON ROLES

You will find that people don't always fall neatly into the categories in this book. Every company, every team is different. Small companies may rely less on committees. Managing the people, process and organization—getting everyone to pull in the same direction—is the priority, regardless of how the team is organized. Also, never forget that the involvement of the business group is essential throughout the entire project life-cycle, no matter who is taking the lead.

THE BUSINESS GROUP'S ROLE IN THE FRONT OFFICE

In the front office, the business group is focused on the content and use of data. They have to analyze data, sometimes huge amounts of it, to keep the company running smoothly. They're examining metrics like profitability, return on investment, inventory levels, and market share. It is this group, not IT, that has to define what a BI solution is going to accomplish in a business context and identify its business value. Sometimes this core purpose of BI is lost to IT when they are too focused on technology and generating reports.

The data and applicable business rules used in the enterprise are the core of a BI project. Without rules and definitions, data is just a bunch of characters and numbers. The business group defines these requirements, which can include:

- **Business events or transactions**, such as sales, employee pay, and website traffic.
- **Dimensions and attributes** that describe these events and transactions. For example, what products sold, who bought them, how many did they buy, how much profit you earned from the sale, etc.

- **Hierarchies and groupings of dimensions** such as geographies, sales, organizations, and product categories.
- **Metrics** that are used to monitor and measure the business.
- **Business rules** that may be used to select, filter, aggregate, and calculate data and metrics.

Although IT may physically define these requirements when implementing them during the project, it is the business people who are responsible for defining what they really mean in a business context.

IT'S ROLE IN THE BACK OFFICE

In the back office, IT is focused on the technical aspects of the data so they can deliver it to the business. This work may or may not require a data warehouse. IT's role includes:

- Determining (after discussing with the business) what data is needed for BI.
- Doing source system analysis or data profiling to determine where the data is located and how to get it.
- Data modeling to enable integration and BI.
- Developing the data and information architecture.
- Physically integrating the data.
- Designing and developing the infrastructure to support all of these efforts.

ROLES THAT SPAN BOTH BUSINESS AND IT

There are some roles that may be filled by either IT or the business group. It often depends on the technical skills of the business people. It's more likely if the business group has power users who have IT skills and are already creating customized BI applications for their coworkers. Typically, if the business group has data shadow systems, these are the people who built them. Some organizations tend to foster more power users, and therefore are more likely to create or customize their own applications rather than always relying on IT

A business or system analyst might be in either an individual business group or a centralized IT group. This is the person who typically works with the business to determine the business and data requirements for BI applications, and creates specifications that IT can use to develop them. Having the analyst in either group can work, but those in the business group tend to have a better understanding of the business operations and needs. It depends on the business structure, and which group has the people with the skills to do this work. What is most important is that someone is in this role, and it's not just assigned to IT developers along with their other tasks.

With the trend toward self-service BI, business customers can modify or create BI applications without always relying on IT As BI becomes more pervasive, even more people learn BI skills. Self-service BI has evolved to include data discovery, easy-to-use dashboards, and, even better, spreadsheet integration, the latter of which is a familiar and popular tool with business people. As the trend of self-service BI evolves, the IT and business roles will continue to overlap.

BUILDING THE BI TEAM

A successful BI project team is like a four-legged table—each leg holds up its share of the weight. Remove one and the project wobbles. The four legs of a team are:

- Project sponsorship and governance
- Project management
- Development team (core team)
- Extended project team

See Figure 17.2 to see where each function fits. While large companies may be able to assign these roles to different people, smaller companies always have people performing multiple roles. The typical size BI project team I have worked with over the years is 6–12. There has been a wide range, as I have worked with a teams with dozens of people and teams of one! Regardless of the size, these are the roles that should be done, but as any small team knows, you prioritize and do the best you can.

PROJECT SPONSORSHIP AND GOVERNANCE

IT and the business should work together to sponsor and govern design, development, deployment, and ongoing support. Although business sponsors obviously need to come up with the money, they also have to commit business resources to work with the BI team throughout the project.

If there is just one BI project on the table, a steering committee will usually suffice. If there are several projects, additional committees may be required, as explained below.

Oversight of One BI Project—the Steering Committee

With just one project, the company's oversight efforts can start small—with the BI project itself. In this situation, a *BI steering committee* is a very effective organizational mechanism to guide and support the project. This committee is composed of the business and IT management that the BI project team reports to. It typically meets biweekly or monthly during a major BI project. The committee hears the status from the BI project's management and discusses issues and concerns.

Its purpose is to keep the BI project on target by talking with the project team, interacting with groups outside the project team when necessary to resolve issues or enlist support, and communicating about the project to the rest of the enterprise. For an individual project, this is a very successful model that monitors the project team and keeps them from being isolated, thereby avoiding project failure.

Oversight of Multiple BI Projects—or a Complete BI Program

With multiple BI projects, oversight gets a bit more complicated. You'll need to expand your organizational and governance mechanisms so the BI steering committee includes business representation from the business sponsors of the individual BI projects and, ideally, from all lines of business (LOBs), business functions, and geographies that are stakeholders any of the projects.

The BI steering committee should be composed of the people who have BI budgetary control. This group will be responsible not only for the individual project's success, but the overall BI program's success. Therefore, they will deal with monitoring projects as well as prioritization and funding across projects.

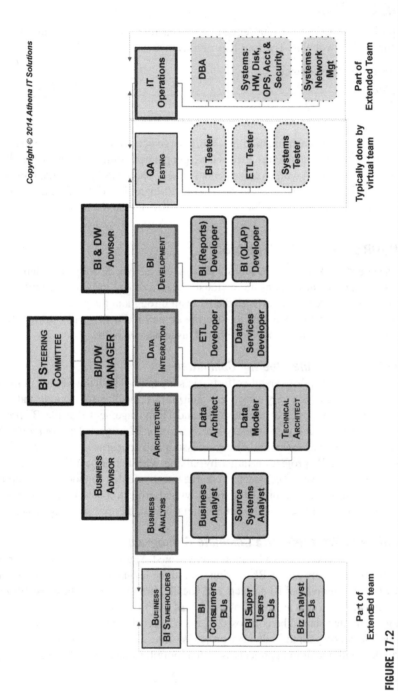

FIGURE 17.2

Business Intelligence (BI) project team.

BI Working Committee

A *BI working committee* is often formed as a bridge between the individual BI projects and the BI steering committee. It can be composed of the individuals managing the BI projects, often their management and their peers from business units who do not have active BI projects. The purpose of this committee, which often meets biweekly or monthly, is cross-project management and issue resolution. This group interacts with the BI steering committee and the individual BI project teams. With a proactive BI working committee, the BI steering committee may shift the frequency of their meetings to monthly or quarterly.

Program Management Office

Truly proactive enterprises will also form program management offices (PMOs) to manage cross-function efforts. In these enterprises, you can think of the BI PMO as being a supersized BI working committee. The PMO is set up to manage an effort that is cross-functional in nature, and within that charter it assists in prioritizing projects, distributing funding, communicating to the various stakeholders, measuring ROI and marketing BI efforts throughout the enterprise. In addition, the PMO sponsors the creation of an overall BI strategy and architecture that ensures that individual BI projects work toward a common goal and infrastructure. It endorses the methodologies and standards to use within BI projects. This framework assists in the reuse of data, functions, and applications across projects, ultimately improving the time-to-market of BI solutions within the enterprise in a cost-effective and flexible manner.

A word of caution: people are usually not indifferent with regard to PMOs—you either love them or hate them. They can be viewed as an excellent cross-functional organization or a bureaucratic entity that thwarts anything constructive. If your situation is the former, then getting a PMO dedicated to the BI program is an absolute necessity from an organizational sponsorship and funding perspective. If it's the latter, then various business units will circumvent the PMO by funding their own BI efforts, often disguised within various business initiatives. This then creates information stovepipes and all the problems they cause (as discussed in Chapter 16).

BI Center of Excellence

An organizational entity that some companies have implemented, and industry analysts are promoting, is the BI competency center or BI center of excellence (COE). The COE is created to gain a more cohesive approach for IT to work within a BI program perspective. (Chapter 19 is devoted to COEs.)

Often, the IT personnel working on a BI project are analysts working for a business unit, either directly as members of that unit or indirectly through business unit funding. Meanwhile, the IT personnel developing the enterprise data warehouse are located in another group, often a central IT group.

The IT analysts and their business unit partners sometimes view the DW group as slow to respond to needs, and this fosters stand-alone (stovepipe) BI applications. The BI COE should include the IT analysts developing the BI applications in the various business units as well as the DW group. This enables the IT analysts to develop a cross-functional viewpoint and gets them to work with the DW and infrastructure efforts. Some proponents of BI COEs suggest combining the IT analysts only. That is good, but not as strong as also including the DW group and getting their unique data perspective into the equation. Data is the glue that binds a BI program and a COE together.

PROJECT MANAGEMENT TEAM

Project management includes managing daily tasks, reporting status, and communicating to the extended project team, steering committee, and affected business people. We discuss project management in detail in Chapter 18.

The project management team needs extensive business knowledge, BI expertise, DW architecture background, and people management, project management, and communications skills. The project management team leadership includes three functions or members:

- Project development manager
- Business advisor
- BI/DW project advisor

Project Development Manager

The project development manager is responsible for deliverables, managing team resources, monitoring tasks, and reporting status and communications. This role requires a hands-on IT manager with a background in iterative development (Chapter 18). The person must understand the changes caused by this approach and the impact on the business, project resources, schedule, and the trade-offs.

The responsibilities include:

- Creating project plans and overseeing scope management processes.
- Organizing the working environment for both core and extended team members.
- Monitoring and reporting on project status.
- Managing project risks and client expectations.
- Promoting communication and coordination at all organizational levels.
- Working with business and IT to identify and obtain resources to fulfill project staffing requirements.
- Helping ensure that milestones are met and quality is delivered.

Business Advisor

The business advisor works within the sponsoring business organization(s). The responsibilities include:

- Monitoring the extended team's involvement and ensuring they meet their commitments.
- Identifying issues, concerns, or risks that could potentially impede deliverables or quality.
- Serving as the business advocate on the project team and the project advocate within the business community.

Often, the business advocate is a project co-manager who defers daily IT tasks to the IT project manager, but oversees the budget and business deliverables.

BI/DW Project Advisor

The project advisor, who might even be an outside consultant, has enough expertise with architectures and technologies to guide the project team on their use. Responsibilities include ensuring that architecture; data models; databases; extract, load and transform (ETL) code; and BI tools are all being used effectively and conform to best practices and standards.

It's especially important to have a project advisor when the project development manager is not very experienced with BI data or technology architectures, or when that person's primary role is managing the people, not the deliverables.

PROJECT DEVELOPMENT TEAM (CORE TEAM)

The project development team performs four core functions (Figure 17.3) and is typically split into corresponding sub-teams:

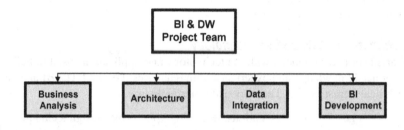

FIGURE 17.3

Project development team—core functions.

- **Business Analysis**—This sub-team may be composed of either business people who understand IT systems, sometimes referred to as "BI power users" or IT people who understand the business. In either case, the team represents the business and their interests. They are responsible for gathering and prioritizing business needs, translating them into data and IT systems requirements, interacting with the business on the data quality and completeness, and ensuring the business provides feedback on how well the solutions deployed meet their needs.
- **Architecture**—This sub-team designs and develops the overall BI architecture, selects the appropriate technology, creates the data models, maps the overall data workflow from source systems to BI analytics, and oversees the ETL and BI development teams from a technical perspective. This sub-team is responsible for the successful deployment of the four architectures: information, data, technology, and product.
- **Data integration (DI) Development**—This sub-team receives: the business, data, and data quality requirements from the business analysis sub-team; data architecture and technology from the architecture sub-team; and target data models to be used by BI analytics to design, develop, and deploy the supporting DI processes. Currently, most development teams are primarily using ETL functionality even if their DI tool offers more capabilities. Often, a system analyst who is an expert in the source systems (such as SAP or Oracle applications) is part of the team to provide knowledge of the data sources, customizations, and data quality. As business requirements get more demanding, real-time integration and complex event processing functionality become part of this team's expanding role.
- **BI Application Development**—This sub-team designs and creates the reports or business analytics that the business customers will interact with to do their jobs. This is typically a very iterative process requiring much interaction with the business people using the BI applications.

This sub-team is responsible for not only meeting the business requirements, but also selecting and deploying the appropriate analytical styles supporting the business workflow.

Table 17.1 shows how the individual roles fit into the four sub-teams described above. A role does not necessarily mean an individual person or job; sometimes one person assumes two or more roles, or there are several people in one role. The ideal size of the project team is dependent on the scope of the BI requirements, complexity of source systems, data volumes, data quality, analytical functionality, and diversity of the BI consumers, along with the skills and experience of the team members. Small firms may have a one-person team, while a large enterprise, in such industries as financial services, may have many dozens of people engaged in a significant BI implementation.

The individual roles are detailed below:

Principal Architect—BI, DW, and/or Technology

The principal architect is experienced with the technology and applications used to build BI systems. This person may need knowledge and experience with databases, DI and ETL, BI and analytics, data design, and technical infrastructure. The responsibilities include:

- Applying knowledge of technology options, technology platforms, design techniques, and approaches across life-cycle phases to design an integrated, quality, and cost-effective solution addressing business requirements.
- System integration of many diverse components and technologies used in the design, construction, testing, deployment, and operation of BI solutions.
- Designing technology infrastructure to support performance, availability, and architecture requirements.
- Supervising the technical aspect of the BI development project team—staff, work deliverables, and issues. The principal architect is the de facto technical leader of the project team.
- Providing input and recommendations on technical issues to the project manager.
- Reviewing and participating in testing of data design, tool design, data extracts, networks, and hardware.

There needs to be a primary architect driving the overall systems design. This role may be referred to as a DW or a BI architect depending on the orientation of the project team and its name, i.e., DW or

Table 17.1 Project Development Sub-teams			
Business Analysis	**Architecture**	**DI Development**	**BI Development**
Business analysis leader	Principal architect	DI leader	BI leader
Business analyst	• Technology	DI developer	BI developer
Source system analyst	• BI	• ETL (or ELT)	• Reporting
	• Data	• Real-time integration	• OLAP
	Data modeler	• Data virtualization	• Data visualization
	• Logical modeling	• MDM	• Data discovery
	• Physical modeling		• Predictive analytics
	DBA		

BI group. If the project team is large enough, there may actually be multiple architecture roles with the primary architect managing the overall system and the BI and DW-specific functions split between multiple architects who specialize in specific functionality.

Data Architect

The data architect determines the source systems' data availability and understands the nature and quality of the data. The role requires an understanding of business processes and data requirements, as well as how to translate the business requirements into an actionable data model. The person in this role should be experienced in the use of various techniques to develop quality data models (e.g., joint application development (JAD) facilitation, interviewing, iterative development/prototyping of conceptual data models). The responsibilities include:

- Reviewing the source systems to understand what is available and if its quality meets analytics requirements.
- Designing the data models for extensibility, scalability, simplicity, consistency, and integrity.
- Working with the principal architect to design and implement databases that support the agreed upon BI architecture and DI workflows.
- Working closely with the DBA to help ensure that the physical design meets the business requirements, meets enterprise technical standards, conforms to security requirements, and adheres to industry standards.

Data Modeler or Designer

The data modeler or designer has a strong understanding of logical modeling techniques: entity relationship diagrams (ERD) and dimensional data modeling. The person should be proficient in using a data modeling tool and have a thorough understanding of physical implementation issues, data strategies, design implications, and performance requirements. He or she also understands the database engine, database structure, and the implications of the physical design. Although a relational database is still the primary database technology used, the data designer needs to be familiar with other technologies that may potentially be used, including columnar, massive parallel processing (MPP), NoSQL, online analytical processing (OLAP), and in-memory, in addition to BI appliances that may use a variety of these technologies along with specialized hardware and/or specific logical and physical data architectures. The role includes working closely with the DBA(s) managing the development and production databases, as well as the data architect.

There are two distinct roles in designing databases for BI and DI:

> Responsibilities may overlap in some situations, particularly when defining, designing, and constructing data structures and databases. Make sure the roles of the data modeler/designer, data architect, and DBA are clearly defined so you can head off any turf battles.

Logical data design. This is the techniques used to represent the data in its business context supporting business relationships, transformations, and rules. This is sometimes referred to as defining business subject areas. Logical design also enables the DI workflow and processes used to conform dimensions, standardize facts and metrics, and transform data to business information.

Physical data design. Logical design needs to be physically implemented, and also leverage database, DI, and BI technologies. If the project team follows the data architecture discussed in Chapter 6, then the data designer will need to physically model separate schemes for DI and BI. Designing relational databases would involve best practice designs for tables, indexes and partitioning, while columnar, in-memory, and other data storage technologies would involve very different physical designs. The variety of data storage technologies are used either to improve access speed, expand the breadth and depth of analytics, or enable various analytical styles such as data visualization, predictive analytics, OLAP, and data discovery.

The responsibilities of the data modeler or designer include:

- Defining, designing, and constructing data structures or databases.
- Working with the data architect to ensure that data structures contain all required data elements.
- Recommending database optimization and physical design changes.
- Conforming to corporate database security and database backup procedures.

Database Administrator (DBA)

The DBA is responsible for the physical databases used by the BI solution across the entire data workflow, from source systems through information consumption by BI consumers. This may include multiple databases and database technologies such as relational, columnar, MPP, NoSQL, OLAP, in-memory, and other emerging data storage technologies.

The responsibilities include:

- Designing, testing, deploying, maintaining, and securing databases used in BI solutions.
- Implementing technology and security standards for databases and collaborating with associated infrastructure resources.
- Supporting the development and testing database environments.
- Supporting production databases (this role is often in an infrastructure oriented group).
- Providing expertise to architects, developers, and data modelers on:
  - Physical database design
  - Database configuration, performance, and tuning
  - Database utilization
  - Database security and privacy

DI Developer

The DI developer is responsible for gathering and integrating data from the source systems to the data structures supporting business analytics. The required DI workflow and supporting DI code will likely require data movement, transformation, and integration with several databases. This work includes designing, developing, testing, and deploying DI code for data profiling, data validation, data cleansing, and data transformation. This person will work with the source data analyst to understand the source system's business rules, both current and historical, to ensure they are accounted for in the DI processes.

Responsibilities include:

- Designing the system components for the DI or conversion of data from source systems to the target application.
- Designing system components that reconcile and audit the results of the DI from source systems throughout the data architecture.

- Constructing the extract, transform, transfer, and audit components of a data warehousing system or data conversion programs through the use of extract development tools or custom developed procedures.
- Defining and managing the manual data load procedures.
- Documentation of above. Many DI tools generate documentation but typically this is very technically oriented and needs to be supplemented with the business, data and quality requirements implemented in the DI code.

DI Leader

The DI leader is responsible for the overall processes that transfer data from the legacy systems to the data warehouse including data validation, data cleansing, data transformation and calculations. This individual will manage all DI developers (see above), as well as participate in the DI work. If the DI sub-team is small, then this individual is likely the senior DI developer and performs hands-on development work while coordinating any others in the group. As the sub-team expands, it is likely this individual will take on a more managerial role with less or even no hands-on development.

BI Developer

The BI analyst has BI tool experience. The analyst may work on BI and reporting tools, OLAP tools, data mining tools, or a variety of other tools for specific types of users. The analyst will ensure data security, user friendly reports, "drill-down" features, as well as a flexible design of data hierarchies and a logical, easy-to-use interface and web enabling of user interfaces for the people who will ultimately use the solution. Additionally, the analyst must ensure the presentation tool provides all functionality supported by the conceptual data model, and that the tool takes advantage of the physical database design features. The responsibilities include:

- Verifying the correctness of the data relationships, mapping, and definitions.
- Verifying the correctness and completeness of the conceptual data model.
- Working closely with business people and the data architect to translate business information requirements into flexible applications.
- Understanding the usage, nuances, and architecture of the presentation tool being used
- Defining, designing, and constructing reports.
- Defining, designing, and constructing system functions.
- Mapping report layouts to data warehouse objects and application software functions and features.

BI Leader

The BI leader is responsible for the design, development, testing, and deployment of all business BI consumer access of the data via reporting or analytical applications. This individual will manage all BI developers (see above), as well as participate in the BI development work. If the BI development sub-team is small, then this individual is likely the senior BI developer and performs hands-on development work while coordinating any others in the group. As the sub-team expands it is likely this individual will take on a more managerial role with less or even no hands-on development.

Business Analyst

The business analyst serves as the advocate for the business with the BI development project team, and as the liaison between business and IT. He or she gathers business needs and translates them into data and IT systems requirements. He or she determines if the business is satisfied with the BI solutions, ensuring that their feedback reaches the development team.

The responsibilities include:

- Gathering business requirements from business stakeholders and working with them to establish priorities.
- Working with principle architect or DI developers to correlate business requirements to data requirements mapped to their source systems.
- Documenting business requirements, including data needs and process flows.
- Translating business requirements into preliminary specifications for both DI and BI development sub-groups.
- Testing and validating DI and BI applications in regards to meeting business requirements.
- Communicating project status, issues and concerns related to business requirements with business stakeholders.
- Coordinating end user acceptance testing (UAT) of BI applications with business stakeholders.

Source Data Analyst

The source data analyst determines the data availability in the source systems. This role often involves reviewing existing load routines, validation programs, and report routines. He or she understands the nature and quality of the data and should provide a data dictionary of the source data (if an accurate data dictionary is not already available). Responsibilities include:

- Reviewing the source system(s) so as to understand the data they contain.
- Determining what data is available from the source system, and its quality.
- Creating/validating a data dictionary of the source system.

Business Analysis Leader

The business analysis leader is responsible for the interaction between the business stakeholders and the BI development project team. He or she will manage all business analysts (see above), as well as participate in the business analysis work. If the business analysis sub-team is small, then he or she is likely the senior business analyst and performs hands-on work while coordinating any others in the group. As the sub-team expands, it is likely that he or she will take on a more managerial role with less or even no hands-on business analysis.

EXTENDED PROJECT TEAM

The extended project team handles several functions required by the project that occur at discrete times and that are performed by people outside of the core development team. The extended team encompasses three primary roles:

- **Players**—A group of business customers are signed up to "play with" or test the BI analytics and reports as they are developed to provide feedback to the core development team. BI solutions developed in an iterative and interactive fashion, often leveraging agile development techniques consistently yield higher business value and adoption than the "old school" waterfall methodology. This is a virtual team that provides focused attention during specific periods of the project. Since business peoples' time is valuable, it is necessary to schedule these times and get business management to commit to allocating people to these tasks.

Communication of project status and any scheduling changes must be managed by the BI project leader.

- **Testers**—A group is gathered, similar to the virtual team just mentioned, to perform more extensive QA testing of the BI analytics, ETL processes and overall systems testing. You may have project members test other members' work, such as the ETL team test the BI analytics and vice versa. Other groups that are often asked to participate are the source system experts to verify DI processes, and BI consumers, particularly "power users," to validate BI applications. These tests include usability, but more importantly are used to reconcile data from source systems and compare results with any legacy reporting systems or data shadow systems.

- **Operators**—IT operations is often separated from the development team, but it is critical that they are involved from the beginning of the project to ensure that the systems are developed and deployed within your company's infrastructure. Key functions are database administration, systems administration, and networks. In addition, this extended team may also include help desk and training resources if they are usually provided outside of development.

TRAINING

One of the biggest mistakes project teams make is in refusing to acknowledge the need for training. This is just one of the ways companies undermine their own efforts to take BI to its full potential.

TYPES OF TRAINING

Getting the right kind of training is important. It's not enough to just learn the software products. Often, software vendors offer courses in addition to their product-specific training, or devote a portion of a class on BI or ETL tools to DW/BI concepts. Although this is useful, it is generally not detailed enough to really give people an understanding of what is involved in developing a BI project, and although the people teaching vendor-sponsored classes are very knowledgeable in their tools, they may not have many years of relevant experience to draw upon in their teaching.

Vendor-agnostic foundational training—It's important to start out with fundamental BI training that explains concepts, architectures, and best practices. This training should include the topics of DI, data modeling, business analysis, project methodology, and analytics. This type of training works best when done in-house with all the business customers who will be using the BI solution.

Tool-specific training—Those who understand the concepts of BI are ready to learn the particular tools their group will be using. This is often taught by the software vendors. On-the-job training can be very effective in relation to tools training if a group has a tool guru who would be able to mentor less experienced peers and create templates or standards for them to follow.

Training with use cases—The best way to expand the use of BI and self-service BI, especially with business consumers, is to train with use cases involving the reports and data they would use in their own jobs. For example, business analysts in the sales group might see use cases related to sales campaigns, ideally with dashboards accessing previous campaigns. Financial analysts might see use cases with analysis of budget forecast to actual expenditures. If business people train with analytics and data they understand, then learning how and when to use analytic tools is much easier to grasp and remember.

So how do you justify getting BI training, especially if you have been involved in your company's BI program? Pitch your training as necessary to increase the business return on investment (ROI) from your company's BI efforts or, even better, explain how you be able to better support the latest business initiative that requires analytics. Your investment of time and expense in really understanding BI and data warehousing will be rewarded when you improve your company's corporate performance management (CPM), BI, or DW efforts in the future.

TRAINING FOR THE IT GROUP

Unfortunately, the IT group tends to skip formal training, or limits it to just the specific tools they're using because they think that prior experience building transactional applications is enough. This is a big mistake, as BI applications are very different. IT people really need to understand not just the mechanics of the tools, but how they're actually used in BI projects.

Working on a BI project can be overwhelming if you don't have a solid grounding in the basics. It's difficult to focus on the goals of the project when you're bogged down by unanswered questions; it's even more dangerous if you don't even know what questions to ask. By arming yourself with foundational training on the concepts, fundamentals, and best practices, you can hit the ground running.

Also, it takes time to become proficient in ETL/BI tools and in BI itself. Too often, project managers plan tasks as if rookies are just as productive as those who have years of experience.

The types of training that IT people tend to need include:

- DW/BI fundamentals and architecture
- Tools used by individuals:
  - ETL
  - BI
  - Database
- Database and SQL programming

TRAINING FOR THE BUSINESS GROUP

Simply sending business people to generic BI vendor training is not effective, although it often happens. The problem is that people generally do not learn how to use a tool effectively if it does not have the context in which they will use it. Business people need to understand what data is available and how that data was transformed before they can use BI effectively and correctly.

A better approach for training the business group includes customized training that uses their own data and BI application. It should take place when both the BI application and the associated data are available (usable, but not necessarily final), allowing the business people to see real-life examples and put things into context. Although this customized training may cost more and be harder to arrange up front, it pays big dividends down the line, and should be considered a requirement.

The content of business training should include:

- BI analytics fundamentals and capabilities
- Types of analytics available and how to use them
- What data is accessible for analytics
- What filters, business transformations and rules are used in BI applications
- How to use the BI tools for specific use cases

Keep these guidelines in mind for training business groups:

Class size—If you have many business users to train, it's best to split them into smaller groups of 6–12 people. Ensure that each person has hands-on access to the BI applications and data during class. The class should be a mixture of slides, demos, and hand-on workshops.

It's a good idea to split classes by business unit so those who use similar data are in the same class and can support one another. Include the group's power users even if they don't think they need training; participation in the class will allow them to support colleagues during in-class workshops, and encourages supportive relationships after the class.

Remember who the audience is—Business group training is different from IT training. The same BI tool is going to look different depending on your perspective. IT professionals tend to focus on a software product's bells and whistles. Business users, on the other hand, are usually just looking to do their jobs, and don't respond to training that doesn't show how they can use a tool to accomplish what they're doing now with spreadsheets.

Use real data—The training should use the company's own data, not generic information. After the initial training session, encourage business people to try out the BI technology and get completely comfortable using it with actual data well before their bosses start asking them for reports. Just have someone ready to hold their hands if needed. Detailed follow-on training should then be made available for the users who really need it.

Customize it—Before starting a training program, get a complete understanding of the software features that business people actually need for their BI usage, and then train them on *that* functionality. It's OK to give them an overview of the entire BI tool, but focus on what they specifically will be using to do their jobs. Get power users to look at the tool and give you feedback on which functions are most useful and which ones aren't needed. Then you should follow the "less is more" approach when it comes to training the rest of the business. If you overwhelm them with mind-numbing talk about features that they don't need, the useful capabilities may be forgotten.

Timing—Most classes should be 2–4 hour sessions with the number of sessions depending on the complexity and variety of BI applications, such as dashboards, they need to learn. Training shouldn't take place too early in the project, because you want business people to be able to use the tools soon afterward, before they forget them.

Bear in mind that effective training takes time. If projects are late, business customer training is often cut or rushed. This becomes a big problem when business people then become frustrated with the BI environment and request constant hand-holding from IT. Also, the work to develop customized business training is often underestimated. It typically it takes 8 hours of development time for 1 hour of training.

Market the project—Among the benefits of business group training is that it's a great marketing tool for the BI efforts. It's an opportunity to connect with BI customers, create and reinforce positive feelings about using the BI solution, and get feedback that may be invaluable in developing future BI applications or improving existing ones.

TRAINING METHODS

There are several training approaches that can work, depending on your situation:

Custom class (for the business group)—As discussed above, vendor-neutral, tailored training on the basics of BI is the best way to get the business group started. Although some lecture slides may be necessary for foundational training, it is critical that each business person attending training has hands-on access to the BI tools.

On the job (for the IT group)—Learning a tool on the job can be effective, especially if experienced consultants are on hand to help out. It's important, however, that people receive foundational BI training first, or they won't fully understand what they're doing with the tool. Developers who have experience with comparable products are in a good position to learn new tools on the job, because they're already familiar with the concepts and how other tools work.

Vendor (for the IT group)—Vendor training is useful if no team members have extensive experience with the products. Not everyone needs this training, but it's a good idea to make sure someone on the team has it, and can then mentor the others. There may be a wider selection of courses on mature BI products, so take advantage of the opportunity to send people to training targeted to their needs, e.g., send the BI developer to development classes and someone else to administration-type classes.

Train the trainer (for the business group)—This approach can work if the business group has power users. In this case, power users get trained by or along with the IT group, then go back to their business groups to teach them. This helps ensure that different business groups get consistent training across the enterprise.

Lunch and learn (for the business group)—If you are simply modifying or expanding an existing BI implementation, the lunch-and-learn approach can work well. Invite business people to lunch or breakfast sessions, introduce them to BI concepts if it's new for them, or jump right into training them on what's new in their BI implementation. It's a great way to get feedback, provide ongoing support, and expand the internal customer base.

DATA GOVERNANCE

More and more companies are recognizing that they're accumulating ever-increasing amounts of data, but not necessarily gaining business insights from it. The missing link is the transformation of data into information that is comprehensive, consistent, correct, and current. That is a problem technology cannot solve for you; it requires people.

The answer is establishing a data governance program to help your organization truly treat its data as a corporate asset and maximize its value. The data governance program will enforce consistent definitions, rules, business metrics, policies, and procedures for areas such as:

- Data creation
- Data movement, transformation, and integration
- Business metrics and data definitions
- BI data models
- Master or reference data
- Use cases for specific BI tools and self-service BI
- Data change management
- Monitoring governance
- Information access and delivery
- Information consumption (reporting and analysis)

Data governance helps ensure that your data is trustworthy and provides business value. The process of governance, however, is becoming more challenging as organizations rely more on data that is unstructured and from the cloud, as well as Big Data.

It is critical that data governance manages not only data creation, but also data consumption. Too often enterprises concentrate solely on creation only to have business and IT people alter data in their spreadmarts or BI applications. It is seemingly pointless to spend all one's efforts to ensure consistent data creation, only to have the data altered, and thus become inconsistent when business people conduct their analytics.

WHO'S RESPONSIBLE, BUSINESS OR IT?

Because data governance is all about how you handle a key corporate asset (data) and not just about technology, the business group, not IT, should be the key driver in data governance efforts. IT often regards data governance sponsorship as business executives writing a check and putting people on a governance committee (see below). While that is, in fact a great first step, the business must also be committed to it.

People from the business side need to create the data definitions, business rules, and key performance indicators (KPIs) for a data governance program; achieve agreement on them across an organization; enforce usage and compliance; and ensure that the definitions, rules, and KPIs are updated on an ongoing basis as business needs evolve and change.

The reality is that in the vast majority of cases, data governance tasks are merely tacked on to the already overloaded schedules of business managers instead of being made a priority, with other responsibilities correspondingly getting taken off their to-do lists. Without a real business-resource commitment, data governance will take a back seat to the daily firefight and will never be implemented effectively. It is critical that both business and IT commit to data governance on an ongoing basis.

GETTING STARTED WITH DATA GOVERNANCE

Ideally, data governance is, eventually, an enterprise-wide effort involving multiple business groups and IT. In most companies, though, it starts with a project or two and then grows. If you're responsible for getting a governance effort launched, start by creating the organization, then focus on defining processes and data.

Start Small, Build for the Future

A typical approach would be to start small and take a tactical approach with a handful of projects that have data issues. The processes you build may be focused on these projects, but they should also be reusable for future projects. The budget, too, should be set with the goal of sustaining the governance effort over the long haul.

A significant trap that many data governance efforts fall into is trying to solve all of an organization's data problems in the initial phase of the project. Or, companies start with their biggest data problems, issues that span the entire enterprise, and are likely to be very political. It's almost impossible to establish a data governance program while at the same time tackling data problems that have taken years to build up. This is a case in which you need to "think globally and act locally." In other words, data problems need to be broken down into incremental deliverables. "Too big, too fast" is a sure recipe for disaster.

Narrow Down the Scope

Another issue that can arise is that the program is too high-level and substantive data issues are never really dealt with; or, the opposite problem, it attempts to create definitions and rules for every data field in every table in every application that an enterprise has—with the result being that the effort gets bogged down in minutiae. There needs to be a happy compromise between those two extremes that enables the data governance initiative to create real business value.

CREATING A DATA GOVERNANCE ORGANIZATION

Before creating the data governance organization, it's important to ensure everyone understands the scope of the data governance effort and their roles and responsibilities. A guaranteed way to stall a data governance initiative and lead the business to lose interest is to prematurely organize the management framework and then realize you need a do-over.

Be mindful of how many people are on the committees. Often, the more people on each committee, the more politics comes into play and the more watered-down governance responsibilities become. To be successful, try to limit the size of committees to between 6 and 12 people and make sure that committee members have the required decision-making authority.

Data Governance Board

Just like a corporate board of directors, the data governance board's purpose is the overall oversight across an enterprise. The members of this board need to have the responsibility and budgetary authority to sponsor data governance and commit the resources to implement it.

Data Governance Task Force

The data governance task force is the working hands-on group. Their mission is to define, implement, and enforce data and reporting governance. The group's responsibilities include:

- Defining the mission and scope of the data governance effort
- Creating a road-map of projects
- Defining priorities and determining which projects from the road-map will be tackled first
- Defining data and reporting governance processes
- Communicating with data stakeholders in the business and IT groups, up to the executive level if necessary, ensuring that they understand the governance concepts and issues
- Working on initial governance projects
- Monitoring and enforcing governance processes on future projects

The group is led by its data governor, who oversees the governance initiatives and coordinates with the BI and DI COEs. The other committee members include data owners and data stewards. See Table 17.2 for an overview of their responsibilities.

WORKING WITH COEs

Ideally, this group works in concert with the BI COE and DI COE (described in Chapter 19). Working together, these teams help provide the enterprise with consistent information and useful business analytics. See Figure 17.4.

Table 17.2 Data Governance Task Force

Data governor

- Establishes and prioritizes data governance requirements
- Coordinates multiple governance projects
- Enables change management in processes and organization
- Coordinates with business, BI COE and DI COE

Data owner

- Assumes business ownership (or co-ownership) of key business metrics and data subject areas
- Defines data and reporting governance processes
- Resolves business metric and data disputes
- Advocates for governance in the business group

Data steward

- Partners with business stakeholders
- Defines business metrics and data definitions
- Defines data and reporting governance processes
- Works on data governance projects
- Resolves data and reporting governance issues
- Must understand business systems analysis, data structures used in DW and applications, and how to query data and use BI tools

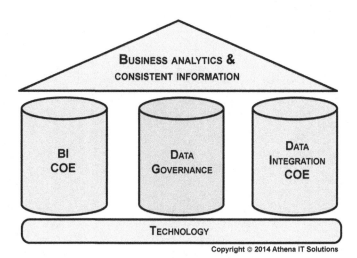

FIGURE 17.4

Data governance and centers of excellence (COEs).

KEEPING DATA GOVERNANCE ON TRACK

What gets organizations in trouble is how they actually go about implementing governance programs. Below are a few things to keep in mind to help you become better positioned for governance success.

Use it or lose it—In order for the data governance effort to produce business value, people have to actually *use* the data definitions, business rules, and KPIs. The governance process needs to be a complete feedback loop in which data is defined, monitored, acted upon, and changed when appropriate.

Keep communicating—Similarly, ongoing communication about governance initiatives should not be forgotten. Without it, business users are more likely to revert to their old habits, causing the data governance program to lose momentum.

Deal with change—If data governance is to be successful, both business and IT processes need to be changed; however, the accompanying need for change management is seldom addressed. People and process issues, and the internal politics resulting from them, are challenges that need to be tackled.

Put technology in its place—Software is not a quick fix, letting you avoid people, process, and political issues. Companies that buy master data management, DI, or data quality software—or a mix of the three—to support their data governance programs sometimes fall prey to the combination of vendor hype and high price tags and forget that it's the internal interactions that make or break a governance effort.

Keep an eye on data shadow systems—A very common governance mistake is to focus on an enterprise's transactional and BI systems, assuming that all the important data can be found there. But often, key information is located in data shadow systems scattered throughout an organization. For example, the "real" BI reports and analytical findings used by business workers often end up in Microsoft Excel spreadsheets. (See Chapter 16.)

PROJECT MANAGEMENT

INFORMATION IN THIS CHAPTER:

* Establishing a BI program
* BI assessments
* Work breakdown structure (WBS)
* Project methodologies
* Project phases
* Project schedule

THE ROLE OF PROJECT MANAGEMENT

Without good project management, IT projects are prone to be late, over budget, low quality and, most important, they fail to meet expectations. The failures occur primarily because the project emphasis is on technology rather than the business need, and because there is poor communication between IT and the business.

Project management is critical for a business intelligence (BI) project's success, yet teams often fail to give it proper attention; they tend to behave as if project management is not their problem. But actually, it's everyone's problem.

The role of the project manager is not trivial. This function carries major responsibility, but too often the person who becomes the project manager does not have the appropriate background or experience. In some cases, the person selected is a project manager without any BI experience; in others, the person is technically proficient but has no project management experience. The problem is especially acute if it is the first time the enterprise has developed a BI solution—a risky scenario because then there are no in-house experts to help.

Managing a BI project can be quite complex, requiring knowledge of project management methodology, an excellent understanding of how BI works, and a thick skin for all the project meetings. Ideally, the project manager has prior experience or there are others in the company who are available for guidance. If not, it may be best to engage an outside expert to help with this task.

The project manager needs to remember that the project is being undertaken for the sake of a business group. The focus is on getting information for the business, not on the technology that makes it happen. Keeping the lines of communication open, asking the right questions, and paying attention to the answers will help keep the business and IT groups on the same page and avoid unpleasant surprises.

BI project managers must not only manage the project team but also serve as primary advocates for the business users, i.e., BI customers, and keep active communications with all stakeholders. BI project managers must handle all the people, process, and political issues that arise throughout the project. They need to introduce and ensure that solid project management processes and best practices are followed by all members of the project team.

In this chapter, we will discuss the following project management subjects:

- BI program management
- Work breakdown structures (WBS)
- Project methodologies
- Project phases

Each of these topics is meant to enable a BI project manager to better plan and manage a BI project. There are cross references to the other sections of this book that discuss the details of the BI project tasks.

ESTABLISHING A BI PROGRAM

Enterprises are managed strategically by their senior management and operationally by business groups or departments such as marketing, sales, finance, and human resources. This division of labor enables specialization and fosters improved productivity. Although the individual business groups may have a considerable amount of autonomy in making tactical decisions, the enterprise must have an overall strategic vision and a set of guidelines under which these groups must operate.

Senior management will lay out a strategic vision and work with the various business groups to develop a plan—typically done at least once a year—to implement that decision. Those plans involve multiple business initiatives that are needed by the enterprise to achieve its strategic vision (see Figure 18.1). Typically, these business initiatives require cross-functional collaboration. Business initiative plans include business objectives and deliverables along with the schedules, budgets, and resources needed. An enterprise's strategic vision and business initiatives are the glue that binds its business groups together.

Business groups within the enterprise need data and analytics to run day-to-day operations, so these groups tend to tactically drive BI projects. Although it is certainly understandable that business groups

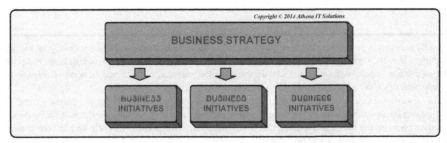

FIGURE 18.1

Enterprise business strategy and business initiatives.

feel the urgency to initiate BI projects to get the data and analytics they need, tactical BI projects tend to create data, application, and technology silos, lost business and IT productivity, redundant or overlapping work and resources, and, quite simply, the inability to achieve success with BI on an enterprise-wide basis.

A *BI program*, as opposed to separate, tactical projects, helps the enterprise achieve several benefits:

- The enterprise has a strategic BI vision
- Data, application, and technology silos are not created
- Business and IT groups are more productive
- Work and resources do not overlap and are not redundant
- Enterprise-wide BI has a greater chance of success

Just as an enterprise needs a strategic vision with an overall program of business initiatives to achieve it, BI needs a strategic vision within its overall BI program. The enterprise's strategic vision will evolve over time and along with its products or services; so too will its data analytics needs. BI is not a "one and done" project, but an ongoing program that supports business needs.

BUSINESS STRATEGY DRIVES THE BI PROGRAM

The chief information officer (CIO) needs to ensure that an overall BI program is established for the enterprise. When you consider that data is an enterprise asset, and analytics the key to leveraging that data, BI efforts can no longer be scattered and uncoordinated throughout an enterprise no matter what its size.

The BI program must support the enterprise's business strategy (see Figure 18.2). In this context, it is clear that the BI program needs to focus on business enablement rather than on technology, which is just the opposite of the orientation of many BI projects.

Historically, when BI projects are driven tactically by individual business groups, each project determines its deliverables and priorities solely in the context of that group. This "bottom-up" approach

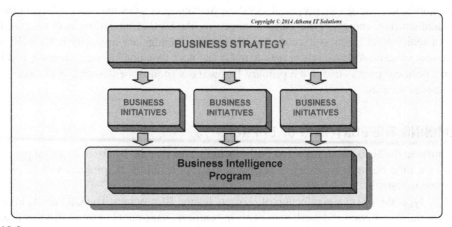

FIGURE 18.2

Business strategy and plans drive business intelligence program.

ignores other groups' priorities and inhibits investments in scope that may be needed in other groups. These missed or shortchanged investments often include important infrastructure or enterprise-wide data management work, such as master data management (MDM).

A BI program needs to use a "top-down" approach that leverages the existing business strategy and priorities. There is no reason for a BI program to independently determine the strategic vision of the enterprise. Keep in mind that using a "top-down" approach to set overall direction for the program does not imply that the program will be managed centrally. The choice of central or decentralized management of the BI program will be based on the enterprise's organization and political culture.

BUSINESS SPONSORS FOR THE BI PROGRAM

Although the initial establishment of a BI program may be driven by the CIO, a key element of success will be finding a strategic business sponsor for that program. Since the primary objective of BI is enabling business rather than implementing technology, the business group needs to sign up to drive this program.

One of the common BI program business sponsors is the CFO. CFOs are the natural candidates because they are responsible for the accuracy and transparency of enterprise information, at least in regard to financial information, for enterprise stakeholders. They are legally responsible for the data that is published outside the enterprise and are subject to regulatory compliance and potential audits regarding the data. This responsibility means that they have a cross-organizational perspective that many of the sponsors may not have. In addition, they are responsible for driving enterprise-wide cost management, so they have keen interest in ensuring that the BI investments are managed appropriately. The CFO's responsibility for driving the overall enterprise's budgetary process enables it to be integrated with the creation and prioritization of the BI program.

Although the CFO is a natural candidate to be the BI program sponsor, there are other senior managers who may take the lead due to the industry of the enterprise or simply because of the political structures in that enterprise. In customer-oriented industries such as financial services, retail, and consumer goods, the senior vice president (SVP) of marketing or sales may be the BI program sponsor. In manufacturing, energy, or the utilities industries, the SVP of operations may take the lead. In all cases, a senior-level business executive with significant budgetary authority is typically the primary business sponsor. Although there may actually be more than one business sponsor, it is imperative from a political perspective that a primary BI business sponsor be designated to ensure that the program moves forward.

DETERMINING THE PORTFOLIO OF BI PROJECTS

After identifying the business strategy and business initiatives that the BI program will support, IT can then work with the business sponsors to determine what portfolio of BI projects will be required to support those initiatives.

The CIO typically drives the selection of projects for the BI program. The CIO needs to be the IT advocate for the BI program and work with peers in senior management to ensure that this is an enterprise-wide effort. The CIO, of all corporate executives, needs to be concerned with both the "what" and "how" of the program—what are its goals and how is it going to accomplish them? The CIO is in the unique position to understand why long-term success—measured in business value and cost effectiveness—comes from developing an overall architecture to guide the short-term BI solutions needed by the business.

The BI portfolio needs to focus on business needs first, not IT needs. Getting the business the information it needs is priority; choosing software tools and other IT-centric issues are important only in terms of how they help achieve the business goals. IT groups too often create their list of projects and priorities based on a logical and mainly technical viewpoint. Their agenda is driven by upgrading hardware and software to take advantage of new capabilities that vendors have built into their products, along with support and maintenance. None of this necessarily matters to the business. Getting information matters to the business. Chances are that every business initiative in the company needs more data, so every project should be directly tied to a priority initiative. (See Figure 18.3.)

If the business needs are not priority, you really cannot expect a high level of business group participation. The business groups are focused on their priority business initiatives, so they cannot commit to a BI program that does not address these needs. And, as we discussed in Chapter 16, if the business group's information needs are not addressed, they tend to create data shadow systems.

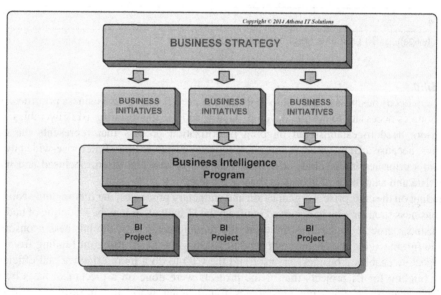

FIGURE 18.3

Business intelligence (BI) program composed of multiple BI projects.

SPONSORSHIP, GOVERNANCE, AND BUSINESS PARTICIPATION

The BI program does not work in a vacuum. It needs to receive direction and influence from certain areas outside the BI team. Part of the project management responsibility is ensuring that three areas, which are particularly important in the BI effort, are in place. These areas are sponsorship, governance, and business group participation. (See Figure 18.4.)

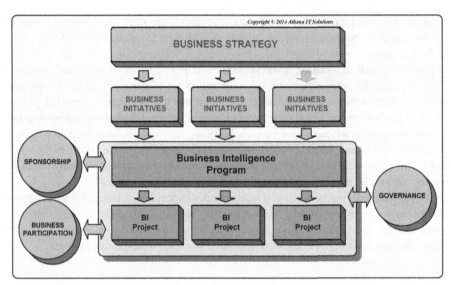

FIGURE 18.4

Business intelligence (BI) programs need business involvement.

Sponsorship

A BI program needs business sponsorship to justify the need for it, set its business priorities, and commit the resources necessary to design, develop, deploy, and use the resulting BI deliverables. The business sponsors need to establish an ongoing prioritization process that represents the enterprise stakeholders, because a BI program and its capabilities evolve over time. Enterprise-wide buy-in of the BI program's priorities is essential; otherwise, business groups feel disenfranchised and will create their own data and analytical silos or data shadow systems.

Depending on the enterprise's organization and budgetary processes, the funding may come directly from the business sponsor's budget, carved out from the IT budget, or may be a pooling of budgets from various business groups. Regardless of where the funding originates, the business sponsors will be responsible for managing the BI program funding. Managing the BI program funding from an enterprise perspective enables a business sponsor and the CIO to do a more effective and efficient job of allocating funding for BI projects than if the projects were done on a piecemeal basis by business groups. This method of financing encourages foundational work and infrastructure investments, because it is shared across the enterprise. In addition, it reduces the likelihood of overlapping or redundant investments because of the enterprise visibility.

Business sponsorship is nearly always discussed in the context of funding. Although this is critical, there are two other areas that are just as essential from a business perspective: governance and business participation.

Program Governance

The BI program needs an overall governance model to ensure that it meets its goals and objectives for all its stakeholders. The governance model defines the accountabilities, responsibilities, roles, and levels of involvement by the stakeholders in the BI program. A common mistake is to concentrate exclusively on the roles and responsibilities of the BI project team rather than the BI program. If the governance model is project-focused, then the program typically does not get the level of business involvement or commitment that is necessary for success. The governance model also involves creating the processes necessary to gather and adjust requirements and priorities based on stakeholder involvement and feedback. These processes need to be transparent and communicated to all stakeholders.

Business Participation

The business needs to provide sponsorship (funding) and governance but it also needs to be actively involved with the BI program and individual BI projects. This participation may involve the following tasks, although they may not apply in every case:

- Providing input on requirements, refinement, validation, and prioritization
- Software evaluation
- Validation and refinement of specifications using techniques such as storyboarding, wireframes, and mock-ups
- Providing iterative feedback on BI design such as dashboards and visualizations
- Working with prototypes or proofs-of-concept (POCs)
- Agile, prototyping, rapid application development (RAD), or other team-developing BI deliverables
- User training
- User acceptance testing (UAT), systems testing, and parallel testing, if applicable

If the business has the personnel resources that can participate as active members of the team, then the probability of success and quality of the deliverables is significantly enhanced. The BI project manager needs to develop schedules and resource plans that include both IT and business. Business participants need to understand what is expected of them, the level of effort required, and when their involvement is planned to happen.

Typically, the most valuable business participants are already overloaded with work and need their manager's commitment to free up their time to work on the BI project. It is the task of the IT group to determine realistically how much the business group really can and will contribute. Sometimes the business group says, with all good intentions, that it will be involved, but then does not have the resources to offer. The BI manager needs to be ever vigilant in monitoring the expected versus actual participation. If there is a variance, take corrective action. Avoid the common pitfall of tracking only IT resources while ignoring business participation. Too many BI projects have been derailed because lack of business participation led to schedule slip and adversely affected deliverables, completely surprising the stakeholders.

BUILD THE BI PROGRAM LIKE A SOFTWARE FIRM

BI is not a one-time effort; you are in it for the long haul. So, the BI program needs to be built iteratively and allowed to grow incrementally. This approach accelerates business value, enables business agility, and ultimately lowers the total cost of ownership. Successful BI programs incrementally add data and analytical capabilities, expand the number of business processes and business BI consumers, and increase the supporting infrastructure and software.

There is often pressure to lay out a very high-level BI program plan quickly and almost immediately jump into BI development. This happens because there is an attitude that getting into hands-on development as soon as possible is desirable, and that people will figure out the details of the BI program as they go along. This approach turns every project into a standalone project needing to define its own infrastructure, data, and analytics capabilities. These standalone projects typically under-invest in infrastructure, short-change architecture, and fail to leverage potentially interconnected or shared work across projects. The BI program needs to plan not just the deliverables, but the "how" of those deliverables. Examining the program holistically enables you to plan the projects, building the long-term BI framework (architecture, data, integration, analytics and skills) incrementally and iteratively in a deliberate manner.

Think of the way a software company builds and updates its product. Just as with a BI program, a software product is going to evolve and expand over time. The software firm will develop and release an initial product V1.0, and follow that with incremental updates that add features and fix bugs. They take customer feedback into account as they decide what new functionality needs to be added. As they move forward, they will announce their product roadmap and software release schedule, laying out the growth in capability and features. Enterprises, therefore, should plan and manage their BI programs as if they were software products: design, schedule, and communicate a program roadmap and release schedule.

Figure 18.5 illustrates a sample template for a BI program release schedule with the following key attributes filled in:

> See the book Web site www.BIguidebook.com for a BI program release planning template you can fill in.

- **Timeframe:** typically the month or quarter that major project or releases are completed
- **Key deliverables** in regard to analytical functionality or reports/dashboards

PROGRAM RELEASE	1.0	2.0	3.0	4.0
Timeframe				
Key Deliverables				
Business Sponsors				
Business Constituency				
Business Processes				
Business Applications				
Data Subjects				
Source Systems				
SLAs				
Applications Retired				
Technology Required				
Budget Allocation				
Project Team (IT & Business)				
Participating Resources (outside direct project team)				

FIGURE 18.5

Business intelligence program release planning template.

- **Business sponsors:** the business groups and executive funding the project
- **Business constituency:** the business groups that will use the resulting deliverables
- **Business process** affected by the release, and whether BI deliverables will be embedded in those processes
- **Business applications** involved in data integration or analytics
- **Data subjects** needed for analytics, extracted or integrated
- **Source systems** from which data is gathered, and extraction frequencies
- **Service level agreements (SLAs)** may be established for such factors as data currency, data load times (occur when there are data loading time periods that are agreed upon with source applications), query performance (typically associated with specific datasets or dashboards), length of time data is available, etc.
- **Applications retired**, if applicable, along with retirement criteria and dependencies
- **Technology required:** includes hardware, software, and cloud services, along with corresponding licenses and versions
- **Budget allocation**, if applicable, with capital, labor, and other expenses
- **Project team (IT and business)**
- **Participating resources** outside of the full-time BI project team

BALANCING A BI PROGRAM

As with any project, there are always trade-offs between the resources and time available in relation to the results desired. Since the luxury of unlimited resources and time are seldom a reality, this balancing act is common. As shown in Figure 18.6, the BI project manager needs to balance along the three

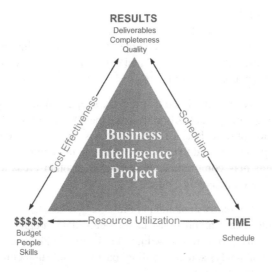

FIGURE 18.6

Business intelligence project—trade-offs.

dimensions of results, resources, and time. But even within these dimensions, further trade-offs can occur:

- **Results:** BI deliverables are a combination of software and data, and as such, much of the deliverables are hidden from the business people. Because of this, a BI project manager can adjust the deliverables of that project from a functional perspective, and can even change the completeness or quality of the deliverables.
- **Resources:** project resources can be adjusted based on labor such as IT staff, consultants, or business people; the quality of that labor, i.e., skills and experience; the budget; and the investment in infrastructure, i.e., hardware, storage, memory, etc.
- **Time:** ironically, this is the one variable that is generally determined even before any other variables. It is very common for the business sponsors to assign a completion date before any planning occurs. In one common scenario, there are particular business events that require the availability of BI deliverables. In this particular case, the BI program manager uses a time-boxed approach where time is fixed in the scope of the deliverables (results) and resources are variable. The second most common scenario, and one that is very reasonable when planning out an entire BI program, is to set up specific time intervals for the BI project release, again another time-boxed approach. BI project results and resources vary; all time is fixed.

A BI project is a very complex application with many factors influencing the scope: resources, results, and schedule. Some of the other key factors affecting the scope of a BI project include:

- Complexity and variety of analytical functionality
- Complexity and number of dashboards, reports, and visualizations
- Amount of data detail
- Amount of historical data
- Data currency or latency
- Complexity and extent of data integration
- Complexity and extent of data quality
- Number, variety, complexity, velocity, and volume of data sources (internal and external)
- Number of supported business users (internal and external) and variety of analytical styles
- Privacy, security, and regulatory requirements

Each of the above factors can be modified to affect the scope. Often, changes to scope are not readily apparent until the business people actually start using the BI deliverables hands-on, and even then it may take an extended period of time. Each of these attributes, therefore, needs to be defined and documented to set business expectations and to effectively manage the BI project.

Unfortunately, BI teams may compromise or short-change other areas to meet resource and time constraints that might not be immediately evident:

- **Testing:** unit, UAT, system, regression, and parallel
- **Documentation:** requirements, architecture, data models, data integration specifications and data mapping, BI specifications, production schedules, application and system workflows
- **Discovery:** source system analysis, data profiling, business and subject matter expert (SME) interviews, and background documents

Just like the scoping factors previously discussed, these areas also need to be defined and the level of effort agreed on to effectively manage the project and avoid unexpected and potentially harmful errors or omissions in the BI deliverables.

INTERNAL MARKETING OF THE BI PROGRAM

An important task for the BI project manager is to create and execute a communication strategy during the life of the project. This includes scheduled status reporting, providing ongoing project information, and enabling stakeholder feedback. Besides scheduling meetings, there are many types of collaboration tools that enable all levels of communication.

It is a mistake to assume that your key players know about current developments taking place in the BI program. There is often a need to increase internal awareness and market the BI program within the company. Business results are key to getting a project staffed and implemented, so an internal awareness and marketing campaign can be essential. Even after the project is approved and budgeted, it is important to engage business sponsors, IT staff, and future program users to promote enthusiasm and involvement in the new endeavor. Otherwise, although your project might be viewed as successful, funding may be cut anyway because of the business perception that it is already "good enough."

The benefits of the program are not always obvious. Business group members may not be "connecting the dots" between what information they ultimately need to do their jobs and the process it will take to get them that information. Someone may have to make crystal clear the business value of the investments necessary for a BI project—and this is not a one-time effort; you may need to have an ongoing plan to assess the success of the BI program by gauging the perceptions and expectations of the business people and sponsors.

Also, just because a business group's "power user" is on board and up-to-speed on the BI program, other critical members of the business group might not be so well informed. There might be a communication gap within the business group.

Before diving into the marketing work, meet with business users and sponsors to determine the perception of the program and future expectations. Then conduct a gap analysis to see where the needs are, and formulate an internal awareness and marketing campaign to increase the likelihood of successfully moving your program forward.

The marketing campaign might consist of a series of presentations, workshops, or training sessions delivered to business sponsors, business group members who will use it (existing or desired), and the IT team. The content should cover the business benefits of the BI program and should include workshops to provide information on what is involved in BI from a business, technology, and project perspective. These workshops should help with knowledge transfer and setting the right expectations for your program.

Effective marketing methods include:

- Enterprise portal, if applicable, where business group or program information is typically posted
- Collaboration tools used to share information, solicit feedback, and communicate information among stakeholders
- Social media, such as blogs
- Case studies or testimonials (just like product vendors)
- Lunch (or breakfast) and learn sessions (in person or web conferencing)
- Tutorials (web videos) posted for learning and understanding what is available

A BI program manager's choices will depend on organizational culture and enterprise standards. The BI program manager must monitor and manage all marketing campaigns. Privacy, security, and governmental regulations all need to be considered.

BI ASSESSMENT

Before kicking off any BI project, there are many questions to be answered. What is the scope? What is the best way to proceed? How long will it take? How much will it cost and how much do we have to spend? Who needs to be involved? What products do we need? And so on. An assessment helps answer these questions and keep a project on track. It can be done either internally or by an outside consultant.

The end result of the BI assessment is a BI roadmap or program to achieve your business and technical objectives in a manner that is as cost and resource efficient as possible. Ideally, the roadmap should include a few potential scenarios providing different capability, timeline, and cost possibilities. To develop the roadmap, you'll need to examine the four subject areas shown in Figure 18.7 in sufficient detail to quantify and qualify the roadmap's plans, budgets, and timeline.

Done before a project begins, the BI assessment will help flesh out the scope and design. With detailed information on feedback and priorities, you can further refine your project schedule, resource plans, and deliverables, while mitigating risk. You will use this information to assess the status of the company in its BI program, where it should be, and what its current capabilities are. These observations will help refine objectives in terms of project, people, processes, and technology.

The high-level depiction of the BI assessment is provided in Figure 18.8. As this shows, the assessment covers these three dimensions:

- Architecture: information, data, technology and product
- Requirements and priorities: business and IT
- People: organization, governance, projects, and skills

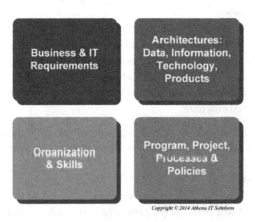

FIGURE 18.7

Business intelligence assessment: four subject areas.

Figure 18.9 shows how to conduct your assessment in three phases: discovery, analysis, and recommendations.

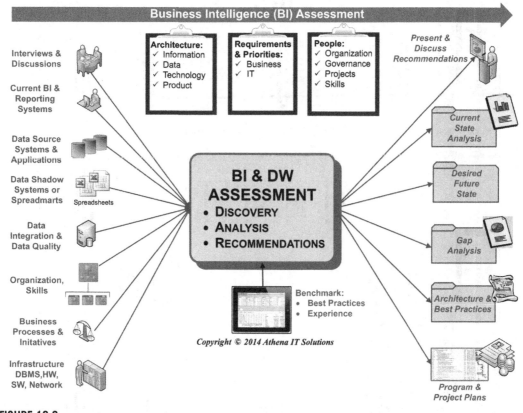

FIGURE 18.8

BI assessment framework.

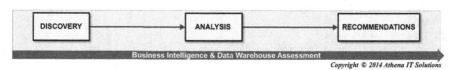

FIGURE 18.9

Three phases of business intelligence assessment.

DISCOVERY PHASE—ASSESS CURRENT ENVIRONMENT

The discovery phase, shown in Figure 18.10, explores the following areas:

- Business and IT requirements
- Organization, partnerships, processes, and skills
- Data, information, technology, and product architectures

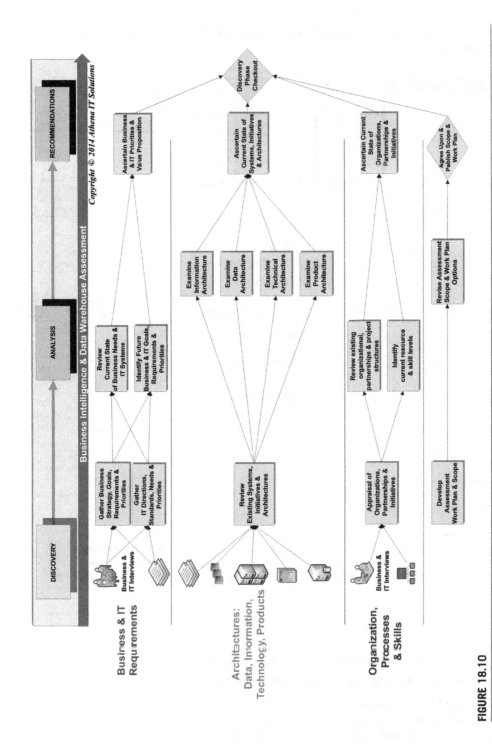

FIGURE 18.10

Business intelligence assessment: discovery tasks.

The figure contains the following labels:

Business Intelligence & Data Warehouse Assessment

DISCOVERY ANALYSIS RECOMMENDATIONS

Copyright © 2014 Athena IT Solutions

Business & IT Requirements

- Business & IT Interviews
- Gather Business Strategy, Goals, Requirements & Priorities
- Gather IT Directions, Standards, Needs & Priorities
- Review Current State of Business Needs & IT Systems
- Identify Future Business & IT Goals, Requirements & Priorities
- Ascertain Business & IT Priorities & Value Proposition

Architectures: Data, Information, Technology, Products

- Review Existing Systems, Initiatives & Architectures
- Examine Information Architecture
- Examine Data Architecture
- Examine Technical Architecture
- Examine Product Architecture
- Ascertain Current State of Systems, Initiatives & Architectures

Organization, Processes & Skills

- Business & IT Interviews
- Appraisal of Organizations, Partnerships & Initiatives
- Review existing organizational, partnerships & project structures
- Identify current resource & skill levels
- Ascertain Current State of Organizations, Partnerships & Initiatives

- Develop Assessment Work Plan & Scope
- Revise Assessment Scope & Work Plan Options
- Agree Upon & Publish Scope & Work Plan

Discovery Phase Checkout

Much of the information gathering for this phase is done through interviews with IT and business people, such as business sponsors, key members of business staff who will likely use the BI environment, and potential business power users. The following list highlights the subjects to discuss with business group members:

- **Desired reporting and analysis:** what capabilities do they need and what data do they need to get?
- **Current reporting and data shortcomings and workarounds:** this information will help you with the gap analysis
- **Priorities:** what is most important for them in terms of the BI project and the information they need for decision-making?
- **Analytical skills:** what skills do they already have?

IT staff to be interviewed include potential project team members, DBAs, project management, and IT management. The IT discussions should include an overview of the existing application and reporting environment and then reviewing more details regarding the architectures, requirements, and future plans. Have the following discussions with IT:

- IT directions/plans, project methodology, product standards, application direction
- Skill level in database, reporting/BI, data modeling, applications
- Review source systems/applications
    - Major business applications: overview, reporting, database/OS
    - Other business applications, spreadsheets, or access databases that are relevant to cross-group reporting
- Demos of reporting applications

Background materials to review during the discovery phase may include data source systems, data models, business and technical requirements, samples of existing reports or analysis conducted that will be replaced by the BI solution, existing technical infrastructure, current IT application plans, and business initiatives driving the need for BI.

ANALYSIS PHASE—IDENTIFY THE GAPS

During the analysis phase, you will review the conversations, discussions, and interviews along with the BI requirements and materials gathered in the discovery phase. The analysis involves examining the architecture, organization, and requirements in terms of where you are now and where you would like to move your BI environment. Determine the gaps between the two, validate your ability to achieve your future end state, and determine what you would need along all three of these dimensions to achieve success.

Figure 18.11 shows an overview of the analysis phase. The tasks for the analysis phase include:

- Developing a list of requirements for areas like enterprise-wide reporting, enterprise-wide shared data, and data cleansing needs
- Creating a list of current reporting capabilities
- Examining the business and IT group's skills and determining what training might be needed

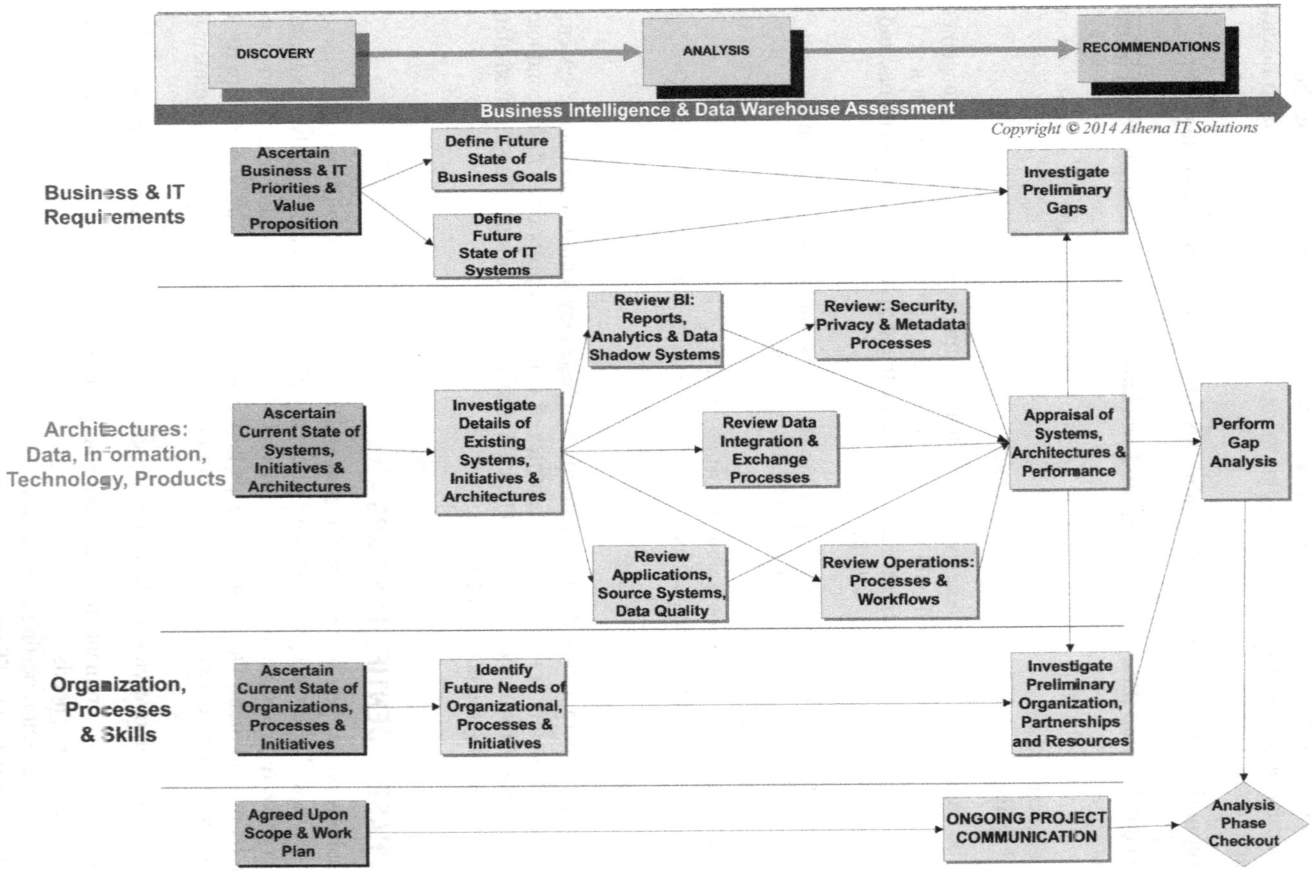
DISCOVERY
ANALYSIS
RECOMMENDATIONS
Business Intelligence & Data Warehouse Assessment
Copyright © 2014 Athena IT Solutions
Business & IT Requirements
Ascertain Business & IT Priorities & Value Proposition
Define Future State of Business Goals
Define Future State of IT Systems
Investigate Preliminary Gaps
Architectures: Data, Information, Technology, Products
Ascertain Current State of Systems, Initiatives & Architectures
Investigate Details of Existing Systems, Initiatives & Architectures
Review BI: Reports, Analytics & Data Shadow Systems
Review: Security, Privacy & Metadata Processes
Review Data Integration & Exchange Processes
Review Applications, Source Systems, Data Quality
Review Operations: Processes & Workflows
Appraisal of Systems, Architectures & Performance
Perform Gap Analysis
Organization, Processes & Skills
Ascertain Current State of Organizations, Processes & Initiatives
Identify Future Needs of Organizational, Processes & Initiatives
Investigate Preliminary Organization, Partnerships and Resources
Agreed Upon Scope & Work Plan
ONGOING PROJECT COMMUNICATION
Analysis Phase Checkout

FIGURE 18.11

Business intelligence assessment: analysis tasks.

- Performing a gap analysis of what is desired, what is reasonable, and what gets added to the to-do list for BI, data integration, data cleansing, and MDM
- Developing a product vendor short list
- Developing product demos for the recommendation phase. This may involve obtaining sample data and reports from the business and asking vendors to create the demos
- Developing a high-level program plan with timeline, costs, and resources
- Developing program and project plans, including high-level timeline, cost, and resources estimates, data sources, and reporting capabilities

RECOMMENDATIONS PHASE—SCOPE, PRIORITIES, AND BUDGET

During the recommendation phase, you will present the results of the analysis phase along with a roadmap that has a vision for the BI program. Ideally, it will also include an iterative series of projects to achieve your overall BI program objectives.

The recommendations phase will involve feedback and recommendations on the current state of your readiness in relation to your requirements and capabilities. These recommendations will involve your architecture (information, data, technology, and product) and your organization (program/project plans, resources/skills/training, and rough cost estimates.) See Figure 18.12 for an overview of the recommendations phase.

The tasks in this phase include:

- Reviewing the program roadmap with the business and IT to go over timeline/budget and the iterative implementation of the BI program
- Marketing the BI program to the business
- Reviewing the skills assessment for business and IT, discussing how it affects the timeline and product selection, and what training is then required
- Reviewing the product and technology roadmap with IT, including product shortlists and demos

WORK BREAKDOWN STRUCTURE

Typically, the project manager is either a technology-oriented person without much project management background or a project manager without much BI experience. When enterprises are new to BI, it is likely that the project manager will not have any BI or project management background.

There is a tendency in BI projects to require the project manager to develop a detailed project schedule before any work gets underway. If the BI project manager has limited or no experience with BI and/or project management, then this is likely an impossible task. This is a difficult task, even if the person has experience in project management, because of the complexity of a BI project. There are often many unknowns or high-level-only requirements at the beginning of the project, making it difficult to create a detailed project schedule. The best project management approach at the beginning of both the BI program and any BI project is to define a WBS prior to developing any project schedule.

See the book Web site at www.BIguidebook.com for a WBS template.

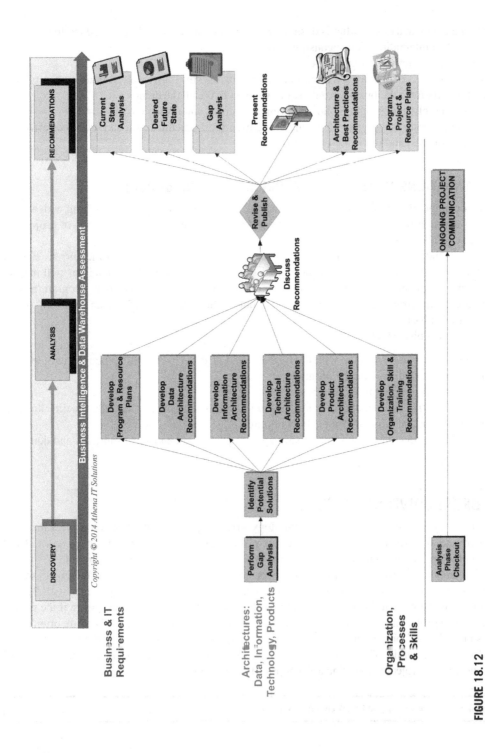

FIGURE 18.12

Business intelligence assessment: recommendations tasks.

WBS DEFINED

The WBS concept was developed by the U.S. Department of Defense in the early 1960s and later documented by the Project Management Institute for use outside the defense industry. WBS is a project management technique that incrementally decomposes a project into smaller components based on its deliverables. It is visually represented as a hierarchical or tree structure.

With WBS you start with the project's ultimate objective, then successively subdivide it into smaller, manageable components that scope out areas such as deliverables, time, resources, cost, and span of responsibility. Each component or node in the tree structure needs to have a defined scope, timeframe, budget, resources, and person responsible for its delivery.

WBS provides a framework to plan, schedule, and manage a BI program and individual BI projects. It is important to note that the primary purpose of the WBS is to decompose the project by deliverables rather than defining a detailed, task-oriented project schedule. Developing a detailed project schedule is a natural follow-on creating a WBS.

When dealing with a systems integrator (SI) or outside contractor, use a WBS to create the statement of work (SOW) for the SI, who then develops a proposal with detailed plans and costs. Even if an SI is not engaged in the BI project, the BI stakeholders should consider the WBS to be its SOW.

WBS DESIGN PRINCIPLES

There are several principles that help with the design and development of the WBS. They use parent-child terminology to describe levels. They are as follows:

- **100-percent rule:** a WBS contains 100% of the work required to deliver all project deliverables. Each level in the hierarchy needs to be equal to 100% of the project, and the children of each parent need to represent the totality of their parent.
- **Mutual exclusivity:** every node in the WBS needs to be exclusive to the parent and not overlap with any other branches in the tree structure. Besides enforcing the 100-percent rule, the purpose of this is to eliminate ambiguity and duplicate work.
- **Plan deliverables:** a WBS is a breakdown of the project's deliverables or scope rather than activities. Concentrating on what will be delivered rather than how it will be delivered keeps a WBS from getting bogged down into too many details and becoming too time-consuming to develop.
- **8/80 rule:** the WBS components at the lowest level of detail should not require fewer than 8 hours of effort, or the WBS will be too detailed. In addition, the most detailed components should not require more than 80 hours of work, otherwise it is assumed that the components are too high-level to manage. The 8/80 rule is not an absolute rule, but rather a "rule of thumb" that experienced, successful project managers follow.

A project may have multiple WBSs representing different views of the project from various stakeholders' perspectives. The two most common WBS structures for an application development project are:

- **Functional-oriented breakdown:** representing the viewpoint of one or more categories of the stakeholders. These categories may be the business sponsors and the business people who will use the resulting BI application.
- **Project-oriented breakdown:** representing the stakeholders involved in the day-to-day management of the project or its execution.

When multiple WBSs are created, each needs to follow the rules specified above and, in addition, needs to be connected to the underlying project plan to ensure completeness and control. Using multiple WBSs enables more effective communication and better program and project management with a diverse project stakeholder community.

MULTIPLE WBSs FOR BI

Using WBSs is a very effective project management tool for planning and developing BI solutions. Too often, the planning and scheduling of a BI project becomes a project unto itself, consuming a large part of the time that was thought to be used for designing, developing and deploying the solution. Because the WBS does not involve creating the project task-oriented schedule, the BI project manager can determine project scope and estimate the time, cost, and resources needed by decomposing deliverables, while not getting bogged down in the minutia of the tasks. In addition, since the WBS is independent of any specific project methodology, the BI project manager is not forced into a one-size-fits-all project approach. The BI project manager can tailor the methodology choice based on the project scope and BI maturity of the enterprise. In fact, for more complex or larger projects, it is recommended to use a hybrid approach for the project methodology. This is described further in this chapter.

There are several WBSs to support the design, development, deployment, and expansion of an enterprise BI solution:

- BI program WBS
- BI project WBS
- BI architecture WBS

BI Program WBS

The WBS is an effective planning tool for an overall BI program. Just as a software firm would plan out its product development over series of releases that incrementally and iteratively expand its functionality, so too should a BI program be planned. The BI program's WBS decomposes the program into a series of releases with their own scope, i.e., deliverables, timeframe, and costs, as depicted in Figure 18.13. Each of the BI releases is then decomposed into the underlying functionality and data that will be delivered.

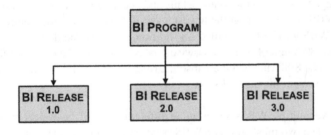

FIGURE 18.13

Work breakdown structure— business intelligence (BI) program.

BI Project WBS

Create a BI program WBS prior to creating the individual BI project WBS. As depicted in Figure 18.14, the BI project WBS is broken down at the highest level by project phases (more on this in the project

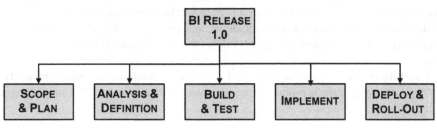

FIGURE 18.14

Work breakdown structure—business intelligence (BI) project by program phase.

task section of this chapter). Each of the phases is then broken down by its key deliverables. Each one of the deliverables is further broken down into more detailed underlying deliverables, but as mentioned previously the decomposition should not go down to task level nor should it get too detailed.

This WBS is an effective planning tool to develop a list of the key deliverables showing their interdependencies, level of effort, estimated cost, planned resources, and milestone dates. This WBS describes what will be built and what resources are needed, but does not yet discuss how it will be built, which is deferred to other project management activities.

This WBS is an effective communication tool between stakeholders because it deals with the "what's" rather than the "how's." The BI project WBS is used to solicit budget and resource commitments along with agreement about schedule milestones.

BI Architecture WBS

The third WBS is tied to the BI architecture, and has proven to be very useful at planning architectural deliverables and components for the BI program and individual BI projects. As depicted in Figure 18.15, the BI program or project is broken into the four BI architectures: information, data, technical, and project. (See the discussion in Part III of this book.)

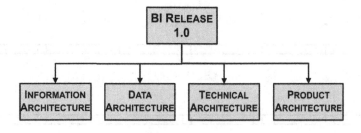

FIGURE 18.15

Work breakdown structure—business intelligence (BI) architecture.

Each of the architectural nodes is further broken down into the deliverables and components of that specific architecture:

- **Information architecture** contains the BI applications that will be developed and then will be broken down further until the lowest level of detail is specific BI dashboards, visualizations, or reports.
- **Data architecture** is broken into data integration deliverables related to data sourcing and the BI data structures used for analytics, such as data warehouses (DWs), data marts, and cubes.

- **Technology architecture** is broken down into the underlying technologies that are used to create the BI deliverables. Technologies may include BI, analytics, data integration, databases, data profiling, data modeling, data cleansing, MDM, source control, job scheduling, storage, and appliances.
- **Project architecture** is broken down by the delivery and availability of specific products. At the highest level, this may include product categories, while at the lowest level it may list specific products.

BI ARCHITECTURAL PLAN

The BI architecture WBS defines the key deliverables and components for the overall BI program, and is the companion to the BI Program WBS that defines the key business BI deliverables for the program. This enables the BI program manager to examine the program deliverables holistically and then determine the best sequence for incrementally developing the architecture. Once this is done, the manager can assign the architectural component to individual projects to design, develop, and deploy. As depicted in Figure 18.16, the four architectures span each phase in the individual BI projects.

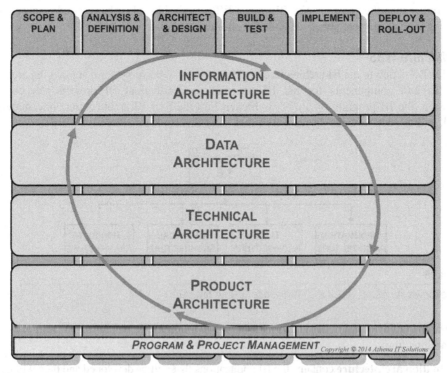

FIGURE 18.16

Business intelligence project phases with four architectures.

The BI program manager should define four architectural plans:

- Information
- Data
- Technical
- Product

The information architecture plan defines what BI functionality needs to be built and what data will be accessed in the context of the business requirements for the BI solution. This plan should detail the following:

- Business applications accessed
- Business processes impacted
- Business and data subjects used
- Business groups and business people defining and using BI solution
- BI and analytic capabilities required

The data architecture plan defines what data is used to support the information architecture. This plan should detail the following:

- Data sources
  - Source applications, databases, and files
  - Subset of data accessed: tables, columns, fields
  - Historical data requirements
- Data integration and transformation
- Data quality and cleansing
  - Processing requirements
  - Metrics and monitoring
- Define requirements for changes in historic data and approaches for:
  - AS-IS, AS-WAS and AS-PLANNED data difference
  - Slowly changing dimensions
- Data currency or latency
- Handling of errors, omissions, and exceptions

The technology architecture plan lists what technology is needed to support the information and data architectures:

- BI and analytic tools
- Data integration or extract, transform, and load (ETL)
- Application integration
- Database
- Data modeling
- Data profiling
- Metadata management
- Application development: source code management, job scheduling, backups, recovery

The product architecture plan lists what products are needed to support the technology architecture above. The products selected should comply with the appropriate enterprise standards, although often the BI project introduces many new technologies and products into the enterprise. If particular technologies and products are not being used by the enterprise, then it is likely that the BI project team will need to conduct a product evaluation and selection process. See Chapter 7 for more details.

BI PROJECTS ARE DIFFERENT

From a high-level perspective, project plans for a BI application look very similar to a typical IT application development project. In fact, the project phases can be identical. However, there are fundamental differences between BI and typical IT applications that significantly affect the selection of the appropriate project methodology and the detailed breakdown of its project plan.

These differences are summarized in Table 18.1.

Whereas most companies standardize their business transactional processing and select enterprise resource planning (ERP) to implement that processing, BI has remained a highly customized application. From a high level, there are BI functions and data subject areas that are common within industry groups or business functions such as finance, sales, or marketing. However, the details and specific implementations of those functions and data structures vary widely from enterprise to enterprise. Business performance metrics and detailed data used in the calculation will vary wildly not only across

Table 18.1 Key Differences between Enterprise Applications and BI Applications		
	Enterprise Applications (Transaction Oriented)	**Business Intelligence and Data Warehouse**
Purpose	Creating and updating data	Querying data
Performance criteria	Transaction throughput	Query response time; data latency may be a criteria
Business focus	Business operations	Business management and planning
Data	• Highly volatile • Process (application) oriented • Current data	• Typically read-only • Subject oriented • Current and historical data
Requirements	Well defined, both in terms of data and functionality	Will change and expand; analytical functionality will expand
Data structures	Nonredundant, normalized, 3NF	Hybrid dimensional schema (best)
Query types	Typically select rows related to a specific business transaction for a specific timeframe	Typically spans (joins) many tables spanning an extended timeframe
Consumers	Business operations	Business at all levels and potentially partners, suppliers, prospects, customers, and other stakeholders
Owners	IT owns and manages enterprise applications	Typically mix of IT and business, but not necessarily coordinated

enterprises, but sometimes across business groups within the same enterprise. Although an enterprise can bring in an expert in a particular ERP application to implement their application with much certainty for business and data requirements, that certainty does not exist when implementing an enterprise-specific BI implementation that is highly customized.

Not only is each BI implementation highly customized at the detail level, but, typically, the details will not be readily apparent at the beginning of the project, regardless of how thorough the discovery processes for business data requirements. Not until the business people actually start using BI applications along with the associated data can the BI team complete the detailed business and data requirements. As we discussed in Chapter 16, much of detail processing that the business is using to gather and analyze data is hidden in undocumented spreadsheets and data silos.

The primary difference between selecting a project methodology and defining a detailed project plan is the uncertainty in the business data requirements at the beginning of the project. This means that the typical waterfall methodology—in which business people communicate their requirements and then IT implements a project to satisfy them—will not work. This one of the key reasons that most BI projects fail to meet business expectations.

PROJECT METHODOLOGIES

A systems development life cycle (SDLC), sometimes called an application development methodology, is the term used by software engineers and IT professionals to describe the process used to plan, design, develop, test, and deploy software applications. Software engineers working within a technology firm will always use an SDLC when developing and maintaining software products that are sold to customers. IT professionals, on the other hand, might not use a formal project methodology when developing their applications. This is especially true in small to medium-sized businesses, but is also evident even in larger enterprises.

The primary reason for the difference between software engineers and IT professionals is that software engineers are developing and maintaining the products that their company sells. These software products are therefore the assets of the technology companies and need to be treated as such. Using a common project methodology is the best way for technology firms to design, maintain, support, and expand their products. Using a methodology enables a technology firm to better manage its resources, makes it easier to plan, and establishes documentation as part of the deliverables.

In contrast, the applications that the IT group develops for its company typically are not viewed as an enterprise asset, and the IT group is often viewed as overhead or a company cost center. In addition, business people want their application ASAP and are typically unconcerned about, or unaware of, how that application has been built. With these viewpoints, it is not surprising that a software development project methodology is typically not high on the priority list of many IT groups.

Another difference between IT and software engineers is the "accidental" application phenomena. It is a very common scenario for a business person to ask IT to develop something for them "quick and dirty" with the intention of the code being a one-off. However, the business person starts using it and then goes back and asks IT to add more to it. This continues, resulting in an application that was never designed because it was never planned in the first place. This is the same phenomenon that occurs when a one-off spreadsheet becomes a full-fledged data shadow system. Under this scenario, IT would never use a formal project methodology to build the application.

Without a software development project methodology, it is common for large projects to be late, over budget, or fail to deliver business value, while smaller projects may produce short-term praise but typically create redundant or fragmented data silos. Other shortcomings from failing to use a methodology are:

- BI applications are typically not documented
- Testing gets short-changed
- The application gets increasingly difficult to support
- The application becomes more costly to expand

To succeed both in the short run managing individual BI projects and in the long run in a sustained and expanding BI program, IT groups need to use software development project methodologies. The key for this to happen is that an enterprise must believe that the information used in analytics is a corporate asset, as are the BI applications that transform data into that business information. When both BI applications and information are considered corporate assets, the need for software development project methodologies becomes clear.

BATTLING PROJECT METHODOLOGIES

There has been a battle in recent years regarding which project methodology an enterprise should use for business intelligence: waterfall versus agile. The *waterfall* methodology has been the traditional approach used in the industry, while *agile* is a newer approach that is especially popular in Web development.

Waterfall

The waterfall methodology uses a sequential or linear approach to software development. The project is broken down into a sequence of tasks, with the highest level grouping referred to as *phases*. A true waterfall approach requires phases that are completed in sequence and have formal exit criteria, typically a sign-off by the project stakeholders. A typical list of waterfall tasks would include:

- Scope and plan project
- Gather and document requirements
- Design application
- Develop application and perform unit tests
- Conduct system testing
- Perform UAT
- Fix application as appropriate
- Deploy application

The waterfall methodology is a formal process, with each phase comprising a list of detail tasks with accompanying documentation and exit criteria. Larger enterprises often require the use of SDLC methodology products, particularly in larger IT application projects. This is also the approach that SIs use when building IT applications for their customers, since budget, resources, deliverables, and scope have to be managed on a very disciplined basis.

The advantages of the waterfall methodology are that:

- Requirements are completed early in the project, enabling the team to define the entire project scope, create a complete schedule, and design the overall application.
- It improves resource utilization because tasks can be split to be worked in parallel or grouped to leverage resource skills.
- It is a better application design because there is a more complete understanding of all the requirements and deliverables.
- The project status is more easily measured based on a complete schedule and resource plan.

The disadvantages of the waterfall methodology are that:

- It is often difficult, particularly in BI, to get complete business requirements up front in a project, because business people have not really thought through in detail what they need, and business requirements can change during the project.
- It requires a very detailed breakdown of the tasks and deliverables for the overall BI application, which may be beyond the project team's capability or experience at the start of the project.
- Although waterfall projects do not inherently have to span lengthy periods of time, it is very common for these projects to span months or quarters because of the emphasis on trying to get everything done at one time, i.e., the "big bang" approach. The likelihood of projects being late, over budget, and failing to meet expectations rises as the timeframe for an IT project significantly increases.

Agile

The primary alternative to waterfall is the agile project methodology. Agile is an iterative team-based approach where requirements and deliverables evolve through cross-functional collaboration. Rather than creating schedules with detail tasks, a list of deliverables is defined, with the team gathering requirements and creating the deliverables in time-boxed phases called *sprints*. Time boxing is a project planning technique where a fixed time period is assigned to deliverables (scope) and resources rather than the traditional, i.e., waterfall, approach that fixes scope and then determines the time and resources necessary to implement. With the typical agile workflow:

- Deliverables are prioritized by the business consumer and assigned to a sprint
- Requirements gathering, design, development, and testing are completed during the sprint
- Business consumers are active in each sprint, reviewing and evaluating work
- Any work not completed is reprioritized for future deliverables
- The work iterates into the next sprint and loops through same sequence

The emphasis of the agile methodology is rapid and iterative development with considerable interaction between the developers and the business people who will be the application customers. This methodology is popular in Web development and garners a lot of enthusiasm from many industry pundits.

The advantages of the agile methodology are:

- By isolating individual deliverables, work is highly focused and time to completion is accelerated
- Customers are highly involved, enabling more interaction in development and greater ownership of results
- Business requirements are communicated during development, rather than up front as with waterfall, due to customer engagement

The disadvantages of the agile methodology are:

- Individual deliverables are time boxed and rapid, but to achieve this, scope might be reduced and quality of deliverables compromised
- If the overall project requires many interdependent deliverables, then the lack of an overall architecture and framework may result in, at best, a suboptimal design and, at worst, a system whose parts do not work together
- With larger projects, there may be wide variance in expectations about project costs, overall functionality, and quality

THE FALSE CHOICE BETWEEN PROJECT METHODOLOGIES

The battle of waterfall versus agile project methodologies is not as clear cut as advocates of each methodology proclaim. There are assumptions about selecting a single methodology that are false or misleading:

- A specific methodology will work on any type of IT application project
- A specific methodology will work on any size project in regard to scope, resources, deliverables, and time
- There are only two choices of methodologies: waterfall or agile
- Only one methodology can be used by an enterprise

Misleading Examples

When debating the use of waterfall versus agile, advocates base their choice on experience with specific types of IT applications. Waterfall advocates base their experience on developing enterprise applications that are transactional oriented, while agile advocates typically use the creation of standalone BI dashboards, reports, or visualizations. The comparison of the project characteristics between these two types of applications is outlined in Table 18.2.

The key take-away from the comparison is that neither application being used for comparison truly reflects a full life-cycle BI project that includes data sourcing, data integration, database design, and likely multiple BI dashboards, reports, or visualizations. The enterprise application does have the same

Table 18.2 Differences between Enterprise and BI Applications		
	Enterprise Applications (Transaction Oriented)	**BI Dashboards, Reports, and Visualizations**
Methodology	Waterfall	Agile
Scope	Business process or enterprise	Typically limited to specific group of business people and processes
Data	Well defined	Assumed in place
Data integration	Not applicable	Not applicable
Functionality	Well defined	Needs to be defined

scope as a BI project; however, the BI project does not have well-defined functionality or data require-ments. The standalone BI dashboard does share the lack of well-defined functional requirements with the BI project; however, it assumes that the data is in place, no data integration is needed, and the scope is typically limited. It appears, based on these characteristics, that neither waterfall nor agile method-ologies are appropriate fits for a BI project.

One Size Does Fit All

BI project teams range from dozens of IT staff with dedicated roles—such as ETL developer, business analyst, or BI developer in a large enterprise—to a two-to-three person team where every person is involved in all types of development roles. Waterfall works well with large teams but not so much with the small team, where people are frequently switching between roles. Agile, on the other hand, works extremely well with small, dedicated, standalone teams, but its strength works against it when many small teams have to work together in an interdisciplinary fashion.

Based on these characteristics, the selection of waterfall versus agile is more influenced by team size and whether many people working in small groups need to interoperate.

More Than Two Choices

Waterfall and agile are not the only methodologies that are available for a project manager to choose from. The various options include:

- **Incremental development:** mix of waterfall and iterative development methodologies
- **Spiral development:** mix of waterfall and prototyping development methodologies
- **Rapid application development (RAD):** iterative development methodology using prototypes
- **Prototyping:** not a formal methodology for large projects but an approach to iteratively develop-ing applications
- **Object oriented:** object-oriented analysis and design methodology
- **Unified process:** an iterative development methodology framework based on unified modeling language (UML)

The agile methodology also has variations such as extreme programming and scrum.

Mixing Project Methodologies

Both incremental and spiral development methodologies are really plans of waterfall and iterative methodologies. With these methodologies, waterfall is used for the overall project framework, with the project divided into subprojects that are developed iteratively. The subprojects may use miniwaterfall, prototyping, RAD, or agile methodologies to complete the deliverables. The overall project is tracked in the more traditional waterfall fashion.

HYBRID BI PROJECT METHODOLOGY

Our recommended BI project methodology is a hybrid approach using the incremental development methodology and some variation of iterative development such as prototyping, RAD, or agile. We will refer to this hybrid as the *BI iterative and incremental development methodology*. The comparison of the hybrid methodology with waterfall and agile is depicted in Table 18.3.

	Enterprise Applications (Transaction Oriented)	BI Dashboards, Reports and Visualizations	BI and DW (with Data Integration) Systems
Methodology	Waterfall	Agile	Hybrid: Iterative and incremental with agile, RAD, prototyping
Scope	Business process or enterprise	Typically limited to specific group of business people and processes	Enterprise, across business groups and processes; may expand to customers, prospects, partners, suppliers, and other stakeholders
Data	Well defined	Assumed in place	Data sources, historical quality and metrics need to be identified and documented; needs will expand
Data integration	Not applicable	Not application	Key functionality includes consistency, cleansing, quality, and MDM
Functionality	Well defined	Needs to be defined	Business requirements need to be defined but will change and expand; analytical functionality will expand

Table 18.3 BI Iterative and Increment Development Methodology

The BI methodology uses:

- Incremental methodology to define the BI program with its releases, i.e., BI projects
- Waterfall methodology to define an overall framework for an individual BI project and establish interdependencies between subprojects
- Iterative approach to design and develop applications within a subproject

The choice of the iterative development approach will be based on the enterprise's project management culture, project teams' experience, and the scope of the subproject. The choice of the specific iterative method is not as critical as commitment by the team to use that approach for that subproject.

See the book Web site at www.BIguidebook.com for an agile BI tasks template.

Regardless of how much time is spent gathering business requirements, it is inherent in the nature of BI development that the business people will either poorly grasp what their analytical and data needs are, or they will change those needs once they start hands-on with the BI application. Many teams following the waterfall methodology are frustrated with business people changing their minds and adding new functionality or modifying requirements, but those changes are inevitable. BI project teams need to understand that business people are BI consumers and these changes increase the business value of the BI applications. Therefore, they should adopt better methodologies to enable application improvements instead of pushing back.

BI PROJECT PHASES

At a high level, a BI project shares the same phases as a typical IT application development project. The project phases, as depicted in Figure 18.17, are:

1. Scope and plan
2. Analyze and define
3. Architect and design
4. Build, test and refine
5. Implement
6. Deploy and roll-out

The recommended BI project phases resemble an IT application development project that follows a waterfall methodology; however, it deviates from that methodology in several key aspects.

First, waterfall-based methodology requires that a phase must be completed before the next phase starts. Our recommended BI project structure has overlapping phases. And as a project is further decomposed into functional groupings that may be performed in parallel, as you will see later in this chapter, there may be several overlapping phases related to specific BI functionality. The functional groups are visually represented by "swim lanes," which is a processing modeling technique used in UML activity diagram modeling and business process modeling notation.

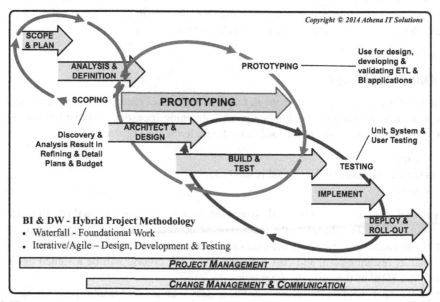

FIGURE 18.17

Project phases.

Second, as opposed to waterfall-based methodology that works sequentially from the start, our recommended BI structure incorporates three feedback or iteration loops. These feedback loops are:

1. **Scoping:** the initial iteration examining business, technical, and budgetary requirements is always performed at a high level. More detail is always necessary to refine those requirements and adjust deliverables, costs, resources, and timetable. Locking in the scope early and without enough details is a sure recipe for slipping schedule, exceeding budget, and ultimately failing to meet expectations. On the other hand, it is essential to establish some bounds on the requirements, costs, and timeframe at the beginning of the project. Building in the scoping feedback loop enables discovery, flexibility, and better buy-in to the project.

2. **Prototyping or development:** it is very common in BI and data warehousing projects to need to actually start working with the data, its integration, and the analytical capability before you get a chance to work on the functional design or truly understand its complexity. Writing complete detailed specs before the developers get hands-on with the data is a fool's exercise. As we discussed previously, the development feedback loop uses an iterative approach that may include the blended use of prototyping, RAD, or an agile methodology. The specific techniques to use are highly dependent on the complexity of the project, as well as the size and experience of the development team. Also, as we discussed in the WBS section, the development activities are split into various swim lanes with feedback loops identifying dependencies across the lanes.

3. **Testing:** this phase includes informal business group feedback and interaction; UAT; user testing; functional testing; system testing; and, potentially, regression or parallel testing. When dealing with the variety and time span of data, it is essential to build the feedback loop to deal with errors, omissions, and surprises. Many of the issues encountered during testing require changing the programs and then retesting. In addition, business people will often identify items that they forgot to ask for during the requirements gathering process. This feedback loop enables some, but not all, of these changes to be incorporated into the deliverables.

SCOPE AND PLAN PHASE

This phase involves defining project scope in terms of high-level requirements, timeframe, resources, and costs. It includes creating the project budget and obtaining sponsorship if that has not already been done. A key decision will be about who will actually undertake the project:

- Internal team
- Internal team augmented with external resources
- External team

If an external team is going to be used, then typically a request for proposal (RFP) process will be completed during this phase to select the team. This selection process will typically involve a written RFP sent out to candidates, who will then submit proposals with an SOW that includes deliverables, project schedule, resource plan, and cost estimates. The exit criteria will be a signed agreement that incorporates the SOW as the basis for the project.

Although the rigor of an RFP process is not necessary if an internal team is performing the BI project, it is still best practice to provide an SOW with the same content that an external vendor will provide (of course, without the sales and marketing materials).

> **WHAT ABOUT SCOPE CREEP?**
>
> BI projects are notorious for scope creep. The best way to manage scope creep is to avoid it. Some tactics for avoiding and managing it are:
>
> - Conduct BI assessments that clarify the requirements, scope, schedule, resources, budget, and products
> - Set realistic expectations, and communicate them clearly
> - Gain agreement on business rules and data definitions
> - Manage with iterative project phases and measurable goals
> - Leave some room in the schedule for changes and problems
> - Create and enforce a process for managing changes
> - Document changes, determining their impact on plan, making the agreed-upon project adjustments and adjusting the project baseline to reflect the revisions
> - Recognize "lily gilding"; sometimes that gold plating simply does not add value
> - Be willing to say "no" or "not yet"
> - Enlist sponsors and/or managers who are willing to back you up
> - Communicate, communicate, communicate on all issues ranging from project status, problems, changes requested, and the impact of those changes

There can be significant risks in this phase if the business and data requirement details are not clear. Analyzing the details may reveal unexpected issues regarding data quality and completeness, or may lead to changes in analytical requirements that will affect the scope and timeline of the project. One of the best practices for BI projects with vague requirements is to undertake a BI assessment. The BI assessment (discussed earlier in this chapter) is a combination of the first two phases of the BI project with an accompanying feedback loop. A BI assessment enables an iterative and stepwise refinement of the requirements, significantly reducing uncertainty and, more formally, revising scope and timelines in the initial phases of the project. This significantly reduces the likelihood that the project will be late and over budget, and better sets expectations for deliverables.

ANALYSIS AND DEFINITION PHASE

The key deliverables in this phase are detailed business, data, and quality requirements derived from the high-level requirements documented in the scope and plan phase. The analysis tasks examine what is being asked for and compare that to the current status of data in reporting. The in-depth comparison results in a gap analysis that reveals what can be leveraged, what needs to be replaced or retired, and what needs to be built.

From the data perspective, source system analysis is the key task to determine:

- what data is being asked for
- the current sources of that data
- most important, the state of the data: consistency, completeness, and quality

It is critical, when profiling data, to examine in detail the state of the data as far back in history as is needed by the business. As we discussed previously, data does not age well. Many BI projects have included unpleasant, last-minute surprises when historical data differed from current data because the project failed to look at that historical data in this phase.

Although IT and business people should be interacting throughout the project, this phase will be the most people-intensive portion of the project. Although there are certainly software tools to assist in profiling data and collaborating with stakeholders, analyzing and defining the detailed requirements includes intensive interaction between business BI consumers in the BI development team.

For more in-depth discussion of this phase, see Chapter 11, and Chapter 14.

ARCHITECT AND DESIGN PHASE

In this phase, the BI development team begins to feel that it is laying the foundations for the BI solutions. The key deliverables are the BI solution blueprints: information, data, technology, and product architectures. These include the design for data integration processing, business intelligence applications, data models, and their technology underpinnings.

This is a reminder that our project methodology is not a strict waterfall where previous phases have to be completed before subsequent phases can start. In our methodology, phases will overlap and will provide feedback for refinement of other phases. In this manner, the architectural blueprints can be designed, if resources are available, while the analysis and definition phase is underway. The architectural frameworks do not need all the details from the analysis phase to be designed. The frameworks are similar to an architect's blueprint of a house that lays out all the critical specifications, but leaves details such as bathroom fixtures and furniture to a later design.

The assumption in this phase is that technology and products have been acquired by the organization and the architectures use these in their design. If new products need to be selected and purchased, then the RFP process (in the scope and plan phase) needs to be expanded to incorporate this selection process.

For more in-depth discussion of this phase, see these other parts and chapters:

- Part III
- Part IV
- Chapter 12
- Chapter 14

BUILD, TEST, AND REFINE PHASE

As the architecture and design phase is underway, the construction phase, i.e., build, test, and refine can start. There have been many advances over the years in the technologies and products used to build, test, and implement BI solutions, as we discussed in Chapter 4 and Chapter 7. These advances have not only expanded BI functionality, but have improved productivity, quality, and time to market.

In addition, current technology has enabled much better interaction between the developers and the BI consumers in the design, testing, and refinement of the BI solutions. There are several alternative project methodologies to encourage this interaction such as agile, prototyping, proof of concept (POC), and RAD. Regardless of which methodology is used, the key to success is getting the business person involved in examining the solutions both from a data and BI functional viewpoint. A crucial mistake made by many projects is to have user involvement in the requirements and then re-engage the BI consumer for UAT. No matter how much time is spent on gathering requirements, business people will add to or modify those requirements once they start interacting with the data in the BI application. It is a fairly common occurrence for the business person to have forgotten detailed steps performed or data needed in the business process supported by the BI application being built. The best way to really get a complete set of process and data requirements is to have the business BI consumer interact with the BI application as it is being built and the data integrated.

For more in-depth discussion of this phase, see the following parts of this book:

- Part V
- Part VI

IMPLEMENTATION PHASE

The implementation phase is the first phase that shifts to primarily IT-oriented deliverables, which are:

- Migrating software and data to testing environments
- UAT
- System testing
- Parallel or regression testing, if applicable
- Migrating software and data into the production environments

In the past, the BI project team would work with the enterprise's in-house production support group to complete these tasks. Nowadays, it is much more common to have one or more components of the BI solution and hosted environments in the cloud rather than just residing in on-premise data centers. When the BI solution or portions thereof reside off-premise, the BI project team will likely coordinate with both their in-house production support and the off-premise production support.

It is critical that the processes are defined and the success criteria documented for each of these tasks. Nothing should be ambiguous regarding the success or failure of any of the testing processes. Before the start of each of these tests, business and IT have to be involved in committing to whatever criteria have been agreed to. The success criteria should be in the form of an SLA between the BI project team and the BI consumers, who are likely represented by the business sponsor.

Both cloud and virtualization technologies have enabled organizations to perform more complete and thorough testing much more cost effectively than they could ever do in the past. Successful testing is absolutely essential prior to deploying BI solutions to obtain BI business value and avoid the business costs of faulty decision making based on faulty BI applications.

For more in-depth discussion of the testing deliverables in this phase, see these parts of the book:

- Part V
- Part VI

Migrating software, sometimes referred to as promoting, from development to test environment and subsequently to a production environment, needs to follow a documented process with a checklist to ensure successful completion. It is recommended that both the application software and data migrate together from one level to another, along with any supporting documentation and procedures. The application software includes all the data integration, BI and any other software involved in moving, transforming, or analyzing data. The software also includes any procedures used to create or modify the data structures. In addition, the data model and applicable metadata should be included.

The primary objective of the implementation phase is to migrate the software and data into the production environment to deploy and roll out the BI solution.

DEPLOY AND ROLL-OUT PHASE

The moment of truth has arrived as the BI system goes into production and business people start using the BI applications in their daily jobs. This phase should be handled just the way a software firm would release a product to its customers, by offering:

- Product communication
- Product training
- Product support
- Product marketing

BI project communication channels—BI portal, collaboration tools, e-mails, social media, and meetings—should transition naturally in the deployment phase to an overall BI program perspective. The communication with the stakeholders should include status, timetables, support mechanisms, and training availability.

Business person BI training should include education on both how to use the BI application and what data is available with it. The BI educational plan developed during the build phase will be executed during this phase. Encourage business people to take the BI education before they use the application, as this will improve their productivity and significantly reduce misuse and misunderstanding of the system data.

The BI program should leverage any existing standard support processes, such as a help desk, that are deployed for IT applications. If not, the BI program needs to establish an effective support structure for its consumers.

It is best practice to provide at least two tiers of support. The first tier handles basic support issues such as gaining access to the software, connectivity issues, and an explanation of basic capabilities. This first tier handles the bulk of the support inquiries regarding BI. If basic instructions are segmented into easy-to-find explanations on a portal or Web site, sometimes even presented in a short video, then business people may be able to more quickly use the BI solution. Of course, a help desk process manned by IT staff will often be necessary because a business person may not even know what questions to ask. Business interaction with help desk personnel may be by phone, e-mail, chat, or a more formal help desk software package.

The second or higher level tiers supply more in-depth support. This high-level tier support is typically provided by the BI project team, the subject matter experts (SMEs) for the system. Typically, a business systems analyst (BSA) from the BI team is the first point of contact by the business person requesting support. In many cases, BSAs can answer the support inquiries, but when that is not possible they will confer with the BI project member whose expertise is needed.

The BI solution needs to be marketed during the deployment stage to the existing business people as well as any business groups and people that are being targeted for the roll out. Business people are busy, and no matter what the value of the BI solution, it will take a commitment of their time to get them trained and started in using it. You need to proactively market the business value to them.

BI PROJECT SCHEDULE

The BI project is composed of the six phases as depicted in Figure 18.17. These phases represent the full life cycle of a project from planning through deployment. An effective approach to creating a BI project schedule is to decompose the BI Project WBS (Figure 18.14) into greater levels of detail until it is sufficient to schedule tasks, assign resources and track progress. The level of detail will vary based on:

- Complexity of the project: more details
- How extensive an interactive methodology is used: fewer details, more milestones
- Enterprise project management standards: likely more details
- Project manager skills and BI knowledge

Divide BI project tasks and milestones into functional groupings. The groupings, which are visually represented by swim lanes in Figure 18.18, are:

- Business intelligence
- Data and database
- Data integration
- Infrastructure
- Program and project management

The functional groups are based on the three major technology categories (BI, data, and data integration) and the two enabling categories of infrastructure and project management. This is very useful in planning and managing related tasks and skills. These groupings serve the purpose of organizing by team skillsets and related tasks. As BI project teams or groups get larger, they will likely be organized along these same skillsets.

The swim lane visually illustrates the sequence of tasks as they iteratively and incrementally progress through a project. From this level of detail, the project manager should construct a detailed BI project plan with tasks, dependencies, and resource allocations. The initial level of detail or key tasks performed within the functional groupings are illustrated in Figure 18.19.

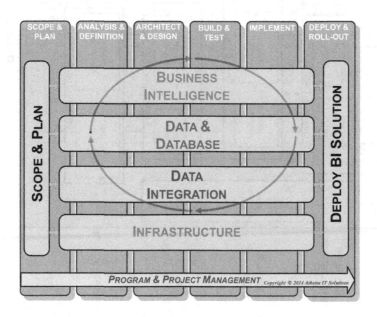

FIGURE 18.18

Business intelligence (BI) project work breakdown structure with functional groupings.

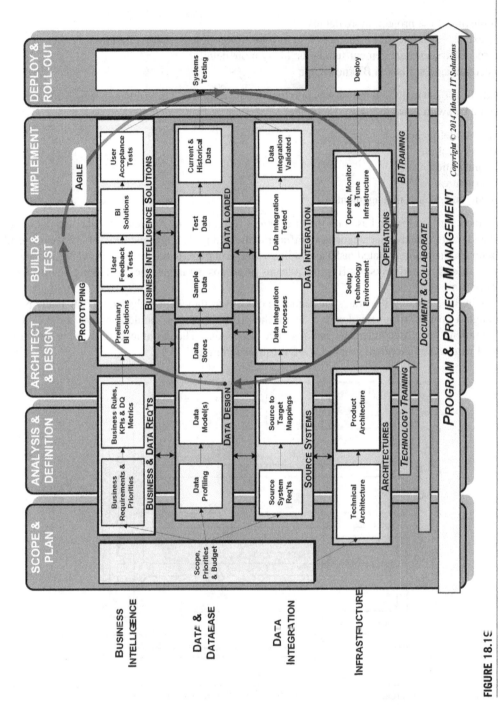

FIGURE 18.15

Business intelligence (BI) project work breakdown structure: functional groups with key tasks.

BI SWIM LANE

The BI functional group contains the primary set of activities (Figure 18.20) in which the BI project team interacts with its customers, i.e., business people. The BI team roles responsible for these tasks are BSA and BI developer. The project manager takes on the supporting role of account manager to the business people who are this project's stakeholders, serving as their advocate to ensure that their views and feedback are properly represented.

> See the book Web site at www.BIguidebook.com for a project schedule template that will help you get started.

This grouping is responsible for the two primary deliverables:

- Business and data requirements
- BI deliverables such as dashboards, visualizations, reports, or advanced analytics

The BSA works with the business BI stakeholders to gather, prioritize, and document business requirements, including analytical capabilities and data needed. The BSA delves into the details such as the business rules, transformations, algorithms, key performance indicators (KPIs), and data quality metric requirements. These requirements are likely to be further refined and modified during the BI development activities.

The BI developer designs, develops, and tests the BI solutions, i.e., the deliverables requested by the BI consumers. If using an iterative methodology such as agile, prototyping, or RAD, the developers work closely with a selected set of business BI consumers throughout this process and use a feedback loop to iteratively develop the BI solution. The four key milestones during this process are:

- Design preliminary BI solutions
- Gather user feedback and perform unit tests
- Refine and publish BI deliverables
- Conduct UAT with selected business BI consumers

If this is a large project supporting multiple business departments, the deliverables are grouped together to reflect their respective business constituencies. With sufficient resources, the subgroups can work independently of each other to improve productivity.

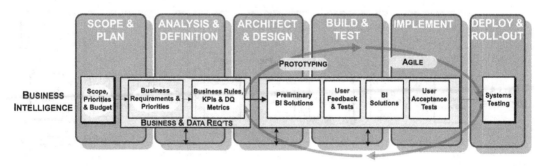

FIGURE 18.20

Business intelligence (BI) functional group.

These activities are dependent on two tasks:

- **Scope-priorities-budget task**, which provides the high-level description of deliverables to be used as the basis for the requirements–discovery activities
- **Data-and-database-task**, which supplies the data schema for BI design and actual data to use in development and testing

DATA AND DATABASE SWIM LANE

The data and database functional group contains the data-focused activities (Figure 18.21) for designing and populating (loading) all data structures needed to support BI. The BI team roles responsible for these tasks are the data architect, data modeler, and database administrator (DBA). The data architect oversees all data-focused activities and coordinates with BI personnel responsible for interdependent activities.

The two primary deliverables from this grouping are:

- Data design: logical and physical
- Data loaded into all relevant BI data structures

The data architect and data modeler examine the business and data requirements to start designing the data architecture and data models. If there is already a BI solution in place, they will examine what data is needed, what data already exists in the DW, and what data is missing in that DW. They will design new BI data structures and modify existing ones to fill in the data gaps they identify. If the enterprise is new to BI, a data architecture will be designed followed by supporting data models.

The key milestones for data design are:

- Data profiling: examine current and historical data sources
- Data models: logically design
- Data stores: physically design and create

This functional group is responsible for supplying the data models and data architecture to the BI, data integration, and infrastructure groups. The group depends on the BI group to supply the business and data requirements, the data integration group to load the data, and the infrastructure group to set up and manage the technology to support the data structures.

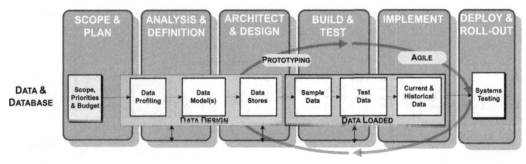

FIGURE 18.21

Data and database functional group.

The data and database functional group validates that the following data loads have completed properly:

- Sample data to be used for prototyping
- Test data to be used for more extensive prototyping and validation
- Current and historical data to be used for development, systems testing, and implementation

DATA INTEGRATION SWIM LANE

The data integration (DI) functional group contains the integration-focused activities (Figure 18.22) that design, develop, test, and deploy all integration-related processing. The BI team roles responsible for these tasks are DI architect and DI developers. The DI architect will oversee all integration-focused activities and coordinate with BI personnel responsible for interdependent activities.

The two primary deliverables from this grouping are:

- Source systems analysis
- Data integration processes

The DI architect and DI developer examine the business and data requirements to determine what source systems need to be integrated. If there is already a BI solution in place, then they determine what data is already sourced compared to the data needed, to identify any data source gaps. If the enterprise is new to BI, they need to examine all the data sources.

The next step is to conduct a source systems analysis. The DI team works with the source systems' SMEs, if available, to gain a better understanding of what is available and its data quality. After those discussions, the DI team should conduct hands-on data profiling to drill into the details of both current and historical data. If there are no SMEs, the team will have to rely totally on data profiling.

After source system analysis, the DI developers use the results to obtain the schemas for the BI data structures from the data-focused group to design the source-to-target mappings and accompanying data workflows. The mappings and workflows are the basis for the DI specifications. In larger projects, either the DI architect or senior-level DI developer creates the DI specifications and provides them to the hands-on DI developers.

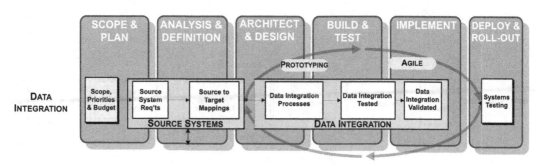

FIGURE 18.22

Data integration functional group.

The source systems milestones are:

- Source systems requirements
- Source-to-target mappings

The DI developers use the specifications to design, develop, and test the integration processes. If this is a large project, the DI development is grouped by business subject and then by data source to improve consistency and productivity. The iterative and incremental approach is best for performing this data integration work, because there are many interdependencies across the code and the developers should heavily rely on common standards, templates, and applets (this is covered in Chapter 12).

The key milestones for data integration are:

- Data integration processes designed and developed
- Data integration processes tested
- Data integration processes validated

The DI team loads the sample, test, and production BI data structures, and works with both the data and BI teams to validate the data. The DI team works with the infrastructure team, obtaining support for the data integration, databases, and technology they need to perform their work.

INFRASTRUCTURE SWIM LANE

The infrastructure functional group is responsible for all the activities involving the care and feeding of the technologies used for BI, as shown in Figure 18.23. Typically, the team is composed of IT staff personnel from an enterprise's systems group. This group manages the enterprise's infrastructure such as networks, hardware (servers, PCs, tablets), storage, and databases. Nowadays, some or all of these may actually be hosted in off-premise cloud environments, in which case this group is the liaison with the outside vendor that provides the hosting solution.

The two primary deliverables from this grouping are:

- **Architectures:** design and implementation of the technology and product architectures
- **Operations:** operating, monitoring, and tuning the BI environment

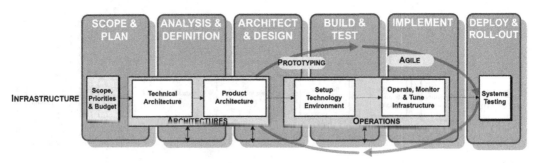

FIGURE 18.23

Infrastructure functional group.

This group's primary interaction with the BI team is with the BI architect. It is that BI architect who will design the initial technology and product architectures. In addition, the BI architect likely handles any product evaluation efforts. The infrastructure group works with the BI architect to develop the detailed technology and product architectures that will be implemented.

After the architectures have been designed and the product selected, the infrastructure group's responsibilities include setting up the technology environments, including such deliverables as:

- Acquiring appropriate products with licenses
- Installation and configuration of the products
- Enabling product access and their usability by the BI project team and appropriate business users
- Ensuring appropriate privacy, security, and regulatory compliance

The infrastructure group is responsible for ongoing operations, including monitoring and performance tuning. This group includes the BI environment in its backups, auditing, and disaster recovery processes.

PROGRAM AND PROJECT MANAGEMENT SWIM LANE

This functional group is responsible for all the BI program and project planning and management activities. The primary responsible individual is the BI project manager. If the BI project is small, this person may also be the BI group manager; in a larger organization, there may be a dedicated project manager. In organizations that have project management offices (PMOs)—typically Fortune 500 companies—the BI project manager would be assigned from the PMO.

It is a best practice for the business sponsor to designate a person responsible for coordinating any activities between business people and the BI project team. In addition, this person manages any deliverables that the business is responsible for. This person is typically considered the peer of the BI project manager and, in some organizations, may be a project co-manager. This person is the project team's business advisor.

Potentially, there is a third individual who forms a project management triad: BI technical advisor. This role is needed when the BI project manager and business advisor are not very knowledgeable about BI itself or if the BI team has many technologists to be managed. The typical candidates for this role are either the BI architect or a very experienced outside consultant. Besides providing BI subject matter expertise to the BI project manager and business advisor, this person manages the day-to-day activities of the technical staff.

The project management related activities include:

- Business justification
- Schedule and resource planning
- Schedule and resource management
- Change management
- Status reporting
- Issues resolution
- Communication with all BI stakeholders
- Coordination between the BI project team and others involved in the project
- Risk management and contingency planning
- Planning for business and IT training

For more in-depth discussions of project management roles, see Chapter 17.

The project manager is also responsible for any coordination necessary between the BI project team and the following organizations or processes, if they exist:

- Data governance
- Analytics and report governance
- BI COE
- DI COE

For more in-depth discussions of these concepts, see these other chapters of the book:

- Chapter 17
- Chapter 19

CENTERS OF EXCELLENCE

THE PURPOSE OF CENTERS OF EXCELLENCE

Teamwork is an essential ingredient in successful BI, as we discussed in Chapter 17. Centers of excellence (COEs) are organizational teams that help companies coordinate similar activities that are taking place in disparate groups all over the company.

COEs are people-oriented solutions that systematically address the problem of disconnected application and data silos across an enterprise. They operate cross-functionally with different business groups along with their supporting processes, applications, and technologies.

COEs enable enterprises to share skills, expertise, and data across applications used in different groups so, as a whole, the enterprise is making better use of the applications, and resources are more easily shared, while investments are maximized. A COE can be an actual organizational unit or a virtual unit.

This chapter will discuss COEs for BI and data integration.

- **The Business Intelligence COE** (BI COE) coordinates and oversees BI activities, including resources and expertise.
- **The Data Integration COE** (DI COE) team focuses specifically on data integration: establishing its scope, defining its architecture and vision, and helping to implement that vision.

Both of these COEs have occasionally been labeled as competency centers: BI competency center (BICC) and integration competency center (ICC). This book uses the term COE versus CC for psychological and marketing reasons. Clients have told me they do not wish to be merely competent, but rather strive for excellence. Creating a CC implies that you are currently incompetent, while creating a COE means you are trying to improve to being excellent (and it does not disparage your current efforts or skills). This distinction may sound humorous, but using the right terminology can help you convince management that the COE is needed and gets business and IT people onboard.

BI COE

The BI COE is a cross-functional team composed of business and IT people representing the BI stake-holders in an enterprise. Its goals are to:

- Expand the use of analytics to better manage and grow the enterprise's business;
- Improve business and IT productivity in the design, development, deployment, and use of analytics;
- Increase business value and ROI from the investments of time, resources, and capital in analytics;

    Based on organizational preferences, the BI COE span of control would be either:

- Advisory—team coordinates and oversees BI projects and activities
- Development—team includes hands-on people from both business and IT groups who design, develop, implement, and support BI applications throughout the enterprise.

    The BI COE pools the skills and expertise of people doing analytical work and allows them to collaborate. The pooling may be in a centralized organization or a virtual team; there are several alternatives for collaboration, which we discuss later in this chapter. As with many of the people-oriented processes developed for BI, it is best to start small, learn from successes and mistakes, and expand to an enterprise-wide solution iteratively.

WHY BUSINESSES NEED BI COEs

The reasons why businesses need BI COEs are deeply ingrained in the way they operate and are organized. These factors are never going to change, so it's almost inevitable that a BI COE is going to be needed.

Organizational Structures Drives Reporting Silos

The need for a BI COE arises from the basic way that companies are organized—as silos. This isn't a bad thing—it's just an observation. Companies are typically organized along business functions such as sales, finance, marketing, and human resources. Companies may further be divided by geographic boundaries or the products or services they offer. Although larger enterprises are likely to have more complex and detached groups, small to midsize enterprises are often organized in this fashion, too.

    Each business group builds or acquires applications to support their unique needs; these applications are different and separate from those in other groups, which have their own unique needs and customized solutions. Although many firms purchase enterprise resource planning (ERP) systems that support business processes, the reality is that even these applications are split into modules geared to specific group needs. Typically, these ERP systems have reporting capabilities that business people use. As their needs get more sophisticated, people may expand the ERP systems' reporting solution, build new custom reporting applications, or use spreadsheets pulling in data from the ERP systems for reporting. Each of these approaches creates or expands the distinct islands, or silos, of applications and data.

    Each group may be doing what is right for them, but as cross-functional, enterprise-wide reporting becomes a higher priority, this approach will become counter-productive. BI should keep pace with and support the cross-functional nature of an enterprise, not hold it back. However, each reporting silo adds to the escalating costs of integrating the data, making it consistent and reconciling differences in reports. BI cannot become truly cross-functional if it is hampered by silos; each silo makes it more difficult to achieve that goal.

Business Preferences Exacerbate the Problem

Many enterprises, both large and small, are using multiple BI tools. It is not uncommon, for example, for a Fortune 1000 company to be using more than a half dozen different BI tools. Some of these BI tools may be the result of different ERP applications bundling different BI tools in their reporting solutions. The business people using a particular ERP system typically have no choice but to use the bundled BI tool, whether they like the tool or not, because that is the only method to gain access to that system's prebuilt reporting.

In addition to the BI tools bundled with ERP systems, it is very common when a customized reporting application is built for business groups to select a different BI tool. Typically, the BI tool selection process is done based on the needs of that business group and is independent of enterprise-wide considerations.

Enterprise IT groups that are driven by efficiency and cost considerations want to establish enterprise-wide standards for the technologies used. Although they have been very effective with technologies related to infrastructure, i.e., things that the typical business person is not all that concerned with (unless it does not work), they have been less successful on standardization when the business person visibly interacts with the technology. BI is one of those areas.

A business group might believe that the BI standard conflicts with what they feel is the best solution to their unique needs. They are focused on solving business problems, and are not really concerned if a BI tool meets IT's criteria for a standard. Their dissatisfaction with the tool may stem from the fact that IT selected it without really understanding what the business needed, or because they have prior experience with another BI tool, or even because they have listened to a vendor claiming that another tool is superior. So for any of these reasons, the tools don't get used, and the business people either use a BI tool they selected or continue using spreadsheets.

Although the business people understand what data they need better than anyone else, they may not be well versed in choosing a BI tool that best helps analyze that data. They're not technology experts, after all. So, a vendor may convince them that their feature-rich product is the answer. However, product features aren't the only things one should evaluate when choosing an application. What about how it meshes with the company's existing architecture and technology strategies? Is it going to just create another silo that only meets a narrow, departmental need but conflicts with the rest of the company's IT solutions?

The trends toward self-service BI also contributes to this problem as business groups assume, and are reassured by product vendors, that their BI needs will be solved by the ease of use and powerful analytical capabilities of the latest BI tool. First, there should always be a disclaimer with these purchases that the self-service BI tool is only as good as the data underneath it; and, second, no matter how self-sufficient a business group feels it is with these tools, they will eventually need to work with other business groups and IT as their analytical needs expand. The initial self-service BI applications look good, but the next silo has just been created and with it all the downsides that we have discussed.

As we covered in Chapter 16, silos are expensive and messy. It's so easy (and tempting) to build them, and so expensive and complicated to solve the problems they create.

BUILDING A BUSINESS CASE FOR A BI COE

A BI COE helps organizations maximize their investments in BI. The benefits of a BI COE are:

- Increased BI business value and ROI
  - BI initiatives are better aligned with the business and become more successful
  - Investments in BI are well-spent
  - Lower total cost of ownership (TCO) over time
- Enterprise-wide BI strategy and road map is agreed upon
  - Processes enable cross-functional input, feedback, and decision-making
  - Strategy and road map are communicated and promoted
- Improved business and IT productivity
  - Enable self-service BI
  - Data silos such as data shadow systems are reduced
- Leveraged BI skills, knowledge, and experiences across enterprise and over time
  - Business groups benefit from one another's BI experiences
  - Maximize use of BI skills throughout the enterprise

For someone who has been involved in BI projects, it may be obvious that a BI COE can benefit your organization, but others may need some help understanding its value, especially if they're being asked to help fund it and commit resources to it. Breaking down organizational silos and working collaboratively in a BI COE often encounters political resistance. This resistance typically is passive-aggressive in nature, meaning that everyone says they are for it, but behind the scenes they are acting like the silos will always exist. To avoid this resistance, it is critical to sell the BI COE, to openly discuss the problems with the status quo, and to get business groups' resource commitments to the COE initiative. It may be helpful to frame it as follows:

1. Explain the value of BI
2. Point out the cost savings
3. Reinforce business and IT objectives
4. Demonstrate the improved alignment of resources

These points are all explained further, below.

Value of BI

If they don't already realize it, executives need to understand the value of BI in the organization before they can even consider a BI COE. With Big Data and analytics so often appearing in the mainstream business press now, BI has gotten a big boost. However, closer to home, executives need to be shown examples of how critical the data from BI projects is to enabling the decision-making necessary to effectively manage and grow the business. Exposing the obvious reliance on BI for business success helps pave the way for funding and support of a COE.

Cost Savings

The silo approach to BI projects wastes money. Each group is on its own, figuring out what approach to use, what tools to buy, and hiring and training resources. No group has a chance to learn from one another's mistakes. The overlapping and redundant nature of the BI projects greatly increases costs, lengthens the time to implement analytical processes, and creates lost business opportunities due to the backlog of analytical needs going unfulfilled.

Inconsistent or missing data across data silos creates a very expensive hidden cost and productivity drain (see Chapter 16). This inconsistency causes many business people to gather and reconcile data across these silos, taking significant time away from business analysis and decision-making.

The BI COE offers immediate cost savings even with just the economies of scale of shared resources, knowledge, and data. Then, it ultimately saves the enterprise money by avoiding unsuccessful, expensive BI projects and eliminating the need to reconcile data across silos.

Business and IT Objectives

With a BI COE, business groups have a formalized process to voice their needs: defining and prioritizing their data and analytical requirements across business groups. The COE team can build a BI strategy and road map that meet the needs of all the groups, and reduce their temptation to build silo-type solutions. The BI road-map is critical to elevate the perspective and timeline beyond individual BI projects.

Likewise, this helps the business groups gain a better understanding of how important it is to have a cohesive, enterprise-wide IT strategy. It reminds them that they don't operate in a vacuum, and they can also learn from the experiences of other departments. The sum of the deliverables from the BI road-map should be greater that what the individual business group could achieve by itself and at a lower aggregate cost.

Monitor BI Performance with BI on BI

How do you know if a BI program is successful? Are the business people actually using the application, or are they returning to their data shadow systems? How easy is it for them to get the answers they need? The BI COE is where you can perform "BI on BI," monitoring the performance and success of the BI program.

A Forrester Research report [1] sheds light on the BI on BI concept by pointing out that "Enterprises still rely largely on intuition and qualitative hearsay assessments of business users' level of satisfaction with BI applications and tools."

Using BI on BI, as the report points out, the BI COE can make recommendations on the following:

- Purchasing or weeding out software—taking into account consolidations, migrations, and upgrades
- Assessing the maturity of the BI environment
- Justifying new BI endeavors
- Confirming adherence to service level agreements (SLAs), clarifying the basis for charge-backs
- Justifying incentive compensation
- Complement governance, risk, and compliance activities
- Gauge BI performance against benchmarks

These efforts can help the BI COE increase the usefulness of a BI program by predicting the requests business people are going to make, and finding hidden data so it can be used for decision-making.

See the book's companion Website www.biguidebook.com for links to relevant industry research.

Improved Alignment of Resources

The BI COE can help the enterprise identify and better align its most skilled and experienced people with BI. Enterprises typically have a shortage of BI-savvy business and IT people, and the push for Big Data only makes that gap more acute. Where relying on ad hoc teams for each BI project would find each group starting from scratch, working with a BI COE would make it easier for groups to find resources—people, standards, processes, and templates—to accelerate the launch of their projects.

It also encourages more coordinated training. Although a single department might not have the budget for in-house, customized training, a BI COE can arrange for training for business people in various groups, ensuring they learn the basics of BI, the specific tools the company has chosen, and how to analyze the new streams of data they'll be receiving. An enterprise-wide approach also enables the COE to establish "train the trainer" or mentoring programs staffed by internal staff, which is something that would not be practical if BI projects remained as silos.

The COE has insight into various business units, so it makes it easier to share data sets and results among them. The business units benefit from the cross-pollination of reports, dashboards, and analysis that this can enable.

BI COE DELIVERABLES

The BI COE's mission is to expand the use and business value of analytics in a cost- and labor-effective manner. The BI COE needs to interact with business groups, the BI development group, and the IT group that supports business application (Figure 19.1). Working with BI subject matter experts (SMEs) in the business groups, the COE determines what the BI consumers need. Working with systems-of-record (SOR) SMEs in the business application group, the COE learns where the data originates.

The process of establishing and operating a COE will include these deliverables:

- Establish processes for business and IT interaction (see Chapter 18)
  - Requirement-gathering and prioritization across business groups
  - Change and scope management
  - Communication and marketing plans on the state of analytics in the enterprise
- Create a BI Portfolio (see Chapter 7 and Chapter 14)
  - Assess analytics needs associated with:
    - Business functions and processes
    - Business people's analytical styles and skills
  - Design BI Portfolio capability and usage road-map
  - Assist in implementing BI Portfolio incrementally
- Formulate policies and adherence standards (see Chapter 4 and Chapter 17)
  - Access, privacy, and security
  - Data governance (in conjunction with data governance team, if one exists)
  - Reporting and analytics governance
- Create common and reusable processes (if there is a hands-on team) (see Chapter 14)
  - Design common templates such as dashboards and reports
  - Enable business self-service BI

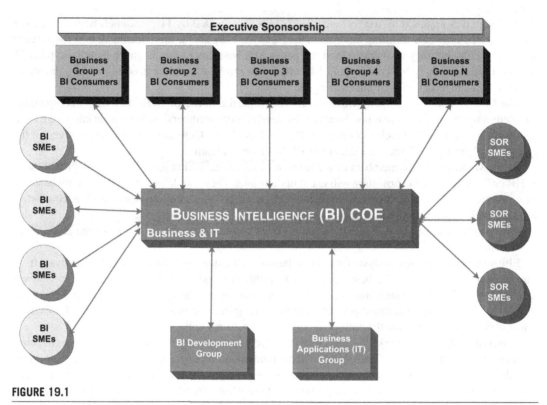

FIGURE 19.1

Business intelligence (BI) COE interactions.

- • Perform ad-hoc query analysis for business peers
- • Work with IT to implement BI monitoring processes
- • Work with IT to implement BI performance tuning processes
- • Expand knowledge and skills (see Chapter 17)
  - • Determine skills, experience and knowledge of business BI consumers
  - • Obtain or deliver targeted business training

SKILLS NEEDED

The BI COE needs people with a variety of skills: technical, business, and analytic. Ideally, you'll have people with combinations of these skills. It is important to have business and IT people working in the COE. The types of skills needed are:

Technical skills—These should include a mastery of the tools in the BI portfolio to access and analyze business data; ability to mentor others in the use of these tools, particularly self-service BI; being able to navigate data models, data relationships, and business metric definitions; understanding how the DW and BI systems work; and the ability to know how to match technology to the analytical needs of the business.

Although it is assumed all the technical skills will be provided by IT personnel, business "power users" are well suited for fulfilling that role in the BI COE. They are far more technical than the average business person, but they also understand the needs of a business group far more than the typical IT person. They are usually better at linking BI functionality to how it can be used in business processes and then explaining that to their business peers.

The BI development team will provide technical expertise to the BI COE, but how it is organized will determine the extent of that involvement. BI development members' participation can range from key members, such as a BI architect or senior BI developer being COE advisors, to the other end of the spectrum, where the COE includes the entire BI development team.

Business skills—Some members of the team must understand what data the business groups, such as HR or finance, need and how they will use it in their jobs. They should be able to work with business BI consumers to determine their requirements and priorities. This may require a level of comfort in working with executives to understand their strategic goals, requirements, and priorities. They also need to be able to translate business requirements from business to technical terms for the BI development team.

Either business systems analysts from IT or business (finance, operational, or other) analysts from various business groups are the best candidates to fulfill this role. Both types of analysts spend their time understanding the business and translating their needs into an analytical context. Typically, these people are already assigned to support specific business groups or processes that enable the COE to select individuals to represent the enterprise via cross-functional collaboration.

Analytic skills—People skilled with analytics are becoming more essential in every enterprise, and especially in the BI COE. These people need to understand business issues and the data required to address those issues; work with IT to determine specific data needed; identify what data is available and its quality; be able to discern patterns, relationships, trends, and anomalies in data; assist in creating analytical processes; and assist business people in using those analytical processes. These people need to be proficient in at least some set of tools in the BI portfolio. The analytical role bridges both the technical and business roles already described, but with the analytical person being able to leverage their skills to create and apply analytical applications to business processes.

The demands of Big Data have created the increased need for a much more sophisticated analytical role: the data scientist. In order to create Big Data analytical applications and predictive models, they need to have skills in statistics, data mining, data aggregation, and potentially some programming skills. To develop the model, they also need to understand their business and industry. It also helps if they understand how to apply customer behavior and economic models.

Although Big Data means "a lot of data," the reality is, in many cases, that data is incomplete and inconsistent. Developing analytical models means dealing with dirty data and gaps. Many "numbers" people have trouble dealing with these conditions.

Data scientists need to have expertise in statistics, economics, and business, in addition to the basic programming skills. Although the ranks of the software engineers and IT is an excellent place to start looking for people with these skills, it helps to broaden the search to reach to people with mathematics, actuarial, statistical, economics, engineering, or business backgrounds.

Fortunately, many business schools have started offering analytical curriculum at both the undergraduate and graduate level. For business people with deep business expertise, it is time to brush up on statistics.

ORGANIZATION AND FUNDING

Someone has to "own" the BI COE, but its success depends on its ability to guide BI in the entire enterprise. In many cases, it makes sense for a BI COE to be organized under the CIO. Ideally, IT already has a strategic role in the company, paving the way for the COE to be accepted and therefore effective in its role.

Alternatively, it could be located in a particular business group if that business drives the direction of the enterprise. For example, a retail company might be very marketing-focused, and that's where their most crucial data resides. In many other enterprises, finance may be the business driver to cross-functional collaboration, so the CFO may sponsor and "host" the COE. If a BI COE is located in a business group, it's essential that internal politics allow the center to represent the whole enterprise.

Because the BI COE can be a virtual group, it can overlap with other centers of excellence, such as the DI COE, also discussed in this chapter. As virtual groups, they can share resources and shift priorities more easily.

Someone also has to fund the COE, which can be complicated because it is designed to benefit many different cost centers. If it's necessary to have its costs covered, its owner, which we'll say is the IT group for this example, could cross-charge each group for their use of the center. This provides an opportunity to demonstrate the economic value of the COE, but on the down side, it can discourage groups on a tight budget from using it.

Another approach is to cross-charge other groups on a subscription basis. This way, groups that have made their annual payment aren't discouraged from making good use of the COE. The more use it gets, the more effective it can be, and the more everyone's investment grows.

Many enterprises use a shared funding approach rather than cross-charging. Using this method, the enterprise executives working with various business groups will agree on the funding level for the BI COE, similar to the way they fund the IT organization.

A BI COE that is funded solely by the CIO who carves out a portion of the IT budget to support the COE raises a red flag in regards to sustainability. Without an explicit commitment by business groups to fund the BI COE, their buy-in is in question and internal politics often hinder BI COE success.

DATA INTEGRATION CENTER OF EXCELLENCE

The data integration COE (DI COE) is an enterprise team driving the design and implementation of data integration to enable enterprise-wide analytics. Its goals:

- Develop data integration standards, best practices, and reusable processes spanning enterprise-wide integration uses within a data integration framework (DIF) (see Chapter 5)
- Improve productivity in the design, development, deployment, and use of data integration
- Increase business value and ROI from the investments of time, resources, and capital in data integration

In contrast to the BI COE, this team is composed primarily of IT personal who specialize in data integration. There's a misconception that the DI COE only involves loading the data warehouse; in actuality, its scope encompasses all integration processing in business applications, business processes,

MDM, BI applications, DW, and inter-application processes. In addition, its scope includes data gathering, exchange, and integration with:

- External stakeholders—partners, supplier, customers, partners
- Big Data—social media, web analytics, machine data
- Unstructured data

The DI COE pools the skills and expertise of people doing data integration work in either a single organization or a virtual team. This chapter covers alternative roles and responsibilities later.

Although this organizational structure is often associated with larger enterprises, it is just as critical for small and midsize enterprises. Smaller organizations may not use the term COE because it seems too pretentious or they don't have many integration people, but the DI COE goals are just as applicable to them as they are to a larger firm.

As with other people-oriented processes developed for BI, it is best to start small, learn from successes and mistakes, and expand to an enterprise-wide solution iteratively as the integration maturity level rises within an enterprise.

WHY BUSINESSES NEED DI COEs

Several factors contribute to the need for a DI COE. The reasons generally have to do with the project-oriented approach toward integration that creates silos, and peoples' tendencies to stick with what they know, assuming it has worked in the past, not the limitations of technology.

Data Sources and Silos Exploding

Enterprises are experiencing an accelerating deluge of data volumes, varieties, and velocities, creating an expanding demand for data integration. Many people point out that the world's data is doubling every year, but whether that is a real statistic or an "urban legend" isn't clear. What is clear is that the problem is not just the explosion of data. It's also the fact that businesses create and expand application, data, and reporting silos—further exacerbating the integration challenges.

Myriad Integration Approaches Make the Problem Worse

Each business group uses its own applications and processes to support its unique needs. These applications, which may be purchased or custom-built, include such systems as ERP; customer relationship management (CRM); supply chain management (SCM); budgeting, planning, and forecasting; sales-force automation; and many more that may be industry-specific or more narrowly supporting a particular business process.

The implementation, customization, and expansion of these applications is done on a project-by-project basis. Inter-application data exchange and integration are also done in projects that are tactical and stand-alone. Each of these integration projects starts with a clean slate:

- Gathering requirements
- Determine if and what type of integration software is needed
  - If yes, select integration software
- Acquiring skilled resources
- Getting training

- Establishing processes, procedures, and standards
- Developing the integration application
- Deploying the integration application

Without a data integration framework, these projects are destined to "reinvent the wheel" each time in terms of defining an architecture, selecting integration software, and developing integration processes. There are myriad different types of integration tools and techniques that provide overlapping data integration processes:

- Business application developers will typically select tools and techniques in the enterprise application integration (EAI) software category as web services in an enterprise service bus (ESB), middleware, or service-oriented architecture (SOA).
- DW developers generally use extract, transform and load (ETL); or extract, load and transform (ELT) tools; and data quality tools, if needed.
- BI developers will use connectivity capabilities built into their BI tools; manually create custom code; or, use enterprise information integration (EII) or data virtualization software
- MDM developers will use MDM applications or use a combination of ETL and data quality tools

The tendency for each of these IT specialists to create their own architectures and select different integration software to essentially perform the same data integration processes results in integration silos. From an enterprise perspective, these silos increase costs, require more resources (with skills in short supply), and reduce productivity. As each silo is established, it creates yet another application that needs to be integrated and makes the problem worse. These silos will create an integration backlog, making it take longer for IT to enable the availability of integrated data needed for analytics.

Silos are Expensive

Each group may be doing what seems right for them, but their parochial approach can be wrong for the enterprise as a whole. Data silos create another version of data instead of actually integrating it. Silos drain company finances in several ways:

- Expense of creating and maintaining various silos
- Waste of overlapping and redundant projects
- Time spent reviewing and reconciling conflicting numbers from the various data silos
- Loss of business confidence in the numbers and their transparency

Even more wasteful and expensive data silos are created when companies undertake projects such as data migrations to support application consolidation. These can be due to corporate mergers, ERP instance consolidations, and master data consolidations (product and customer reference data). Although these are data integration projects, they are treated as stand-alone, one-off projects—further fragmenting already constrained resources and budgets.

When Data Integration Problems become Hard to Ignore

Many companies are blind to their data integration problems. All they see are their investments in ERP, CRM, SCM, and DW systems, and the terabytes of data stored in them. Smug with the knowledge that they have all the data that the business needs, they're not even aware of the data silos surrounding them.

At some point, they start noticing inconsistent data, which is a symptom of a data integration problem. However, because they don't understand the cause, they focus on relieving the symptoms with quick-hit solutions. For example, they may try to consolidate BI tools. While this may be a worthy goal unto itself, using a single BI tool will do nothing about the fact that the underlying data is coming from many disparate systems (ERP, CRM, SCM, data warehouses, data marts, etc.). The business is not getting different numbers because it is using different tools, but rather because each tool is associated with a *different* database where the data had been transformed differently than the other databases. The BI tool used is the tip of the iceberg; the data integration issue is what is below the waterline.

BUILDING A BUSINESS CASE FOR A DI COE

You now understand how issues with people, politics, and process have established integration silos throughout an enterprise that are costly, inefficient, and inhibit the use of data as an enterprise asset. How do you stop the madness? The key deliverables to breaking the silos and establishing an enterprise-wide integration initiative are:

1. Create the business case
2. Enlist sponsorship
3. Establish an integration investment portfolio
4. Create DI COE

An enterprise needs to create a DI COE to enable enterprise-wide integration. Too often, people assume that a COE has to be a centralized group within a company controlling and staffing all integration projects. Although that is one model that can be used, there are other alternatives that can be implemented based on the circumstances within an enterprise.

Build the Business Case

You have to establish the business and technical case for an enterprise-wide integration approach. It should clearly explain that the project-by-project, start-from-scratch approach is too costly, too inefficient from time and resource perspectives, and too ineffective, because each project is reinventing the wheel.

However, the justification isn't just that a DI COE will save money and time in the long-run; more importantly, it's that a DI COE is the key ingredient to truly implementing the consistent, comprehensive, and current data needed by the business. The business value of the integrated data is the primary selling point, with cost savings and efficiency secondary.

The business case needs to answer these questions:

- What business problems or opportunities are being addressed by the DI COE?
- Who will use it?
- What are the anticipated business benefits?

Enlist Sponsorship

The goal of the justification is to enlist sponsorship, both from your business and IT leadership. Although many initiatives start from the bottom in order to establish success and credibility, at some point, to truly achieve an enterprise-wide approach, your CFO and CIO have to become sponsors. The

CFO is necessary both from a budget and a data governance (ownership) perspective, and your CIO has to commit the IT organization to approaching integration from an enterprise-wide perspective, not just on a tactical project basis.

The business is investing in projects and applications that require data integration, but historically, these are disjointed projects that have created data silos scattered across the enterprise. Someone needs to recognize that this is a systemic problem that needs to be addressed in order to better use IT investments and, more importantly, get the information needed by the business to manage the enterprise. The data integration problem needs an out-of-the-box approach that looks at the problem in a holistic manner.

The task of enlisting sponsorship involves three types of people or groups:

- **The Evangelist**—The first step in this journey is getting help from someone who sees the forest, not just the trees—someone who recognizes the need for change. This is usually an IT person involved in existing data integration efforts who sees the redundancy in data integration projects and understands the business benefit of eliminating it. This person becomes the data integration evangelist who preaches that there is a problem and that something must be done about it. Not having significant budgetary authority and being located deep in the IT organization means that the evangelist generally cannot single-handedly change the momentum of the company. Often, this IT person is someone with architectural responsibility.
- **The Champion**—The next person in the chain to keep the fire going is a champion—someone higher in the organization visible to and respected by either the CIO or CFO. The evangelist enlists the champion to continue selling the vision further up the organizational hierarchy. The champion also may lack significant budgetary authority, but is often the person who creates the business and IT case for budget submissions to the CIO or CFO. The champion needs to justify the solid business case of establishing data integration as an infrastructure program, just as e-mail and networks are treated in most enterprises today.
- **Sponsors**—Finally, the crucial link to success is getting the sponsors, with both the CIO and CFO signed on, to treat data integration as an investment portfolio. There is a wide range of organizational approaches to this—from actually having a single data integration budget to a more realistic approach of budgetary reviews of all projects with data integration components. The budgetary reviews would eliminate redundant or conflicting efforts and, possibly, combine the data integration of multiple projects to enable more expansive and complete coverage.

Establish a Data Integration Investment Portfolio

With multiple projects vying for the same budget, you need to evaluate and manage the data integration components by creating a data integration strategy and architecture, i.e., data integration framework (DIF). (The DIF is covered in detail in Chapter 5.) Although the DIF is a prerequisite to guiding the data integration program, it is crucial to make sure that you have funding.

The Portfolio Approach

The best way to ensure funding for the right projects is a data integration investment portfolio. With this approach, you examine each project to determine if a data integration component exists. If so, you position it within your DIF to classify what data integration functionality is being performed. Then you examine that component in the context of all the other data integration components of other projects.

This review will determine if there are any overlapping or complementary aspects between projects, thereby eliminating redundant expenditures and leveraging work across projects.

Looking at data integration efforts from an enterprise perspective often enhances these efforts because you are no longer sub-optimizing the data integration efforts of each project to fit within that individual project's budget and resource constraints. You can undertake a more robust effort when the enterprise is being used as a focus. In addition, you can modify some aspects that may have hindered the effort put into other projects in order to reach a better solution.

Money talks. You absolutely must have financial incentives such as budgeting to get buy-in for data integration projects. Enterprise-wide data integration, while appealing to many in the IT industry, is just an esoteric concept that will be overshadowed by short-term and parochial projects unless backed up by budgetary allocation and review.

Establishing the Portfolio

Creating the integration portfolio involves assessing where you are, determining where you want to be, and how you are going to close the gap.

First, you need to take an inventory of what data integration is already occurring in an enterprise. Existing IT projects may be under these labels:

- Performance management
- Customer data integration (CDI)
- Big Data
- Predictive analytics
- MDM
- Data warehousing
- BI

In addition to these IT labeled projects, it is a safe assumption that most, if not all, key business initiatives have integration components to gather the data and generate the business metrics needed.

The technologies that may be used include:

- ETL or ELT
- Data virtualization (formerly enterprise information integration (EII)
- Web or data services—evolved form of EAI
- Data quality
- MDM
- Data shadow systems or spreadmarts that are used extensively across enterprises using SQL scripts, ODBC/JDBC, Microsoft Access, and Microsoft Excel to "integrate" data

When assessing this inventory, examine what has the most significant impact on the enterprise, either in terms of business benefit or IT cost. You are not going to be able to solve all the problems at first, so concentrate on the areas that provide the best rate of return for your efforts and make the biggest impact.

After taking inventory, you need to determine what you want your integration portfolio to be in the future. You cannot succeed unless you have an agreed upon goal, i.e., architecture, that supports the information needs of the business. The integration portfolio needs to be an integral part of your information architecture and systems.

Finally, you need to create an integration road-map to move from your existing data silos to your desired information architecture. This will involve integration initiatives providing new capabilities along with projects that renovate or replace existing silos.

ORGANIZATIONAL MODELS FOR BUILDING THE DI COE

There are several approaches to organizing the role and responsibilities of a DI COE. The approach you take depends on your enterprise's people, politics, and processes. Too often, people assume that a DI COE has to be a centralized group within a company controlling and staffing all integration projects. Although that is one model that can be used, there are other alternatives that may be more advantageous based on the circumstances within an enterprise. Another incorrect assumption people make is that only large corporations need DI COEs.

The four organizational models most often used to implement DI COEs are:

- Best practices
- Technology standards
- Shared services
- Centralized services

Although the DI COE organizational choices above are listed in an increasing level of control, scope, and size, it is neither necessary nor recommended for an enterprise to step up the DI COE organization ladder. The organizational approach that best fits an enterprise depends on its unique situation, rather than some esoteric, one-size-fits-all model. These four models are explained in more detail in the following sections.

Sharing Best Practices Organizational Model

The simplest form of DI COE organization is a virtual team that documents and shares best practices among data integration projects. This allows each project to leverage past work without reinventing the wheel. Like all organizational models, it has pros and cons.

The pros of this approach are that it saves time, reduces costs, and enables each project team to concentrate on expanding the overall enterprise's integration expertise, thereby contributing new or improved practices based on what they've learned. In this manner, enterprise integration expertise continues to grow project-by-project rather than being lost as each project is completed and resources inevitably scatter.

In addition, there is a considerable amount of industry knowledge gained from successful and unsuccessful integration projects, which has formed a set of data integration best practices. Tapping into that pool of best practices should improve an enterprise's integration efforts and help avoid many of the learning mistakes everyone new encounters. Just to set expectations: there is no single recipe that applies to all situations, but rather a data integration cookbook of best practices that an enterprise needs to pick which recipes apply to them.

Very few corporate cultures lend themselves to this approach, however. The people on the virtual team are often doing this work on a voluntary basis in addition to their primary jobs. In difficult economic times, most people are already working many more hours than they did in the past and may not have the opportunity to invest the time that is needed. Virtual team members are often drawn back into their primary jobs as priorities change or crises emerge.

Enterprises must recognize the level of efforts that each contributor needs to make for the common good. If the investment in people is recognized and encouraged—by incorporating as objectives in employee reviews and substituting this work for lower priority work—then this approach can be very effective. If, however, this activity is just thrown on top of everyone's already too-large workload, then this model will not be effective.

Another issue that can arise with this model is that each project team generally feels empowered to do their project their own way and figures they will do it better than others. New project teams may not have the bandwidth to study and use other projects' best practices. In fact, they might not even know how they apply. Although this is a very appealing approach from a practical standpoint, it often has little effect on enterprise-wide data integration efforts.

Common Technology Organizational Model

The second DI COE organizational approach is to have a virtual team that not only publishes best practices, but also determines and recommends a common technology platform. The benefit of this approach is that it goes beyond sharing ideas by creating a technology platform that each independent integration project can tap into. This approach avoids the costly and time-consuming tool evaluation and selection process; avoids the cost of redundant or overlapping software and supporting infrastructure; and, if the integration standard is followed, provides the potential for a common pool of expertise in the enterprise that might be enlisted to work on various projects.

Standardizing on integration technology enables the integration projects to concentrate on creating business value rather than continually tying up resources in the evaluation, selection, purchase, training, development, and deployment of multiple integration technologies.

There are some concerns with this approach, however:

- First, how will the DI COE team make its selection without using various projects for requirements input?
- Second, the team often does not have the budget or resources to adequately pick a technology platform. This approach means that an additional budget item must be allocated to a pure IT technology project—often a difficult sell when budgets are tight.
- Third, while the team is examining the technology options, other projects are moving forward without the guidance that it can provide. In other words, more data silos may be built just as the DI COE looks at ways to prevent them.
- Finally, what are the real incentives for each project to adopt the common technology platform? Many corporate cultures will allow new projects to pick another platform anyway, because these projects must still deliver their objectives in addition to picking up the requirements of the technology platform. Many projects will justify moving forward on their own because of their limited budget, resources, and expertise.

Shared Services Organizational Model

The third organizational approach is to create a DI COE where a group of dedicated people develop the data integration components of individual projects. In this services model, the DI COE operates as a subcontractor within the individual projects. It determines the strategy, designs the architecture, and selects the technology platform as prerequisites to its development efforts. The shared services model allows companies to leverage work and resources across projects to develop an enterprise-wide data integration program. This organization enables the enterprise to develop deep data integration skills because the DI COE specializes in that area. This approach works extremely well, especially when reinforced by strong business and IT sponsorship along with supporting budgetary investments.

The individual integration project teams are still responsible for the development activities and deliverables; however, the DI COE assigns resources from their common pool of talent to work on those projects.

This is a terrific approach to developing and nurturing integration talent and expertise (from an employee perspective) and a very productive way to leverage individual skills, thus reducing costs (from an enterprise perspective).

This approach works extremely well, especially when reinforced by strong business and IT sponsorship, along with supporting budgetary investments. The main caution is that decentralized companies may be reluctant to use the shared services approach. However, with strong financial incentives and recognition that many IT services already operate in this manner, initial resistance can be overcome.

Centralized Services Organizational Model

The final organizational model, which requires the highest levels of skills and experience, is a completely centralized DI COE operation. Data integration is elevated as a primary program; projects are independent of the other IT and business application projects. The data integration projects are executed to build a data infrastructure supporting other business projects. All data integration components are pulled out of projects and placed into the data integration program. Just as with the shared services model, the DI COE determines the strategy, designs the architecture, and selects the technology platform as prerequisites to its development efforts. However, unlike the previous model, the DI COE operates the entire data integration project.

This is an extremely effective model if the corporate culture supports centralized development and control. However, in a decentralized culture, the shared services model will have a better chance of success.

DI COE DELIVERABLES

The DI COE facilitates the design, implementation, and support of a data integration framework (DIF) that enables the integration of comprehensive, clean, consistent, and current data for the business in a cost- and resource-effective manner. The best practices to follow during this process include:

- Create DIF (see Chapter 5)
  - Classify data integration needs by category and functionality
  - Document DI use cases
  - Design data integration architecture
- Create common and reusable processes (see Chapter 11)
  - Design common standards and templates
  - Design common data quality processes and standards
  - Design common communications, "logging," and alerts
  - Design DI monitoring processes
  - Design BI performance tuning processes

- Leverage integration software (see Chapter 13)
  - Use a common set of data integration software
  - Use DI software rather than manually coding
- Expand integration knowledge and skills (see Chapter 17)
  - Determine skills, experience, and knowledge
  - Obtain fundamentals training
  - Obtain tools training

SKILLS NEEDED

There is an ongoing shortage of experienced data integration professionals. The skills gap is getting larger with the data deluge and growing integration backlog. Most people gain their data integration experience while manually building custom-coded processes; however, it's limited. These manually coded projects have not provided an opportunity to learn data integration architectures, best practices, standards, and how to use sophisticated data integration software, never mind learn data integration fundamentals.

A skilled data integration specialist needs expertise in the following:

- Data modeling
- Database design
- Data profiling
- ETL, ELT, or data integration suites
- SQL
- Web and data services
- MDM
- DW design
- BI and analytics design
- Data and technical architectures
- Software development methodology

A good data integration specialist will have extensive data and software skills across a variety of integration uses. But the IT industry is in a quandary because as long as manually coded integration processes dominate projects then data integration specialists will not learn how to implement more sophisticated integration software that will break through the integration backlog. (Chapter 12)

How do we close the skills gap?

- Invest in training and ongoing education on integration fundamentals and tools
- Accept lower productivity in initial integration projects as an investment in gaining skills for the long term
- Create an on-the-job mentoring program with senior integration specialists as the mentors. (This means the senior staff time shifts from development to mentoring—another investment in the future with the associated short-term drop in productivity.)
- Create a DIF with its architecture, best practices, and standards as a way for integration specialists skills to grow over time
- Create a DI COE!

ENABLING A DATA-DRIVEN ENTERPRISE

Organizationally, the best approach to implement a sustained enterprise data management strategy is to establish a data governance program along with the BI and data integration COEs. The three-pillar approach to data management is a best practice for enterprises of all sizes, with the differences being that larger organizations will actually have three organizations, while smaller enterprises will have three processes.

The benefits of the data management trilogy:

- Leverages analytics to create business value
- Improves the productivity of both business and IT people
- In the long-term, it is the cost-effective approach to becoming a data-driven enterprise

The three organizations in the data management trilogy, as depicted in Figure 19.2, support each other's goals and objectives. The data governance program will work with the DI COE to gather the data definitions from the SORs and with the BI COE to define the data and metrics used in BI applications. The data governance program will then work with the COEs to implement and enforce (or strongly encourage) the use of these definitions in the enterprise's data integration and BI applications. There is an overlap in skills across the trilogy and, except possibly in the largest enterprises, there is also a sharing of people and resource commitments.

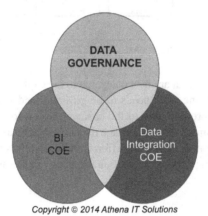

Copyright © 2014 Athena IT Solutions

FIGURE 19.2

Three data-management processes.

An organizational view of the trilogy is illustrated in Figure 19.3. The ideal or long-term goal is to have executive sponsorship support an enterprise-wide data-governance board that then drives both the BI COE and DI COE. The reality is that the most successful data management programs have started small and grown iteratively based on each tactical success story. Data management is not a goal unto itself, but rather an enabler to better analytics and better decision-making. It is merely an esoteric concept until it can be proved to provide business value.

The data governance board should leverage the COEs as the intermediaries and specialists who work directly with the SMEs for SORs and business intelligence applications. Data management involves very

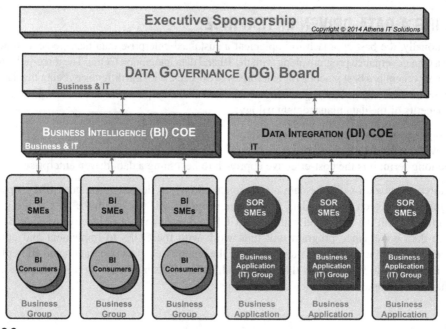

FIGURE 19.3

Data-management organizational interconnections.

detailed and time-consuming tasks that are best delegated to the COEs. The data governance board needs to sift through that detail, determine what needs to be governed and what is not worth the investment, work with the executives and representatives of the business groups to prioritize these needs, work with the business groups on how to enforce and encourage data governance use in analytics, establish ongoing communication across the enterprise, market the efforts, and keep refreshing the program as the business changes and evolves. The most important contribution the trilogy makes is managing the politics that data management always evokes.

REFERENCE

[1] Evelson Boris, Powers Stephen, Kister Holger, Bennet Martha, Coyne Shannon. BI on BI: how to manage the performance of BI initiatives. Forrester Research; May 2, 2013. [PDF].

Index

Note: Page numbers with "f" and "t" denote figures and tables, respectively.

A

Access services, 312
Accidental architecture. *See also* Analytical data architecture
(ADA); Information architecture; Technical architecture.
  addiction signs, 82
  avoiding accidents, 81–83
  BI, 115–116
  recovering from, 83
Accumulating fact tables, 218–219
ACID. *See* Atomicity, consistency, isolation, and durability
Ad hoc analysis, 150, 406
ADA. *See* Analytical data architecture
Additive facts, 202–203
Adopters, 312
Advanced analytics, 375b. *See also* Big Data analytics;
Predictive analytics.
  in action, 376–377
  analytical hubs, 384–387
  analytical sandboxes, 383–384
  architecture, 381f
  data mining, 377–383
  data visualization, 401–402
  overview and background, 375–377
  past and predictive analytics, 376
  predictive analytics, 377–383
  roadblocks to success, 382–383
  skills, 382t, 399t
  techniques and examples, 381t
  window to future, 376
Advanced dimensional modeling, 237. *See also* Dimensional
modeling.
  approaches, 270
    custom dimension groups, 271–272, 272f
    hot swappable dimension, 270–271, 271f
  causal dimension, 262–263, 263f
  heterogeneous products, 269–270
  hierarchies, 237, 238f
    balanced, 238–240
    ragged, 240–241, 240f
    unbalanced, 241, 241f
    variable-depth, 241–244
  junk dimension, 265–267
  multivalued dimension, 263–265
  outrigger tables, 244, 245f
  SCD, 245–262
  too few dimensions, 272
  too many dimensions, 272
  value band reporting, 268–269, 268f

Aggregation subservice, 323–324, 324f
Agile methodology, 475–476
AJAX. *See* Asynchronous JavaScript and XML
Alternate key (AK), 187
Analysts, 341–342
Analytical data architecture (ADA), 120, 123, 124f.
  See also Information architecture; Technical
  architecture.
  BI sources, 127
  data marts, 125
  data schemas, 125–126
  EDW, 125
  enhanced hub-and-spoke model, 124–125
  physical data store combinations, 128
Analytical hubs, 384–387, 386f
  advice for, 394–395
  architecture options, 388, 389f
    advanced analytics layers, 388–391
    business analytics, 388–391
    data access and integration, 393–394
    platforms, 391–392
    predictive modeling with, 392–393
  design principles, 387–388
Analytical sandboxes, 383–384, 385f
  advice for, 394–395
  architecture options, 388, 390f
    advanced analytics layers, 388–391
    business analytics, 388–391
    data access and integration, 393–394
    platforms, 391–392
  design principles, 387–388
Analytics, 225
  challenges, 7–8
  deluge, 6–8
  importance, 7
  strategy, 8
API. *See* Application programming interface
Application development methodology. *See* Systems
  development life cycle (SDLC)
Application programming interface (API), 109
Application vendor, 101
Architecture framework
  accidental architecture, 81
    addiction signs, 82
    recovering from, 83
  action plan, 84t
  architectural blueprints, 65–66
  BI framework, 66, 67f